Special Edition

Using

Using

Visual C++® 6

201 West 103rd Street, Indianapolis, Indiana 46290

Kate Gregory

Special Edition Using Visual C++® 6

Trademarks

Warning and Disclaimer

Contents at a Glance

Table of Contents

III Improving Your User Interface

9 Status Bars and Toolbars   185

10 Common Controls   205

11 Help   243

Credits

EXECUTIVE EDITOR
Bradley L. Jones

ACQUISITIONS EDITOR
Kelly Marshall

DEVELOPMENT EDITOR
Matt Purcell

MANAGING EDITOR
Jodi Jensen

SENIOR EDITOR
Susan Ross Moore

COPY EDITORS
Susan M. Dunn
Kate O. Givens
Kate Talbot

INDEXER
Greg Pearson

TECHNICAL EDITOR
Olaf Meding

SOFTWARE DEVELOPMENT SPECIALIST
Andrea Duvall

PRODUCTION
Carol Bowers
Mona Brown
Ayanna Lacey
Gene Redding

About the Author

Kate Gregory is a founding partner of Gregory Consulting Limited (**www.gregcons.com**), which has been providing consulting and development services throughout North America since 1986. Her experience with C++ stretches back to before Visual C++ existed—she enthusiastically converted upon seeing the first release. Gregory Consulting develops software and Web sites and specializes in combining software development with Web site development to create active sites. They build quality custom and off-the-shelf software components for Web pages and other applications.

Dedication

To my children, Beth and Kevin, who keep me connected to the world away from the keyboard, and remind me every day how good it feels to learn new things.

Acknowledgments

Writng a book is hard, hard work. What makes it possible is the support I get from those around me. First, as always, my family, Brian, Beth, and Kevin, who know it's only temporary. Brian does double duty as both supportive husband and world's best technical editor. This time around I was lucky enough to have Bryan Oliver helping, shooting figures, testing code, finding bugs, and generally pitching in. Thanks, Bryan.

There's an army of editors, proofers, indexers, illustrators, and general saints who turn my Word documents into the book you hold in your hand. Many of the team members this time have been involved in other Que projects with me, and I know that I landed the "good ones" for this book. Special mention has to go to Olaf Meding, who provided a terrific tech edit based on a fast-changing product. Joe Massoni and Mike Blaszczak at Microsoft have also earned my gratitude during this release cycle.

While I cheerfully share the credit for the accurate and educational aspects of this book, the mistakes and omissions I have to claim as mine alone. Please bring them to my attention so that they can be corrected in subsequent printings and editions. I am as grateful as ever to readers who have done so in the past, and improved this book in the process.

Tell Us What You Think!

As the reader of this book, *you* are our most important critic and commentator. We value your opinion and want to know what we're doing right, what we could do better, what areas you'd like to see us publish in, and any other words of wisdom you're willing to pass our way.

As the Executive Editor for the Programming team at Macmillan Computer Publishing, I welcome your comments. You can fax, email, or write me directly to let me know what you did or didn't like about this book—as well as what we can do to make our books stronger.

Please note that I cannot help you with technical problems related to the topic of this book, and that due to the high volume of mail I receive, I might not be able to reply to every message.

When you write, please be sure to include this book's title and author as well as your name and phone or fax number. I will carefully review your comments and share them with the author and editors who worked on the book.

Fax: 317-817-7070

Email: **adv_prog@mcp.com**

Mail: Executive Editor
          Programming
          Macmillan Computer Publishing
          201 West 103rd Street
          Indianapolis, IN 46290 USA

Introduction

Visual C++ is a powerful and complex tool for building 32-bit applications for Window 95 and Windows NT. These applications are much larger and more complex than their predecessors for 16-bit Windows or older programs that didn't use a graphical user interface. Yet, as program size and complexity has increased, programmer effort has decreased, at least for programmers who are using the right tools.

Visual C++ is one of the right tools. With its code-generating wizards, it can produce the shell of a working Windows application in seconds. The class library included with Visual C++, the Microsoft Foundation Classes (MFC), has become the industry standard for Windows software development in a variety of C++ compilers. The visual editing tools make layout of menus and dialogs a snap. The time you invest in learning to use this product will pay for itself on your first Windows programming project.

Who Should Read This Book?

This book teaches you how to use Visual C++ to build 32-bit Windows applications, including database applications, Internet applications, and applications that tap the power of the ActiveX technology. That's a tall order, and to fit all that in less than a thousand pages, some things have to go. This book does not teach you the following:

- *The C++ programming language*: You should already be familiar with C++. Appendix A, "C++ Review and Object-Oriented Concepts," is a review for those whose C++ skills need a boost.
- *How to use Windows applications*: You should be a proficient Windows user, able to resize and move windows, double-click, and recognize familiar toolbar buttons, for example.
- *How to use Visual C++ as a C compiler*: If you already work in C, you can use Visual C++ as your compiler, but new developers should take the plunge into C++.
- *Windows programming without MFC*: This, too, is okay for those who know it, but not something to learn now that MFC exists.
- *The internals of ActiveX programming*: This is referred to in the ActiveX chapters, which tell you only what you need to know to make it work.

You should read this book if you fit one of these categories:

- You know some C++ and some Windows programming techniques and are new to Visual C++. You will learn the product much more quickly than you would if you just tried writing programs.
- You've been working with previous versions of Visual C++. Many times users learn one way to do things and end up overlooking some of the newer productivity features.
- You've been working with Visual C++ 6 for a while and are beginning to suspect you're doing things the hard way. Maybe you are.
- You work in Visual C++ 6 regularly, and you need to add a feature to your product. For tasks like Help, printing, and threading, you'll find a "hand up" to get started.

Before You Start Reading

You need a copy of Visual C++ 6 and must have it installed. The installation process is simple and easy to follow, so it's not covered in this book.

Before you buy Visual C++ 6, you need a 32-bit Windows operating system: Windows 95, Windows 98, or Windows NT Server or Workstation. That means your machine must be reasonably powerful and modern—say, a 486 or better for your processor, at least 16MB of RAM and 500MB of disk space, and a screen that can do 800 × 600 pixel displays or even finer resolutions. The illustrations in this book were all prepared at a resolution of 800 × 600 and, as you will see, at times things become a little crowded. The sample code is all available on the Web, so following along will be simpler if you also have a modem and access to the Web.

Finally, you need to make a promise to yourself—that you will follow along in Visual C++ as you read this book, clicking and typing and trying things out. You don't need to type all the code if you don't want to: It's all on the Web site for you to look at. However, you should be ready to open the files and look at the code as you go.

What This Book Covers

A topic such as Windows programming in Visual C++ covers a lot of ground. This book contains 28 chapters and 6 reference appendixes (A to F). Be sure to look over the titles of the appendixes now and turn to them whenever you are unsure how to do something. They provide valuable references for the following:

- Appendix A, "C++ Review and Object-Oriented Concepts," reminds you of the basics of the C++ language and the principles and benefits of object-oriented programming.
- Appendix B, "Windows Programming Review and a Look Inside CWnd," covers the specifics of Windows programming that are now hidden from you by MFC classes such as CWnd.
- Appendix C, "The Visual Studio User Interface, Menus, and Toolbars," explains all the menus, toolbars, editing areas on the screens, shortcuts, and so on, that make up the highly complicated and richly powerful interface between you and Visual Studio.
- Appendix D, "Debugging," explains the extra menus, windows, toolbars, and commands involved in debugging a running application.
- Appendix E, "MFC Macros and Globals," summarizes the many preprocessor macros and global variables and functions sprinkled throughout code generated by the Developer Studio wizards.
- Appendix F, "Useful Classes," describes the classes used throughout the book to manipulate dates, strings, and collections of objects.

Depending on your background and willingness to poke around in menus and the online help, you might just skim these appendixes once and never return, or you might fill them full of bookmarks and yellow stickies. Although they don't lead you through the sample applications, they will teach you a lot.

The mainstream of the book is in Chapters 1 through 28. Each chapter teaches you an important programming task or sometimes two closely related tasks, such as building a taskbar or adding Help to an application. Detailed instructions show you how to build a working application, or several working applications, in each chapter.

The first nine chapters cover concepts found in almost every Windows application; after that, the tasks become less general. Here's a brief overview of some of the work that is covered.

Dialogs and Controls

What Windows program doesn't have a dialog box? an edit box? a button? Dialog boxes and controls are vital to Windows user interfaces, and all of them, even the simple button or piece of static text, are windows. The common controls enable you to take advantage of the learning time users have devoted to other programs and the programming time developers have put in on the operating system in order to use the same File Open dialog box as everybody else, the same hierarchical tree control, and so on. Learn more about all these controls in Chapters 2, "Dialogs and Controls," and 10, "Windows 95 Common Controls."

Messages and Commands

Messages form the heart of Windows programming. Whenever anything happens on a Windows machine, such as a user clicking the mouse or pressing a key, a message is triggered and sent to one or more windows, which do something about it. Visual C++ makes it easy for you to write code that catches these messages and acts on them. Chapter 3, "Messages and Commands," explains the concept of messages and how MFC and other aspects of Visual C++ enable you to deal with them.

The View/Document Paradigm

A *paradigm* is a model, a way of looking at things. The designers of MFC chose to design the framework based on the assumption that every program has something it wants to save in a file. That collection of information is referred to as the *document*. A *view* is one way of looking at a document. There are many advantages to separating the view and the document, explained further in Chapter 4, "Documents and Views." MFC provides classes from which to inherit your document class and your view class, so that common programming tasks such as implementing scrollbars are no longer your problem.

Drawing Onscreen

No matter how smart your Windows program is, if you can't tell the user what's going on by putting some words or pictures onscreen, no one will know what the program has done. A remarkable amount of the work is automatically done by your view classes (one of the advantages of adopting the document/view paradigm), but at times you have to do the drawing yourself. You learn about device contexts, scrolling, and more in Chapter 5, "Drawing on the Screen."

Printing on Paper

Adding printing capabilities to your program is sometimes the simplest thing in the world because the code you use to draw onscreen can be reused to draw on paper. If more than one page of information is involved, though, things become tricky. Chapter 6, "Printing and Print Preview," explains all this, as well as mapping modes, headers and footers, and more.

Persistence and File I/O

Some good things are meant to be only temporary, such as the display of a calculator or an online chat window. However, most programs can save their documents to a file and open and load that file to re-create a document that has been stored. MFC simplifies this by using archives and extending the use of the stream I/O operators >> and <<. You learn all about reading and writing to files in Chapter 7, "Persistence and File I/O."

ActiveX Programming

ActiveX is the successor to OLE, and it's the technology that facilitates communication between applications at the object level, enabling you to embed a Word document in an Excel spreadsheet or to embed any of hundreds of kinds of objects in any ActiveX application. ActiveX chapters include Chapters 13, "ActiveX Concepts," 14, "Building an ActiveX Container Application," 15, "Building an ActiveX Server Application," 16, "Building an Automation Server," and 17, "Building an ActiveX Control."

The Internet

Microsoft recognizes that distributed computing, in which work is shared between two or more computers, is becoming more and more common. Programs need to talk to each other, people need to send messages across a LAN or around the world, and MFC has classes that support these kinds of communication. The four Internet chapters in this book are Chapter 18, "Sockets, MAPI, and the Internet," Chapter 19, "Internet Programming with the WinInet Classes," Chapter 20, "Building an Internet ActiveX Control," and Chapter 21, "The Active Template Library."

Database Access

Database programming keeps getting easier. ODBC, Microsoft's Open DataBase Connectivity package, enables your code to call API functions that access a huge variety of database files— Oracle, DBase, an Excel spreadsheet, a plain text file, old legacy mainframe systems using SQL, whatever! You call a standard name function, and the API provided by the database vendor or a third party handles the translation. The details are in Chapters 22, "Database Access," and 23, "SQL and the Enterprise Edition."

Advanced Material

For developers who have mastered the basics, this book features some advanced chapters to move your programming skills forward. You will learn how to prevent memory leaks, find bottlenecks, and locate bugs in your code with the techniques discussed in Chapter 24, "Improving Your Application's Performance."

Reuse is a hugely popular concept in software development at the moment, especially with managers who see a chance to lower their development budget. If you'd like to write reusable code and components, Chapter 25, "Achieving Reuse with the Gallery and Your Own AppWizards," will take you there.

Often C++ programmers are so busy learning the basics of how to make programs work that they miss the features that make C++ truly powerful. You will learn in Chapter 26, "Exceptions and Templates," how to catch errors efficiently and how to use one set of code in many different situations.

As user demands for high-performance software continue to multiply, developers must learn entirely new techniques to produce powerful applications that provide fast response times. For many developers, writing multithreaded applications is a vital technique. Learn about threading in Chapter 27, "Multitasking with Windows Threads."

Chapter 28, "Future Explorations," introduces you to topics that are definitely not for beginners. Learn how to create console applications, use and build your own DLLs, and work with Unicode.

Conventions Used in This Book

One thing this book has plenty of is code. Sometimes you need to see only a line or two, so the code is mixed in with the text, like this:

```
int SomeFunction( int x, int y);
{
    return x+y;
}
```

You can tell the difference between code and regular text by the fonts used for each. Sometimes, you'll see a piece of code that's too large to mix in with the text: You will find an example in Listing 0.1.

Listing 0.1

```
CHostDialog dialog(m_pMainWnd);
    if (dialog.DoModal() == IDOK)
    {
        AppSocket = new CSocket();
        if (AppSocket->Connect(dialog.m_hostname,119))
        {
            while (AppSocket->GetStatus() == CONNECTING)
            {
                YieldControl();
            }
            if (AppSocket->GetStatus() == CONNECTED)
            {
             CString response = AppSocket->GetLine();
                SocketAvailable = TRUE;
            }
        }
    }
    if (!SocketAvailable)
    {
        AfxMessageBox("Can't connect to server. Please
➥ quit.",MB_OK¦MB_ICONSTOP);
    }
```

The character on the next-to-last line (➥) is called the *code continuation character*. It indicates a place where a line of code had to be broken to fit it on the page, but in reality the line doesn't break there. If you're typing code from the book, don't break the line there—keep going. If you're reading along in code that was generated for you by Visual C++, don't be confused when the line doesn't break there.

Remember, the code is in the book so that you can understand what's going on, not for you to type it. All the code is on the companion Web site as well. Sometimes you will work your way through the development of an application and see several versions of a block of code as you go—the final version is on the Web site. You'll find the site by going to **www.mcp.com/info** or **www.gregcons.com/uvc6.htm**.

 This is a Tip: a shortcut or an interesting feature you might want to know about.

N O T E This is a Note: It explains a subtle but important point. Don't skip Notes, even if you're the kind who skips Tips. ▪

CAUTION

This is a Caution, and it's serious. It warns you of the horrible consequences if you make a false step, so be sure to read all of these that you come across.

When a word is being defined or emphasized, it's in *italic*. The names of variables, functions, and C++ classes are all in `monospaced` font. Internet URLS and things you should type are in **bold**. Remember, an URL never ends with punctuation, so ignore any comma or period after the URL.

Time to Get Started

That about wraps up things for the introduction. You've learned what you need to get started, including some advanced warning about the notations used throughout the book. Jump right in, learn all about writing Windows applications with MFC, and then get started on some development of your own! Good luck and have fun.

Getting Started with Visual C++

Building Your First Windows Application

In this chapter

Creating a Windows Application

Visual C++ doesn't just compile code; it generates code. You can create a Windows application in minutes with a tool called AppWizard. In this chapter you'll learn how to tell AppWizard to make you a starter app with all the Windows boilerplate code you want. AppWizard is a very effective tool. It copies into your application the code that almost all Windows applications require. After all, you aren't the first programmer to need an application with resizable edges, minimize and maximize buttons, a File menu with Open, Close, Print Setup, Print, and Exit options, are you?

AppWizard can make many kinds of applications, but what most people want, at least at first, is an executable (.exe) program. Most people also want AppWizard to produce boilerplate code—the classes, objects, and functions that have to be in every program. To create a program like this, Choose File, New and click the Projects tab in the New dialog box, as shown in Figure 1.1.

FIG. 1.1
The Projects tab of the New dialog box is where you choose the kind of application you want to build.

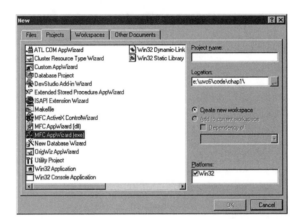

Choose MFC AppWizard (EXE) from the list box on the left, fill in a project name, and click OK. AppWizard will work through a number of steps. At each step, you make a decision about what kind of application you want and then click Next. At any time, you can click Back to return to a previous decision, Cancel to abandon the whole process, Help for more details, or Finish to skip to the end and create the application without answering any more questions (not recommended before the last step). The following sections explain each step.

N O T E   An MFC application uses MFC, the Microsoft Foundation Classes. You will learn more about MFC throughout this book. ■

Deciding How Many Documents the Application Supports

The first decision to communicate to AppWizard, as shown in Figure 1.2, is whether your application should be MDI, SDI, or dialog based. AppWizard generates different code and classes for each of these application types.

FIG. 1.2

The first step in building a typical application with AppWizard is choosing the interface.

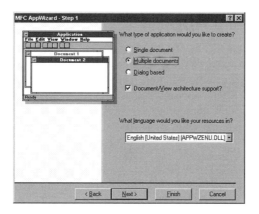

The three application types to choose from are as follows:

- A *single document interface* (SDI) application, such as Notepad, has only one document open at a time. When you choose File, Open, the currently open file is closed before the new one is opened.

- A *multiple document interface* (MDI) application, such as Excel or Word, can open many documents (typically files) at once. There is a Window menu and a Close item on the File menu. It's a quirk of MFC that if you like multiple views on a single document, you must build an MDI application.

- A *dialog-based* application, such as the Character Map utility that comes with Windows and is shown in Figure 1.3, does not have a document at all. There are no menus. (If you'd like to see Character Map in action, it's usually in the Accessories folder, reached by clicking Start. You may need to install it by using Add/Remove programs under Control Panel.)

FIG. 1.3

Character Map is a dialog-based application.

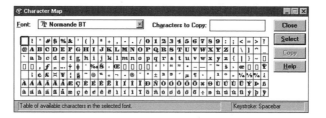

As you change the radio button selection, the picture on the left of the screen changes to demonstrate how the application appears if you choose this type of application.

N O T E   Dialog-based applications are quite different from MDI or SDI applications. The AppWizard dialogs are different when you're creating a dialog-based application. They are presented later in the section "Creating a Dialog-Based Application." ▪

Beneath these choices is a checkbox for you to indicate whether you want support for the Document/View architecture. This framework for your applications is explained in Chapter 4, "Documents and Views." Experienced Visual C++ developers, especially those who are porting an application from another development system, might choose to turn off this support. You should leave the option selected.

Lower on the screen is a drop-down box to select the language for your resources. If you have set your system language to anything other than the default, English[United States], make sure you set your resources to that language, too. If you don't, you will encounter unexpected behavior from ClassWizard later. (Of course, if your application is for users who will have their language set to U.S. English, you might not have a choice. In that case, change your system language under Control Panel.) Click Next after you make your choices.

Databases

The second step in creating an executable Windows program with AppWizard is to choose the level of database support, as shown in Figure 1.4.

FIG. 1.4

The second step to building a typical application with AppWizard is to set the database options you will use.

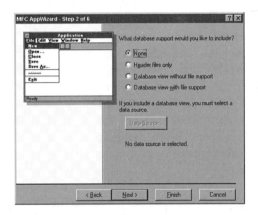

There are four choices for database support:

- If you aren't writing a database application, choose None.
- If you want to have access to a database but don't want to derive your view from CFormView or have a Record menu, choose Header Files Only.
- If you want to derive your view from CFormView and have a Record menu but don't need to serialize a document, choose Database View Without File Support. You can update database records with CRecordset, an MFC class discussed in more detail in Chapter 22, "Database Access."
- If you want to support databases as in the previous option but also need to save a document on disk (perhaps some user options), choose Database View With File Support.

Chapter 22 clarifies these choices and demonstrates database programming with MFC. If you choose to have a database view, you must specify a data source now. Click the Data Source button to set this up.

As you select different radio buttons, the picture on the left changes to show you the results of your choice. Click Next to move to the next step.

Compound Document Support

The third step in running AppWizard to create an executable Windows program is to decide on the amount of compound document support you want to include, as shown in Figure 1.5. OLE (object linking and embedding) has been officially renamed ActiveX to clarify the recent technology shifts, most of which are hidden from you by MFC. ActiveX and OLE technology are jointly referred to as *compound document technology*. Chapter 13, "ActiveX Concepts," covers this technology in detail.

FIG. 1.5

The third step of building a typical application with AppWizard is to set the compound document support you will need.

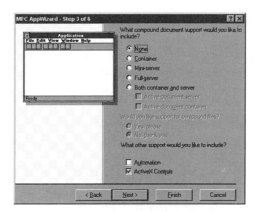

There are five choices for compound document support:

- If you are not writing an ActiveX application, choose None.

- If you want your application to contain embedded or linked ActiveX objects, such as Word documents or Excel worksheets, choose Container. You learn to build an ActiveX container in Chapter 14, "Building an ActiveX Container Application."

- If you want your application to serve objects that can be embedded in other applications, but it never needs to run as a standalone application, choose Mini Server.

- If your application serves documents and also functions as a standalone application, choose Full Server. In Chapter 15, "Building an ActiveX Server Application," you learn to build an ActiveX full server.

- If you want your application to have the capability to contain objects from other applications and also to serve its objects to other applications, choose Both Container and Server.

If you choose to support compound documents, you can also support *compound files*. Compound files contain one or more ActiveX objects and are saved in a special way so that one of the objects can be changed without rewriting the whole file. This spares you a great deal of time. Use the radio buttons in the middle of this Step 3 dialog box to say Yes, Please, or No, Thank You to compound files.

If you want your application to surrender control to other applications through automation, check the Automation check box. (Automation is the subject of Chapter 16, "Building an Automation Server.") If you want your application to use ActiveX controls, select the ActiveX Controls check box. Click Next to move to the next step.

N O T E   If you want your application to *be* an ActiveX control, you don't create a typical .exe application as described in this section. Creating ActiveX controls with the ActiveX ControlWizard is covered in Chapter 17, "Building an ActiveX Control." ▤

Appearance and Other Options

The fourth step in running AppWizard to create an executable Windows program (see Figure 1.6) is to determine some of the interface appearance options for your application. This Step 4 dialog box contains a number of independent check boxes. Check them if you want a feature; leave them unchecked if you don't.

FIG. 1.6
The fourth step of building a typical application with AppWizard is to set some interface options.

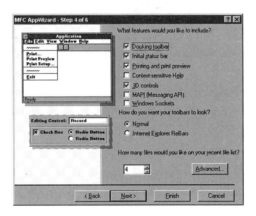

The following are the options that affect your interface's appearance:

- ▪ *Docking Toolbar.* AppWizard sets up a toolbar for you. You can edit it to remove unwanted buttons or to add new ones linked to your own menu items. This is described in Chapter 9, "Status Bars and Toolbars."

- ▪ *Initial Status Bar.* AppWizard creates a status bar to display menu prompts and other messages. Later, you can write code to add indicators and other elements to this bar, as described in Chapter 9.

■ *Printing and Print Preview.* Your application will have Print and Print Preview options on the File menu, and much of the code you need in order to implement printing will be generated by AppWizard. Chapter 6, "Printing and Print Preview," discusses the rest.

■ *Context-Sensitive Help.* Your Help menu will gain Index and Using Help options, and some of the code needed to implement Help will be provided by AppWizard. This decision is hard to change later because quite a lot of code is added in different places when implementing Context-Sensitive Help. Chapter 11, "Help," describes Help implementation.

■ *3D Controls.* Your application will look like a typical Windows 95 application. If you don't select this option, your dialog boxes will have a white background, and there will be no shadows around the edges of edit boxes, check boxes, and other controls.

■ *MAPI(Messaging API).* Your application will be able to use the Messaging API to send fax, email, or other messages. Chapter 18, "Sockets, MAPI, and the Internet," discusses the Messaging API.

■ *Windows Sockets.* Your application can access the Internet directly, using protocols like FTP and HTTP (the World Wide Web protocol). Chapter 18 discusses sockets. You can produce Internet programs without enabling socket support if you use the new WinInet classes, discussed in Chapter 19, "Internet Programming with the WinInet Classes."

You can ask AppWizard to build applications with "traditional" toolbars, like those in Word or Visual C++ itself, or with toolbars like those in Internet Explorer. You can read more about this in Chapter 9.

You can also set how many files you want to appear on the recent file list for this application. Four is the standard number; change it only if you have good reason to do so.

Clicking the Advanced button at the bottom of this Step 4 dialog box brings up the Advanced Options dialog box, which has two tabs. The Document Template Strings tab is shown in Figure 1.7. AppWizard builds many names and prompts from the name of your application, and sometimes it needs to abbreviate your application name. Until you are familiar with the names AppWizard builds, you should check them on this Document Template Strings dialog box and adjust them, if necessary. You can also change the mainframe caption, which appears in the title bar of your application. The file extension, if you choose one, will be incorporated into filenames saved by your application and will restrict the files initially displayed when the user chooses File, Open.

The Window Styles tab is shown in Figure 1.8. Here you can change the appearance of your application quite dramatically. The first check box, Use Split Window, adds all the code needed to implement splitter windows like those in the code editor of Developer Studio. The remainder of the Window Styles dialog box sets the appearance of your *main frame* and, for an MDI application, of your *MDI child frames*. Frames hold windows; the system menu, title bar, minimize and maximize boxes, and window edges are all frame properties. The main frame holds your entire application. An MDI application has a number of MDI child frames—one for each document window, inside the main frame.

FIG. 1.7

The Document Template Strings tab of the Advanced Options dialog box lets you adjust the way names are abbreviated.

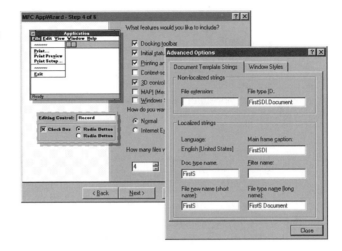

FIG. 1.8

The Window Styles tab of the Advanced Options dialog box lets you adjust the appearance of your windows.

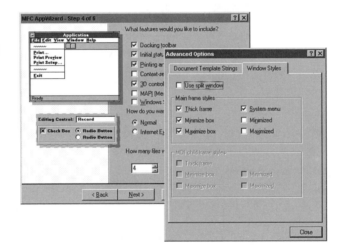

Here are the properties you can set for frames:

- *Thick Frame.* The frame has a visibly thick edge and can be resized in the usual Windows way. Uncheck this to prevent resizing.

- *Minimize Box.* The frame has a minimize box in the top-right corner.

- *Maximize Box.* The frame has a maximize box in the top-right corner.

- *System Menu.* The frame has a system menu in the top-left corner.

- *Minimized.* The frame is minimized when the application starts. For SDI applications, this option will be ignored when the application is running under Windows 95.

- *Maximized.* The frame is maximized when the application starts. For SDI applications, this option will be ignored when the application is running under Windows 95.

When you have made your selections, click Close to return to step 4 and click Next to move on to the next step.

Other Options

The fifth step in running AppWizard to create an executable Windows program (see Figure 1.9) asks the leftover questions that are unrelated to menus, OLE, database access, or appearance. Do you want comments inserted in your code? You certainly do. That one is easy.

FIG. 1.9

The fifth step of building an application with AppWizard is to decide on comments and the MFC library.

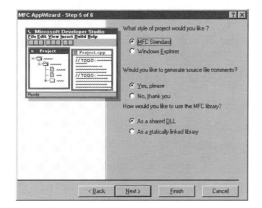

The next question isn't as straightforward. Do you want the MFC library as a shared DLL or statically linked? A *DLL* (dynamic link library) is a collection of functions used by many different applications. Using a DLL makes your programs smaller but makes the installation a little more complex. Have you ever moved an executable to another directory, or another computer, only to find it won't run anymore because it's missing DLLs? If you statically link the MFC library into your application, it is larger, but it is easier to move and copy around.

If your users are likely to be developers themselves and own at least one other application that uses the MFC DLL or aren't intimidated by the need to install DLLs as well as the program itself, choose the shared DLL option. The smaller executable is convenient for all. If your users are not developers, choose the statically linked option. It reduces the technical support issues you have to face with inexperienced users. If you write a good install program, you can feel more confident about using shared DLLs.

After you've made your Step 5 choices, click Next to move to Step 6.

Filenames and Classnames

The final step in running AppWizard to create an executable Windows program is to confirm the classnames and the filenames that AppWizard creates for you, as shown in Figure 1.10. AppWizard uses the name of the project (FirstSDI in this example) to build the classnames and filenames. You should not need to change these names. If your application includes a view class, you can change the class from which it inherits; the default is `CView`, but many developers prefer to use another view, such as `CScrollView` or `CEditView`. The view classes are discussed in Chapter 4. Click Finish when this Step 6 dialog box is complete.

 T I P   Objects, classes, and inheritance are reviewed in Appendix A, "C++ Review and Object-Oriented Concepts."

FIG. 1.10

The final step of building a typical application with AppWizard is to confirm filenames and classnames.

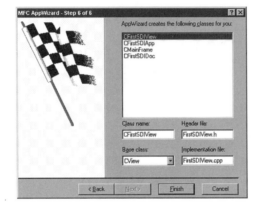

Creating the Application

After you click Finish, AppWizard shows you what is going to be created in a dialog box, similar to Figure 1.11. If anything here is wrong, click Cancel and work your way back through AppWizard with the Back buttons until you reach the dialog box you need to change. Move forward with Next, Finish; review this dialog box again; and click OK to actually create the application. This takes a few minutes, which is hardly surprising because hundreds of code lines, menus, dialog boxes, help text, and bitmaps are being generated for you in as many as 20 files. Let it work.

FIG. 1.11

When AppWizard is ready to build your application, you get one more chance to confirm everything.

Try It Yourself

If you haven't started Developer Studio already, do so now. If you've never used it before, you may find the interface intimidating. There's a full explanation of all the areas, toolbars, menus, and shortcuts in Appendix C, "The Visual Studio User Interface, Menus, and Toolbars."

Bring up AppWizard by choosing File, New and clicking the Projects tab. On the Projects tab, fill in a folder name where you would like to keep your applications; AppWizard will make a new folder for each project. Fill in **FirstSDI** for the project name; then move through the six AppWizard steps. Choose an SDI application at Step 1, and on all the other steps simply leave the selections as they are and click Next. When AppWizard has created the project, choose Build, Build from the Developer Studio menu to compile and link the code.

When the build is complete, choose Build, Execute. You have a real, working Windows application, shown in Figure 1.12. Play around with it a little: Resize it, minimize it, maximize it.

FIG. 1.12

Your first application looks like any full-fledged Windows application.

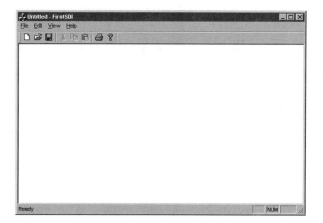

Try out the File menu by choosing File, Open; bring up the familiar Windows File Open dialog (though no matter what file you choose, nothing seems to happen); and then choose File, Exit to close the application. Execute the program again to continue exploring the capabilities that have been automatically generated for you. Move the mouse cursor over one of the toolbar buttons and pause; a ToolTip will appear, reminding you of the toolbar button's purpose. Click the Open button to confirm that it is connected to the File Open command you chose earlier. Open the View menu and click Toolbar to hide the toolbar; then choose View Toolbar again to restore it. Do the same thing with the status bar. Choose Help, About, and you'll see it even has an About box with its own name and the current year in the copyright date (see Figure 1.13).

Repeat these steps to create an MDI application called *FirstMDI*. The creation process will differ only on Step 0, where you specify the project name, and Step 1, where you choose an MDI application. Accept the defaults on all the other steps, create the application, build it, and execute it. You'll see something similar to Figure 1.14, an MDI application with a single document open. Try out the same operations you tried with FirstSDI.

FIG. 1.13

You even get an About box in this start application.

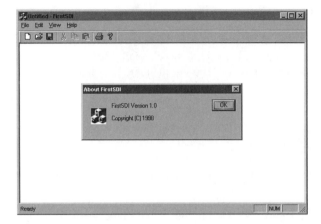

FIG. 1.14

An MDI application can display a number of documents at once.

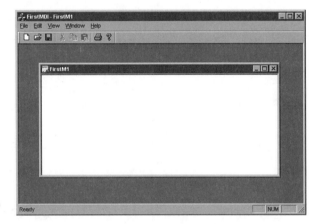

Choose File, New, and a second window, FirstM2, appears. Try minimizing, maximizing, and restoring these windows. Switch among them using the Window menu. All this functionality is yours from AppWizard, and you don't have to write a single line of code to get it.

Creating a Dialog-Based Application

A dialog-based application has no menus other than the system menu, and it cannot save or open a file. This makes it good for simple utilities like the Windows Character Map. The AppWizard process is a little different for a dialog-based application, primarily because such applications can't have a document and therefore can't support database access or compound documents. To create a dialog-based application, start AppWizard as you did for the SDI or MDI application, but in Step 1 choose a dialog-based application, as shown in Figure 1.15. Call this application **FirstDialog**.

FIG. 1.15
To create a dialog-based application, specify your preference in Step 1 of the AppWizard process.

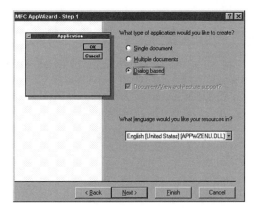

Choose Dialog Based and click Next to move to Step 2, shown in Figure 1.16.

FIG. 1.16
Step 2 of the AppWizard process for a dialog-based application involves choosing Help, Automation, ActiveX, and Sockets settings.

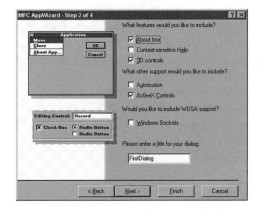

If you would like an About item on the system menu, select the About Box item. To have AppWizard lay the framework for Help, select the Context-Sensitive Help option. The third check box, 3D Controls, should be selected for most Windows 95 and Windows NT applications. If you want your application to surrender control to other applications through automation, as discussed in Chapter 16, select the Automation check box. If you want your application to contain ActiveX controls, select the ActiveX Controls check box. If you are planning to have this application work over the Internet with sockets, check the Windows Sockets box. (Dialog-based apps can't use MAPI because they have no document.) Click Next to move to the third step, shown in Figure 1.17.

As with the SDI and MDI applications created earlier, you want comments in your code. The decision between static linking and a shared DLL is also the same as for the SDI and MDI applications. If your users are likely to already have the MFC DLLs (because they are developers or because they have another product that uses the DLL) or if they won't mind installing the DLLs as well as your executable, go with the shared DLL to make a smaller executable file and a faster link. Otherwise, choose As A Statically Linked Library. Click Next to move to the final step, shown in Figure 1.18.

FIG. 1.17
Step 3 of the AppWizard process for a dialog-based application deals with comments and the MFC library.

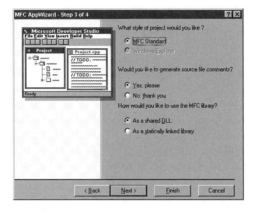

FIG. 1.18
Step 4 of the AppWizard process for a dialog-based application gives you a chance to adjust filenames and classnames.

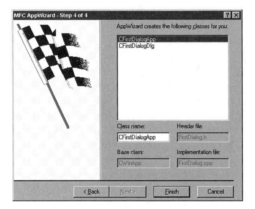

In this step you can change the names AppWizard chooses for files and classes. This is rarely a good idea because it will confuse people who maintain your code if the filenames can't be easily distinguished from the classnames, and vice versa. If you realize after looking at this dialog that you made a poor choice of project name, use Back to move all the way back to the New Project Workspace dialog, change the name, click Create, and then use Next to return to this dialog. Click Finish to see the summary of the files and classes to be created, similar to that in Figure 1.19.

If any information on this dialog isn't what you wanted, click Cancel and then use Back to move to the appropriate step and change your choices. When the information is right, click OK and watch as the application is created.

To try it yourself, create an empty dialog-based application yourself, call it *FirstDialog*, and accept the defaults for each step of AppWizard. When it's complete, choose Build, Build to compile and link the application. Choose Build, Execute to see it in action. Figure 1.20 shows the empty dialog-based application running.

FIG. 1.19
AppWizard confirms the files and classes before creating them.

Part

I

Ch

1

FIG. 1.20
A starter dialog application includes a reminder of the work ahead of you.

Clicking the OK or Cancel button, or the X in the top-right corner, makes the dialog disappear. Clicking the system menu in the top-left corner gives you a choice of Move, Close, or About. Figure 1.21 shows the About box that was generated for you.

FIG. 1.21
The same About box is generated for SDI, MDI, and dialog-based applications.

Creating DLLs, Console Applications, and More

Although most people use AppWizard to create an executable program, it can make many other kinds of projects. You choose File, New and then the Projects tab, as discussed at the start of this chapter, but choose a different wizard from the list on the left of the New dialog box, shown in Figure 1.1. The following are some of the other projects AppWizard can create:

- ATL COM AppWizard
- Custom AppWizard
- Database Project
- DevStudio Add-In Wizard
- Extended Stored Procedure AppWizard
- ISAPI Extension Wizard
- Makefile
- MFC ActiveX ControlWizard
- MFC AppWizard (dll)
- Utility Project
- Win32 Application
- Win32 Console Application
- Win32 Dynamic Link Library
- Win32 Static Library

These projects are explained in the following sections.

ATL COM AppWizard

ATL is the Active Template Library, and it's used to write small ActiveX controls. It's generally used by developers who have already mastered writing MFC ActiveX controls, though an MFC background is not required to learn ATL. Chapter 17 introduces important control concepts while demonstrating how to build an MFC control; Chapter 21, "The Active Template Library," teaches you ATL.

Custom AppWizard

Perhaps you work in a large programming shop that builds many applications. Although AppWizard saves a lot of time, your programmers may spend a day or two at the start of each project pasting in your own *boilerplate*, which is material that is the same in every one of your projects. You may find it well worth your time to build a Custom AppWizard, a wizard of your very own that puts in your boilerplate as well as the standard MFC material. After you have done this, your application type is added to the list box on the left of the Projects tab of the New dialog box shown in Figure 1.1. Creating and using Custom AppWizards is discussed in Chapter 25, "Achieving Reuse with the Gallery and Your Own AppWizards."

Database Project

If you have installed the Enterprise Edition of Visual C++, you can create a database project. This is discussed in Chapter 23, "SQL and the Enterprise Edition."

DevStudio Add-In Wizard

Add-ins are like macros that automate Developer Studio, but they are written in C++ or another programming language; macros are written in VBScript. They use automation to manipulate Developer Studio.

ISAPI Extension Wizard

ISAPI stands for Internet Server API and refers to functions you can call to interact with a running copy of Microsoft Internet Information Server, a World Wide Web server program that serves out Web pages in response to client requests. You can use this API to write DLLs used by programs that go far beyond browsing the Web to sophisticated automatic information retrieval. This process is discussed in Chapter 18.

Makefile

If you want to create a project that is used with a different make utility than Developer Studio, choose this wizard from the left list in the New Project Workspace dialog box. No code is generated. If you don't know what a make utility is, don't worry—this wizard is for those who prefer to use a standalone tool to replace one portion of Developer Studio.

MFC ActiveX ControlWizard

ActiveX controls are controls you write that can be used on a Visual C++ dialog, a Visual Basic form, or even a Web page. These controls are the 32-bit replacement for the VBX controls many developers were using to achieve intuitive interfaces or to avoid reinventing the wheel on every project. Chapter 17 guides you through building a control with this wizard.

MFC AppWizard (DLL)

If you want to collect a number of functions into a DLL, and these functions use MFC classes, choose this wizard. (If the functions don't use MFC, choose Win32 Dynamic Link Library, discussed a little later in this section.) Building a DLL is covered in Chapter 28, "Future Explorations." AppWizard generates code for you so you can get started.

Win32 Application

There are times when you want to create a Windows application in Visual C++ that doesn't use MFC and doesn't start with the boilerplate code that AppWizard produces for you. To create such an application, choose the Win32 Application wizard from the left list in the Projects tab, fill in the name and folder for your project, and click OK. You are not asked any questions; AppWizard simply creates a project file for you and opens it. You have to create all your code from scratch and insert the files into the project.

Win32 Console Application

A *console application* looks very much like a DOS application, though it runs in a resizable window. (Console applications are 32-bit applications that won't run under DOS, however.) It has a strictly character-based interface with cursor keys instead of mouse movement. You use the Console API and character-based I/O functions such as `printf()` and `scanf()` to interact with the user. Some very rudimentary boilerplate code can be generated for you, or you can have just an empty project. Chapter 28 discusses building and using console applications.

Win32 Dynamic Link Library

If you plan to build a DLL that does not use MFC and does not need any boilerplate, choose the Win32 Dynamic Link Library option instead of MFC AppWizard (dll). You get an empty project created right away with no questions.

Win32 Static Library

Although most code you reuse is gathered into a DLL, you may prefer to use a static library because that means you don't have to distribute the DLL with your application. Choose this wizard from the left list in the New Project Workspace dialog box to create a project file into which you can add object files to be linked into a static library, which is then linked into your applications.

Changing Your AppWizard Decisions

Running AppWizard is a one-time task. Assuming you are making a typical application, you choose File, New; click the Projects tab; enter a name and folder; choose MFC Application (exe); go through the six steps; create the application starter files; and then never touch AppWizard again. However, what if you choose not to have online Help and later realize you should have included it?

AppWizard, despite the name, isn't really magic. It pastes in bits and pieces of code you need, and you can paste in those very same bits yourself. Here's how to find out what you need to paste in.

First, create a project with the same options you used in creating the project whose settings you want to change, and don't add any code to it. Second, in a different folder create a project with the same name and all the same settings, except the one thing you want to change (Context-Sensitive Help in this example). Compare the files, using WinDiff, which comes with Visual C++. Now you know what bits and pieces you need to add to your full-of-code project to implement the feature you forgot to ask AppWizard for.

Some developers, if they discover their mistake soon enough, find it quicker to create a new project with the desired features and then paste their own functions and resources from the partially built project into the new empty one. It's only a matter of taste, but after you go through either process for changing your mind, you probably will move a little more slowly through those AppWizard dialog boxes.

Understanding AppWizard's Code

The code generated by AppWizard may not make sense to you right away, especially if you haven't written a C++ program before. You don't need to understand this code in order to write your own simple applications. Your programs will be better ones, though, if you know what they are doing, so a quick tour of AppWizard's boilerplate code is a good idea. You'll see the core of an SDI application, an MDI application, and a dialog-based application.

You'll need the starter applications FirstSDI, FirstMDI, and FirstDialog, so if you didn't create them earlier, do so now. If you're unfamiliar with the Developer Studio interface, glance through Appendix C to learn how to edit code and look at classes.

A Single Document Interface Application

An SDI application has menus that the user uses to open one document at a time and work with that document. This section presents the code that is generated when you create an SDI application with no database or compound document support, with a toolbar, a status bar, Help, 3D controls, source file comments, and with the MFC library as a shared DLL—in other words, when you accept all the AppWizard defaults after Step 1.

Five classes have been created for you. For the application FirstSDI, they are as follows:

- CAboutDlg, a dialog class for the About dialog box
- CFirstSDIApp, a CWinApp class for the entire application
- CFirstSDIDoc, a document class
- CFirstSDIView, a view class
- CMainFrame, a frame class

Dialog classes are discussed in Chapter 2, "Dialogs and Controls." Document, view, and frame classes are discussed in Chapter 4. The header file for CFirstSDIApp is shown in Listing 1.1. The easiest way for you to see this code is to double-click on the classname, CFirstDSIApp, in the ClassView pane. This will edit the header file for the class.

Listing 1.1   FirstSDI.h—Main Header File for the FirstSDI Application

```
// FirstSDI.h : main header file for the FIRSTSDI application
//

#if !defined(AFX_FIRSTSDI_H__CDF38D8A_8718_11D0_B02C_0080C81A3AA2__INCLUDED_)
#define AFX_FIRSTSDI_H__CDF38D8A_8718_11D0_B02C_0080C81A3AA2__INCLUDED_

#if _MSC_VER >= 1000
#pragma once
#endif // _MSC_VER >= 1000

#ifndef __AFXWIN_H__
    #error include 'stdafx.h' before including this file for PCH
#endif
```

continues

Listing 1.1   Continued

```
#include "resource.h"        // main symbols

//////////////////////////////////////////////////////////////////////////
// CFirstSDIApp:
// See FirstSDI.cpp for the implementation of this class
//
class CFirstSDIApp : public CWinApp
{
public:
    CFirstSDIApp();

// Overrides
    // ClassWizard generated virtual function overrides
    //{{AFX_VIRTUAL(CFirstSDIApp)
    public:
    virtual BOOL InitInstance();
    //}}AFX_VIRTUAL

// Implementation

    //{{AFX_MSG(CFirstSDIApp)
    afx_msg void OnAppAbout();
        // NOTE - The ClassWizard will add and remove member functions here.
        //    DO NOT EDIT what you see in these blocks of generated code!
    //}}AFX_MSG
    DECLARE_MESSAGE_MAP()
};


//////////////////////////////////////////////////////////////////////////

//{{AFX_INSERT_LOCATION}}
// Microsoft Developer Studio will insert additional declarations
// immediately before the previous line.

#endif //!defined(AFX_FIRSTSDI_H__CDF38D8A_8718_11D0_B02C_0080C81A3AA2__INCLUDED_)
```

This code is confusing at the beginning. The #if(!defined) followed by the very long string (yours will be different) is a clever form of include guarding. You may have seen a code snippet like this before:

```
#ifndef test_h
#include "test.h"
#define test_h
#endif
```

This guarantees that the file test.h will never be included more than once. Including the same file more than once is quite likely in C++. Imagine that you define a class called Employee, and it uses a class called Manager. If the header files for both Employee and Manager include, for example, BigCorp.h, you will get error messages from the compiler about "redefining" the symbols in BigCorp.h the second time it is included.

There is a problem with this approach: If someone includes test.h but forgets to set `test_h`, your code will include test.h the second time. The solution is to put the test and the definition in the header file instead, so that test.h looks like this:

```
#ifndef test_h
... the entire header file
#define test_h
#endif
```

All AppWizard did was generate a more complicated variable name than `test_h` (this wild name prevents problems when you have several files, in different folders and projects, with the same name) and use a slightly different syntax to check the variable. The `#pragma once` code is also designed to prevent multiple definitions if this file is ever included twice.

The actual meat of the file is the definition of the class `CFirstSDIApp`. This class inherits from `CWinApp`, an MFC class that provides most of the functionality you need. AppWizard has generated some functions for this class that override the ones inherited from the base class. The section of code that begins `//Overrides` is for virtual function overrides. AppWizard generated the odd-looking comments that surround the declaration of `InitInstance()`: ClassWizard will use these to simplify the job of adding other overrides later, if they are necessary. The next section of code is a message map and declares there is a function called `OnAppAbout`. You can learn all about message maps in Chapter 3, "Messages and Commands."

AppWizard generated the code for the `CFirstSDIApp` constructor, `InitInstance()`, and `OnAppAbout()` in the file firstsdi.cpp. Here's the constructor, which initializes a `CFirstSDIApp` object as it is created:

```
CFirstSDIApp::CFirstSDIApp()
{
    // TODO: add construction code here,
    // Place all significant initialization in InitInstance
}
```

This is a typical Microsoft constructor. Because constructors don't return values, there's no easy way to indicate that there has been a problem with the initialization. There are several ways to deal with this. Microsoft's approach is a two-stage initialization, with a separate initializing function so that construction does no initialization. For an application, that function is called `InitInstance()`, shown in Listing 1.2.

Listing 1.2 *CFirstSDIApp::InitInstance()*

```
BOOL CFirstSDIApp::InitInstance()
{
    AfxEnableControlContainer();

    // Standard initialization
    // If you are not using these features and want to reduce the size
    //  of your final executable, you should remove from the following
    //  the specific initialization routines you don't need.
```

continues

Listing 1.2 Continued

```
#ifdef _AFXDLL
    Enable3dControls();        // Call this when using MFC in a shared DLL
#else
    Enable3dControlsStatic();  // Call this when linking to MFC statically
#endif

    // Change the registry key under which our settings are stored.
    // You should modify this string to be something appropriate,
    // such as the name of your company or organization.
    SetRegistryKey(_T("Local AppWizard-Generated Applications"));

    LoadStdProfileSettings();  // Load standard INI file options (including
                               // MRU)

    // Register the application's document templates. Document templates
    //  serve as the connection between documents, frame windows, and views.

    CSingleDocTemplate* pDocTemplate;
    pDocTemplate = new CSingleDocTemplate(
        IDR_MAINFRAME,
        RUNTIME_CLASS(CFirstSDIDoc),
        RUNTIME_CLASS(CMainFrame),        // main SDI frame window
        RUNTIME_CLASS(CFirstSDIView));
    AddDocTemplate(pDocTemplate);

    // Parse command line for standard shell commands, DDE, file open
    CCommandLineInfo cmdInfo;
    ParseCommandLine(cmdInfo);

    // Dispatch commands specified on the command line
    if (!ProcessShellCommand(cmdInfo))
        return FALSE;

    // The one and only window has been initialized, so show and update it.
    m_pMainWnd->ShowWindow(SW_SHOW);
    m_pMainWnd->UpdateWindow();

    return TRUE;
}
```

InitInstance gets applications ready to go. This one starts by enabling the application to contain ActiveX controls with a call to AfxEnableControlContainer() and then turns on 3D controls. It then sets up the Registry key under which this application will be registered. (The Registry is introduced in Chapter 7, "Persistence and File I/O." If you've never heard of it, you can ignore it for now.)

InitInstance() goes on to register single document templates, which is what makes this an SDI application. Documents, views, frames, and document templates are all discussed in Chapter 4.

Following the comment about parsing the command line, InitInstance() sets up an empty CCommandLineInfo object to hold any parameters that may have been passed to the application when it was run, and it calls ParseCommandLine() to fill that. Finally, it calls ProcessShellCommand() to do whatever those parameters requested. This means your application can support command-line parameters to let users save time and effort, without effort on your part. For example, if the user types at the command line **FirstSDI fooble**, the application starts and opens the file called *fooble*. The command-line parameters that ProcessShellCommand() supports are the following:

Parameter	Action
None	Start app and open new file.
Filename	Start app and open file.
/p filename	Start app and print file to default printer.
/pt filename printer driver port	Start app and print file to the specified printer.
/dde	Start app and await DDE command.
/Automation	Start app as an OLE automation server.
/Embedding	Start app to edit an embedded OLE item.

If you would like to implement other behavior, make a class that inherits from CCommandLineInfo to hold the parsed command line; then override CWinApp:: ParseCommandLine() and CWinApp::ProcessShellCommand() in your own App class.

 T I P You may already know that you can invoke many Windows programs from the command line; for example, typing **Notepad blah.txt** at a DOS prompt will open blah.txt in Notepad. Other command line options work, too, so typing **Notepad /p blah.txt** will open blah.txt in Notepad, print it, and then close Notepad.

That's the end of InitInstance(). It returns TRUE to indicate that the rest of the application should now run.

The message map in the header file indicated that the function OnAppAbout() handles a message. Which one? Here's the message map from the source file:

```
BEGIN_MESSAGE_MAP(CFirstSDIApp, CWinApp)
    //{{AFX_MSG_MAP(CFirstSDIApp)
    ON_COMMAND(ID_APP_ABOUT, OnAppAbout)
        // NOTE - The ClassWizard will add and remove mapping macros here.
        //    DO NOT EDIT what you see in these blocks of generated code!
    //}}AFX_MSG_MAP
    // Standard file-based document commands
    ON_COMMAND(ID_FILE_NEW, CWinApp::OnFileNew)
    ON_COMMAND(ID_FILE_OPEN, CWinApp::OnFileOpen)
    // Standard print setup command
    ON_COMMAND(ID_FILE_PRINT_SETUP, CWinApp::OnFilePrintSetup)
END_MESSAGE_MAP()
```

This message map catches commands from menus, as discussed in Chapter 3. When the user chooses Help About, `CFirstSDIApp::OnAppAbout()` will be called. When the user chooses File New, File Open, or File Print Setup, functions from `CWinApp` will handle that work for you. (You would override those functions if you wanted to do something special for those menu choices.) `OnAppAbout()` looks like this:

```
void CFirstSDIApp::OnAppAbout()
{
    CAboutDlg aboutDlg;
    aboutDlg.DoModal();
}
```

This code declares an object that is an instance of `CAboutDlg`, and calls its `DoModal()` function to display the dialog onscreen. (Dialog classes and the `DoModal()` function are both covered in Chapter 2.) There's no need to handle OK or Cancel in any special way—this is just an About box.

Other Files

If you selected Context-Sensitive Help, AppWizard generates an .HPJ file and a number of .RTF files to give some context-sensitive help. These files are discussed in Chapter 11 in the "Components of the Help System" section.

AppWizard also generates a README.TXT file that explains what all the other files are and what classes have been created. Read this file if all the similar filenames become confusing.

There are also a number of project files used to hold your settings and options, to speed build time by saving partial results, and to keep information about all your variables and functions. These files have extensions like .ncb, .aps, .dsw, and so on. You can safely ignore these files because you will not be using them directly.

Understanding a Multiple Document Interface Application

A multiple document interface application also has menus, and it enables the user to have more than one document open at once. This section presents the code that is generated when you choose an MDI application with no database or compound document support, but instead with a toolbar, a status bar, Help, 3D controls, source file comments, and the MFC library as a shared DLL. As with the SDI application, these are the defaults after Step 1. The focus here is on what differs from the SDI application in the previous section.

Five classes have been created for you. For the application FirstMDI, they are

- `CAboutDlg`, a dialog class for the About dialog box
- `CFirstMDIApp`, a `CWinApp` class for the entire application
- `CFirstMDIDoc`, a document class
- `CFirstMDIView`, a view class
- `CMainFrame`, a frame class

The App class header is shown in Listing 1.3.

Listing 1.3 FirstMDI.h—Main Header File for the FirstMDI Application

```
// FirstMDI.h : main header file for the FIRSTMDI application
//

#if !defined(AFX_FIRSTMDI_H__CDF38D9E_8718_11D0_B02C_0080C81A3AA2__INCLUDED_)
#define AFX_FIRSTMDI_H__CDF38D9E_8718_11D0_B02C_0080C81A3AA2__INCLUDED_

#if _MSC_VER >= 1000
#pragma once
#endif // _MSC_VER >= 1000

#ifndef __AFXWIN_H__
     #error include 'stdafx.h' before including this file for PCH
#endif

#include "resource.h"        // main symbols

/////////////////////////////////////////////////////////////////////////////
// CFirstMDIApp:
// See FirstMDI.cpp for the implementation of this class
//

class CFirstMDIApp : public CWinApp
{
public:
     CFirstMDIApp();

// Overrides
     // ClassWizard generated virtual function overrides
     //{{AFX_VIRTUAL(CFirstMDIApp)
     public:
     virtual BOOL InitInstance();
     //}}AFX_VIRTUAL

// Implementation

     //{{AFX_MSG(CFirstMDIApp)
     afx_msg void OnAppAbout();
          // NOTE - The ClassWizard will add and remove member functions here.
          //    DO NOT EDIT what you see in these blocks of generated code !
     //}}AFX_MSG
     DECLARE_MESSAGE_MAP()
};


/////////////////////////////////////////////////////////////////////////////

//{{AFX_INSERT_LOCATION}}
// Microsoft Developer Studio will insert additional declarations immediately
// before the previous line.

#endif //!defined(AFX_FIRSTMDI_H__CDF38D9E_8718_11D0_B02C_0080C81A3AA2__INCLUDED_)
```

How does this differ from FirstSDI.h? Only in the classnames. The constructor is also the same as before. OnAppAbout() is just like the SDI version. How about InitInstance()? It is in Listing 1.4.

Listing 1.4   *CFirstMDIApp::InitInstance()*

```
BOOL CFirstMDIApp::InitInstance()
{
    AfxEnableControlContainer();

    // Standard initialization
    // If you are not using these features and want to reduce the size
    //  of your final executable, you should remove from the following
    //  the specific initialization routines you don't need.

#ifdef _AFXDLL
    Enable3dControls();          // Call this when using MFC in a shared DLL
#else
    Enable3dControlsStatic();    // Call this when linking to MFC statically
#endif

    // Change the registry key under which your settings are stored.
    // You should modify this string to be something appropriate,
    // such as the name of your company or organization.
    SetRegistryKey(_T("Local AppWizard-Generated Applications"));

    LoadStdProfileSettings();    // Load standard INI file options (including
                                 // MRU)

    // Register the application's document templates. Document templates
    //  serve as the connection between documents, frame windows, and views.

    CMultiDocTemplate* pDocTemplate;
    pDocTemplate = new CMultiDocTemplate(
        IDR_FIRSTMTYPE,
        RUNTIME_CLASS(CFirstMDIDoc),
        RUNTIME_CLASS(CChildFrame), // custom MDI child frame
        RUNTIME_CLASS(CFirstMDIView));
    AddDocTemplate(pDocTemplate);

    // create main MDI Frame window
    CMainFrame* pMainFrame = new CMainFrame;
    if (!pMainFrame->LoadFrame(IDR_MAINFRAME))
        return FALSE;
    m_pMainWnd = pMainFrame;

    // Parse command line for standard shell commands, DDE, file open
    CCommandLineInfo cmdInfo;
    ParseCommandLine(cmdInfo);

    // Dispatch commands specified on the command line
    if (!ProcessShellCommand(cmdInfo))
```

```
        return FALSE;

    // The main window has been initialized, so show and update it.
    pMainFrame->ShowWindow(m_nCmdShow);
    pMainFrame->UpdateWindow();

    return TRUE;
}
```

What's different here? Using WinDiff can help. WinDiff is a tool that comes with Visual C++ and is reached from the Tools menu. (If WinDiff isn't on your Tools menu, see the "Tools" section of Appendix C.) Using WinDiff to compare the FirstSDI and FirstMDI versions of InitInstance() confirms that, other than the classnames, the differences are

■ The MDI application sets up a CMultiDocTemplate and the SDI application sets up a CSingleDocTemplate, as discussed in Chapter 4.

■ The MDI application sets up a mainframe window and then shows it; the SDI application does not.

This shows a major advantage of the Document/View paradigm: It enables an enormous design decision to affect only a small amount of the code in your project and hides that decision as much as possible.

Understanding the Components of a Dialog-Based Application

Dialog applications are much simpler than SDI and MDI applications. Create one called *FirstDialog*, with an About box, no Help, 3D controls, no automation, ActiveX control support, no sockets, source file comments, and MFC as a shared DLL. In other words, accept all the default options.

Three classes have been created for you for the application called *FirstMDI*:

■ CAboutDlg, a dialog class for the About dialog box

■ CFirstDialogApp, a CWinApp class for the entire application

■ CFirstDialogDlg, a dialog class for the entire application

The dialog classes are the subject of Chapter 2. Listing 1.5 shows the header file for CFirstDialogApp.

Listing 1.5   dialog16.h—Main Header File

```
// FirstDialog.h : main header file for the FIRSTDIALOG application
//

#if !defined(AFX_FIRSTDIALOG_H__CDF38DB4_8718_11D0_B02C_0080C81A3AA2__INCLUDED_)
```

continues

Listing 1.5 Continued

```
#define AFX_FIRSTDIALOG_H__CDF38DB4_8718_11D0_B02C_0080C81A3AA2__INCLUDED_

#if _MSC_VER >= 1000
#pragma once
#endif // _MSC_VER >= 1000

#ifndef __AFXWIN_H__
    #error include 'stdafx.h' before including this file for PCH
#endif

#include "resource.h"          // main symbols

/////////////////////////////////////////////////////////////////////////////
// CFirstDialogApp:
// See FirstDialog.cpp for the implementation of this class
//

class CFirstDialogApp : public CWinApp
{
public:
    CFirstDialogApp();

// Overrides
    // ClassWizard generated virtual function overrides
    //{{AFX_VIRTUAL(CFirstDialogApp)
    public:
    virtual BOOL InitInstance();
    //}}AFX_VIRTUAL

// Implementation

    //{{AFX_MSG(CFirstDialogApp)
        // NOTE - The ClassWizard will add and remove member functions here.
        //    DO NOT EDIT what you see in these blocks of generated code !
    //}}AFX_MSG
    DECLARE_MESSAGE_MAP()
};


/////////////////////////////////////////////////////////////////////////////

//{{AFX_INSERT_LOCATION}}
// Microsoft Developer Studio will insert additional declarations immediately
// before the previous line.

#endif // !defined(AFX_FIRSTDIALOG_H__CDF38DB4_8718_11D0_B02C_0080C81A3AA2
➥__INCLUDED_)
```

CFirstDialogApp inherits from CWinApp, which provides most of the functionality. CWinApp has
a constructor, which does nothing, as did the SDI and MDI constructors earlier in this chapter,
and it overrides the virtual function InitInstance(), as shown in Listing 1.6.

Listing 1.6   FirstDialog.cpp—*CDialog16App::InitInstance()*

```
BOOL CFirstDialogApp::InitInstance()
{
    AfxEnableControlContainer();

    // Standard initialization
    // If you are not using these features and want to reduce the size
    // of your final executable, you should remove from the following
    // the specific initialization routines you don't need.

#ifdef _AFXDLL
    Enable3dControls();            // Call this when using MFC in a shared DLL
#else
    Enable3dControlsStatic();   // Call this when linking to MFC statically
#endif

    CFirstDialogDlg dlg;
    m_pMainWnd = &dlg;
    int nResponse = dlg.DoModal();
    if (nResponse == IDOK)
    {
        // TODO: Place code here to handle when the dialog is
        //   dismissed with OK
    }
    else if (nResponse == IDCANCEL)
    {
        // TODO: Place code here to handle when the dialog is
        //  dismissed with Cancel
    }

    // Because the dialog has been closed, return FALSE so that you exit the
    //  application, rather than start the application's message pump.
    return FALSE;
}
```

This enables 3D controls, because you asked for them, and then puts up the dialog box that is the entire application. To do that, the function declares an instance of CDialog16Dlg, dlg, and then calls the DoModal() function of the dialog, which displays the dialog box onscreen and returns IDOK if the user clicks OK, or IDCANCEL if the user clicks Cancel. (This process is discussed further in Chapter 2.) It's up to you to make that dialog box actually do something. Finally, InitInstance() returns FALSE because this is a dialog-based application and when the dialog box is closed, the application is ended. As you saw earlier for the SDI and MDI applications, InitInstance() usually returns TRUE to mean "everything is fine—run the rest of the application" or FALSE to mean "something went wrong while initializing." Because there is no "rest of the application," dialog-based apps always return FALSE from their InitInstance().

Reviewing AppWizard Decisions and This Chapter

AppWizard asks a lot of questions and starts you down a lot of roads at once. This chapter explains InitInstance and shows some of the code affected by the very first AppWizard decision: whether to have AppWizard generate a dialog-based, SDI, or MDI application. Most of the other AppWizard decisions are about topics that take an entire chapter. The following table summarizes those choices and where you can learn more:

Step	Decision	Chapter	Dialog
0	MFC DLL or non-MFC DLL	28, Future Explorations	
0	OCX Control	17, Building an ActiveX Control	
0	Console Application	28, Future Explorations	
0	Custom AppWizards	25, Achieving Reuse with the Gallery and Your Own AppWizard	
0	ISAPI Extension	18, Sockets, MAPI, and the Internet Wizard	
1	Language Support	28, Future Explorations	Yes
2	Database Support	22, Database Access	
3	Compound Document Container	14, Building an ActiveX Container Application	
3	Compound Document Mini-Server	15, Building an ActiveX Server Application	
3	Compound Document Full Server	15, Building an ActiveX Server Application	
3	Compound Files	14, Building an ActiveX Container Application	
3	Automation	16, Building an Automation Server	Yes
3	Using ActiveX Controls	17, Building an ActiveX Control	Yes
4	Docking Toolbar	9, Status Bars and Toolbars	
4	Status Bar	9, Status Bars and Toolbars	
4	Printing and Print Preview	6, Printing and Print Preview	
4	Context-Sensitive Help	11, Help	Yes
4	3D Controls	—	Yes

Step	Decision	Chapter	Dialog
4	MAPI	18, Sockets, MAPI, and the Internet	
4	Windows Sockets	18, Sockets, MAPI, and the Internet	Yes
4	Files in MRU list	—	
5	Comments in code	—	Yes
5	MFC library	—	Yes
6	Base class for View	4, Documents and Views	

Because some of these questions are not applicable for dialog-based applications, this table has a Dialog column *Yes* that indicates this decision applies to dialog-based applications, too. An entry of — in the Chapter column means that this decision doesn't really warrant discussion. These topics get a sentence or two in passing in this chapter or elsewhere.

By now you know how to create applications that don't do much of anything. To make them do something, you need menus or dialog controls that give commands, and you need other dialog controls that gather more information. These are the subject of the next chapter, Chapter 2, "Dialogs and Controls." ●

2

Dialogs and Controls

Understanding Dialog Boxes

Windows programs have a graphical user interface. In the days of DOS, the program could simply print a prompt onscreen and direct the user to enter whatever value the program needed. With Windows, however, getting data from the user is not as simple, and most user input is obtained from dialog boxes. For example, a user can give the application details about a request by typing in edit boxes, choosing from list boxes, selecting radio buttons, checking or unchecking check boxes, and more. These components of a dialog box are called *controls*.

Chances are that your Windows application will have several dialog boxes, each designed to retrieve a specific type of information from your user. For each dialog box that appears onscreen, there are two entities you need to develop: a *dialog box resource* and a *dialog box class*.

The dialog box resource is used to draw the dialog box and its controls onscreen. The class holds the values of the dialog box, and it is a member function of the class that causes the dialog box to be drawn onscreen. They work together to achieve the overall effect: making communication with the program easier for your user.

You build a dialog box resource with the resource editor, adding controls to it and arranging them to make the control easy to use. Class Wizard then helps you to create a dialog box class, typically derived from the MFC class CDialog, and to connect the resource to the class. Usually, each control on the dialog box resource corresponds to one member variable in the class. To display the dialog box, you call a member function of the class. To set the control values to defaults before displaying the dialog box, or to determine the values of the controls after the user is finished with the box, you use the member variables of the class.

Creating a Dialog Box Resource

The first step in adding a dialog box to your MFC application is creating the dialog box resource, which acts as a sort of template for Windows. When Windows sees the dialog box resource in your program, it uses the commands in the resource to construct the dialog box for you.

In this chapter you learn to work with dialog boxes by adding one to a simple application. Create an SDI application just as you did in Chapter 1, "Building Your First Windows Application," calling it simply SDI. You will create a dialog box resource and a dialog box class for the application, write code to display the dialog box, and write code to use the values entered by the user.

To create a dialog box resource, first open the application. Choose Insert, Resource from Developer Studio's menu bar. The Insert Resource dialog box, shown in Figure 2.1, appears. Double-click Dialog in the Resource Type box. The dialog box editor appears, as shown in Figure 2.2.

Bring up the Properties dialog box for the new dialog box by choosing View, Properties. Change the caption to **Sample Dialog**, as shown in Figure 2.3. You'll be using the Properties dialog box quite a lot as you work on this dialog box resource, so pin it to the screen by clicking the pushpin in the upper-left corner.

FIG. 2.1

Double-click Dialog on the Insert Resource dialog box.

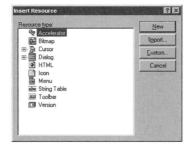

Part

I

Ch

2

FIG. 2.2

A brand new dialog box resource has a title, an OK button, and a Cancel button.

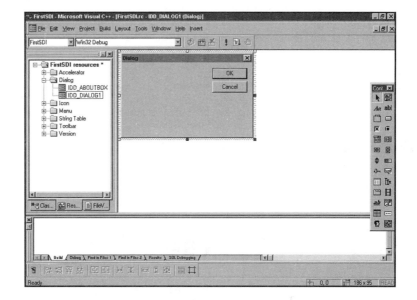

FIG. 2.3

Use the Dialog Properties dialog box to change the title of the new dialog box.

The control palette shown at the far right of Figure 2.2 is used to add controls to the dialog box resource. Dialog boxes are built and changed with a very visual WYSIWYG interface. If you need a button on your dialog box, you grab one from the control palette, drop it where you want it, and change the caption from Button1 to Lookup, or Connect, or whatever you want the button to read. All the familiar Windows controls are available for your dialog boxes:

- *Static text.* Not really a control, this is used to label other controls such as edit boxes.

- *Edit box.* Single line or multiline, this is a place for users to type strings or numbers as input to the program. Read-only edit boxes are used to display text.

- *Button.* Every dialog box starts with OK and Cancel buttons, but you can add as many of your own as you want.

- *Check box.* You use this control to set options on or off; each option can be selected or deselected independently.

- *Radio button.* You use this to select only one of a number of related options. Selecting one button deselects the rest.

- *List box.* You use this box type to select one item from a list hardcoded into the dialog box or filled in by the program as the dialog box is created. The user cannot type in the selection area.

- *Combo box.* A combination of an edit box and a list box, this control enables users to select from a list or type their response, if the one they want isn't on the list.

The sample application in this chapter is going to have a dialog box with a selection of controls on it, to demonstrate the way they are used.

Defining Dialog Box and Control IDs

Because dialog boxes are often unique to an application (with the exception of the common dialog boxes), you almost always create your own IDs for both the dialog box and the controls it contains. You can, if you want, accept the default IDs that the dialog box editor creates for you. However, these IDs are generic (for example, IDD_DIALOG1, IDC_EDIT1, IDC_RADIO1, and so on), so you'll probably want to change them to something more specific. In any case, as you can tell from the default IDs, a dialog box's ID usually begins with the prefix IDD, and control IDs usually begin with the prefix IDC. You change these IDs in the Properties dialog box: Click the control (or the dialog box background to select the entire background), and choose View, Properties unless the Properties dialog box is already pinned in place; then change the resource ID to a descriptive name that starts with IDD for a dialog and IDC for a control.

Creating the Sample Dialog Box

Click the Edit box button on the control palette, and then click in the upper-left corner of the dialog box to place the edit box. If necessary, grab a moving handle and move it until it is in approximately the same place as the edit box in Figure 2.4. Normally, you would change the ID from Edit1, but for this sample leave it unchanged.

FIG. 2.4
You can build a simple dialog box quickly in the resource editor.

 TIP If you aren't sure which control palette button inserts an edit box (or any other type of control), just hold the pointer still over one of the buttons for a short time. A ToolTip will appear, reminding you of the name of the control associated with the button. Move the pointer from button to button until you find the one for the edit box.

Add a check box and three radio buttons to the dialog box so that it resembles Figure 2.4. Change the captions on the radio buttons to **One**, **Two**, and **Three**. To align all these controls, click one, and then while holding down the Ctrl key, click each of the rest of them. Choose Layout, Align, Left, and if necessary drag the stack of controls over with the mouse while they are all selected. Then choose Layout, Space Evenly, Down, to adjust the vertical spacing.

 TIP The commands on the Layout menu are also on the Dialog toolbar, which appears at the bottom of your screen while you are using the resource editor. The toolbar symbols are repeated on the menu to help you learn which button is associated with each menu item.

Click the One radio button again and bring up the Properties dialog box. Select the Group check box. This indicates that this is the first of a group of buttons. When you select a radio button, all the other buttons in the group are deselected.

Add a list box to the dialog box, to the right of the radio buttons, and resize it to match Figure 2.4. With the list box highlighted, choose View, Properties to bring up the Properties dialog box if it is not still pinned in place. Select the Styles tab and make sure that the Sort box is not selected. When this box is selected, the strings in your list box are automatically presented in alphabetical order. For this application, they should be presented in the order that they are added.

Writing a Dialog Box Class

When the resource is complete, bring up ClassWizard by choosing View, ClassWizard. ClassWizard recognizes that this new dialog box resource does not have a class associated with it and offers to build one for you, as shown in Figure 2.5. Leave the Create a New Class radio button selected, and click OK. The New Class dialog box appears, as shown in Figure 2.6. Fill in the classname as **CSdiDialog** and click OK. ClassWizard creates a new class, prepares the source file (SdiDialog.cpp) and header file (SdiDialog.h), and adds them to your project.

FIG. 2.5

ClassWizard makes
sure you don't forget to
create a class to go
with your new dialog
box resource.

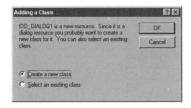

 You connect the dialog box resources to your code with the Member Variables tab of ClassWizard, shown in Figure 2.7. Click IDC_CHECK1 and then click the Add Variable button. This brings up the Add Member Variable dialog box, shown in Figure 2.8.

FIG. 2.6

Creating a dialog box
class is simple with
ClassWizard.

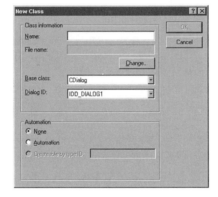

FIG. 2.7

The Member Variables
tab of ClassWizard
connects dialog box
controls to dialog box
class member variables.

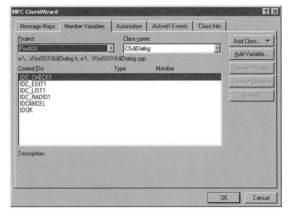

A member variable in the new dialog box class can be connected to a control's value or to the control. This sample demonstrates both kinds of connection. For IDC_CHECK1, fill in the variable name as **m_check**, and make sure that the Category drop-down box has Value selected. If you open the Variable Type drop-down box, you will see that the only possible choice is BOOL. Because a check box can be either selected or not selected, it can be connected only to a BOOL variable, which holds the value TRUE or FALSE. Click OK to complete the connection.

FIG. 2.8

You choose the name for the member variable associated with each control.

Here are the data types that go with each control type:

- *Edit box.* Usually a string but also can be other data types, including int, float, and long
- *Check box.* int
- *Radio button.* int
- *List box.* String
- *Combo box.* String
- *Scrollbar.* int

Connect IDC_EDIT1 in the same way, to a member variable called m_edit of type CString as a Value. Connect IDC_LIST1 as a Control to a member variable called m_listbox of type CListBox. Connect IDC_RADIO_1, the first of the group of radio buttons, as a Value to an int member variable called m_radio.

After you click OK to add the variable, ClassWizard offers, for some kinds of variables, the capability to validate the user's data entry. For example, when an edit control is selected, a field under the variables list allows you to set the maximum number of characters the user can enter into the edit box (see Figure 2.9). Set it to 10 for m_edit. If the edit box is connected to a number (int or float), this area of ClassWizard is used to specify minimum or maximum values for the number entered by the user. The error messages asking the user to try again are generated automatically by MFC with no work on your part.

FIG. 2.9

Enter a number in the Maximum Characters field to limit the length of a user's entry.

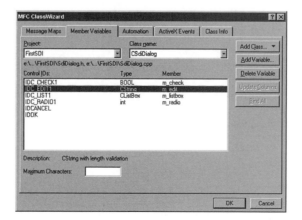

Using the Dialog Box Class

Now that you have your dialog box resource built and your dialog box class written, you can create objects of that class within your program and display the associated dialog box element. The first step is to decide what will cause the dialog box to display. Typically, it is a menu choice, but because adding menu items and connecting them to code are not covered until Chapter 8, "Building a Complete Application: ShowString," you can simply have the dialog box display when the application starts running. To display the dialog box, you call the `DoModal()` member function of the dialog box class.

Modeless Dialog Boxes

Most of the dialog boxes you will code will be modal dialog boxes. A modal dialog box is on top of all the other windows in the application: The user must deal with the dialog box and then close it before going on to other work. An example of this is the dialog box that comes up when the user chooses File, Open in any Windows application.

A modeless dialog box enables the user to click the underlying application and do some other work and then return to the dialog box. An example of this is the dialog box that comes up when the user chooses Edit, Find in many Windows applications.

Displaying a modeless dialog box is more difficult than displaying a modal one. The dialog box object, the instance of the dialog box class, must be managed carefully. Typically, it is created with `new` and destroyed with `delete` when the user closes the dialog box with Cancel or OK. You have to override a number of functions within the dialog box class. In short, you should be familiar and comfortable with modal dialog boxes before you attempt to use a modeless dialog box. When you're ready, look at the Visual C++ sample called MODELESS that comes with Developer Studio. The fastest way to open this sample is by searching for MODELESS in InfoViewer. Searching in InfoViewer is covered in Appendix C, "The Visual Studio User Interface, Menus, and Toolbars."

Arranging to Display the Dialog Box

Select the ClassView in the project workspace pane, expand the SDI Classes item, and then expand CSdiApp. Double-click the `InitInstance()` member function. This function is called whenever the application starts. Scroll to the top of the file, and after the other `#include` statements, add this directive:

```
#include "sdidialog.h"
```

This ensures that the compiler knows what a CSdiDialog class is when it compiles this file.

Double-click `InitInstance()` in the ClassView again to bring the cursor to the beginning of the function. Scroll down to the end of the function, and just before the return at the end of the function, add the lines in Listing 2.1.

Listing 2.1 SDI.CPP—Lines to Add at the End of *CSdiApp::InitInstance()*

```
CSdiDialog dlg;
dlg.m_check = TRUE;
dlg.m_edit = "hi there";
CString msg;
if (dlg.DoModal() == IDOK)
{
    msg = "You clicked OK. ";
}
else
{
    msg = "You cancelled. ";
}
msg += "Edit box is: ";
msg += dlg.m_edit;
AfxMessageBox (msg);
```

Part

I

Ch

2

Entering Code

As you enter code into this file, you may want to take advantage of a feature that makes its debut in this version of Visual C++: Autocompletion. Covered in more detail in Appendix C, Autocompletion saves you the trouble of remembering all the member variables and functions of a class. If you type dlg. and then pause, a window will appear, listing all the member variables and functions of the class CSdiDialog, including those it inherited from its base class. If you start to type the variable you want—for example, typing m_—the list will scroll to variables starting with m_. Use the arrow keys to select the one you want, and press Space to select it and continue typing code. You are sure to find this feature a great time saver. If the occasional pause as you type bothers you, Autocompletion can be turned off by choosing Tools, Options and clicking the Editor tab. Deselect the parts of Autocompletion you no longer want.

This code first creates an instance of the dialog box class. It sets the check box and edit box to simple default values. (The list box and radio buttons are a little more complex and are added later in this chapter, in "Using a List Box Control" and "Using Radio Buttons.") The dialog box displays onscreen by calling its DoModal() function, which returns a number represented by IDOK if the user clicks OK and IDCANCEL if the user clicks Cancel. The code then builds a message and displays it with the AfxMessageBox function.

N O T E The CString class has a number of useful member functions and operator overloads. As you see here, the += operator tacks characters onto the end of a string. For more about the CString class, consult Appendix F, "Useful Classes." ■

Build the project by choosing Build, Build or by clicking the Build button on the Build toolbar. Run the application by choosing Build, Execute or by clicking the Execute Program button on the Build toolbar. You will see that the dialog box displays with the default values you just coded, as shown in Figure 2.10. Change them, and click OK. You should get a message box telling you what you did, such as the one in Figure 2.11. Now the program sits there, ready to go, but because there is no more for it to do, you can close it by choosing File, Exit or by clicking the – in the top-right corner.

FIG. 2.10

Your application displays the dialog box when it first runs.

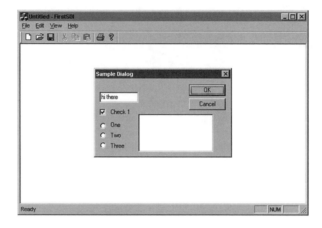

FIG. 2.11

After you click OK, the application echoes the contents of the edit control.

Run it again, change the contents of the edit box, and this time click Cancel on the dialog box. Notice in Figure 2.12 that the edit box is reported as still hi there. This is because MFC does not copy the control values into the member variables when the user clicks Cancel. Again, just close the application after the dialog box is gone.

FIG. 2.12

When you click Cancel, the application ignores any changes you made.

Be sure to try entering more characters into the edit box than the 10 you specified with ClassWizard. You will find you cannot type more than 10 characters—the system just beeps at you. If you try to paste in something longer than 10 characters, only the first 10 characters appear in the edit box.

Behind the Scenes

You may be wondering what's going on here. When you click OK on the dialog box, MFC arranges for a function called OnOK() to be called. This function is inherited from CDialog, the base class for CSdiDialog. Among other things, it calls a function called DoDataExchange(), which ClassWizard wrote for you. Here's how it looks at the moment:

```
void CSdiDialog::DoDataExchange(CDataExchange* pDX)
{
    CDialog::DoDataExchange(pDX);
    //{{AFX_DATA_MAP(CSdiDialog)
    DDX_Control(pDX, IDC_LIST1, m_listbox);
    DDX_Check(pDX, IDC_CHECK1, m_check);
    DDX_Text(pDX, IDC_EDIT1, m_edit);
    DDV_MaxChars(pDX, m_edit, 10);
    DDX_Radio(pDX, IDC_RADIO1, m_radio);
    //}}AFX_DATA_MAP
}
```

Part

I

Ch

2

The functions with names that start with DDX all perform data exchange: Their second parameter is the resource ID of a control, and the third parameter is a member variable in this class. This is the way that ClassWizard connected the controls to member variables—by generating this code for you. Remember that ClassWizard also added these variables to the dialog box class by generating code in the header file that declares them.

There are 34 functions whose names begin with DDX: one for each type of data that might be exchanged between a dialog box and a class. Each has the type in its name. For example, DDX_Check is used to connect a check box to a BOOL member variable. DDX_Text is used to connect an edit box to a CString member variable. ClassWizard chooses the right function name when you make the connection.

> **N O T E** Some DDX functions are not generated by ClassWizard. For example, when you connect a list box as a Value, your only choice for type is CString. Choosing that causes ClassWizard to generate a call to DDX_LBString(), which connects the selected string in the list box to a CString member variable. There are cases when the integer index into the list box might be more useful, and there is a DDX_LBIndex() function that performs that exchange. You can add code to DoDataExchange(), outside the special ClassWizard comments, to make this connection. If you do so, remember to add the member variable to the class yourself. You can find the full list of DDX functions in the online documentation. ▪

Functions with names that start with DDV perform data validation. ClassWizard adds a call to DDV_MaxChars right after the call to DDX_Text that filled m_edit with the contents of IDC_EDIT1. The second parameter of the call is the member variable name, and the third is the limit: how many characters can be in the string. If a user ever managed to get extra characters into a length-validated string, the DDV_MaxChars() function contains code that puts up a warning box and gets the user to try again. You can just set the limit and count on its being enforced.

Using a List Box Control

Dealing with the list box is more difficult because only while the dialog box is onscreen is the list box control a real window. You cannot call a member function of the list box control class unless the dialog box is onscreen. (This is true of any control that you access as a control rather than as a value.) This means that you must initialize the list box (fill it with strings) and use it (determine which string is selected) in functions that are called by MFC while the dialog box is onscreen.

When it is time to initialize the dialog box, just before it displays onscreen, a CDialog function named OnInitDialog() is called. Although the full explanation of what you are about to do will have to wait until Chapter 3, "Messages and Commands," follow the upcoming steps to add the function to your class.

In ClassView, right-click CSdiDialog and choose Add Windows Message Handler. The New Windows Message and Event Handlers dialog box shown in Figure 2.13 appears. Choose WM_INITDIALOG from the list and click Add Handler. The message name disappears from the left list and appears in the right list. Click it and then click Edit Existing to see the code.

FIG. 2.13

The New Windows
Message and Event
Handlers dialog box
helps you override
OnInitDialog().

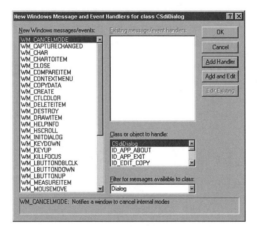

Remove the TODO comment and add calls to the member functions of the list box so that the function is as shown in Listing 2.2.

Listing 2.2   SDIDIALOG.CPP—*CSdiDialog::OnInitDialog()*

```
BOOL CSdiDialog::OnInitDialog()
{
    CDialog::OnInitDialog();

    m_listbox.AddString("First String");
    m_listbox.AddString("Second String");
    m_listbox.AddString("Yet Another String");
    m_listbox.AddString("String Number Four");
```

```
m_listbox.SetCurSel(2);

return TRUE;  // return TRUE unless you set the focus to a control
              // EXCEPTION: OCX Property Pages should return FALSE
}
```

This function starts by calling the base class version of `OnInitDialog()` to do whatever behind-the-scenes work MFC does when dialog boxes are initialized. Then it calls the list box member function `AddString()` which, as you can probably guess, adds a string to the list box. The strings will be displayed to the user in the order that they were added with `AddString()`. The final call is to `SetCurSel()`, which sets the current selection. As you see when you run this program, the index you pass to `SetCurSel()` is zero based, which means that item 2 is the third in the list, counting 0, 1, 2.

Part

I

Ch

2

> **N O T E**   Usually, the strings of a list box are not hardcoded like this. To set them from elsewhere in your program, you have to add a `CStringArray` member variable to the dialog box class and a function to add strings to that array. The `OnInitDialog()` would use the array to fill the list box. Alternatively, you can use another one of MFC's collection classes or even fill the list box from a database. For more about `CStringArray` and other MFC collection classes, consult Appendix F. Database programming is covered in Chapter 22, "Database Access." ■

In order to have the message box display some indication of what was selected in the list box, you have to add another member variable to the dialog box class. This member variable will be set as the dialog box closes and can be accessed after it is closed. In ClassView, right-click `CSdiDialog` and choose Add Member Variable. Fill in the dialog box, as shown in Figure 2.14, and then click OK. This adds the declaration of the `CString` called `m_selected` to the header file for you. (If the list box allowed multiple selections, you would have to use a `CStringArray` to hold the list of selected items.) Strictly speaking, the variable should be private, and you should either add a public accessor function or make `CSdiApp::InitInstance()` a friend function to `CSdiDialog` in order to be truly object oriented. Here you take an excusable shortcut. The general rule still holds: Member variables should be private.

FIG. 2.14
Add a `CString` to your class to hold the string that was selected in the list box.

> **T I P**   Object-oriented concepts (such as accessor functions), friend functions, and the reasoning behind private member variables are discussed in Appendix A, "C++ Review and Object-Oriented Concepts."

This new member variable is used to hold the string that the user selected. It is set when the user clicks OK or Cancel. To add a function that is called when the user clicks OK, follow these steps:

1. Right-click `CSdiDialog` in the ClassView, and choose Add Windows Message Handler.
2. In the New Windows Message and Event Handlers dialog box, shown in Figure 2.15, highlight ID_OK in the list box at the lower right, labeled Class or Object to Handle.

FIG. 2.15

Add a function to handle the user's clicking OK on your dialog box.

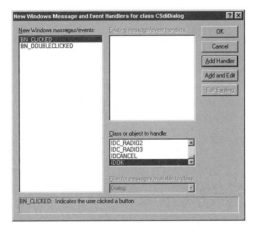

3. In the far right list box, select BN_CLICKED. You are adding a function to handle the user's clicking the OK button once.
4. Click the Add Handler button. The Add Member Function dialog box shown in Figure 2.16 appears.

FIG. 2.16

ClassWizard suggests a very good name for this event handler: Do not change it.

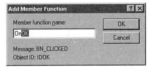

5. Accept the suggested name, `OnOK()`, by clicking OK.
6. Click the Edit Existing button to edit the code, and add lines as shown in Listing 2.3.

Listing 2.3   SDIDIALOG.CPP—*CSdiDialog::OnOK()*

```
void CSdiDialog::OnOK()
{
    int index = m_listbox.GetCurSel();
    if (index != LB_ERR)
    {
        m_listbox.GetText(index, m_selected);
    }
```

```
else
{
    m_selected = "";
}


CDialog::OnOK();
}
```

This code calls the list box member function GetCurSel(), which returns a constant represented by LB_ERR if there is no selection or if more than one string has been selected. Otherwise, it returns the zero-based index of the selected string. The GetText() member function fills m_selected with the string at position index. After filling this member variable, this function calls the base class OnOK() function to do the other processing required.

In a moment you will add lines to CSdiApp::InitInstance() to mention the selected string in the message box. Those lines will execute whether the user clicks OK or Cancel, so you need to add a function to handle the user's clicking Cancel. Simply follow the numbered steps for adding OnOK, except that you choose ID_CANCEL from the top-right box and agree to call the function OnCancel. The code, as shown in Listing 2.4, resets m_selected because the user canceled the dialog box.

Listing 2.4 SDIDIALOG.CPP—*CSdiDialog::OnCancel()*

```
void CSdiDialog::OnCancel()
{
    m_selected = "";
    CDialog::OnCancel();
}
```

Add these lines to CSdiApp::InitInstance() just before the call to AfxMessageBox():

```
msg += ". List Selection: ";
msg += dlg.m_selected;
```

Build the application, run it, and test it. Does it work as you expect? Does it resemble Figure 2.17?

FIG. 2.17

Your application now displays strings in the list box.

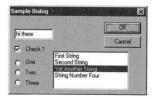

[handwritten] code for buttons are added as member handles for specific classes they are in

Using Radio Buttons

You may have already noticed that when the dialog box first appears onscreen, none of the radio buttons are selected. You can arrange for one of them to be selected by default: Simply add two lines to `CSdiDialog::OnInitDialog()`. These lines set the second radio button and save the change to the dialog box:

```
m_radio = 1;
UpdateData(FALSE);
```

You may recall that `m_radio` is the member variable to which the group of radio buttons is connected. It is a zero-based index into the group of buttons, indicating which one is selected. Button 1 is the second button. The call to `UpdateData()` refreshes the dialog box controls with the member variable values. The parameter indicates the direction of transfer: `UpdateData(TRUE)` would refresh the member variables with the control values, wiping out the setting of `m_radio` you just made.

Unlike list boxes, a group of radio buttons can be accessed after the dialog box is no longer onscreen, so you won't need to add code to `OnOK()` or `OnCancel()`. However, you have a problem: how to convert the integer selection into a string to tack on the end of `msg`. There are lots of approaches, including the `Format()` function of `CString`, but in this case, because there are not many possible selections, a `switch` statement is readable and quick. At the end of `CSdiApp::InitInstance()`, add the lines in Listing 2.5 just before the call to `AfxMessageBox()`.

Listing 2.5   SDIDIALOG.CPP—Lines to Add to *CSdiApp::InitInstance()*

```
msg += "\r\n";
msg += "Radio Selection: ";

switch (dlg.m_radio)
{
case 0:
    msg += "0";
    break;
case 1:
    msg += "1";
    break;
case 2:
    msg += "2";
    break;
default:
    msg += "none";
    break;
}
```

\r = return
\n = new line

The first new line adds two special characters to the message. *Return*, represented by \r, and *new line*, represented by \n, combine to form the Windows end-of-line marker. This adds a line break after the part of the message you have built so far. The rest of `msg` will appear on the second line of the message box. The `switch` statement is an ordinary piece of C++ code, which was also present in C. It executes one of the `case` statements, depending on the value of `dlg.m_radio`.

Once again, build and test the application. Any surprises? It should resemble Figure 2.18. You are going to be building and using dialog boxes throughout this book, so take the time to understand how this application works and what it does. You may want to step through it with the debugger and watch it in action. You can read all about debugging in Chapter 24, "Improving Your Application's Performance," and in Appendix D, "Debugging."

FIG. 2.18

Your application now selects Button Two by default.

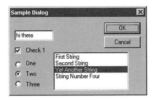

Messages and Commands

Understanding Message Routing

If there is one thing that sets Windows programming apart from other kinds of programming, it is messages. Most DOS programs, for example, relied on watching (sometimes called *polling*) possible sources of input like the keyboard or the mouse to await input from them. A program that wasn't polling the mouse would not react to mouse input. In contrast, everything that happens in a Windows program is mediated by messages. A message is a way for the operating system to tell an application that something has happened—for example, the user has typed, clicked, or moved the mouse, or the printer has become available. A window (and every screen element is a window) can also send a message to another window, and typically most windows react to messages by passing a slightly different message along to another window. MFC has made it much easier to deal with messages, but you must understand what is going on beneath the surface.

Messages are all referred to by their names, though the operating system uses integers to refer to them. An enormous list of #define statements connects names to numbers and lets Windows programmers talk about WM_PAINT or WM_SIZE or whatever message they need to talk about. (The WM stands for Window Message.) An excerpt from that list is shown in Listing 3.1.

Listing 3.1   Excerpt from winuser.h Defining Message Names

```
#define WM_SETFOCUS              0x0007
#define WM_KILLFOCUS             0x0008
#define WM_ENABLE                0x000A
#define WM_SETREDRAW             0x000B
#define WM_SETTEXT               0x000C
#define WM_GETTEXT               0x000D
#define WM_GETTEXTLENGTH         0x000E
#define WM_PAINT                 0x000F
#define WM_CLOSE                 0x0010
#define WM_QUERYENDSESSION       0x0011
#define WM_QUIT                  0x0012
#define WM_QUERYOPEN             0x0013
#define WM_ERASEBKGND            0x0014
#define WM_SYSCOLORCHANGE        0x0015
#define WM_ENDSESSION            0x0016
```

As well as a name, a message knows what window it is for and can have up to two parameters. (Often, several different values are packed into these parameters, but that's another story.)

Different messages are handled by different parts of the operating system or your application. For example, when the user moves the mouse over a window, the window receives a WM_MOUSEMOVE message, which it almost certainly passes to the operating system to deal with. The operating system redraws the mouse cursor at the new location. When the left button is clicked over a button, the button (which is a window) receives a WM_LBUTTONDOWN message and handles it, often generating another message to the window that contains the button, saying, in effect, "I was clicked."

MFC has enabled many programmers to completely ignore low-level messages such as WM_MOUSEMOVE and WM_LBUTTONDOWN. Instead, programmers deal only with higher level messages that mean things like "The third item in this list box has been selected" or "The Submit button has been clicked." All these kinds of messages move around in your code and the operating system code in the same way as the lower level messages. The only difference is what piece of code chooses to handle them. MFC makes it much simpler to announce, at the individual class's level, which messages each class can handle. The old C way, which you will see in the next section, made those announcements at a higher level and interfered with the object-oriented approach to Windows programming, which involves hiding implementation details as much as possible inside objects.

Understanding Message Loops

Part

I

Ch

3

The heart of any Windows program is the message loop, typically contained in a WinMain() routine. The WinMain() routine is, like the main() in DOS or UNIX, the function called by the operating system when you run the program. You won't write any WinMain() routines because it is now hidden away in the code that AppWizard generates for you. Still, there is a WinMain(), just as there is in Windows C programs. Listing 3.2 shows a typical WinMain().

Listing 3.2   Typical *WinMain()* Routine

```
int APIENTRY WinMain(HINSTANCE hInstance,
             HINSTANCE hPrevInstance,
             LPSTR lpCmdLine,
             int nCmdShow)
{

    MSG msg;
    if (! InitApplication (hInstance))
     return (FALSE);

    if (! InitInstance (hInstance, nCmdShow))
     return (FALSE);

    while (GetMessage (&msg, NULL, 0, 0)){
     TranslateMessage (&msg);
     DispatchMessage (&msg);
    }
    return (msg.wParam);
}
```

In a Windows C program like this, InitApplication() typically calls RegisterWindow(), and InitInstance() typically calls CreateWindow(). (More details on this are in Appendix B, "Windows Programming Review and a Look Inside Cwnd.") Then comes the message loop, the while loop that calls GetMessage(). The API function GetMessage() fills msg with a message destined for this application and almost always returns TRUE, so this loop runs over and over until the program is finished. The only thing that makes GetMessage() return FALSE is if the message it receives is WM_QUIT.

`TranslateMessage()` is an API function that streamlines dealing with keyboard messages. Most of the time, you don't need to know that "the A key just went down" or "the A key just went up," and so on. It's enough to know that "the user pressed A." `TranslateMessage()` deals with that. It catches the `WM_KEYDOWN` and `WM_KEYUP` messages and usually sends a `WM_CHAR` message in their place. Of course, with MFC, most of the time you don't care that the user pressed A. The user types into an edit box or similar control, and you can retrieve the entire string out of it later, when the user has clicked OK. Don't worry too much about `TranslateMessage()`.

The API function `DispatchMessage()` calls the `WndProc` for the window that the message is headed for. The `WndProc()` function for a Windows C program is a huge `switch` statement with one case for each message the programmer planned to catch, such as the one in Listing 3.3.

Listing 3.3   Typical *WndProc()* Routine

```
LONG APIENTRY MainWndProc (HWND hWnd, // window handle
                   UINT message, // type of message
                   UINT wParam, // additional information
                   LONG lParam) // additional information
{
    switch (message) {
    case WM_MOUSEMOVE:
        //handle mouse movement
    break;

    case WM_LBUTTONDOWN:
        //handle left click
    break;

    case WM_RBUTTONDOWN:
        //handle right click
    break;

    case WM_PAINT:
        //repaint the window
    break;

    case WM_DESTROY: // message: window being destroyed
    PostQuitMessage (0);
    break;

    default:
    return (DefWindowProc (hWnd, message, wParam, lParam));
    }

    return (0);
}
```

As you can imagine, these `WndProcs` become very long in a hurry. Program maintenance can be a nightmare. MFC solves this problem by keeping information about message processing close to the functions that handle the messages, freeing you from maintaining a giant `switch` statement that is all in one place. Read on to see how it's done.

Reading Message Maps

Message maps are part of the MFC approach to Windows programming. Instead of writing a `WinMain()` function that sends messages to your `WindProc` and then writing a `WindProc` that checks which kind of message this is and then calls another of your functions, you just write the function that will handle the message, and you add a message map to your class that says, in effect, "I will handle this sort of message." The framework handles whatever routing is required to send that message to you.

T I P If you've worked in Microsoft Visual Basic, you should be familiar with event procedures, which handle specific events such as a mouse click. The message-handling functions you will write in C++ are equivalent to event procedures. The message map is the way that events are connected to their handlers.

Message maps come in two parts: one in the .h file for a class and one in the corresponding .cpp. Typically, they are generated by wizards, although in some circumstances you will add entries yourself. Listing 3.4 shows the message map from the header file of one of the classes in a simple application called ShowString, presented in Chapter 8, "Building a Complete Application: ShowString."

Listing 3.4   Message Map from showstring.h

```
//{{AFX_MSG(CShowStringApp)
    afx_msg void OnAppAbout();
        // NOTE - the ClassWizard will add and remove member functions here.
        // DO NOT EDIT what you see in these blocks of generated code !
    //}}AFX_MSG
    DECLARE_MESSAGE_MAP()
```

This declares a function called `OnAppAbout()`. The specially formatted comments around the declarations help ClassWizard keep track of which messages are caught by each class. `DECLARE_MESSAGE_MAP()` is a macro, expanded by the C++ compiler's preprocessor, that declares some variables and functions to set up some of this magic message catching.

The message map in the source file, as shown in Listing 3.5, is quite similar.

Listing 3.5   Message Map from Chapter 8's showstring.cpp

```
BEGIN_MESSAGE_MAP(CShowStringApp, CWinApp)
    //{{AFX_MSG_MAP(CShowStringApp)
    ON_COMMAND(ID_APP_ABOUT, OnAppAbout)
        // NOTE - the ClassWizard will add and remove mapping macros here.
        //    DO NOT EDIT what you see in these blocks of generated code!
    //}}AFX_MSG_MAP
    // Standard file based document commands
    ON_COMMAND(ID_FILE_NEW, CWinApp::OnFileNew)
    ON_COMMAND(ID_FILE_OPEN, CWinApp::OnFileOpen)
    // Standard print setup command
    ON_COMMAND(ID_FILE_PRINT_SETUP, CWinApp::OnFilePrintSetup)
END_MESSAGE_MAP()
```

Message Map Macros

BEGIN_MESSAGE_MAP and END_MESSAGE_MAP are macros that, like DECLARE_MESSAGE_MAP in the include file, declare some member variables and functions that the framework can use to navigate the maps of all the objects in the system. A number of macros are used in message maps, including these:

- DECLARE_MESSAGE_MAP—Used in the include file to declare that there will be a message map in the source file.

- BEGIN MESSAGE MAP—Marks the beginning of a message map in the source file.

- END MESSAGE MAP—Marks the end of a message map in the source file.

- ON_COMMAND—Used to delegate the handling of a specific command to a member function of the class.

- ON_COMMAND_RANGE—Used to delegate the handling of a group of commands, expressed as a range of command IDs, to a single member function of the class.

- ON_CONTROL—Used to delegate the handling of a specific custom control–notification message to a member function of the class.

- ON_CONTROL_RANGE—Used to delegate the handling of a group of custom control–notification messages, expressed as a range of control IDs, to a single member function of the class.

- ON_MESSAGE—Used to delegate the handling of a user-defined message to a member function of the class.

- ON_REGISTERED_MESSAGE—Used to delegate the handling of a registered user-defined message to a member function of the class.

- ON_UPDATE_COMMAND_UI—Used to delegate the updating for a specific command to a member function of the class.

- ON_COMMAND_UPDATE_UI_RANGE—Used to delegate the updating for a group of commands, expressed as a range of command IDs, to a single member function of the class.

- ON_NOTIFY—Used to delegate the handling of a specific control-notification message with extra data to a member function of the class.

- ON_NOTIFY_RANGE—Used to delegate the handling of a group of control-notification messages with extra data, expressed as a range of child identifiers, to a single member function of the class. The controls that send these notifications are child windows of the window that catches them.

- ON_NOTIFY_EX—Used to delegate the handling of a specific control-notification message with extra data to a member function of the class that returns TRUE or FALSE to indicate whether the notification should be passed on to another object for further reaction.

- ON_NOTIFY_EX_RANGE—Used to delegate the handling of a group of control-notification messages with extra data, expressed as a range of child identifiers, to a single member function of the class that returns TRUE or FALSE to indicate whether the notification should be passed on to another object for further reaction. The controls that send these notifications are child windows of the window that catches them.

In addition to these, there are about 100 macros, one for each of the more common messages, that direct a single specific message to a member function. For example, ON_CREATE delegates the WM_CREATE message to a function called OnCreate(). You cannot change the function names in these macros. Typically, these macros are added to your message map by ClassWizard, as demonstrated in Chapter 8.

How Message Maps Work

The message maps presented in Listings 3.3 and 3.4 are for the CShowStringApp class of the ShowString application. This class handles application-level tasks such as opening a new file or displaying the About box. The entry added to the header file's message map can be read as "there is a function called OnAppAbout() that takes no parameters." The entry in the source file's map means "when an ID_APP_ABOUT command message arrives, call OnAppAbout()." It shouldn't be a big surprise that the OnAppAbout() member function displays the About box for the application.

If you don't mind thinking of all this as magic, it might be enough to know that adding the message map entry causes your code to run when the message is sent. Perhaps you're wondering just how message maps really work. Here's how. Every application has an object that inherits from CWinApp, and a member function called Run(). That function calls CWinThread::Run(), which is far longer than the simple WinMain() presented earlier but has the same message loop at its heart: call GetMessage(), call TranslateMessage(), call DispatchMessage(). Almost every window object uses the same old-style Windows class and the same WindProc, called AfxWndProc(). The WindProc, as you've already seen, knows the handle, hWnd, of the window the message is for. MFC keeps something called a *handle map*, a table of window handles and pointers to objects, and the framework uses this to send a pointer to the C++ object, a CWnd*. Next, it calls WindowProc(), a virtual function of that object. Buttons or views might have different WindowProc() implementations, but through the magic of polymorphism, the right function is called.

Part
I

Ch
3

Polymorphism

Virtual functions and polymorphism are important C++ concepts for anyone working with MFC. They arise only when you are using pointers to objects and when the class of objects to which the pointers are pointing is derived from another class. Consider as an example a class called CDerived that is derived from a base class called CBase, with a member function called Function() that is declared in the base class and overridden in the derived class. There are now two functions: One has the full name CBase::Function(), and the other is CDerived::Function().

If your code has a pointer to a base object and sets that pointer equal to the address of the derived object, it can then call the function, like this:

```
CDerived derivedobject;
CBase* basepointer;
basepointer = &derivedobject;
basepointer->Function();
```

In this case, CBase::Function() will be called. However, there are times when that is not what you want—when you have to use a CBase pointer, but you really want CDerived::Function() to be called. To indicate this, in CBase, Function() is declared to be virtual. Think of it as an instruction to the compiler to override this function, if there is any way to do it.

When Function() is declared to be virtual in the base class, CBase, the code fragment above would actually call CDerived::Function(), as desired. That's polymorphism, and that shows up again and again when using MFC classes. You use a pointer to a window, a CWnd*, that really points to a CButton or a CView or some other class derived from CWnd, and when a function such as WindowProc() is called, it will be the derived function—CButton::WindowProc() for example— that is called.

N O T E You might wonder why the messages can't just be handled by virtual functions. This would make the virtual tables enormous, and slow the application too much. The message map system is a much faster approach. ■

WindowProc() calls OnWndMsg(), the C++ function that really handles messages. First, it checks to see whether this is a message, a command, or a notification. Assuming it's a message, it looks in the message map for the class, using the member variables and functions set up by DECLARE_MESSAGE_MAP, BEGIN_MESSAGE_MAP, and END_MESSAGE_MAP. Part of what those macros arrange is to enable access to the message map entries of the base class by the functions that search the message map of the derived class. That means that if a class inherits from CView and doesn't catch a message normally caught by CView, that message will still be caught by the same CView function as inherited by the derived class. This message map inheritance parallels the C++ inheritance but is independent of it and saves a lot of trouble carrying virtual functions around.

The bottom line: You add a message map entry, and when a message arrives, the functions called by the hidden message loop look in these tables to decide which of your objects, and which member function of the object, should handle the message. That's what's really going on behind the scenes.

Messages Caught by MFC Code

The other great advantage of MFC is that the classes already catch most of the common messages and do the right thing, without any coding on your part at all. For example, you don't need to catch the message that tells you that the user has chosen File, Save As—MFC classes catch it, put up the dialog box to obtain the new filename, handle all the behind-the-scenes work, and finally call one of your functions, which must be named Serialize(), to actually write out the document. (Chapter 7, "Persistence and File I/O," explains the Serialize() function.) You need only to add message map entries for behavior that is not common to all applications.

Learning How ClassWizard Helps You Catch Messages

Message maps may not be simple to read, but they are simple to create if you use ClassWizard. There are two ways to add an entry to a message map in Visual C++ 6.0: with the main ClassWizard dialog box or with one of the new dialog boxes that add message handlers or virtual functions. This section shows you these dialog boxes for ShowString, rather than work you through creating a sample application.

The ClassWizard Tabbed Dialog Box

The main ClassWizard dialog box is displayed by choosing View, ClassWizard or by pressing Ctrl+W. ClassWizard is a tabbed dialog box, and Figure 3.1 shows the Message Maps tab. At the top of the dialog box are two drop-down list boxes, one that reminds you which project you are working on (ShowString in this case) and the other that reminds you which class owns the message map you are editing. In this case, it is the CShowStringApp class, whose message map you have already seen.

FIG. 3.1

ClassWizard makes catching messages simple.

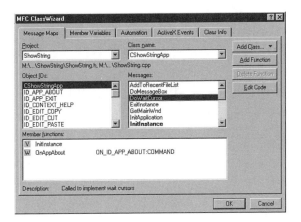

Below those single-line boxes is a pair of multiline boxes. The one on the left lists the class itself and all the commands that the user interface can generate. Commands are discussed in the "Commands" section later in this chapter. With the classname highlighted, the box on the right lists all the Windows messages this class might catch. It also lists a number of virtual functions that catch common messages.

To the right of those boxes are buttons where you can add a new class to the project, add a function to the class to catch the highlighted message, remove a function that was catching a message, or open the source code for the function that catches the highlighted message. Typically, you select a class, select a message, and click Add Function to catch the message. Here's what the Add Function button sets in motion:

- Adds a skeleton function to the bottom of the source file for the application
- Adds an entry to the message map in the source file
- Adds an entry to the message map in the include file
- Updates the list of messages and member functions in the dialog box

After you add a function, clicking Edit Code makes it simple to start filling in the behavior of that function. If you prefer, double-click the function name in the Member Functions list box.

Below the Object IDs and Messages boxes is a list of the member functions of this class that are related to messages. This class has two such functions:

- `InitInstance()`—Overrides a virtual function in `CWinApp`, the base class for `CShowStringApp`, and is labeled with a `V` (for *virtual* function) in the list.
- `OnAppAbout()`—Catches the `ID_APP_ABOUT` command and is labeled with a `W` (for Windows message) in the list.

The `InitInstance` function is called whenever an application first starts. You don't need to understand this function to see that ClassWizard reminds you the function has been overridden.

Finally, under the Member Functions box is a reminder of the meaning of the highlighted message. `called to implement wait cursors` is a description of the `DoWaitCursor` virtual function.

The Add Windows Message Handler Dialog Box

In release 5.0 of Visual C++, a new way of catching messages was added. Rather than opening ClassWizard and then remembering to set the right classname in a drop-down list box, you right-click on the classname in `ClassView` and then choose Add Windows Message Handler from the shortcut menu that appears. Figure 3.2 shows the dialog box that appears when you make this choice.

FIG. 3.2

The New Windows Message and Event Handlers dialog box is another way to catch messages.

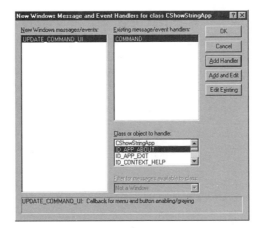

This dialog box doesn't show any virtual functions that were listed in the main ClassView dialog box. It is easy to see that this class catches the command ID_APP_ABOUT but doesn't catch the command update. (Commands and command updating are discussed in more detail later in this chapter.) To add a new virtual function, you right-click on the class in ClassView and choose Add New Virtual Function from the shortcut menu. Figure 3.3 shows this dialog box.

FIG. 3.3

The New Virtual Override dialog box simplifies implementing virtual functions.

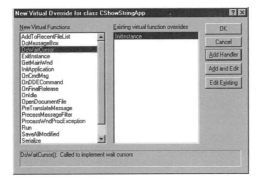

You can see in Figure 3.3 that CShowStringApp already overrides the InitInstance() virtual function, and you can see what other functions are available to be overridden. As in the tabbed dialog box, a message area at the bottom of the dialog box reminds you of the purpose of each function: In fact, the text—Called to implement wait cursors—is identical to that in Figure 3.1.

Part

I

Ch

3

Which Class Should Catch the Message?

The only tricky part of message maps and message handling is deciding which class should catch the message. That's a decision you can't make until you understand all the different message and command targets that make up a typical application. The choice is usually one of the following:

- The active view
- The document associated with the active view
- The frame window that holds the active view
- The application object

Views, documents, and frames are discussed in Chapter 4, "Documents and Views."

Recognizing Messages

There are almost 900 Windows messages, so you won't find a list of them all in this chapter. Usually, you arrange to catch messages with ClassWizard and are presented with a much shorter list that is appropriate for the class you are catching messages with. Not every kind of window can receive every kind of message. For example, only classes that inherit from CListBox receive list box messages such as LB_SETSEL, which directs the list box to move the highlight to a specific list item. The first component of a message name indicates the kind of window this message is destined for, or coming from. These window types are listed in Table 3.1.

Table 3.1   Windows Message Prefixes and Window Types

Prefix	Window Type
ABM, ABN	Appbar
ACM, ACN	Animation control
BM, BN	Button
CB, CBN	Combo box
CDM, CDN	Common dialog box
CPL	Control Panel application
DBT	Any application (device change message)
DL	Drag list box
DM	Dialog box
EM, EN	Edit box
FM, FMEVENT	File Manager
HDM, HDN	Header control

Prefix	Window Type
HKM	HotKey control
IMC, IMN	IME window
LB, LBN	List box
LVM, LVN	List view
NM	Any parent window (notification message)
PBM	Progress bar
PBT	Any application (battery power broadcast)
PSM, PSN	Property sheet
SB	Status bar
SBM	Scrollbar
STM, STN	Static control
TB, TBN	Toolbar
TBM	Track bar
TCM, TCN	Tab control
TTM, TTN	ToolTip
TVM, TVN	Tree view
UDM	Up Down control
WM	Generic window

Part
I

Ch
3

What's the difference between, say, a BM message and a BN message? A BM message is a message to a button, such as "act as though you were just clicked." A BN message is a notification from a button to the window that owns it, such as "I was clicked." The same pattern holds for all the prefixes that end with M or N in the preceding table.

Sometimes the message prefix does not end with M; for example CB is the prefix for a message to a combo box, whereas CBN is the prefix for a notification from a combo box to the window that owns it. Another example is CB_SETCURSEL, a message to a combo box directing it to select one of its strings, whereas CBN_SELCHANGE is a message sent from a combo box, notifying its parent that the user has changed which string is selected.

Understanding Commands

What is a command? It is a special type of message. Windows generates a command whenever a user chooses a menu item, clicks a button, or otherwise tells the system to do something. In older versions of Windows, both menu choices and button clicks generated a WM_COMMAND message; these days you receive a WM_COMMAND for a menu choice and a WM_NOTIFY for a control notification such as button clicking or list box selecting. Commands and notifications are passed around by the operating system just like any other message, until they get into the top of OnWndMsg(). At that point, Windows message passing stops and MFC command routing starts.

Command messages all have, as their first parameter, the resource ID of the menu item that was chosen or the button that was clicked. These resource IDs are assigned according to a standard pattern—for example, the menu item File, Save has the resource ID ID_FILE_SAVE.

Command routing is the mechanism OnWndMsg() uses to send the command (or notification) to objects that can't receive messages. Only objects that inherit from CWnd can receive messages, but all objects that inherit from CCmdTarget, including CWnd and CDocument, can receive commands and notifications. That means a class that inherits from CDocument can have a message map. There won't be any entries in it for messages, only for commands and notifications, but it's still a message map.

How do the commands and notifications get to the class, though? By command routing. (This becomes messy, so if you don't want the inner details, skip this paragraph and the next.) OnWndMsg() calls CWnd::OnCommand() or CWnd::OnNotify(). OnCommand() checks all sorts of petty stuff (such as whether this menu item was grayed after the user selected it but before this piece of code started to execute) and then calls OnCmdMsg(). OnNotify() checks different conditions and then it, too, calls OnCmdMsg(). OnCmdMsg() is virtual, which means that different command targets have different implementations. The implementation for a frame window sends the command to the views and documents it contains.

This is how something that started out as a message can end up being handled by a member function of an object that isn't a window and therefore can't really catch messages.

Should you care about this? Even if you don't care how it all happens, you should care that you can arrange for the right class to handle whatever happens within your application. If the user resizes the window, a WM_SIZE message is sent, and you may have to rescale an image or do some other work inside your view. If the user chooses a menu item, a command is generated, and that means your document can handle it if that's more appropriate. You see examples of these decisions at work in Chapter 4.

Understanding Command Updates

This under-the-hood tour of how MFC connects user actions such as window resizing or menu choices to your code is almost finished. All that's left is to handle the graying of menus and buttons, a process called *command updating*.

Imagine you are designing an operating system, and you know it's a good idea to have some menu items grayed to show they can't be used right now. There are two ways you can go about implementing this.

One is to have a huge table with one entry for every menu item and a flag to indicate whether it's available. Whenever you have to display the menu, you can quickly check the table. Whenever the program does anything that makes the item available or unavailable, it updates the table. This is called the *continuous-update approach.*

The other way is not to have a table but to check all the conditions just before your program displays the menu. This is called the *update-on-demand approach* and is the approach taken in Windows. In the old C way of doing things—to check whether each menu option should be grayed—the system sent a WM_INITMENUPOPUP message, which means "I'm about to display a menu." The giant switch in the WindProc caught that message and quickly enabled or disabled each menu item. This wasn't very object-oriented though. In an object-oriented program, different pieces of information are stored in different objects and aren't generally made available to the entire program.

When it comes to updating menus, different objects know whether each item should be grayed. For example, the document knows whether it has been modified since it was last saved, so it can decide whether File, Save should be grayed. However, only the view knows whether some text is currently highlighted; therefore, it can decide if Edit, Cut and Edit, Copy should be grayed. This means that the job of updating these menus should be parcelled out to various objects within the application rather than handled within the WindProc.

The MFC approach is to use a little object called a CCmdUI, a command user interface, and give this object to whoever catches a CN_UPDATE_COMMAND_UI message. You catch those messages by adding (or getting ClassWizard to add) an ON_UPDATE_COMMAND_UI macro in your message map. If you want to know what's going on behind the scenes, it's this: The operating system still sends WM_INITMENUPOPUP; then the MFC base classes such as CFrameWnd take over. They make a CCmdUI, set its member variables to correspond to the first menu item, and call one of that object's own member functions, DoUpdate(). Then, DoUpdate() sends out the CN_COMMAND_UPDATE_UI message with a pointer to itself as the CCmdUI object the handlers use. The same CCmdUI object is then reset to correspond to the second menu item, and so on, until the entire menu is ready to be displayed. The CCmdUI object is also used to gray and ungray buttons and other controls in a slightly different context.

CCmdUI has the following member functions:

- Enable()—Takes a TRUE or FALSE (defaults to TRUE). This grays the user interface item if FALSE and makes it available if TRUE.
- SetCheck()—Checks or unchecks the item.
- SetRadio()—Checks or unchecks the item as part of a group of radio buttons, only one of which can be set at any time.
- SetText()—Sets the menu text or button text, if this is a button.
- DoUpdate()—Generates the message.

Part

I

Ch

3

Determining which member function you want to use is usually clear-cut. Here is a shortened version of the message map from an object called CWhoisView, a class derived from CFormView that is showing information to a user. This form view contains several edit boxes, and the user may want to paste text into one of them. The message map contains an entry to catch the update for the ID_EDIT_PASTE command, like this:

```
BEGIN_MESSAGE_MAP(CWhoisView, CFormView)
    ...
    ON_UPDATE_COMMAND_UI(ID_EDIT_PASTE, OnUpdateEditPaste)
    ...
END_MESSAGE_MAP()
```

The function that catches the update, OnUpdateEditPaste(), looks like this:

```
void CWhoisView::OnUpdateEditPaste(CCmdUI* pCmdUI)
{
 pCmdUI->Enable(::IsClipboardFormatAvailable(CF_TEXT));
}
```

This calls the API function ::IsClipboardFormatAvailable() to see whether there is text in the Clipboard. Other applications may be able to paste in images or other nontext Clipboard contents, but this application cannot and grays the menu item if there is no text available to paste. Most command update functions look just like this: They call Enable() with a parameter that is a call to a function that returns TRUE or FALSE, or perhaps a simple logical expression. Command update handlers must be fast because five to ten of them must run between the moment the user clicks to display the menu and the moment before the menu is actually displayed.

Learning How ClassWizard Helps You Catch Commands and Command Updates

The ClassWizard dialog box shown in Figure 4.1 has the classname highlighted in the box labeled Object IDs. Below that are resource IDs of every resource (menu, toolbar, dialog box controls, and so on) that can generate a command or message when this object (view, dialog, and so on) is on the screen. If you highlight one of those, the list of messages associated with it is much smaller, as you see in Figure 3.4.

Only two messages are associated with each resource ID: COMMAND and UPDATE_COMMAND_UI. The first enables you to add a function to handle the user selecting the menu option or clicking the button—that is, to catch the command. The second enables you to add a function to set the state of the menu item, button, or other control just as the operating system is about to display it—that is, to update the command. (The COMMAND choice is boldface in Figure 3.4 because this class already catches that command.)

FIG. 3.4

ClassWizard enables you to catch or update commands.

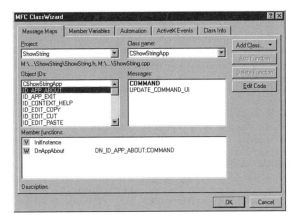

Clicking Add Function to add a function that catches or updates a command involves an extra step. ClassWizard gives you a chance to change the default function name, as shown in Figure 3.5. This is almost never appropriate. There is a regular pattern to the suggested names, and experienced MFC programmers come to count on function names that follow that pattern. Command handler functions, like message handlers, have names that start with On. Typically, the remainder of the function name is formed by removing the ID and the underscores from the resource ID and capitalizing each word. Command update handlers have names that start with OnUpdate and use the same conventions for the remainder of the function name. For example, the function that catches ID_APP_EXIT should be called OnAppExit(), and the function that updates ID_APP_EXIT should be called OnUpdateAppExit().

Naming

FIG. 3.5

It's possible, but not wise, to change the name for your command handler or command update handler from the name suggested by ClassWizard.

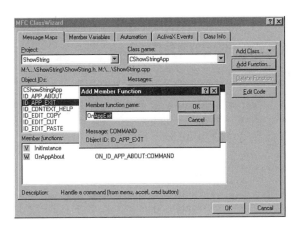

Not every command needs an update handler. The framework does some very nice work graying and ungraying for you automatically. Say you have a menu item—Network, Send—whose command is caught by the document. When there is no open document, this menu item is grayed by the framework, without any coding on your part. For many commands, it's enough

Part

I

Ch

3

that an object that can handle them exists, and no special updating is necessary. For others, you may want to check that something is selected or highlighted or that no errors are present before making certain commands available. That's when you use command updating. If you'd like to see an example of command updating at work, there's one in Chapter 8 in the "Command Updating" section. ●

Getting Information from Your Applications

CHAPTER 4

Documents and Views

In this chapter

Understanding the Document Class

When you generate your source code with AppWizard, you get an application featuring all the bells and whistles of a commercial 32-bit Windows application, including a toolbar, a status bar, ToolTips, menus, and even an About dialog box. However, in spite of all those features, the application really doesn't do anything useful. In order to create an application that does more than look pretty on your desktop, you need to modify the code that AppWizard generates. This task can be easy or complex, depending on how you want your application to look and act.

Probably the most important set of modifications are those related to the *document*—the information the user can save from your application and restore later—and to the *view*—the way that information is presented to the user. MFC's document/view architecture separates an application's data from the way the user actually views and manipulates that data. Simply, the document object is responsible for storing, loading, and saving the data, whereas the view object (which is just another type of window) enables the user to see the data onscreen and to edit that data in a way that is appropriate to the application. In this chapter, you learn the basics of how MFC's document/view architecture works.

SDI and MDI applications created with AppWizard are document/view applications. That means that AppWizard generates a class for you derived from CDocument, and delegates certain tasks to this new document class. It also creates a view class derived from CView and delegates other tasks to your new view class. Let's look through an AppWizard starter application and see what you get.

Choose File, New, and select the Projects tab. Fill in the project name as **App1** and fill in an appropriate directory for the project files. Make sure that MFC AppWizard (exe) is selected. Click OK.

Move through the AppWizard dialog boxes, changing the settings to match those in the following table, and then click Next to continue:

> Step 1: Multiple documents
>
> Step 2: Don't change the defaults presented by AppWizard
>
> Step 3: Don't change the defaults presented by AppWizard
>
> Step 4: Deselect all check boxes except Printing and Print Preview
>
> Step 5: Don't change the defaults presented by AppWizard
>
> Step 6: Don't change the defaults presented by AppWizard

After you click Finish on the last step, the New project information box summarizes your work. Click OK to create the project. Expand the App1 classes in ClassView, and you see that six classes have been created: CAboutDlg, CApp1App, CApp1Doc, CApp1View, CChildFrame, and CMainframe.

CApp1Doc represents a document; it holds the application's document data. You add storage for the document by adding data members to the CApp1Doc class. To see how this works, look at Listing 4.1, which shows the header file AppWizard creates for the CApp1Doc class.

Listing 4.1   APP1DOC.H—The Header File for the *CApp1Doc* Class

```
// App1Doc.h : interface of the CApp1Doc class
//
/////////////////////////////////////////////////////////////////////////////

#if !defined(AFX_APP1DOC_H__43BB481D_64AE_11D0_9AF3_0080C81A397C__INCLUDED_)
#define AFX_APP1DOC_H__43BB481D_64AE_11D0_9AF3_0080C81A397C__INCLUDED_
#if _MSC_VER > 1000
#pragma once
#endif // _MSC_VER > 1000
class CApp1Doc : public CDocument
{
protected: // create from serialization only
    CApp1Doc();
    DECLARE_DYNCREATE(CApp1Doc)

// Attributes
public:

// Operations
public:

// Overrides
    // ClassWizard generated virtual function overrides
    //{{AFX_VIRTUAL(CApp1Doc)
    public:
    virtual BOOL OnNewDocument();
    virtual void Serialize(CArchive& ar);
    //}}AFX_VIRTUAL

// Implementation
public:
    virtual ~CApp1Doc();
#ifdef _DEBUG
    virtual void AssertValid() const;
    virtual void Dump(CDumpContext& dc) const;
#endif

protected:

// Generated message map functions
protected:
    //{{AFX_MSG(CApp1Doc)
        // NOTE - the ClassWizard will add and remove member functions here.
        //    DO NOT EDIT what you see in these blocks of generated code !
    //}}AFX_MSG
    DECLARE_MESSAGE_MAP()
};

/////////////////////////////////////////////////////////////////////////////
```

continues

Listing 4.1   Continued

```
//{{AFX_INSERT_LOCATION}}
// Microsoft Visual C++ will insert additional declarations
// immediately before the previous line.

#endif // !defined(AFX_APP1DOC_H__43BB481D_64AE_11D0_9AF3
[ccc]    _0080C81A397C__INCLUDED_)
```

Near the top of the listing, you can see the class declaration's Attributes section, which is followed by the `public` keyword. This is where you declare the data members that will hold your application's data. In the program that you create a little later in this chapter, the application must store an array of `CPoint` objects as the application's data. That array is declared as a member of the document class like this:

```
// Attributes
public:
    CPoint points[100];
```

`CPoint` is an MFC class that encapsulates the information relevant to a point on the screen, most importantly the x and y coordinates of the point.

Notice also in the class's header file that the `CApp1Doc` class includes two virtual member functions called `OnNewDocument()` and `Serialize()`. MFC calls the `OnNewDocument()` function whenever the user selects the File, New command (or its toolbar equivalent, if a New button has been implemented in the application). You can use this function to perform whatever initialization must be performed on your document's data. In an SDI application, which has only a single document open at any time, the open document is closed and a new blank document is loaded into the same object; in an MDI application, which can have multiple documents open, a blank document is opened in addition to the documents that are already open. The `Serialize()` member function is where the document class loads and saves its data. This is discussed in Chapter 7, "Persistence and File I/O."

Understanding the View Class

As mentioned previously, the view class displays the data stored in the document object and enables the user to modify this data. The view object keeps a pointer to the document object, which it uses to access the document's member variables in order to display or modify them. Listing 4.2 is the header file for `Capp1View`, as generated by AppWizard.

 TIP Most MFC programmers add public member variables to their documents to make it easy for the view class to access them. A more object-oriented approach is to add private or protected member variables, and then add public functions to get or change the values of these variables. The reasoning behind these design principles is explored in Appendix A, " C++ Review and Object-Oriented Concepts."

Listing 4.2   APP1VIEW.H—The Header File for the *CApp1View* Class

```
// App1View.h : interface of the CApp1View class
//
/////////////////////////////////////////////////////////////////////

#if !defined(AFX_APP1VIEW_H__43BB481F_64AE_11D0_9AF3
[ccc]_0080C81A397C__INCLUDED_)
#define AFX_APP1VIEW_H__43BB481F_64AE_11D0_9AF3_0080C81A397C__INCLUDED_

#if _MSC_VER > 1000
#pragma once
#endif // _MSC_VER > 1000

class CApp1View : public CView
{
protected: // create from serialization only
    CApp1View();
    DECLARE_DYNCREATE(CApp1View)

// Attributes
public:
    CApp1Doc* GetDocument();

// Operations
public:

// Overrides
    // ClassWizard generated virtual function overrides
    //{{AFX_VIRTUAL(CApp1View)
    public:
    virtual void OnDraw(CDC* pDC);  // overridden to draw this view
virtual BOOL PreCreateWindow(CREATESTRUCT& cs);
    protected:
    virtual BOOL OnPreparePrinting(CPrintInfo* pInfo);
    virtual void OnBeginPrinting(CDC* pDC, CPrintInfo* pInfo);
    virtual void OnEndPrinting(CDC* pDC, CPrintInfo* pInfo);
    //}}AFX_VIRTUAL

// Implementation
public:
    virtual ~CApp1View();
#ifdef _DEBUG
    virtual void AssertValid() const;
    virtual void Dump(CDumpContext& dc) const;
#endif

protected:

// Generated message map functions
protected:
    //{{AFX_MSG(CApp1View)
        // NOTE - the ClassWizard will add and remove member functions here.
```

Part

II

Ch

4

continues

Listing 4.2 Continued

```
        //    DO NOT EDIT what you see in these blocks of generated code !
    //}}AFX_MSG
    DECLARE_MESSAGE_MAP()
};

#ifndef _DEBUG  // debug version in App1View.cpp
inline CApp1Doc* CApp1View::GetDocument()
   { return (CApp1Doc*)m_pDocument; }
#endif


/////////////////////////////////////////////////////////////////////////////

//{{AFX_INSERT_LOCATION}}
// Microsoft Visual C++ will insert additional declarations
// immediately before the previous line.

#endif // !defined(AFX_APP1VIEW_H__43BB481F_64AE_11D0_9AF3
[ccc] _0080C81A397C__INCLUDED_)
```

Near the top of the listing, you can see the class's public attributes, where it declares the
GetDocument() function as returning a pointer to a CApp1Doc object. Anywhere in the view class
that you need to access the document's data, you can call GetDocument() to obtain a pointer to
the document. For example, to add a CPoint object to the aforementioned array of CPoint
objects stored as the document's data, you might use the following line:

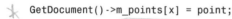

```
GetDocument()->m_points[x] = point;
```

You also can do this a little differently, of course, by storing the pointer returned by
GetDocument() in a local pointer variable and then using that pointer variable to access the
document's data, like this:

```
pDoc = GetDocument();
pDoc->m_points[x] = point;
```

The second version is more convenient when you need to use the document pointer in several
places in the function, or if using the less clear GetDocument()->variable version makes the
code hard to understand.

N O T E In release versions of your program, the GetDocument() function is inline, which means
there is no performance advantage to saving the pointer like this, but it does improve
readability. Inline functions are expanded into your code like macros, but offer type checking and other
advantages, as discussed in Appendix A. ■

Notice that the view class, like the document class, overrides a number of virtual functions
from its base class. As you'll soon see, the OnDraw() function, which is the most important of
these virtual functions, is where you paint your window's display. As for the other functions,
MFC calls PreCreateWindow() before the window element (that is, the actual Windows window) is created and attached to the MFC window class, giving you a chance to modify the

window's attributes (such as size and position). These two functions are discussed in more detail in Chapter 5, "Drawing on the Screen." OnPreparePrinting() is used to modify the Print dialog box before it displays for the user; the OnBeginPrinting() function gives you a chance to create GDI objects like pens and brushes that you need to handle the print job; and OnEndPrinting() is where you can destroy any objects you might have created in OnBeginPrinting(). These three functions are discussed in Chapter 6, "Printing and Print Preview."

N O T E When you first start using an application framework like MFC, it's easy to get confused about the difference between an object instantiated from an MFC class and the Windows element it represents. For example, when you create an MFC frame-window object, you're actually creating two things: the MFC object that has member functions and member variables, and a Windows window that you can manipulate using the functions of the MFC object. The window element is associated with the MFC class, but is also an entity unto itself. ■

Creating the Rectangles Application

Now that you've had an introduction to documents and views, a little hands-on experience should help you better understand how these classes work. In the steps that follow, you build the Rectangles application, which demonstrates the manipulation of documents and views. When you first run this application, it will draw an empty window. Wherever you click in the window, a small rectangle will be drawn. You can resize the window, or minimize and restore it, and the rectangles will be redrawn at all the coordinates where you clicked, because Rectangles keeps an array of coordinate points in the document and uses that array in the view.

Part

II

Ch

4

First, use AppWizard to create the basic files for the Rectangles program, selecting the options listed in the following table. (AppWizard is first discussed in Chapter 1, "Building Your First Windows Application." When you're done, the New Project Information dialog box appears; it should look like Figure 4.1. Click the OK button to create the project files.

Dialog Box Name	Options to Select
New Project	Name the project **recs** and set the project path to the directory into which you want to store the project's files. Leave the other options set to their defaults.
Step 1	Select Single Document.
Step 2 of 6	Leave default settings.
Step 3 of 6	Leave default settings.
Step 4 of 6	Turn off all application features except Printing and Print Preview.
Step 5 of 6	Leave default settings.
Step 6 of 6	Leave default settings.

FIG. 4.1
When you create an SDI
application with
AppWizard, the project
information summary
confirms your settings.

Now that you have a starter application, it's time to add code to the document and view classes in order to create an application that actually does something. This application will draw many rectangles in the view and save the coordinates of the rectangles in the document.

Follow these steps to add the code that modifies the document class to handle the application's data, which is an array of CPoint objects that determine where rectangles should be drawn in the view window:

1. Click the ClassView tab to display the ClassView in the project workspace window at the left of the screen.

2. Expand the recs classes by clicking the + sign before them.

3. Right-click the CRecsDoc class and choose Add Member Variable from the shortcut menu that appears.

4. Fill in the Add Member Variable dialog box. For Variable Type, enter **CPoint**. For Variable Name, enter **m_points[100]**. Make sure the Public radio button is selected. Click OK.

5. Again, right-click the CRecsDoc class and choose Add Member Variable.

6. For Variable Type, enter **UINT**. For Variable Name, enter **m_pointIndex**. Make sure the Public radio button is selected. Click OK.

7. Click the + next to CRecsDoc in ClassView to see the member variables and functions. The two member variables you added are now listed.

The m_points[] array holds the locations of rectangles displayed in the view window. The m_pointIndex data member holds the index of the next empty element of the array.

T I P   If you've programmed in C++ before and are not used to the ClassView, you can open RecsDoc.h from the FileView and add (after a public: specifier) the two lines of code that declare these variables:

```
UINT m_pointIndex;
CPoint m_points[100];
```

Now you need to get these variables initialized to appropriate values and then use them to draw the view. MFC applications that use the document/view paradigm initialize document data in a function called OnNewDocument(), which is called automatically when the application first runs and whenever the user chooses File, New.

The list of member variables and functions of CRecsDoc should still be displayed in ClassView. Double-click OnNewDocument() in that list to edit the code. Using Listing 4.3 as a guide, remove the comments left by AppWizard and initialize m_pointIndex to zero.

Listing 4.3   RECSDOC.CPP—*CRecsDoc::OnNewDocument()*

```
BOOL CRecsDoc::OnNewDocument()
{
    if (!CDocument::OnNewDocument())
        return FALSE;

    m_pointIndex = 0;

    return TRUE;
}
```

There is no need to initialize the array of points because the index into the array will be used to ensure no code tries to use an uninitialized element of the array. At this point your modifications to the document class are complete. As you'll see in Chapter 7, there are a few simple changes to make if you want this information actually saved in the document. In order to focus on the way documents and views work together, you will not be making those changes to the recs application.

Now turn your attention to the view class. It will use the document data to draw rectangles onscreen. A full discussion of the way that drawing works must wait for Chapter 5. For now it is enough to know that the OnDraw() function of your view class does the drawing. Expand the CRecsView class in ClassView and double-click OnDraw(). Using Listing 4.4 as a guide, remove the comments left by AppWizard and add code to draw a rectangle at each point in the array.

Listing 4.4   RECSVIEW.CPP—*CRecsView::OnDraw()*

```
void CRecsView::OnDraw(CDC* pDC)
{
    CRecsDoc* pDoc = GetDocument();
    ASSERT_VALID(pDoc);

    UINT pointIndex = pDoc->m_pointIndex;

    for (UINT i=0; i<pointIndex; ++i)
    {
        UINT x = pDoc->m_points[i].x;
        UINT y = pDoc->m_points[i].y;
        pDC->Rectangle(x, y, x+20, y+20);
    }
}
```

Part

II

Ch

4

Your modifications to the starter application generated by AppWizard are almost complete. You have added member variables to the document, initialized those variables in the document's `OnNewDocument()` function, and used those variables in the view's `OnDraw()` function. All that remains is to enable the user to add points to the array. As discussed in Chapter 3, "Messages and Commands," you catch the mouse message with ClassWizard and then add code to the message handler. Follow these steps:

1. Choose View, ClassWizard. The ClassWizard dialog box appears.

2. Make sure that `CRecsView` is selected in the Class Name and Object IDs boxes. Then, double-click `WM_LBUTTONDOWN` in the Messages box to add the `OnLButtonDown()` message-response function to the class. Whenever the application receives a `WM_LBUTTONDOWN` message, it will call `OnLButtonDown()`.

3. Click the Edit Code button to jump to the `OnLButtonDown()` function in your code. Then, add the code shown in Listing 4.5 to the function.

Listing 4.5   RECSVIEW.CPP—*CRecsView::OnLButtonDown()*

```
void CRecsView::OnLButtonDown(UINT nFlags, CPoint point)
{
    CRecsDoc *pDoc = GetDocument();

    // don't go past the end of the 100 points allocated
    if (pDoc->m_pointIndex == 100)
        return;

    //store the click location
    pDoc->m_points[pDoc->m_pointIndex] = point;
    pDoc->m_pointIndex++;

    pDoc->SetModifiedFlag();
    Invalidate();

    CView::OnLButtonDown(nFlags, point);
}
```

The new `OnLButtonDown()` adds a point to the document's point array each time the user clicks the left mouse button over the view window. It increments `m_pointIndex` so that the next click goes into the point on the array after this one.

The call to `SetModifiedFlag()` marks this document as modified, or "dirty." MFC automatically prompts the user to save any dirty files on exit. (The details are found in Chapter 7.) Any code you write that changes any document variables should call `SetModifiedFlag()`.

N O T E   Earlier in this chapter you were reminded that public access functions in the document have some advantages. One such advantage: Any document member function that changed a variable also could call `SetModifiedFlag()`, thus guaranteeing no programmer could forget it. ▪

Finally, the call to `Invalidate()` causes MFC to call the `OnDraw()` function, where the window's display is redrawn with the new data. `Invalidate()` takes a single parameter (with the default value `TRUE`) that determines if the background is erased before calling `OnDraw()`. On rare occasions you may choose to call `Invalidate(FALSE)` so that `OnDraw()` draws over whatever was already onscreen.

Finally, a call to the base class `OnLButtonDown()` takes care of the rest of the work involved in handling a mouse click.

You've now finished the complete application. Click the toolbar's Build button, or choose Build, Build from the menu bar, to compile and link the application. After you have the Rectangles application compiled and linked, run it by choosing Build, Execute. When you do, you see the application's main window. Place your mouse pointer over the window's client area and click. A rectangle appears. Go ahead and keep clicking. You can place up to 100 rectangles in the window (see Figure 4.2).

FIG. 4.2
The Rectangles application draws rectangles wherever you click.

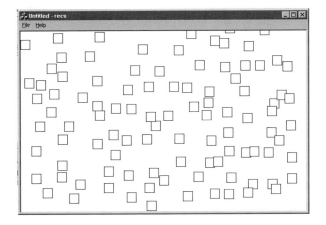

Other View Classes

The view classes generated by AppWizard in this chapter's sample applications have been derived from MFC's `CView` class. There are cases, however, when it is to your advantage to derive your view class from one of the other MFC view classes derived from `CView`. These additional classes provide your view window with special capabilities such as scrolling and text editing. Table 4.1 lists the various view classes along with their descriptions.

Table 4.1   View Classes

Class	Description
CView	The base view class from which the specialized view classes are derived
CCtrlView	A base class from which view classes that implement 32-bit Windows common controls (such as the ListView, TreeView, and RichEdit controls) are derived
CDaoRecordView	Same as CRecordView, except used with the OLE DB database classes
CEditView	A view class that provides basic text-editing features
CFormView	A view class that implements a form-like window using a dialog box resource
CHtmlView	A view class that can display HTML, with all the capabilities of Microsoft Internet Explorer
CListView	A view class that displays a ListView control in its window
COleDBRecordView	Same as CRecordView, except used with the DAO database classes
CRecordView	A view class that can display database records along with controls for navigating the database
CRichEditView	A view class that provides more sophisticated text-editing capabilities by using the RichEdit control
CScrollView	A view class that provides scrolling capabilities
CTreeView	A view class that displays a TreeView control in its window

To use one of these classes, substitute the desired class for the CView class in the application's project. When using AppWizard to generate your project, you can specify the view class you want in the wizard's Step 6 of 6 dialog box, as shown in Figure 4.3. When you have the desired class installed as the project's view class, you can use the specific class's member functions to control the view window. Chapter 5 demonstrates using the CScrollView class to implement a scrolling view.

A CEditView object, on the other hand, gives you all the features of a Windows edit control in your view window. Using this class, you can handle various editing and printing tasks, including find-and-replace. You can retrieve or set the current printer font by calling the GetPrinterFont() or SetPrinterFont() member function or get the currently selected text by calling GetSelectedText(). Moreover, the FindText() member function locates a given text string, and OnReplaceAll() replaces all occurrences of a given text string with another string.

FIG. 4.3
You can use AppWizard to select your application's base view class.

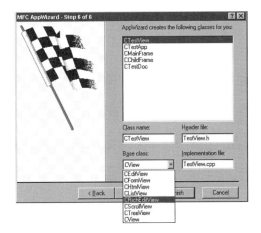

The `CRichEditView` class adds many features to an edit view, including paragraph formatting (such as centered, right-aligned, and bulleted text), character attributes (including underlined, bold, and italic), and the capability to set margins, fonts, and paper size. As you might have guessed, the `CRichEditView` class features a rich set of methods you can use to control your application's view object.

Figure 4.4 shows how the view classes fit into MFC's class hierarchy. Describing these various view classes fully is beyond the scope of this chapter. However, you can find plenty of information about them in your Visual C++ online documentation.

Part
II

Ch
4

FIG. 4.4
The view classes all trace their ancestry back to `CView`.

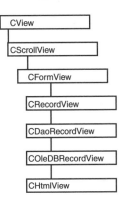

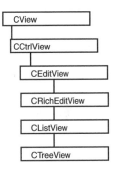

Document Templates, Views, and Frame Windows

Because you've been working with AppWizard-generated applications in this chapter, you've taken for granted a lot of what goes on in the background of an MFC document/view program. That is, much of the code that enables the frame window (your application's main window), the document, and the view window to work together is automatically generated by AppWizard and manipulated by MFC.

For example, if you look at the InitInstance() method of the Rectangles application's CRecsApp class, you see (among other things) the lines shown in Listing 4.6.

Listing 4.6 RECS.CPP—Initializing an Application's Document

```
CSingleDocTemplate* pDocTemplate;
pDocTemplate = new CSingleDocTemplate(
     IDR_MAINFRAME,
     RUNTIME_CLASS(CRecsDoc),
     RUNTIME_CLASS(CMainFrame),
     RUNTIME_CLASS(CRecsView));
AddDocTemplate(pDocTemplate);
```

In Listing 4.6, you discover one secret that makes the document/view system work. In that code, the program creates a document-template object. These document templates have nothing to do with C++ templates, discussed in Chapter 26, "Exceptions and Templates." A document template is an older concept, named before C++ templates were implemented by Microsoft, that pulls together the following objects:

- A resource ID identifying a menu resource—IDR_MAINFRAME in this case
- A document class—CRecsDoc in this case
- A frame window class—always CMainFrame
- A view class—CRecsView in this case

Notice that you are not passing an object or a pointer to an object. You are passing the *name* of the class to a macro called RUNTIME_CLASS. It enables the framework to create instances of a class at runtime, which the application object must be able to do in a program that uses the document/view architecture. In order for this macro to work, the classes that will be created dynamically must be declared and implemented as such. To do this, the class must have the DECLARE_DYNCREATE macro in its declaration (in the header file) and the IMPLEMENT_DYNCREATE macro in its implementation. AppWizard takes care of this for you.

For example, if you look at the header file for the Rectangles application's CMainFrame class, you see the following line near the top of the class's declaration:

```
DECLARE_DYNCREATE(CMainFrame)
```

As you can see, the DECLARE_DYNCREATE macro requires the class's name as its single argument.

Now, if you look near the top of CMainFrame's implementation file (MAINFRM.CPP), you see this line:

```
IMPLEMENT_DYNCREATE(CMainFrame, CFrameWnd)
```

The IMPLEMENT_DYNCREATE macro requires as arguments the name of the class and the name of the base class.

If you explore the application's source code further, you find that the document and view classes also contain the DECLARE_DYNCREATE and IMPLEMENT_DYNCREATE macros.

If you haven't heard of frame windows before, you should know that they contain all the windows involved in the applications—this means control bars as well as views. They also route messages and commands to views and documents, as discussed in Chapter 3.

The last line of Listing 4.6 calls AddDocTemplate() to pass the object on to the application object, CRecsApp, which keeps a list of documents. AddDocTemplate() adds this document to this list and uses the document template to create the document object, the frame, and the view window.

Because this is a Single Document Interface, a single document template (CSingleDocTemplate) is created. Multiple Document Interface applications use one CMultiDocTemplate object for each kind of document they support. For example, a spreadsheet program might have two kinds of documents: tables and graphs. Each would have its own view and its own set of menus. Two instances of CMultiDocTemplate would be created in InitInstance(), each pulling together the menu, document, and view that belong together. If you've ever seen the menus in a program change as you switched from one view or document to another, you know how you can achieve the same effect: Simply associate them with different menu resource IDs as you build the document templates. ●

Part

II

Ch

4

Drawing on the Screen

Understanding Device Contexts

Most applications need to display some type of data in their windows. You'd think that, because Windows is a device-independent operating system, creating window displays would be easier than luring a kitten with a saucer of milk. However, it's exactly Windows' device independence that places a little extra burden on a programmer's shoulders. Because you can never know in advance exactly what type of devices may be connected to a user's system, you can't make many assumptions about display capabilities. Functions that draw to the screen must do so indirectly through something called a *device context* (DC).

Although device independence forces you, the programmer, to deal with data displays indirectly, it helps you by ensuring that your programs run on all popular devices. In most cases, Windows handles devices for you through the device drivers that users have installed on the system. These device drivers intercept the data that the application needs to display and then translates the data appropriately for the device on which it will appear, whether that's a screen, a printer, or some other output device.

To understand how all this device independence works, imagine an art teacher trying to design a course of study appropriate for all types of artists. The teacher creates a course outline that stipulates the subject of a project, the suggested colors to be used, the dimensions of the finished project, and so on. What the teacher doesn't stipulate is the surface on which the project will be painted or the materials needed to paint on that surface. In other words, the teacher stipulates only general characteristics. The details of how these characteristics are applied to the finished project are left to each specific artist.

For example, an artist using oil paints will choose canvas as his drawing surface and oil paints, in the colors suggested by the instructor, as the paint. On the other hand, an artist using watercolors will select watercolor paper and will, of course, use watercolors instead of oils for paint. Finally, the charcoal artist will select the appropriate drawing surface for charcoal and will use a single color.

The instructor in this scenario is much like a Windows programmer. The programmer has no idea who may eventually use the program and what kind of system that user may have. The programmer can recommend the colors in which data should be displayed and the coordinates at which the data should appear, for example, but it's the device driver—the Windows artist—who ultimately decides how the data appears.

A system with a VGA monitor may display data with fewer colors than a system with a Super VGA monitor. Likewise, a system with a monochrome monitor displays the data in only a single color. High-resolution monitors can display more data than lower-resolution monitors. The device drivers, much like the artists in the imaginary art school, must take the display requirements and fine-tune them to the device on which the data will actually appear. And it's a data structure known as a *device context* that links the application to the device's driver.

A device context (DC) is little more than a data structure that keeps track of the attributes of a window's drawing surface. These attributes include the currently selected pen, brush, and font that will be used to draw onscreen. Unlike an artist, who can have many brushes and pens with which to work, a DC can use only a single pen, brush, or font at a time. If you want to use a pen that draws wider lines, for example, you need to create the new pen and then replace the DC's old pen with the new one. Similarly, if you want to fill shapes with a red brush, you must create the brush and *select it into the DC*, which is how Windows programmers describe replacing a tool in a DC.

A window's client area is a versatile surface that can display anything a Windows program can draw. The client area can display any type of data because everything displayed in a window—whether it be text, spreadsheet data, a bitmap, or any other type of data—is displayed graphically. MFC helps you display data by encapsulating Windows' GDI functions and objects into its DC classes.

Introducing the Paint1 Application

In this chapter, you will build the Paint1 application, which demonstrates fonts, pens, and brushes. Paint1 will use the document/view paradigm discussed in Chapter 4, "Documents and Views," and the view will handle displaying the data. When run, the application will display text in several different fonts. When users click the application, it displays lines drawn with several different pens. After another click, it displays boxes filled with a variety of brushes.

The first step in creating Paint1 is to build an empty shell with AppWizard, as first discussed in Chapter 1, "Building Your First Windows Application." Choose File, New, and select the Projects tab. As shown in Figure 5.1, fill in the project name as **Paint1** and fill in an appropriate directory for the project files. Make sure that MFC AppWizard (exe) is selected. Click OK.

FIG. 5.1
Start an AppWizard project workspace called Paint1.

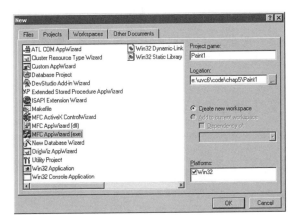

Move through the AppWizard dialog boxes, change the settings to match those in the list that follows, and then click Next to move to the next step.

Step 1: Select Single Document.

Step 2: Use default settings.

Step 3: Use default settings.

Step 4: Deselect all check boxes.

Step 5: Use default settings.

Step 6: Use default settings.

After you click Finish on the last step, the New Project Information box should resemble Figure 5.2. Click OK to create the project.

FIG. 5.2

The starter application for Paint1 is very simple.

Now that you have a starter application, it's time to add code to make it demonstrate some ways an MFC program can display data onscreen. By the time you get to the end of this chapter, the words *display context* won't make you scratch your head in perplexity.

N O T E   Your starter application has menus, but you will ignore them completely. It would be quite a bit of work to remove them; just pretend they aren't there. ■

Building the Paint1 Application

To build the Paint1 application, you first need to understand how painting and drawing work in an MFC program. Then you can set up the skeleton code to handle user clicks and the three different kinds of display. Finally, you'll fill in the code for each kind of display in turn.

Painting in an MFC Program

In Chapter 3, "Messages and Commands," you learned about message maps and how you can tell MFC which functions to call when it receives messages from Windows. One important message that every Windows program with a window must handle is WM_PAINT. Windows sends the WM_PAINT message to an application's window when the window needs to be redrawn. Several events cause Windows to send a WM_PAINT message:

- When users simply run the program: In a properly written Windows application, the application's window receives a WM_PAINT message almost immediately after being run, to ensure that the appropriate data is displayed from the very start.

- When the window has been resized or has recently been uncovered (fully or partially) by another window: Part of the window that wasn't visible before is now onscreen and must be updated.

- When a program indirectly sends itself a WM_PAINT message by invalidating its client area: This capability ensures that an application can change its window's contents almost any time it wants. For example, a word processor might invalidate its window after users paste some text from the Clipboard.

When you studied message maps, you learned to convert a message name to a message-map macro and function name. You now know, for example, that the message-map macro for a WM_PAINT message is ON_WM_PAINT(). You also know that the matching message-map function should be called OnPaint(). This is another case where MFC has already done most of the work of matching a Windows message with its message-response function. (If all this message-map stuff sounds unfamiliar, you might want to review Chapter 3.)

You might guess that your next step is to catch the WM_PAINT message or to override the OnPaint() function that your view class inherited from CView, but you won't do that. Listing 5.1 shows the code for CView::OnPaint(). As you can see, WM_PAINT is already caught and handled for you.

Listing 5.1 *CView::OnPaint()*

```
void CView::OnPaint()
{
    // standard paint routine
    CPaintDC dc(this);        ptr to current window
    OnPrepareDC(&dc);         constructs dc
    OnDraw(&dc);
}
```

CPaintDC is a special class for managing *paint DCs*—device contexts used only when responding to WM_PAINT messages. An object of the CPaintDC class does more than just create a DC; it also calls the BeginPaint() Windows API function in the class's constructor and calls EndPaint() in its destructor. When a program responds to WM_PAINT messages, calls to BeginPaint() and EndPaint() are required. The CPaintDC class handles this requirement without your having to get involved in all the messy details. As you can see, the CPaintDC constructor takes a single argument, which is a pointer to the window for which you're creating the DC. The this pointer points to the current view, so it's passed to the constructor to make a DC for the current view.

OnPrepareDC() is a CView function that prepares a DC for use. You'll learn more about it in Chapter 6, "Printing and Print Preview."

OnDraw() does the actual work of visually representing the document. In most cases you will write the OnDraw() code for your application and never touch OnPaint().

Switching the Display

View class

The design for Paint1 states that when you click the application's window, the window's display changes. This seemingly magical feat is actually easy to accomplish. You add a member variable to the view to store what kind of display is being done and then change it when users click the window. In other words, the program routes WM_LBUTTONDOWN messages to the OnLButtonDown() message-response function, which sets the m_display flag as appropriate.

First, add the member variable. You must add it by hand rather than through the shortcut menu because the type includes an enum declaration. Open Paint1View.h from the FileView and add these lines after the //Attributes comment:

```
protected:
    enum {Fonts, Pens, Brushes} m_Display;
```

TIP This is an *anonymous* or unnamed enum. You can learn more about enum types in Appendix A, "C++ Review and Object-Oriented Concepts."

Choose ClassView in the Project Workspace pane, expand the classes, expand CPaint1View, and then double-click the constructor CPaint1View(). Add this line of code in place of the TODO comment:

```
m_Display = Fonts;
```

This initializes the display selector to the font demonstration. You use the display selector in the OnDraw() function called by CView::OnPaint(). AppWizard has created CPaint1View::OnDraw(), but it doesn't do anything at the moment. Double-click the function name in ClassView and add the code in Listing 5.2 to the function, removing the TODO comment left by AppWizard.

Listing 5.2 *CPaint1View::OnDraw()*

```
void CPaint1View::OnDraw(CDC* pDC)
{
    CPaint1Doc* pDoc = GetDocument();
    ASSERT_VALID(pDoc);

    switch (m_Display)
    {
        case Fonts:
            ShowFonts(pDC);                    we write fns
            break;
        case Pens:
            ShowPens(pDC);
            break;
        case Brushes:
            ShowBrushes(pDC);
```

```
            break;
    }
}
```

You will write the three functions ShowFonts(), ShowPens(), and ShowBrushes() in upcoming sections of this chapter. Each function uses the same DC pointer that was passed to OnDraw() by OnPaint(). Add them to the class now by following these steps:

1. Right-click the CPaint1View class in ClassView and select Add Member Function.

2. Enter **void** for the Function Type.

3. Enter **ShowFonts(CDC* pDC)** for the Function Declaration.

4. Change the access to protected. Click OK.

5. Repeat steps 1 through 4 for ShowPens(CDC* pDC) and ShowBrushes(CDC* pDC).

The last step in arranging for the display to switch is to catch left mouse clicks and write code in the message handler to change m_display.

Right-click CPaint1View in the ClassView and select Add Windows Message Handler from the shortcut menu that appears. Double-click WM_LBUTTONDOWN in the New Windows Messages/ Events list box. ClassWizard adds a function called OnLButtonDown() to the view and adds entries to the message map so that this function will be called whenever users click the left mouse button over this view.

Click Edit Existing to edit the OnLButtonDown() you just created, and add the code shown in Listing 5.3.

Listing 5.3 *CPaint1View::OnLButtonDown()*

```
void CPaint1View::OnLButtonDown(UINT nFlags, CPoint point)
{
    if (m_Display == Fonts)
        m_Display = Pens;
    else if (m_Display == Pens)
        m_Display = Brushes;
    else
        m_Display = Fonts;

    Invalidate();

    CView::OnLButtonDown(nFlags, point);
}
```

Part

II

Ch

5

As you can see, depending on its current value, m_display is set to the next display type in the series. Of course, just changing the value of m_display doesn't accomplish much; the program still needs to redraw the contents of its window. The call to Invalidate() tells Windows that all of the window needs to be repainted. This causes Windows to generate a WM_PAINT message for the window, which means that eventually OnDraw() will be called and the view will be redrawn as a font, pen, or brush demonstration.

Using Fonts

Changing the font used in a view is a technique you'll want to use in various situations. It's not as simple as you might think because you can never be sure that any given font is actually installed on the user's machine. You set up a structure that holds information about the font you want, attempt to create it, and then work with the font you actually have, which might not be the font you asked for.

A Windows font is described in the LOGFONT structure outlined in Table 5.1. The LOGFONT structure uses 14 fields to hold a complete description of the font. Many fields can be set to 0 or the default values, depending on the program's needs.

Table 5.1   *LOGFONT* Fields and Their Descriptions

Field	Description
lfHeight	Font height in logical units
lfWidth	Font width in logical units
lfEscapement	Angle at which to draw the text
lfOrientation	Character tilt in tenths of a degree
lfWeight	Font weight
lfItalic	A nonzero value indicates italics
lfUnderline	A nonzero value indicates an underlined font
lfStrikeOut	A nonzero value indicates a strikethrough font
lfCharSet	Font character set
lfOutPrecision	How to match requested font to actual font
lfClipPrecision	How to clip characters that run over clip area
lfQuality	Print quality of the font
lfPitchAndFamily	Pitch and font family
lfFaceName	Typeface name

Some terms in Table 5.1 need a little explanation. The first is *logical units*. How high is a font with a height of 8 logical units, for example? The meaning of a logical unit depends on the *mapping mode* you're using, as shown in Table 5.2. The default mapping mode is MM_TEXT, which means that one logical unit is equal to 1 pixel. Mapping modes are discussed in more detail in Chapter 6.

Table 5.2   Mapping Modes

Mode	Unit
MM_HIENGLISH	0.001 inch
MM_HIMETRIC	0.01 millimeter
MM_ISOTROPIC	Arbitrary
MM_LOENGLISH	0.01 inch
MM_LOMETRIC	0.1 millimeter
MM_TEXT	Device pixel
MM_TWIPS	1/1440 inch

default — (handwritten note next to MM_TEXT)

Escapement refers to writing text along an angled line. *Orientation* refers to writing angled text along a flat line. The font weight refers to the thickness of the letters. A number of constants have been defined for use in this field: FW_DONTCARE, FW_THIN, FW_EXTRALIGHT, FW_ULTRALIGHT, FW_LIGHT, FW_NORMAL, FW_REGULAR, FW_MEDIUM, FW_SEMIBOLD, FW_DEMIBOLD, FW_BOLD, FW_EXTRABOLD, FW_ULTRABOLD, FW_BLACK, and FW_HEAVY. Not all fonts are available in all weights. Four character sets are available (ANSI_CHARSET, OEM_CHARSET, SYMBOL_CHARSET, and UNICODE_CHARSET), but for writing English text you'll almost always use ANSI_CHARSET. (Unicode is discussed in Chapter 28, "Future Explorations.") The last field in the LOGFONT structure is the face name, such as Courier or Helvetica.

Listing 5.4 shows the code you need to add to the empty ShowFonts() function you created earlier.

Part
II
Ch
5

Listing 5.4   *CPaint1View::ShowFonts()*

```
void CPaint1View::ShowFonts(CDC * pDC)
{
    // Initialize a LOGFONT structure for the fonts.
    LOGFONT logFont;
    logFont.lfHeight = 8;
    logFont.lfWidth = 0;
    logFont.lfEscapement = 0;
    logFont.lfOrientation = 0;
    logFont.lfWeight = FW_NORMAL;
    logFont.lfItalic = 0;
    logFont.lfUnderline = 0;
    logFont.lfStrikeOut = 0;
    logFont.lfCharSet = ANSI_CHARSET;
    logFont.lfOutPrecision = OUT_DEFAULT_PRECIS;
    logFont.lfClipPrecision = CLIP_DEFAULT_PRECIS;
    logFont.lfQuality = PROOF_QUALITY;
    logFont.lfPitchAndFamily = VARIABLE_PITCH | FF_ROMAN;
    strcpy(logFont.lfFaceName, "Times New Roman");
```

continues

Listing 5.4   Continued

```
        // Initialize the position of text in the window.
        UINT position = 0;

        // Create and display eight example fonts.
        for (UINT x=0; x<8; ++x)
        {
            // Set the new font's height.
            logFont.lfHeight = 16 + (x * 8);

            // Create a new font and select it into the DC.
            CFont font;
            font.CreateFontIndirect(&logFont);
            CFont* oldFont = pDC->SelectObject(&font);

            // Print text with the new font.
            position += logFont.lfHeight;        // move to next line
            pDC->TextOut(20, position, "A sample font.");

            // Restore the old font to the DC.     Old font = 1st params
            pDC->SelectObject(oldFont);
        }
    }
```

ShowFonts() starts by setting up a Times Roman font 8 pixels high, with a width that best matches the height and all other attributes set to normal defaults.

To show the many fonts displayed in its window, the Paint1 application creates its fonts in a for loop, modifying the value of the LOGFONT structure's lfHeight member each time through the loop, using the loop variable x to calculate the new font height:

```
logFont.lfHeight = 16 + (x * 8);
```

Because x starts at 0, the first font created in the loop will be 16 pixels high. Each time through the loop, the new font will be 8 pixels higher than the previous one.

After setting the font's height, the program creates a CFont object and calls its CreateFontIndirect() function, which attempts to create a CFont object corresponding to the LOGFONT you created. It will change the LOGFONT to describe the CFont that was actually created, given the fonts installed on the user's machine.

After ShowFonts() calls CreateFontIndirect(), the CFont object is associated with a Windows font. Now you can select it into the DC. Selecting objects into device contexts is a crucial concept in Windows output programming. You can't use any graphical object, such as a font, directly; instead, you select it into the DC and then use the DC. You always save a pointer to the old object that was in the DC (the pointer is returned from the SelectObject() call) and use it to restore the device context by selecting the old object again when you're finished. The same function, SelectObject(), is used to select various objects into a device context: the font you're using in this section, a pen, a brush, or a number of other drawing objects.

After selecting the new font into the DC, you can use the font to draw text onscreen. The local variable position holds the vertical position in the window at which the next line of text should be printed. This position depends on the height of the current font. After all, if there's not enough space between the lines, the larger fonts will overlap the smaller ones. When Windows created the new font, it stored the font's height (most likely the height that you requested, but maybe not) in the LOGFONT structure's lfHeight member. By adding the value stored in lfHeight, the program can determine the next position at which to display the line of text. To make the text appear onscreen, ShowFonts() calls TextOut().

TextOut()'s first two arguments are the X and Y coordinates at which to print the text. The third argument is the text to print. Having printed the text, you restore the old font to the DC in case this is the last time through the loop.

Build the application and run it. It should resemble Figure 5.3. If you click the window, it will go blank because the ShowPens() routine doesn't draw anything. Click again and it's still blank, this time because the ShowBrushes() routine doesn't draw anything. Click a third time and you are back to the fonts screen.

FIG. 5.3
The font display shows different types of text output.

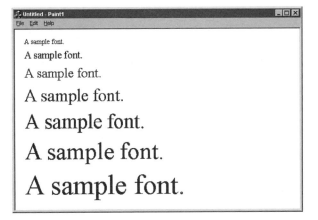

Sizing and Positioning the Window

As you can see in Figure 5.3, Paint1 doesn't display eight different fonts at 800×600 screen settings—only seven can fit in the window. To correct this, you need to set the size of the window a little larger than the Windows default. In an MFC program, you do this in the mainframe class PreCreateWindow() function. This is called for you just before the mainframe window is created. The mainframe window surrounds the entire application and governs the size of the view.

PreCreateWindow() takes one parameter, a reference to a CREATESTRUCT structure. The CREATESTRUCT structure contains essential information about the window that's about to be created, as shown in Listing 5.5.

Part
II

Ch
5

Listing 5.5 The *CREATESTRUCT* Structure

```
typedef struct tagCREATESTRUCT {
    LPVOID     lpCreateParams;
    HANDLE     hInstance;
    HMENU      hMenu;
    HWND       hwndParent;
    int        cy;
    int        cx;
    int        y;
    int        x;
    LONG       style;
    LPCSTR     lpszName;
    LPCSTR     lpszClass;
    DWORD      dwExStyle;
} CREATESTRUCT;
```

If you've programmed Windows without application frameworks such as MFC, you'll recognize the information stored in the CREATESTRUCT structure. You used to supply much of this information when calling the Windows API function CreateWindow() to create your application's window. Of special interest to MFC programmers are the cx, cy, x, and y members of this structure. By changing cx and cy, you can set the window width and height, respectively. Similarly, modifying x and y changes the window's position. By overriding PreCreateWindow(), you have a chance to fiddle with the CREATESTRUCT structure before Windows uses it to create the window.

AppWizard created a CMainFrame::PreCreateWindow() function. Expand CMainFrame in ClassView, double-click PreCreateWindow() to edit it, and add lines to obtain the code shown in Listing 5.6. This sets the application's height and width. It also prevents users from resizing the application by using the bitwise and operator (&) to turn off the WS_SIZEBOX style bit.

Listing 5.6 *CMainFrame::PreCreateWindow()*

```
BOOL CMainFrame::PreCreateWindow(CREATESTRUCT& cs)
{
    cs.cx = 440;
    cs.cy = 480;

    cs.style &= ~WS_SIZEBOX;

    if( !CFrameWnd::PreCreateWindow(cs) )

            return FALSE;
    return TRUE;

}
```

It's important that after your own code in PreCreateWindow(), you call the base class's PreCreateWindow(). Failure to do this will leave you without a valid window because MFC never gets a chance to pass the CREATESTRUCT structure on to Windows, so Windows never creates your window. When overriding class member functions, you usually need to call the base class's version.

Build and run Paint1 to confirm that all eight fonts fit in the application's window. Now you're ready to demonstrate pens.

Using Pens

You'll be pleased to know that pens are much easier to deal with than fonts, mostly because you don't have to fool around with complicated data structures like LOGFONT. In fact, to create a pen, you need to supply only the pen's line style, thickness, and color. The Paint1 application's ShowPens() function displays in its window the lines drawn by using different pens created within a for loop. Listing 5.7 shows the code.

Listing 5.7 CPaint1View::ShowPens()

```
void CPaint1View::ShowPens(CDC * pDC)
{
    // Initialize the line position.
    UINT position = 10;

    // Draw sixteen lines in the window.
    for (UINT x=0; x<16; ++x)
    {
        // Create a new pen and select it into the DC.
        CPen pen(PS_SOLID, x*2+1, RGB(0, 0, 255));
        CPen* oldPen = pDC->SelectObject(&pen);

        // Draw a line with the new pen.
        position +=  x * 2 + 10;
        pDC->MoveTo(20, position);
        pDC->LineTo(400, position);  ← draw line

        // Restore the old pen to the DC.
        pDC->SelectObject(oldPen);
    }
}
```

Within the loop, ShowPens() first creates a custom pen. The constructor takes three parameters. The first is the line's style, one of the styles listed in Table 5.3. (You can draw only solid lines with different thicknesses. If you specify a pattern and a thickness greater than 1 pixel, the pattern is ignored and a solid line is drawn.) The second argument is the line thickness, which increases each time through the loop. The third argument is the line's color. The RGB macro takes three values for the red, green, and blue color components and converts them to a valid Windows color reference. The values for the red, green, and blue color components can be anything from 0 to 255—the higher the value, the brighter that color component. This code creates a bright blue pen. If all the color values were 0, the pen would be black; if the color values were all 255, the pen would be white.

Table 5.3   Pen Styles

Style	Description
PS_DASH	A pen that draws dashed lines
PS_DASHDOT	A pen that draws dash-dot patterned lines
PS_DASHDOTDOT	A pen that draws dash-dot-dot patterned lines
PS_DOT	A pen that draws dotted lines
PS_INSIDEFRAME	A pen that's used with shapes, in which the line's thickness must not extend outside the shape's frame
PS_NULL	A pen that draws invisible lines
PS_SOLID	A pen that draws solid lines

Alternate pen

N O T E   If you want to control the style of a line's end points or create your own custom patterns for pens, you can use the alternative CPen constructor, which requires a few more arguments than the CPen constructor described in this section. To learn how to use this alternative constructor, look up CPen in your Visual C++ online documentation. ▇

After creating the new pen, ShowPens() selects it into the DC, saving the pointer to the old pen. The MoveTo() function moves the pen to an X,Y coordinate without drawing as it moves; the LineTo() function moves the pen while drawing. The style, thickness, and color of the pen are used. Finally, you select the old pen into the DC.

T I P   There are a number of line drawing functions other than LineTo(), including Arc(), ArcTo(), AngleArc(), and PolyDraw().

Build and run Paint1 again. When the font display appears, click the window. You will see a pen display similar to the one in Figure 5.4.

Using Brushes

A pen draws a line of a specified thickness onscreen. A brush fills a shape onscreen. You can create solid and patterned brushes and even brushes from bitmaps that contain your own custom fill patterns. Paint1 will display both patterned and solid rectangles in the ShowBrushes() function, shown in Listing 5.8.

FIG. 5.4

The pen display shows the effect of setting line thickness.

Listing 5.8 CPaint1View::ShowBrushes()

```
void CPaint1View::ShowBrushes(CDC * pDC)
     // Initialize the rectangle position.
     UINT position = 0;

     // Select pen to use for rectangle borders
     CPen pen(PS_SOLID, 5, RGB(255, 0, 0));
     CPen* oldPen = pDC->SelectObject(&pen);

     // Draw seven rectangles.
     for (UINT x=0; x<7; ++x)
     {
         CBrush* brush;

         // Create a solid or hatched brush.
         if (x == 6)
             brush = new CBrush(RGB(0,255,0));
         else
             brush = new CBrush(x, RGB(0,160,0));

         // Select the new brush into the DC.
         CBrush* oldBrush = pDC->SelectObject(brush);

         // Draw the rectangle.
         position += 50;
         pDC->Rectangle(20, position, 400, position + 40);

         // Restore the DC and delete the brush.
         pDC->SelectObject(oldBrush);
         delete brush;
     }
```

continues

Listing 5.8 Continued

```
    // Restore the old pen to the DC.
    pDC->SelectObject(oldPen);
}
```

The rectangles painted with the various brushes in this routine will all be drawn with a border. To arrange this, create a pen (this one is solid, 5 pixels thick, and bright red) and select it into the DC. It will be used to border the rectangles without any further work on your part. Like ShowFonts() and ShowPens(), this routine creates its graphical objects within a for loop. Unlike those two functions, ShowBrushes() creates a graphical object (in this routine, a brush) with a call to new. This enables you to call the one-argument constructor, which creates a solid brush, or the two-argument constructor, which creates a hatched brush.

In Listing 5.8, the first argument to the two-argument constructor is just the loop variable, x. Usually, you don't want to show all the hatch patterns but want to select a specific one. Use one of these constants for the hatch style:

- HS_HORIZONTAL—Horizontal
- HS_VERTICAL—Vertical
- HS_CROSS—Horizontal and vertical
- HS_FDIAGONAL—Forward diagonal
- HS_BDIAGONAL—Backward diagonal
- HS_DIAGCROSS—Diagonal in both directions

In a pattern that should be familiar by now, ShowBrushes() selects the brush into the DC, determines the position at which to work, uses the brush by calling Rectangle(), and then restores the old brush. When the loop is complete, the old pen is restored as well.

Rectangle()is just one of the shape-drawing functions that you can call. Rectangle() takes as arguments the coordinates of the rectangle's upper-left and lower-right corners. Some others of interest are Chord(), DrawFocusRect(), Ellipse(), Pie(), Polygon(), PolyPolygon(), Polyline(), and RoundRect(), which draws a rectangle with rounded corners.

Again, build and run Paint1. Click twice, and you will see the demonstration of brushes, as shown in Figure 5.5.

N O T E Remember the call to Invalidate() in CPaint1View::OnLButtonDown()? Invalidate() actually takes a Boolean argument with a default value of TRUE. This argument tells Windows whether to erase the window's background. If you use FALSE for this argument, the background isn't erased. In Figure 5.6, you can see what happens to the Paint1 application if Invalidate() is called with an argument of FALSE. ∎

FIG. 5.5
The brushes display shows several patterns inside thick-bordered rectangles.

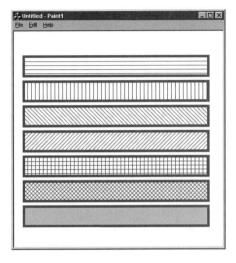

FIG. 5.6
Without erasing the background, the Paint1 application's windows appear messy.

Scrolling Windows

Those famous screen rectangles known as *windows* enable you to partition screen space between various applications and documents. Also, if a document is too large to completely fit within a window, you can view portions of it and scroll through it a bit at a time. The Windows operating system and MFC pretty much take care of the partitioning of screen space. However, if you want to enable users to view portions of a large document, you must create scrolling windows.

Adding scrollbars to an application from scratch is a complicated task. Luckily for Visual C++ programmers, MFC handles many of the details involved in scrolling windows over documents. If you use the document/view architecture and derive your view window from MFC's CScrollView class, you have scrolling capabilities almost for free. I say "almost" because you still must handle a few details, which you learn about in the following sections.

N O T E   If you create your application with AppWizard, you can specify that you want to use
CScrollView as the base class for your view class. To do this, in the Step 6 of 6 dialog box displayed by AppWizard, select your view window in the class list and then select CScrollView in the Base Class dialog box, as shown in Figure 5.7. ■

FIG. 5.7

You can create a scrolling window from within AppWizard.

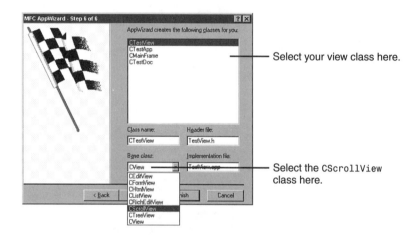

Select your view class here.

Select the CScrollView class here.

Building the Scroll Application

In this section, you'll build a sample program called Scroll to experiment with a scrolling window. When Scroll first runs, it displays five lines of text. Each time you click the window, five lines of text are added to the display. When you have more lines of text than fit in the window, a vertical scrollbar appears, enabling you to scroll to the parts of the documents that you can't see.

As usual, building the application starts with AppWizard. Choose File, New, and select the Projects tab. Fill in the project name as **Scroll** and fill in an appropriate directory for the project files. Make sure that MFC AppWizard (exe) is selected. Click OK.

Complete the AppWizard steps, selecting the following options:

    Step 1: Select Single Document.

    Step 2: Use default settings

    Step 3: Use default settings.

    Step 4: Deselect all check boxes.

Step 5: Use default settings.

Step 6: Select `CScrollView` from the Base Class drop-down box, as in Figure 5.7.

The New Project Information dialog box should resemble Figure 5.8. Click OK to create the project.

FIG. 5.8

Create a scroll application with AppWizard.

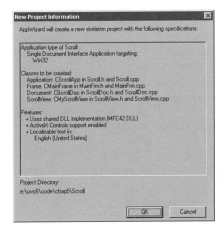

This application generates very simple lines of text. You need to keep track only of the number of lines in the scrolling view at the moment. To do this, add a variable to the document class by following these steps:

1. In ClassView, expand the classes and right-click `CScrollDoc`.
2. Choose Add Member Variable from the shortcut menu.
3. Fill in `int` as the variable type.
4. Fill in `m_NumLines` as the variable declaration.
5. Select Public for the Access.

Variables associated with a document are initialized in `OnNewDocument()`, as discussed in Chapter 4. In ClassView, expand `CScrollDoc` and double-click `OnNewDocument()` to expand it. Replace the TODO comments with this line of code:

```
m_NumLines = 5;
```

To arrange for this variable to be saved with the document and restored when the document is loaded, you must serialize it as discussed in Chapter 7, "Persistence and File I/O." Edit `CScrollDoc::Serialize()` as shown in Listing 5.9.

Listing 5.9 *CScrollDoc::Serialize()*

```
void CScrollDoc::Serialize(CArchive& ar)
{
    if (ar.IsStoring())
    {
        ar << m_NumLines;
    }
    else
    {
        ar >> m_NumLines;
    }
}
```

Store

Load

Now all you need to do is use m_NumLines to draw the appropriate number of lines. Expand the view class, CMyScrollView, in ClassView and double-click OnDraw(). Edit it until it's the same as Listing 5.10. This is very similar to the ShowFonts() code from the Paint1 application earlier in this chapter.

Listing 5.10 *CMyScrollView::OnDraw()*

```
void CMyScrollView::OnDraw(CDC* pDC)
{
    CScrollDoc* pDoc = GetDocument();
    ASSERT_VALID(pDoc);

    // get the number of lines from the document
    int numLines = pDoc->m_NumLines;

    // Initialize a LOGFONT structure for the fonts.
    LOGFONT logFont;
    logFont.lfHeight = 24;
    logFont.lfWidth = 0;
    logFont.lfEscapement = 0;
    logFont.lfOrientation = 0;
    logFont.lfWeight = FW_NORMAL;
    logFont.lfItalic = 0;
    logFont.lfUnderline = 0;
    logFont.lfStrikeOut = 0;
    logFont.lfCharSet = ANSI_CHARSET;
    logFont.lfOutPrecision = OUT_DEFAULT_PRECIS;
    logFont.lfClipPrecision = CLIP_DEFAULT_PRECIS;
    logFont.lfQuality = PROOF_QUALITY;
    logFont.lfPitchAndFamily = VARIABLE_PITCH | FF_ROMAN;
    strcpy(logFont.lfFaceName, "Times New Roman");

    // Create a new font and select it into the DC.
    CFont* font = new CFont();
    font->CreateFontIndirect(&logFont);
    CFont* oldFont = pDC->SelectObject(font);

    // Initialize the position of text in the window.
    UINT position = 0;
```

```
// Create and display eight example lines.
for (int x=0; x<numLines; ++x)
{
    // Create the string to display.
    char s[25];
    wsprintf(s, "This is line #%d", x+1);

    // Print text with the new font.
    pDC->TextOut(20, position, s);
    position += logFont.lfHeight;
}

// Restore the old font to the DC, and
// delete the font the program created.
pDC->SelectObject(oldFont);
delete font;
}
```

Build and run the Scroll application. You will see a display similar to that in Figure 5.9. No scrollbars appear because all the lines fit in the window.

FIG. 5.9

At first, the scroll application displays five lines of text and no scrollbars.

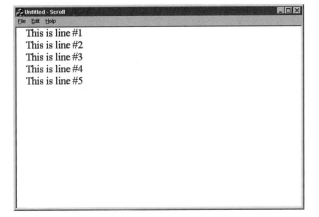

Part
II

Ch
5

Adding Code to Increase Lines

To increase the number of lines whenever users click the window, you need to add a message handler to handle left mouse clicks and then write the code for the handler. Right-click CMyScrollView in ClassView and choose Add Windows Message Handler. Double-click WM_LBUTTONDOWN to add a handler and click the Edit Existing button to change the code. Listing 5.11 shows the completed handler. It simply increases the number of lines and calls Invalidate() to force a redraw. Like so many message handlers, it finishes by passing the work on to the base class version of this function.

Listing 5.11 *CMyScrollView::OnLButtonDown()*

```
void CMyScrollView::OnLButtonDown(UINT nFlags, CPoint point)
{
    CScrollDoc* pDoc = GetDocument();
    ASSERT_VALID(pDoc);

    // Increase number of lines to display.
    pDoc->m_NumLines += 5;

    // Redraw the window.
    Invalidate();

    CScrollView::OnLButtonDown(nFlags, point);
}
```

Adding Code to Decrease Lines

So that you can watch scrollbars disappear as well as appear, why not implement a way for users to decrease the number of lines in the window? If left-clicking increases the number of lines, it makes sense that right-clicking would decrease it. Add a handler for WM_RBUTTONDOWN just as you did for WM_LBUTTONDOWN, and edit it until it's just like Listing 5.12. This function is a little more complicated because it ensures that the number of lines is never negative.

Listing 5.12 *CMyScrollView::OnRButtonDown()*

```
void CMyScrollView::OnRButtonDown(UINT nFlags, CPoint point)
{
    CScrollDoc* pDoc = GetDocument();
    ASSERT_VALID(pDoc);

    // Decrease number of lines to display.
    pDoc->m_NumLines -= 5;

    if (pDoc->m_NumLines < 0)
    {
        pDoc->m_NumLines = 0;
    }

    // Redraw the window.
    Invalidate();

    CScrollView::OnRButtonDown(nFlags, point);
}
```

If you build and run Scroll now and click the window, you can increase the number of lines, but scrollbars don't appear. You need to add some lines to OnDraw() to make that happen. Before you do, review the way that scrollbars work. You can click three places on a vertical scrollbar: the thumb (some people call it the elevator), above the thumb, or below it. Clicking the thumb does nothing, but you can click and hold to drag it up or down. Clicking above it moves you one page (screenful) up within the data. Clicking below it moves you one page down. What's more, the size of the thumb is a visual representation of the size of a page in proportion to the entire document. Clicking the up arrow at the top of the scrollbar moves you up one line in the document; clicking the down arrow at the bottom moves you down one line.

What all this means is that the code that draws the scrollbar and handles the clicks needs to know the size of the entire document, the page size, and the line size. You don't have to write code to draw scrollbars or to handle clicks on the scrollbar, but you do have to pass along some information about the size of the document and the current view. The lines of code you need to add to OnDraw() are in Listing 5.13; add them after the for loop and before the old font is selected back into the DC.

Cn View

Listing 5.13   Lines to Add to *OnDraw()*

```
// Calculate the document size.
CSize docSize(100, numLines*logFont.lfHeight);

// Calculate the page size.
   CRect rect;
GetClientRect(&rect);
CSize pageSize(rect.right, rect.bottom);

// Calculate the line size.
CSize lineSize(0, logFont.lfHeight);

// Adjust the scrollers.
SetScrollSizes(MM_TEXT, docSize, pageSize, lineSize);
```

This new code must determine the document, page, and line sizes. The document size is the width and height of the screen area that could hold the entire document. This is calculated by using the number of lines in the entire document and the height of a line. (CSize is an MFC class created especially for storing the widths and heights of objects.) The page size is simply the size of the client rectangle of this view, and the line size is the height of the font. By setting the horizontal component of the line size to 0, you prevent horizontal scrolling. *not true for*
WIN XP

These three sizes must be passed along to implement scrolling. Simply call SetScrollSizes(), which takes the mapping mode, document size, page size, and line size. MFC will set the scrollbars properly for any document and handle user interaction with the scrollbars.

Build and run Scroll again and generate some more lines. You should see a scrollbar like the one in Figure 5.10. Add even more lines and you will see the thumb shrink as the document size grows. Finally, resize the application horizontally so that the text won't all fit. Notice how no horizontal scrollbars appear, because you set the horizontal line size to 0.

Part
II

Ch
5

FIG. 5.10

After displaying more lines than fit in the window, the vertical scrollbar appears.

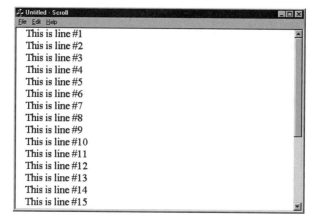

Printing and Print Preview

Understanding Basic Printing and Print Preview with MFC

If you brought together 10 Windows programmers and asked them what part of creating Windows applications they thought was the hardest, probably at least half of them would choose printing documents. Although the device-independent nature of Windows makes it easier for users to get peripherals working properly, programmers must take up some of the slack by programming all devices in a general way. At one time, printing from a Windows application was a nightmare that only the most experienced programmers could handle. Now, however, thanks to application frameworks such as MFC, the job of printing documents from a Windows application is much simpler.

MFC handles so much of the printing task for you that, when it comes to simple one-page documents, you have little to do on your own. To see what I mean, follow these steps to create a basic MFC application that supports printing and print preview:

1. Choose File, New; select the Projects tab and start a new AppWizard project workspace called Print1 (see Figure 6.1).

FIG. 6.1
Start an AppWizard project workspace called Print1.

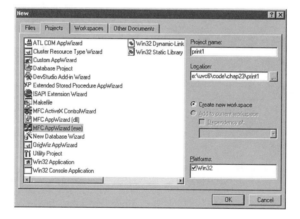

2. Give the new project the following settings in the AppWizard dialog boxes. The New Project Information dialog box should then look like Figure 6.2.

Step 1: Choose Single Document.

Step 2: Don't change the defaults presented by AppWizard.

Step 3: Don't change the defaults presented by AppWizard.

Step 4: Turn off all features except Printing and Print Preview.

Step 5: Don't change the defaults presented by AppWizard.

Step 6: Don't change the defaults presented by AppWizard.

FIG. 6.2

The New Project Information dialog box.

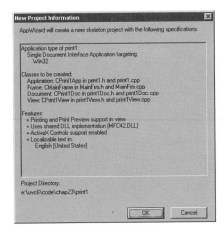

3. Expand the classes in ClassView, expand `CPrint1View`, double-click the `OnDraw()` function, and add the following line of code to it, right after the comment `TODO: add draw code for native data here:`

```
pDC->Rectangle(20, 20, 220, 220);
```

You've seen the `Rectangle()` function twice already: in the Recs app of Chapter 4, "Documents and Views," and the Paint1 app of Chapter 5, "Drawing on the Screen." Adding this function to the `OnDraw()` function of an MFC program's view class causes the program to draw a rectangle. This one is 200 pixels by 200 pixels, located 20 pixels down from the top of the view and 20 pixels from the left edge.

If you haven't read Chapter 5 and aren't comfortable with device contexts, go back and read it now. Also, if you didn't read Chapter 4 and aren't comfortable with the document/view paradigm, you should read it, too. In this chapter, you override a number of virtual functions in your view class and work extensively with device contexts.

Believe it or not, you've just created a fully print-capable application that can display its data (a rectangle) not only in its main window but also in a print preview window and on the printer. To run the Print1 application, first compile and link the source code by choosing Build, Build or by pressing F7. Then, choose Build, Execute to run the program. You will see the window shown in Figure 6.3. This window contains the application's output data, which is simply a rectangle. Next, choose File, Print Preview. You see the print preview window, which displays the document as it will appear if you print it (see Figure 6.4). Go ahead and print the document (choose File, Print). These commands have been implemented for you because you chose support for printing and print preview when you created this application with AppWizard.

Part
II

Ch
6

FIG. 6.3

Print1 displays a rectangle when you first run it.

FIG. 6.4

The Print1 application automatically handles print previewing, thanks to the MFC AppWizard.

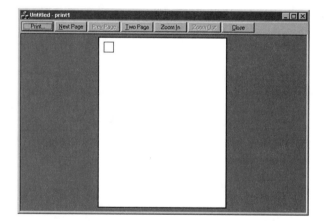

Scaling

One thing you may notice about the printed document and the one displayed onscreen is that, although the screen version of the rectangle takes up a fairly large portion of the application's window, the printed version is tiny. That's because the pixels onscreen and the dots on your printer are different sizes. Although the rectangle is 200 dots square in both cases, the smaller printer dots yield a rectangle that appears smaller. This is how the default Windows MM_TEXT graphics mapping mode works. If you want to scale the printed image to a specific size, you might want to choose a different mapping mode. Table 6.1 lists the mapping modes from which you can choose.

Table 6.1 Mapping Modes

Mode	Unit	X	Y
MM_HIENGLISH	0.001 inch	Increases right	Increases up
MM_HIMETRIC	0.01 millimeter	Increases right	Increases up
MM_ISOTROPIC	User-defined	User-defined	User-defined
MM_LOENGLISH	0.01 inch	Increases right	Increases up
MM_LOMETRIC	0.1 millimeter	Increases right	Increases up
MM_TEXT	Device pixel	Increases right	Increases down
MM_TWIPS	1/1440 inch	Increases right	Increases up

Working with graphics in MM_TEXT mode causes problems when printers and screens can accommodate a different number of pixels per page. A better mapping mode for working with graphics is MM_LOENGLISH, which uses a hundredth of an inch, instead of a dot or pixel, as a unit of measure. To change the Print1 application so that it uses the MM_LOENGLISH mapping mode, replace the line you added to the OnDraw() function with the following two lines:

```
pDC->SetMapMode(MM_LOENGLISH);
pDC->Rectangle(20, -20, 220, -220);
```

The first line sets the mapping mode for the device context. The second line draws the rectangle by using the new coordinate system. Why the negative values? If you look at MM_LOENGLISH in Table 6.1, you see that although X coordinates increase to the right as you expect, Y coordinates increase upward rather than downward. Moreover, the default coordinates for the window are located in the lower-right quadrant of the Cartesian coordinate system, as shown in Figure 6.5. Figure 6.6 shows the print preview window when the application uses the MM_LOENGLISH mapping mode. When you print the document, the rectangle is exactly 2 inches square because a unit is now 1/100 of an inch and the rectangle is 200 units square.

FIG. 6.5
The MM_LOENGLISH mapping mode's default coordinates derive from the Cartesian coordinate system.

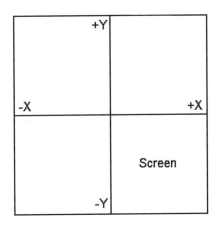

FIG. 6.6

The rectangle to be printed matches the rectangle onscreen when you use `MM_LOENGLISH` as your mapping mode.

Printing Multiple Pages

When your application's document is as simple as Print1's, adding printing and print previewing capabilities to the application is virtually automatic. This is because the document is only a single page and requires no pagination. No matter what you draw in the document window (except bitmaps), MFC handles all the printing tasks for you. Your view's `OnDraw()` function is used for drawing onscreen, printing to the printer, and drawing the print preview screen. Things become more complex, however, when you have larger documents that require pagination or some other special handling, such as the printing of headers and footers.

To get an idea of the problems with which you're faced with a more complex document, modify Print1 so that it prints lots of rectangles—so many that they can't fit on a single page. This will give you an opportunity to deal with pagination. Just to make things more interesting, add a member variable to the document class to hold the number of rectangles to be drawn, and allow the users to increase or decrease the number of rectangles by left- or right-clicking. Follow these steps:

1. Expand `CPrint1Doc` in ClassView, right-click it, and choose Add Member Variable from the shortcut menu. The variable type is `int`, the declaration is `m_numRects`, and the access should be public. This variable will hold the number of rectangles to display.

2. Double-click the `CPrint1Doc` constructor and add this line to it:

   ```
   m_numRects = 5;
   ```

   This line arranges to display five rectangles in a brand new document.

3. Use ClassWizard to catch mouse clicks (`WM_LBUTTONDOWN` messages) by adding an `OnLButtonDown()` function to the view class (see Figure 6.7).

4. Click the Edit Code button to edit the new `OnLButtonDown()` function. It should resemble Listing 6.1. Now the number of rectangles to be displayed increases each time users click the left mouse button.

FIG. 6.7

Use ClassWizard to add the OnLButtonDown() function.

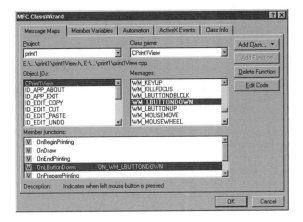

Listing 6.1 print1View.cpp —*CPrint1View::OnLButtonDown()*

```
void CPrint1View::OnLButtonDown(UINT nFlags, CPoint point)
{
    CPrint1Doc* pDoc = GetDocument();
    ASSERT_VALID(pDoc);

    pDoc->m_numRects++;
    Invalidate();

    CView::OnLButtonDown(nFlags, point);
}
```

5. Use ClassWizard to add the OnRButtonDown() function to the view class, as shown in Figure 6.8.

FIG. 6.8

Use ClassWizard to add the OnRButtonDown() function.

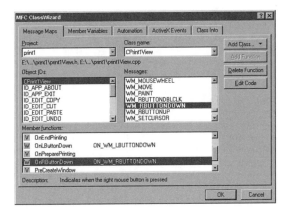

Part
II

Ch
6

6. Click the Edit Code button to edit the new `OnRButtonDown()` function. It should resemble Listing 6.2. Now the number of rectangles to be displayed decreases each time users right-click.

Listing 6.2 print1View.cpp —*CPrint1View::OnRButtonDown()*

```
void CPrint1View::OnRButtonDown(UINT nFlags, CPoint point)
{
    CPrint1Doc* pDoc = GetDocument();
    ASSERT_VALID(pDoc);

    if (pDoc->m_numRects > 0)
    {
        pDoc->m_numRects--;
        Invalidate();
    }

    CView::OnRButtonDown(nFlags, point);
}
```

7. Rewrite the view's `OnDraw()` to draw many rectangles (refer to Listing 6.3). Print1 now draws the selected number of rectangles one below the other, which may cause the document to span multiple pages. It also displays the number of rectangles that have been added to the document.

Listing 6.3 print1View.cpp —*CPrint1View::OnDraw()*

```
void CPrint1View::OnDraw(CDC* pDC)
{
    CPrint1Doc* pDoc = GetDocument();
    ASSERT_VALID(pDoc);

    // TODO: add draw code for native data here
    pDC->SetMapMode(MM_LOENGLISH);

    char s[10];
    wsprintf(s, "%d", pDoc->m_numRects);
    pDC->TextOut(300, -100, s);

    for (int x=0; x<pDoc->m_numRects; ++x)
    {
        pDC->Rectangle(20, -(20+x*200),
            200, -(200+x*200));
    }
}
```

When you run the application now, you see the window shown in Figure 6.9. The window not only displays the rectangles but also displays the rectangle count so that you can see how many rectangles you've requested. When you choose File, Print Preview, you see the print preview window. Click the Two Page button to see the window shown in Figure 6.10. The five rectangles display properly on the first page, with the second page blank.

FIG. 6.9

Print1 now displays multiple rectangles.

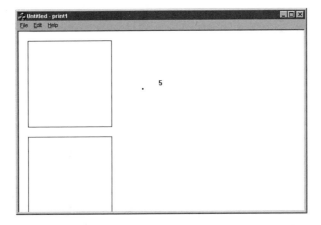

FIG. 6.10

Five rectangles are previewed properly; they will print on a single page.

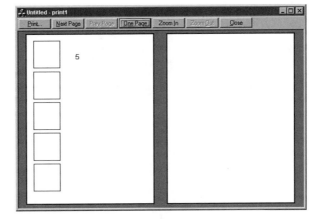

Now, go back to the application's main window and click inside it three times to add three more rectangles. Right-click to remove one. (The rectangle count displayed in the window should be seven.) After you add the rectangles, choose File, Print Preview again to see the two-page print preview window. Figure 6.11 shows what you see. The program hasn't a clue how to print or preview the additional page. The sixth rectangle runs off the bottom of the first page, but nothing appears on the second page.

The first step is to tell MFC how many pages to print (or preview) by calling the SetMaxPage() function in the view class's OnBeginPrinting() function. AppWizard gives you a skeleton OnBeginPrinting() that does nothing. Modify it so that it resembles Listing 6.4.

Part
II

Ch
6

FIG. 6.11

Seven rectangles do not yet appear correctly on multiple pages.

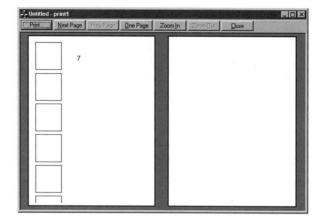

Listing 6.4   print1View.cpp —*CPrint1View::OnBeginPrinting()*

```
void CPrint1View::OnBeginPrinting(CDC* pDC, CPrintInfo* pInfo)
{
    CPrint1Doc* pDoc = GetDocument();
    ASSERT_VALID(pDoc);

    int pageHeight = pDC->GetDeviceCaps(VERTRES);
    int logPixelsY = pDC->GetDeviceCaps(LOGPIXELSY);
    int rectHeight = (int)(2.2 * logPixelsY);
    int numPages = pDoc->m_numRects * rectHeight / pageHeight + 1;
    pInfo->SetMaxPage(numPages);
}
```

OnBeginPrinting() takes two parameters: a pointer to the printer device context and a pointer to a CPrintInfo object. Because the default version of OnBeginPrinting() doesn't refer to these two pointers, the parameter names are commented out to avoid compilation warnings, like this:

```
void CPrint1View::OnBeginPrinting(CDC* /*pDC*/ , CPrintInfo* /*pInfo*/)
```

However, to set the page count, you need to access both the CDC and CPrintInfo objects, so your first task is to uncomment the function's parameters.

Now you need to get some information about the device context (which, in this case, is a printer device context). Specifically, you need to know the page height (in single dots) and the number of dots per inch. You obtain the page height with a call to GetDeviceCaps(), which gives you information about the capabilities of the device context. You ask for the vertical resolution (the number of printable dots from the top of the page to the bottom) by passing the constant VERTRES as the argument. Passing HORZRES gives you the horizontal resolution. There are 29 constants you can pass to GetDeviceCaps(), such as NUMFONTS for the number of fonts that are supported and DRIVERVERSION for the driver version number. For a complete list, consult the online Visual C++ documentation.

Print1 uses the MM_LOENGLISH mapping mode for the device context, which means that the printer output uses units of 1/100 of an inch. To know how many rectangles will fit on a page, you have to know the height of a rectangle in dots so that you can divide dots per page by dots per rectangle to get rectangles per page. (You can see now why your application must know all about your document to calculate the page count.) You know that each rectangle is 2 inches high with 20/100 of an inch of space between each rectangle. The total distance from the start of one rectangle to the start of the next, then, is 2.2 inches. The call to GetDeviceCaps() with an argument of LOGPIXELSY gives the dots per inch of this printer; multiplying by 2.2 gives the dots per rectangle.

You now have all the information to calculate the number of pages needed to fit the requested number of rectangles. You pass that number to SetMaxPage(), and the new OnBeginPrinting() function is complete.

Again, build and run the program. Increase the number of rectangles to seven by clicking twice in the main window. Now choose File, Print Preview and look at the two-page print preview window (see Figure 6.12). Whoops! You obviously still have a problem somewhere. Although the application is previewing two pages, as it should with seven rectangles, it's printing exactly the same thing on both pages. Obviously, page two should take up where page one left off, rather than redisplay the same data from the beginning. There's still some work to do.

FIG. 6.12
The Print1 application still doesn't display multiple pages correctly.

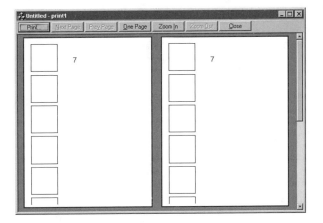

Setting the Origin

To get the second and subsequent pages to print properly, you have to change where MFC believes the top of the page to be. Currently, MFC just draws the pages exactly as you told it to do in CPrint1View::OnDraw(), which displays all seven rectangles from the top of the page to the bottom. To tell MFC where the new top of the page should be, you first need to override the view class's OnPrepareDC() function.

Part

II

Ch

6

Bring up ClassWizard and choose the Message Maps tab. Ensure that CPrintView is selected in the Class Name box, as shown in Figure 6.13. Click CPrintView in the Object IDs box and OnPrepareDC in the Messages box, and then click Add Function. Click the Edit Code button to edit the newly added function. Add the code shown in Listing 6.5.

FIG. 6.13

Use ClassWizard to override the OnPrepareDC() function.

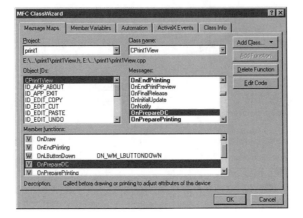

Listing 6.5   print1View.cpp —CPrint1View::OnPrepareDC()

```
void CPrint1View::OnPrepareDC(CDC* pDC, CPrintInfo* pInfo)
{    if (pDC->IsPrinting())
    {
        int pageHeight = pDC->GetDeviceCaps(VERTRES);
        int originY = pageHeight * (pInfo->m_nCurPage - 1);
        pDC->SetViewportOrg(0, -originY);
    }

    CView::OnPrepareDC(pDC, pInfo);
}
```

The MFC framework calls OnPrepareDC() right before it displays data onscreen or before it prints the data to the printer. (One strength of the device context approach to screen display is that the same code can often be used for display and printing.) If the application is about to display data, you (probably) don't want to change the default processing performed by OnPrepareDC(). So, you must check whether the application is printing data by calling IsPrinting(), a member function of the device context class.

If the application is printing, you must determine which part of the data belongs on the current page. You need the height in dots of a printed page, so you call GetDeviceCaps() again.

Next, you must determine a new viewport origin (the position of the coordinates 0,0) for the display. Changing the origin tells MFC where to begin displaying data. For page one, the origin is zero; for page two, it's moved down by the number of dots on a page. In general, the vertical component is the page size times the current page minus one. The page number is a member variable of the CPrintInfo class.

After you calculate the new origin, you only need to give it to the device context by calling `SetViewportOrg()`. Your changes to `OnPrepareDC()` are complete.

To see your changes in action, build and run your new version of Print1. When the program's main window appears, click twice in the window to add two rectangles to the display. (The displayed rectangle count should be seven.) Again, choose File, Print Preview and look at the two-page print preview window (see Figure 6.14). Now the program previews the document correctly. If you print the document, it will look the same in hard copy as it does in the preview.

FIG. 6.14
Print1 finally previews and prints properly.

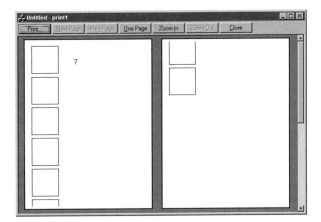

MFC and Printing

Now you've seen MFC's printing and print preview support in action. As you added more functionality to the Print1 application, you modified several member functions that were overridden in the view class, including `OnDraw()`, `OnBeginPrinting()`, and `OnPrepareDC()`. These functions are important to the printing and print preview processes. However, other functions also enable you to add even more printing power to your applications. Table 6.2 describes the functions important to the printing process.

Table 6.2 Printing Functions of a View Class

Function	Description
OnBeginPrinting()	Override this function to create resources, such as fonts, that you need for printing the document. You also set the maximum page count here.
OnDraw()	This function serves triple duty, displaying data in a frame window, a print preview window, or on the printer, depending on the device context sent as the function's parameter.

continues

Table 6.2   Continued

Function	Description
OnEndPrinting()	Override this function to release resources created in OnBeginPrinting().
OnPrepareDC()	Override this function to modify the device context used to display or print the document. You can, for example, handle pagination here.
OnPreparePrinting()	Override this function to provide a maximum page count for the document. If you don't set the page count here, you should set it in OnBeginPrinting().
OnPrint()	Override this function to provide additional printing services, such as printing headers and footers, not provided in OnDraw().

To print a document, MFC calls the functions listed in Table 6.2 in a specific order. First it calls OnPreparePrinting(), which simply calls DoPreparePrinting(), as shown in Listing 6.6. DoPreparePrinting() is responsible for displaying the Print dialog box and creating the printer DC.

Listing 6.6   print1View.cpp —*CPrint1View::OnPreparePrinting()* as Generated by AppWizard

```
BOOL CPrint1View::OnPreparePrinting(CPrintInfo* pInfo)
{
    // default preparation
    return DoPreparePrinting(pInfo);
}
```

As you can see, OnPreparePrinting() receives as a parameter a pointer to a CPrintInfo object. By using this object, you can obtain information about the print job as well as initialize attributes such as the maximum page number. Table 6.3 describes the most useful data and function members of the CPrintInfo class.

Table 6.3   Members of the *CPrintInfo* Class

Member	Description
SetMaxPage()	Sets the document's maximum page number.
SetMinPage()	Sets the document's minimum page number.
GetFromPage()	Gets the number of the first page that users selected for printing.

Member	Description
GetMaxPage()	Gets the document's maximum page number, which may be changed in OnBeginPrinting().
GetMinPage()	Gets the document's minimum page number, which may be changed in OnBeginPrinting().
GetToPage()	Gets the number of the last page users selected for printing.
m_bContinuePrinting	Controls the printing process. Setting the flag to FALSE ends the print job. *For cancelling print Job*
m_bDirect	Indicates whether the document is being directly printed.
m_bPreview	Indicates whether the document is in print preview.
m_nCurPage	Holds the current number of the page being printed.
m_nNumPreviewPages	Holds the number of pages (1 or 2) being displayed in print preview.
m_pPD	Holds a pointer to the print job's CPrintDialog object.
m_rectDraw	Holds a rectangle that defines the usable area for the current page.
m_strPageDesc	Holds a page-number format string.

MFC Printing Process

When the DoPreparePrinting() function displays the Print dialog box, users can set the value of many data members of the CPrintInfo class. Your program then can use or set any of these values. Usually, you'll at least call SetMaxPage(), which sets the document's maximum page number, before DoPreparePrinting() so that the maximum page number displays in the Print dialog box. If you can't determine the number of pages until you calculate a page length based on the selected printer, you have to wait until you have a printer DC for the printer.

After OnPreparePrinting(), MFC calls OnBeginPrinting(), which is not only another place to set the maximum page count but also the place to create resources, such as fonts, that you need to complete the print job. OnPreparePrinting() receives as parameters a pointer to the printer DC and a pointer to the associated CPrintInfo object.

Next, MFC calls OnPrepareDC() for the first page in the document. This is the beginning of a print loop that's executed once for each page in the document. OnPrepareDC() is the place to control what part of the whole document prints on the current page. As you saw previously, you handle this task by setting the document's viewport origin.

After OnPrepareDC(), MFC calls OnPrint() to print the actual page. Normally, OnPrint() calls OnDraw() with the printer DC, which automatically directs OnDraw()'s output to the printer rather than onscreen. You can override OnPrint() to control how the document is printed. You can print headers and footers in OnPrint() and then call the base class's version (which in turn calls OnDraw()) to print the body of the document, as demonstrated in Listing 6.7. (The footer will appear below the body, even though PrintFooter() is called before OnPrint()—don't worry.) To prevent the base class version from overwriting your header and footer area, restrict the printable area by setting the m_rectDraw member of the CPrintInfo object to a rectangle that doesn't overlap the header or footer.

Listing 6.7   Possible *OnPrint()* with Headers and Footers

```
void CPrint1View::OnPrint(CDC* pDC, CPrintInfo* pInfo)
{
    // TODO: Add your specialized code here and/or call the base class

    // Call local functions to print a header and footer.
    PrintHeader();
    PrintFooter();

    CView::OnPrint(pDC, pInfo);
}
```

Alternatively, you can remove OnDraw() from the print loop entirely by doing your own printing in OnPrint() and not calling OnDraw() at all (see Listing 6.8).

Listing 6.8   Possible *OnPrint()* Without *OnDraw()*

```
void CPrint1View::OnPrint(CDC* pDC, CPrintInfo* pInfo)
{
    // TODO: Add your specialized code here and/or call the base class

    // Call local functions to print a header and footer.
    PrintHeader();
    PrintFooter();

    // Call a local function to print the body of the document.
    PrintDocument();
}
```

As long as there are more pages to print, MFC continues to call OnPrepareDC() and OnPrint() for each page in the document. After the last page is printed, MFC calls OnEndPrinting(), where you can destroy any resources you created in OnBeginPrinting(). Figure 6.15 summarizes the entire printing process.

FIG. 6.15
MFC calls various member functions during the printing process.

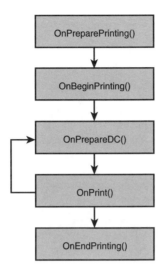

OnPreparePrinting()

OnBeginPrinting()

OnPrepareDC()

OnPrint()

OnEndPrinting()

Persistence and File I/O

Understanding Objects and Persistence

One of the most important things a program must do is save users' data after that data is changed in some way. Without the capability to save edited data, the work a user performs with an application exists only as long as the application is running, vanishing the instant the user exits the application. Not a good way to get work done! In many cases, especially when using AppWizard to create an application, Visual C++ provides much of the code necessary to save and load data. However, in some cases—most notably when you create your own object types—you have to do a little extra work to keep your users' files up to date.

When you're writing an application, you deal with a lot of different object types. Some data objects might be simple types, such as integers and characters. Other objects might be instances of classes, such as strings from the CString class or even objects created from your own custom classes. When using objects in applications that must create, save, and load documents, you need a way to save and load the state of those objects so that you can re-create them exactly as users left them at the end of the last session.

An object's capability to save and load its state is called *persistence*. Almost all MFC classes are persistent because they're derived directly or indirectly from MFC's CObject class, which provides the basic functionality for saving and loading an object's state. The following section reviews how MFC makes a document object persistent.

Examining the File Demo Application

When you use Visual C++'s AppWizard to create a program, you get an application that uses document and view classes to organize, edit, and display its data. As discussed in Chapter 4, "Documents and Views," the document object, derived from the CDocument class, is responsible for holding the application's data during a session and for saving and loading the data so that the document persists from one session to another.

In this chapter, you'll build the File Demo application, which demonstrates the basic techniques behind saving and loading data of an object derived from CDocument. File Demo's document is a single string containing a short message, which the view displays.

Three menu items are relevant in the File Demo application. When the program first begins, the message is automatically set to the string Default Message. Users will change this message by choosing Edit, Change Message. The File, Save menu option saves the document, as you'd expect, and File, Open reloads it from disk.

A Review of Document Classes

Anyone who's written a program has experienced saving and opening files—object persistence from the user's point of view. In this chapter you'll learn how persistence works. Although you had some experience with document classes in Chapter 4, you'll now review the basic concepts with an eye toward extending those concepts to your own custom classes.

When working with an application created by AppWizard, you must complete several steps to enable your document to save and load its state. Those steps are discussed in this section. The steps are as follows:

1. Define the member variables that will hold the document's data.
2. Initialize the member variables in the document class's `OnNewDocument()` member function.
3. Display the current document in the view class's `OnDraw()` member function.
4. Provide member functions in the view class that enable users to edit the document.
5. Add to the document class's `Serialize()` member function the code needed to save and load the data that comprises the document.

When your application can handle multiple documents, you need to do a little extra work to be sure that you use, change, or save the correct document. Luckily, most of that work is taken care of by MFC and AppWizard.

Building the File Demo Application

To build the File Demo application, start by using AppWizard to create an SDI application. All the other AppWizard choices should be left at their default values, so you can speed things up by clicking Finish on Step 1 after selecting SDI and making sure that Document/View support is selected.

Double-click `CFileDemoDoc` in ClassView to edit the header file for the document class. In the Attributes section add a `CString` member variable called `m_message`, so that the Attributes section looks like this:

```
// Attributes
public:
    CString m_message;
```

In this case, the document's storage is nothing more than a single string object. Usually, your document's storage needs are much more complex. This single string, however, is enough to demonstrate the basics of a persistent document. It's very common for MFC programmers to use public variables in their documents, rather than a private variable with public access functions. It makes it a little simpler to write the code in the view class that will access the document variables. It will, however, make future enhancements a little more work. These tradeoffs are discussed in more detail in Appendix A, "C++ Review and Object-Oriented Concepts."

This string, like all the document's data, must be initialized. The `OnNewDocument()` member function is the place to do it. Expand `CFileDemoDoc` in ClassView and double-click `OnNewDocument()` to edit it. Add a line of code to initialize the string so that the function looks like Listing 7.1. You should remove the TODO comments because you've done what they were reminding you to do.

Part

II

Ch

7

Listing 7.1   Initializing the Document's Data

```
BOOL CFileDemoDoc::OnNewDocument()
{
    if (!CDocument::OnNewDocument())
        return FALSE;

    m_message = "Default Message";

    return TRUE;
}
```

With the document class's m_message data member initialized, the application can display the data in the view window. You just need to edit the view class's OnDraw() function (see Listing 7.2). Expand CFileDemoView in ClassView and double-click OnDraw() to edit it. Again, you're just adding one line of code and removing the TODO comment.

Listing 7.2   Displaying the Document's Data

```
void CFileDemoView::OnDraw(CDC* pDC)
{
    CFileDoc* pDoc = GetDocument();
    ASSERT_VALID(pDoc);

    pDC->TextOut(20, 20, pDoc->m_message);
}
```

Getting information onscreen, using device contexts, and the TextOut() function are all discussed in Chapter 5, "Drawing on the Screen."

Build File Demo now, to make sure there are no typos, and run it. You should see Default Message appear onscreen.

Now, you need to allow users to edit the application's document by changing the string. In theory, the application should display a dialog box to let the user enter any desired string at all. For our purposes, you're just going to have the Edit, Change Message menu option assign the string a different, hard-coded value. ShowString, the subject of Chapter 8, "Building a Complete Application: ShowString," shows how to create a dialog box such as the one File Demo might use.

Click the Resource tab to switch to ResourceView, expand the resources, expand Menus, and double-click IDR_MAINFRAME to edit it. Click once on the Edit item in the menu you are editing to drop it down. Click the blank item at the end of the list and type **Change &Message**. This will add another item to the menu.

Choose View, ClassWizard to make the connection between this menu item and your code. You should see ID_EDIT_CHANGEMESSAGE highlighted already; if not, click it in the box on the left to highlight it. Choose CFileDemoView from the drop-down box on the upper right. Click COMMAND in the lower-right box and then click the Add Function button. Accept the suggested name, OnEditChangemessage(), by clicking OK on the dialog that appears. Click Edit Code to open the new function in the editor and edit it to match Listing 7.3.

Listing 7.3 Changing the Document's Data

```
void CFileDemoView::OnEditChangemessage()
{
    CTime now = CTime::GetCurrentTime();
    CString changetime = now.Format("Changed at %B %d %H:%M:%S");
    GetDocument()->m_message = changetime;
    GetDocument()->SetModifiedFlag();
    Invalidate();
}
```

Time Access

redraw screen brings up dialog to save changes

This function, which responds to the application's Edit, Change Message command, builds a string from the current date and time and transfers it to the document's data member. (The CTime class and its Format() function are discussed in Appendix F, "Useful Classes.") The call to the document class's SetModifiedFlag() function notifies the object that its contents have been changed. The application will warn about exiting with unsaved changes as long as you remember to call SetModifiedFlag() everywhere there might be a change to the data. Finally, this code forces a redraw of the screen by calling Invalidate(), as discussed in Chapter 4.

TIP If m_message was a private member variable of the document class, you could have a public SetMessage() function that called SetModifiedFlag() and be guaranteed no programmer would ever forget to call it. That's one of the advantages of writing truly object-oriented programs.

The document class's Serialize() function handles the saving and loading of the document's data. Listing 7.4 shows the empty shell of Serialize() generated by AppWizard.

File handle

Listing 7.4 FILEVIEW.CPP—The Document Class *Serialize()* Function

```
void CFileDoc::Serialize(CArchive& ar)
{
    if (ar.IsStoring())
    {
        // TODO: add storing code here
    }
    else
    {
        // TODO: add loading code here
    }
}
```

Part

II

Ch

7

Simple data types [handwritten]

Because the `CString` class (of which m_message is an object) defines the >> and << operators for transferring strings to and from an archive, it's a simple task to save and load the document class's data. Simply add this line where the comment reminds you to add storing code:

Store string [handwritten]

```
ar << m_message;
```

Load string [handwritten]

Add this similar line where the loading code belongs:

```
ar >> m_message;
```

The << operator sends the `CString` m_message to the archive; the >> operator fills m_message from the archive. As long as all the document's member variables are simple data types such as integers or characters, or MFC classes such as `CString` with these operators already defined, it's easy to save and load the data. The operators are defined for these simple data types:

- BYTE
- WORD
- int
- LONG
- DWORD
- float
- double

Build File Demo and run it. Choose Edit, Change Message, and you should see the new string onscreen, as shown in Figure 7.1. Choose File, Save and enter a filename you can remember. Now change the message again. Choose File, New and you'll be warned about saving your current changes first, as in Figure 7.2. Choose File, Open and browse to your file, or just find your filename towards the bottom of the File menu to re-open it, and you'll see that File Demo can indeed save and reload a string.

FIG. 7.1

File Demo changes the string on command.

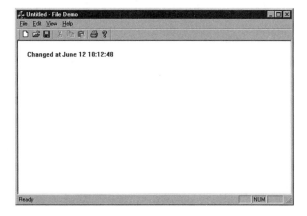

FIG. 7.2

Your users will never lose unsaved data again.

N O T E If you change the file, save it, change it again, and re-open it, File Demo will not ask Revert to saved document? as some applications do. Instead, it will bail out of the File Open process partway through and leave you with your most recent changes. This behavior is built in to MFC. If the name of the file you are opening matches the name of the file that is already open, you will not revert to the saved document. ■

Creating a Persistent Class

What if you've created your own custom class for holding the elements of a document? How can you make an object of this class persistent? You find the answers to these questions in this section.

Suppose that you now want to enhance the File Demo application so that it contains its data in a custom class called CMessages. The member variable is now called m_messages and is an instance of CMessages. This class holds three CString objects, each of which must be saved and loaded for the application to work correctly. One way to arrange this is to save and load each individual string, as shown in Listing 7.5.

Listing 7.5   One Possible Way to Save the New Class's Strings

```
void CFileDoc::Serialize(CArchive& ar)
{
    if (ar.IsStoring())
    {
        ar << m_messages.m_message1;
        ar << m_messages.m_message2;
        ar << m_messages.m_message3;
    }
    else
    {
```

Part

II

Ch

7

continues

Listing 7.5   Continued

```
        ar >> m_messages.m_message1;
        ar >> m_messages.m_message2;
        ar >> m_messages.m_message3;
    }
    }
```

You can write the code in Listing 7.5 only if the three member variables of the CMessages class are public and if you know the implementation of the class itself. Later, if the class is changed in any way, this code also has to be changed. It's more object oriented to delegate the work of storing and loading to the CMessages class itself. This requires some preparation. The following basic steps create a class that can serialize its member variables:

1. Derive the class from CObject.
2. Place the DECLARE_SERIAL() macro in the class declaration.
3. Place the IMPLEMENT_SERIAL() macro in the class implementation.
4. Override the Serialize() function in the class.
5. Provide an empty, default constructor for the class.

In the following section, you build an application that creates persistent objects in just this way.

The File Demo 2 Application

The next sample application, File Demo 2, demonstrates the steps you take to create a class from which you can create persistent objects. It will have an Edit, Change Messages command that changes all three strings. Like File Demo, it will save and reload the document when the user chooses File, Save or File, Open.

Build an SDI application called MultiString just as you built File Demo. Add a member variable to the document, as before, so that the Attributes section of MultiStringDoc.h reads

```
// Attributes
public:
    CMessages m_messages;
```

The next step is to write the CMessages class.

Looking at the *CMessages* Class

Before you can understand how the document class manages to save and load its contents successfully, you have to understand how the CMessages class, of which the document class's m_messages data member is an object, works. As you work with this class, you will see how to implement the preceding five steps for creating a persistent class.

To create the CMessages class, first choose Insert, New Class. Change the class type to generic class and name it **CMessages**. In the area at the bottom of the screen, enter **CObject** as the base class name and leave the As column set to public, as shown in Figure 7.3.

FIG. 7.3

Create a new class to hold the messages.

This will create two files: messages.h for the header and messages.cpp for the code. It also adds some very simple code to these files for you. (You may get a warning about not being able to find the header file for CObject: just click OK and ignore it because CObject, like all MFC files, is available to you without including extra headers.)

Switch back to Multistringdoc.h and add this line before the class definition:

```
#include "Messages.h"
```

This will ensure the compiler knows about the CMessages class when it compiles the document class. You can build the project now if you want to be sure you haven't forgotten anything. Now switch back to Messages.h and add these lines:

```
    DECLARE_SERIAL(CMessages)

protected:
    CString m_message1;
    CString m_message2;
    CString m_message3;

public:
    void SetMessage(UINT msgNum, CString msg);
    CString GetMessage(UINT msgNum);
    void Serialize(CArchive& ar);
```

The DECLARE_SERIAL() macro provides the additional function and member variable declarations needed to implement object persistence.

Next come the class's data members, which are three objects of the CString class. Notice that they are protected member variables. The public member functions are next. SetMessage(), whose arguments are the index of the string to set and the string's new value, changes a data member. GetMessage() is the complementary function, enabling a program to retrieve the current value of any of the strings. Its single argument is the number of the string to retrieve.

Part

II

Ch

7

Finally, the class overrides the `Serialize()` function, where all the data saving and loading takes place. The `Serialize()` function is the heart of a persistent object, with each persistent class implementing it in a different way. Listing 7.6 shows the code for each of these new member functions. Add it to messages.cpp.

Listing 7.6 MESSAGES.CPP—The *CMessages* Class Implementation File

```
void CMessages::SetMessage(UINT msgNum, CString msg)
{
    switch (msgNum)
    {
    case 1:
        m_message1 = msg;
        break;

    case 2:
        m_message2 = msg;
        break;

    case 3:
        m_message3 = msg;
        break;
    }
    SetModifiedFlag();
}

CString CMessages::GetMessage(UINT msgNum)
{
    switch (msgNum)
    {
        case 1:
            return m_message1;
        case 2:
            return m_message2;
        case 3:
            return m_message3;
        default:
            return "";
    }
}

void CMessages::Serialize(CArchive& ar)
{
    CObject::Serialize(ar);

    if (ar.IsStoring())
    {
        ar << m_message1 << m_message2 << m_message3;
    }
    else
    {
        ar >> m_message1 >> m_message2 >> m_message3;
    }
}
```

There's nothing tricky about the SetMessage() and GetMessage() functions, which perform their assigned tasks precisely. The Serialize() function, however, may inspire a couple of questions. First, note that the first line of the body of the function calls the base class's Serialize() function. This is a standard practice for many functions that override functions of a base class. In this case, the call to CObject::Serialize() doesn't do much because the CObject class's Serialize() function is empty. Still, calling the base class's Serialize() function is a good habit to get into because you may not always be working with classes derived directly from CObject.

After calling the base class's version of the function, Serialize() saves and loads its data in much the same way a document object does. Because the data members that must be serialized are CString objects, the program can use the >> and << operators to write the strings to the disk.

Towards the top of messages.cpp, after the include statements, add this line:

```
IMPLEMENT_SERIAL(CMessages, CObject, 0)
```

The IMPLEMENT_SERIAL() macro is partner to the DECLARE_SERIAL() macro, providing implementation for the functions that give the class its persistent capabilities. The macro's three arguments are the name of the class, the name of the immediate base class, and a schema number, which is like a version number. In most cases, you use 0 or 1 for the schema number.

Using the *CMessages* Class in the Program

Now that CMessages is defined and implemented, member functions of the MultiString document and view classes can work with it. First, expand CMultiStringDoc and double-click OnNewDocument() to edit it. Add these lines in place of the TODO comments.

```
m_messages.SetMessage(1, "Default Message 1");
m_messages.SetMessage(2, "Default Message 2");
m_messages.SetMessage(3, "Default Message 3");
```

Because the document class can't directly access the data object's protected data members, it initializes each string by calling the CMessages class's SetMessage() member function.

Expand CMultiStringView and double-click OnDraw() to edit it. Here's how it should look when you're finished:

```
void CMultiStringView::OnDraw(CDC* pDC)
{
        CMultiStringDoc* pDoc = GetDocument();
        ASSERT_VALID(pDoc);

    pDC->TextOut(20, 20, pDoc->m_messages.GetMessage(1));
    pDC->TextOut(20, 40, pDoc->m_messages.GetMessage(2));
    pDC->TextOut(20, 60, pDoc->m_messages.GetMessage(3));
}
```

As you did for File Demo, add a "Change Messages" item to the Edit menu. Connect it to a view function called OnEditChangemessages. This function will change the data by calling the CMessages object's member functions, as in Listing 7.7. The view class's OnDraw() function also calls the GetMessage() member function to access the CMessages class's strings.

Listing 7.7 Editing the Data Strings

```
void CMultiStringView::OnEditChangemessages()
{
    CMultiStringDoc* pDoc = GetDocument();
    CTime now = CTime::GetCurrentTime();
    CString changetime = now.Format("Changed at %B %d %H:%M:%S");

    pDoc->m_messages.SetMessage(1, CString("String 1 ") + changetime);
    pDoc->m_messages.SetMessage(2, CString("String 2 ") + changetime);
    pDoc->m_messages.SetMessage(3, CString("String 3 ") + changetime);
    pDoc->SetModifiedFlag();
    Invalidate();

}
```

All that remains is to write the document class's Serialize() function, where the m_messages data object is serialized out to disk. You just delegate the work to the data object's own Serialize() function, as in Listing 7.8.

Listing 7.8 Serializing the Data Object

```
void CMultiStringDoc::Serialize(CArchive& ar)
{
    m_messages.Serialize(ar);
        if (ar.IsStoring())
        {
        }
        else
        {
        }
}
```

As you can see, after serializing the m_messages data object, not much is left to do in the document class's Serialize() function. Notice that the call to m_messages.Serialize() passes the archive object as its single parameter. Build MultiString now and test it as you tested File Demo. It should do everything you expect.

Reading and Writing Files Directly

Although using MFC's built-in serialization capabilities is a handy way to save and load data, sometimes you need more control over the file-handling process. For example, you might need to deal with your files nonsequentially, something the Serialize() function and its associated CArchive object can't handle because they do stream I/O. In this case, you can handle files almost exactly as they're handled by non-Windows programmers: creating, reading, and writing files directly. Even when you need to dig down to this level of file handling, MFC offers help. Specifically, you can use the CFile class and its derived classes to handle files directly.

The *CFile* Class

MFC's CFile class encapsulates all the functions you need to handle any type of file. Whether you want to perform common sequential data saving and loading or construct a random access file, the CFile class gets you there. Using the CFile class is a lot like handling files the old-fashioned C-style way, except that the class hides some of the busy-work details from you so that you can get the job done quickly and easily. For example, you can create a file for reading with only a single line of code. Table 7.1 shows the CFile class's member functions and their descriptions.

Table 7.1   Member Functions of the *CFile* Class

Function	Description
CFile	Creates the CFile object. If passed a filename, it opens the file.
Destructor	Cleans up a CFile object that's going out of scope. If the file is open, it closes that file.
Abort()	Immediately closes the file with no regard for errors.
Close()	Closes the file.
Duplicate()	Creates a duplicate file object.
Flush()	Flushes data from the stream.
GetFileName()	Gets the file's filename.
GetFilePath()	Gets the file's full path.
GetFileTitle()	Gets the file's title (the filename without the extension).
GetLength()	Gets the file's length.
GetPosition()	Gets the current position within the file.
GetStatus()	Gets the file's status.
LockRange()	Locks a portion of the file.
Open()	Opens the file.
Read()	Reads data from the file.
Remove()	Deletes a file.
Rename()	Renames the file.
Seek()	Sets the position within the file.
SeekToBegin()	Sets the position to the beginning of the file.
SeekToEnd()	Sets the position to the end of the file.
SetFilePath()	Sets the file's path.

Part
II

Ch
7

continues

Table 7.1 Continued

Function	Description
SetLength()	Sets the file's length.
SetStatus()	Sets the file's status.
UnlockRange()	Unlocks a portion of the file.
Write()	Writes data to the file.

As you can see from Table 7.1, the CFile class offers plenty of file-handling power. This section demonstrates how to call a few of the CFile class's member functions. However, most of the other functions are just as easy to use.

Here's a sample snippet of code that creates and opens a file, writes a string to it, and then gathers some information about the file:

```
// Create the file.
CFile file("TESTFILE.TXT", CFile::modeCreate | CFile::modeWrite);

// Write data to the file.
CString message("Hello file!");
int length = message.GetLength();
file.Write((LPCTSTR)message, length);

// Obtain information about the file.
CString filePath = file.GetFilePath();
Int fileLength = file.GetLength();
```

Notice that you don't have to explicitly open the file when you pass a filename to the constructor, whose arguments are the name of the file and the file access mode flags. You can use several flags at a time simply by ORing their values together, as in the little snippet above. These flags, which describe how to open the file and which specify the types of valid operations, are defined as part of the CFile class and are described in Table 7.2.

Table 7.2 The File Mode Flags

Flag	Description
CFile::modeCreate	Creates a new file or truncates an existing file to length 0
CFile::modeNoInherit	Disallows inheritance by a child process
CFile::modeNoTruncate	When creating the file, doesn't truncate the file if it already exists
CFile::modeRead	Allows read operations only
CFile::modeReadWrite	Allows both read and write operations
CFile::modeWrite	Allows write operations only

Flag	Description
CFile::shareCompat	Allows other processes to open the file
CFile::shareDenyNone	Allows other processes read or write operations on the file
CFile::shareDenyRead	Disallows read operations by other processes
CFile::shareDenyWrite	Disallows write operations by other processes
CFile::shareExclusive	Denies all access to other processes
CFile::typeBinary	Sets binary mode for the file
CFile::typeText	Sets text mode for the file

CFile::Write() takes a pointer to the buffer containing the data to write and the number of bytes to write. Notice the LPCTSTR casting operator in the call to Write(). This operator is defined by the CString class and extracts the string from the class.

One other thing about the code snippet: There is no call to Close()—the CFile destructor closes the file automatically when file goes out of scope.

Reading from a file isn't much different from writing to one:

```
// Open the file.
CFile file("TESTFILE.TXT", CFile::modeRead);

// Read data from the file.
char s[81];
int bytesRead = file.Read(s, 80);
s[bytesRead] = 0;
CString message = s;
```

This time the file is opened by the CFile::modeRead flag, which opens the file for read operations only, after which the code creates a character buffer and calls the file object's Read() member function to read data into the buffer. The Read() function's two arguments are the buffer's address and the number of bytes to read. The function returns the number of bytes actually read, which in this case is almost always less than the 80 requested. By using the number of bytes read, the program can add a 0 to the end of the character data, thus creating a standard C-style string that can be used to set a CString variable.

The code snippets you've just seen use a hard-coded filename. To get filenames from your user with little effort, be sure to look up the MFC class CFileDialog in the online help. It's simple to use and adds a very nice touch to your programs.

Creating Your Own *CArchive* Objects

Although you can use CFile objects to read from and write to files, you can also go a step farther and create your own CArchive object and use it exactly as you use the CArchive object in the Serialize() function. This lets you take advantage of Serialize functions already written for other objects, passing them a reference to your own archive object.

Part
II

Ch
7

To create an archive, create a CFile object and pass it to the CArchive constructor. For example, if you plan to write out objects to a file through an archive, create the archive like this:

```
CFile file("FILENAME.EXT", CFile::modeWrite);
CArchive ar(&file, CArchive::store);
```

After creating the archive object, you can use it just like the archive objects that MFC creates for you, for example, calling Serialize() yourself and passing the archive to it. Because you created the archive with the CArchive::store flag, any calls to IsStoring() return TRUE, and the code that dumps objects to the archive executes. When you're through with the archive object, you can close the archive and the file like this:

```
ar.Close();
file.Close();
```

If the objects go out of scope soon after you're finished with them, you can safely omit the calls to Close() because both CArchive and CFile have Close() calls in the destructor.

Using the Registry — *Central, storage, access, initialize*

In the early days of Windows programming, applications saved settings and options in initialization files, typically with the .INI extension. The days of huge WIN.INI files or myriad private .INI files are now gone—when an application wants to store information about itself, it does so by using a centralized system Registry. Although the Registry makes sharing information between processes easier, it can make things more confusing for programmers. In this section, you uncover some of the mysteries of the Registry and learn how to manage it in your applications.

How the Registry Is Set Up

Unlike .INI files, which are plain text files that can be edited with any text editor, the Registry contains binary and ASCII information that can be edited only by using the Registry Editor or special API function calls created specifically for managing the Registry. If you've ever used the Registry Editor to browse your system's Registry, you know that it contains a huge amount of information that's organized into a tree structure. Figure 7.4 shows how the Registry appears when you first run the Registry Editor. (On Windows 95, you can find the Registry Editor, REGEDIT.EXE, in your main Windows folder, or you can run it from the Start menu by choosing Run, typing **regedit**, and then clicking OK. Under Windows NT, it's REGEDT32.EXE.)

The far left window lists the Registry's predefined keys. The plus marks next to the keys in the tree indicate that you can open the keys and view more detailed information associated with them. Keys can have subkeys, and subkeys themselves can have subkeys. Any key or subkey may or may not have a value associated with it. If you explore deep enough in the hierarchy, you see a list of values in the far right window. In Figure 7.5, you can see the values associated with the current user's screen appearance. To see these values yourself, browse from HKEY_CURRENT_USER to Control Panel to Appearance to Schemes, and you'll see the desktop schemes installed on your system.

FIG. 7.4
The Registry Editor displays the Registry.

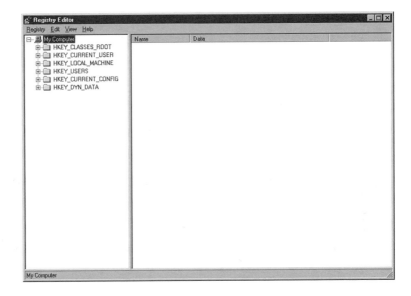

FIG. 7.5
The Registry is structured as a tree containing a huge amount of information.

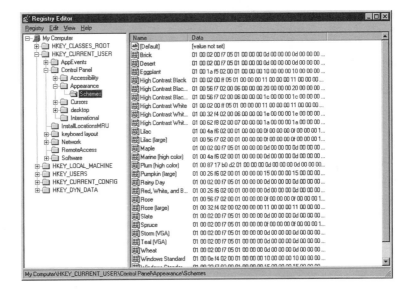

The Predefined Keys

To know where things are stored in the Registry, you need to know about the predefined keys and what they mean. From Figure 7.4, you can see that the six predefined keys are

- HKEY_CLASSES_ROOT
- HKEY_CURRENT_USER

- HKEY_LOCAL_MACHINE
- HKEY_USERS
- HKEY_CURRENT_CONFIG
- HKEY_DYN_DATA

The HKEY_CLASSES_ROOT key holds document types and properties, as well as class information about the various applications installed on the machine. For example, if you explored this key on your system, you'd probably find an entry for the .DOC file extension, under which you'd find entries for the applications that can handle this type of document (see Figure 7.6).

FIG. 7.6
The
HKEY_CLASSES_ROOT
key holds document
information.

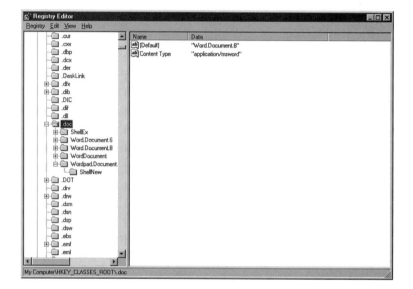

The HKEY_CURRENT_USER key contains all the system settings the current user has established, including color schemes, printers, and program groups. The HKEY_LOCAL_MACHINE key, on the other hand, contains status information about the computer, and the HKEY_USERS key organizes information about each user of the system, as well as the default configuration. Finally, the HKEY_CURRENT_CONFIG key holds information about the hardware configuration, and the HKEY_DYN_DATA key contains information about dynamic Registry data, which is data that changes frequently. (You may not always see this key on your system.)

Using the Registry in an MFC Application

Now that you know a little about the Registry, let me say that it would take an entire book to explain how to fully access and use it. As you may imagine, the Win32 API features many functions for manipulating the Registry. If you're going to use those functions, you had better know what you're doing! Invalid Registry settings can crash your machine, make it unbootable, and perhaps force you to reinstall Windows to recover.

However, you can easily use the Registry with your MFC applications to store information that the application needs from one session to another. To make this task as easy as possible, MFC provides the CWinApp class with the SetRegistryKey() member function, which creates (or opens) a key entry in the Registry for your application. All you have to do is supply a key name (usually a company name) for the function to use, like this:

```
SetRegistryKey("MyCoolCompany");
```

You should call SetRegistryKey() in the application class's InitInstance() member function, which is called once at program startup.

After you call SetRegistryKey(), your application can create the subkeys and values it needs by calling one of two functions. The WriteProfileString() function adds string values to the Registry, and the WriteProfileInt() function adds integer values to the Registry. To get values from the Registry, you can use the GetProfileString() and GetProfileInt() functions. (You also can use RegSetValueEx() and RegQueryValueEx() to set and retrieve Registry values.)

> **N O T E** When they were first written, the WriteProfileString(), WriteProfileInt(), GetProfileString(), and GetProfileInt() functions transferred information to and from an .INI file. Used alone, they still do. But when you call SetRegistryKey() first, MFC reroutes these profile functions to the Registry, making using the Registry an almost painless process. ■

The Sample Applications Revisited

In this chapter, you've already built applications that used the Registry. Here's an excerpt from CMultiStringApp::InitInstance()—this code was generated by AppWizard and is also in CFileDemoApp::InitInstance().

```
// Change the registry key under which our settings are stored.
// You should modify this string to be something appropriate
// such as the name of your company or organization.
SetRegistryKey(_T("Local AppWizard-Generated Applications"));

LoadStdProfileSettings();  // Load standard INI file options (including MRU)
```

MRU stands for *Most Recently Used* and refers to the list of files that appears on the File menu after you open files with an application. Figure 7.7 shows the Registry Editor displaying the key that stores this information, HKEY_CURRENT_USER\Software\Local AppWizard-Generated Applications\MultiString\Recent File List. In the foreground, MultiString's File menu shows the single entry in the MRU list.

Part

II

Ch

7

FIG. 7.7

The most recently used files list is stored in the Registry automatically.

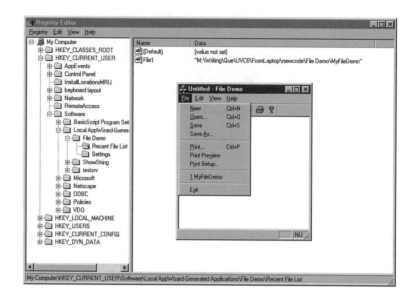

Building a Complete Application: ShowString

Building an Application That Displays a String

In this chapter you pull together the concepts demonstrated in previous chapters to create an application that really does something. You add a menu, a menu item, a dialog box, and persistence to an application that draws output based on user settings. In subsequent chapters this application serves as a base for more advanced work.

The sample application you will build is very much like the traditional "Hello, world!" of C programming. It simply displays a text string in the main window. The *document* (what you save in a file) contains the string and a few settings. There is a new menu item to bring up a dialog box to change the string and the settings, which control the string's appearance. This is a deliberately simple application so that the concepts of adding menu items and adding dialogs are not obscured by trying to understand the actual brains of the application. So, bring up Developer Studio and follow along.

Creating an Empty Shell with AppWizard

First, use AppWizard to create the starter application. (Chapter 1, "Building Your First Windows Application," covers AppWizard and creating starter applications.) Choose File, New and the Project tab. Select an MFC AppWizard (exe) application, name the project ShowString so that your classnames will match those shown throughout this chapter, and click OK.

In Step 1 of AppWizard, it doesn't matter much whether you choose SDI or MDI, but MDI will enable you to see for yourself how little effort is required to have multiple documents open at once. So, choose MDI. Choose U.S. English, and then click Next.

The ShowString application needs no database support and no compound document support, so click Next on Step 2 and Step 3 without changing anything. In AppWizard's Step 4 dialog box, select a docking toolbar, initial status bar, printing and print preview, context-sensitive help, and 3D controls, and then click Next. Choose source file comments and shared DLL, and then click Next. The classnames and filenames are all fine, so click Finish. Figure 8.1 shows the final confirmation dialog box. Click OK.

FIG. 8.1

AppWizard summarizes the design choices for ShowString.

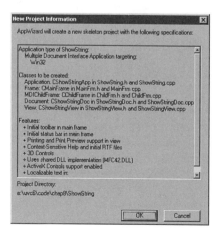

Displaying a String

The ShowString application displays a string that will be kept in the document. You need to add a member variable to the document class, `CShowStringDoc`, and add loading and saving code to the `Serialize()` function. You can initialize the string by adding code to `OnNewDocument()` for the document and, in order to actually display it, override `OnDraw()` for the view. Documents and views are introduced in Chapter 4, "Documents and Views."

Member Variable and Serialization   Add a private variable to the document and a public function to get the value by adding these lines to ShowStringDoc.h:

```
private:
    CString string;
public:
    CString GetString() {return string;}
```

The inline function gives other parts of your application a copy of the string to use whenever necessary but makes it impossible for other parts to change the string.

Next, change the skeleton `CShowStringDoc::Serialize()` function provided by AppWizard to look like Listing 8.1. (Expand `CShowStringDoc` in ClassView and double-click `Serialize()` to edit the code.) Because you used the MFC `CString` class, the archive has operators << and >> already defined, so this is a simple function to write. It fills the archive from the string when you are saving the document and fills the string from the archive when you are loading the document from a file. Chapter 7, "Persistence and File I/O," introduces serialization.

Listing 8.1   SHOWSTRINGDOC.CPP—*CShowStringDoc::Serialize()*

```cpp
void CShowStringDoc::Serialize(CArchive& ar)
{
    if (ar.IsStoring())
    {
        ar << string;
    }
    else
    {
        ar >> string;
    }
}
```

Initializing the String   Whenever a new document is created, you want your application to initialize `string` to `"Hello, world!"`. A new document is created when the user chooses File, New. This message is caught by `CShowStringApp` (the message map is shown in Listing 8.2, you can see it yourself by scrolling toward the top of ShowString.cpp) and handled by `CWinApp::OnFileNew()`. (Message maps and message handlers are discussed in Chapter 3, "Messages and Commands.") Starter applications generated by AppWizard call `OnFileNew()` to create a blank document when they run. `OnFileNew()` calls the document's `OnNewDocument()`, which actually initializes the member variables of the document.

Listing 8.2   SHOWSTRING.CPP—Message Map

```
BEGIN_MESSAGE_MAP(CShowStringApp, CWinApp)
    //{{AFX_MSG_MAP(CShowStringApp)
    ON_COMMAND(ID_APP_ABOUT, OnAppAbout)
        // NOTE - The ClassWizard will add and remove mapping macros here.
        //    DO NOT EDIT what you see in these blocks of generated code!
    //}}AFX_MSG_MAP
    // Standard file-based document commands
    ON_COMMAND(ID_FILE_NEW, CWinApp::OnFileNew)
    ON_COMMAND(ID_FILE_OPEN, CWinApp::OnFileOpen)
    // Standard print setup command
    ON_COMMAND(ID_FILE_PRINT_SETUP, CWinApp::OnFilePrintSetup)
END_MESSAGE_MAP()
```

AppWizard gives you the simple OnNewDocument() shown in Listing 8.3. To see yours in the editor, double-click OnNewDocument() in ClassView—you may have to expand CshowStringDoc first.

Listing 8.3   SHOWSTRINGDOC.CPP—*CShowStringDoc::OnNewDocument()*

```
BOOL CShowStringDoc::OnNewDocument()
{
    if (!CDocument::OnNewDocument())
        return FALSE;

    // TODO: add reinitialization code here
    // (SDI documents will reuse this document)

    return TRUE;
}
```

Take away the comments and add this line in their place:

```
string = "Hello, world!";
```

(What else could it say, after all?) Leave the call to CDocument::OnNewDocument() because that will handle all other work involved in making a new document.

Getting the String Onscreen   As you learned in Chapter 5, "Drawing on the Screen," a view's OnDraw() function is called whenever that view needs to be drawn, such as when your application is first started, resized, or restored or when a window that had been covering it is taken away. AppWizard has provided a skeleton, shown in Listing 8.4. To edit this function, expand CShowStringView in ClassView and then double-click OnDraw().

Listing 8.4   SHOWSTRINGVIEW.CPP—*CShowStringView::OnDraw()*

```
void CShowStringView::OnDraw(CDC* pDC)
{
    CShowStringDoc* pDoc = GetDocument();
```

```
    ASSERT_VALID(pDoc);

    // TODO: add draw code for native data here
}
```

OnDraw() takes a pointer to a device context, as discussed in Chapter 5. The device context class, CDC, has a member function called DrawText() that draws text onscreen. It is declared like this:

```
int DrawText( const CString& str, LPRECT lpRect, UINT nFormat )
```

▶ **See** "Understanding Device Contexts," **p. 98**

The CString to be passed to this function is going to be the string from the document class, which can be accessed as pDoc->GetString(). The lpRect is the client rectangle of the view, returned by GetClientRect(). Finally, nFormat is the way the string should display; for example, DT_CENTER means that the text should be centered from left to right within the view. DT_VCENTER means that the text should be centered up and down, but this works only for single lines of text that are identified with DT_SINGLELINE. Multiple format flags can be combined with ¦, so DT_CENTER¦DT_VCENTER¦DT_SINGLELINE is the nFormat that you want. The drawing code to be added to CShowStringView::OnDraw() looks like this:

```
CRect rect;
GetClientRect(&rect);
pDC->DrawText(pDoc->GetString(), &rect, DT_CENTER¦DT_VCENTER¦DT_SINGLELINE);
```

This sets up a CRect and passes its address to GetClientRect(), which sets the CRect to the client area of the view. DrawText() draws the document's string in the rectangle, centered vertically and horizontally.

At this point, the application should display the string properly. Build and execute it, and you will see something like Figure 8.2. You have a lot of functionality—menus, toolbars, status bar, and so on—but nothing that any other Windows application doesn't have, yet. Starting with the next section, that changes.

FIG. 8.2

ShowString starts simply, with the usual greeting.

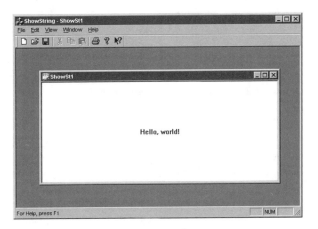

Building the ShowString Menus

AppWizard creates two menus for you, shown in the ResourceView window in Figure 8.3. IDR_MAINFRAME is the menu shown when no file is open; IDR_SHOWSTTYPE is the menu shown when a ShowString document is open. Notice that IDR_MAINFRAME has no Window menus and that the File menu is much shorter than the one on the IDR_SHOWSTTYPE menu, with only New, Open, Print Setup, recent files, and Exit items.

FIG. 8.3

AppWizard creates two menus for ShowString.

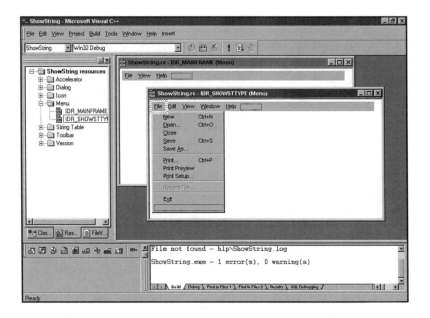

You are going to add a menu item to ShowString, so the first decision is where to add it. The user will be able to edit the string that displays and to set the string's format. You could add a Value item to the Edit menu that brings up a small dialog box for only the string and then create a Format menu with one item, Appearance, that brings up the dialog box to set the appearance. The choice you are going to see here, though, is to combine everything into one dialog box and then put it on a new Tools menu, under the Options item.

NOTE You may have noticed already that more and more Windows applications are standardizing Tools, Options as the place for miscellaneous settings. ▪

Do you need to add the item to both menus? No. When there is no document open, there is nowhere to save the changes made with this dialog box. So only IDR_SHOWSTTYPE needs to have a menu added. Open the menu by double-clicking it in the ResourceView window. At the far right of the menu, after Help, is an empty menu. Click it and type **&Tools**. The Properties dialog box appears; pin it to the background by clicking the pushpin. The Caption box contains &Tools. The menu at the end becomes the Tools menu, with an empty item underneath it; another empty menu then appears to the right of the Tools menu, as shown in Figure 8.4.

FIG. 8.4

Adding the Tools menu is easy in the ResourceView window.

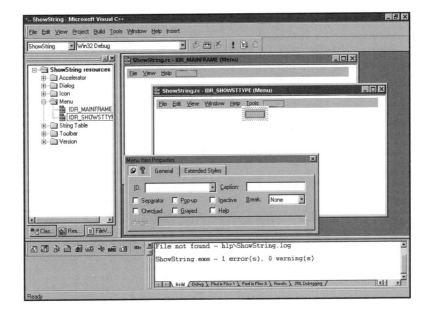

Click the new Tools menu and drag it between the View and Window menus, corresponding to the position of Tools in products like Developer Studio and Microsoft Word. Next, click the empty sub-item. The Properties dialog box changes to show the blank properties of this item; change the caption to **&Options** and enter a sensible prompt, as shown in Figure 8.5. The prompt will be shown on the status bar when the user pauses the mouse over the menu item or moves the highlight over it with the cursor.

 TIP The & in the Caption edit box precedes the letter that serves as the mnemonic key for selecting that menu with the keyboard (for example, Alt+T in the case of Tools). This letter appears underlined in the menu. There is no further work required on your part. You can opt to select a different mnemonic key by moving the & so that it precedes a different letter in the menu or menu item name (for example, T&ools changes the key from *T* to *o*). You should not use the same mnemonic letter for two menus or for two items on the same menu.

All menu items have a resource ID, and this resource ID is the way the menu items are connected to your code. Developer Studio will choose a good one for you, but it doesn't appear right away in the Properties dialog box. Click some other menu item, and then click Options again; you see that the resource ID is ID_TOOLS_OPTIONS. Alternatively, press Enter when you are finished, and the highlight moves down to the empty menu item below Options. Press the up-arrow cursor key to return the highlight to the Options item.

If you'd like to provide an accelerator, like the Ctrl+C for Edit, Copy that the system provides, this is a good time to do it. Click the + next to Accelerator in the ResourceView window and then double-click IDR_MAINFRAME, the only Accelerator table in this application. At a glance, you can see what key combinations are already in use. Ctrl+O is already taken, but Ctrl+T is available. To connect Ctrl+T to Tools, Options, follow these steps:

FIG. 8.5

The menu command
Tools, Options controls
everything that
ShowString does.

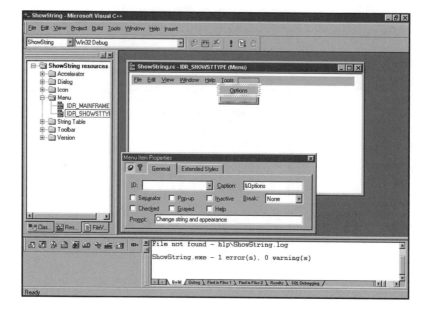

1. Click the empty line at the bottom of the Accelerator table. If you have closed the Properties dialog box, bring it back by choosing View, Properties and then pin it in place. (Alternatively, double-click the empty line to bring up the Properties dialog box.)

2. Click the drop-down list box labeled ID and choose ID_TOOLS_OPTIONS from the list, which is in alphabetical order. (There are a lot of entries before ID_TOOLS_OPTIONS; drag the elevator down to almost the bottom of the list or start typing the resource ID—by the time you type **ID_TO**, the highlight will be in the right place.)

3. Type **T** in the Key box; then make sure that the Ctrl check box is selected and that the Alt and Shift boxes are deselected. Alternatively, click the Next Key Typed button and then type **Ctrl+T**, and the dialog box will be filled in properly.

4. Click another line in the Accelerator table to commit the changes.

Figure 8.6 shows the Properties dialog box for this accelerator after again clicking the newly entered line.

What happens when the user chooses this new menu item, Tools, Options? A dialog box displays. So, tempting as it may be to start connecting this menu to code, it makes more sense to build the dialog box first.

Building the ShowString Dialog Boxes

Chapter 2, "Dialogs and Controls," introduces dialog boxes. This section builds on that background. ShowString is going to have two custom dialog boxes: one brought up by Tools, Options and also an About dialog box. An About dialog box has been provided by AppWizard, but it needs to be changed a little; you build the Options dialog box from scratch.

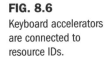

FIG. 8.6
Keyboard accelerators are connected to resource IDs.

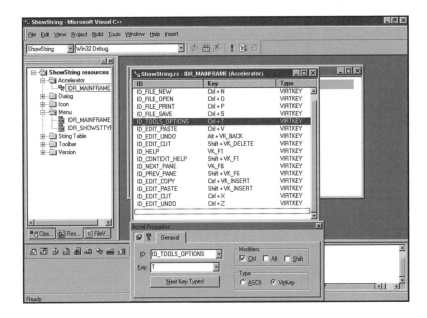

ShowString's About Dialog Box

Figure 8.7 shows the About dialog box that AppWizard makes for you; it contains the application name and the current year. To view the About dialog box for ShowString, click the ResourceView tab in the project workspace window, expand the Dialogs list by clicking the + icon next to the word *Dialogs*, and then double-click IDD_ABOUTBOX to bring up the About dialog box resource.

FIG. 8.7
AppWizard makes an About dialog box for you.

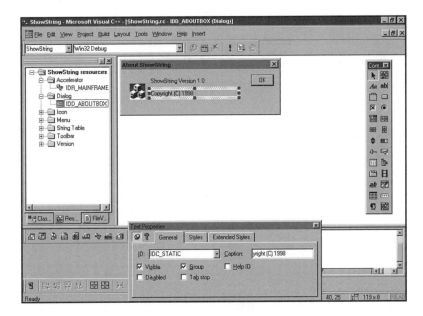

You might want to add a company name to your About dialog box. Here's how to add **Que Books,** as an example. Click the line of text that reads Copyright© 1998, and it will be surrounded by a selection box. Bring up the Properties dialog box, if it isn't up. Edit the caption to add **Que Books** at the end; the changes are reflected immediately in the dialog box.

T I P If the rulers you see in Figure 8.7 don't appear when you open IDD_ABOUTBOX in Developer Studio, you can turn them on by choosing Layout, Guide Settings and then selecting the Rulers and Guides radio button in the top half of the Guide Settings dialog box.

I decided to add a text string to remind users what book this application is from. Here's how to do that:

1. Size the dialog box a little taller by clicking the whole dialog box to select it, clicking the sizing square in the middle of the bottom border, and dragging the bottom border down a little. (This visual editing is what gave Visual C++ its name when it first came out.)

2. In the floating toolbar called Controls, click the button labeled *Aa* to get a *static control,* which means a piece of text that the user cannot change, perfect for labels like this. Click within the dialog box under the other text to insert the static text there.

3. In the Properties dialog box, change the caption from Static to **Using Visual C++ 6.** The box automatically resizes to fit the text.

4. Hold down the Ctrl key and click the other two static text lines in the dialog box. Choose Layout, Align Controls, Left, which aligns the edges of the three selected controls. The one you select last stays still, and the others move to align with it.

5. Choose Layout, Space Evenly, Down. These menu options can save you a great deal of dragging, squinting at the screen, and then dragging again.

The About dialog box will resemble Figure 8.8.

FIG. 8.8

In a matter of minutes, you can customize your About dialog box.

T I P All the Layout menu items are on the Dialog toolbar.

ShowString's Options Dialog Box

The Options dialog box is simple to build. First, make a new dialog box by choosing Insert, Resource and then double-clicking Dialog. An empty dialog box called Dialog1 appears, with an OK button and a Cancel button, as shown in Figure 8.9.

FIG. 8.9

A new dialog box always has OK and Cancel buttons.

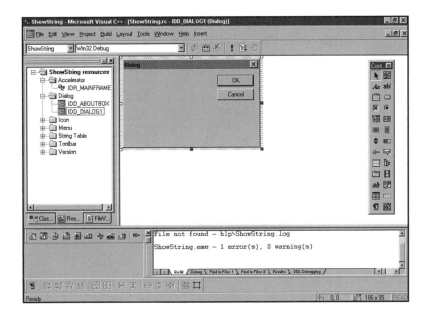

Next, follow these steps to convert the empty dialog box into the Options dialog box:

1. Change the ID to **IDD_OPTIONS** and the caption to **Options**.

2. In the floating toolbar called Controls, click the button labeled abl to get an edit box in which the user can enter the new value for the string. Click inside the dialog box to place the control and then change the ID to **IDC_OPTIONS_STRING**. (Control IDs should all start with **IDC** and then mention the name of their dialog box and an identifier that is unique to that dialog box.)

3. Drag the sizing squares to resize the edit box as wide as possible.

4. Add a static label above the edit box and change that caption to **String:**.

You will revisit this dialog box later, when adding the appearance capabilities, but for now it's ready to be connected. It will look like Figure 8.10.

FIG. 8.10

The Options dialog box is the place to change the string.

Making the Menu Work

When the user chooses Tools, Options, the Options dialog box should display. You use ClassWizard to arrange for one of your functions to be called when the item is chosen, and then you write the function, which creates an object of your dialog box class and then displays it.

The Dialog Box Class

ClassWizard makes the dialog box class for you. While the window displaying the IDD_OPTIONS dialog box has focus, choose View, ClassWizard. ClassWizard realizes there is not yet a class that corresponds to this dialog box and offers to create one, as shown in Figure 8.11.

FIG. 8.11

Create a C++ class to go with the new dialog box.

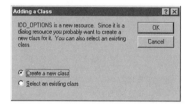

Leave Create a New Class selected and then click OK. The New Class dialog box, shown in Figure 8.12, appears.

FIG. 8.12

The dialog box class inherits from CDialog.

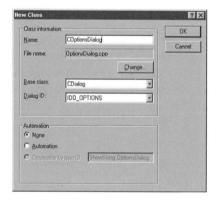

Fill in the dialog box as follows:

1. Choose a sensible name for the class, one that starts with C and contains the word Dialog; this example uses COptionsDialog.

2. The base class defaults to CDialog, which is perfect for this case.

3. Click OK to create the class.

The ClassWizard dialog box has been waiting behind these other dialog boxes, and now you use it. Click the Member Variables tab and connect IDC_OPTIONS_STRING to a CString called m_string, just as you connected controls to member variables of the dialog box class in Chapter 2. Click OK to close ClassWizard.

Perhaps you're curious about what code was created for you when ClassWizard made the class. The header file is shown in Listing 8.5.

Listing 8.5 OPTIONSDIALOG.H—Header File for *COptionsDialog*

```cpp
// OptionsDialog.h : header file
//


/////////////////////////////////////////////////////////////////////////////
// COptionsDialog dialog

class COptionsDialog : public CDialog
{
// Construction
public:
    COptionsDialog(CWnd* pParent = NULL);   // standard constructor

// Dialog Data
    //{{AFX_DATA(COptionsDialog)
    enum { IDD = IDD_OPTIONS };
    CString     m_string;
    //}}AFX_DATA
// Overrides
    // ClassWizard generated virtual function overrides
    //{{AFX_VIRTUAL(COptionsDialog)
    protected:
    virtual void DoDataExchange(CDataExchange* pDX);    // DDX/DDV support
    //}}AFX_VIRTUAL
// Implementation
protected:
    // Generated message map functions
    //{{AFX_MSG(COptionsDialog)
        // NOTE: The ClassWizard will add member functions here
    //}}AFX_MSG
    DECLARE_MESSAGE_MAP()
};
```

There are an awful lot of comments here to help ClassWizard find its way around in the file when the time comes to add more functionality, but there is only one member variable, m_string; one constructor; and one member function, DoDataExchange(), which gets the control value into the member variable, or vice versa. The source file isn't much longer; it's shown in Listing 8.6.

Listing 8.6 OPTIONSDIALOG.CPP—Implementation File for *COptionsDialog*

```cpp
// OptionsDialog.cpp : implementation file
//

#include "stdafx.h"
#include "ShowString.h"
#include "OptionsDialog.h"
```

continues

Listing 8.6   Continued

```
#ifdef _DEBUG
#define new DEBUG_NEW
#undef THIS_FILE
static char THIS_FILE[] = __FILE__;
#endif
////////////////////////////////////////////////////////////////////////////
// COptionsDialog dialog
COptionsDialog::COptionsDialog(CWnd* pParent /*=NULL*/)
    : CDialog(COptionsDialog::IDD, pParent)
{
    //{{AFX_DATA_INIT(COptionsDialog)
    m_string = _T("");
    //}}AFX_DATA_INIT
}
void COptionsDialog::DoDataExchange(CDataExchange* pDX)
{
    CDialog::DoDataExchange(pDX);
    //{{AFX_DATA_MAP(COptionsDialog)
    DDX_Text(pDX, IDC_OPTIONS_STRING, m_string);
    //}}AFX_DATA_MAP
}
BEGIN_MESSAGE_MAP(COptionsDialog, CDialog)
    //{{AFX_MSG_MAP(COptionsDialog)
        // NOTE: The ClassWizard will add message map macros here
    //}}AFX_MSG_MAP
END_MESSAGE_MAP()
```

The constructor sets the string to an empty string; this code is surrounded by special ClassWizard comments that enable it to add other variables later. The DoDataExchange() function calls DDX_Text() to transfer data from the control with the resource ID IDC_OPTIONS_STRING to the member variable m_string, or vice versa. This code, too, is surrounded by ClassWizard comments. Finally, there is an empty message map because COptionsDialog doesn't catch any messages.

Catching the Message

The next step in building ShowString is to catch the command message sent when the user chooses Tools, Options. There are seven classes in ShowString: CAboutDlg, CChildFrame, CMainFrame, COptionsDialog, CShowStringApp, CShowStringDoc, and CShowStringView. Which one should catch the command? The string and the options will be saved in the document and displayed in the view, so one of those two classes should handle the changing of the string. The document owns the private variable and will not let the view change the string unless you implement a public function to set the string. So, it makes the most sense to have the document catch the message.

N O T E   Often the hardest part of catching these messages is deciding which class should catch them. The decision between View and Document is frequently a very difficult one. If the message handler will need access to a private member of either class, that's the class to catch the message. ▪

To catch the message, follow these steps:

1. Open ClassWizard (if it isn't already open).
2. Click the Message Maps tab.
3. Select `CShowStringDoc` from the Class Name drop-down list box.
4. Select `ID_TOOLS_OPTIONS` from the Object IDs list box on the left, and select `COMMAND` from the Messages list box on the right.
5. Click Add Function to add a function to handle this command.
6. The Add Member Function dialog box, shown in Figure 8.13, appears, giving you an opportunity to change the function name from the usual one. Do not change it; just click OK.

FIG. 8.13
ClassWizard suggests a good name for the message-catching function.

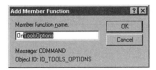

 You should almost never change the names that ClassWizard suggests for message catchers. If you find that you have to (perhaps because the suggested name is too long or conflicts with another function name in the same object), be sure to choose a name that starts with *On*. Otherwise the next developer to work on your project is going to have a very hard time finding the message handlers.

Click Edit Code to close ClassWizard and edit the newly added function. What happened to `CShowStringDoc` when you arranged for the `ID_TOOLS_OPTIONS` message to be caught? The new message map in the header file is shown in Listing 8.7.

Listing 8.7 SHOWSTRINGDOC.H—Message Map for *CShowStringDoc*

```
// Generated message map functions
protected:
    //{{AFX_MSG(CShowStringDoc)
    afx_msg void OnToolsOptions();
    //}}AFX_MSG
    DECLARE_MESSAGE_MAP()
```

This is just declaring the function. In the source file, ClassWizard changed the message maps shown in Listing 8.8.

Listing 8.8 SHOWSTRINGDOC.CPP—Message Map for *CShowStringDoc*

```
BEGIN_MESSAGE_MAP(CShowStringDoc, CDocument)
    //{{AFX_MSG_MAP(CShowStringDoc)
    ON_COMMAND(ID_TOOLS_OPTIONS, OnToolsOptions)
    //}}AFX_MSG_MAP
END_MESSAGE_MAP()
```

This arranges for OnToolsOptions() to be called when the command ID_TOOLS_OPTIONS is sent. ClassWizard also added a skeleton for OnToolsOptions():

```
void CShowStringDoc::OnToolsOptions()
{
    // TODO: Add your command handler code here

}
```

Making the Dialog Box Work

OnToolsOptions() should initialize and display the dialog box and then do something with the value that the user provided. (This process was first discussed in Chapter 2. You have already connected the edit box to a member variable, m_string, of the dialog box class. You initialize this member variable before displaying the dialog box and use it afterwards.

OnToolsOptions(), shown in Listing 8.9, displays the dialog box. Add this code to the empty function ClassWizard generated for you when you arranged to catch the message.

Listing 8.9 SHOWSTRINGDOC.CPP—*OnToolsOptions()*

```
void CShowStringDoc::OnToolsOptions()
{
    COptionsDialog dlg;
    dlg.m_string = string;
    if (dlg.DoModal() == IDOK)
    {
        string = dlg.m_string;
        SetModifiedFlag();
        UpdateAllViews(NULL);
    }

}
```

This code fills the member variable of the dialog box with the document's member variable (ClassWizard added m_string as a public member variable of COptionsDialog, so the document can change it) and then brings up the dialog box by calling DoModal(). If the user clicks OK, the member variable of the document changes, the modified flag is set (so that the user is prompted to save the document on exit), and the view is asked to redraw itself with a call to UpdateAllViews(). For this to compile, of course, the compiler must know what a COptionsDialog is, so add this line at the beginning of ShowStringDoc.cpp:

```
#include "OptionsDialog.h"
```

At this point, you can build the application and run it. Choose Tools, Options and change the string. Click OK and you see the new string in the view. Exit the application; you are asked whether to save the file. Save it, restart the application, and open the file again. The default "Hello, world!" document remains open, and the changed document is open with a different string. The application works, as you can see in Figure 8.14 (the windows are resized to let them both fit in the figure).

FIG. 8.14
ShowString can change the string, save it to a file, and reload it.

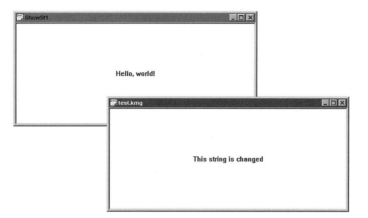

Adding Appearance Options to the Options Dialog Box

ShowString doesn't have much to do, just demonstrate menus and dialog boxes. However, the only dialog box control that ShowString uses is an edit box. In this section, you add a set of radio buttons and check boxes to change the way the string is drawn in the view.

Changing the Options Dialog Box

It is quite simple to incorporate a full-fledged Font dialog box into an application, but the example in this section is going to do something much simpler. A group of radio buttons will give the user a choice of several colors. One check box will enable the user to specify that the text should be centered horizontally, and another that the text be centered vertically. Because these are check boxes, the text can be either, neither, or both.

Open the IDD_OPTIONS dialog box by double-clicking it in the ResourceView window, and then add the radio buttons by following these steps:

1. Stretch the dialog box taller to make room for the new controls.

2. Click the radio button in the Controls floating toolbar, and then click the Options dialog box to drop the control.

3. Choose View, Properties and then pin the Properties dialog box in place.

4. Change the resource ID of the first radio button to **IDC_OPTIONS_BLACK**, and change the caption to **&Black**.

5. Select the Group box to indicate that this is the first of a group of radio buttons.

6. Add another radio button with resource ID **IDC_OPTIONS_RED** and **&Red** as the caption. Do not select the Group box because the Red radio button doesn't start a new group but is part of the group that started with the Black radio button.

7. Add a third radio button with resource ID **IDC_OPTIONS_GREEN** and **&Green** as the caption. Again, do not select Group.

8. Drag the three radio buttons into a horizontal arrangement, and select all three by clicking on one and then holding Ctrl while clicking the other two.

9. Choose Layout, Align Controls, Bottom (to even them up).

10. Choose Layout, Space Evenly, Across to space the controls across the dialog box.

Next, add the check boxes by following these steps:

1. Click the check box in the Controls floating toolbar and then click the Options dialog box, dropping a check box onto it.

2. Change the resource ID of this check box to **IDC_OPTIONS_HORIZCENTER** and the caption to **Center &Horizontally**.

3. Select the Group box to indicate the start of a new group after the radio buttons.

4. Drop another check box onto the dialog box as in step 1 and give it the resource ID **IDC_OPTIONS_VERTCENTER** and the caption **Center &Vertically**.

5. Arrange the check boxes under the radio buttons.

6. Click the Group box on the Controls floating toolbar, and then click and drag a group box around the radio buttons. Change the caption to **Text Color**.

7. Move the OK and Cancel buttons down to the bottom of the dialog box.

8. Select each horizontal group of controls and use Layout, Center in Dialog, Horizontal to make things neater.

9. Choose Edit, Select All, and then drag all the controls up toward the top of the dialog box. Shrink the dialog box to fit around the new controls. It should now resemble Figure 8.15.

FIG. 8.15
The Options dialog box for ShowString has been expanded.

 TIP If you don't recognize the icons on the Controls toolbar, use the ToolTips. If you hold the cursor over any of the toolbar buttons, a tip pops up after a few seconds, telling you what control the button represents.

Finally, set the tab order by choosing Layout, Tab Order and then clicking the controls, in this order:

1. IDC_OPTIONS_STRING

2. IDC_OPTIONS_BLACK

3. IDC_OPTIONS_RED

4. IDC_OPTIONS_GREEN

5. IDC_OPTIONS_HORIZCENTER

6. IDC_OPTIONS_VERTCENTER

7. IDOK

8. IDCANCEL

Then click away from the dialog box to leave the two static text controls as positions 9 and 10.

Adding Member Variables to the Dialog Box Class

Having added controls to the dialog box, you need to add corresponding member variables to the COptionsDialog class. Bring up ClassWizard, select the Member Variable tab, and add member variables for each control. Figure 8.16 shows the summary of the member variables created. The check boxes are connected to BOOL variables; these member variables are TRUE if the box is selected and FALSE if it isn't. The radio buttons are handled differently. Only the first—the one with the Group box selected in its Properties dialog box—is connected to a member variable. That integer is a zero-based index that indicates which button is selected. In other words, when the Black button is selected, m_color is 0; when Red is selected, m color is 1; and when Green is selected, m_color is 2.

FIG. 8.16

Member variables in the dialog box class are connected to individual controls or the group of radio buttons.

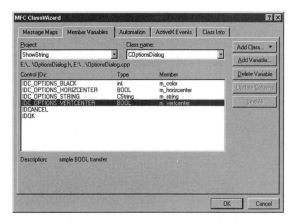

Adding Member Variables to the Document

The variables to be added to the document are the same ones that were added to the dialog box. You add them to the CShowStringDoc class definition in the header file, to OnNewDocument(), and to Serialize(). Add the lines in Listing 8.10 at the top of the CShowStringDoc definition in ShowStringDoc.h, replacing the previous definition of string and GetString(). Make sure that the variables are private and the functions are public.

Listing 8.10   SHOWSTRINGDOC.H—*CShowStringDoc* Member Variables

```
private:
    CString string;
    int     color;
    BOOL horizcenter;
    BOOL vertcenter;
public:
    CString GetString() {return string;}
    int     GetColor() {return color;}
    BOOL GetHorizcenter() {return horizcenter;}
    BOOL GetVertcenter() {return vertcenter;}
```

As with `string`, these are private variables with public `get` functions but no `set` functions. All these options should be serialized; the new `Serialize()` is shown in Listing 8.11. Change your copy by double-clicking the function name in ClassView and adding the new code.

Listing 8.11   SHOWSTRINGDOC.CPP—*Serialize()*

```
void CShowStringDoc::Serialize(CArchive& ar)
{
    if (ar.IsStoring())
    {
        ar << string;
        ar << color;
        ar << horizcenter;
        ar << vertcenter;
    }
    else
    {
        ar >> string;
        ar >> color;
        ar >> horizcenter;
        ar >> vertcenter;
    }
}
```

Finally, you need to initialize these variables in `OnNewDocument()`. What are good defaults for these new member variables? Black text, centered in both directions, was the old behavior, and it makes sense to use it as the default. The new `OnNewDocument()` is shown in Listing 8.12.

Listing 8.12   SHOWSTRINGDOC.CPP—*OnNewDocument()*

```
BOOL CShowStringDoc::OnNewDocument()
{
    if (!CDocument::OnNewDocument())
        return FALSE;

    string = "Hello, world!";
    color = 0;      //black
    horizcenter = TRUE;
```

```
        vertcenter = TRUE;

        return TRUE;
}
```

Of course, at the moment, users cannot change these member variables from the defaults. To allow the user to change the variables, you have to change the function that handles the dialog box.

Changing *OnToolsOptions()*

The OnToolsOptions() function sets the values of the dialog box member variables from the document member variables and then displays the dialog box. If the user clicks OK, the document member variables are set from the dialog box member variables and the view is redrawn. Having just added three member variables to the dialog box and the document, you have three lines to add before the dialog box displays and then three more to add in the block that's called after OK is clicked. The new OnToolsOptions() is shown in Listing 8.13.

Listing 8.13   SHOWSTRINGDOC.CPP—*OnToolsOptions()*

```
void CShowStringDoc::OnToolsOptions()
{
    COptionsDialog dlg;
    dlg.m_string = string;
    dlg.m_color = color;
    dlg.m_horizcenter = horizcenter;
    dlg.m_vertcenter = vertcenter;

    if (dlg.DoModal() == IDOK)
    {
        string = dlg.m_string;
        color = dlg.m_color;
        horizcenter = dlg.m_horizcenter;
        vertcenter = dlg.m_vertcenter;
        SetModifiedFlag();
        UpdateAllViews(NULL);
    }

}
```

What happens when the user opens the dialog box and changes the value of a control, say, by deselecting Center Horizontally? The framework—through Dialog Data Exchange (DDX), as set up by ClassWizard—changes the value of COptionsDialog::m_horizcenter to FALSE. This code in OnToolsOptions() changes the value of CShowStringDoc::horizcenter to FALSE. When the user saves the document, Serialize() saves horizcenter. This is all good, but none of this code actually changes the way the view is drawn. That involves OnDraw().

Changing *OnDraw()*

The single call to `DrawText()` in `OnDraw()` becomes a little more complex now. The document member variables are used to set the view's appearance. Edit `OnDraw()` by expanding `CShowStringView` in the ClassView and double-clicking `OnDraw()`.

The color is set with `CDC::SetTextColor()` before the call to `DrawText()`. You should always save the old text color and restore it when you are finished. The parameter to `SetTextColor()` is a `COLORREF`, and you can directly specify combinations of red, green, and blue as hex numbers in the form `0x00bbggrr`, so that, for example, `0x000000FF` is bright red. Most people prefer to use the `RGB` macro, which takes hex numbers from `0x0` to `0xFF`, specifying the amount of each color; bright red is `RGB(FF,0,0)`, for instance. Add the lines shown in Listing 8.14 before the call to `DrawText()` to set up everything.

Listing 8.14   SHOWSTRINGDOC.CPP—*OnDraw()* Additions Before *DrawText()* Call

```
COLORREF oldcolor;
switch (pDoc->GetColor())
{
case 0:
    oldcolor = pDC->SetTextColor(RGB(0,0,0)); //black
    break;
case 1:
    oldcolor = pDC->SetTextColor(RGB(0xFF,0,0)); //red
    break;
case 2:
    oldcolor = pDC->SetTextColor(RGB(0,0xFF,0)); //green
    break;
}
```

Add this line after the call to `DrawText()`:

```
pDC->SetTextColor(oldcolor);
```

There are two approaches to setting the centering flags. The brute-force way is to list the four possibilities (neither, horizontal, vertical, and both) and have a different `DrawText()` statement for each. If you were to add other settings, this would quickly become unworkable. It's better to set up an integer to hold the `DrawText()` flags and `OR` in each flag, if appropriate. Add the lines shown in Listing 8.15 before the call to `DrawText()`.

Listing 8.15   SHOWSTRINGDOC.CPP—*OnDraw()* Additions After *DrawText()* Call

```
int DTflags = 0;
if (pDoc->GetHorizcenter())
{
    DTflags |= DT_CENTER;
}
if (pDoc->GetVertcenter())
{
    DTflags |= (DT_VCENTER|DT_SINGLELINE);
}
```

The call to DrawText() now uses the DTflags variable:

```
pDC->DrawText(pDoc->GetString(), &rect, DTflags);
```

Now the settings from the dialog box have made their way to the dialog box class, to the document, and finally to the view, to actually affect the appearance of the text string. Build and execute ShowString and then try it. Any surprises? Be sure to change the text, experiment with various combinations of the centering options, and try all three colors. ●

Improving Your User Interface

Status Bars and Toolbars

Building a good user interface is half the battle of programming a Windows application. Luckily, Visual C++ and its AppWizard supply an amazing amount of help in creating an application that supports all the expected user-interface elements, including menus, dialog boxes, toolbars, and status bars. The subjects of menus and dialog boxes are covered in Chapters 2, "Dialogs and Controls," and 8, "Building a Complete Application: ShowString." In this chapter, you learn how to get the most out of toolbars and status bars.

Working with Toolbars

The buttons on a toolbar correspond to commands, just as the items on a menu do. Although you can add a toolbar to your application with AppWizard, you still need to use a little programming polish to make things just right. This is because every application is different and AppWizard can create only the most generally useful toolbar for most applications. When you create your own toolbars, you will probably want to add or delete buttons to support your application's unique command set.

For example, when you create a standard AppWizard application with a toolbar, AppWizard creates the toolbar shown in Figure 9.1. This toolbar provides buttons for the commonly used commands in the File and Edit menus, as well as a button for displaying the About dialog box. What if your application doesn't support these commands? It's up to you to modify the default toolbar to fit your application.

FIG. 9.1
The default toolbar provides buttons for commonly used commands.

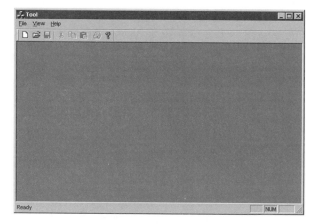

Deleting Toolbar Buttons

Create a multiple document interface application with a toolbar by choosing File, New; selecting the Project tab; highlighting MFC AppWizard (exe); naming the application **Tool**; and accepting the defaults in every dialog box. If you like, you can click the Finish button in step 1 to speed up the process. AppWizard provides a docking toolbar by default. Build and run the application, and you should see a toolbar of your own, just like Figure 9.1.

Before moving on, play with this toolbar a little. On the View menu, you can toggle whether the toolbar is displayed. Turn it off and then on again. Now click and hold on the toolbar between buttons and pull it down into the working area of your application. Let it go, and it's a floating palette. Drag it around and drop it at the bottom of the application or one of the sides—it will dock against any side of the main window. Watch the tracking rectangle change shape to show you it will dock if you drop it. Drag it back off again so that it's floating and close it by clicking the small x in the upper-right corner. Bring it back with the View menu and notice that it comes back right where you left it. All this functionality is yours free from AppWizard and MFC.

The first step in modifying the toolbar is to delete buttons you no longer need. To do this, first select the ResourceView tab to display your application's resources by clicking on the + next to Tool Resources. Click the + next to Toolbar and double-click the IDR_MAINFRAME toolbar resource to edit it, as shown in Figure 9.2. (The Graphics and Colors palettes, shown floating in Figure 9.2, are docked by default. You can move them around by grabbing the wrinkles at the top.)

FIG. 9.2
Use the toolbar editor to customize your application's toolbar.

Toolbar being edited

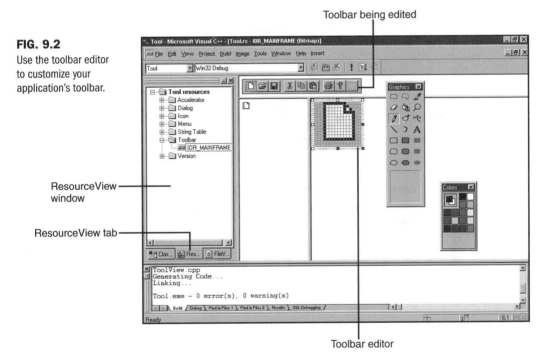

ResourceView window

ResourceView tab

Toolbar editor

After you have the toolbar editor on the screen, deleting buttons is as easy as dragging the unwanted buttons from the toolbar. Place your mouse pointer on the button, hold down the left mouse button, and drag the unwanted button away from the toolbar. When you release the mouse button, the toolbar button disappears. In the Tool application, delete all the buttons except the Help button with a yellow question mark. Figure 9.3 shows the edited toolbar with only the Help button remaining. The single blank button template is only a starting point for the next button you want to create. If you leave it blank, it doesn't appear in the final toolbar.

FIG. 9.3

This edited toolbar has only a single button left (not counting the blank button template).

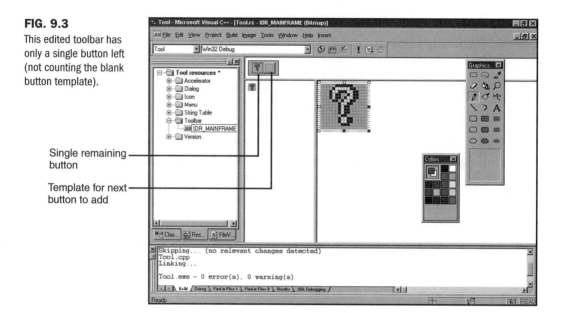

Single remaining button

Template for next button to add

Adding Buttons to a Toolbar

Adding buttons to a toolbar is a two-step process: First you draw the button's icon, and then you match the button with its command. To draw a new button, first click the blank button template in the toolbar. The blank button appears enlarged in the edit window, as shown in Figure 9.4.

FIG. 9.4

Click the button template to open it in the button editor.

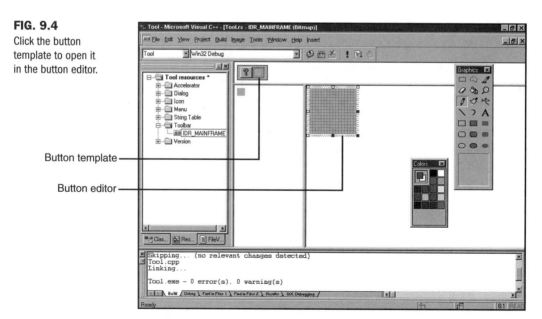

Button template

Button editor

Suppose you want to create a toolbar button that draws a red circle in the application's window. Draw a red circle on the blank button with the Ellipse tool, and you've created the button's icon. Open the properties box and give the button an appropriate ID, such as ID_CIRCLE in this case.

Now you need to define the button's description and ToolTip. The description appears in the application's status bar. In this case, a description of "Draws a red circle in the window" might be good. The ToolTip appears whenever the user leaves the mouse pointer over the button for a second or two, acting as a reminder of the button's purpose. A ToolTip of *Circle* would be appropriate for the circle button. Type these two text strings into the Prompt box. The description comes first, followed by the newline character (\n) and the ToolTip, as shown in Figure 9.5.

FIG. 9.5

After drawing the button, specify its properties.

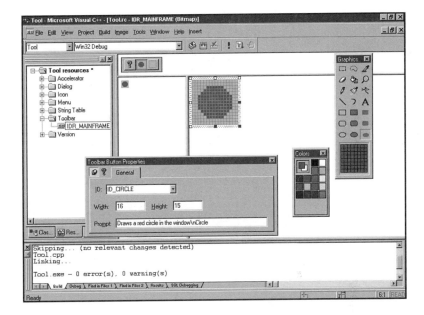

You've now defined a command ID for your new toolbar button. Usually, you use the command ID of an existing menu item already connected to some code. In these cases, simply choose the existing command ID from the drop-down box, and your work is done. The prompt is taken from the properties of the menu item, and the message handler has already been arranged for the menu item. You will already be handling the menu item, and that code will handle the toolbar click, too. In this application, the toolbar button doesn't mirror a menu item, so you will associate the ID with a message-handler function that MFC automatically calls when the user clicks the button.

To do this, follow these steps:

1. Make sure the button for which you want to create a message handler is selected in the custom toolbar, and then open ClassWizard.

2. The MFC ClassWizard property sheet appears, with the button's ID already selected (see Figure 9.6). To add the message-response function, select in the Class Name box the class to which you want to add the function (the sample application uses the view class).

3. Double-click the COMMAND selection in the Messages box.

4. Accept the function name that MFC suggests in the next message box, and you're all set. Click OK to finalize your changes.

> **N O T E**   If you haven't defined a message-response function for a toolbar button, or if there is no instance of the class that catches the message, MFC disables the button when you run the application. For example, if the message is caught by the document or view in an MDI application and there is no open document, the button is disabled. The same is true for menu commands—in fact, for all intents and purposes, toolbar buttons *are* menu commands. ■

FIG. 9.6

You can use ClassWizard to catch messages from your toolbar buttons.

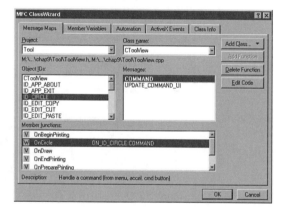

> **N O T E**   Ordinarily, toolbar buttons duplicate menu commands, providing a quicker way for the user to select commonly used commands in the menus. In that case, the menu item and the toolbar button both represent the exact same command, and you give both the same ID. Then the same message-response function is called, whether the user selects the command from the menu bar or the toolbar. ■

If you compile and run the application now, you will see the window shown in Figure 9.7. In the figure, you can see the new toolbar button, as well as its ToolTip and description line. The toolbar looks sparse in this example, but you can add as many buttons as you like.

You can create as many buttons as you need; just follow the same procedure for each. After you have created the buttons, you're through with the toolbar resources and ready to write the code that responds to the buttons. For example, in the previous example, a circle button was added to the toolbar, and a message-response function, called OnCircle(), was added to the program. MFC calls that message-response function whenever the user clicks the associated button. However, right now, that function doesn't do anything, as shown in Listing 9.1.

FIG. 9.7
The new toolbar button shows its ToolTip and description.

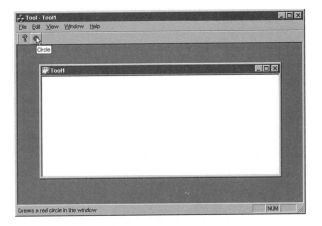

Listing 9.1 An Empty Message-Response Function

```
void CToolView::OnCircle()
{
    // TODO: Add your command handler code here

}
```

Although the circle button is supposed to draw a red circle in the window, you can see that the OnCircle() function is going to need a little help accomplishing that task. Add the lines shown in Listing 9.2 to the function so that the circle button will do what it's supposed to do, as shown in Figure 9.8. This drawing code makes a brush, selects it into the DC, draws an ellipse with it, and then restores the old brush. The details of drawing are discussed in Chapter 5, "Drawing on the Screen."

Listing 9.2 *CToolView::OnCircle()*

```
void CToolView::OnCircle()
{
    CClientDC clientDC(this);
    CBrush newBrush(RGB(255,0,0));
    CBrush* oldBrush = clientDC.SelectObject(&newBrush);
    clientDC.Ellipse(20, 20, 200, 200);
    clientDC.SelectObject(oldBrush);
}
```

The *CToolBar* Class's Member Functions

In most cases, after you have created your toolbar resource and associated its buttons with the appropriate command IDs, you don't need to bother any more with the toolbar. The code generated by AppWizard creates the toolbar for you, and MFC takes care of calling the buttons' response functions for you. However, at times you might want to change the toolbar's default behavior or appearance in some way. In those cases, you can call on the CToolBar class's member functions, which are listed in Table 9.1 along with their descriptions. The toolbar is accessible from the CMainFrame class as the m_wndToolBar member variable. Usually, you change the toolbar behavior in CMainFrame::OnCreate().

FIG. 9.8

After adding code to OnCircle(), the new toolbar button actually does something.

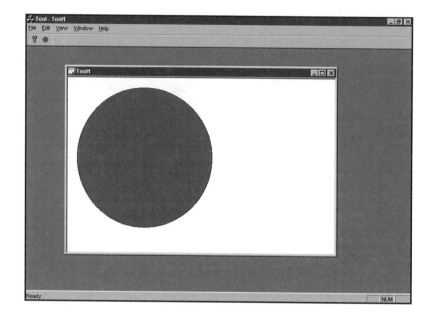

Table 9.1   Member Functions of the *CToolBar* Class

Function	Description
CommandToIndex()	Obtains the index of a button, given its ID
Create()	Creates the toolbar
GetButtonInfo()	Obtains information about a button
GetButtonStyle()	Obtains a button's style
GetButtonText()	Obtains a button's text label
GetItemID()	Obtains the ID of a button, given its index
GetItemRect()	Obtains an item's display rectangle, given its index
GetToolBarCtrl()	Obtains a reference to the CToolBarCtrl object represented by the CToolBar object
LoadBitmap()	Loads the toolbar's button images
LoadToolBar()	Loads a toolbar resource

Function	Description
SetBitmap()	Sets a new toolbar button bitmap
SetButtonInfo()	Sets a button's ID, style, and image number
SetButtons()	Sets the IDs for the toolbar buttons
SetButtonStyle()	Sets a button's style
SetButtonText()	Sets a button's text label
SetHeight()	Sets the toolbar's height
SetSizes()	Sets the button sizes

Normally, you don't need to call the toolbar's methods, but you can achieve some unusual results when you do, such as the extra high toolbar shown in Figure 9.9. (The buttons are the same size, but the toolbar window is bigger.) This toolbar resulted from a call to the toolbar object's SetHeight() member function. The CToolBar class's member functions enable you to perform this sort of toolbar trickery, but use them with great caution.

FIG. 9.9
You can use a toolbar object's member functions to change how the toolbar looks and acts.

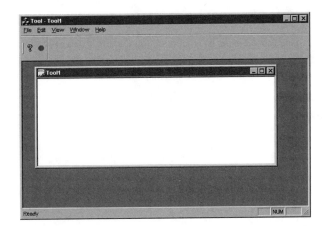

Working with Status Bars

Status bars are mostly benign objects that sit at the bottom of your application's window, doing whatever MFC instructs them to do. This consists of displaying command descriptions and the status of various keys on the keyboard, including the Caps Lock and Scroll Lock keys. In fact, status bars are so mundane from the programmer's point of view (at least they are in an AppWizard application) that they aren't even represented by a resource that you can edit like a toolbar. When you tell AppWizard to incorporate a status bar into your application, there's not much left for you to do.

Or is there? A status bar, just like a toolbar, must reflect the interface needs of your specific application. For that reason, the CStatusBar class features a set of methods with which you can customize the status bar's appearance and operation. Table 9.2 lists the methods along with brief descriptions.

Table 9.2   Methods of the *CStatusBar* Class

Method	Description
CommandToIndex()	Obtains an indicator's index, given its ID
Create()	Creates the status bar
GetItemID()	Obtains an indicator's ID, given its index
GetItemRect()	Obtains an item's display rectangle, given its index
GetPaneInfo()	Obtains information about an indicator
GetPaneStyle()	Obtains an indicator's style
GetPaneText()	Obtains an indicator's text
GetStatusBarCtrl()	Obtains a reference to the CStatusBarCtrl object represented by the CStatusBar object
SetIndicators()	Sets the indicators' IDs
SetPaneInfo()	Sets the indicators' IDs, widths, and styles
SetPaneStyle()	Sets an indicator's style
SetPaneText()	Sets an indicator's text

When you create a status bar as part of an AppWizard application, you see a window similar to that shown in Figure 9.10. (To make your own, create a project called **Status** and accept all the defaults, as you did for the Tool application.) The status bar has several parts, called *panes*, that display certain information about the status of the application and the system. These panes, which are marked in Figure 9.10, include indicators for the Caps Lock, Num Lock, and Scroll Lock keys, as well as a message area for showing status text and command descriptions. To see a command description, place your mouse pointer over a button on the toolbar (see Figure 9.11).

The most common way to customize a status bar is to add new panes. To add a pane to a status bar, complete these steps:

1. Create a command ID for the new pane.
2. Create a default string for the pane.
3. Add the pane's command ID to the status bar's indicators array.
4. Create a command-update handler for the pane.

The following sections cover these steps in detail.

FIG. 9.10

The default MFC status bar contains a number of informative panes.

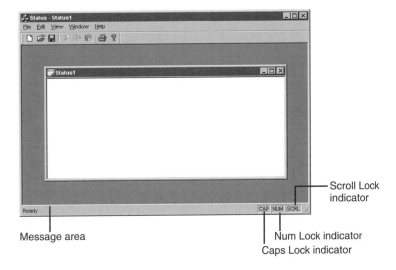

Scroll Lock indicator

Message area

Num Lock indicator

Caps Lock indicator

FIG. 9.11

The message area is mainly used for command descriptions.

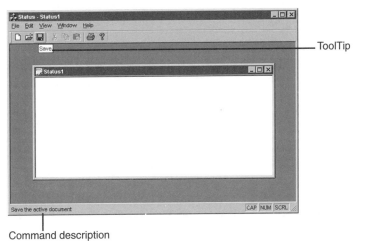

ToolTip

Command description

Creating a New Command ID

This step is easy, thanks to Visual C++'s symbol browser. To add the command ID, start by choosing View, Resource Symbols. When you do, you see the Resource Symbols dialog box (see Figure 9.12), which displays the currently defined symbols for your application's resources. Click the New button, and the New Symbol dialog box appears. Type the new ID, **ID_MYNEWPANE**, into the Name box (see Figure 9.13). Usually, you can accept the value that MFC suggests for the ID.

FIG. 9.12

Use the Resource
Symbols dialog box to
add new command IDs
to your application.

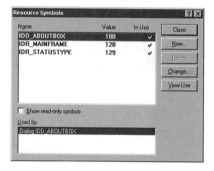

FIG. 9.13

Type the new ID's name
and value into the New
Symbol dialog box.

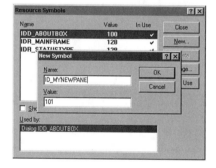

Click the OK and Close buttons to finalize your selections, and your new command ID is
defined.

Creating the Default String

You have now defined a resource ID, but it isn't being used. To represent a status bar pane, the
ID must have a default string defined for it. To define the string, first go to the ResourceView
window (by clicking the ResourceView tab in the workspace pane) and double-click the String
Table resource to open it in the string table editor, as shown in Figure 9.14.

Now, choose Insert, New String to open the String Properties dialog box. Type the new pane's
command ID **ID_MYNEWPANE** into the ID box (or choose it from the drop-down list) and the
default string (**Default string** in this case) into the Caption box (see Figure 9.15).

Adding the ID to the Indicators Array

When MFC constructs your status bar, it uses an array of IDs to determine which panes to
display and where to display them. This array of IDs is passed as an argument to the status
bar's SetIndicators() member function, which is called in the CMainFrame class's OnCreate()
function. You find this array of IDs, shown in Listing 9.3, near the top of the MainFrm.cpp file.
One way to reach these lines in the source code editor is to switch to ClassView, expand
CMainFrame, double-click OnCreate(), and scroll up one page. Alternatively, you could use
FileView to open MainFrm.cpp and scroll down to this code.

FIG. 9.14

Define the new pane's default string in the string table.

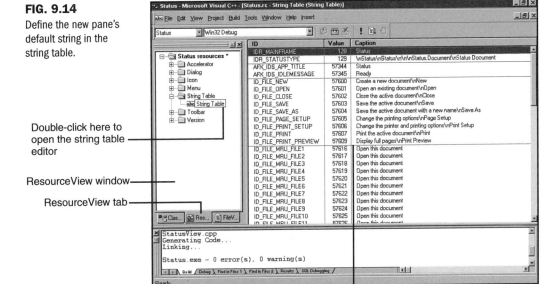

Double-click here to open the string table editor

ResourceView window

ResourceView tab

String table editor

FIG. 9.15

Use the String Properties dialog box to define the new pane's default string.

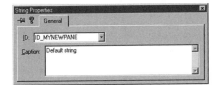

Listing 9.3 MainFrm.cpp—The Indicator Array

```
static UINT indicators[] =
{
    ID_SEPARATOR,            // status line indicator
    ID_INDICATOR_CAPS,
    ID_INDICATOR_NUM,
    ID_INDICATOR_SCRL,
};
```

To add your new pane to the array, type the pane's ID into the array at the position in which you want it to appear in the status bar, followed by a comma. (The first pane, ID_SEPARATOR, should always remain in the first position.) Listing 9.4 shows the indicator array with the new pane added.

Listing 9.4   MainFrm.cpp—The Expanded Indicator Array

```
static UINT indicators[] =
{
    ID_SEPARATOR,              // status line indicator
    ID_MYNEWPANE,
    ID_INDICATOR_CAPS,
    ID_INDICATOR_NUM,
    ID_INDICATOR_SCRL,
};
```

Creating the Pane's Command-Update Handler

MFC doesn't automatically enable new panes when it creates the status bar. Instead, you must create a command-update handler for the new pane and enable the pane yourself. (You first learned about command-update handlers in Chapter 4, "Messages and Commands.") Also, for most applications, the string displayed in the pane is calculated on-the-fly—the default string you defined in an earlier step is only a placeholder.

Normally, you use ClassWizard to arrange for messages to be caught, but ClassWizard doesn't help you catch status bar messages. You must add the handler entries to the message map yourself and then add the code for the handler. You add entries to the message map in the header file and the map in the source file, and you add them outside the special AFX_MSG_MAP comments used by ClassWizard.

Double-click CMainFrame in ClassView to open the header file, and scroll to the bottom. Edit the message map so that it resembles Listing 9.5. When you write your own applications, you will use a variety of function names to update status bar panes, but the rest of the declaration will always be the same.

Listing 9.5   MainFrm.h—Message Map

```
// Generated message map functions
protected:
    //{{AFX_MSG(CMainFrame)
    afx_msg int OnCreate(LPCREATESTRUCT lpCreateStruct);
        // NOTE - the ClassWizard will add and remove member functions here.
        //    DO NOT EDIT what you see in these blocks of generated code!
    //}}AFX_MSG
    afx_msg void OnUpdateMyNewPane(CCmdUI *pCmdUI);
    DECLARE_MESSAGE_MAP()
```

Next, you add the handler to the source message map to associate the command ID with the handler. Open any CMainFrame function and scroll upwards until you find the message map; then edit it so that it looks like Listing 9.6.

Listing 9.6 MainFrm.cpp—Message Map

```
BEGIN_MESSAGE_MAP(CMainFrame, CFrameWnd)
    //{{AFX_MSG_MAP(CMainFrame)
        // NOTE - the ClassWizard will add and remove mapping macros here.
        //    DO NOT EDIT what you see in these blocks of generated code !
    ON_WM_CREATE()
    //}}AFX_MSG_MAP
    ON_UPDATE_COMMAND_UI(ID_MYNEWPANE, OnUpdateMyNewPane)
END_MESSAGE_MAP()
```

You have now arranged for the CMainFrame member function OnUpdateMyNewPane() to be called whenever the status bar pane ID_MYNEWPANE needs to be updated.

Now you're ready to write the new command-update handler. In the handler, you will enable the new pane and set its contents. Listing 9.7 shows the command-update handler for the new pane; add this code to mainfrm.cpp. As you can see, it uses a member variable called m_paneString. Update handlers should be very quick—the job of making sure that m_paneString holds the right string should be tackled in a function that is called less often.

 TIP Command update handlers are discussed in Chapter 3, "Messages and Commands," in the "Understanding Command Updates" section. They have to be quick because the system calls them whenever it refreshes the display.

Listing 9.7 CMainFrame::OnUpdateMyNewPane()

```
void CMainFrame::OnUpdateMyNewPane(CCmdUI *pCmdUI)
{
    pCmdUI->Enable();
    pCmdUI->SetText(m_paneString);
}
```

Setting the Status Bar's Appearance

To add the last touch to your status bar demonstration application, you will want a way to set m_paneString. To initialize it, double-click on the CMainFrame constructor to edit it, and add this line:

```
m_paneString = "Default string";
```

The value you entered in the string table is only to assure Visual Studio that the resource ID you created is in use. Right-click CMainFrame in ClassView and choose Add Member Variable to add m_paneString as a private member variable. The type should be CString.

To set up the status bar for the first time, add these lines to `CMainFrame::OnCreate()`, just before the `return` statement:

```
CClientDC dc(this);
SIZE size = dc.GetTextExtent(m_paneString);
int index = m_wndStatusBar.CommandToIndex(ID_MYNEWPANE);
m_wndStatusBar.SetPaneInfo(index,ID_MYNEWPANE, SBPS_POPOUT, size.cx);
```

These lines set the text string and the size of the pane. You set the size of the pane with a call to `SetPaneInfo()`, which needs the index of the pane and the new size. `CommandToIndex()` obtains the index of the pane, and `GetTextExtent()` obtains the size. As a nice touch, the call to `SetPaneInfo()` uses the `SBPS_POPOUT` style to create a pane that seems to stick out from the status bar, rather than be indented.

The user will change the string by making a menu selection. Open the `IDR_STATUSTYPE` menu in the resource editor and add a Change String item to the File menu. (Working with menus is discussed for the first time in Chapter 8.) Let Developer Studio assign it the resource ID `ID_FILE_CHANGESTRING`.

Open ClassWizard and add a handler for this command; it should be caught by `CMainFrame` because that's where the `m_paneString` variable is kept. ClassWizard offers to call the handler `OnFileChangestring()`, and you should accept this name. Click OK twice to close ClassWizard.

Insert a new dialog box into the application and call it **IDD_PANEDLG**. The title should be **Change Pane String**. Add a single edit box, stretched the full width of the dialog box, and leave the ID as `IDC_EDIT1`. Add a static text item just above the edit box with the caption **New String:**. With the dialog box open in the resource editor, open ClassWizard. Create a new class for the dialog box called `CPaneDlg`, and associate the edit control, `IDC_EDIT1`, with a `CString` member variable of the dialog class called `m_paneString`.

 TIP Adding dialog boxes to applications and associating them with classes are discussed in more depth in several earlier chapters, including Chapters 2 and 8.

Switch to ClassView, expand `CMainFrame`, and double-click `OnFileChangeString()` to edit it. Add the code shown in Listing 9.8.

Listing 9.8   *CMainFrame::OnFileChangestring()*

```
void CMainFrame::OnFileChangestring()
{
    CPaneDlg dialog(this);
    dialog.m_paneString = m_paneString;

    int result = dialog.DoModal();

    if (result == IDOK)
    {
```

```
        m_paneString = dialog.m_paneString;
        CClientDC dc(this);
        SIZE size = dc.GetTextExtent(m_paneString);
        int index = m_wndStatusBar.CommandToIndex(ID_MYNEWPANE);
        m_wndStatusBar.SetPaneInfo(index,
            ID_MYNEWPANE, SBPS_POPOUT, size.cx);
    }
}
```

This code displays the dialog box, and, if the user exits the dialog box by clicking OK, changes the text string and resets the size of the pane. The code is very similar to the lines you added to OnCreate(). Scroll up to the top of MainFrm.cpp and add this line:

```
#include "panedlg.h"
```

This tells the compiler what the CPaneDlg class is. Build and run the Status application, and you should see the window shown in Figure 9.16. As you can see, the status bar contains an extra panel displaying the text Default string. If you choose File, Change String, a dialog box appears into which you can type a new string for the panel. When you exit the dialog box via the OK button, the text appears in the new panel, and the panel resizes itself to accommodate the new string (see Figure 9.17).

FIG. 9.16

The Status Bar Demo application shows how to add and manage a status bar panel.

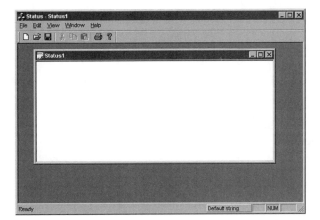

Working with Rebars

Rebars are toolbars that contain controls other than toolbar buttons. It was possible to add other controls to normal toolbars in the past, but difficult. With rebars, it's simple.

Start by using AppWizard to make a project call ReBar. Accept all the defaults on each step, or click Finish on step 1 to speed the process a little. When the project is generated, double-click CMainFrame in ClassView to edit the header file. This frame holds the open documents and is where a classic toolbar goes. The rebar for this sample will go here, too. Add the rebar as a public member variable:

```
CReBar m_rebar;
```

FIG. 9.17

The panel resizes itself to fit the new string.

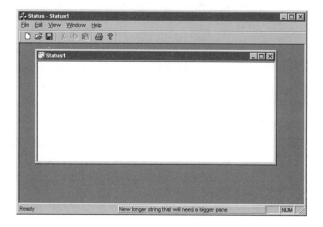

In this sample application, you will add a check box to the bar—you can add any kind of control at all. A check box, a radio button, and a command button (like the OK or Cancel button on a dialog) are all represented by the CButton class, with slightly different styles. Add the check box to the header file right after the rebar, like this:

```
CButton m_check;
```

You saw in the previous section that an application's toolbar is created and initialized in the OnCreate() function of the mainframe class. The same is true for rebars. Expand CMainFrame in ClassView, and double-click OnCreate() to edit it. Add these lines just before the final return statement:

```
if (!m_rebar.Create(this) )
{
    TRACE0("Failed to create rebar\n");
    return -1;      // fail to create
}
```

The check box control will need a resource ID. When you create a control with the dialog editor, the name you give the control is automatically associated with a number. This control will be created in code, so you will have to specify the resource ID yourself, as you did for the new pane in the status bar earlier in this chapter. Choose View, Resource Symbols and click the New button. Type the name **IDC_CHECK** and accept the number suggested. This adds a line to resource.h, defining IDC_CHECK, and assures you that other controls will not reuse this resource ID.

Back in CMainFrame::OnCreate(), add these lines to create the check box (note the styles carefully):

```
if (!m_check.Create("Check Here",
        WS_CHILD¦WS_VISIBLE¦BS_AUTOCHECKBOX,
```

```
        CRect(0,0,20,20), this, IDC_CHECK)  )
{
    TRACE0("Failed to create checkbox\n");
    return -1;        // fail to create
}
```

Finally, add this line to add a band containing the check box control to the rebar:

```
m_rebar.AddBar(&m_check, "On The Bar", NULL,
                RBBS_BREAK ¦ RBBS_GRIPPERALWAYS);
```

AddBar() takes four parameters: a pointer to the control that will be added, some text to put next to it, a pointer to a bitmap to use for the background image on the rebar, and a rebar style, made by combining any of these style flags:

- RBBS_BREAK puts the band on a new line, even if there's room for it at the end of an existing line.

- RBBS_CHILDEDGE puts the band against a child window of the frame.

- RBBS_FIXEDBMP prevents moving the bitmap if the band is resized by the user.

- RBBS_FIXEDSIZE prevents the user from resizing the band.

- RBBS_GRIPPERALWAYS guarantees sizing wrinkles are present.

- RBBS_HIDDEN hides the band.

- RBBS_NOGRIPPER suppresses sizing wrinkles.

- RBBS_NOVERT hides the band when the rebar is vertical.

- RBBS_VARIABLEHEIGHT enables the band to be resized by the rebar.

At this point, you can build the project and run it. You should see your rebar, as in Figure 9.18. The check box works in that you can select and deselect it, but nothing happens when you do.

FIG. 9.18

The rebar contains a check box.

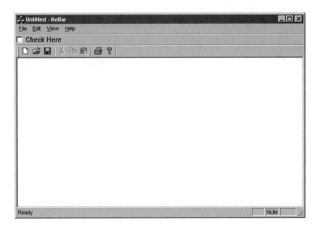

To react when the user clicks the button, you need to catch the message and do something based on the message. The simplest thing to do is change what is drawn in the view's OnDraw(), so the view should catch the message. Double click CRebarView in ClassView to edit the header file, and scroll to the message map. Between the closing AFX_MSG and the DECLARE_MESSAGE_MAP, add this line:

```
afx_msg void OnClick();
```

Expand CRebarView in ClassView and double-click OnDraw(), which you will edit in a moment. After it, add this function:

```
void CRebarView::OnClick()
{
    Invalidate();
}
```

This causes the view to redraw whenever the user selects or deselects the check box. Scroll up in the file until you find the message map, and add (after the three entries related to printing) this line:

```
ON_BN_CLICKED(IDC_CHECK, OnClick)
```

At the top of the file, after the other include statements, add this one:

```
#include "mainFrm.h"
```

Now add these lines to OnDraw() in place of the TODO comment:

```
CString message;
if ( ((CMainFrame*)(AfxGetApp()->m_pMainWnd))->m_check.GetCheck())
    message = "The box is checked";
else
    message = "The box is not checked";
pDC->TextOut(20,20,message);
```

The if statement obtains a pointer to the main window, casts it to a CMainFrame*, and asks the check box whether it is selected. Then the message is set appropriately.

Build the project and run it. As you select and deselect the check box, you should see the message change, as in Figure 9.19.

FIG. 9.19

Clicking the check box changes the view.

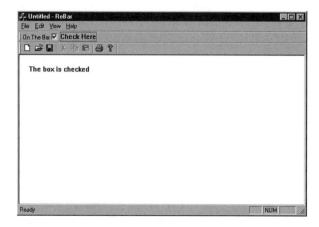

Common Controls

As a Windows user, you're accustomed to seeing controls such as buttons, list boxes, menus, and edit boxes. As Windows developed, however, Microsoft noticed that developers routinely create other types of controls in their programs: toolbars, status bars, progress bars, tree views, and others. To make life easier for Windows programmers, Microsoft included these popular controls as part of the operating environment of Windows 95 (as well as later versions of Windows NT and then Windows 98). Now Windows programmers no longer need to create from scratch their own versions of these controls. This chapter introduces you to many of the 32-bit Windows common controls. The toolbar and status bar controls are covered in Chapter 9, "Status Bars and Toolbars," and property sheets are covered in Chapter 12, "Property Pages and Sheets."

This chapter's sample program is called Common. It demonstrates nine of the Windows 95 common controls: the progress bar, slider, up-down, list view, tree view, rich edit, IP address, date picker, and month calendar controls, all of which are shown in Figure 10.1. In the following sections, you learn the basics of creating and using these controls in your own applications.

FIG. 10.1

The Common sample application demonstrates nine Windows 95 common controls.

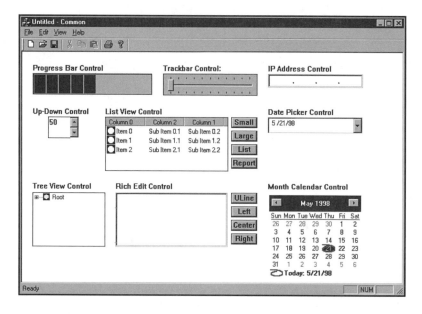

To make Common, create a new project with AppWizard and name it **Common**. Choose a single-document interface (SDI) application in Step 1 and accept all the defaults until Step 6. Drop down the Base Class box and choose CScrollView from the list. This ensures that users can see all the controls in the view, even if they have to scroll to do so. Click Finish and then OK to complete the process.

The controls themselves are declared as data members of the view class. Double-click CCommonView in ClassView to edit the header file and add the lines in Listing 10.1 in the Attributes section. As you can see, the progress bar is an object of the CProgressCtrl class. It's discussed in the next section, and the other controls are discussed in later sections of this chapter.

Listing 10.1   CommonView.h—Declaring the Controls

```
protected:
    //Progress Bar
     CProgressCtrl m_progressBar;

    //Trackbar or Slider
     CSliderCtrl m_trackbar;
     BOOL m_timer;

    // Up-Down or Spinner
     CSpinButtonCtrl m_upDown;
     CEdit m_buddyEdit;

    // List View
     CListCtrl m_listView;
     CImageList m_smallImageList;
     CImageList m_largeImageList;
     CButton m_smallButton;
     CButton m_largeButton;
     CButton m_listButton;
     CButton m_reportButton;

    // Tree View
     CTreeCtrl m_treeView;
     CImageList m_treeImageList;

    // Rich Edit
     CRichEditCtrl m_richEdit;
     CButton m_boldButton;
     CButton m_leftButton;
     CButton m_centerButton;
     CButton m_rightButton;
    // IP Address
    CIPAddressCtrl m_ipaddress;
    // Date Picker
    CDateTimeCtrl m_date;
    // Month Calendar
    CMonthCalCtrl m_month;
```

Part
III

Ch
10

Expand the CCommonView class. Double-click CCommonView::OnDraw() in ClassView and replace the TODO comment with these lines:

```
pDC->TextOut(20, 22, "Progress Bar Control");
pDC->TextOut(270, 22, "Trackbar Control:");
pDC->TextOut(20, 102, "Up-Down Control");
pDC->TextOut(160, 102, "List View Control");
pDC->TextOut(20, 240, "Tree View Control");
pDC->TextOut(180, 240, "Rich Edit Control");
pDC->TextOut(470, 22, "IP Address Control");
pDC->TextOut(470, 102, "Date Picker Control");
pDC->TextOut(470, 240, "Month Calendar Control");
```

These label the controls that you will add to CCommonView in this chapter.

The Progress Bar Control

The common control that's probably easiest to use is the progress bar, which is nothing more than a rectangle that slowly fills in with colored blocks. The more colored blocks that are filled in, the closer the task is to being complete. When the progress bar is completely filled in, the task associated with the progress bar is also complete. You might use a progress bar to show the status of a sorting operation or to give the user visual feedback about a large file that's being loaded.

Creating the Progress Bar

Before you can use a progress bar, you must create it. Often in an MFC program, the controls are created as part of a dialog box. However, Common displays its controls in the application's main window, the view of this single-document interface (SDI) application. Documents and views are introduced in Chapter 4, "Documents and Views." All the controls are created in the view class OnCreate() function, which responds to the WM_CREATE Windows message. To set up this function, right-click CCommonView in ClassView and choose Add Windows Message Handler. Choose WM_CREATE from the list on the left and click Add and Edit. Add this line in place of the TODO comment:

```
CreateProgressBar();
```

Right-click CCommonView in ClassView again and this time choose Add Member Function. Enter **void** for the Function Type and enter **CreateProgressBar()** for the Function Declaration. Leave the access as Public. Click OK to add the function; then add the code in Listing 10.2.

Listing 10.2   CommonView.cpp—*CCommonView::CreateProgressBar()*

```
void CCommonView::CreateProgressBar()
{
    m_progressBar.Create(WS_CHILD | WS_VISIBLE | WS_BORDER,
        CRect(20, 40, 250, 80), this, IDC_PROGRESSBAR);

    m_progressBar.SetRange(1, 100);
    m_progressBar.SetStep(10);
    m_progressBar.SetPos(50);
    m_timer = FALSE;

}
```

CreateProgressBar() first creates the progress bar control by calling the control's Create() function. This function's four arguments are the control's style flags, the control's size (as a CRect object), a pointer to the control's parent window, and the control's ID. The resource ID, IDC_PROGRESSBAR, is added by hand. To add resource symbols to your own applications, choose View, Resource Symbols and click the New button. Type in a resource ID Name, such as IDC_PROGRESSBAR, and accept the default Value Visual Studio provides.

The style constants are the same constants that you use for creating any type of window (a control is nothing more than a special kind of window, after all). In this case, you need at least the following:

- ▪ `WS_CHILD` Indicates that the control is a child window
- ▪ `WS_VISIBLE` Ensures that the user can see the control

The `WS_BORDER` is a nice addition because it adds a dark border around the control, setting it off from the rest of the window.

Initializing the Progress Bar

To initialize the control, `CCommonView::CreateProgressBar()` calls `SetRange()`, `SetStep()`, and `SetPos()`. Because the range and the step rate are related, a control with a range of 1–10 and a step rate of 1 works almost identically to a control with a range of 1–100 and a step rate of 10.

When this sample application starts, the progress bar is already half filled with colored blocks. (This is purely for aesthetic reasons. Usually a progress bar begins its life empty.) It's half full because `CreateProgressBar()` calls `SetPos()` with the value of 50, which is the midpoint of the control's range.

Manipulating the Progress Bar

Normally you update a progress bar as a long task moves toward completion. In this sample, you will fake it by using a timer. When the user clicks in the background of the view, start a timer that generates `WM_TIMER` messages periodically. Catch these messages and advance the progress bar. Here's what to do:

1. Open ClassWizard. Make sure that `CCommonView` is selected in the upper-right drop-down box.
2. Scroll most of the way through the list box on the right until you find `WM_LBUTTONDOWN`, the message generated when the user clicks on the view. Select it.
3. Click Add Function; then click Edit Code.
4. Edit `OnLButtonDown()` so that it looks like this:

```
void CCommonView::OnLButtonDown(UINT nFlags, CPoint point)
{
    if (m_timer)
    {
        KillTimer(1);
        m_timer = FALSE;
    }
    else
    {
        SetTimer(1, 500, NULL);
        m_timer = TRUE;
    }

    CView::OnLButtonDown(nFlags, point);
}
```

Part
III

Ch
10

This code enables users to turn the timer on or off with a click. The parameter of 500 in the `SetTimer` call is the number of milliseconds between `WM_TIMER` messages: This timer will send a message twice a second.

5. In case a timer is still going when the view closes, you should override `OnDestroy()` to kill the timer. Right-click `CCommonView` in ClassView yet again and choose Add Windows Message Handler. Select `WM_DESTROY` and click Add and Edit. Replace the `TODO` comment with this line:

   ```
   KillTimer(1);
   ```

6. Now, catch the timer messages. Open ClassWizard and, as before, scroll through the list of messages in the far right list box. `WM_TIMER` is the second-to-last message in the alphabetic list, so drag the elevator all the way to the bottom and select `WM_TIMER`. Click Add Function and then click Edit Code. Replace the `TODO` comment with this line:

   ```
   m_progressBar.StepIt();
   ```

The `StepIt()` function increments the progress bar control's value by the step rate, causing new blocks to be displayed in the control as the control's value setting counts upward. When the control reaches its maximum, it automatically starts over.

N O T E   Notice that no `CProgressCtrl` member functions control the size or number of blocks that will fit into the control. These attributes are indirectly controlled by the size of the control.

Build Common and execute it to see the progress bar in action. Be sure to try stopping the timer as well as starting it.

The Slider Control

Many times in a program you might need the user to enter a value within a specific range. For this sort of task, you use MFC's `CSliderCtrl` class to create a slider (also called *trackbar*) control. For example, suppose you need the user to enter a percentage. In this case, you want the user to enter values only in the range of 0–100. Other values would be invalid and could cause problems in your program.

By using the slider control, you can force the user to enter a value in the specified range. Although the user can accidentally enter a wrong value (a value that doesn't accomplish what the user wants to do), there is no way to enter an invalid value (one that brings your program crashing down like a stone wall in an earthquake).

For a percentage, you create a slider control with a minimum value of 0 and a maximum value of 100. Moreover, to make the control easier to position, you might want to place tick marks at each setting that's a multiple of 10, providing 11 tick marks in all (including the one at 0). Common creates exactly this type of slider.

To use a slider, the user clicks the slider's slot. This moves the slider forward or backward, and often the selected value appears near the control. When a slider has the focus, the user can also control it with the Up and Down arrow keys and the Page Up and Page Down keys.

Creating the Trackbar

You are going to need a resource symbol for the trackbar control, so just as you did for the progress bar, choose View, Resource Symbols and click New. Enter IDC_TRACKBAR for the resource ID Name and accept the suggested Value. In CCommonView::OnCreate(), add a call to CreateTrackbar(). Then add the new member function as you added CreateProgressBar() and type in the code in Listing 10.3.

Listing 10.3   CommonView.cpp—*CCommonView::CreateTrackBar()*

```
void CCommonView::CreateTrackbar()
{
    m_trackbar.Create(WS_CHILD | WS_VISIBLE | WS_BORDER |
        TBS_AUTOTICKS | TBS_BOTH | TBS_HORZ,
        CRect(270, 40, 450, 80), this, IDC_TRACKBAR);
    m_trackbar.SetRange(0, 100, TRUE);
    m_trackbar.SetTicFreq(10);
    m_trackbar.SetLineSize(1);
    m_trackbar.SetPageSize(10);
}
```

Part
III

Ch
10

As with the progress bar, the first step is to create the slider control by calling its Create() member function. This function's four arguments are the control's style flags, the control's size (as a CRect object), a pointer to the control's parent window, and the control's ID. The style constants include the same constants that you would use for creating any type of window, with the addition of special styles used with sliders. Table 10.1 lists these special styles.

Table 10.1   Slider Styles

Style	Description
TBS_AUTOTICKS	Enables the slider to automatically draw its tick marks
TBS_BOTH	Draws tick marks on both sides of the slider
TBS_BOTTOM	Draws tick marks on the bottom of a horizontal slider
TBS_ENABLESELRANGE	Enables a slider to display a subrange of values
TBS_HORZ	Draws the slider horizontally
TBS_LEFT	Draws tick marks on the left side of a vertical slider
TBS_NOTICKS	Draws a slider with no tick marks
TBS_RIGHT	Draws tick marks on the right side of a vertical slider
TBS_TOP	Draws tick marks on the top of a horizontal slider
TBS_VERT	Draws a vertical slider

Initializing the Trackbar

Usually, when you create a slider control, you want to set the control's range and tick frequency. If the user is going to use the control from the keyboard, you also need to set the control's line and page size. In Common, the program initializes the trackbar with calls to `SetRange()`, `SetTicFreq()`, `SetLineSize()`, and `SetPageSize()`, as you saw in Listing 10.3. The call to `SetRange()` sets the trackbar's minimum and maximum values to 0 and 100. The arguments are the minimum value, the maximum value, and a Boolean value indicating whether the slider should redraw itself after setting the range. Notice that the tick frequency and page size are then set to be the same. This isn't absolutely required, but it's a very good idea. Most people assume that the tick marks indicate the size of a page, and you will confuse your users if the tick marks are more or less than a page apart.

A number of other functions can change the size of your slider, the size of the thumb, the current selection, and more. You can find all the details in the online documentation.

Manipulating the Slider

A slider is really just a special scrollbar control. When the user moves the slider, the control generates `WM_HSCROLL` messages, which you will arrange to catch. Open ClassWizard, select the Message Maps tab, make sure `CCommonView` is selected in the upper-right box, and find `WM_HSCROLL` in the list on the right. Select it, click Add Function, and then click Edit Code. Type in the code in Listing 10.4.

Listing 10.4   CommonView.cpp—*CCommonView::OnHScroll()*

```
void CCommonView::OnHScroll(UINT nSBCode, UINT nPos, CScrollBar* pScrollBar)
{
    CSliderCtrl* slider = (CSliderCtrl*)pScrollBar;
    int position = slider->GetPos();
    char s[10];
    wsprintf(s, "%d   ", position);
    CClientDC clientDC(this);
    clientDC.TextOut(390, 22, s);
    CScrollView::OnHScroll(nSBCode, nPos, pScrollBar);
}
```

Looking at this code, you see that the control itself doesn't display the current position as a number nearby; it's the `OnHScroll()` function that displays the number. Here's how it works:

1. `OnHScroll()`'s fourth parameter is a pointer to the scroll object that generated the `WM_HSCROLL` message.

2. The function first casts this pointer to a `CSliderCtrl` pointer; then it gets the current position of the trackbar's slider by calling the `CSliderCtrl` member function `GetPos()`.

3. After the program has the slider's position, it converts the integer to a string and displays that string in the window with `TextOut()`.

To learn how to make text appear onscreen, refer to Chapter 5, "Drawing on the Screen." Before moving on to the next control, build Common and test it. Click around on the slider and watch the number change.

 T I P If you have Windows set to Large Fonts (perhaps because you have a high screen resolution), the current slider value might not be displayed in quite the right place because the string "Trackbar Control" takes up more space on the screen with large fonts. If this happens, simply change the TextOut call to write the current slider value a little farther to the right.

The Up-Down Control

The trackbar control isn't the only way you can get a value in a predetermined range from the user. If you don't need the trackbar for visual feedback, you can use an up-down control, which is little more than a couple of arrows that the user clicks to increase or decrease the control's setting. Typically, an edit control next to the up-down control, called a *buddy edit* control or just a *buddy* control, displays the value to the user.

In the Common application, you can change the setting of the up-down control by clicking either of its arrows. When you do, the value in the attached edit box changes, indicating the up-down control's current setting. After the control has the focus, you can also change its value by pressing your keyboard's Up and Down arrow keys.

Creating the Up-Down Control

Add another call to CCommonView::OnCreate(), this time calling it **CreateUpDownCtrl()**. Add the member function and the code in Listing 10.5. Also add resource symbols for IDC_BUDDYEDIT and IDC_UPDOWN.

> **Listing 10.5   CommonView.cpp—*CCommonView::CreateUpDownCtrl()***

```
void CCommonView::CreateUpDownCtrl()
{
    m_buddyEdit.Create(WS_CHILD ¦ WS_VISIBLE ¦ WS_BORDER,
        CRect(50, 120, 110, 160), this, IDC_BUDDYEDIT);
    m_upDown.Create(WS_CHILD ¦ WS_VISIBLE ¦ WS_BORDER ¦
        UDS_ALIGNRIGHT ¦ UDS_SETBUDDYINT ¦ UDS_ARROWKEYS,
        CRect(0, 0, 0, 0), this, IDC_UPDOWN);
    m_upDown.SetBuddy(&m_buddyEdit);
    m_upDown.SetRange(1, 100);
    m_upDown.SetPos(50);
}
```

The program creates the up-down control by first creating the associated buddy control to which the up-down control communicates its current value. In most cases, including this one, the buddy control is an edit box, created by calling the CEdit class's Create() member function. This function's four arguments are the control's style flags, the control's size, a pointer to the control's parent window, and the control's ID. If you recall the control declarations, m_buddyEdit is an object of the CEdit class.

Now that the program has created the buddy control, it can create the up-down control in much the same way, by calling the object's Create() member function. As you can probably guess by now, this function's four arguments are the control's style flags, the control's size, a pointer to the control's parent window, and the control's ID. As with most controls, the style constants include the same constants that you use for creating any type of window. The CSpinButtonCtrl class, of which m_upDown is an object, however, defines special styles to be used with up-down controls. Table 10.2 lists these special styles.

Table 10.2 Up-Down Control Styles

Styles	Description
UDS_ALIGNLEFT	Places the up-down control on the left edge of the buddy control
UDS_ALIGNRIGHT	Places the up-down control on the right edge of the buddy control
UDS_ARROWKEYS	Enables the user to change the control's values by using the keyboard's Up and Down arrow keys
UDS_AUTOBUDDY	Makes the previous window the buddy control
UDS_HORZ	Creates a horizontal up-down control
UDS_NOTHOUSANDS	Eliminates separators between each set of three digits
UDS_SETBUDDYINT	Displays the control's value in the buddy control
UDS_WRAP	Causes the control's value to wrap around to its minimum when the maximum is reached, and vice versa

This chapter's sample application establishes the up-down control with calls to SetBuddy(), SetRange(), and SetPos(). Thanks to the UDS_SETBUDDYINT flag passed to Create() and the call to the control's SetBuddy() member function, Common doesn't need to do anything else for the control's value to appear on the screen. The control automatically handles its buddy. Try building and testing now.

You might want up-down controls that move faster or slower than in this sample or that use hex numbers rather than base-10 numbers. Look at the member functions of this control in the online documentation, and you will see how to do that.

The Image List Control

Often you need to use images that are related in some way. For example, your application might have a toolbar with many command buttons, each of which uses a bitmap for its icon. In a case like this, it would be great to have some sort of program object that could not only hold the bitmaps but also organize them so that they can be accessed easily. That's exactly what an image list control does for you—it stores a list of related images. You can use the images any way that you see fit in your program. Several common controls rely on image lists. These controls include the following:

- List view controls
- Tree view controls
- Property pages
- Toolbars

You will undoubtedly come up with many other uses for image lists. You might, for example, have an animation sequence that you'd like to display in a window. An image list is the perfect storage place for the frames that make up an animation, because you can easily access any frame just by using an index.

If the word *index* makes you think of arrays, you're beginning to understand how an image list stores images. An image list is very similar to an array that holds pictures rather than integers or floating-point numbers. Just as with an array, you initialize each "element" of an image list and thereafter can access any part of the "array" by using an index.

You won't, however, see an image list control in your running application in the same way that you can see a status bar or a progress bar control. This is because (again, similar to an array) an image list is only a storage structure for pictures. You can display the images stored in an image list, but you can't display the image list itself. Figure 10.2 shows how an image list is organized.

Part III

Ch 10

FIG. 10.2
An image list is much like an array of pictures.

Picture 1   Picture 2   Picture 3   Picture 4   Picture 5

Creating the Image List

In the Common Controls App application, image lists are used with the list view and tree view controls, so the image lists for the controls are created in the `CreateListView()` and `CreateTreeView()` local member functions and are called from `CCommonView::OnCreate()`. Just as with the other controls, add calls to these functions to `OnCreate()` and then add the functions to the class. You will see the full code for those functions shortly, but because they are long, this section presents the parts that are relevant to the image list.

A list view uses two image lists: one for small images and the other for large ones. The member variables for these lists have already been added to the class, so start coding `CreateListView()` with a call to each list's `Create()` member function, like this:

```
m_smallImageList.Create(16, 16, FALSE, 1, 0);
m_largeImageList.Create(32, 32, FALSE, 1, 0);
```

The `Create()` function's five arguments are

- The width of the pictures in the control
- The height of the pictures
- A Boolean value indicating whether the images contain a mask
- The number of images initially in the list
- The number of images by which the list can dynamically grow

This last value is 0 to indicate that the list isn't allowed to grow during runtime. The `Create()` function is overloaded in the `CImageList` class so that you can create image lists in various ways. You can find the other versions of `Create()` in your Visual C++ online documentation.

Initializing the Image List

After you create an image list, you will want to add images to it. After all, an empty image list isn't of much use. The easiest way to add the images is to include the images as part of your application's resource file and load them from there. Add these four lines to `CreateListView()` to fill each list with images:

```
HICON hIcon = ::LoadIcon (AfxGetResourceHandle(),
    MAKEINTRESOURCE(IDI_ICON1));
m_smallImageList.Add(hIcon);
hIcon = ::LoadIcon (AfxGetResourceHandle(),
    MAKEINTRESOURCE(IDI_ICON2));
m_largeImageList.Add(hIcon);
```

Here the program first gets a handle to the icon. Then it adds the icon to the image list by calling the image list's `Add()` member function. (In this case, the list includes only one icon. In other applications, you might have a list of large icons for folders, text files, and so on, as well as another list of small icons for the same purposes.) To create the first icon, choose Insert, Resource and double-click Icon. Then edit the new blank icon in the Resource Editor. (It will automatically be called `IDI_ICON1`.) Click the New Device Image toolbar button next to the drop-down box that says Standard (32×32) and choose Small (16×16) on the dialog that appears; click OK. You can spend a long time making a beautiful icon or just quickly fill in the whole grid with black and then put a white circle on it with the Ellipse tool. Add another icon, `IDI_ICON2`, and leave it as 32×32. Draw a similar symbol on this icon.

You can use many member functions to manipulate an object of the `CImageList` class, adjusting colors, removing images, and much more. The online documentation provides more details on these member functions.

You can write the first few lines of `CreateTreeView()` now. It uses one image list that starts with three images. Here's the code to add:

```
m_treeImageList.Create(13, 13, FALSE, 3, 0);
HICON hIcon = ::LoadIcon(AfxGetResourceHandle(),
    MAKEINTRESOURCE(IDI_ICON3));
m_treeImageList.Add(hIcon);
hIcon = ::LoadIcon(AfxGetResourceHandle(),
    MAKEINTRESOURCE(IDI_ICON4));
```

```
m_treeImageList.Add(hIcon);
hIcon = ::LoadIcon(AfxGetResourceHandle(),
    MAKEINTRESOURCE(IDI_ICON5));
m_treeImageList.Add(hIcon);
```

Create IDI_ICON3, IDI_ICON4, and IDI_ICON5 the same way you did the first two icons. All three are 32×32. Draw circles as before. If you leave the background the same murky green you started with, rather than fill it with black, the circles will appear on a transparent background—a nice effect.

The List View Control

A list view control simplifies the job of building an application that works with lists of objects and organizes those objects in such a way that the program's user can easily determine each object's attributes. For example, consider a group of files on a disk. Each file is a separate object associated with a number of attributes, including the file's name, size, and the most recent modification date. When you explore a folder, you see files either as icons in a window or as a table of entries, each entry showing the attributes associated with the files. You have full control over the way that the file objects are displayed, including which attributes are shown and which are unlisted. The common controls include something called a *list view control*, so you can organize lists in exactly the same way. If you'd like to see an example of a full-fledged list view control, open the Windows Explorer (see Figure 10.3). The right side of the window shows how the list view control can organize objects in a window. (The left side of the window contains a tree view control, which you will learn about later in this chapter in the section titled "The Tree View Control.") In the figure, the list view is currently set to the report view, in which each object in the list receives its own line, showing not only the object's name but also the attributes associated with that object.

Part

III

Ch

10

FIG. 10.3

Windows Explorer uses a list view control to organize file information.

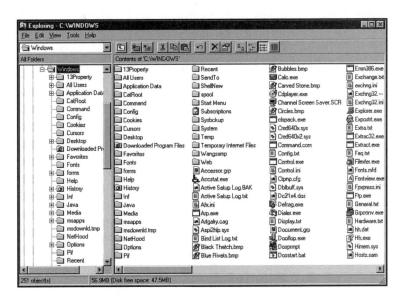

The user can change the way objects are organized in a list view control. Figure 10.4, for example, shows the list view portion of the Explorer set to the large-icon setting, and Figure 10.5 shows the small-icon setting, which enables the user to see more objects (in this case, files) in the window. With a list view control, the user can edit the names of objects in the list and in the report view can sort objects, based on data displayed in a particular column.

FIG. 10.4

Here's Explorer's list view control set to large icons.

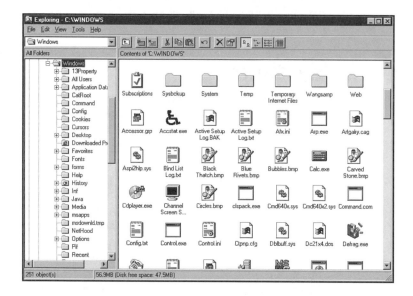

FIG. 10.5

Here's Explorer's list view control set to small icons.

Common will also sport a list view control, although not as fancy as Explorer's. You will add a list view and some buttons to switch between the small-icon, large-icon, list, and report views.

Creating the List View

How does all this happen? Well, it does require more work than the progress bar, trackbar, or up-down controls (it could hardly take less). You will write the rest of `CreateListView()`, which performs the following tasks:

1. Creates and fills the image list controls
2. Creates the list view control itself
3. Associates the image lists with the list view
4. Creates the columns
5. Sets up the columns
6. Creates the items
7. Sets up the items
8. Creates the buttons

After creating the image lists, `CreateListView()` goes on to create the list view control by calling the class's `Create()` member function, as usual. Add these lines to `CreateListView()`:

```
// Create the List View control.
    m_listView.Create(WS_VISIBLE | WS_CHILD | WS_BORDER |
        LVS_REPORT | LVS_NOSORTHEADER | LVS_EDITLABELS,
        CRect(160, 120, 394, 220), this, IDC_LISTVIEW);
```

The `CListCtrl` class, of which `m_listView` is an object, defines special styles to be used with list view controls. Table 10.3 lists these special styles and their descriptions.

Table 10.3   List View Styles

Style	Description
LVS_ALIGNLEFT	Left-aligns items in the large-icon and small-icon views
LVS_ALIGNTOP	Top-aligns items in the large-icon and small-icon views
LVS_AUTOARRANGE	Automatically arranges items in the large-icon and small-icon views
LVS_EDITLABELS	Enables the user to edit item labels
LVS_ICON	Sets the control to the large-icon view
LVS_LIST	Sets the control to the list view
LVS_NOCOLUMNHEADER	Shows no column headers in report view
LVS_NOITEMDATA	Stores only the state of each item
LVS_NOLABELWRAP	Disallows multiple-line item labels

continues

Table 10.3   Continued

Style	Description
LVS_NOSCROLL	Turns off scrolling
LVS_NOSORTHEADER	Turns off the button appearance of column headers
LVS_OWNERDRAWFIXED	Enables owner-drawn items in report view
LVS_REPORT	Sets the control to the report view
LVS_SHAREIMAGELISTS	Prevents the control from destroying its image lists when the control no longer needs them
LVS_SINGLESEL	Disallows multiple selection of items
LVS_SMALLICON	Sets the control to the small-icon view
LVS_SORTASCENDING	Sorts items in ascending order
LVS_SORTDESCENDING	Sorts items in descending order

The third task in CreateListView() is to associate the control with its image lists with two calls to SetImageList(). Add these lines to CreateListView():

```
m_listView.SetImageList(&m_smallImageList, LVSIL_SMALL);
m_listView.SetImageList(&m_largeImageList, LVSIL_NORMAL);
```

This function takes two parameters: a pointer to the image list and a flag indicating how the list is to be used. Three constants are defined for this flag: LVSIL_SMALL (which indicates that the list contains small icons), LVSIL_NORMAL (large icons), and LVSIL_STATE (state images). The SetImageList() function returns a pointer to the previously set image list, if any.

Creating the List View's Columns

The fourth task is to create the columns for the control's report view. You need one main column for the item itself and one column for each sub-item associated with an item. For example, in Explorer's list view, the main column holds file and folder names. Each additional column holds the sub-items for each item, such as the file's size, type, and modification date. To create a column, you must first declare a LV_COLUMN structure. You use this structure to pass information to and from the system. After you add the column to the control with InsertColumn(), you can use the structure to create and insert another column. Listing 10.6 shows the LV_COLUMN structure.

Listing 10.6   The *LV_COLUMN* Structure, Defined by MFC

```
typedef struct _LV_COLUMN
{
    UINT mask;        // Flags indicating valid fields
    int fmt;          // Column alignment
    int cx;           // Column width
```

```
    LPSTR pszText;      // Address of string buffer
    int cchTextMax;     // Size of the buffer
    int iSubItem;       // Subitem index for this column
} LV_COLUMN;
```

The mask member of the structure tells the system which members of the structure to use and which to ignore. The flags you can use are

- LVCF_FMT   fmt is valid.
- LVCF_SUBITEM   iSubItem is valid.
- LVCF_TEXT   pszText is valid.
- LVCF_WIDTH   cx is valid.

The fmt member denotes the column's alignment and can be LVCFMT_CENTER, LVCFMT_LEFT, or LVCFMT_RIGHT. The alignment determines how the column's label and items are positioned in the column.

Part III
Ch 10

N O T E   The first column, which contains the main items, is always aligned to the left. The other columns in the report view can be aligned however you like.

The cx field specifies the width of each column, whereas pszText is the address of a string buffer. When you're using the structure to create a column (you also can use this structure to obtain information about a column), this string buffer contains the column's label. The cchTextMax member denotes the size of the string buffer and is valid only when retrieving information about a column.

CreateListView() creates a temporary LV_COLUMN structure, sets the elements, and then inserts it into the list view as column 0, the main column. This process is repeated for the other two columns. Add these lines to CreateListView():

```
// Create the columns.
    LV_COLUMN lvColumn;
    lvColumn.mask = LVCF_FMT ¦ LVCF_WIDTH ¦ LVCF_TEXT ¦ LVCF_SUBITEM;
    lvColumn.fmt = LVCFMT_CENTER;
    lvColumn.cx = 75;

    lvColumn.iSubItem = 0;
    lvColumn.pszText = "Column 0";
    m_listView.InsertColumn(0, &lvColumn);
    lvColumn.iSubItem = 1;
    lvColumn.pszText = "Column 1";
    m_listView.InsertColumn(1, &lvColumn);
    lvColumn.iSubItem = 2;
    lvColumn.pszText = "Column 2";
    m_listView.InsertColumn(1, &lvColumn);
```

Creating the List View's Items

The fifth task in CreateListView() is to create the items that will be listed in the columns when the control is in its report view. Creating items is not unlike creating columns. As with columns, Visual C++ defines a structure that you must initialize and pass to the function that creates the items. This structure is called LV_ITEM and is defined as shown in Listing 10.7.

Listing 10.7   The *LV_ITEM* Structure, Defined by MFC

```
typedef struct _LV_ITEM
{
    UINT    mask;           // Flags indicating valid fields
    int     iItem;          // Item index
    int     iSubItem;       // Sub-item index
    UINT    state;          // Item's current state
    UINT    stateMask;      // Valid item states.
    LPSTR   pszText;        // Address of string buffer
    int     cchTextMax;     // Size of string buffer
    int     iImage;         // Image index for this item
    LPARAM  lParam;         // Additional information as a 32-bit value
} LV_ITEM;
```

In the LV_ITEM structure, the mask member specifies the other members of the structure that are valid. The flags you can use are

- ▪ LVIF_IMAGE   iImage is valid.
- ▪ LVIF_PARAM   lParam is valid.
- ▪ LVIF_STATE   state is valid.
- ▪ LVIF_TEXT   pszText is valid.

The iItem member is the index of the item, which you can think of as the row number in report view (although the items' position can change when they're sorted). Each item has a unique index. The iSubItem member is the index of the sub-item, if this structure is defining a sub-item. You can think of this value as the number of the column in which the item will appear. For example, if you're defining the main item (the first column), this value should be 0.

The state and stateMask members hold the item's current state and its valid states, which can be one or more of the following:

- ▪ LVIS_CUT   The item is selected for cut and paste.
- ▪ LVIS_DROPHILITED   The item is a highlighted drop target.
- ▪ LVIS_FOCUSED   The item has the focus.
- ▪ LVIS_SELECTED   The item is selected.

The pszText member is the address of a string buffer. When you use the LV_ITEM structure to create an item, the string buffer contains the item's text. When you are obtaining information about the item, pszText is the buffer where the information will be stored, and cchTextMax is the size of the buffer. If pszText is set to LPSTR_TEXTCALLBACK, the item uses the callback mechanism. Finally, the iImage member is the index of the item's icon in the small-icon and large-icon image lists. If set to I_IMAGECALLBACK, the iImage member indicates that the item uses the callback mechanism.

`CreateListView()` creates a temporary `LV_ITEM` structure, sets the elements, and then inserts it into the list view as item 0. Two calls to `SetItemText()` add sub-items to this item so that each column has some text in it, and the whole process is repeated for two other items. Add these lines:

```
// Create the items.
    LV_ITEM lvItem;
    lvItem.mask = LVIF_TEXT | LVIF_IMAGE | LVIF_STATE;
    lvItem.state = 0;
    lvItem.stateMask = 0;
    lvItem.iImage = 0;

    lvItem.iItem = 0;
    lvItem.iSubItem = 0;
    lvItem.pszText = "Item 0";
    m_listView.InsertItem(&lvItem);
    m_listView.SetItemText(0, 1, "Sub Item 0.1");
    m_listView.SetItemText(0, 2, "Sub Item 0.2");

    lvItem.iItem = 1;
    lvItem.iSubItem = 0;
    lvItem.pszText = "Item 1";
    m_listView.InsertItem(&lvItem);
    m_listView.SetItemText(1, 1, "Sub Item 1.1");
    m_listView.SetItemText(1, 2, "Sub Item 1.2");

    lvItem.iItem = 2;
    lvItem.iSubItem = 0;
    lvItem.pszText = "Item 2";
    m_listView.InsertItem(&lvItem);
    m_listView.SetItemText(2, 1, "Sub Item 2.1");
    m_listView.SetItemText(2, 2, "Sub Item 2.2");
```

Now you have created a list view with three columns and three items. Normally the values wouldn't be hard-coded, as this was, but instead would be filled in with values calculated by the program.

Manipulating the List View

You can set a list view control to four different types of views: small icon, large icon, list, and report. In Explorer, for example, the toolbar features buttons that you can click to change the view, or you can select the view from the View menu. Although Common doesn't have a snazzy toolbar like Explorer, it will include four buttons (labeled Small, Large, List, and Report) that you can click to change the view. Those buttons are created as the sixth step in `CreateListView()`. Add these lines to complete the function:

```
// Create the view-control buttons.
    m_smallButton.Create("Small", WS_VISIBLE | WS_CHILD | WS_BORDER,
        CRect(400, 120, 450, 140), this, IDC_LISTVIEW_SMALL);
    m_largeButton.Create("Large", WS_VISIBLE | WS_CHILD | WS_BORDER,
        CRect(400, 145, 450, 165), this, IDC_LISTVIEW_LARGE);
    m_listButton.Create("List", WS_VISIBLE | WS_CHILD | WS_BORDER,
        CRect(400, 170, 450, 190), this, IDC_LISTVIEW_LIST);
    m_reportButton.Create("Report", WS_VISIBLE | WS_CHILD | WS_BORDER,
        CRect(400, 195, 450, 215), this, IDC_LISTVIEW_REPORT);
```

TIP If you're using large fonts, these buttons will need to be more than 50 pixels wide. This code creates each button from position 400 to 450—make the second number larger to widen the buttons.

Edit the message map in CommonView.h to declare the handlers for each of these buttons so that it looks like this:

```
// Generated message map functions
protected:
        //{{AFX_MSG(CCommonView)
        afx_msg int OnCreate(LPCREATESTRUCT lpCreateStruct);
        afx_msg void OnLButtonDown(UINT nFlags, CPoint point);
        afx_msg void OnDestroy();
        afx_msg void OnTimer(UINT nIDEvent);
        afx_msg void OnHScroll(UINT nSBCode, UINT nPos, CScrollBar* pScrollBar);
        //}}AFX_MSG
        afx_msg void OnSmall();
        afx_msg void OnLarge();
        afx_msg void OnList();
        afx_msg void OnReport();
        DECLARE_MESSAGE_MAP()
};
```

Edit the message map in CommonView.cpp to associate the messages with the functions:

```
BEGIN_MESSAGE_MAP(CCommonView, CScrollView)
    //{{AFX_MSG_MAP(CCommonView)
    ON_WM_CREATE()
    ON_WM_LBUTTONDOWN()
    ON_WM_DESTROY()
    ON_WM_TIMER()
    ON_WM_HSCROLL()
    //}}AFX_MSG_MAP
    ON_COMMAND(IDC_LISTVIEW_SMALL, OnSmall)
    ON_COMMAND(IDC_LISTVIEW_LARGE, OnLarge)
    ON_COMMAND(IDC_LISTVIEW_LIST, OnList)
    ON_COMMAND(IDC_LISTVIEW_REPORT, OnReport)
    // Standard printing commands
    ON_COMMAND(ID_FILE_PRINT, CScrollView::OnFilePrint)
    ON_COMMAND(ID_FILE_PRINT_DIRECT, CScrollView::OnFilePrint)
    ON_COMMAND(ID_FILE_PRINT_PREVIEW, CScrollView::OnFilePrintPreview)
END_MESSAGE_MAP()
```

Choose View, Resource Symbols and click New to add new IDs for each constant referred to in this new code:

- IDC_LISTVIEW
- IDC_LISTVIEW_SMALL
- IDC_LISTVIEW_LARGE
- IDC_LISTVIEW_LIST
- IDC_LISTVIEW_REPORT

The four handlers will each call `SetWindowLong()`, which sets a window's attribute. Its arguments are the window's handle, a flag that specifies the value to be changed, and the new value. For example, passing `GWL_STYLE` as the second value means that the window's style should be changed to the style given in the third argument. Changing the list view control's style (for example, to `LVS_SMALLICON`) changes the type of view that it displays. With that in mind, add the four handler functions to the bottom of CommonView.cpp:

```
void CCommonView::OnSmall()
{
    SetWindowLong(m_listView.m_hWnd, GWL_STYLE,
        WS_VISIBLE | WS_CHILD | WS_BORDER |
        LVS_SMALLICON | LVS_EDITLABELS);
}

void CCommonView::OnLarge()
{
    SetWindowLong(m_listView.m_hWnd, GWL_STYLE,
        WS_VISIBLE | WS_CHILD | WS_BORDER |
        LVS_ICON | LVS_EDITLABELS);
}

void CCommonView::OnList()
{
    SetWindowLong(m_listView.m_hWnd, GWL_STYLE,
        WS_VISIBLE | WS_CHILD | WS_BORDER |
        LVS_LIST | LVS_EDITLABELS);
}

void CCommonView::OnReport()
{
    SetWindowLong(m_listView.m_hWnd, GWL_STYLE,
        WS_VISIBLE | WS_CHILD | WS_BORDER |
        LVS_REPORT | LVS_EDITLABELS);
}
```

Part

III

Ch

10

In addition to changing the view, you can program a number of other features for your list view controls. When the user does something with the control, Windows sends a `WM_NOTIFY` message to the parent window. The most common notifications sent by a list view control are the following:

- **LVN_COLUMNCLICK**   Indicates that the user clicked a column header
- **LVN_BEGINLABELEDIT**   Indicates that the user is about to edit an item's label
- **LVN_ENDLABELEDIT**   Indicates that the user is ending the label-editing process

Why not have Common allow editing of the first column in this list view? You start by overriding the virtual function `OnNotify()` that was inherited by `CCommonView` from `CScrollView`. Right-click `CCommonView` in ClassView and choose Add Virtual Function. Select `OnNotify()` from the list on the left and click Add and Edit; then add these lines of code at the beginning of the function, replacing the `TODO` comment:

```
LV_DISPINFO* lv_dispInfo = (LV_DISPINFO*) lParam;

    if (lv_dispInfo->hdr.code == LVN_BEGINLABELEDIT)
    {
        CEdit* pEdit = m_listView.GetEditControl();
        // Manipulate edit control here.
    }
    else if (lv_dispInfo->hdr.code == LVN_ENDLABELEDIT)
    {
        if ((lv_dispInfo->item.pszText != NULL) &&
            (lv_dispInfo->item.iItem != -1))
        {
            m_listView.SetItemText(lv_dispInfo->item.iItem,
                0, lv_dispInfo->item.pszText);
        }
    }
```

The three parameters received by OnNotify() are the message's WPARAM and LPARAM values and a pointer to a result code. In the case of a WM_NOTIFY message coming from a list view control, the WPARAM is the list view control's ID. If the WM_NOTIFY message is the LVN_BEGINLABELEDIT or LVN_ENDLABELEDIT notification, the LPARAM is a pointer to an LV_DISPINFO structure, which itself contains NMHDR and LV_ITEM structures. You use the information in these structures to manipulate the item that the user is trying to edit.

If the notification is LVN_BEGINLABELEDIT, your program can do whatever pre-editing initialization it needs to do, usually by calling GetEditControl() and then working with the pointer returned to you. This sample application shows you only how to get that pointer.

When handling label editing, the other notification to watch out for is LVN_ENDLABELEDIT, which means that the user has finished editing the label, by either typing the new label or canceling the editing process. If the user has canceled the process, the LV_DISPINFO structure's item.pszText member will be NULL, or the item.iItem member will be –1. In this case, you need do nothing more than ignore the notification. If, however, the user completed the editing process, the program must copy the new label to the item's text, which OnNotify() does with a call to SetItemText(). The CListCtrl object's SetItemText() member function requires three arguments: the item index, the sub-item index, and the new text.

At this point you can build Common again and test it. Click each of the four buttons to change the view style. Also, try editing one of the labels in the first column of the list view.

Figure 10.1 already showed you the report view for this list view. Figure 10.6 shows the application's list view control displaying small icons, and Figure 10.7 shows the large icons. (Some controls in these figures have yet to be covered in this chapter.)

You can do a lot of other things with a list view control. A little time invested in exploring and experimenting can save you a lot of time writing your user interface.

FIG. 10.6

Here's the sample application's list view control set to small icons.

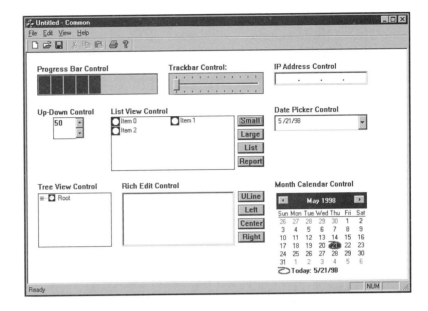

FIG. 10.7

Here's the sample application's list view control set to large icons.

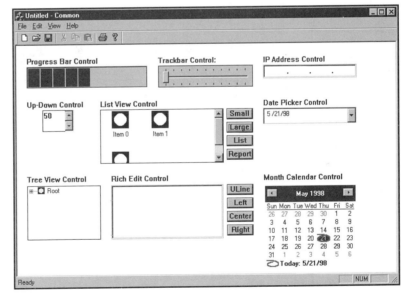

The Tree View Control

In the preceding section, you learned how to use the list view control to organize the display of many items in a window. The list view control enables you to display items both as objects in a window and objects in a report organized into columns. Often, however, the data you'd like to organize for your application's user is best placed in a hierarchical view. That is, elements of the data are shown as they relate to one other. A good example of a hierarchical display is the directory tree used by Windows to display directories and the files that they contain.

MFC provides this functionality in the `CTreeCtrl` class. This versatile control displays data in various ways, all the while retaining the hierarchical relationship between the data objects in the view.

If you'd like to see an example of a tree view control, revisit Windows Explorer (see Figure 10.8). The left side of the window shows how the tree view control organizes objects in a window. (The right side of the window contains a list view control, which you learned about in the preceding section). In the figure, the tree view displays not only the storage devices on the computer but also the directories and files stored on those devices. The tree clearly shows the hierarchical relationship between the devices, directories, and files, and it enables the user to open and close branches on the tree to explore different levels.

FIG. 10.8

A tree view control displays a hierarchical relationship between items.

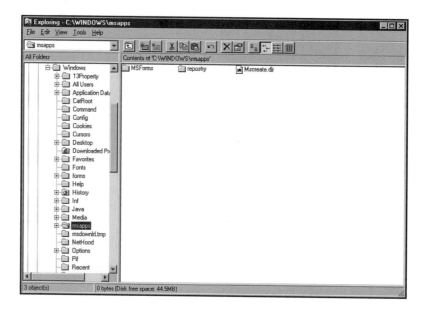

Creating the Tree View

Tree views are a little simpler than list views. You will write the rest of `CreateTreeView()`, which performs the following tasks:

1. Creates an image list
2. Creates the tree view itself
3. Associates the image list with the list view
4. Creates the root item
5. Creates child items

Creating the image list, creating the tree control, and associating the control with the image list are very similar to the steps completed for the image list. You've already written the code to create the image list, so add these lines to CreateTreeView():

```
// Create the Tree View control.
    m_treeView.Create(WS_VISIBLE | WS_CHILD | WS_BORDER |
        TVS_HASLINES | TVS_LINESATROOT | TVS_HASBUTTONS |
        TVS_EDITLABELS, CRect(20, 260, 160, 360), this,
        IDC_TREEVIEW);
    m_treeView.SetImageList(&m_treeImageList, TVSIL_NORMAL);
```

(Remember to add a resource ID for IDC_TREEVIEW.) The CTreeCtrl class, of which m_treeView is an object, defines special styles to be used with tree view controls. Table 10.4 lists these special styles.

Table 10.4   Tree View Control Styles

Style	Description
TVS_DISABLEDRAGDROP	Disables drag-and-drop operations
TVS_EDITLABELS	Enables the user to edit labels
TVS_HASBUTTONS	Gives each parent item a button
TVS_HASLINES	Adds lines between items in the tree
TVS_LINESATROOT	Adds a line between the root and child items
TVS_SHOWSELALWAYS	Forces a selected item to stay selected when losing focus
TVS_NOTOOLTIPS	Suppresses ToolTips for the tree items
TVS_SINGLEEXPAND	Expands or collapses tree items with a single click rather than a double click

Creating the Tree View's Items

Creating items for a tree view control is much like creating items for a list view control. As with the list view, Visual C++ defines a structure that you must initialize and pass to the function that creates the items. This structure is called TVITEM and is defined in Listing 10.8.

Listing 10.8   The *TVITEM* Structure, Defined by MFC

```
typedef struct _TVITEM
{
    UINT      mask;
    HTREEITEM hItem;
    UINT      state;
    UINT      stateMask;
    LPSTR     pszText;
    int       cchTextMax;
```

continues

Listing 10.8   Continued

```
    int       iImage;
    int       iSelectedImage;
    int       cChildren;
    LPARAM    lParam;
} TV_ITEM;
```

In the TVITEM structure, the mask member specifies the other structure members that are valid. The flags you can use are as follows:

- TVIF_CHILDREN   cChildren is valid.
- TVIF_HANDLE   hItem is valid.
- TVIF_IMAGE   iImage is valid.
- TVIF_PARAM   lParam is valid.
- TVIF_SELECTEDIMAGE   iSelectedImage is valid.
- TVIF_STATE   state and stateMask are valid.
- TVIF_TEXT   pszText and cchTextMax are valid.

The hItem member is the handle of the item, whereas the state and stateMask members hold the item's current state and its valid states, which can be one or more of TVIS_BOLD, TVIS_CUT, TVIS_DROPHILITED, TVIS_EXPANDED, TVIS_EXPANDEDONCE, TVIS_FOCUSED, TVIS_OVERLAYMASK, TVIS_SELECTED, TVIS_STATEIMAGEMASK, and TVIS_USERMASK.

The pszText member is the address of a string buffer. When using the TVITEM structure to create an item, the string buffer contains the item's text. When obtaining information about the item, pszText is the buffer where the information will be stored, and cchTextMax is the size of the buffer. If pszText is set to LPSTR_TEXTCALLBACK, the item uses the callback mechanism. Finally, the iImage member is the index of the item's icon in the image list. If set to I_IMAGECALLBACK, the iImage member indicates that the item uses the callback mechanism.

The iSelectedImage member is the index of the icon in the image list that represents the item when the item is selected. As with iImage, if this member is set to I_IMAGECALLBACK, the iSelectedImage member indicates that the item uses the callback mechanism. Finally, cChildren specifies whether there are child items associated with the item.

In addition to the TVITEM structure, you must initialize a TVINSERTSTRUCT structure that holds information about how to insert the new structure into the tree view control. That structure is declared in Listing 10.9.

Listing 10.9   The *TVINSERTSTRUCT* Structure, Defined by MFC

```
typedef struct tagTVINSERTSTRUCT {
    HTREEITEM hParent;
    HTREEITEM hInsertAfter;
#if (_WIN32_IE >= 0x0400)
    union
```

```
    {
        TVITEMEX itemex;
        TVITEM item;
    } DUMMYUNIONNAME;
#else
    TVITEM item;
#endif
} TVINSERTSTRUCT, FAR *LPTVINSERTSTRUCT;
```

In this structure, hParent is the handle to the parent tree-view item. A value of NULL or TVI_ROOT specifies that the item should be placed at the root of the tree. The hInsertAfter member specifies the handle of the item after which this new item should be inserted. It can also be one of the flags TVI_FIRST (beginning of the list), TVI_LAST (end of the list), or TVI_SORT (alphabetical order). Finally, the item member is the TVITEM structure containing information about the item to be inserted into the tree.

Common first initializes the TVITEM structure for the root item (the first item in the tree). Add these lines:

```
// Create the root item.
    TVITEM tvItem;
    tvItem.mask =
        TVIF_TEXT | TVIF_IMAGE | TVIF_SELECTEDIMAGE;
    tvItem.pszText = "Root";
    tvItem.cchTextMax = 4;
    tvItem.iImage = 0;
    tvItem.iSelectedImage = 0;
    TVINSERTSTRUCT tvInsert;
    tvInsert.hParent = TVI_ROOT;
    tvInsert.hInsertAfter = TVI_FIRST;
    tvInsert.item = tvItem;
    HTREEITEM hRoot = m_treeView.InsertItem(&tvInsert);
```

The CTreeCtrl member function InsertItem() inserts the item into the tree view control. Its single argument is the address of the TVINSERTSTRUCT structure.

CreateTreeView() then inserts the remaining items into the tree view control. Add these lines to insert some hard-coded sample items into the tree view:

```
// Create the first child item.
    tvItem.pszText = "Child Item 1";
    tvItem.cchTextMax = 12;
    tvItem.iImage = 1;
    tvItem.iSelectedImage = 1;
    tvInsert.hParent = hRoot;
    tvInsert.hInsertAfter = TVI_FIRST;
    tvInsert.item = tvItem;
    HTREEITEM hChildItem = m_treeView.InsertItem(&tvInsert);

    // Create a child of the first child item.
    tvItem.pszText = "Child Item 2";
    tvItem.cchTextMax = 12;
    tvItem.iImage = 2;
    tvItem.iSelectedImage = 2;
```

Part

III

Ch

10

```
tvInsert.hParent = hChildItem;
tvInsert.hInsertAfter = TVI_FIRST;
tvInsert.item = tvItem;
m_treeView.InsertItem(&tvInsert);

// Create another child of the root item.
tvItem.pszText = "Child Item 3";
tvItem.cchTextMax = 12;
tvItem.iImage = 1;
tvItem.iSelectedImage = 1;
tvInsert.hParent = hRoot;
tvInsert.hInsertAfter = TVI_LAST;
tvInsert.item = tvItem;
m_treeView.InsertItem(&tvInsert);
```

Manipulating the Tree View

Just as with the list view control, you can edit the labels of the items in Common's tree view. Also, like the list view control, this process works because the tree view sends WM_NOTIFY messages that trigger a call to the program's OnNotify() function.

OnNotify() handles the tree-view notifications in almost exactly the same way as the list-view notifications. The only difference is in the names of the structures used. Add these lines to OnNotify() before the return statement:

```
TV_DISPINFO* tv_dispInfo = (TV_DISPINFO*) lParam;

    if (tv_dispInfo->hdr.code == TVN_BEGINLABELEDIT)
    {
        CEdit* pEdit = m_treeView.GetEditControl();
        // Manipulate edit control here.
    }
    else if (tv_dispInfo->hdr.code == TVN_ENDLABELEDIT)
    {
        if (tv_dispInfo->item.pszText != NULL)
        {
            m_treeView.SetItemText(tv_dispInfo->item.hItem,
                tv_dispInfo->item.pszText);
        }
    }
```

The tree view control sends a number of other notification messages, including TVN_BEGINDRAG, TVN_BEGINLABELEDIT, TVN_BEGINRDRAG, TVN_DELETEITEM, TVN_ENDLABELEDIT, TVN_GETDISPINFO, TVN_GETINFOTIP, TVN_ITEMEXPANDED, TVN_ITEMEXPANDING, TVN_KEYDOWN, TVN_SELCHANGED, TVN_SELCHANGING, TVN_SETDISPINFO, and TVN_SINGLEEXPAND. Check your Visual C++ online documentation for more information about handling these notification messages.

Now is a good time to again build and test Common. Be sure to try expanding and collapsing the levels of the tree and editing a label. If you can't see all the control, maximize the application and adjust your screen resolution if you can. The application will eventually scroll but not just yet.

The Rich Edit Control

If you took all the energy expended on writing text-editing software and you concentrated that energy on other, less mundane programming problems, computer science would probably be a decade ahead of where it is now. Although that might be an exaggeration, it is true that when it comes to text editors, a huge amount of effort has been dedicated to reinventing the wheel. Wouldn't it be great to have one piece of text-editing code that all programmers could use as the starting point for their own custom text editors?

With Visual C++'s CRichEditCtrl control, you get a huge jump on any text-editing functionality that you need to install in your applications. The rich edit control is capable of handling fonts, paragraph styles, text color, and other types of tasks that are traditionally found in text editors. In fact, a rich edit control (named for the fact that it handles text in Rich Text Format) provides a solid starting point for any text-editing tasks that your application must handle. Your users can

- Type text.
- Edit text, using cut-and-paste and sophisticated drag-and-drop operations.
- Set text attributes such as font, point size, and color.
- Apply underline, bold, italic, strikethrough, superscript, and subscript properties to text.
- Format text, using various alignments and bulleted lists.
- Lock text from further editing.
- Save and load files.

As you can see, a rich edit control is powerful. It is, in fact, almost a complete word-processor-in-a-box that you can plug into your program and use immediately. Of course, because a rich edit control offers so many features, there's a lot to learn. This section gives you a quick introduction to creating and manipulating a rich edit control.

Creating the Rich Edit Control

Add a call to CreateRichEdit() to the view class's OnCreate() function and then add the function to the class. Listing 10.10 shows the code you should add to the function. Add resource IDs for IDC_RICHEDIT, IDC_RICHEDIT_ULINE, IDC_RICHEDIT_LEFT, IDC_RICHEDIT_CENTER, and IDC_RICHEDIT_RIGHT.

Listing 10.10   CommonView.cpp—*CCommonView::CreateRichEdit()*

```
void CCommonView::CreateRichEdit()
{
    m_richEdit.Create(WS_CHILD | WS_VISIBLE | WS_BORDER |
        ES_AUTOVSCROLL | ES_MULTILINE,
        CRect(180, 260, 393, 360), this, IDC_RICHEDIT);

    m_boldButton.Create("ULine", WS_VISIBLE | WS_CHILD | WS_BORDER,
        CRect(400, 260, 450, 280), this, IDC_RICHEDIT_ULINE);
```

continues

Listing 10.10 Continued

```
    m_leftButton.Create("Left", WS_VISIBLE | WS_CHILD | WS_BORDER,
        CRect(400, 285, 450, 305), this, IDC_RICHEDIT_LEFT);
    m_centerButton.Create("Center", WS_VISIBLE | WS_CHILD | WS_BORDER,
        CRect(400, 310, 450, 330), this, IDC_RICHEDIT_CENTER);
    m_rightButton.Create("Right", WS_VISIBLE | WS_CHILD | WS_BORDER,
        CRect(400, 335, 450, 355), this, IDC_RICHEDIT_RIGHT);
}
```

As usual, things start with a call to the control's `Create()` member function. The style constants include the same constants that you would use for creating any type of window, with the addition of special styles used with rich edit controls. Table 10.5 lists these special styles.

Table 10.5 Rich Edit Styles

Style	Description
ES_AUTOHSCROLL	Automatically scrolls horizontally
ES_AUTOVSCROLL	Automatically scrolls vertically
ES_CENTER	Centers text
ES_LEFT	Left-aligns text
ES_LOWERCASE	Lowercases all text
ES_MULTILINE	Enables multiple lines
ES_NOHIDESEL	Doesn't hide selected text when losing the focus
ES_OEMCONVERT	Converts from ANSI characters to OEM characters and back to ANSI
ES_PASSWORD	Displays characters as asterisks
ES_READONLY	Disables editing in the control
ES_RIGHT	Right-aligns text
ES_UPPERCASE	Uppercases all text
ES_WANTRETURN	Inserts return characters into text when Enter is pressed

Initializing the Rich Edit Control

The rich edit control is perfectly usable as soon as it is created. Member functions manipulate the control extensively, formatting and selecting text, enabling and disabling many control features, and more. As always, check your online documentation for all the details on these member functions.

Manipulating the Rich Edit Control

This sample application shows you the basics of using the rich edit control by setting character attributes and paragraph formats. When you include a rich edit control in an application, you will probably want to give the user some control over its contents. For this reason, you usually create menu and toolbar commands for selecting the various options that you want to support in the application. In Common, the user can click four buttons to control the rich edit control.

You've already added the code to create these buttons. Add lines to the message map in the header file to declare the handlers:

```
afx_msg void OnULine();
afx_msg void OnLeft();
afx_msg void OnCenter();
afx_msg void OnRight();
```

Similarly, add these lines to the message map in the source file:

```
ON_COMMAND(IDC_RICHEDIT_ULINE, OnULine)
ON_COMMAND(IDC_RICHEDIT_LEFT, OnLeft)
ON_COMMAND(IDC_RICHEDIT_CENTER, OnCenter)
ON_COMMAND(IDC_RICHEDIT_RIGHT, OnRight)
```

Each of these functions is simple. Add them each to CommonView.cpp. OnULine() looks like this:

```
void CCommonView::OnULine()
{
    CHARFORMAT charFormat;
    charFormat.cbSize = sizeof(CHARFORMAT);
    charFormat.dwMask = CFM_UNDERLINE;
    m_richEdit.GetSelectionCharFormat(charFormat);

    if (charFormat.dwEffects & CFM_UNDERLINE)
        charFormat.dwEffects = 0;
    else
        charFormat.dwEffects = CFE_UNDERLINE;

    m_richEdit.SetSelectionCharFormat(charFormat);
    m_richEdit.SetFocus();
}
```

OnULine() creates and initializes a CHARFORMAT structure, which holds information about character formatting and is declared in Listing 10.11.

Part

III

Ch

10

Listing 10.11   The *CHARFORMAT* Structure, Defined by MFC

```
typedef struct _charformat
{
    UINT     cbSize;
    _WPAD    _wPad1;
    DWORD    dwMask;
    DWORD    dwEffects;
    LONG     yHeight;
```

continues

Listing 10.11 Continued

```
    LONG      yOffset;
    COLORREF  crTextColor;
    BYTE      bCharSet;
    BYTE      bPitchAndFamily;
    TCHAR     szFaceName[LF_FACESIZE];
    _WPAD     _wPad2;
} CHARFORMAT;
```

In a CHARFORMAT structure, cbSize is the size of the structure. dwMask indicates which members of the structure are valid (can be a combination of CFM_BOLD, CFM_CHARSET, CFM_COLOR, CFM_FACE, CFM_ITALIC, CFM_OFFSET, CFM_PROTECTED, CFM_SIZE, CFM_STRIKEOUT, and CFM_UNDERLINE). dwEffects is the character effects (can be a combination of CFE_AUTOCOLOR, CFE_BOLD, CFE_ITALIC, CFE_STRIKEOUT, CFE_UNDERLINE, and CFE_PROTECTED). yHeight is the character height, and yOffset is the character baseline offset (for super- and subscript characters). crTextColor is the text color. bCharSet is the character set value (see the ifCharSet member of the LOGFONT structure). bPitchAndFamily is the font pitch and family, and szFaceName is the font name.

After initializing the CHARFORMAT structure, as needed, to toggle underlining, OnULine() calls the control's GetSelectionCharFormat() member function. This function, whose single argument is a reference to the CHARFORMAT structure, fills the character format structure. OnULine() checks the dwEffects member of the structure to determine whether to turn underlining on or off. The bitwise and operator, &, is used to test a single bit of the variable.

Finally, after setting the character format, OnULine() returns the focus to the rich edit control. By clicking a button, the user has removed the focus from the rich edit control. You don't want to force the user to keep switching back manually to the control after every button click, so you do it by calling the control's SetFocus() member function.

Common also enables the user to switch between the three types of paragraph alignment. This is accomplished similarly to toggling character formats. Listing 10.12 shows the three functions—OnLeft(), OnRight(), and OnCenter()—that handle the alignment commands. Add the code for these functions to CommonView.cpp. As you can see, the main difference is the use of the PARAFORMAT structure instead of CHARFORMAT and the call to SetParaFormat() instead of SetSelectionCharFormat().

Listing 10.12 CommonView.cpp—Changing Paragraph Formats

```cpp
void CCommonView::OnLeft()
{
    PARAFORMAT paraFormat;
    paraFormat.cbSize = sizeof(PARAFORMAT);
    paraFormat.dwMask = PFM_ALIGNMENT;
    paraFormat.wAlignment = PFA_LEFT;
    m_richEdit.SetParaFormat(paraFormat);
    m_richEdit.SetFocus();
}
```

```
void CCommonView::OnCenter()
{
    PARAFORMAT paraFormat;
    paraFormat.cbSize = sizeof(PARAFORMAT);
    paraFormat.dwMask = PFM_ALIGNMENT;
    paraFormat.wAlignment = PFA_CENTER;
    m_richEdit.SetParaFormat(paraFormat);
    m_richEdit.SetFocus();
}
void CCommonView::OnRight()
{
    PARAFORMAT paraFormat;
    paraFormat.cbSize = sizeof(PARAFORMAT);
    paraFormat.dwMask = PFM_ALIGNMENT;
    paraFormat.wAlignment = PFA_RIGHT;
    m_richEdit.SetParaFormat(paraFormat);
    m_richEdit.SetFocus();
}
```

After adding all that code, it's time to build and test again. First, click in the text box to give it the focus. Then, start typing. Want to try out character attributes? Click the ULine button to add underlining to either selected text or the next text you type. To try out paragraph formatting, click the Left, Center, or Right button to specify paragraph alignment. (Again, if you're using large text, adjust the button size if the labels don't fit.) Figure 10.9 shows the rich edit control with some different character and paragraph styles used.

FIG. 10.9
A rich edit control is almost a complete word processor.

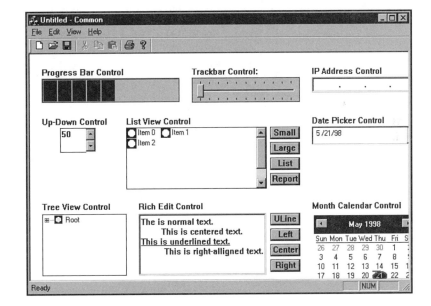

IP Address Control

If you're writing an Internet-aware program, you might have already wondered how you're going to validate certain kinds of input from your users. One thing you could ask for is an IP address, like this one:

```
205.210.40.1
```

IP addresses always have four parts, separated by dots, and each part is always a number between 1 and 255. The IP address picker guarantees that the user will give you information that meets this format.

To try it out, add yet another line to OnCreate(), this time a call to CreateIPAddress(). Add the function to the class. The code is really simple; just add a call to Create():

```
void CCommonView::CreateIPAddress()
{
   m_ipaddress.Create(WS_CHILD | WS_VISIBLE | WS_BORDER,
        CRect(470,40,650,65), this, IDC_IPADDRESS);
}
```

Remember to add a resource ID for IDC_IPADDRESS. No special styles are related to this simple control. There are some useful member functions to get, set, clear, or otherwise manipulate the address. Check them out in the online documentation.

Build and run Common, and try entering numbers or letters into the parts of the field. Notice how the control quietly fixes bad values (enter **999** into one part, for example) and how it moves you along from part to part as you enter the third digit or type a dot. It's a simple control, but if you need to obtain IP addresses from the user, this is the only way to fly.

The Date Picker Control

How many different applications ask users for dates? It can be annoying to have to type a date according to some preset format. Many users prefer to click on a calendar to select a day. Others find this very slow and would rather type the date, especially if they're merely changing an existing date. The date picker control, in the MFC class CDateTimeCtrl, gives your users the best of both worlds.

Start, as usual, by adding a call to CreateDatePicker() to CCommonView::OnCreate() and then adding the function to the class. Add the resource ID for IDC_DATE. Like the IP Address control, the date picker needs only to be created. Add this code to CommonView.cpp:

```
void CCommonView::CreateDatePicker()
{
   m_date.Create(WS_CHILD | WS_VISIBLE | DTS_SHORTDATEFORMAT,
        CRect(470,120,650,150), this, IDC_DATE);
}
```

The CDateTimeCtrl class, of which m_date is an object, defines special styles to be used with date picker controls. Table 10.6 lists these special styles.

Table 10.6   Date Picker Control Styles

Style	Description
DTS_APPCANPARSE	Instructs the date control to give more control to your application while the user edits dates.
DTS_LONGDATEFORMAT	After the date is picked, displays it like Monday, May 18, 1998 or whatever your locale has defined for long dates.
DTS_RIGHTALIGN	Aligns the calendar with the right edge of the control (if you don't specify this style, it will align with the left edge).
DTS_SHOWNONE	A date is optional: A check box indicates that a date has been selected.
DTS_SHORTDATEFORMAT	After the date is picked, displays it like 5/18/98 or whatever your locale has defined for short dates.
DTS_TIMEFORMAT	Displays the time as well as the date.
DTS_UPDOWN	Uses an up-down control instead of a calendar for picking.

Part
III

Ch
10

There are a number of member functions that you might use to set colors and fonts for this control, but the most important function is GetTime(), which gets you the date and time entered by the user. It fills in a COleDateTime or CTime object, or a SYSTEMTIME structure, which you can access by individual members. Here's the declaration of SYSTEMTIME:

```
typedef struct _SYSTEMTIME {
 WORD wYear;
 WORD wMonth;
 WORD wDayOfWeek;
 WORD wDay;
 WORD wHour;
 WORD wMinute;
 WORD wSecond;
 WORD wMilliseconds;
} SYSTEMTIME;
```

If you want to do anything with this date, you're probably going to find it easier to work with as a CTime object. The CTime class is discussed in Appendix F, "Useful Classes."

For now, you probably just want to see how easy it is to use the control, so build and test Common yet again. Click the drop-down box next to the short date, and you will see how the date picker got its name. Choose a date and see the short date change. Edit the date and then drop the month down again, and you will see that the highlight has moved to the day you entered. Notice, also, that today's date is circled on the month part of this control.

This month calendar is a control of its own. One is created by the date picker, but you will create another one in the next section.

Month Calendar Control

The month calendar control used by the date picker is compact and neat. Putting one into Common is very simple. Add a call to `CreateMonth()` to `CCommonView::OnCreate()` and add the function to the class. Add a resource ID for `IDC_MONTH`, too; then add the code for `CreateMonth()`. Here it is:

```
void CCommonView::CreateMonth()
{
    m_month.Create(WS_CHILD | WS_VISIBLE | DTS_SHORTDATEFORMAT,
        CRect(470,260,650,420), this, IDC_MONTH);
}
```

You can use many of the `DTS_` styles when creating your month calendar control. In addition, the `CMonthCalCtrl` class, of which `m_month` is an object, defines special styles to be used with month calendar controls. Table 10.7 lists these special styles.

Table 10.7 Month Calendar Control Styles

Style	Description
MCS_DAYSTATE	Instructs the control to send MCN_GETDAYSTATE messages to the application so that special days (such as holidays) can be displayed in bold.
MCS_MULTISELECT	Enables the user to choose a range of dates.
MCS_NOTODAY	Suppresses the Today date at the bottom of the control. The user can display today's date by clicking the word *Today*.
MCS_NOTODAY_CIRCLE	Suppresses the circling of today's date.
MCS_WEEKNUMBERS	Numbers each week in the year from 1 to 52 and displays the numbers at the left of the calendar.

A number of member functions enable you to customize the control, setting the colors, fonts, and whether weeks start on Sunday or Monday. You will be most interested in `GetCurSel()`, which fills a `COleDateTime`, `CTime`, or `LPSYSTEMTIME` with the currently selected date.

Build and test Common again and really exercise the month control this time. (Make the window larger if you can't see the whole control.) Try moving from month to month. If you're a long way from today's date, click the Today down at the bottom to return quickly. This is a neat control and should quickly replace the various third-party calendars that so many developers have been using.

Scrolling the View

After adding all these controls, you might find that they don't all fit in the window. As Figure 10.10 shows, no scrollbars appear, even though `CCommonView` inherits from `CScrollView`. You need to set the scroll sizes in order for scrolling to work properly.

FIG. 10.10

The view doesn't automatically gain scrollbars as more controls are added.

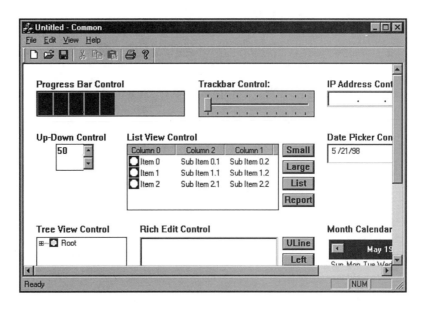

Expand CCommonView and double-click OnInitialUpdate() in ClassView. Edit it so that it looks like this:

```
void CCommonView::OnInitialUpdate()
{
        CScrollView::OnInitialUpdate();

        CSize sizeTotal;
        sizeTotal.cx = 700;
        sizeTotal.cy = 500;

        SetScrollSizes(MM_TEXT, sizeTotal);
}
```

The last control you added, the month calendar, ran from the coordinates (470, 260) to (650, 420). This code states that the entire document is 700×500 pixels, so it leaves a nice white margin between that last control and the edge of the view. When the displayed window is less than 700×500, you get scrollbars. When it's larger, you don't. The call to SetScrollSizes() takes care of all the work involved in making scrollbars, sizing them to represent the proportion of the document that is displayed, and dealing with the user's scrollbar clicks. Try it yourself—build Common one more time and experiment with resizing it and scrolling around. (The scrollbars weren't there before because the OnInitialUpdate() generated by AppWizard stated that the app was 100×100 pixels, which wouldn't require scrollbars.)

So, what's going on? Vertical scrolling is fine, but horizontal scrolling blows up your application, right? You can use the techniques described in Appendix D, "Debugging," to find the cause. The problem is in OnHScroll(), which assumed that any horizontal scrolling was related to the slider control and acted accordingly. Edit that function so that it looks like this:

Part
III

Ch
10

```
void CCommonView::OnHScroll(UINT nSBCode, UINT nPos, CScrollBar* pScrollBar)
{
    CSliderCtrl* slider = (CSliderCtrl*)pScrollBar;
    if (slider == &m_trackbar)
    {
        int position = slider->GetPos();
        char s[10];
        wsprintf(s, "%d   ", position);
        CClientDC clientDC(this);
        clientDC.TextOut(390, 22, s);
    }

    CScrollView::OnHScroll(nSBCode, nPos, pScrollBar);
}
```

Now the slider code is executed only when the scrollbar that was clicked is the one kept in m_trackbar. The rest of the time, the work is simply delegated to the base class. For the last time, build and test Common—everything should be perfect now. ●

Help

Too many programmers entirely neglect online Help. Even those who add Help to an application tend to leave it to the end of a project, and when the inevitable time squeeze comes, guess what? There's no time to write the Help text or make the software adjustments that arrange for that text to display when the user requests Help. One reason people do this is because they believe implementing Help is really hard. With Visual C++, though, it's a lot easier than you might anticipate. Visual C++ even writes some of your Help text for you! This chapter is going to add Help, after the fact, to the ShowString application built in Chapter 8, "Building a Complete Application: ShowString."

Different Kinds of Help

You can characterize Help in a variety of ways. This section presents four different questions you might ask about Help:

- How does the user invoke it?
- How does it look onscreen?
- What sort of answers does the user want?
- How does the developer implement it in code?

None of these questions has a single answer. There are at least nine different ways for a user to invoke Help, three standard Help appearances, and three different programming tasks you must implement in order to display Help. These different ways of looking at Help can help you understand why the implementation involves a number of different techniques, which can be confusing at first.

Getting Help

The first way of characterizing Help is to ask "How does the user open it up?" There are a number of ways to open Help:

- By choosing an item from the Help menu, such as Help, Contents (choosing What's This? or About doesn't open Help immediately)
- By pressing the F1 key
- By clicking the Help button on a dialog box
- By clicking a What's This? button on a toolbar and then clicking something else
- By choosing What's This? from the Help menu (the System menu for dialog box–based applications) and then clicking something
- By clicking a Question button on a dialog box and then clicking part of the dialog box
- By right-clicking something and choosing What's This? from the pop-up menu
- In some older applications, by pressing Shift+F1 and then clicking something
- Outside the application completely, by double-clicking the HLP file

For the first three actions in this list, the user does one thing (chooses a menu item, presses F1, or clicks a button), and Help appears immediately. For the next five actions, there are two steps: typically, one click to go into Help mode (more formally called What's This? mode) and another to indicate which Help is required. Users generally divide Help into single-step Help and two-step Help, accordingly.

N O T E You will become confused if you try to use Visual Studio to understand Help, in general. Much of the information is presented as HTML Help in a separate product, typically MSDN, though there are some circumstances under which more traditional Help appears. Use simple utilities and accessories that come with your operating system or use your operating system itself to follow along. ▪

HTML Help

Until fairly recently, all Help files were built from RTF files, as described in this chapter, and displayed with the Microsoft Help engine. Microsoft has now started to use HTML files for its Help, and has released a number of tools to simplify the job of creating and maintaining HTML Help.

There are a number of advantages to an HTML Help system: Your Help files can contain links to Internet resources, for example. You can incorporate any active content that your browser understands, including ActiveX controls, Java applets, and scripting. Many developers find attractive Help systems quicker to build in HTML.

Unfortunately, there are also disadvantages. The interface is not as rich as the traditional Help interface, for example. Many developers take one look at the HTML Help provided with Visual Studio and vow never to produce HTML Help files for their own products.

If you would like to use HTML Help rather than the traditional Help files discussed in this chapter, start by visiting **http://www.microsoft.com/workshop/author/htmlhelp** to get a copy of the HTML Help Workshop and plenty of documentation and examples.

Most of the work involved in creating HTML Help is the same as the traditional Help techniques presented here, but involves, for example, calling HTMLHelp() instead of ::WinHelp(). Instead of editing RTF files with Word, you edit HTML files with the HTML Help Workshop editor.

Part

III

Ch

11

Presenting Help

The second way of characterizing Help is to ask, "How does it look?" You can display Help in several ways:

- ▪ *Help Topics dialog box.* As shown in Figure 11.1, this dialog box enables users to scroll through an index, look at a table of contents, or find a word within the Help text. (To open this dialog on Windows, choose Start, Help.)

- ▪ *Ordinary Help window.* As shown in Figure 11.2, this window has buttons such as Help Topics, Back, and Options. It can be resized, minimized, maximized, or closed and in many cases is always on top, like the system clock and other popular utilities. (To see this one, open the calculator, usually by choosing Start, Programs, Accessories, Calculator; then press F1. Expand a closed book by double-clicking it; then double-click a topic from the list that appears. Finding Out What a Calculator Button Does appears under Tips and Tricks.)

■ *Pop-up windows.* As shown in Figure 11.3, pop-up windows are relatively small and don't have buttons or menus. They disappear when you click outside them, cannot be resized or moved, and are perfect for a definition or quick explanation. To re-create Figure 11.3, right-click the MC button and choose What's This?

FIG. 11.1

The Help Topics dialog box enables users to go through the contents or index or search the Help text with Find.

FIG. 11.2

An ordinary Help window has buttons and sometimes menus. It can be treated like any other window.

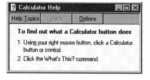

FIG. 11.3

A pop-up Help topic window gives the user far less control and should be used only for short explanations.

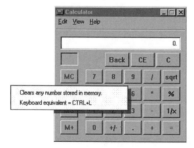

Using Help

A third way of characterizing Help is according to the user's reasons for invoking it. In the book *The Windows Interface Guidelines for Software Design,* Microsoft categorizes Help in this way and lists these kinds of Help:

■ *Contextual user assistance* answers questions such as What does this button do? or What does this setting mean?

- *Task-oriented Help* explains how to accomplish a certain task, such as printing a document. (It often contains numbered steps.)
- *Reference Help* looks up function parameters, font names, or other material that expert users need to refer to from time to time.
- *Wizards* walk a user through a complicated task, just as AppWizard walks you through creating an application.

These describe the content of the material presented to the user. Although these content descriptions are important to a Help designer and writer, they're not very useful from a programming point of view.

 TIP The book mentioned previously is provided with the MSDN CDs included with Visual Studio. In Visual Studio, press F1 to bring up MSDN. On the Contents tab of MSDN, expand the Books item, then expand the interface guidelines book. Chapter 12, "User Assistance," gives Help guidelines.

Programming Help

The final way of characterizing Help, and perhaps the most important to a developer, is by examining the code behind the scenes. Three Windows messages are sent when the user invokes Help:

- `WM_COMMAND`
- `WM_HELP`
- `WM_CONTEXTMENU`

N O T E Windows messages are discussed in Chapter 3, "Messages and Commands." ■

When the user chooses a Help item from a menu or clicks the Help button on a dialog box, the system sends a `WM_COMMAND` message, as always. To display the associated Help, you catch these messages and call the WinHelp system.

When the user right-clicks an element of your application, a `WM_CONTEXTMENU` message is sent. You catch the message and build a shortcut menu on the spot. Because in most cases you will want a shortcut menu with only one item on it, What's This?, you can use a prebuilt menu with only that item and delegate the display of that menu to the Help system—more on this later in the "Programming for Context Help" section.

When the user opens Help in any other way, the framework handles most of it. You don't catch the message that puts the application into What's This? mode, you don't change the cursor, and you don't deal with clicks while in that mode. You catch a `WM_HELP` message that identifies the control, dialog box, or menu for which Help is required, and you provide that Help. Whether the user pressed F1 or went into What's This? mode and clicked the item doesn't matter. In fact, you can't tell from within your application.

The WM_HELP and WM_CONTEXTMENU messages are handled almost identically, so from the point of view of the developer, there are two kinds of help. We'll call these *command help* and *context help*. Each is discussed later in this chapter in the "Programming for Command Help" and "Programming for Context Help" sections, but keep in mind that there's no relationship between this split (between command and context help) and the split between one-step and two-step Help that users think of.

Components of the Help System

As you might expect, a large number of files interact to make online Help work. The final product, which you deliver to your user, is the Help file, with the .hlp extension. It is built from component files. In the list that follows, *appname* refers to the name of your application's .exe file. If no name appears, there might be more than one file with a variety of names. The component files produced by AppWizard are as follows:

.h	These Header files define resource IDs and Help topic IDs for use within your C++ code.
.hm	These Help Mapping files define Help topic IDs. appname.hm is generated every time you build your application—don't change it yourself.
.rtf	These Rich Text Format files contain the Help text for each Help topic.
appname.cnt	You use this table of contents file to create the Contents tab of the Help Topics dialog box. (You should distribute this contents file with your application in addition to the Help file.)
appname.hpj	This Help ProJect file pulls together .hm and .rtf files to produce, when compiled, a .hlp file.

While being used, the Help system generates other files. When you uninstall your application from the user's hard disk, be sure to look for and remove the following files, in addition to the .hlp and .cnt files:

- *appname.gid* is a configuration file, typically hidden.
- *appname.fts* is a full text search file, generated when your user does a Find through your Help text.
- *appname.ftg* is a full text search group list, also generated when your user does a Find.

Help topic IDs are the connection between your Help text and the Help system. Your program eventually directs the Help system to display a Help topic, using a name such as HID_FILE_OPEN, and the system looks for this Help topic ID in the Help file, compiled from the .rtf files, including the .rtf file that contains your Help text for that Help topic ID. (This process is illustrated in Figure 11.4.) These topic IDs have to be defined twice—once for use by the Help system and once for use by your program. When the Help system is displaying a topic or the Help Topics dialog box, it takes over displaying other Help topics as the user requests them, with no work on your part.

FIG. 11.4
Your program, the Help system, and your Help files all work together to display a topic.

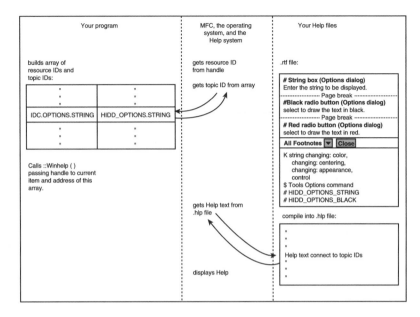

Help Support from AppWizard

When you build an MDI application (no database or OLE support) with AppWizard and choose the Context-Sensitive Help option (in Step 4), here's what you find:

- Message map entries are added to catch the commands `ID_HELP_FINDER`, `ID_HELP`, `ID_CONTEXT_HELP`, and `ID_DEFAULT_HELP`. No code is added to handle these; they are passed to `CMDIFrameWnd` member functions.

- A What's This? button is added to the toolbar.

- A Help Topics item is added to the Help menu for both menus provided by AppWizard: the one used when a file is open and the smaller one used when no files are open.

- Accelerators for F1 (`ID_HELP`) and Shift+F1 (`ID_CONTEXT_HELP`) are added.

- The default message in the status bar is changed from `Ready` to `For Help, press F1`.

- A status bar prompt is added, to be displayed while in What's This? mode: `Select an object on which to get Help`.

- Status bar prompts are added for the Help menu and its items.

- afxcore.rtf, a Help text file for standard menu items such as File, Open, is copied into the project.

- afxprint.rtf, a Help text file for printing and print previewing, is copied into the project. (These files are added separately because not all projects include printing and print previewing. If this project has database- or OLE-related features, more help is provided.)

- Twenty-two .bmp files, included as illustrations in Help for topics such as File, Open, are copied into the project.

Part
III

Ch
11

With this solid foundation, the task of implementing Help for this application breaks down into three steps:

1. You must plan your Help. Do you intend to provide reference material only, task-oriented instructions only, or both? To what extent will you supplement these with context pop-ups?

2. You must provide the programming hooks that will result in the display of the Help topics you have designed. This is done differently for command and context Help, as you will see in the sections that follow.

3. You must build the .rtf files with the Help topic IDs and text to explain your application. If you have designed the Help system well and truly understand your application, this should be simple, though time-consuming.

N O T E On large projects, often a technical writer rather than a programmer writes the Help text. This requires careful coordination: For example, you have to provide topic IDs to the Help writer, and you might have to explain some functions so that they can be described in the Help. You have to work closely together throughout a project like this and respect each other's area of expertise. ▪

Planning Your Help Approach

Developing Help is like developing your software. You shouldn't do it without a plan. Strictly speaking, you shouldn't do it last. A famous experiment decades ago split a programming class into two groups. One group was required to hand in a completed user manual for a program before writing the program, the other to finish the program before writing the manual. The group who wrote the manual first produced better programs: They noticed design errors early, before the errors were carved in code, and they found writing programs much easier as well.

If your application is of any size, the work involved in developing a Help system for it would fill a book. If you need further information on how to do this, consider the book *Designing Windows 95 Help: A Guide to Creating Online Documents*, written by Mary Deaton and Cheryl Lockett Zubak, published by Que. In this section, there is room for only a few basic guidelines.

The result of this planning process is a list of Help topics and the primary way they will be reached. The topics you plan are likely to include the following:

▪ A page or so of Help on each menu item, reached by getting into What's This? mode and clicking the item (or by pressing F1 on a highlighted menu item).

▪ A page, reachable from the Contents, that lists all the menus and their menu items, with links to the pages for those items.

▪ A page, reachable from the Contents, for each major task that a user might perform with the application. This includes examples or tutorials.

▪ Context Help for the controls on all dialog boxes.

Although that might seem like a lot of work, remember that all the boilerplate resources have been documented already in the material provided by AppWizard. This includes menu items, common dialog boxes, and more.

After you have a complete list of material and the primary way each page is reached, think about links between pages (for example, the AppWizard-supplied Help for File, Open mentions using File, New and vice versa) and pop-up definitions for jargon and keywords.

In this section, you plan Help for ShowString, the application introduced in Chapter 8. This simple application displays a string that the user can set. The string can be centered vertically or horizontally, and it can be black, green, or red. A new menu (Tools) with one item (Options) opens a dialog box on which the user can set all these options at once. The Help tasks you need to tackle include the following:

- Changing AppWizard's placeholder strings to ShowString or other strings specific to this application
- Adding a topic about the Tools menu and the Options item
- Adding a topic about each control on the Options dialog box
- Adding a Question button to the Options dialog box
- Changing the text supplied by AppWizard and displayed when the user requests context Help about the view
- Adding an Understanding Centering topic to the Help menu and writing it
- Adjusting the Contents to point to the new pages

The remainder of this chapter tackles this list of tasks.

Part
III

Ch

11

Programming for Command Help

Command Help is simple from a developer's point of view. (Of course, you probably still have to write the explanations, so don't relax too much.) As you've seen, AppWizard added the Help Topics menu item and the message map entries to catch it, and the MFC class CMDIChildFrame has the member function to process it, so you have no work to do for that. However, if you choose to add another menu item to your Help menu, you do so just like any other menu, using the ResourceView. Then, have your application class, CShowStringApp, catch the message.

Say, for example, that ShowString deserves an item named Understanding Centering on the Help menu. Here's how to make that happen:

1. Open ShowString, either your own copy from working along with Chapter 8 or a copy you have downloaded from the book's Web site, in Visual Studio. You may want to make a copy of the old project before you start, because ShowString is the foundation for many of the projects in this book.

 If you aren't familiar with editing menus and dialogs or catching messages, you should read Chapter 9 before this one.

2. Open the IDR_MAINFRAME menu by switching to ResourceView, expanding Menus, and double-clicking IDR_MAINFRAME. Add the Understanding Centering item to the Help menu (just below Help Topics) and let Developer Studio assign it the resource ID ID_HELP_UNDERSTANDINGCENTERING. This is one occasion when a slightly shorter resource ID wouldn't hurt, but this chapter presents it with the longer ID.

3. Add the item to the other menu, IDR_SHOWSTTYPE, as well. Use the same resource ID.

4. Use ClassWizard to arrange for CShowStringApp to catch this message, as discussed in Chapter 8. Add the code for the new function, which looks like this:

```
void CShowStringApp::OnHelpUnderstandingcentering()
{
    WinHelp(HID_CENTERING);
}
```

This code fires up the Help system, passing it the Help topic ID HID_CENTERING. For this to compile, that Help topic ID has to be known to the compiler, so in ShowString.h add this line:

#define HID_CENTERING 0x01

The Help topic IDs in the range 0x0000 to 0xFFFF are reserved for user-defined Help topics, so 0x01 is a fine choice. Now the C++ compiler is happy, but when this runs, the call to WinHelp() isn't going to find the topic that explains centering. You need to add a *help mapping entry*. This should be done in a new file named ShowStringx.hm. (The *x* is for extra, because extra Help mapping entries are added here.) Choose File, New; select the Files tab; highlight Text File; fill in the filename as ShowStringx.hm; and click OK. In the new file, type this line:

HID_CENTERING   0x01

Save the file. Next, you need to edit the Help project file, ShowString.hpj. If you double-click this from a folder such as Windows 95 Explorer, the Help Compiler opens it. In this case, you want to edit it as text, so you should open it with Developer Studio by double-clicking it in the FileView (and you wondered what the FileView was good for). Add this line at the very bottom:

#include <ShowStringX.hm>

Press Enter at the end of this line so that there's a blank line after this last directive. The Help compiler can be weird if there isn't a blank line after the last include.

Now, both the Help system and the compiler know about this new Help topic ID. Later in this chapter, when you write the Help text, you will add a section that explains centering and connect it to this Help topic ID.

The other common use of command Help is to add a Help button to a dialog box that gives an overview of the dialog box. This used to be standard behavior but is now recommended only for large dialog boxes, especially those with complex interactions between the various controls. For simple boxes, the What's This? Help is a better choice, because the information comes up in a small pop-up rather than an entire page of explanations. To add a Help button to a dialog, follow the same process steps you followed to add the menu item Help, Understanding

Centering, but add a button to a dialog rather than an item to a menu. You wouldn't create a new .hm file; add the button's Help topic ID to ShowStringX.hm, which continues to grow in the next section.

Programming for Context Help

Your first task in arranging for context Help is to get a Question button onto the Options dialog box, because AppWizard already added one to the toolbar. Open the Options dialog box by double-clicking it in the ResourceView and then choose View, Properties. Click the Extended Styles tab and then make sure that the Context Help check box is selected, as shown in Figure 11.5.

FIG. 11.5
Turn on the Question box on the Options dialog box of ShowString.

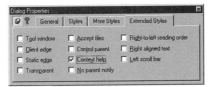

As mentioned earlier, two messages are relevant to context Help: WM_HELP when a user clicks something while in What's This? mode, and WM_CONTEXTMENU when a user right-clicks something. You need to arrange for your dialog box class, COptionsDialog, to catch these messages. Because ClassWizard doesn't include them in the list of messages it will catch, you will add entries outside the special ClassWizard comments. The message map in OptionsDialog.h should look like this:

```
// Generated message map functions
//{{AFX_MSG(COptionsDialog)
    // NOTE: the ClassWizard will add member functions here
//}}AFX_MSG
afx_msg BOOL OnHelpInfo(HELPINFO* lpHelpInfo);
afx_msg void OnContextMenu(CWnd* pWnd, CPoint point);
 DECLARE_MESSAGE_MAP()
```

The message map in OptionsDialog.cpp should look like this:

```
BEGIN_MESSAGE_MAP(COptionsDialog, CDialog)
    //{{AFX_MSG_MAP(COptionsDialog)
        // NOTE: the ClassWizard will add message map macros here
    //}}AFX_MSG_MAP
    ON_WM_HELPINFO()
    ON_WM_CONTEXTMENU()
END_MESSAGE_MAP()
```

These macros arrange for WM_HELP to be caught by OnHelpInfo() and for WM_CONTEXTMENU to be caught by OnContextMenu(). The next step is to write these functions. They both need to use a table to connect resource IDs to Help topic IDs. To create this table, add these lines at the beginning of OptionsDialog.cpp, after the comment block that reads // COptionsDialog dialog:

```
static DWORD aHelpIDs[] =
{
    IDC_OPTIONS_STRING, HIDD_OPTIONS_STRING,
    IDC_OPTIONS_BLACK, HIDD_OPTIONS_BLACK,
    IDC_OPTIONS_RED, HIDD_OPTIONS_RED,
    IDC_OPTIONS_GREEN, HIDD_OPTIONS_GREEN,
    IDC_OPTIONS_HORIZCENTER, HIDD_OPTIONS_HORIZCENTER,
    IDC_OPTIONS_VERTCENTER, HIDD_OPTIONS_VERTCENTER,
    IDOK, HIDD_OPTIONS_OK,
    IDCANCEL, HIDD_OPTIONS_CANCEL,
    0, 0
};
```

The Help system uses this array (you pass the address to the `WinHelp()` function) to connect resource IDs and Help topic IDs. The compiler, however, has never heard of `HIDD_OPTIONS_STRING`, so add these lines to OptionsDialog.h before the definition of the `COptionsDialog` class:

```
#define HIDD_OPTIONS_STRING 2
#define HIDD_OPTIONS_BLACK 3
#define HIDD_OPTIONS_RED 4
#define HIDD_OPTIONS_GREEN 5
#define HIDD_OPTIONS_HORIZCENTER 6
#define HIDD_OPTIONS_VERTCENTER 7
#define HIDD_OPTIONS_OK 8
#define HIDD_OPTIONS_CANCEL 9
```

The numbers are chosen arbitrarily. Now, after the two functions are written, the compiler will be happy because all these constants are defined. The Help system, however, doesn't know what's going on because these topics aren't in the Help mapping file yet. Therefore, add these lines to ShowStringX.hm:

```
HIDD_OPTIONS_STRING        0x02
HIDD_OPTIONS_BLACK         0x03
HIDD_OPTIONS_RED      0x04
HIDD_OPTIONS_GREEN         0x05
HIDD_OPTIONS_HORIZCENTER        0x06
HIDD_OPTIONS_VERTCENTER         0x07
HIDD_OPTIONS_OK      0x08
HIDD_OPTIONS_CANCEL        0x09
```

Be sure to use the same numbers as in the `#define` statements in OptionsDialog.h. The stage is set; all that remains is to add the code for the functions at the end of OptionsDialog.cpp. Here's what `OnHelpInfo()` looks like:

```
BOOL COptionsDialog::OnHelpInfo(HELPINFO *lpHelpInfo)
{
    if (lpHelpInfo->iContextType == HELPINFO_WINDOW) // must be for a control
    {
        // have to call SDK WinHelp not CWinApp::WinHelp
        // because CWinApp::WinHelp doesn't take a
        // handle as a parameter.
        ::WinHelp((HWND)lpHelpInfo->hItemHandle,
            AfxGetApp()->m_pszHelpFilePath,
            HELP_WM_HELP, (DWORD)aHelpIDs);
```

```
    }
    return TRUE;
}
```

This function calls the SDK `WinHelp()` function and passes the handle to the control, the path to the Help file, the command `HELP_WM_HELP` to request a context-sensitive pop-up Help topic, and the table of resource IDs and Help topic IDs built earlier. There's no other work for your function to do after kicking `WinHelp()` into action.

T I P If you've never seen the `::` scope resolution operator used without a classname before it, it means "call the function that isn't in any class," and in Windows programming, that generally means the SDK function.

N O T E The third parameter of this call to `WinHelp()` directs the Help system to put up a certain style of Help window. `HELP_WM_HELP` gives you a pop-up menu, as does `HELP_WM_CONTEXTMENU`. `HELP_CONTEXT` produces an ordinary Help window, which can be resized and moved, and enables Help navigation. `HELP_FINDER` opens the Help Topics dialog box. `HELP_CONTENTS` and `HELP_INDEX` are obsolete and should be replaced with `HELP_FINDER` if you maintain code that uses them. ■

`OnContextMenu()` is even simpler. Add this code at the end of OptionsDialog.cpp:

```
void COptionsDialog::OnContextMenu(CWnd *pWnd, CPoint /*point*/)
{
    ::WinHelp((HWND)*pWnd, AfxGetApp()->m_pszHelpFilePath,
        HELP_CONTEXTMENU, (DWORD)aHelpIDs);
}
```

This function doesn't need to check that the right-click is on a control as `OnHelpInfo()` did, so it just calls the SDK `WinHelp()`. `WinHelp()` takes care of displaying the shortcut menu with only a What's This item and then displays Help when that item is chosen.

To check your typing, build the project by choosing Build, Build and then compile the Help file by giving focus to ShowString.hpj and choosing Build, Compile. (You can also right-click ShowString.hpj in the FileView of the Project Workspace window and choose Compile from the shortcut menu.) There's not much point in testing it, though; the AppWizard stuff is sure to work, and without Help content connected to those topics, none of the code you just added can succeed in displaying content.

Writing Help Text

You write Help text in an RTF file, using special formatting codes that mean something rather different than they usually do. The traditional way to do this has been in Microsoft Word, but a large crop of Help authoring tools have sprung up that are far easier to use than Word. Rather than teach you yet another tool, this section presents instructions for writing Help text in Word. However, do keep in mind that there are easier ways, and on a project of a decent size, you easily save the time and money you invest in a Help authoring tool. An entire chapter in *Designing Windows 95 Help* discusses choosing an authoring tool.

Part
III

Ch
11

TIP You can open Word documents from within Developer Studio. Simply choose File, Open and select the file—the starter RTF files for ShowString are in the HLP folder. The Word menus and toolbars will appear. This works because Word documents are ActiveX Document Objects, discussed in Chapter 15, "Building an ActiveX Server Application." Most developers prefer to switch from Word to Developer Studio with the taskbar rather than have a number of files open in Developer Studio and switch among them with the Window menu, so the explanations in this section assume that you are running Word separately. If you would rather work entirely within Developer Studio, feel free to so do.

Figure 11.6 shows afxcore.rtf open in Word. Choose View, Footnotes to display the footnotes across the bottom of the screen—they are vital. This is how the text connects to the Help topic IDs. Choose Tools, Options; select the View tab; and make sure the Hidden Text check box is selected. This is how links between topics are entered. The topics are separated by page breaks.

FIG. 11.6

Help text, such as this boilerplate provided by AppWizard, can be edited in Word.

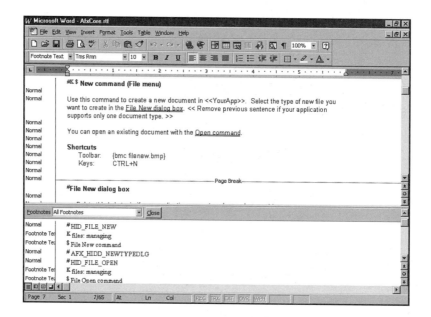

There are eight kinds of footnotes, each with a different meaning. Only the first three footnote types in the following list are in general use:

- #, *the Help topic ID*. The SDK `WinHelp` function looks for this topic ID when displaying Help.

- $, *the topic title*. This title displays in search results.

- K, *keywords*. These appear in the Index tab of the Help Topics dialog box.

- A, *A-keyword*. These keywords can be jumped to but don't appear in the Index tab of the Help Topics dialog box.

- +, *browse code.* This marks the topic's place in a sequence of topics.
- !, *macro entry.* This makes the topic a macro to be run when the user requests the topic.
- *, *build tag.* You use this to include certain tags only in certain builds of the Help file.
- >, *window type.* This overrides the type of window for this topic.

The double-underlined text, followed by hidden text, identifies a jump to another Help topic. If a user clicks to follow the link, this Help topic leaves the screen. If the text before the hidden text was single-underlined, following the link opens a pop-up over this Help topic, perfect for definitions and notes. (You can also see Help text files in which strikethrough text is used; this is exactly the same as double-underlined—a jump to another topic.) In all three cases, the hidden text is the topic ID of the material to be jumped to or popped up.

Figure 11.7 shows how the File, New Help material appears from within ShowString. To display it yourself, run ShowString by choosing Build, Execute from within Developer Studio and then choose Help, Help Topics in ShowString. Open the menus book, double-click the File menu topic, and click New. Alternatively, choose the File menu, and while the highlight is on New, press F1.

FIG. 11.7
ShowString displays the boilerplate Help generated by AppWizard.

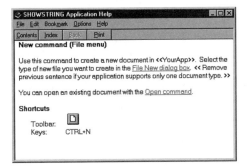

With the programming out of the way, it's time to tackle the list of Help tasks for ShowString from the "Planning Your Help Approach" section earlier in this chapter. These instructions assume you are using Word.

Changing Placeholder Strings

To change the placeholder strings left behind by AppWizard in the boilerplate Help files, open afxcore.rtf in Word if it isn't already open. (It's in the hlp folder of the ShowString project folder.) Then follow these steps:

1. Position the cursor at the very beginning of the document and choose Edit, Replace.
2. Enter **<<YourApp>>** in the Find What box and **ShowString** in the Replace With box.
3. Click Replace All.

Open afxprint.rtf and repeat these steps.

Switch back to afxcore.rtf and look through the text for << characters (use Edit, Find and remember that Shift+F4 is the shortcut to repeat your previous Find). These identify places where you must make a change or a decision. For ShowString, the changes in afxcore.rtf are these:

1. The first section in the file is the ShowString Help Index. Remove the How To section and the reminder to add some How To topics. In a real application, you add topics here.

2. The next section, after the page break, is a table describing the items on the File menu. Because there's no Send item on ShowString's File menu, remove the Send row of the File menu table.

3. The third section is a table listing the items on the Edit menu. Remove the Paste Link, Insert New Object, and Links rows.

4. The fourth section is for the View menu and doesn't need any changes.

5. The fifth section is for the Window menu. Remove the Split row from the Window menu table.

6. The sixth section is for the Help menu and doesn't need any changes.

7. The seventh section is for the New command (File menu). Remove the sentence about choosing a file type and the reminder to remove it.

8. Entirely delete the eighth section, the File New dialog box topic, including the page break before or after it, but not both. Whenever you remove a section, remove one of the breaks so that the file doesn't contain two consecutive page breaks.

9. The next topic is for the File, Open command and doesn't need any changes.

10. Moving on to the File Open dialog box topic, edit the text to mention that the List Files of Type list box contains only All Files.

11. Continue down the file until you find the File, Send topic and remove it entirely, including one page break either before or after it.

12. In the File Save As topic, remove the suggestion to describe other options because there are none.

13. When you reach the Edit Undo topic, you start to see why programs written after their manuals are better programs. The way ShowString was written in Chapter 8, the Undo item will never be enabled, nor will Cut, Copy, or Paste. You could remove the Help topics about these unsupported menu items, but it's probably better to plan on adding support for the menu items to a later version of ShowString. Add some text to all these topics, explaining that they aren't implemented in this version of the product. Leave the shortcuts sections there so that users can find out why Ctrl+Z does nothing.

14. Continue down through the file to the Toolbar topic, where you find this reminder: `<< Add or remove toolbar buttons from the list below according to which ones your application offers. >>` Remove the reminder and delete the references to the Cut, Copy, Paste, Undo, First Record, Previous Record, Next Record, and Last Record buttons.

15. About halfway down the file is a topic for the `Split` command (Window menu). Remove the entire topic.

16. Move down to the `Index` command (Help menu) topic and remove it. Also remove the `Using Help` command (Help menu) and `About` command (Help menu) topics.

17. In the Title Bar topic, remove the directive to insert a graphic. If you would rather follow the directive, create a bitmap in a .bmp file of the title bar with screen shot software, cropping the shot down to just the title bar, and insert the graphic with the `bmc` directive, just as the bullet.bmp graphic is inserted a few lines lower in the file.

18. Because the ShowString view doesn't inherit from `CScrollView`, it doesn't scroll. Remove the Scrollbars Help topic and its page break.

19. In the Close command topic (not the File Close topic, which was much earlier in the file) the shortcut for Alt+F4 should be described like this: `closes ShowString`.

20. Remove the Ruler, Choose Font, Choose Color, Edit Find, Find Dialog, Edit Replace, Replace Dialog Box, Edit Repeat, Edit Clear, Edit Clear All, Next Pane, and Previous Pane topics.

21. Skip the How To Modify Text topic for now and leave it unchanged.

22. Remove the final directive about tailoring the `No Help Available` messages to each message box (don't remove the two No Help Available topics).

Part
III
Ch
11

That completes the extensive changes required to the boilerplate afxcore.rtf file generated by AppWizard. In the other boilerplate file, afxprint.rtf, scroll to the bottom and remove the Page Setup topic.

Would you like to test all this work? Save afxcore.rtf and afxprint.rtf within Word. Switch to Developer Studio and choose Build, Build to bring the project up to date. Then open ShowString.hpj and choose Build, Compile. This pulls all the .rtf files together into ShowString.hlp. Choose Build, Execute to run ShowString, and choose Help, Help Topics from the ShowString menus. As you can see in Figure 11.8, the Window menu topic is now substantially shorter. You can check that your other changes have been made, as well.

FIG. 11.8

After saving the .rtf files and compiling the Help project, you can test to see that your changes have been made successfully.

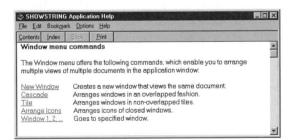

Adding Topics

When you are adding new topics, you don't add new topics to the boilerplate files that were provided. Those files should stay untouched unless you want to change the description of File,

Open or other boilerplate topics. Instead, create a new file by choosing File, New in Word and saving it in the hlp folder of the ShowString project folder as ShowString.rtf. (Make sure to change the Save File As Type list box selection to Rich Text Format.) If this were a large project, you could divide it up into several .rtf files, but one will suffice for ShowString. In Developer Studio, open ShowString.hpj by double-clicking it in the FileView tab and find the section headed [FILES]. Add this line at the end of that section:

```
showstring.rtf
```

The Tools Menu   Back in Word, switch to afxcore.rtf and copy the topic for the File menu into the Clipboard; then switch back to ShowString.rtf and paste it in. (Don't forget to include the page break after the topic in the selection when you copy.) Choose View, Footnotes to display the footnotes, and Tools, Options, View tab, Hidden Text to display the hidden text. Now you are going to edit the copied File topic to make it the Tools topic. Change the footnotes first. They are as follows:

- The # footnote is the topic ID. The Help system uses this to find this topic from the Contents page. Change it to **menu_tools**.

- The K footnote is the keyword entry. Although the Options dialog box probably deserves several keywords, this menu doesn't, so remove that footnote by selecting the letter *K* in the Help topic and pressing Delete. You must select the letter; it isn't enough to click just before it. The footnote is deleted at the same time.

- The $ footnote is the topic title. Change it to **Tools menu commands**.

In the topic, change File to **Tools** on the first two lines, and delete all the rows of the table but one. Change the underlined text of that row to **Options**, the hidden text immediately following to **HID_TOOLS_OPTIONS**, and the right column of that row to **Changes string, color, and centering**. Figure 11.9 shows the way ShowString.rtf looks in Word after these changes.

FIG. 11.9
Change the ShowString.rtf file to explain the new menu item.

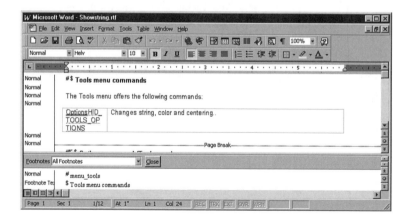

TIP If you can't remember the Help topic IDs your project is using, check your .hm files. The ones added by Developer Studio, such as `HID_TOOLS_OPTIONS` for the menu item with resource ID `ID_TOOLS_OPTIONS`, are in ShowString.hm, whereas ShowStringx.hm contains the Help topic IDs added by hand for context Help.

The Tools, Options Menu Item   Switch back to afxcore, copy the File New topic, and paste it into ShowString.rtf, as before. The topic and its footnotes are copied together. Watch carefully to be sure you are working with the footnotes for the Tools Options topic and not the ones for the Tools menu. Follow these steps:

1. Change the # footnote to **`HID_TOOLS_OPTIONS`**.
2. Change the K keyword. Several keywords should lead here, and each needs to be separated from the next by a semicolon (;). Some need to be two-level keywords with the levels separated by commas. A good first start is **string, changing;color, changing;centering, changing;appearance, controlling**.
3. Change the $ keyword to **Tools Options command**.
4. Change the first line of the topic to **Options command (Tools menu)**.
5. Delete the rest of the topic and replace it with a short description of this menu item. The following text is okay:

   ```
   Use this command to change the appearance of the ShowString
   display with the Options dialog box. The string being displayed,
   color of the text, and vertical and horizontal centering are
   all controlled from this dialog.
   ```

If you want to test this, too, save the files in Word, compile the Help project, run ShowString, and choose Tools. Highlight the Options item by moving the highlight with the cursor keys, but don't click Options to select it; press F1 instead. Figure 11.10 shows the Help window that displays.

FIG. 11.10
The new Tools Options Help is reached by pressing F1 while the item is highlighted on the menu.

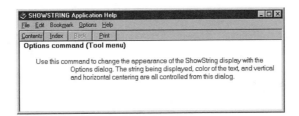

Each Control on the Options Dialog   Copy the File New topic into ShowString.rtf again and cut it down drastically. To do this, follow these steps:

1. Remove the K and $ footnotes.
2. Change the # footnote to **`HIDD_OPTIONS`**.
3. Change the first line to **(Options dialog)**.
4. Delete the other text in the topic.

Copy this block into the Clipboard and paste it in seven more times so that you have a skeleton for each control on the dialog box. Remember to copy the page break before or after the topic, too. Then, edit each skeleton to document the following topic IDs:

- HIDD_OPTIONS_STRING
- HIDD_OPTIONS_BLACK
- HIDD_OPTIONS_RED
- HIDD_OPTIONS_GREEN
- HIDD_OPTIONS_HORIZCENTER
- HIDD_OPTIONS_VERTCENTER
- HIDD_OPTIONS_OK
- HIDD_OPTIONS_CANCEL

Change the topic ID and add a sentence or two of text. Be consistent. The examples included with this chapter are each a single sentence that starts with an imperative verb like *Click* or *Select* and ends with a period (.). If you would rather choose a different style for your pop-up boxes, use the same style for all of them. It confuses the user when pop-up boxes are inconsistent and tends to make them believe your coding is sloppy, too.

To test your work, compile ShowString.hpj again, run ShowString, and choose Tools, Options. Click the Question button and then click somewhere on the dialog box. Explore each of the controls to be sure you have entered the correct text. Figure 11.11 shows the context Help for the String edit box.

FIG. 11.11

Display Help for a dialog box control by clicking the Question button in the upper-right corner and then clicking a control.

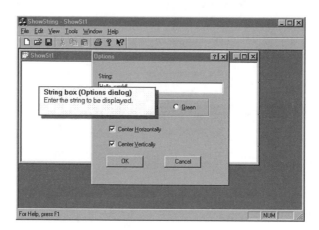

Understanding Centering In ShowString.rtf, paste in another copy of the File New topic. Make the following changes:

1. Change the # footnote to **HID_CENTERING** (the topic ID you added to ShowStringx.hm and called in CShowStringApp::OnHelpUnderstandingcentering()).
2. Change the K footnote to **centering**.
3. Change the $ footnote to **Understanding Centering**.

4. Change the title on the first line to **Understanding Centering**.

5. Replace the text with a short explanation of centering, like this:

```
ShowString can center the displayed string within the view. The two
options, "center horizontally" and "center vertically", can be set
independently on the Options dialog box, reached by choosing the Options
item on the Tools menu. Text that is not centered horizontally is
displayed at the left edge of the window. Text that is not centered
vertically is displayed at the top of the window.
```

6. Add links from the word *Tools* to the menu_tools topic and from the word *Options* to HID_TOOLS_OPTIONS, as before. Remember to watch for extra spaces.

Test this change in the usual way, and when you choose Help, Understanding Centering from the ShowString menus, you should see something like Figure 11.12. Try following the links; you can use the Back button to return to the centering topic.

FIG. 11.12

Display a teaching Help topic by choosing it from the Help menu.

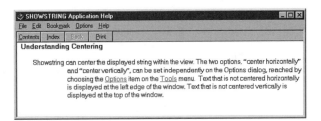

Changing the How to Modify Text Topic

AppWizard already provided a How to Modify Text topic at the bottom of afxcore.rtf that needs to be edited to explain how ShowString works. It displays when the user selects the view area for context Help. Replace the text with a much shorter explanation that tells the user to choose Tools, Options. To add a link to that topic (short though it is), type **HID_TOOLS_OPTIONS** immediately after the word *Options* in the Help topic. While you're at it, type **menu_tools** immediately after the word *Tools*. Select the word *Options* and press Ctrl+Shift+D to double-underline it; then do the same for *Tools*. Select HID_TOOLS_OPTIONS and press Ctrl+Shift+H to hide it; then do the same for menu_tools.

 If you've reassigned these keys, you can do the formatting the long way. To double-underline text, select it and choose Format, Font. Drop down the Underline box and choose Double; then click OK. To hide text, select it and choose Format, Font; then select the Hidden box and click OK.

 There can't be any spaces between the double-underlined text and the hidden text or at the end of the hidden text. Word can give you some trouble about this because the Smart Cut and Paste feature that works so nicely with words can insert extra spaces where you don't want them or can make it impossible to select only half a word. You can turn off the feature in Word by choosing Tools, Options, the Edit tab and by deselecting the When Selecting, Automatically Select Entire Word and Use Smart Cut and Paste check boxes.

Ready to test again? Save the files in Word, compile the Help project file, and execute ShowString; then click the What's This? button on the toolbar and click in the main view. Your new How to Modify Text entry should display.

Adjustments to the Contents

This tiny little application is almost entirely documented now. You need to add the Tools menu and Understanding Centering to the Contents and to check the index. The easiest way to tackle the Contents is with Help Workshop. Close all the Help-related files that are open in Developer Studio and Word and open Help Workshop by choosing Start, Programs, Microsoft Visual Studio 6.0, Microsoft Visual Studio 6.0 Tools, Help Workshop. Open ShowString.cnt by choosing File, Open and working your way through the Open dialog box. (If you can't find the contents file, be sure to change the File Type drop-down. It's probably in your Debug directory.) This is the Contents file for ShowString.

In the first open book, click the View Menu item and then click the Add Below button. (Alternatively, click the Window Menu item and then the Add Above button.) The Edit Contents Tab Entry dialog box, shown in Figure 11.13, appears. Fill it in as shown; by leaving the last two entries blank, the default Help File and Window Type are used. Click OK.

FIG. 11.13

Add entries to the Contents tab with Help Workshop's Edit Contents Tab Entry dialog box.

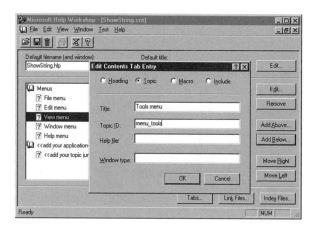

Click the placeholder book named <<add your application-specific topics here>> and click Add Above again. When the Edit Contents Tab Entry dialog box appears, select the Heading radio button from the list across the top. As shown in Figure 11.14, you can change only the title here. Don't use Understanding Centering because that's the title of the only topic under this heading. Enter **Displaying a string** and click OK.

Add a topic below the new heading for Understanding Centering, whose ID is HID_CENTERING, and remove the placeholder heading and topic. Save your changes, close Help Workshop, compile ShowString.hpj in Developer Studio again, and test your Help. Choose Help, Help Topics and expand each heading. You will see something like Figure 11.15.

FIG. 11.14

Add headings to the Contents tab with Help Workshop's Edit Contents Tab Entry dialog box.

FIG. 11.15

After saving the .cnt file and compiling the .hpj file, display the new table of contents by choosing Help, Help Topics.

While you have the Help Topics dialog box open, click the Index tab. Figure 11.16 shows how the K footnotes you entered throughout this section have all been added to the index. If it looks a little sparse, you can always go to the .rtf files and add more keywords, remembering to separate them with semicolons.

FIG. 11.16

The index has been built from the K footnotes in the .rtf files.

Part

III

Ch

11

Now the Help file for this application is complete, and you've arranged for the relevant sections of the file to be displayed when the user requests online Help. You can apply these concepts to your own application, and never again deliver an undocumented product. ●

CHAPTER 12

Property Pages and Sheets

In this chapter

Introducing Property Sheets

One of the newest types of graphical objects is the tabbed dialog box, also known as a *property sheet.* A property sheet is a dialog box with two or more pages. Windows and NT are loaded with property sheets, which organize the many options that users can modify. You flip the pages by clicking labeled tabs at the top of the dialog box. Using such dialog boxes to organize complex groups of options enables users to more easily find the information and settings they need. As you've probably guessed, Visual C++ 6 supports property sheets, with the classes CPropertySheet and CPropertyPage.

Similar to property sheets are *wizards,* which use buttons instead of tabs to move from one page to another. You've seen a lot of wizards, too. These special types of dialog boxes guide users step by step through complicated processes. For example, when you use AppWizard to generate source code for a new project, the wizard guides you through the entire process. To control the wizard, you click buttons labeled Back, Next, and Finish.

Finding a sample property sheet is as easy as finding sand at the beach. Just click virtually any Properties command or bring up an Options dialog in most applications. For example, Figure 12.1 shows the dialog box that you see when you choose Tools, Options from within Visual C++. This property sheet contains 12 pages in all, each covering a different set of options.

FIG. 12.1

The Options properties sheet contains many tabbed pages.

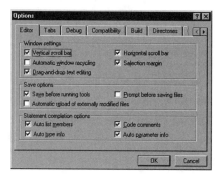

N O T E   Many people forget the difference between a property sheet and a property page. A *property sheet* is a window that contains property pages. *Property pages* are windows that hold controls. They appear on the property sheet. ■

As you can see, property sheets are a great way to organize many types of related options. Gone are the days of dialog boxes so jam-packed with options that you needed a college-level course just to figure them out. In the following sections, you'll learn to program your own tabbed property sheets by using MFC's CPropertySheet and CPropertyPage classes.

Creating the Property Sheet Demo Application

Now that you've had an introduction to property sheets, it's time to learn how to build an application that uses these handy specialized dialog boxes. You're about to build the Property Sheet Demo application, which demonstrates the creation and manipulation of property sheets. Follow the steps in the following sections to create the basic application and modify its resources.

Creating the Basic Files

First, use AppWizard to create the basic files for the Property Sheet Demo program, selecting the options listed in the following table. When you're done, the New Project Information dialog box appears; it will look like Figure 12.2. Click OK to create the project files.

Dialog Box Name	Options to Select
New, Project tab	Name the project Propsheet and then set the project path to the directory in which you want to store the project's files. Make sure that MFC AppWizard (exe) is highlighted. Leave the other options set to their defaults.
Step 1	Select Single Document.
Step 2 of 6	Leave set to defaults.
Step 3 of 6	Leave set to defaults.
Step 4 of 6	Turn off all application features.
Step 5 of 6	Leave set to defaults.
Step 6 of 6	Leave set to defaults.

FIG. 12.2
Your New Project Information dialog box looks like this.

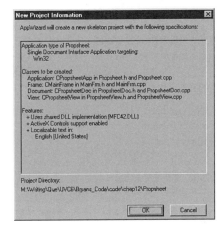

Part
III

Ch
12

Editing the Resources

Now you'll edit the resources in the application generated for you by AppWizard, removing unwanted menus and accelerators, editing the About box, and most importantly, adding a menu item that will bring up a property sheet. Follow these steps:

1. Select the ResourceView tab in the project workspace window. Developer Studio displays the ResourceView window (see Figure 12.3).

FIG. 12.3

The ResourceView tab displays the ResourceView window.

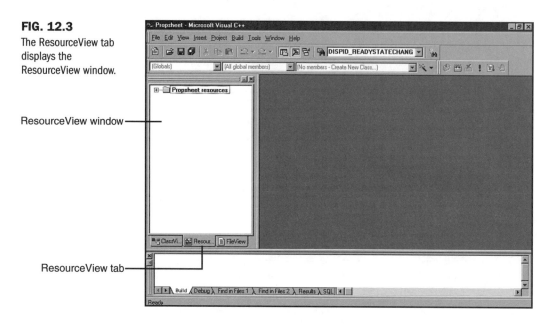

2. In the ResourceView window, click the plus sign next to Propsheet Resources to display the application's resources. Click the plus sign next to Menu and then double-click the `IDR_MAINFRAME` menu ID. Visual C++'s menu editor appears, displaying the `IDR_MAINFRAME` menu generated by AppWizard.

3. Click the Property Sheet Demo application's Edit menu (not Visual C++'s Edit menu) and then press Delete to delete the Edit menu. A dialog box asks for verification of the Delete command; click OK.

4. Double-click the About Propsheet... item in the Help menu to bring up its properties dialog box. Change the caption to **&About Property Sheet Demo**. Pin the properties dialog box in place by clicking the pushpin in the upper-left corner.

5. On the application's File menu, delete all menu items except Exit.

6. Select the blank menu item at the end of the File menu, and change the caption to **&Property Sheet...** and the command ID to `ID_PROPSHEET` (see Figure 12.4). Then use your mouse to drag the new command above the Exit command so that it's the first command in the File menu.

FIG. 12.4

Add a Property Sheet command to the File menu.

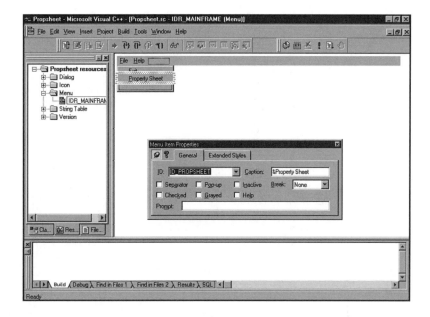

7. Click the + next to Accelerator in the ResourceView window and highlight the IDR_MAINFRAME accelerator ID. Press Delete to delete all accelerators from the application.

8. Click the + next to Dialog in the ResourceView window. Double-click the IDD_ABOUTBOX dialog box ID to bring up the dialog box editor.

9. Modify the dialog box by clicking the title so that the properties box refers to the whole dialog box. Change the caption to **About Property Sheet Demo**.

10. Click the first static text string and change the caption to **Property Sheet Demo, Version 1.0**. Click the second and add **Que Books** to the end of the copyright string.

11. Add a third static string with the text **Special Edition Using Visual C++ 6** so that your About box resembles the one in Figure 12.5. Close the dialog box editor.

12. Click the + next to String Table in the ResourceView window. Double-click the String Table ID to bring up the string table editor.

13. Double-click the IDR_MAINFRAME string and then change the first segment of the string to **Property Sheet Demo** (see Figure 12.6). The meanings of these strings are discussed in Chapter 15, "Building an ActiveX Server Application," in the "Shortcomings of This Server" section. The one you just changed is the Window Title, used in the title bar of the application.

Part

III

Ch

12

FIG. 12.5
The About box looks like this.

FIG. 12.6
The first segment of the IDR_MAINFRAME string appears in your main window's title bar.

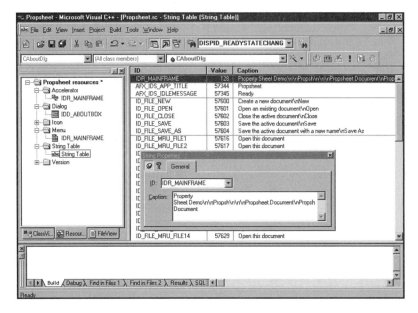

Adding New Resources

Now that you have the application's basic resources the way you want them, it's time to add the resources that define the application's property sheet. This means creating dialog box resources for each page in the property sheet. Follow these steps:

1. Click the New Dialog button on the Resource toolbar, or press Ctrl+1, to create a new dialog box resource. The new dialog box, IDD_DIALOG1, appears in the dialog box editor. This dialog box, when set up properly, will represent the first page of the property sheet.

2. Delete the OK and Cancel buttons by selecting each with your mouse and then pressing Delete.

3. If the Properties box isn't still up, bring it up by choosing View, Properties. Change the ID of the dialog box to **IDD_PAGE1DLG** and the caption to **Page 1** (see Figure 12.7).

FIG. 12.7

Change the caption and resource ID of the new dialog box.

4. Click the Styles tab of the dialog box's property sheet. In the Style drop-down box select Child, and in the Border drop-down box select Thin. Turn off the System Menu check box. Your properties dialog box will resemble Figure 12.8.

The Child style is necessary because the property page will be a child window of the property sheet. The property sheet itself will provide the container for the property pages.

FIG. 12.8

A property page uses styles different from those used in regular dialog boxes.

5. Add an edit box to the property page, as shown in Figure 12.9. In most applications you would change the resource ID from IDC_EDIT1, but for this demonstration application, leave it unchanged.

6. Create a second property page by following steps 1 through 5 again. For this property page, use the ID IDD_PAGE2DLG, a caption of Page 2, and add a check box rather than an edit control (see Figure 12.10).

Part

III

Ch

12

FIG. 12.9

A property page can hold whatever controls you like.

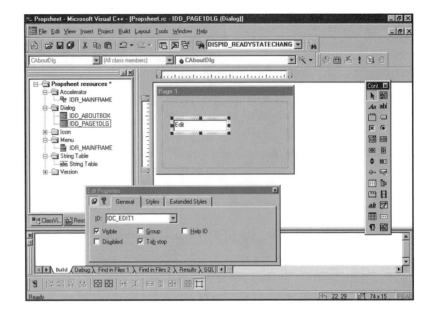

FIG. 12.10

The second property page looks like this.

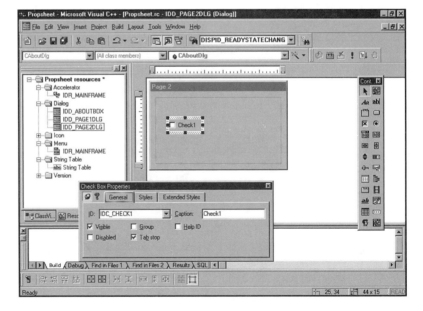

Associating Your Resources with Classes

You now have all your resources created. Next, associate your two new property-page resources with C++ classes so that you can control them in your program. You also need a class for your property sheet, which will hold the property pages that you've created. Follow these steps to create the new classes:

1. Make sure that the Page 1 property page is visible in the dialog box edit area and then double-click it. If you prefer, choose View, ClassWizard from the menu bar. The MFC ClassWizard property sheet appears, displaying the Adding a Class dialog box first discussed in Chapter 2, "Dialogs and Controls."

2. Select the Create New Class option and then click OK. The New Class dialog box appears.

3. In the Name box, type **CPage1**. In the Base Class box, select CPropertyPage. (Don't accidentally select CPropertySheet.) Then click OK to create the class.

   You've now associated the property page with an object of the CPropertyPage class, which means that you can use the object to manipulate the property page as needed. The CPropertyPage class will be especially important when you learn about wizards.

4. Select the Member Variables tab of the MFC ClassWizard property sheet. With IDC_EDIT1 highlighted, click the Add Variable button. The Add Member Variable dialog box appears.

5. Name the new member variable **m_edit**, as shown in Figure 12.11, and then click OK. ClassWizard adds the member variable, which will hold the value of the property page's control, to the new CPage1 class.

FIG 12.11

ClassWizard makes it easy to connect controls on a dialog box to member variables of the class representing the dialog box.

6. Click OK on the MFC ClassWizard properties sheet to finalize the creation of the CPage1 class.

7. Follow steps 1 through 6 for the second property sheet. Name the class **CPage2** and add a Boolean member variable called m_check for the IDC_CHECK1 control, as shown in Figure 12.12.

FIG. 12.12
The second property page needs a Boolean member variable called `m_checkbox`.

Creating a Property Sheet Class

At this point, you've done all the resource editing and don't need to have so many windows open. Choose Window, Close All from the menu bar and close the properties box. You'll now create a property sheet class that displays the property pages already created. Follow these steps:

1. Bring up ClassWizard and click the Add Class button. A tiny menu appears below the button; choose New. The New Class dialog box appears.

2. In the Name box, type **CPropSheet**, select `CPropertySheet` in the Base Class box, and then click OK.

3. ClassWizard creates the `CPropSheet` class. Click the MFC ClassWizard Properties sheet's OK button to finalize the class.

Mow you have three new classes—CPage1, CPage2, and CPropSheet—in your program. The first two classes are derived from MFC's `CPropertyPage` class, and the third is derived from `CPropertySheet`. Although ClassWizard has created the basic source-code files for these new classes, you still have to add code to the classes to make them work the way you want. Follow these steps to complete the Property Sheet Demo application:

1. Click the ClassView tab to display the ClassView window. Expand the `Propsheet` classes, as shown Figure 12.13.

2. Double-click `CPropSheet` to open the header file for your property sheet class. Because the name of this class (`CPropSheet`) is so close to the name of the application as a whole (PropSheet), you'll find `CPropSheet` in PropSheet1.h, generated by ClassWizard when you created the new class.

3. Add the following lines near the middle of the file, right before the `CPropSheet` class declaration:

```
#include "page1.h"
#include "page2.h"
```

These lines give the `CPropSheet` class access to the `CPage1` and `CPage2` classes so that the property sheet can declare member variables of these property page classes.

FIG. 12.13

The ClassView window lists the classes that make up your project.

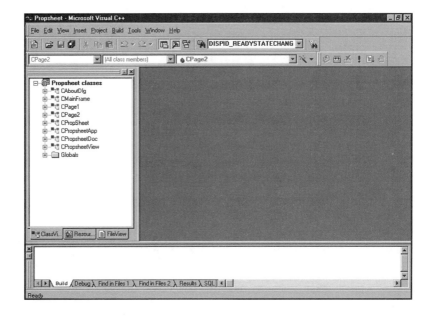

4. Add the following lines to the CPropSheet class's //Attributes section, right after the public keyword:

```
CPage1 m_page1;
CPage2 m_page2;
```

These lines declare the class's data members, which are the property pages that will be displayed in the property sheet.

5. Expand the CPropSheet class in the ClassView pane, and double-click the first constructor, CPropSheet. Add these lines to it:

```
AddPage(&m_page1);
AddPage(&m_page2);
```

This will add the two property pages to the property sheet whenever the sheet is constructed.

6. The second constructor is right below the first; add the same lines there.

7. Double-click CPropsheetView in ClassView to edit the header file, and add the following lines to the //Attributes section, right after the line CPropsheetDoc* GetDocument();:

```
protected:
    CString m_edit;
    BOOL m_check;
```

These lines declare two data members of the view class to hold the selections made in the property sheet by users.

8. Add the following lines to the CPropsheetView constructor:

```
m_edit = "Default";
m_check = FALSE;
```

Part
III

Ch
12

These lines initialize the class's data members so that when the property sheet appears, these default values can be copied into the property sheet's controls. After users change the contents of the property sheet, these data members will always hold the last values from the property sheet, so those values can be restored to the sheet when needed.

9. Edit `CPropsheetView::OnDraw()` so that it resembles Listing 12.1. The new code displays the current selections from the property sheet. At the start of the program, the default values are displayed.

Listing 12.1 *CPropsheetView::OnDraw()*

```
void CPropsheetView::OnDraw(CDC* pDC)
{
    CPropsheetDoc* pDoc = GetDocument();
    ASSERT_VALID(pDoc);

    pDC->TextOut(20, 20, m_edit);
    if (m_check)
        pDC->TextOut(20, 50, "TRUE");
    else
        pDC->TextOut(20, 50, "FALSE");
}
```

10. At the top of PropsheetView.cpp, after the `#include` of propsheet.h, add another `include` statement:

```
#include "propsheet1.h"
```

11. Bring up ClassWizard, click the Message Maps tab, and make sure that `CPropsheetView` is selected in the Class Name box. In the Object IDs box, select `ID_PROPSHEET`, which is the ID of the new item you added to the File menu. In the Messages box, select `COMMAND`. Click Add Function to add a function that will handle the command message generated when users choose this menu item. Name the function `OnPropsheet()`, as shown in Figure 12.14.

FIG. 12.14

Use ClassWizard to add the `OnPropsheet()` member function.

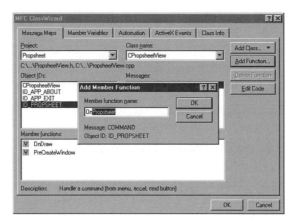

The OnPropsheet() function is now associated with the Property Sheet command that you previously added to the File menu. That is, when users select the Property Sheet command, MFC calls OnPropsheet(), where you can respond to the command.

12. Click the Edit Code button to jump to the OnPropsheet() function, and add the lines shown in Listing 12.2.

Listing 12.2   *CPropsheetView::OnPropsheet()*

```
void CPropsheetView::OnPropsheet()
{
    CPropSheet propSheet("Property Sheet", this, 0);
    propSheet.m_page1.m_edit = m_edit;
    propSheet.m_page2.m_checkbox = m_check;
    int result = propSheet.DoModal();
    if (result == IDOK)
    {
        m_edit = propSheet.m_page1.m_edit;
        m_check = propSheet.m_page2.m_checkbox;
        Invalidate();
    }

}
```

The code segment in Listing 12.2, discussed in more detail later in this chapter, creates an instance of the CPropSheet class and sets the member variables of each of its pages. It displays the sheet by using the familiar DoModal function first discussed in Chapter 2, "Dialogs and Controls." If users click OK, it updates the view member variables to reflect the changes made on each page and forces a redraw with a call to Invalidate().

Running the Property Sheet Demo Application

Part
III

Ch
12

You've finished the complete application. Click the Build button on the Build minibar (or choose Build, Build) to compile and link the application. Run it by choosing Build, Execute or by clicking the Execute button on the Build minibar. When you do, you see the window shown in Figure 12.15.

As you can see, the window displays two values—the default values for the controls in the application's property sheet. You can change these values by using the property sheet. Choose File, Property Sheet; the property sheet appears (see Figure 12.16). The property sheet contains two pages, each of which holds a single control. When you change the settings of these controls and click the property sheet's OK button, the application's window displays the new values. Try it!

FIG. 12.15

When it first starts, the Property Sheet Demo application displays default values for the property sheet's controls.

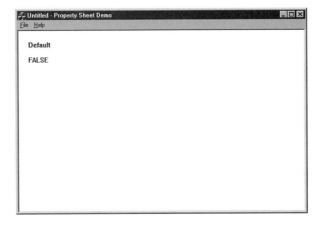

FIG. 12.16

The application's property sheet contains two pages.

Adding Property Sheets to Your Applications

To add a property sheet to one of your own applications, you follow steps very similar to those you followed in the previous section to create the demo application:

1. Create a dialog box resource for each page in the property sheet. These resources should have the Child and Thin styles and should have no system menu.

2. Associate each property page resource with an object of the CPropertyPage class. You can do this easily with ClassWizard. Connect controls on the property page to members of the class you create.

3. Create a class for the property sheet, deriving the class from MFC's CPropertySheet class. You can generate this class by using ClassWizard.

4. In the property sheet class, add member variables for each page you'll be adding to the property sheet. These member variables must be instances of the property page classes that you created in step 2.

5. In the property sheet's constructor, call AddPage() for each page in the property sheet.

6. To display the property sheet, call the property sheet's constructor and then call the property sheet's DoModal() member function, just as you would with a dialog box.

After you write your application and define the resources and classes that represent the property sheet (or sheets—you can have more than one), you need a way to enable users to display the property sheet when it's needed. In Property Sheet Demo, this is done by associating a menu item with a message-response function. However you handle the command to display the property sheet, the process of creating the property sheet is the same. First, you must call the property sheet class's constructor, which Property Sheet Demo does like this:

```
CPropSheet propSheet("Property Sheet", this, 0);
```

Here, the program creates an instance of the CPropSheet class. This instance (or object) is called propSheet. The three arguments are the property sheet's title string, a pointer to the parent window (which, in this case, is the view window), and the zero-based index of the first page to display. Because the property pages are created in the property sheet's constructor, creating the property sheet also creates the property pages.

After you create the property sheet object, you can initialize the data members that hold the values of the property page's controls, which Property Sheet Demo does like this:

```
propSheet.m_page1.m_edit = m_edit;
propSheet.m_page2.m_checkbox = m_check;
```

Now it's time to display the property sheet, which you do just as though it were a dialog box, by calling the property sheet's DoModal() member function:

```
int result = propSheet.DoModal();
```

DoModal() doesn't take any arguments, but it does return a value indicating which button users clicked to exit the property sheet. In a property sheet or dialog box, you'll usually want to process the information entered into the controls only if users clicked OK, which is indicated by a return value of IDOK. If users exit the property sheet by clicking the Cancel button, the changes are ignored and the view or document member variables aren't updated.

Part
III

Ch
12

Changing Property Sheets to Wizards

Here's a piece of information that surprises most people: A wizard is just a special property sheet. Instead of tabbed pages on each sheet that allow users to fill in the information in any order or to skip certain pages entirely, a wizard has Back, Next, and Finish buttons to move users through a process in a certain order. This forced sequence makes wizards terrific for guiding your application's users through the steps needed to complete a complex task. You've already seen how AppWizard in Visual C++ makes it easy to start a new project. You can create your own wizards suited to whatever application you want to build. In the following sections, you'll see how easy it is to convert a property sheet to a wizard.

Running the Wizard Demo Application

To understand Wizards, this section will show you the Wizard Demo application, which is built in much the same way as the Property Sheet Demo application that you created earlier in this chapter. This chapter won't present step-by-step instructions to build Wizard Demo. You will be able to build it yourself if you want, using the general steps presented earlier and the code snippets shown here.

When you run the Wizard Demo application, the main window appears, looking very much like the Property Sheet Demo main window. The File menu now includes a Wizard item; choosing File Wizard brings up the wizard shown in Figure 12.17.

FIG. 12.17

The Wizard Demo application displays a wizard rather than a property sheet.

The wizard isn't too fancy, but it does demonstrate what you need to know to program more complex wizards. As you can see, this wizard has three pages. On the first page is an edit control and three buttons: Back, Next, and Cancel. The Back button is disabled because there's no previous page to go back to. The Cancel button enables users to dismiss the wizard at any time, canceling whatever process the wizard was guiding users through. The Next button causes the next page in the wizard to appear.

You can change whatever is displayed in the edit control if you like. However, the magic really starts when you click the Next button, which displays Page 2 of the wizard (see Figure 12.18). Page 2 contains a check box and the Back, Next, and Cancel buttons. Now the Back button is enabled, so you can return to Page 1 if you want to. Go ahead and click the Back button. The wizard tells you that the check box must be checked (see Figure 12.19). As you'll soon see, this feature of a wizard enables you to verify the contents of a specific page before allowing users to advance to another step.

FIG. 12.18

In Page 2 of the wizard, the Back button is enabled.

After checking the check box, you can click the Back button to move back to Page 1 or click Next to advance to Page 3. Assuming that you advance to Page 3, you see the display shown in Figure 12.20. Here, the Next button has changed to the Finish button because you are on the wizard's last page. If you click the Finish button, the wizard disappears.

FIG. 12.19
You must select the check box before the wizard will let you leave Page 2.

FIG. 12.20
This is the last page of the Wizard Demo Application's wizard.

Creating Wizard Pages

As far as your application's resources go, you create wizard pages exactly as you create property sheet pages—by creating dialog boxes and changing the dialog box styles. The dialog titles—Page 1 of 3, Page 2 of 3, and Page 3 of 3—are hardcoded onto each dialog box. You associate each dialog box resource with an object of the `CPropertyPage` class. Then, to take control of the pages in your wizard and keep track of what users are doing with the wizard, you override the `OnSetActive()`, `OnWizardBack()`, `OnWizardNext()`, and `OnWizardFinish()` functions of your property page classes. Read on to see how to do this.

Displaying a Wizard

The File, Wizard command is caught by `CWizView`'s `OnFileWizard()` function. It's very similar to the `OnPropSheet()` function in the Property Sheet demo, as you can see from Listing 12.3. The first difference is the call to `SetWizardMode()` before the call to `DoModal()`. This function call tells MFC that it should display the property sheet as a wizard rather than as a conventional property sheet. The only other difference is that users arrange for property sheet changes to be accepted by clicking Finish, not OK, so this code checks for `ID_WIZFINISH` rather than `IDOK` as a return from `DoModal()`.

Part
III

Ch
12

Listing 12.3 *CWizView::OnFileWizard()*

```
void CWizView::OnFileWizard()
{
    CWizSheet wizSheet("Sample Wizard", this, 0);
    wizSheet.m_page1.m_edit = m_edit;
```

continues

Listing 12.3   Continued

```
    wizSheet.m_page2.m_check = m_check;
    wizSheet.SetWizardMode();
    int result = wizSheet.DoModal();
    if (result == ID_WIZFINISH)
    {
        m_edit = wizSheet.m_page1.m_edit;
        m_check = wizSheet.m_page2.m_check;
        Invalidate();
    }
}
```

Setting the Wizard's Buttons

MFC automatically calls the OnSetActive() member function immediately upon displaying a specific page of the wizard. So, when the program displays Page 1 of the wizard, the CPage1 class's OnSetActive() function is called. You add code to this function that makes the wizard behave as you want. CPage1::OnSetActive() looks like Listing 12.4.

Listing 12.4   *CPage1::OnSetActive()*

```
BOOL CPage1::OnSetActive()
{
    CPropertySheet* parent = (CPropertySheet*)GetParent();
    parent->SetWizardButtons(PSWIZB_NEXT);
    return CPropertyPage::OnSetActive();
}
```

OnSetActive() first gets a pointer to the wizard's property sheet window, which is the page's parent window. Then the program calls the wizard's SetWizardButtons() function, which determines the state of the wizard's buttons. SetWizardButtons() takes a single argument, which is a set of flags indicating how the page should display its buttons. These flags are PSWIZB_BACK, PSWIZB_NEXT, PSWIZB_FINISH, and PSWIZB_DISABLEDFINISH. Because the call to SetWizardButtons() in Listing 12.4 includes only the PSWIZB_NEXT flag, only the Next button in the page will be enabled.

Because the CPage2 class represents Page 2 of the wizard, its call to SetWizardButtons() enables the Back and Next buttons by combining the appropriate flags with the bitwise OR operator (¦), like this:

```
parent->SetWizardButtons(PSWIZB_BACK ¦ PSWIZB_NEXT);
```

Because Page 3 of the wizard is the last page, the CPage3 class calls SetWizardButtons() like this:

```
parent->SetWizardButtons(PSWIZB_BACK ¦ PSWIZB_FINISH);
```

This set of flags enables the Back button and provides a Finish button instead of a Next button.

Responding to the Wizard's Buttons

In the simplest case, MFC takes care of everything that needs to be done in order to flip from one wizard page to the next. That is, when users click a button, MFC springs into action and performs the Back, Next, Finish, or Cancel command. However, you'll often want to perform some action of your own when users click a button. For example, you may want to verify that the information that users entered into the currently displayed page is correct. If there's a problem with the data, you can force users to fix it before moving on.

To respond to the wizard's buttons, you override the `OnWizardBack()`, `OnWizardNext()`, and `OnWizardFinish()` member functions. Use the Message Maps tab of ClassWizard to do this; you'll find the names of these functions in the Messages window when a property page class is selected in the Class Name box. When users click a wizard button, MFC calls the matching function which does whatever is needed to process that page. An example is the way the wizard in the Wizard Demo application won't let you leave Page 2 until you've checked the check box. This is accomplished by overriding the functions shown in Listing 12.5.

Listing 12.5 Responding to Wizard Buttons

```
LRESULT CPage2::OnWizardBack()
{
    CButton *checkBox = (CButton*)GetDlgItem(IDC_CHECK1);
    if (!checkBox->GetCheck())
    {
        MessageBox("You must check the box.");
        return -1;
    }
    return CPropertyPage::OnWizardBack();
}

LRESULT CPage2::OnWizardNext()
{
    UpdateData();
    if (!m_check)
    {
        MessageBox("You must check the box.");
        return -1;
    }
    return CPropertyPage::OnWizardNext();
}
```

Part
III

Ch
12

These functions demonstrate two ways to examine the check box on Page 2. `OnWizardBack()` gets a pointer to the page's check box by calling the `GetDlgItem()` function. With the pointer in hand, the program can call the check box class's `GetCheck()` function, which returns a 1 if the check box is checked. `OnWizardNext()` calls `UpdateData()` to fill all the `CPage2` member variables with values from the dialog box controls and then looks at `m_check`. In both functions, if the box isn't checked, the program displays a message box and returns -1 from the function. Returning -1 tells MFC to ignore the button click and not change pages. As you can see, it is simple to arrange for different conditions to leave the page in the Back or Next direction. ●

ActiveX Applications and ActiveX Controls

ActiveX Concepts

The Purpose of ActiveX

This chapter covers the theory and concepts of ActiveX, which is built on the Component Object Model (COM). Until recently, the technology built on COM was called OLE, and OLE still exists, but the emphasis now is on ActiveX. Most new programmers have found OLE intimidating, and the switch to ActiveX is unlikely to lessen that. However, if you think of ActiveX technology as a way to use code already written and tested by someone else, and as a way to save yourself the trouble of reinventing the wheel, you'll see why it's worth learning. Developer Studio and MFC make ActiveX much easier to understand and implement by doing much of the groundwork for you. There are four chapters in Part V, "Internet Programming," and together they demonstrate what ActiveX has become. In addition, ActiveX controls, which to many developers represent the way of the future, are discussed in Chapter 20, "Building an Internet ActiveX Control," and Chapter 21, "The Active Template Library." These are best read after Chapters 18 and 19.

Windows has always been an operating system that allows several applications running at once, and right from the beginning, programmers wanted to have a way for those applications to exchange information while running. The Clipboard was a marvelous innovation, though, of course, the user had to do a lot of the work. DDE (Dynamic Data Exchange) allowed applications to "talk" to each other but had some major limitations. Then came OLE 1 (Object Linking and Embedding). Later there was OLE 2, and then Microsoft just called it OLE, until it moved so far beyond its original roots that it was renamed ActiveX.

N O T E Experienced Windows users will probably be familiar with the examples presented in the early part of this chapter. If you know what ActiveX can do for users and are interested in why it works jump ahead to the "Component Object Model" section, which looks under the hood a little. ▓

ActiveX lets users and applications be document-centered, and this is probably the most important thing about it. If a user wants to create an annual report, by choosing ActiveX-enabled applications, the user stays focused on that annual report. Perhaps parts of it are being done with Word and parts with Excel, but, to the user, these applications are not really the point. This shift in focus is happening on many fronts and corresponds to a more object-oriented way of thinking among many programmers. It seems more natural now to share work among several different applications and arrange for them to communicate than to write one huge application that can do everything.

Here's a simple test to see whether you are document centered or application centered: How is your hard drive organized?

The directory structure in Figure 13.1 is application centered: The directories are named for the applications that were used to create the documents they hold. All Word documents are together, even though they might be for very different clients or projects.

FIG. 13.1

An application-centered directory structure arranges documents by type.

```
Microsoft Office
  Word
    Building Internet Apps
    Using Visual C++
    Acme Corp
      Training
      Web Pages
  Excel
    Journal
    Sales estimates
    Invoices
  ABC Inc
    Payroll System
    Inventory System
Microsoft Developer Studio
  ABC Inc Payroll System
  ABC Inc Inventory System
```

The directory structure in Figure 13.2 is document centered: The directories are named for the client or project involved. All the sales files are together, even though they can be accessed with a variety of different applications.

FIG. 13.2

A document-centered directory structure arranges documents by meaning or content.

```
Clients
  Acme Corp
    Training
    Web Pages
    Invoices
  ABC Inc
    Payroll System
    Inventory System
    Invoices
Books
  Building Internet Apps
  Using Visual C++
    ...
Overhead
  Accounting
  Sales
```

If you've been using desktop computers long enough, you remember when using a program involved a program disk and a data disk. Perhaps you remember installing software that demanded to know the data directory where you would keep all the files created with that product. That was application-centered thinking, and it's fast being supplanted by document-centered thinking.

Why? What's wrong with application-centered thinking? Well, where do you put the documents that are used with two applications equally often? There was a time when each product could read its own file formats and no others. But these days, the lines between applications are blurring; a document created in one word processor can easily be read into another, a spreadsheet file can be used as a database, and so on. If a client sends you a WordPerfect document and you don't have WordPerfect, do you make a \WORDPERFECT\DOCS directory to put it in, or add it to your \MSOFFICE\WORD\DOCS directory? If you have your hard drive arranged in a more document-centered manner, you can just put it in the directory for that client.

The Windows 95 interface, now incorporated into Windows NT as well, encourages document-centered thinking by having users double-click documents to automatically launch the applications that created them. This wasn't new—File Manager had that capability for years—but it feels very different to double-click an icon that's just sitting on the desktop than it does to start an application and then double-click an entry in a list box. More and more it doesn't matter what application or applications were involved in creating this document; you just want to see and change your data, and you want to do that quickly and simply.

After you become document-centered, you see the appeal of *compound documents*—files created with more than one application. If your report needs an illustration, you create it in some graphic program and then stick it in with your text when it's done. If your annual report needs a table, and you already have the numbers in a spreadsheet, you don't retype them into the table feature of your word processor or even import them; you incorporate them as a spreadsheet excerpt, right in the middle of your text. This isn't earth-shatteringly new, of course. Early desktop publishing programs such as Ventura pulled together text and graphics from a variety of sources into one complex compound document. What's exciting is being able to do it simply, intuitively, and with so many different applications.

Object Linking

Figure 13.3 shows a Word document with an Excel spreadsheet linked into it.

Follow these steps to create a similar document yourself:

1. Start Word and enter your text.
2. Click where you want the table to go.
3. Choose Insert, Object.
4. Select the Create from File tab.
5. Enter or select the filename as though this were a File Open dialog box.
6. Be sure to check the Link to File box.
7. Click OK.

The entire file appears in your document. If you make a change in the file on disk, the change is reflected in your document. You can edit the file in its own application by double-clicking it within Word. The other application is launched to edit it, as shown in Figure 13.4. If you delete the file from disk, your Word document still displays what the file last looked like, but you aren't able to edit it.

FIG. 13.3
A Microsoft Word document can contain a link to an Excel file.

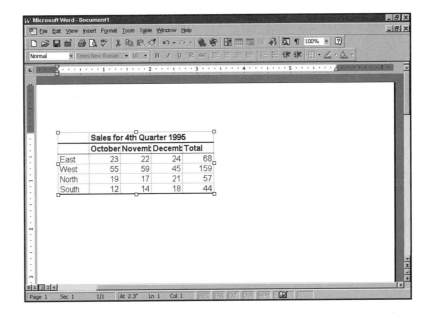

FIG. 13.4
Double-clicking a linked object launches the application that created it.

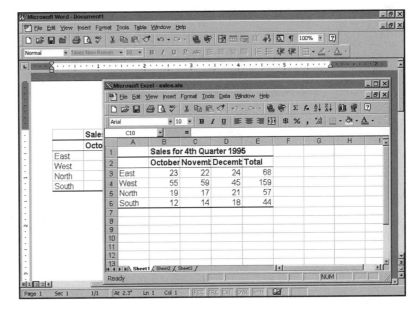

You link files into your documents if you plan to use the same file in many documents and contexts, because your changes to that file are automatically reflected everywhere that you have linked it. Linking doesn't increase the size of your document files dramatically because only the location of the file and a little bit of presentation information needs to be kept in your document.

Object Embedding

Embedding is similar to linking, but a copy of the object is made and placed into your document. If you change the original, the changes aren't reflected in your document. You can't tell by looking whether the Excel chart you see in your Word document is linked or embedded. Figure 13.5 shows a spreadsheet embedded within a Word document.

FIG. 13.5

A file embedded within another file looks just like a linked file.

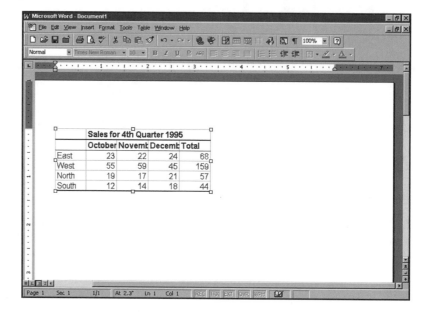

Follow these steps to create a similar document yourself:

1. Start Word and enter your text.
2. Click where you want the table to go.
3. Choose Insert, Object.
4. Select the Create from File tab.
5. Enter or select the filename as though this were a File Open dialog box.
6. Do not check the Link to File box.
7. Click OK.

What's the difference? You'll see when you double-click the object to edit it. The Word menus and toolbars disappear and are replaced with their Excel equivalents, as shown in Figure 13.6. Changes you make here aren't made in the file you originally embedded. They are made in the copy of that file that has become part of your Word document.

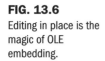

FIG. 13.6
Editing in place is the
magic of OLE
embedding.

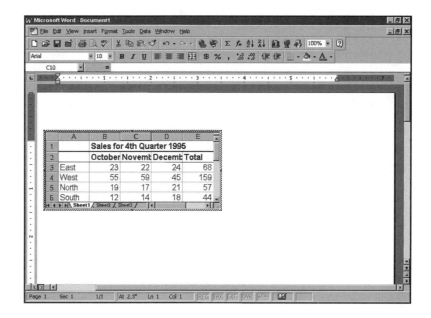

You embed files into your documents if you plan to build a compound document and then use it as a self-contained whole, without using the individual parts again. Changes you make don't affect any other files on your disk, not even the one you copied from in the first place. Embedding makes your document much larger than it was, but you can delete the original if space is a problem.

Containers and Servers

To embed or link one object into another, you need a *container* and a *server*. The container is the application into which the object is linked or embedded—Word in these examples. The server is the application that made them, and that can be launched (perhaps in place) when the object is double-clicked—Excel in these examples.

Why would you develop a container application? To save yourself work. Imagine you have a product already developed and in the hands of your users. It does a specific task like organize a sales team, schedule games in a league sport, or calculate life insurance rates. Then your users tell you that they wish it had a spreadsheet capability so they could do small calculations on-the-fly. How long will it take you to add that functionality? Do you really have time to learn how spreadsheet programs parse the functions that users type?

If your application is a container app, it doesn't take any time at all. Tell your users to link or embed in an Excel sheet and let Excel do the work. If they don't own a copy of Excel, they need some spreadsheet application that can be an ActiveX server. You get to piggyback on the effort of other developers.

Part
IV

Ch
13

It's not just spreadsheets, either. What if users want a scratch pad, a place to scribble a few notes? Let them embed a Word document. (What about bitmaps and other illustrations? Microsoft Paint, or a more powerful graphics package if they have one, and it can act as an ActiveX server.) You don't have to concern yourself with adding functionality like this to your programs because you can just make your application a container and your users can embed whatever they want without any more work on your part.

Why would you develop a server application, then? Look back over the reasons for writing a container application. A lot of users are going to contact developers asking for a feature to be added, and be told they can have that feature immediately—they just need an application that does spreadsheets, text, pictures, or whatever, and can act as an ActiveX server. If your application is an ActiveX server, people will buy it so that they can add its functionality to their container apps.

Together, container and server apps enable users to build the documents they want. They represent a move toward building-block software and a document-centered approach to work. If you want your application to carry the Windows 95 logo, it must be a server, a container, or both. But there is much more to ActiveX than linking and embedding.

Toward a More Intuitive User Interface

What if the object you want to embed is not in a file but is part of a document you have open at the moment? You may have already discovered that you can use the Clipboard to transfer ActiveX objects. For example, to embed part of an Excel spreadsheet into a Word document, you can follow these steps:

1. Open the spreadsheet in Excel.
2. Open the document in Word.
3. In Excel, select the portion you want to copy.
4. Choose Edit, Copy to copy the block onto the Clipboard.
5. Switch to Word and choose Edit, Paste Special.
6. Select the Paste radio button.
7. Select Microsoft Excel Worksheet Object from the list box.
8. Make sure that Display as Icon is not selected.
9. The dialog box should look like Figure 13.7. Click OK.

A copy of the block is now embedded into the document. If you choose Paste Link, changes in the spreadsheet are reflected immediately in the Word document, not just when you save them. (You might have to click the selection in Word to update it.) This is true even if the spreadsheet has no name and has never been saved. Try it yourself! This is certainly better than saving dummy files just to embed them into compound documents and then deleting them, isn't it?

FIG. 13.7

The Paste Special dialog box is used to link or embed selected portions of a document.

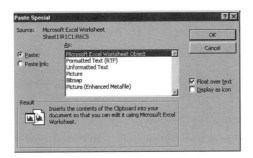

Another way to embed part of a document into another is drag and drop. This is a user-interface paradigm that works in a variety of contexts. You click something (an icon, a high-lighted block of text, a selection in a list box) and hold the mouse button down while moving it. The item you clicked moves with the mouse, and when you let go of the mouse button, it drops to the new location. That's very intuitive for moving or resizing windows, but now you can use it to do much, much more. For example, here's how that Excel-in-Word example would be done with drag and drop:

1. Open Word and size it to less than full screen.
2. Open Excel and size it to less than full screen. If you can arrange the Word and Excel windows so they don't overlap, that's great.
3. In Excel, select the portion you want to copy by highlighting it with the mouse or cursor keys.
4. Click the border of the selected area (the thick black line) and hold.
5. Drag the block into the Word window and let go.

The selected block is embedded into the Word document. If you double-click it, you are editing in place with Excel. Drag and drop also works within a document to move or copy a selection.

 TIP The block is moved by default, which means it is deleted from the Excel sheet. If you want a copy, hold down the Ctrl key while dragging, and release the mouse button before the Ctrl key.

You can also use drag and drop with icons. On your desktop, if you drag a file to a folder, it is moved there. (Hold down Ctrl while dragging to copy it.) If you drag it to a program icon, it is opened with that program. This is very useful when you have a document you use with two applications. For example, pages on the World Wide Web are HTML documents, often created with an HTML editor but viewed with a World Wide Web browser such as Netscape Navigator or Microsoft Internet Explorer. If you double-click an HTML document icon, your browser is launched to view it. If you drag that icon onto the icon for your HTML editor, the editor is launched and opens the file you dragged. After you realize you can do this, you will find your work speeds up dramatically.

All of this is ActiveX, and all of this requires a little bit of work from programmers to make it happen. So what's going on?

Part

IV

Ch

13

The Component Object Model

The heart of ActiveX is the Component Object Model (COM). This is an incredibly complex topic that deserves a book of its own. Luckily, the Microsoft Foundation Classes and the Visual C++ AppWizard do much of the behind-the-scenes work for you. The discussion in these chapters is just what you need to know to use COM as a developer.

COM is a binary standard for Windows objects. That means that the executable code (in a DLL or EXE) that describes an object can be executed by other objects. Even if two objects were written in different languages, they are able to interact using the COM standard.

> **N O T E**   Because the code in a DLL executes in the same process as the calling code, it's the fastest way for applications to communicate. When two separate applications communicate through COM, function calls from one application to another must be *marshaled*: COM gathers up all the parameters and invokes the function itself. A standalone server (EXE) is therefore slower than an in-process server (DLL). ▨

How do they interact? Through an *interface*. An ActiveX interface is a collection of functions, or really just function names. It's a C++ class with no data, only pure virtual functions. Your objects inherit from this class and provide code for the functions. (Remember, as discussed in Appendix A, "C++ Review and Object-Oriented Concepts," a class that inherits a pure virtual function doesn't inherit code for that function.) Other programs get to your code by calling these functions. All ActiveX objects must have an interface named IUnknown (and most have many more, all with names that start with I, the prefix for interfaces).

The IUnknown interface has only one purpose: finding other interfaces. It has a function called QueryInterface() that takes an interface ID and returns a pointer to that interface for this object. All the other interfaces inherit from IUnknown, so they have a QueryInterface() too, and you have to write the code—or you would if there was no MFC. MFC implements a number of macros that simplify the job of writing interfaces and their functions, as you will shortly see. The full declaration of IUnknown is in Listing 13.1. The macros take care of some of the work of declaring an interface and won't be discussed here. There are three functions declared: QueryInterface(), AddRef(), and Release(). These latter two functions are used to keep track of which applications are using an interface. All three functions are inherited by all interfaces and must be implemented by the developer of the interface.

Listing 13.1   *IUnknown*, Defined in \Program Files\Microsoft Visual Studio\VC98\Include\unknwn.h

```
MIDL_INTERFACE("00000000-0000-0000-C000-000000000046")
    IUnknown
    {
    public:
        BEGIN_INTERFACE
        virtual HRESULT STDMETHODCALLTYPE QueryInterface(
```

```
        /* [in] */ REFIID riid,
        /* [iid_is][out] */ void __RPC_FAR *__RPC_FAR *ppvObject) = 0;

    virtual ULONG STDMETHODCALLTYPE AddRef( void) = 0;

    virtual ULONG STDMETHODCALLTYPE Release( void) = 0;

#if (_MSC_VER >= 1200)    // VC6 or greater
    template <class Q>
    HRESULT STDMETHODCALLTYPE QueryInterface(Q** pp)
    {
        return QueryInterface(__uuidof(Q), (void**)pp);
    }
#endif

    END_INTERFACE
};
```

Automation

An Automation server lets other applications tell it what to do. It *exposes* functions and data, called *methods* and *properties*. For example, Microsoft Excel is an Automation server, and programs written in Visual C++ or Visual Basic can call Excel functions and set properties like column widths. That means you don't need to write a scripting language for your application any more. If you expose all the functions and properties of your application, any programming language that can control an Automation server can be a scripting language for your application. Your users may already know your scripting language. They essentially will have no learning curve for writing macros to automate your application (although they will need to learn the names of the methods and properties you expose).

The important thing to know about interacting with automation is that one program is always in control, calling the methods or changing the properties of the other running application. The application in control is called an Automation controller. The application that exposes methods and functions is called an Automation server. Excel, Word, and other members of the Microsoft Office suite are Automation servers, and your programs can use the functions of these applications to really save you coding time.

For example, imagine being able to use the function called by the Word menu item Format, Change Case to convert the blocks of text your application uses to all uppercase, all lowercase, sentence case (the first letter of the first word in each sentence is uppercase, the rest are not), or title case (the first letter of every word is uppercase; the rest are not).

The description of how automation really works is far longer and more complex than the interface summary of the previous section. It involves a special interface called IDispatch, a simplified interface that works from a number of different languages, including those like Visual Basic that can't use pointers. The declaration of IDispatch is shown in Listing 13.2.

Part

IV

Ch

13

> **Listing 13.2** *IDispatch*, Defined in \Program Files\Microsoft Visual
> Studio\VC98\Include\oaidl.h

```
MIDL_INTERFACE("00020400-0000-0000-C000-000000000046")
    IDispatch : public IUnknown
    {
    public:
        virtual HRESULT STDMETHODCALLTYPE GetTypeInfoCount(
            /* [out] */ UINT __RPC_FAR *pctinfo) = 0;

        virtual HRESULT STDMETHODCALLTYPE GetTypeInfo(
            /* [in] */ UINT iTInfo,
            /* [in] */ LCID lcid,
            /* [out] */ ITypeInfo __RPC_FAR *__RPC_FAR *ppTInfo) = 0;

        virtual HRESULT STDMETHODCALLTYPE GetIDsOfNames(
            /* [in] */ REFIID riid,
            /* [size_is][in] */ LPOLESTR __RPC_FAR *rgszNames,
            /* [in] */ UINT cNames,
            /* [in] */ LCID lcid,
            /* [size_is][out] */ DISPID __RPC_FAR *rgDispId) = 0;

        virtual /* [local] */ HRESULT STDMETHODCALLTYPE Invoke(
            /* [in] */ DISPID dispIdMember,
            /* [in] */ REFIID riid,
            /* [in] */ LCID lcid,
            /* [in] */ WORD wFlags,
            /* [out][in] */ DISPPARAMS __RPC_FAR *pDispParams,
            /* [out] */ VARIANT __RPC_FAR *pVarResult,
            /* [out] */ EXCEPINFO __RPC_FAR *pExcepInfo,
            /* [out] */ UINT __RPC_FAR *puArgErr) = 0;

    };
```

Although IDispatch seems more complex than IUnknown, it declares only a few more functions: GetTypeInfoCount(), GetTypeInfo(), GetIDsOfNames(), and Invoke(). Because it inherits from IUnknown, it has also inherited QueryInterface(), AddRef(), and Release(). They are all pure virtual functions, so any COM class that inherits from IDispatch must implement these functions. The most important of these is Invoke(), used to call functions of the Automation server and to access its properties.

ActiveX Controls

ActiveX controls are tiny little Automation servers that load *in process*. This means they are remarkably fast. They were originally called OLE Custom Controls and were designed to replace VBX controls, 16-bit controls written for use in Visual Basic and Visual C++. (There are a number of good technical reasons why the VBX technology could not be extended to the 32-bit world.) Because OLE Custom Controls were traditionally kept in files with the extension .OCX, many people referred to an OLE Custom Control as an OCX control or just an OCX. Although the OLE has been supplanted by ActiveX, ActiveX controls produced by Visual C++ 6.0 are still kept in files with the .OCX extension.

The original purpose of VBX controls was to allow programmers to provide unusual interface controls to their users. Controls that looked like gas gauges or volume knobs became easy to develop. But almost immediately, VBX programmers moved beyond simple controls to modules that involved significant amounts of calculation and processing. In the same way, many ActiveX controls are far more than just controls; they are *components* that can be used to build powerful applications quickly and easily.

N O T E   If you have built an OCX in earlier versions of Visual C++, you might think it is a difficult thing to do. The Control Developer Kit, now integrated into Visual C++, takes care of the ActiveX aspects of the job and allows you to concentrate on the calculations, display, or whatever else it is that makes your control worth using. The ActiveX Control Wizard makes getting started with an empty ActiveX control simple. ▪

Because controls are little Automation servers, they need to be used by an Automation controller, but the terminology is too confusing if there are controls and controllers, so we say that ActiveX controls are used by *container* applications. Visual C++ and Visual Basic are both container applications, as are many members of the Office suite and many non-Microsoft products.

In addition to properties and methods, ActiveX controls have *events*. To be specific, a control is said to *fire* an event, and it does so when there is something that the container needs to be aware of. For example, when the user clicks a portion of the control, the control deals with it, perhaps changing its appearance or making a calculation, but it may also need to pass on word of that click to the container application so that a file can be opened or some other container action can be performed.

This chapter has given you a brief tour through the concepts and terminology used in ActiveX technology, and a glimpse of the power you can add to your applications by incorporating ActiveX into them. The remainder of the chapters in this part lead you through the creation of ActiveX applications, using MFC and the wizards in Visual C++. ●

Building an ActiveX Container Application

You can obtain a rudimentary ActiveX container by asking AppWizard to make you one, but it will have a lot of shortcomings. A far more difficult task is to understand how an ActiveX container works and what you have to do to really use it. In this chapter, by turning the ShowString application of earlier chapters into an ActiveX container and then making it a truly functional container, you get a backstage view of ActiveX in action. Adding drag-and-drop support brings your application into the modern age of intuitive, document-centered user interface design. If you have not yet read Chapter 13, "ActiveX Concepts," it would be a good idea to read it before this one. As well, this chapter will not repeat all the instructions of Chapter 8, "Building a Complete Application: ShowString," so you should have read that chapter or be prepared to refer to it as you progress through this one.

Changing ShowString

ShowString was built originally in Chapter 8, "Building a Complete Application: ShowString," and has no ActiveX support. You could make the changes by hand to implement ActiveX container support, but there would be more than 30 changes. It's quicker to build a new ShowString application—this time asking for ActiveX container support—and then make changes to that code to get the ShowString functionality again.

AppWizard-Generated ActiveX Container Code

Build the new ShowString in a different directory, making almost exactly the same AppWizard choices you used when you built it in the "Creating an Empty Shell with AppWizard" section of Chapter 8. Name the project ShowString, choose an MDI Application, No Database Support, compound document support: Container, a Docking Toolbar, Initial Status Bar, Printing and Print Preview, Context Sensitive Help, and 3D Controls. Finally, select Source File Comments and a Shared DLL. Finish AppWizard and, if you want, build the project.tm1713714470

> **N O T E**   Even though the technology is now called ActiveX, the AppWizard dialog boxes refer to compound document support. Also, many of the classnames that are used throughout this chapter have Ole in their names, and comments refer to OLE. Although Microsoft has changed the name of the technology, it has not propagated that change throughout Visual C++ yet. You have to live with these contradictions for a while. ∎

There are many differences between the application you just built and a do-nothing application without ActiveX container support. The remainder of this section explains these differences and their effects.

Menus   There's another menu, called IDR_SHOWSTTYPE_CNTR_IP, shown in Figure 14.1. The name refers to a container whose *contained* object is being edited *in place*. During in-place editing, the menu bar is built from the container's in-place menu and the server's in-place menu. The pair of vertical bars in the middle of IDR_SHOWSTTYPE_CNTR_IP are separators; the server menu items will be put between them. This is discussed in more detail in Chapter 15, "Building an ActiveX Server Application."

FIG. 14.1
AppWizard adds
another menu for
editing in place.

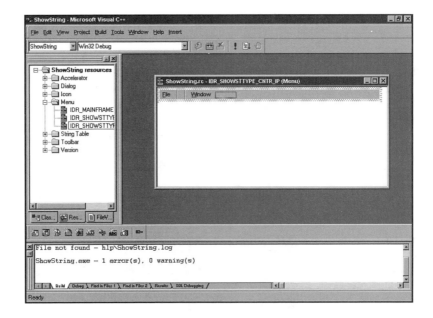

The IDR_SHOWSTTYPE Edit menu, shown in Figure 14.2, has four new items:

FIG. 14.2
AppWizard adds items
to the Edit menu of the
IDR_SHOWSTTYPE
resource.

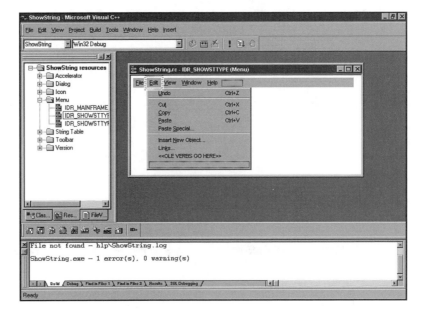

■ **Paste Special.** The user chooses this item to insert an item into the container from the Clipboard.

■ **Insert New Object.** Choosing this item opens the Insert Object dialog box, shown in Figures 14.3 and 14.4, so the user can insert an item into the container.

FIG. 14.3

The Insert Object dialog box can be used to embed new objects.

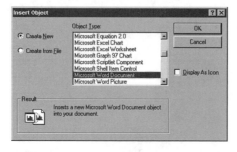

FIG. 14.4

The Insert Object dialog box can be used to embed or link objects that are in a file.

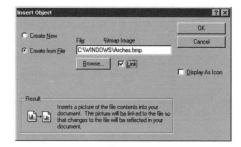

■ **Links.** When an object has been linked into the container, choosing this item opens the Links dialog box, shown in Figure 14.5, to allow control of how the copy of the object is updated after a change is saved to the file.

■ **<<OLE VERBS GO HERE>>.** Each kind of item has different verbs associated with it, like Edit, Open, or Play. When a contained item has focus, this spot on the menu is replaced by an object type like those in the Insert Object dialog box, with a menu cascading from it that lists the verbs for this type, like the one shown in Figure 14.6.

CShowStringApp CShowStringApp::InitInstance() has several changes from the InitInstance() method provided by AppWizard for applications that aren't ActiveX containers. The lines in Listing 14.1 initialize the ActiveX (OLE) libraries.

Listing 14.1   Excerpt from ShowString.cpp—Library Initialization

```
// Initialize OLE libraries
if (!AfxOleInit())
{
    AfxMessageBox(IDP_OLE_INIT_FAILED);
    return FALSE;
}
```

FIG. 14.5

The Links dialog box controls the way linked objects are updated.

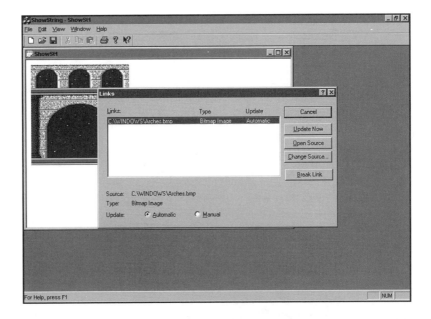

FIG. 14.6

Each object type adds a cascading menu item to the Edit menu when it has focus.

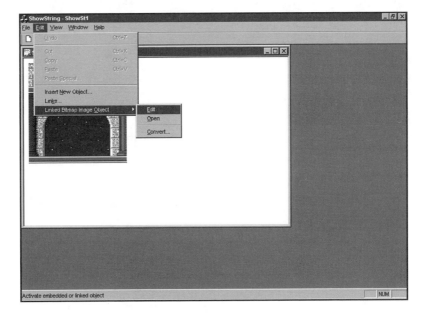

Still in `CShowStringApp::InitInstance()`, after the `MultiDocTemplate` is initialized but before the call to `AddDocTemplate()`, this line is added to register the menu used for in-place editing:

```
pDocTemplate->SetContainerInfo(IDR_SHOWSTTYPE_CNTR_IP);
```

CShowStringDoc   The document class, CShowStringDoc, now inherits from COleDocument rather than CDocument. This line is also added at the top of ShowStringDoc.cpp:

```
#include "CntrItem.h"
```

CntrItem.h describes the container item class, CShowStringCntrItem, discussed later in this chapter. Still in ShowStringDoc.cpp, the macros in Listing 14.2 have been added to the message map.

Listing 14.2   Excerpt from ShowString.cpp—Message Map Additions

```
    ON_UPDATE_COMMAND_UI(ID_EDIT_PASTE,
➥COleDocument::OnUpdatePasteMenu)
    ON_UPDATE_COMMAND_UI(ID_EDIT_PASTE_LINK,
➥COleDocument::OnUpdatePasteLinkMenu)
    ON_UPDATE_COMMAND_UI(ID_OLE_EDIT_CONVERT,
➥COleDocument::OnUpdateObjectVerbMenu)
    ON_COMMAND(ID_OLE_EDIT_CONVERT,
➥COleDocument::OnEditConvert)
    ON_UPDATE_COMMAND_UI(ID_OLE_EDIT_LINKS,
➥COleDocument::OnUpdateEditLinksMenu)
    ON_COMMAND(ID_OLE_EDIT_LINKS,
➥COleDocument::OnEditLinks)
    ON_UPDATE_COMMAND_UI(ID_OLE_VERB_FIRST, ID_OLE_VERB_LAST,
➥COleDocument::OnUpdateObjectVerbMenu)
```

These commands enable and disable the following menu items:

- Edit, Paste
- Edit, Paste Link
- Edit, Links
- The OLE verbs section, including the Convert verb

The new macros also handle Convert and Edit, Links. Notice that the messages are handled by functions of COleDocument and don't have to be written by you.

The constructor, CShowStringDoc::CShowStringDoc(), has a line added:

```
    EnableCompoundFile();
```

This turns on the use of compound files. CShowStringDoc::Serialize() has a line added as well:

```
    COleDocument::Serialize(ar);
```

This call to the base class Serialize() takes care of serializing all the contained objects, with no further work for you.

CShowStringView   The view class, CShowStringView, includes CntrItem.h just as the document does. The view class has these new entries in the message map:

```
ON_WM_SETFOCUS()
ON_WM_SIZE()
```

```
    ON_COMMAND(ID_OLE_INSERT_NEW, OnInsertObject)
    ON_COMMAND(ID_CANCEL_EDIT_CNTR, OnCancelEditCntr)
```

These are in addition to the messages caught by the view before it was a container. These catch WM_SETFOCUS, WM_SIZE, the menu item Edit, Insert New Object, and the cancellation of editing in place. An accelerator has already been added to connect this message to the Esc key.

In ShowStringView.h, a new member variable has been added, as shown in Listing 14.3.

Listing 14.3 Excerpt from ShowStringView.h—*m_pSelection*

```
// m_pSelection holds the selection to the current
// CShowStringCntrItem. For many applications, such
// a member variable isn't adequate to represent a
// selection, such as a multiple selection or a selection
// of objects that are not CShowStringCntrItem objects.
// This selection mechanism is provided just to help you
// get started.

// TODO: replace this selection mechanism with one appropriate
// to your app.
CShowStringCntrItem* m_pSelection;
```

This new member variable shows up again in the view constructor, Listing 14.4, and the revised OnDraw(), Listing 14.5.

Listing 14.4 ShowStringView.cpp—Constructor

```
CShowStringView::CShowStringView()
{
    m_pSelection = NULL;
    // TODO: add construction code here
}
```

Listing 14.5 ShowStringView.cpp—*CShowStringView::OnDraw()*

```
void CShowStringView::OnDraw(CDC* pDC)
{
    CShowStringDoc* pDoc = GetDocument();
    ASSERT_VALID(pDoc);

    // TODO: add draw code for native data here
    // TODO: also draw all OLE items in the document

    // Draw the selection at an arbitrary position.  This code should be
    //   removed once your real drawing code is implemented.  This position
    //   corresponds exactly to the rectangle returned by CShowStringCntrItem,
    //   to give the effect of in-place editing.
```

Part

IV

Ch

14

continues

Listing 14.5   Continued

```
        // TODO: remove this code when final draw code is complete.

        if (m_pSelection == NULL)
        {
            POSITION pos = pDoc->GetStartPosition();
            m_pSelection = (CShowStringCntrItem*)pDoc->GetNextClientItem(pos);
        }
        if (m_pSelection != NULL)
            m_pSelection->Draw(pDC, CRect(10, 10, 210, 210));
    }
```

The code supplied for OnDraw() draws only a single contained item. It doesn't draw any native data—in other words, elements of ShowString that are not contained items. At the moment there is no native data, but after the string is added to the application, OnDraw() is going to have to draw it. What's more, this code only draws one contained item, and it does so in an arbitrary rectangle. OnDraw() is going to see a lot of changes as you work through this chapter.

The view class has gained a lot of new functions. They are as follows:

- OnInitialUpdate()
- IsSelected()
- OnInsertObject()
- OnSetFocus()
- OnSize()
- OnCancelEditCntr()

Each of these new functions is discussed in the subsections that follow.

OnInitialUpdate()   OnInitialUpdate()is called just before the very first time the view is to be displayed. The boilerplate code (see Listing 14.6) is pretty dull.

Listing 14.6   ShowStringView.cpp—*CShowStringView::OnInitialUpdate()*

```
void CShowStringView::OnInitialUpdate()
{
    CView::OnInitialUpdate();

    // TODO: remove this code when final selection
    // model code is written
    m_pSelection = NULL;    // initialize selection

}
```

The base class OnInitialUpdate() calls the base class OnUpdate(), which calls Invalidate(), requiring a full repaint of the client area.

IsSelected()   IsSelected() currently isn't working because the selection mechanism is so rudimentary. Listing 14.7 shows the code that was generated for you. Later, when you have implemented a proper selection method, you will improve how this code works.

Listing 14.7   ShowStringView.cpp—*CShowStringView::IsSelected()*

```
BOOL CShowStringView::IsSelected(const CObject* pDocItem) const
{
    // The implementation below is adequate if your selection consists of
    //  only CShowStringCntrItem objects.  To handle different selection
    //  mechanisms, the implementation here should be replaced.

    // TODO: implement this function that tests for a selected OLE
    // client item

    return pDocItem == m_pSelection;
}
```

This function is passed a pointer to a container item. If that pointer is the same as the current selection, it returns TRUE.

OnInsertObject()   OnInsertObject()is called when the user chooses Edit, Insert New Object. It's quite a long function, so it is presented in parts. The overall structure is presented in Listing 14.8.

Listing 14.8   ShowStringView.cpp—*CShowStringView::OnInsertObject()*

```
void CShowStringView::OnInsertObject()
{
    // Display the Insert Object dialog box.

    CShowStringCntrItem* pItem = NULL;
    TRY
    {
        // Create a new item connected to this document.
        // Initialize the item.
        // Set selection and update all views.
    }
    CATCH(CException, e)
    {
        // Handle failed create.
    }
    END_CATCH

    // Tidy up.
}
```

Each comment here is replaced with a small block of code, discussed in the remainder of this section. The TRY and CATCH statements, by the way, are on old-fashioned form of exception handling, discussed in Chapter 26, "Exceptions and Templates."

First, this function displays the Insert Object dialog box, as shown in Listing 14.9.

Listing 14.9 ShowStringView.cpp—Display the Insert Object Dialog Box

```
// Invoke the standard Insert Object dialog box to obtain information
//  for new CShowStringCntrItem object.
COleInsertDialog dlg;
if (dlg.DoModal() != IDOK)
    return;
BeginWaitCursor();
```

If the user clicks Cancel, this function returns and nothing is inserted. If the user clicks OK, the cursor is set to an hourglass while the rest of the processing occurs.

To create a new item, the code in Listing 14.10 is inserted.

Listing 14.10 ShowStringView.cpp—Create a New Item

```
// Create new item connected to this document.
CShowStringDoc* pDoc = GetDocument();
ASSERT_VALID(pDoc);
pItem = new CShowStringCntrItem(pDoc);
ASSERT_VALID(pItem);
```

This code makes sure there is a document, even though the menu item is enabled only if there is one, and then creates a new container item, passing it the pointer to the document. As you see in the CShowStringCntrItem section, container items hold a pointer to the document that contains them.

The code in Listing 14.11 initializes that item.

Listing 14.11 ShowStringView.cpp—Initializing the Inserted Item

```
// Initialize the item from the dialog data.
if (!dlg.CreateItem(pItem))
    AfxThrowMemoryException();  // any exception will do
ASSERT_VALID(pItem);
// If item created from class list (not from file) then launch
//  the server to edit the item.
if (dlg.GetSelectionType() == COleInsertDialog::createNewItem)
    pItem->DoVerb(OLEIVERB_SHOW, this);

ASSERT_VALID(pItem);
```

The code in Listing 14.11 calls the `CreateItem()` function of the dialog class, `COleInsertDialog`. That might seem like a strange place to keep such a function, but the function needs to know all the answers that were given on the dialog box. If it was a member of another class, it would have to interrogate the dialog for the type and filename, find out whether it was linked or embedded, and so on. It calls member functions of the container item like `CreateLinkFromFile()`, `CreateFromFile()`, `CreateNewItem()`, and so on. So it's not that the code has to actually fill the object from the file that is in the dialog box, but rather that the work is partitioned between the objects instead of passing information back and forth between them.

Then, one question is asked of the dialog box: Was this a new item? If so, the server is called to edit it. Objects created from a file can just be displayed.

Finally, the selection is updated and so are the views, as shown in Listing 14.12.

Listing 14.12 ShowStringView.cpp—Update Selection and Views

```
// As an arbitrary user interface design, this sets the selection
//  to the last item inserted.

// TODO: reimplement selection as appropriate for your application

m_pSelection = pItem;    // set selection to last inserted item
pDoc->UpdateAllViews(NULL);
```

If the creation of the object failed, execution ends up in the CATCH block, shown in Listing 14.13.

Listing 14.13 ShowStringView.cpp—*CATCH* Block

```
CATCH(CException, e)
{
    if (pItem != NULL)
    {
        ASSERT_VALID(pItem);
        pItem->Delete();
    }
    AfxMessageBox(IDP_FAILED_TO_CREATE);
}
END_CATCH
```

This deletes the item that was created and gives the user a message box.

Finally, that hourglass cursor can go away:

```
EndWaitCursor();
```

OnSetFocus() `OnSetFocus()`, shown in Listing 14.14, is called whenever this view gets focus.

Part

IV

Ch

14

Listing 14.14   ShowStringView.cpp—*CShowStringView::OnSetFocus()*

```
void CShowStringView::OnSetFocus(CWnd* pOldWnd)
{
    COleClientItem* pActiveItem = GetDocument()->GetInPlaceActiveItem(this);
    if (pActiveItem != NULL &&
        pActiveItem->GetItemState() == COleClientItem::activeUIState)
    {
        // need to set focus to this item if it is in the same view
        CWnd* pWnd = pActiveItem->GetInPlaceWindow();
        if (pWnd != NULL)
        {
            pWnd->SetFocus();   // don't call the base class
            return;
        }
    }

    CView::OnSetFocus(pOldWnd);
}
```

If there is an active item and its server is loaded, that active item gets focus. If not, focus remains with the old window, and it appears to the user that the click was ignored.

OnSize()   OnSize(), shown in Listing 14.15, is called when the application is resized by the user.

Listing 14.15   ShowStringView.cpp—*CShowStringView::OnSize()*

```
void CShowStringView::OnSize(UINT nType, int cx, int cy)
{
    CView::OnSize(nType, cx, cy);
    COleClientItem* pActiveItem = GetDocument()->GetInPlaceActiveItem(this);
    if (pActiveItem != NULL)
        pActiveItem->SetItemRects();
}
```

This resizes the view using the base class function, and then, if there is an active item, tells it to adjust to the resized view.

OnCancelEditCntr()   OnCancelEditCntr() is called when a user who has been editing in place presses Esc. The server must be closed, and the object stops being active. The code is shown in Listing 14.16.

Listing 14.16   ShowStringView.cpp—*CShowStringView::OnCancelEditCntr()*

```
void CShowStringView::OnCancelEditCntr()
{
    // Close any in-place active item on this view.
    COleClientItem* pActiveItem =
        GetDocument()->GetInPlaceActiveItem(this);
```

```
    if (pActiveItem != NULL)
    {
        pActiveItem->Close();
    }
    ASSERT(GetDocument()->GetInPlaceActiveItem(this) == NULL);
}
```

CShowStringCntrItem   The container item class is a completely new addition to ShowString. It describes an item that is contained in the document. As you've already seen, the document and the view use this object quite a lot, primarily through the m_pSelection member variable of CShowStringView. It has no member variables other than those inherited from the base class, COleClientItem. It has overrides for a lot of functions, though. They are as follows:

- A constructor
- A destructor
- GetDocument()
- GetActiveView()
- OnChange()
- OnActivate()
- OnGetItemPosition()
- OnDeactivateUI()
- OnChangeItemPosition()
- AssertValid()
- Dump()
- Serialize()

The constructor simply passes the document pointer along to the base class. The destructor does nothing. GetDocument() and GetActiveView() are inline functions that return member variables inherited from the base class by calling the base class function with the same name and casting the result.

OnChange() is the first of these functions that has more than one line of code (see Listing 14.17).

Listing 14.17   CntrItem.cpp—*CShowStringCntrItem::OnChange()*

```
void CShowStringCntrItem::OnChange(OLE_NOTIFICATION nCode,
    DWORD dwParam)
{
    ASSERT_VALID(this);

    COleClientItem::OnChange(nCode, dwParam);

    // When an item is being edited (either in-place or fully open)
    //   it sends OnChange notifications for changes in the state of the
    //   item or visual appearance of its content.

    // TODO: invalidate the item by calling UpdateAllViews
    //   (with hints appropriate to your application)

    GetDocument()->UpdateAllViews(NULL);
        // for now just update ALL views/no hints
}
```

Part
IV

Ch

14

Actually, there are only three lines of code. The comments are actually more useful than the code. When the user changes the contained item, the server notifies the container. Calling UpdateAllViews() is a rather drastic way of refreshing the screen, but it gets the job done.

OnActivate() (shown in Listing 14.18) is called when a user double-clicks an item to activate it and edit it in place. ActiveX objects are usually *outside-in*, which means that a single click of the item selects it but doesn't activate it. Activating an outside-in object requires a double-click, or a single click followed by choosing the appropriate OLE verb from the Edit menu.

Listing 14.18   Cntrltem.cpp—*CShowStringCntrltem::OnActivate()*

```
void CShowStringCntrItem::OnActivate()
{
    // Allow only one in-place activate item per frame
    CShowStringView* pView = GetActiveView();
    ASSERT_VALID(pView);
    COleClientItem* pItem = GetDocument()->GetInPlaceActiveItem(pView);
    if (pItem != NULL && pItem != this)
        pItem->Close();

    COleClientItem::OnActivate();
}
```

This code makes sure that the current view is valid, closes the active items, if any, and then activates this item.

OnGetItemPosition() (shown in Listing 14.19) is called as part of the in-place activation process.

Listing 14.19   Cntrltem.cpp—*CShowStringCntrltem::OnGetItemPosition()*

```
void CShowStringCntrItem::OnGetItemPosition(CRect& rPosition)
{
    ASSERT_VALID(this);

    // During in-place activation,
    // CShowStringCntrItem::OnGetItemPosition
    // will be called to determine the location of this item.
    // The default implementation created from AppWizard simply
    // returns a hard-coded rectangle.  Usually, this rectangle
    // would reflect the current position of the item relative
    // to the view used for activation. You can obtain the view
    // by calling CShowStringCntrItem::GetActiveView.

    // TODO: return correct rectangle (in pixels) in rPosition

    rPosition.SetRect(10, 10, 210, 210);
}
```

Like OnChange(), the comments are more useful than the actual code. At the moment, the View's OnDraw() function draws the contained object in a hard-coded rectangle, so this function returns that same rectangle. You are instructed to write code that asks the active view where the object is.

OnDeactivateUI() (see Listing 14.20) is called when the object goes from being active to inactive.

Listing 14.20   CntrItem.cpp—*CShowStringCntrItem::OnDeactivateUI()*

```
void CShowStringCntrItem::OnDeactivateUI(BOOL bUndoable)
{
    COleClientItem::OnDeactivateUI(bUndoable);

    // Hide the object if it is not an outside-in object
    DWORD dwMisc = 0;
    m_lpObject->GetMiscStatus(GetDrawAspect(), &dwMisc);
    if (dwMisc & OLEMISC_INSIDEOUT)
        DoVerb(OLEIVERB_HIDE, NULL);
}
```

Although the default behavior for contained objects is outside-in, as discussed earlier, you can write *inside-out objects*. These are activated simply by moving the mouse pointer over them; clicking the object has the same effect that clicking that region has while editing the object. For example, if the contained item is a spreadsheet, clicking might select the cell that was clicked. This can be really nice for the user, who can completely ignore the borders between the container and the contained item, but it is harder to write.

OnChangeItemPosition() is called when the item is moved during in-place editing. It, too, contains mostly comments, as shown in Listing 14.21.

Listing 14.21   CntrItem.cpp—*CShowStringCntrItem::OnChangeItemPosition()*

```
BOOL CShowStringCntrItem::OnChangeItemPosition(const CRect& rectPos)
{
    ASSERT_VALID(this);

    // During in-place activation
    // CShowStringCntrItem::OnChangeItemPosition
    // is called by the server to change the position
    // of the in-place window.  Usually, this is a result
    // of the data in the server document changing such that
    // the extent has changed or as a result of in-place resizing.
    //
    // The default here is to call the base class, which will call
    //  COleClientItem::SetItemRects to move the item
    //  to the new position.
```

Part
IV

Ch

14

continues

Listing 14.21 Continued

```
    if (!COleClientItem::OnChangeItemPosition(rectPos))
        return FALSE;

    // TODO: update any cache you may have of the item's rectangle/extent

    return TRUE;
}
```

This code is supposed to handle moving the object, but it doesn't really. That's because OnDraw() always draws the contained item in the same place.

AssertValid() is a debug function that confirms this object is valid; if it's not, an ASSERT will fail. ASSERT statements are discussed in Chapter 24, "Improving Your Application's Performance." The last function in CShowStringCntrItem is Serialize(), which is called by COleDocument::Serialize(), which in turn is called by the document's Serialize(), as you've already seen. It is shown in Listing 14.22.

Listing 14.22 CntrItem.cpp—*CShowStringCntrItem::Serialize()*

```
void CShowStringCntrItem::Serialize(CArchive& ar)
{
    ASSERT_VALID(this);

    // Call base class first to read in COleClientItem data.
    // Because this sets up the m_pDocument pointer returned from
 //   CShowStringCntrItem::GetDocument, it is a good idea to call
    //   the base class Serialize first.
    COleClientItem::Serialize(ar);

    // now store/retrieve data specific to CShowStringCntrItem
    if (ar.IsStoring())
    {
        // TODO: add storing code here
    }
    else
    {
        // TODO: add loading code here
    }
}
```

All this code does at the moment is call the base class function. COleDocument::Serialize() stores or loads a number of counters and numbers to keep track of several different contained items, and then calls helper functions such as WriteItem() or ReadItem() to actually deal with the item. These functions and the helper functions they call are a bit too "behind-the-scenes" for most people, but if you'd like to take a look at them, they are in the MFC source folder (C:\Program Files\Microsoft Visual Studio\VC98\MFC\SRC on many installations) in the file olecli1.cpp. They do their job, which is to serialize the contained item for you.

Shortcomings of This Container   This container application isn't ShowString yet, of course, but it has more important things wrong with it. It isn't a very good container, and that's a direct result of all those TODO tasks that haven't been accomplished. Still, the fact that it is a functioning container is a good measure of the power of the MFC classes COleDocument and COleClientItem. So why not build the application now and run it? After it's running, choose Edit, Insert New Object and insert a bitmap image. Now that you've seen the code, it shouldn't be a surprise that Paint is immediately launched to edit the item in place, as you see in Figure 14.7.

FIG. 14.7

The boilerplate container can contain items and activate them for in-place editing, like this bitmap image being edited in Paint.

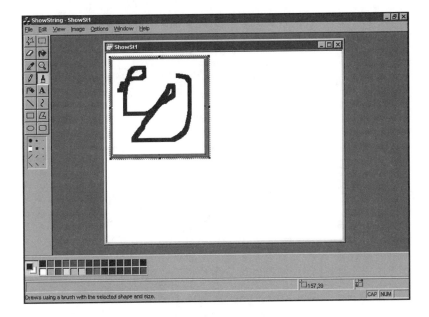

Click outside the bitmap to deselect the item and return control to the container; you see that nothing happens. Click outside the document, and again nothing happens. You're probably asking yourself, "Am I still in ShowString?" Choose File, New, and you see that you are. The Paint menus and toolbars go away, and a new ShowString document is created. Click the bitmap item again, and you are still editing it in Paint. How can you insert another object into the first document when the menus are those of Paint? Press Esc to cancel in-place editing so the menus become ShowString menus again. Insert an Excel chart into the container, and the bitmap disappears as the new Excel chart is inserted, as shown in Figure 14.8. Obviously, this container leaves a lot to be desired.

Press Esc to cancel the in-place editing, and notice that the view changes a little, as shown in Figure 14.9. That's because CShowStringView::OnDraw() draws the contained item in a 200×200 pixel rectangle, so the chart has to be squeezed a little to fit into that space. It is the server—Excel, in this case—that decides how to fit the item into the space given to it by the container.

Part

IV

Ch

14

FIG. 14.8

Inserting an Excel chart gets you a default chart, but it completely covers the old bitmap.

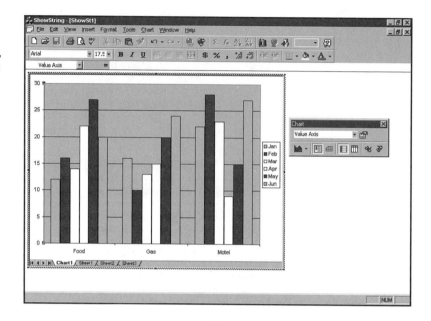

FIG. 14.9

Items can look quite different when they are not active.

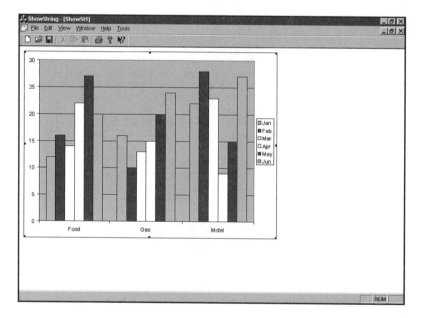

As you can see, there's a lot to be done to make this feel like a real container. But first, you have to turn it back into ShowString.

Returning the ShowString Functionality

This section provides a quick summary of the steps presented in Chapter 8, "Building a Complete Application: ShowString." Open the files from the old ShowString as you go so that you can copy code and resources wherever possible. Follow these steps:

1. In ShowStringDoc.h, add the private member variables and public Get functions to the class.

2. In CShowStringDoc::Serialize(), paste the code that saves or restores these member variables. Leave the call to COleDocument::Serialize() in place.

3. In CShowStringDoc::OnNewDocument(), paste the code that initializes the member variables.

4. In CShowStringView::OnDraw(), add the code that draws the string before the code that handles the contained items. Remove the TODO task about drawing native data.

5. Copy the Tools menu from the old ShowString to the new container ShowString. Choose File, Open to open the old ShowString.rc, open the IDR_SHOWSTTYPE menu, click the Tools menu, and choose Edit, Copy. Open the new ShowString's IDR_SHOWSTTYPE menu, click the Window menu, and choose Edit, Paste. Don't paste it into the IDR_SHOWSTTYPE_CNTR_IP menu.

6. Add the accelerator Ctrl+T for ID_TOOLS_OPTIONS as described in Chapter 8, "Building a Complete Application: ShowString." Add it to the IDR_MAINFRAME accelerator only.

7. Delete the IDD_ABOUTBOX dialog box from the new ShowString. Copy IDD_ABOUTBOX and IDD_OPTIONS from the old ShowString to the new.

8. While IDD_OPTIONS has focus, choose View, Class Wizard. Create the COptionsDialog class as in the original ShowString.

9. Use the Class Wizard to connect the dialog controls to COptionsDialog member variables, as described in Chapter 10.

10. Use the Class Wizard to arrange for CShowStringDoc to catch the ID_TOOLS_OPTIONS command.

11. In ShowStringDoc.cpp, replace the Class Wizard version of CShowStringDoc::OnToolsOptions() with the OnToolsOptions() from the old ShowString, which puts up the dialog box.

12. In ShowStringDoc.cpp, add **#include "OptionsDialog.h"** after the #include statements already present.

Build the application, fix any typos or other simple errors, and then execute it. It should run as before, saying Hello, world! in the center of the view. Convince yourself that the Options dialog box still works and that you have restored all the old functionality. Then resize the application and the view as large as possible, so that when you insert an object it doesn't land on the string. Insert an Excel chart as before, and press Esc to stop editing in place. There you have it: A version of ShowString that is also an ActiveX container. Now it's time to get to work making it a *good* container.

Part

IV

Ch

14

Moving, Resizing, and Tracking

The first task you want to do, even when there is only one item contained in ShowString, is to allow the user to move and resize that item. It makes life simpler for the user if you also provide a *tracker rectangle*, a hashed line around the contained item. This is easy to do with the MFC class CRectTracker.

The first step is to add a member variable to the container item (CShowStringCntrItem) definition in CntrItem.h, to hold the rectangle occupied by this container item. Right-click CShowStringCntrItem in ClassView and choose Add Member Variable. The variable type is CRect, the declaration is m_rect; leave the access public.

m_rect needs to be initialized in a function that is called when the container item is first used and then never again. Whereas view classes have OnInitialUpdate() and document classes have OnNewDocument(), container item classes have no such called-only-once function except the constructor. Initialize the rectangle in the constructor, as shown in Listing 14.23.

Listing 14.23   CntrItem.cpp—*Constructor*

```
CShowStringCntrItem::CShowStringCntrItem(CShowStringDoc* pContainer)
    : COleClientItem(pContainer)
{
    m_rect = CRect(10,10,210,210);
}
```

The numerical values used here are those in the boilerplate OnDraw() provided by AppWizard. Now you need to start using the m rect member variable and setting it. The functions affected are presented in the same order as in the earlier section, CShowStringView.

First, change CShowStringView::OnDraw(). Find this line:

```
    m_pSelection->Draw(pDC, CRect(10, 10, 210, 210));
```

Replace it with this:

```
    m_pSelection->Draw(pDC, m_pSelection->m_rect);
```

Next, change CShowStringCntrItem::OnGetItemPosition(), which needs to return this rectangle. Take away all the comments and the old hardcoded rectangle (leave the ASSERT_VALID macro call), and add this line:

```
    rPosition = m_rect;
```

The partner function

```
CShowStringCntrItem::OnChangeItemPosition()
```

is called when the user moves the item. This is where `m_rect` is changed from the initial value. Remove the comments and add code immediately after the call to the base class function, `COleClientItem::OnChangeItemPosition()`. The code to add is:

```
    m_rect = rectPos;
    GetDocument()->SetModifiedFlag();
    GetDocument()->UpdateAllViews(NULL);
```

Finally, the new member variable needs to be incorporated into `CShowStringCntrItem::Serialize()`. Remove the comments and add lines in the storing and saving blocks so that the function looks like Listing 14.24.

Listing 14.24   CntrItem.cpp—*CShowStringCntrItem::Serialize()*

```
void CShowStringCntrItem::Serialize(CArchive& ar)
{
    ASSERT_VALID(this);

    // Call base class first to read in COleClientItem data.
    // Because this sets up the m_pDocument pointer returned from
    // CShowStringCntrItem::GetDocument, it is a good idea to call
    // the base class Serialize first.
    COleClientItem::Serialize(ar);

    // now store/retrieve data specific to CShowStringCntrItem
    if (ar.IsStoring())
    {
        ar << m_rect;
    }
    else
    {
        ar >> m_rect;
    }
}
```

Build and execute the application, insert a bitmap, and scribble something in it. Press Esc to cancel editing in place, and your scribble shows up in the top-right corner, next to `Hello, world!`. Choose Edit, Bitmap Image Object and then Edit. (Choosing Open allows you to edit it in a different window.) Use the resizing handles that appear to drag the image over to the left, and then press Esc to cancel in-place editing. The image is drawn at the new position, as expected.

Now for the tracker rectangle. The Microsoft tutorials recommend writing a helper function, `SetupTracker()`, to handle this. Add these lines to `CShowStringView::OnDraw()`, just after the call to `m_pSelection->Draw()`:

```
        CRectTracker trackrect;
        SetupTracker(m_pSelection,&trackrect);
        trackrect.Draw(pDC);
```

CAUTION

The one-line statement after the `if` was not in brace brackets before; don't forget to add them. The entire `if` statement should look like this:

```
if (m_pSelection != NULL)
{
    m_pSelection->Draw(pDC, m_pSelection->m_rect);
    CRectTracker trackrect;
    SetupTracker(m_pSelection,&trackrect);
    trackrect.Draw(pDC);
}
```

Add the following public function to ShowStringView.h (inside the class definition):

```
void SetupTracker(CShowStringCntrItem* item,
CRectTracker* track);
```

Add the code in Listing 14.25 to ShowStringView.cpp immediately after the destructor.

Listing 14.25   ShowStringView.cpp—*CShowStringView::SetupTracker()*

```
void CShowStringView::SetupTracker(CShowStringCntrItem* item,
    CRectTracker* track)
{
    track->m_rect = item->m_rect;

    if (item == m_pSelection)
    {
        track->m_nStyle |= CRectTracker::resizeInside;
    }

    if (item->GetType() == OT_LINK)
    {
        track->m_nStyle |= CRectTracker::dottedLine;
    }
    else
    {
        track->m_nStyle |= CRectTracker::solidLine;
    }
    if (item->GetItemState() == COleClientItem::openState ||
        item->GetItemState() == COleClientItem::activeUIState)
    {
        track->m_nStyle |= CRectTracker::hatchInside;
    }
}
```

This code first sets the tracker rectangle to the container item rectangle. Then it adds styles to the tracker. The styles available are as follows:

- `solidLine`—Used for an embedded item.
- `dottedLine`—Used for a linked item.

- ■ `hatchedBorder`—Used for an in-place active item.
- ■ `resizeInside`—Used for a selected item.
- ■ `resizeOutside`—Used for a selected item.
- ■ `hatchInside`—Used for an item whose server is open.

This code first compares the pointers to this item and the current selection. If they are the same, this item is selected and it gets resize handles. It's up to you whether these handles go on the inside or the outside. Then this code asks the item whether it is linked (dotted line) or not (solid line.) Finally, it adds hatching to active items.

Build and execute the application, and try it out. You still cannot edit the contained item by double-clicking it; choose Edit from the cascading menu added at the bottom of the Edit menu. You can't move and resize an inactive object, but if you activate it, you can resize it while active. Also, when you press Esc, the inactive object is drawn at its new position.

Handling Multiple Objects and Object Selection

The next step is to catch mouse clicks and double-clicks so that the item can be resized, moved, and activated more easily. This involves testing to see whether a click is on a contained item.

Hit Testing

You need to write a helper function that returns a pointer to the contained item that the user clicked, or NULL if the user clicked an area of the view that has no contained item. This function runs through all the items contained in the document. Add the code in Listing 14.26 to ShowStringView.cpp immediately after the destructor.

Listing 14.26   ShowStringView.cpp—*CShowStringView::SetupTracker()*

```
CShowStringCntrItem* CShowStringView::HitTest(CPoint point)
{
    CShowStringDoc* pDoc = GetDocument();
    CShowStringCntrItem* pHitItem = NULL;

    POSITION pos = pDoc->GetStartPosition();
    while (pos)
    {
        CShowStringCntrItem* pCurrentItem =
            (CShowStringCntrItem*) pDoc->GetNextClientItem(pos);
        if ( pCurrentItem->m_rect.PtInRect(point) )
        {
            pHitItem = pCurrentItem;
        }
    }

    return pHitItem;
}
```

Part

IV

Ch

14

T I P   Don't forget to add the declaration of this public function to the header file.

This function is given a CPoint that describes the point on the screen where the user clicked. Each container item has a rectangle, m_rect, as you saw earlier, and the CRect class has a member function called PtInRect() that takes a CPoint and returns TRUE if the point is in the rectangle or FALSE if it is not. This code simply loops through the items in this document, using the OLE document member function GetNextClientItem(), and calls PtInRect() for each.

What happens if there are several items in the container, and the user clicks at a point where two or more overlap? The one on top is selected. That's because GetStartPosition() returns a pointer to the bottom item, and GetNextClientItem() works its way up through the items. If two items cover the spot where the user clicked, pHitItem is set to the lower one first, and then on a later iteration of the while loop, it is set to the higher one. The pointer to the higher item is returned.

Drawing Multiple Items

While that code to loop through all the items is still fresh in your mind, why not fix CShowStringView::OnDraw() so it draws all the items? Leave all the code that draws the string, and replace the code in Listing 14.27 with that in Listing 14.28.

Listing 14.27   ShowStringView.cpp—Lines in _OnDraw()_ to Replace

```
// Draw the selection at an arbitrary position.  This code should
// be removed once your real drawing code is implemented.  This
// position corresponds exactly to the rectangle returned by
// CShowStringCntrItem, to give the effect of in-place editing.

// TODO: remove this code when final draw code is complete.

if (m_pSelection == NULL)
{
    POSITION pos = pDoc->GetStartPosition();
    m_pSelection = (CShowStringCntrItem*)pDoc->GetNextClientItem(pos);
}
if (m_pSelection != NULL)
{
    m_pSelection->Draw(pDC, m_pSelection->m_rect);
    CRectTracker trackrect;
    SetupTracker(m_pSelection,&trackrect);
    trackrect.Draw(pDC);
}
```

Listing 14.28   ShowStringView.cpp—New Lines in *OnDraw()*

```
POSITION pos = pDoc->GetStartPosition();
while (pos)
{
    CShowStringCntrItem* pCurrentItem =
        (CShowStringCntrItem*) pDoc->GetNextClientItem(pos);
    pCurrentItem->Draw(pDC, pCurrentItem->m_rect);

    if (pCurrentItem == m_pSelection )
    {
        CRectTracker trackrect;
        SetupTracker(pCurrentItem,&trackrect);
        trackrect.Draw(pDC);
    }
}
```

Now each item is drawn, starting from the bottom and working up, and if it is selected, it gets a tracker rectangle.

Handling Single Clicks

When the user clicks the client area of the application, a `WM_LBUTTONDOWN` message is sent. This message should be caught by the view. Right-click `CShowStringView` in ClassView, and choose Add Windows Message Handler from the shortcut menu. Click `WM_LBUTTONDOWN` in the New Windows Messages/Events box on the left (see Figure 14.10), and then click Add and Edit to add a handler function and edit the code immediately.

FIG. 14.10

Add a function to handle left mouse button clicks.

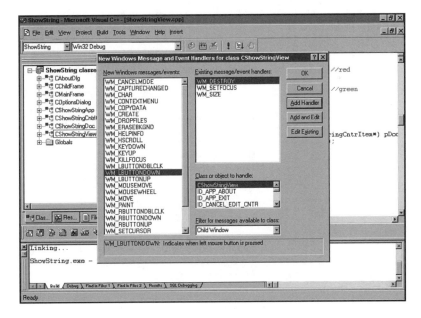

Add the code in Listing 14.29 to the empty OnLButtonDown() that Add Windows Message Handler generated.

Listing 14.29   ShowStringView.cpp—*CShowStringView::OnLButtonDown()*

```
void CShowStringView::OnLButtonDown(UINT nFlags, CPoint point)
{
    CShowStringCntrItem* pHitItem = HitTest(point);
    SetSelection(pHitItem);
    if (pHitItem == NULL)
        return;

    CRectTracker track;
    SetupTracker(pHitItem, &track);
    UpdateWindow();
    if (track.Track(this,point))
        {
            Invalidate();
            pHitItem->m_rect = track.m_rect;
            GetDocument()->SetModifiedFlag();
        }
}
```

This code determines which item has been selected and sets it. (SetSelection() isn't written yet.) Then, if something has been selected, it draws a tracker rectangle around it and calls CRectTracker::Track(), which allows the user to resize the rectangle. After the resizing, the item is sized to match the tracker rectangle and is redrawn.

SetSelection() is pretty straightforward. Add the definition of this public member function to the header file, ShowStringView.h, and the code in Listing 14.30 to ShowStringView.cpp.

Listing 14.30   ShowStringView.cpp—*CShowStringView::SetSelection()*

```
void CShowStringView::SetSelection(CShowStringCntrItem* item)
{
    // if an item is being edited in place, close it
    if ( item == NULL || item != m_pSelection)
    {
        COleClientItem* pActive =
            GetDocument()->GetInPlaceActiveItem(this);
        if (pActive != NULL && pActive != item)
        {
            pActive->Close();
        }
    }
    Invalidate();
    m_pSelection = item;
}
```

When the selection is changed, any item that is being edited in place should be closed. `SetSelection()` checks that the item passed in represents a change, and then gets the active object from the document and closes that object. Then it calls for a redraw and sets `m_pSelection`. Build and execute ShowString, insert an object, and press Esc to stop in-place editing. Click and drag to move the inactive object, and insert another. You should see something like Figure 14.11. Notice the resizing handles around the bitmap, indicating that it is selected.

FIG. 14.11

ShowString can now hold multiple items, and the user can move and resize them intuitively.

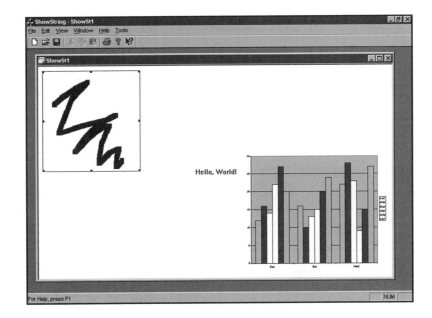

You might have noticed that the cursor doesn't change as you move or resize. That's because you didn't tell it to. Luckily, it's easy to tell it this: `CRectTracker` has a `SetCursor()` member function, and all you need to do is call it when a `WM_SETCURSOR` message is sent. Again, it should be the view that catches this message; right-click `CShowStringView` in ClassView, and choose Add Windows Message Handler from the shortcut menu. Click `WM_SETCURSOR` in the New Windows Messages/Events box on the left; then click Add and Edit to add a handler function and edit the code immediately. Add the code in Listing 14.31 to the empty function that was generated for you.

Listing 14.31   ShowStringView.cpp—*CShowStringView::OnSetCursor()*

```
BOOL CShowStringView::OnSetCursor(CWnd* pWnd, UINT nHitTest,
    UINT message)
{
    if (pWnd == this && m_pSelection != NULL)
    {
        CRectTracker track;
```

continues

Part
IV

Ch
14

Listing 14.31 Continued

```
        SetupTracker(m_pSelection, &track);
        if (track.SetCursor(this, nHitTest))
        {
            return TRUE;
        }
    }

    return CView::OnSetCursor(pWnd, nHitTest, message);
}
```

This code does nothing unless the cursor change involves this view and there is a selection. It gives the tracking rectangle's SetCursor() function a chance to change the cursor because the tracking object knows where the rectangle is and whether the cursor is over a boundary or sizing handle. If SetCursor() didn't change the cursor, this code lets the base class handle it. Build and execute ShowString, and you should see cursors that give you feedback as you move and resize.

Handling Double-Clicks

When a user double-clicks a contained item, the *primary verb* should be called. For most objects, the primary verb is to Edit in place, but for some, such as sound files, it is Play. Arrange as before for CShowStringView to catch the WM_LBUTTONDBLCLK message, and add the code in Listing 14.32 to the new function.

Listing 14.32 ShowStringView.cpp—*CShowStringView::OnLButtonDblClk()*

```
void CShowStringView::OnLButtonDblClk(UINT nFlags, CPoint point)
{
    OnLButtonDown(nFlags, point);

    if( m_pSelection)
    {
        if (GetKeyState(VK_CONTROL) < 0)
        {
            m_pSelection->DoVerb(OLEIVERB_OPEN, this);
        }
        else
        {
            m_pSelection->DoVerb(OLEIVERB_PRIMARY, this);
        }
    }

    CView::OnLButtonDblClk(nFlags, point);
}
```

First, this function handles the fact that this item has been clicked; calling OnLButtonDown() draws the tracker rectangle, sets m_pSelection, and so on. Then, if the user holds down Ctrl while double-clicking, the item is opened; otherwise, the primary verb is called. Finally, the base class function is called. Build and execute ShowString and try double-clicking. Insert an object, press Esc to stop editing it, move it, resize it, and double-click it to edit in place.

Implementing Drag and Drop

The last step to make ShowString a completely up-to-date ActiveX container application is to implement drag and drop. The user should be able to grab a contained item and drag it out of the container, or hold down Ctrl while dragging to drag out a copy and leave the original behind. The user should also be able to drag items from elsewhere and drop them into this container just as though they had been inserted through the Clipboard. In other words, the container should operate as a *drag source* and a *drop target*.

Implementing a Drag Source

Because CShowStringCntrItem inherits from COleClientItem, implementing a drag source is really easy. By clicking a contained object, edit these lines at the end of CShowStringView::OnLButtonDown() so that it resembles Listing 14.33. The new lines are in bold type.

Listing 14.33 *CShowStringView::OnLButtonDown()*—Implementing a Drag Source

```
void CShowStringView::OnLButtonDown(UINT nFlags, CPoint point)
{
    CShowStringCntrItem* pHitItem = HitTest(point);
    SetSelection(pHitItem);
    if (pHitItem == NULL)
        return;

    CRectTracker track;
    SetupTracker(pHitItem, &track);
    UpdateWindow();

    if (track.HitTest(point) == CRectTracker::hitMiddle)
    {
        CRect rect =  pHitItem->m_rect;
        CClientDC dc(this);
        OnPrepareDC(&dc);
        dc.LPtoDP(&rect); // convert logical rect to device rect
        rect.NormalizeRect();
        CPoint newpoint = point - rect.TopLeft();

        DROPEFFECT dropEffect = pHitItem->DoDragDrop(rect, newpoint);
        if (dropEffect == DROPEFFECT_MOVE)
        {
            Invalidate();
            if (pHitItem == m_pSelection)
            {
```

Part

IV

Ch

14

continues

Listing 14.33 Continued

```
                m_pSelection = NULL;
            }
            pHitItem->Delete();
        }
    }
    else
    {
        if (track.Track(this,point))
        {
            Invalidate();
            pHitItem->m_rect = track.m_rect;
            GetDocument()->SetModifiedFlag();
        }
    }
}
```

This code first confirms that the mouse click was inside the tracking rectangle, rather than on the sizing border. It sets up a temporary CRect object that will be passed to DoDragDrop() after some coordinate scheme conversions are complete. The first conversion is from logical to device units, and is accomplished with a call to CDC::LPtoDP(). In order to call this function, the new code must create a temporary device context based on the CShowStringView for which OnLButtonDown() is being called. Having converted rect to device units, the new code normalizes it and calculates the point within the rectangle where the user clicked.

Then the new code calls the DoDragDrop() member function of CShowStringCntrItem, inherited from COleClientItem and not overridden. It passes in the converted rect and the offset of the click. If DoDragDrop() returns DROPEFFECT_MOVE, the item was moved and needs to be deleted. The code to handle a drop, which is not yet written, will create a new container item and set it as the current selection. This means that if the object was dropped elsewhere in the container, the current selection will no longer be equal to the hit item. If these two pointers are still equal, the object must have been dragged away. If it was dragged away, this code sets m_pSelection to NULL. In either case, pHitItem should be deleted.

Build and execute ShowString, insert a new object, press Esc to stop editing in place, and then drag the inactive object to an ActiveX container application such as Microsoft Excel. You can also try dragging to the desktop. Be sure to try dragging an object down to the taskbar and pausing over the icon of a minimized container application, and then waiting while the application is restored so that you can drop the object.

Implementing a Drop Target

It is harder to make ShowString a drop target (it could hardly be easier). If you dragged a contained item out of ShowString and dropped it into another container, try dragging that item back into ShowString. The cursor changes to a circle with a slash through it, meaning "you can't drop that here." In this section, you make the necessary code changes that allow you to drop it there after all.

You need to register your view as a place where items can be dropped. Next, you need to handle the following four events that can occur:

- An item might be dragged across the boundaries of your view. This action will require a cursor change or other indication you will take the item.

- In the view, the item will be dragged around within your boundaries, and you should give the user feedback about that process.

- That item might be dragged out of the window again, having just passed over your view on the way to its final destination.

- The user may drop the item in your view.

Registering the View as a Drop Target

To register the view as a drop target, add a `COleDropTarget` member variable to the view. In ShowStringView.h, add this line to the class definition:

```
COleDropTarget m_droptarget;
```

To handle registration, override `OnCreate()` for the view, which is called when the view is created. Arrange for `CShowStringView` to catch the `WM_CREATE` message. Add the code in Listing 14.34 to the empty function generated for you.

Listing 14.34   ShowStringView.cpp—*CShowStringView::OnCreate()*

```
int CShowStringView::OnCreate(LPCREATESTRUCT lpCreateStruct)
{
    if (CView::OnCreate(lpCreateStruct) == -1)
        return -1;

    if (m_droptarget.Register(this))
    {
        return 0;
    }
    else
    {
        return -1;
    }
}
```

`OnCreate()` returns `0` if everything is going well and `-1` if the window should be destroyed. This code calls the base class function and then uses `COleDropTarget::Register()` to register this view as a place to drop items.

Setting Up Function Skeletons and Adding Member Variables

The four events that happen in your view correspond to four virtual functions you must override: `OnDragEnter()`, `OnDragOver()`, `OnDragLeave()`, and `OnDrop()`. Right-click `CShowStringView` in ClassView and choose Add Virtual Function to add overrides of these functions. Highlight OnDragEnter() in the New Virtual Functions list, click Add Handler, and repeat for the other three functions.

OnDragEnter() sets up a *focus rectangle* that shows the user where the item would go if it were dropped here. This is maintained and drawn by OnDragOver(). But first, a number of member variables related to the focus rectangle must be added to CShowStringView. Add these lines to ShowStringView.h, in the public section:

```
CPoint m_dragpoint;
CSize m_dragsize;
CSize m_dragoffset;
```

A data object contains a great deal of information about itself, in various formats. There is, of course, the actual data as text, *device independent bitmap (DIB)*, or whatever other format is appropriate. But there is also information about the object itself. If you request data in the Object Descriptor format, you can find out the size of the item and where on the item the user originally clicked, and the offset from the mouse to the upper-left corner of the item. These formats are generally referred to as *Clipboard formats* because they were originally used for Cut and Paste via the Clipboard.

To ask for this information, call the data object's GetGlobalData() member function, passing it a parameter that means "Object Descriptor, please." Rather than build this parameter from a string every time, you build it once and store it in a static member of the class. When a class has a static member variable, every instance of the class looks at the same memory location to see that variable. It is initialized (and memory is allocated for it) once, outside the class.

Add this line to ShowStringView.h:

```
static CLIPFORMAT m_cfObjectDescriptorFormat;
```

In ShowStringView.cpp, just before the first function, add these lines:

```
CLIPFORMAT CShowStringView::m_cfObjectDescriptorFormat =
    (CLIPFORMAT) ::RegisterClipboardFormat("Object Descriptor");
```

This makes a CLIPFORMAT from the string "Object Descriptor" and saves it in the static member variable for all instances of this class to use. Using a static member variable speeds up dragging over your view.

Your view doesn't accept any and all items that are dropped on it. Add a BOOL member variable to the view that indicates whether it accepts the item that is now being dragged over it:

```
BOOL m_OKtodrop;
```

There is one last member variable to add to CShowStringView. As the item is dragged across the view, a focus rectangle is repeatedly drawn and erased. Add another BOOL member variable that tracks the status of the focus rectangle:

```
BOOL m_FocusRectangleDrawn;
```

Initialize m_FocusRectangleDrawn, in the view constructor, to FALSE:

```
CShowStringView::CShowStringView()
{
```

```
        m_pSelection = NULL;
        m_FocusRectangleDrawn = FALSE;
}
```

OnDragEnter()

OnDragEnter() is called when the user first drags an item over the boundary of the view. It sets up the focus rectangle and then calls OnDragOver(). As the item continues to move, OnDragOver() is called repeatedly until the user drags the item out of the view or drops it in the view. The overall structure of OnDragEnter() is shown in Listing 14.35.

Listing 14.35   ShowStringView.cpp—*CShowStringView::OnDragEnter()*

```
DROPEFFECT CShowStringView::OnDragEnter(COleDataObject* pDataObject,
    DWORD dwKeyState, CPoint point)
{
    ASSERT(!m_FocusRectangleDrawn);

    // check that the data object can be dropped in this view
    // set dragsize and dragoffset with call to GetGlobalData
    // convert sizes with a scratch dc
    // hand off to OnDragOver
    return OnDragOver(pDataObject, dwKeyState, point);
}
```

First, check that whatever pDataObject carries is something from which you can make a COleClientItem (and therefore a CShowsStringCntrItem). If not, the object cannot be dropped here, and you return DROPEFFECT_NONE, as shown in Listing 14.36.

Listing 14.36   ShowStringView.cpp—Can the Object Be Dropped?

```
    // check that the data object can be dropped in this view
    m_OKtodrop = FALSE;
    if (!COleClientItem::CanCreateFromData(pDataObject))
        return DROPEFFECT_NONE;

    m_OKtodrop = TRUE;
```

Now the weird stuff starts. The GetGlobalData() member function of the data item that is being dragged into this view is called to get the object descriptor information mentioned earlier. It returns a handle of a global memory block. Then the SDK function GlobalLock() is called to convert the handle into a pointer to the first byte of the block and to prevent any other object from allocating the block. This is cast to a pointer to an object descriptor structure (the undyingly curious can check about 2,000 lines into oleidl.h, in the \Program Files\Microsoft Visual Studio\VC98\Include folder for most installations, to see the members of this structure) so that the sizel and pointl elements can be used to fill the \m_dragsize and m_dragoffset member variables.

T I P That is not a number 1 at the end of those structure elements, but a lowercase letter L. The elements of the `sizel` structure are cx and cy, but the elements of the `pointl` structure are x and y. Don't get carried away cutting and pasting.

Finally, `GlobalUnlock()` reverses the effects of `GlobalLock()`, making the block accessible to others, and `GlobalFree()` frees the memory. It ends up looking like Listing 14.37.

Listing 14.37   ShowStringView.cpp—Set *dragsize* and *dragoffset*

```
// set dragsize and dragoffset with call to GetGlobalData
HGLOBAL hObjectDescriptor = pDataObject->GetGlobalData(
    m_cfObjectDescriptorFormat);
if (hObjectDescriptor)
{
    LPOBJECTDESCRIPTOR pObjectDescriptor =
        (LPOBJECTDESCRIPTOR) GlobalLock(hObjectDescriptor);
    ASSERT(pObjectDescriptor);
    m_dragsize.cx = (int) pObjectDescriptor->sizel.cx;
    m_dragsize.cy = (int) pObjectDescriptor->sizel.cy;
    m_dragoffset.cx = (int) pObjectDescriptor->pointl.x;
    m_dragoffset.cy = (int) pObjectDescriptor->pointl.y;
    GlobalUnlock(hObjectDescriptor);
    GlobalFree(hObjectDescriptor);
}
else
{
    m_dragsize = CSize(0,0);
    m_dragoffset = CSize(0,0);
}
```

N O T E Global memory, also called *shared application memory*, is allocated from a different place than the memory available from your process space. It is the memory to use when two different processes need to read and write the same memory, and so it comes into play when using ActiveX.

For some ActiveX operations, global memory is too small—imagine trying to transfer a 40MB file through global memory! There is a more general function than `GetGlobalData()`, called (not surprisingly) `GetData()`, which can transfer the data through a variety of storage medium choices. Because the object descriptors are small, asking for them in global memory is a sensible approach. ■

If the call to `GetGlobalData()` didn't work, set both member variables to zero by zero rectangles. Next, convert those rectangles from OLE coordinates (which are device independent) to pixels:

```
// convert sizes with a scratch dc
    CClientDC dc(NULL);
    dc.HIMETRICtoDP(&m_dragsize);
    dc.HIMETRICtoDP(&m_dragoffset);
```

HIMETRICtoDP() is a very useful function that happens to be a member of CClientDC, which inherits from the familiar CDC of Chapter 5, "Drawing on the Screen." You create an instance of CClientDC just so you can call the function.

OnDragEnter() closes with a call to OnDragOver(), so that's the next function to write.

OnDragOver()

This function returns a DROPEFFECT. As you saw earlier in the "Implementing a Drag Source" section, if you return DROPEFFECT_MOVE, the source deletes the item from itself. Returning DROPEFFECT_NONE rejects the copy. It is OnDragOver() that deals with preparing to accept or reject a drop. The overall structure of the function looks like this:

```
DROPEFFECT CShowStringView::OnDragOver(COleDataObject* pDataObject,
    DWORD dwKeyState, CPoint point)
{
    // return if dropping is already rejected
    // determine drop effect according to keys depressed
    // adjust focus rectangle
}
```

First, check to see whether OnDragEnter() or an earlier call to OnDragOver() already rejected this possible drop:

```
// return if dropping is already rejected
if (!m_OKtodrop)
{
    return DROPEFFECT_NONE;
}
```

Next, look at the keys that the user is holding down now, available in the parameter passed to this function, dwKeyState. The code you need to add (see Listing 14.38) is straightforward.

Listing 14.38 ShowStringView.cpp—Determine the Drop Effect

```
// determine drop effect according to keys depressed
DROPEFFECT dropeffect = DROPEFFECT_NONE;

if ((dwKeyState & (MK_CONTROL¦MK_SHIFT) )
    == (MK_CONTROL¦MK_SHIFT))
{
    // Ctrl+Shift force a link
    dropeffect = DROPEFFECT_LINK;
}

else if ((dwKeyState & MK_CONTROL)     == MK_CONTROL)
{
    // Ctrl forces a copy
    dropeffect = DROPEFFECT_COPY;
}
```

Part
IV

Ch
14

continues

Listing 14.38 Continued

```
else if ((dwKeyState & MK_ALT) == MK_ALT)
{
    // Alt forces a move
    dropeffect = DROPEFFECT_MOVE;
}
else
{
    // default is to move
    dropeffect = DROPEFFECT_MOVE;
}
```

N O T E This code has to be a lot more complex if the document might be smaller than the view, as can happen when you are editing a bitmap in Paint, and especially if the view can scroll. The Microsoft ActiveX container sample, DRAWCLI, (included on the Visual C++ CD) handles these contingencies. Look in the CD folder \Vc98\Samples\Mcl\Mfc\Ole\DrawCli for the file drawvw.cpp and compare that code for `OnDragOver()` to this code.

If the item has moved since the last time `OnDragOver()` was called, the focus rectangle has to be erased and redrawn at the new location. Because the focus rectangle is a simple XOR of the colors, drawing it a second time in the same place removes it. The code to adjust the focus rectangle is in Listing 14.39.

Listing 14.39 ShowStringView.cpp—Adjust the Focus Rectangle

```
// adjust focus rectangle

point -= m_dragoffset;
if (point == m_dragpoint)
{
    return dropeffect;
}

CClientDC dc(this);

if (m_FocusRectangleDrawn)
{
    dc.DrawFocusRect(CRect(m_dragpoint, m_dragsize));
    m_FocusRectangleDrawn = FALSE;
}

if (dropeffect != DROPEFFECT_NONE)
{
    dc.DrawFocusRect(CRect(point, m_dragsize));
    m_dragpoint = point;
    m_FocusRectangleDrawn = TRUE;
}
```

To test whether the focus rectangle should be redrawn, this code adjusts the point where the user clicked by the offset into the item to determine the top-left corner of the item. It can then compare that location to the top-left corner of the focus rectangle. If they are the same, there is no need to redraw it. If they are different, the focus rectangle might need to be erased.

N O T E The first time OnDragOver() is called, m_dragpoint is uninitialized. That doesn't matter because m_FocusRectangleDrawn is FALSE, and an ASSERT in OnDragEnter() guarantees it. When m_FocusRectangleDrawn is set to TRUE, m_dragpoint gets a value at the same time. ■

Finally, replace the return statement that was generated for you with one that returns the calculated DROPEFFECT:

```
return dropeffect;
```

OnDragLeave()

Sometimes a user drags an item right over your view and out the other side. OnDragLeave() just tidies up a little by removing the focus rectangle, as shown in Listing 14.40.

Listing 14.40 ShowStringView.cpp—*ShowStringView::OnDragLeave()*

```
void CShowStringView::OnDragLeave()
{
    CClientDC dc(this);
    if (m_FocusRectangleDrawn)
    {
        dc.DrawFocusRect(CRect(m_dragpoint, m_dragsize));
        m_FocusRectangleDrawn = FALSE;
    }
}
```

OnDragDrop()

If the user lets go of an item that is being dragged over ShowString, the item lands in the container and OnDragDrop() is called. The overall structure is in Listing 14.41.

Listing 14.41 ShowStringView.cpp—Structure of *OnDrop()*

```
BOOL CShowStringView::OnDrop(COleDataObject* pDataObject,
    DROPEFFECT dropEffect, CPoint point)
{
    ASSERT_VALID(this);
    // remove focus rectangle
    // paste in the data object
    // adjust the item dimensions, and make it the current selection
    // update views and set modified flag
    return TRUE;
}
```

Removing the focus rectangle is simple, as shown in Listing 14.42.

Listing 14.42   ShowStringView.cpp—Removing the Focus Rectangle

```
// remove focus rectangle
CClientDC dc(this);
if (m_FocusRectangleDrawn)
{
    dc.DrawFocusRect(CRect(m_dragpoint, m_dragsize));
    m_FocusRectangleDrawn = FALSE;
}
```

Next, create a new item to hold the data object, as shown in Listing 14.43. Note the use of the bitwise and (&) to test for a link.

Listing 14.43   ShowStringView.cpp—Paste the Data Object

```
// paste the data object
CShowStringDoc* pDoc = GetDocument();
CShowStringCntrItem* pNewItem = new CShowStringCntrItem(pDoc);
ASSERT_VALID(pNewItem);
if (dropEffect & DROPEFFECT_LINK)
{
    pNewItem->CreateLinkFromData(pDataObject);
}
else
{
    pNewItem->CreateFromData(pDataObject);
}
ASSERT_VALID(pNewItem);
```

The size of the container item needs to be set, as shown in Listing 14.44.

Listing 14.44   ShowStringView.cpp—Adjust Item Dimensions

```
// adjust the item dimensions, and make it the current selection
CSize size;
pNewItem->GetExtent(&size, pNewItem->GetDrawAspect());
dc.HIMETRICtoDP(&size);
point -= m_dragoffset;
pNewItem->m_rect = CRect(point,size);
m_pSelection = pNewItem;
```

Notice that this code adjusts the place where the user drops the item (point) by m_dragoffset, the coordinates into the item where the user clicked originally.

Finally, make sure the document is saved on exit, because pasting in a new container item changes it, and redraw the view:

```
// update views and set modified flag
pDoc->SetModifiedFlag();
pDoc->UpdateAllViews(NULL);
return TRUE;
```

This function always returns TRUE because there is no error checking at the moment that might require a return of FALSE. Notice, however, that most problems have been prevented; for example, if the data object cannot be used to create a container item, the DROPEFFECT would have been set to DROPEFFECT_NONE in OnDragEnter() and this code would never have been called. You can be confident this code works.

Testing the Drag Target

All the confidence in the world is no substitute for testing. Build and execute ShowString, and try dragging something into it. To test both the drag source and drop target aspects at once, drag something out and then drag it back in. Now this is starting to become a really useful container. There's only one task left to do.

Deleting an Object

You can remove an object from your container by dragging it away somewhere, but it makes sense to implement deleting in a more obvious and direct way. The menu item generally used for this is Edit, Delete, so you start by adding this item to the IDR_SHOWSTTYPE menu before the Insert New Object item. Don't let Developer Studio set the ID to ID_EDIT_DELETE; instead, change it to ID_EDIT_CLEAR, the traditional resource ID for the command that deletes a contained object. Move to another menu item and then return to Edit, Delete, and you see that the prompt has been filled in for you as Erase the selection\nErase automatically.

The view needs to handle this command, so add a message handler as you have done throughout this chapter. Follow these steps:

1. Right-click CShowStringView in ClassView and choose Add Windows Message Handler.
2. Choose ID_EDIT_CLEAR from the Class or Object to Handle drop-down box at the lower right.
3. Choose COMMAND from the New Windows Messages/Events box that appears when you click the ID_EDIT_CLEAR box.
4. Click Add Handler.
5. Click OK to accept the suggested name.
6. Choose UPDATE_COMMAND_UI from the New Windows Messages/Events box and click Add Handler again.
7. Accept the suggested name.
8. Click OK on the large dialog to complete the process.

The code for these two handlers is very simple. Because the update handler is simpler, add code to it first:

Part

IV

Ch

14

```
void CShowStringView::OnUpdateEditClear(CCmdUI* pCmdUI)
{
    pCmdUI->Enable(m_pSelection != NULL);
}
```

If there is a current selection, it can be deleted. If there is not a current selection, the menu item is disabled (grayed). The code to handle the command isn't much longer: it's in Listing 14.45.

Listing 14.45   ShowStringView.cpp—*CShowStringView::OnEditClear()*

```
void CShowStringView::OnEditClear()
{
    if (m_pSelection)
    {
        m_pSelection->Delete();
        m_pSelection = NULL;
        GetDocument()->SetModifiedFlag();
        GetDocument()->UpdateAllViews(NULL);
    }
}
```

This code checks that there is a selection (even though the menu item is grayed when there is no selection) and then deletes it, sets it to NULL so that there is no longer a selection, makes sure the document is marked as modified so that the user is prompted to save it when exiting, and gets the view redrawn without the deleted object.

Build and execute ShowString, insert something, and delete it by choosing Edit, Delete. Now it's an intuitive container that does what you expect a container to do. ●

Building an ActiveX Server Application

Just as AppWizard builds ActiveX containers, it also builds ActiveX servers. However, unlike containers, the AppWizard code is complete, so there isn't much work to do for improving the AppWizard code. This chapter builds a version of ShowString that is only a server and discusses how to build another version that is both a container and a server. You also learn about ActiveX documents and how they can be used in other applications.

Adding Server Capabilities to ShowString

Like Chapter 14, "Building an ActiveX Container Application," this chapter starts by building an ordinary server application with AppWizard and then adds the functionality that makes it ShowString. This is far quicker than adding ActiveX functionality to ShowString because ShowString doesn't have much code and can be written quickly.

AppWizard's Server Boilerplate

Build the new ShowString in a different directory, making almost exactly the same AppWizard choices as when you built versions of ShowString in Chapter 8, "Building a Complete Application: ShowString," and Chapter 14. Call it ShowString, and choose an MDI application with no database support. In AppWizard's Step 3, select full server as your compound document support. This enables the check box for ActiveX document support. Leave this deselected for now. Later in this chapter you see the consequences of selecting this option. Continue the AppWizard process, selecting a docking toolbar, initial status bar, printing and print preview, context sensitive Help, and 3D controls. Finally, select source file comments and a shared DLL. Finish AppWizard and, if you want, build the project.

> **N O T E**   Even though the technology is now called ActiveX, the AppWizard dialog boxes refer to compound document support. Many of the class names that are used throughout this chapter have Ole in their names as well. Although Microsoft has changed the name of the technology, it has not propagated that change throughout Visual C++ yet. You will have to live with these contradictions for awhile. ▪

There are many differences between the application you have just generated and a do-nothing application without ActiveX server support. These differences are explained in the next few sections.

Menus   There are two new menus in an ActiveX server application. The first, called IDR_SHOWSTTYPE_SRVR_IP, is shown in Figure 15.1. When an item is being edited in place, the container in-place menu (called IDR_SHOWSTTYPE_CNTR_IP in the container version of ShoeString) is combined with the server in-place menu, IDR_SHOWSTTYPE_SRVR_IP, to build the in-place menu as shown in Figure 15.2. The double separators in each partial menu show where the menus are joined.

FIG. 15.1

AppWizard adds
another menu for
editing in place.

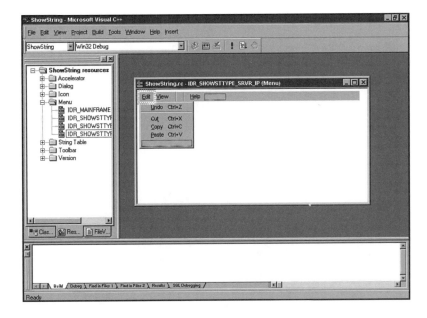

FIG. 15.2

The container and
server in-place menus
are interlaced during in-
place editing.

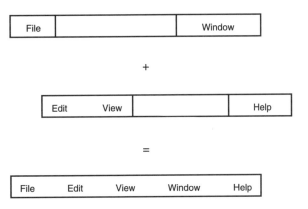

The second new menu is IDR_SHOWSTTYPE_SRVR_EMB, used when an embedded item is being edited in a separate window. Figure 15.3 shows this new menu next to the more familiar IDR_SHOWSTTYPE menu, which is used when ShowString is acting not as a server but as an ordinary application. The File menus have different items: IDR_SHOWSTTYPE_SRVR_EMB has Update in place of Save, and Save Copy As in place of Save As. This is because the item the user is working on in the separate window is not a document of its own, but is embedded in another document. File, Update updates the embedded item; File, Save Copy As doesn't save the whole document, just a copy of this embedded portion.

FIG. 15.3

The embedded menu has different items under File than the usual menu.

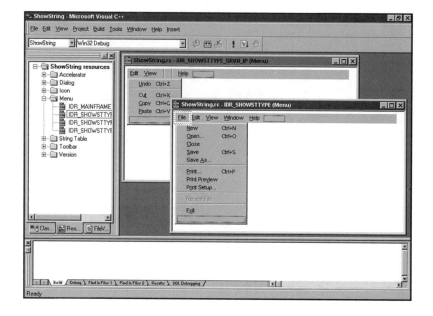

CShowStringApp   Another member variable has been added to this class. It is declared in ShowString.h as:

```
COleTemplateServer m_server;
```

`COleTemplateServer` handles the majority of the work involved in connecting documents to code, as you will see.

The following line is added at the top of ShowString.cpp:

```
#include "IpFrame.h"
```

This sets up the class `CInPlaceFrame`, discussed later in this chapter. Just before `InitInstance()`, the lines shown in Listing 15.1 are added.

Listing 15.1   Excerpt from ShowString.cpp—CLSID

```
// This identifier was generated to be statistically unique for
// your app. You may change it if you prefer to choose a specific
// identifier.

// {0B1DEE40-C373-11CF-870C-00201801DDD6}
static const CLSID clsid =
{ 0xb1dee40, 0xc373, 0x11cf,
    { 0x87, 0xc, 0x0, 0x20, 0x18, 0x1, 0xdd, 0xd6 } };
```

The numbers will be different in your code. This Class ID identifies your server application and document type. Applications that support several kinds of documents (for example, text and graphics) use a different CLSID for each type of document.

As it did for the OLE container version of ShowString, `CShowStringApp::InitInstance()` has several changes from the non-ActiveX ShowString you developed in Chapter 8. The code in Listing 15.2 initializes the ActiveX (OLE) libraries.

Listing 15.2 Excerpt from ShowString.cpp—Initializing Libraries

```
// Initialize OLE libraries
if (!AfxOleInit())
{
    AfxMessageBox(IDP_OLE_INIT_FAILED);
    return FALSE;
}
```

While still in `CShowStringApp::InitInstance()`, after the `CMultiDocTemplate` is initialized but before the call to `AddDocTemplate()`, the following line is added to register the menu used for in-place editing and for separate-window editing:

```
pDocTemplate->SetServerInfo(
        IDR_SHOWSTTYPE_SRVR_EMB, IDR_SHOWSTTYPE_SRVR_IP,
        RUNTIME_CLASS(CInPlaceFrame));
```

A change that was not in the container version is connecting the template for the document to the class ID, like this:

```
// Connect the COleTemplateServer to the document template.
    //  The COleTemplateServer creates new documents on behalf
    //  of requesting OLE containers by using information
    //  specified in the document template.
    m_server.ConnectTemplate(clsid, pDocTemplate, FALSE);
```

Now when a user chooses Create New when inserting an object, the document used for that creation will be available.

When a server application is launched to edit an item in place or in a separate window, the system DLLs add `/Embedding` to the invoking command line. But if the application is already running, and it is an MDI application, a new copy is not launched. Instead, a new MDI window is opened in that application. That particular piece of magic is accomplished with one function call, as shown in Listing 15.3.

Listing 15.3 Excerpt from ShowString.cpp—Registering Running MDI Apps

```
// Register all OLE server factories as running.  This enables the
    //  OLE libraries to create objects from other applications.
    COleTemplateServer::RegisterAll();
    // Note: MDI applications register all server objects without regard
    //  to the /Embedding or /Automation on the command line.
```

After parsing the command line, the AppWizard boilerplate code checks to see if this application is being launched as an embedded (or automation) application. If so, there is no need to continue with the initialization, so this function returns, as shown in Listing 15.4.

Listing 15.4   Excerpt from ShowString.cpp—Checking How the App was Launched

```
// Check to see if launched as OLE server
if (cmdInfo.m_bRunEmbedded || cmdInfo.m_bRunAutomated)
{
    // Application was run with /Embedding or /Automation.
    // Don't show the main window in this case.
    return TRUE;
}
```

If the application is being run standalone, execution continues with a registration update:

```
// When a server application is launched standalone, it is a good idea
    //  to update the system Registry in case it has been damaged.
    m_server.UpdateRegistry(OAT_INPLACE_SERVER);
```

ActiveX information is stored in the Registry. (The Registry is discussed in Chapter 7, "Persistence and File I/O.") When a user chooses Insert, Object or Edit, Insert Object, the Registry provides the list of object types that can be inserted. Before ShowString can appear in such a list, it must be registered. Many developers add code to their install programs to register their server applications, and MFC takes this one step further, registering the application every time it is run. If the application files are moved or changed, the registration is automatically updated the next time the application is run standalone.

CShowStringDoc   The document class, CShowStringDoc, now inherits from COleServerDoc rather than CDocument. As well, the following line is added at the top of ShowStringdoc.cpp:

```
#include "SrvrItem.h"
```

This header file describes the server item class, CShowStringSrvrItem, discussed in the CShowStringSrvrItem subsection of this section. The constructor, CShowStringDoc::CShowStringDoc(), has the following line added:

```
    EnableCompoundFile();
```

This turns on the use of compound files.

There is a new public function inlined in the header file so that other functions can access the server item:

```
CShowStringSrvrItem* GetEmbeddedItem()
        { return (CShowStringSrvrItem*)COleServerDoc::GetEmbeddedItem(); }
```

This calls the base class GetEmbeddedItem(), which in turn calls the virtual function OnGetEmbeddedItem(). That function must be overridden in the ShowString document class as shown in Listing 15.5.

Listing 15.5 ShowStringDoc.cpp—*CShowStringDoc::OnGetEmbeddedItem()*

```
COleServerItem* CShowStringDoc::OnGetEmbeddedItem()
{
    // OnGetEmbeddedItem is called by the framework to get the
    // COleServerItem that is associated with the document.
    // It is only called when necessary.

    CShowStringSrvrItem* pItem = new CShowStringSrvrItem(this);
    ASSERT_VALID(pItem);
    return pItem;
}
```

This makes a new server item from this document and returns a pointer to it.

CShowStringView   The view class has a new entry in the message map:

```
ON_COMMAND(ID_CANCEL_EDIT_SRVR, OnCancelEditSrvr)
```

This catches ID_CANCEL_EDIT_SRVR, and the cancellation of editing is in place. An accelerator has already been added to connect this message to Esc. The function that catches it looks like this:

```
void CShowStringView::OnCancelEditSrvr()
{
    GetDocument()->OnDeactivateUI(FALSE);
}
```

This function simply deactivates the item. There are no other view changes—server views are so much simpler than container views.

CShowStringSrvrItem   The server item class is a completely new addition to ShowString. It provides an interface between the container application that launches ShowString to and opens a ShowString document. It describes an entire ShowString document that is embedded into another document, or a portion of a ShowString document that is linked to part of a container document. It has no member variables other than those inherited from the base class, COleServerItem. It has overrides for eight functions. They are as follows:

- A constructor
- A destructor
- GetDocument()
- AssertValid()
- Dump()
- Serialize()
- OnDraw()
- OnGetExtent()

The constructor simply passes the document pointer along to the base class. The destructor does nothing. `GetDocument()` is an inline function that calls the base class function with the same name and casts the result. `AssertValid()` and `Dump()` are debug functions that simply call the base class functions. `Serialize()` actually does some work, as shown in Listing 15.6.

Listing 15.6   Srvrltem.cpp—*CShowStringSrvrItem::Serialize()*

```
void CShowStringSrvrItem::Serialize(CArchive& ar)
{
    // CShowStringSrvrItem::Serialize will be called by the framework if
    //  the item is copied to the clipboard.  This can happen automatically
    //  through the OLE callback OnGetClipboardData.  A good default for
    //  the embedded item is simply to delegate to the document's Serialize
    //  function.  If you support links, then you will want to serialize
    //  just a portion of the document.

    if (!IsLinkedItem())
    {
        CShowStringDoc* pDoc = GetDocument();
        ASSERT_VALID(pDoc);
        pDoc->Serialize(ar);
    }
}
```

There is no need to duplicate effort here. If the item is embedded, it is an entire document, and that document has a perfectly good `Serialize()` that can handle the work. AppWizard doesn't provide boilerplate to handle serializing a linked item because it is application-specific. You would save just enough information to describe what part of the document has been linked in, for example, cells A3 to D27 in a spreadsheet. This doesn't make sense for ShowString, so don't add any code to `Serialize()`.

You may feel that `OnDraw()` is out of place here. It is normally thought of as a view function. But this `OnDraw()` draws a depiction of the server item when it is inactive. It should look very much like the view when it is active, and it makes sense to share the work between `CShowStringView::OnDraw()` and `CShowStringSrvrItem::OnDraw()`. The boilerplate that AppWizard provides is in Listing 15.7.

Listing 15.7   Srvrltem.cpp—*CShowStringSrvrItem::OnDraw()*

```
BOOL CShowStringSrvrItem::OnDraw(CDC* pDC, CSize& rSize)
{
    CShowStringDoc* pDoc = GetDocument();
    ASSERT_VALID(pDoc);

    // TODO: set mapping mode and extent
    //  (The extent is usually the same as the size returned from OnGetExtent)
    pDC->SetMapMode(MM_ANISOTROPIC);
    pDC->SetWindowOrg(0,0);
    pDC->SetWindowExt(3000, 3000);
```

```
// TODO: add drawing code here.  Optionally, fill in the HIMETRIC extent.
// All drawing takes place in the metafile device context (pDC).

    return TRUE;
}
```

This will change a great deal, but it's worth noting now that unlike
CShowStringView::OnDraw(), this function takes two parameters. The second is the size in
which the inactive depiction is to be drawn. The extent, as mentioned in the boilerplate comments, typically comes from OnGetExtent(), which is shown in Listing 15.8.

Listing 15.8 Srvritem.cpp—*CShowStringSrvrItem:: OnGetExtent()*

```
BOOL CShowStringSrvrItem::OnGetExtent(DVASPECT dwDrawAspect, CSize& rSize)
{
    // Most applications, like this one, only handle drawing the content
    //  aspect of the item.  If you wish to support other aspects, such
    //  as DVASPECT_THUMBNAIL (by overriding OnDrawEx), then this
    //  implementation of OnGetExtent should be modified to handle the
    //  additional aspect(s).

    if (dwDrawAspect != DVASPECT_CONTENT)
        return COleServerItem::OnGetExtent(dwDrawAspect, rSize);

    // CShowStringSrvrItem::OnGetExtent is called to get the extent in
    //  HIMETRIC units of the entire item.  The default implementation
    //  here simply returns a hard-coded number of units.

    CShowStringDoc* pDoc = GetDocument();
    ASSERT_VALID(pDoc);

    // TODO: replace this arbitrary size

    rSize = CSize(3000, 3000);    // 3000 x 3000 HIMETRIC units

    return TRUE;
}
```

You will replace this with real code very shortly.

CInPlaceFrame   The in-place frame class, which inherits from COleIPFrameWnd, handles the
frame around the server item and the toolbars, status bars, and dialog-box bars, collectively
known as *control bars*, that it displays. It has the following three protected member variables:

```
CToolBar     m_wndToolBar;
COleResizeBar   m_wndResizeBar;
COleDropTarget m_dropTarget;
```

The CToolBar class is discussed in Chapter 9, "Status Bars and Toolbars." COleDropTarget is
discussed in the drag and drop section of Chapter 14. COleResizeBar looks just like a
CRectTracker, which was used extensively in Chapter 14, but allows the resizing of a server
item rather than a container item.

The following are the seven member functions of `CInPlaceFrame`:

- A constructor
- A destructor
- `AssertValid()`
- `Dump()`
- `OnCreate()`
- `OnCreateControlBars()`
- `PreCreateWindow()`

The constructor and destructor do nothing. `AssertValid()` and `Dump()` are debug functions that simply call the base class functions. `OnCreate()` actually has code, shown in Listing 15.9.

Listing 15.9   IPFrame.cpp—*CInPlaceFrame::OnCreate()*

```
int CInPlaceFrame::OnCreate(LPCREATESTRUCT lpCreateStruct)
{
    if (COleIPFrameWnd::OnCreate(lpCreateStruct) == -1)
        return -1;

    // CResizeBar implements in-place resizing.
    if (!m_wndResizeBar.Create(this))
    {
        TRACE0("Failed to create resize bar\n");
        return -1;        // fail to create
    }

    // By default, it is a good idea to register a drop-target that does
    //   nothing with your frame window.  This prevents drops from
    //   "falling through" to a container that supports drag-drop.
    m_dropTarget.Register(this);

    return 0;
}
```

This function catches the `WM_CREATE` message that is sent when an in-place frame is created and drawn onscreen. It calls the base class function and then creates the resize bar. Finally, it registers a drop target so that if anything is dropped over this in-place frame, it is dropped on this server rather than the underlying container.

When a server document is activated in place, `COleServerDoc::ActivateInPlace()` calls `CInPlaceFrame::OnCreateControlBars()`, which is shown in Listing 15.10.

Listing 15.10   IPFrame.cpp—*CInPlaceFrame::OnCreateControlBars()*

```
BOOL CInPlaceFrame::OnCreateControlBars(CFrameWnd* pWndFrame,
                                        CFrameWnd* pWndDoc)
{
    // Set owner to this window, so messages are delivered to correct app
    m_wndToolBar.SetOwner(this);

    // Create toolbar on client's frame window
    if (!m_wndToolBar.Create(pWndFrame) ||
        !m_wndToolBar.LoadToolBar(IDR_SHOWSTTYPE_SRVR_IP))

    {
        TRACE0("Failed to create toolbar\n");
        return FALSE;
    }

    // TODO: Remove this if you don't want tool tips or a resizeable toolbar
    m_wndToolBar.SetBarStyle(m_wndToolBar.GetBarStyle() |
        CBRS_TOOLTIPS | CBRS_FLYBY | CBRS_SIZE_DYNAMIC);

    // TODO: Delete these three lines if you don't want the toolbar to
    //   be dockable
    m_wndToolBar.EnableDocking(CBRS_ALIGN_ANY);
    pWndFrame->EnableDocking(CBRS_ALIGN_ANY);
    pWndFrame->DockControlBar(&m_wndToolBar);

    return TRUE;
}
```

This function creates a docking, resizable toolbar with ToolTips, docked against the edge of the main frame window for the application.

TIP If you are developing an MDI application and prefer the toolbar against the document frame, use pWndDoc instead of PWndFrame, in the call to m_wndToolBar.Create() but be sure to check that it is not NULL.

The last function in CInPlaceFrame is PreCreateWindow(). At the moment, it just calls the base class, as shown in Listing 15.11.

Listing 15.11   IPFrame.cpp—*CInPlaceFrame::PreCreateWindow()*

```
BOOL CInPlaceFrame::PreCreateWindow(CREATESTRUCT& cs)
{
    // TODO: Modify the Window class or styles here by modifying
    //   the CREATESTRUCT cs

    return COleIPFrameWnd::PreCreateWindow(cs);
}
```

This function is called before `OnCreate()` and sets up the styles for the frame window through a `CREATESTRUCT`.

> **CAUTION**
>
> Modifying these styles is not for the faint of heart. The Microsoft documentation recommends reading the source code for all the classes in the hierarchy of your `CInPlaceFrame` (`Cwnd`, `CFrameWnd`, `COleIPFrameWnd`) to see what `CREATESTRUCT` elements are already set before making any changes. For this sample application, don't change the `CREATESTRUCT`.

Shortcomings of This Server   Apart from the fact that the starter application from AppWizard doesn't show a string, what's missing from this server? The `OnDraw()` and `GetExtent()`TODOs are the only significant tasks left for you by AppWizard. Try building ShowString, and then run it once standalone just to register it.

Figure 15.4 shows the Object dialog box in Microsoft Word, reached by choosing Insert, Object. ShowString appears in this list as ShowSt Document—not surprising considering the menu name was `IDR_SHOWSTTYPE`. Developer Studio calls this document a ShowSt document. This setting could have been overridden in AppWizard by choosing the Advanced button in Step 4 of AppWizard. Figure 15.5 shows this dialog box and the long and short names of the file type.

FIG. 15.4

The ShowString document type, called ShowSt document, now appears in the Object dialog box when inserting a new object into a Word document.

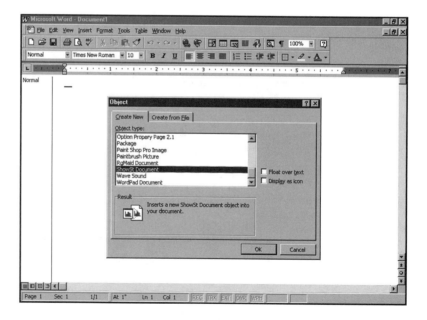

FIG. 15.5
The Advanced Options dialog box of Step 4 in AppWizard provides an opportunity to change the name of the file type.

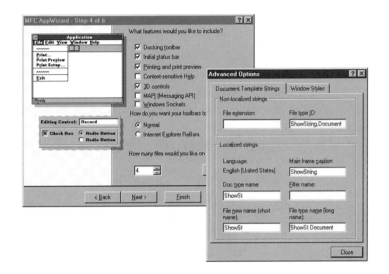

So, the file type names used by the Registry have been set incorrectly for this project. The next few pages take you on a tour of the way file type names are stored and show you how difficult they are to change.

The file type name has been stored in the string table. It is the caption of the IDR_SHOWSTTYPE resource, and AppWizard has set it to:

\nShowSt\nShowSt\n\n\nShowString.Document\nShowSt Document

To look at this string, choose String Table from the Resource View, open the only string table there, click IDR_SHOWSTTYPE once to highlight it, and choose View, Properties (or double-click the string). This string is saved in the document template when a new one is constructed in CShowStringApp::InitInstance(), like this:

Listing 15.12   ShowString.cpp—Excerpt from *ShowStringApp::InitInstance()*

```
pDocTemplate = new CMultiDocTemplate(
    IDR_SHOWSTTYPE,
    RUNTIME_CLASS(CShowStringDoc),
    RUNTIME_CLASS(CChildFrame), // custom MDI child frame
    RUNTIME_CLASS(CShowStringView));
```

The caption of the menu resource holds seven strings, and each is used by a different part of the framework. They are separated by the newline character \n. The seven strings, their purposes, and the values provided by AppWizard for ShowString are as follows:

■ **Window Title**—Used by SDI apps in the title bar. For ShowString: not provided.

■ **Document Name**—Used as the root for default document names. For ShowString: ShowSt, so that new documents will be ShowSt1, ShowSt2, and so on.

- **File New Name**—Prompt in the File New dialog box for file type. (For example, in Developer Studio there are eight file types, including Text File and Project Workspace.) For ShowString: `ShowSt`.

- **Filter Name**—An entry for the drop-down box Files of Type in the File Open dialog box. For ShowString: not provided.

- **Filter Extension**—The extension that matches the filter name. For ShowString: not provided.

- **Registry File Type ID**—A short string to be stored in the Registry. For ShowString: `ShowString.Document`.

- **Registry File Type Name**—A longer string that shows in dialog boxes involving the Registry. For ShowString: `ShowSt Document`.

Look again at Figure 15.5 and you can see where these values came from. Try changing the last entry. In the Properties dialog box, change the caption so that the last element of the string is `ShowString Document` and press Enter. Build the project. Run it once and exit. In the output section of Developer Studio, you see these messages:

```
Warning: Leaving value 'ShowSt Document' for key 'ShowString.Document'
 in registry
 intended value was 'ShowString Document'.
Warning: Leaving value 'ShowSt Document' for key
 'CLSID\{0B1DEE40-C373-11CF-870C-00201801DDD6}' in registry
 intended value was 'ShowString Document'.
```

This means that the call to `UpdateRegistry()` did not change these two keys. There is a way to provide parameters to `UpdateRegistry()` to insist that the keys be updated, but it's even more complicated than the route you will follow. Because no code has been changed from that provided by AppWizard, it's much quicker to delete the ShowString directory and create it again, this time setting the long file type to ShowString Document.

CAUTION

Always test AppWizard-generated code before you add changes of your own. Until you are familiar with every default you are accepting, it is worth a few moments to see what you have before moving on. Rerunning AppWizard is easy, but if you've made several hours worth of changes and then decide to rerun it, it's not such a simple task.

Close Visual Studio, delete the ShowString folder entirely, and generate a new application with AppWizard as before. This time, in Step 4, click the Advanced button and change the file type names as shown in Figure 15.6. After you click Finish, AppWizard asks whether you wish to reuse the existing CLSID, as shown in Figure 15.7. Click Yes and then OK to create the project. This makes a new showstring.reg file for you with the correct Registry values.

FIG. 15.6
The Advanced Options dialog box of Step 4 of AppWizard is the place to improve the file type names.

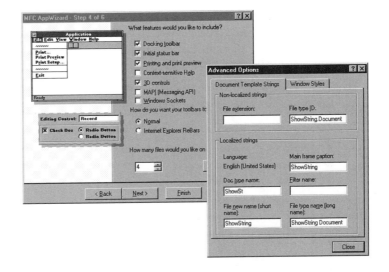

FIG. 15.7
AppWizard makes sure that you don't accidentally reuse a CLSID.

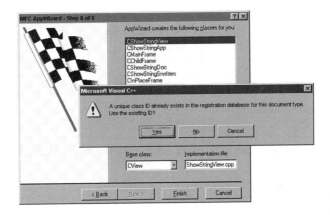

This changes the string table as well as the showstring.reg file, so you might be tempted to build and run the application to make this fix complete. It's true, when you run the application, it will update the Registry for you, using the values from the new string table. Alas, the registration update will fail yet again. If you were to try it, these messages would appear in the output window:

```
Warning: Leaving value 'ShowSt Document' for key
  'ShowString.Document' in registry
  intended value was 'ShowString Document'.
Warning: Leaving value 'ShowSt Document' for key
  'CLSID\{0B1DEE40-C373-11CF-870C-00201801DDD6}' in registry
  intended value was 'ShowString Document'.
Warning: Leaving value 'ShowSt' for key
  'CLSID\{0B1DEE40-C373-11CF-870C-00201801DDD6}\AuxUserType\2'
  in registry
  intended value was 'ShowString'.
```

So, how do you get out of this mess? You have to edit the Registry. If that doesn't sound intimidating, it should. Messing with the Registry can leave your system unusable. But you are not going to go in by hand and change keys; instead, you are going to use the Registry file that AppWizard generated for you. Here's what to do:

1. Choose Start, Run.

2. Type **regedit** and press Enter.

3. Choose Registry, Import Registry File from the Registry Editor menu.

4. Using the Import Registry File dialog box, move through your folders until you reach the one where the replacement ShowString server was just generated by AppWizard, as shown in Figure 15.8. Click Open.

5. A success message is shown. Click OK.

6. Close the Registry Editor.

FIG. 15.8

Registry files generated by AppWizard have the extension .reg.

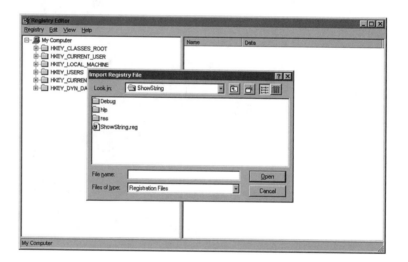

Now if you run ShowString again, those error messages don't appear. Run Word again and choose Insert, Object. The Object dialog box now has a more meaningful ShowString entry, as shown in Figure 15.9.

> **N O T E** There are three morals to this side trip. The first is that you should think really carefully before clicking Finish on the AppWizard dialog box. The second is that you cannot ignore the Registry if you are an ActiveX programmer. The third is that anything can be changed if you have the nerve for it. ■

Click OK on the Object dialog box to insert a ShowString object into the Word document. You can immediately edit it in place, as shown in Figure 15.10. You can see that the combined server and container in-place menus are being used. There's not much you can do to the embedded object at this point because the ShowString code that actually shows a string has not been added. Press Esc to finish editing in place, and the menus return to the usual Word menus, as shown in Figure 15.11.

FIG. 15.9

The updated long file type name appears in the Object dialog box of other applications.

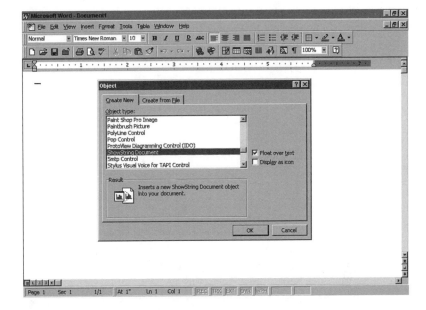

FIG. 15.10

While editing in place, the in-place menus replace the Word menus.

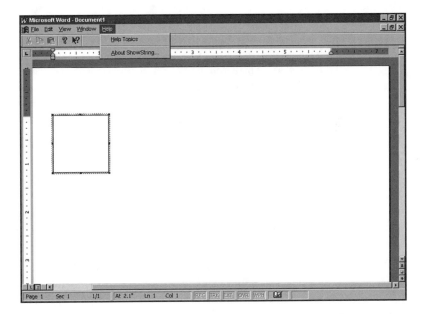

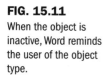

FIG. 15.11

When the object is inactive, Word reminds the user of the object type.

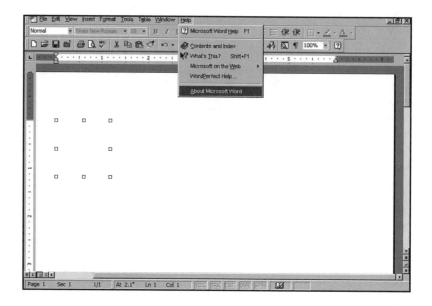

Although this server doesn't do anything, it is a perfectly good server. You can resize and move the embedded item while it is active or inactive, and everything operates exactly as you expect. All that remains is to restore the ShowString functionality.

Showing a String Again

As you did in Chapter 14, it is time to add the ShowString functionality to this version of the program. If you went through this process before, it will be even quicker this time. Remember to open the ShowString files from Chapter 8, so that you can copy code and resources from the functional ShowString to the do-nothing ActiveX server you have just created and explored. (If you didn't code along in Chapter 8, you can get the completed code on the Web at **www.mcp.com/info** or **www.gregcons.com/uvc6.htm**.) Here's what to do:

1. In ShowStringDoc.h, add the private member variables and public Get functions to the class.

2. In CShowStringDoc::Serialize(), paste in the code that saves or restores these member variables.

3. In CShowStringDoc::OnNewDocument(), paste in the code that initializes the member variables. Change the default values of horizcenter and vertcenter to FALSE. You'll see why towards the end of the chapter.

4. Copy the entire Tools menu from the old ShowString to the new server ShowString. Choose File, Open to open the old ShowString.rc, open the IDR_SHOWSTTYPE menu, click the Tools menu, and choose Edit, Copy. Open the new ShowString's IDR_SHOWSTTYPE menu, click the Window menu, and choose Edit, Paste.

5. Paste the Tools menu into the `IDR_SHOWSTTYPE_SRVR_IP` (before the separator bars) and `IDR_SHOWSTTYPE_SRVR_EMB` menus in the same way.

6. Add the accelerator Ctrl+T for `ID_TOOLS_OPTIONS` as described in Chapter 8. Add it to all three accelerators.

7. Delete the `IDD_ABOUTBOX` dialog box from the new ShowString. Copy `IDD_ABOUTBOX` and `IDD_OPTIONS` from the old ShowString to the new.

8. While `IDD_OPTIONS` has focus, choose View, ClassWizard. Create the `COptionsDialog` class as in the original ShowString.

9. Use ClassWizard to arrange for `CShowStringDoc` to catch the `ID_TOOLS_OPTIONS` command.

10. In ShowStringDoc.cpp, replace the ClassWizard version of `CShowStringDoc::OnToolsOptions()` with the one that puts up the dialog box.

11. In ShowStringDoc.cpp, add **`#include "OptionsDialog.h"`** after the #include statements already present.

12. Use ClassWizard to connect the dialog box controls to `COptionsDialog` member variables as before. Connect `IDC_OPTIONS_BLACK` to m_color, `IDC_OPTIONS_HORIZCENTER` to m_horizcenter, `IDC_OPTIONS_STRING` to m_string, and `IDC_OPTIONS_VERTCENTER` to m_vertcenter.

To confirm you've made all the changes correctly, build the project—there should be no errors.

You haven't restored `CShowStringView::OnDraw()` yet because there are actually going to be two `OnDraw()` functions. The first is in the view class, shown in Listing 15.13. It draws the string when ShowString is running standalone and when the user is editing in place, and it's the same as in the old version of ShowString. Just copy it into the new one.

Listing 15.13 ShowStringView.cpp—*CShowStringView::OnDraw()*

```
void CShowStringView::OnDraw(CDC* pDC)
{
    CShowStringDoc* pDoc = GetDocument();
    ASSERT_VALID(pDoc);

    COLORREF oldcolor;
    switch (pDoc->GetColor())
    {
    case 0:
        oldcolor = pDC->SetTextColor(RGB(0,0,0)); //black
        break;
    case 1:
        oldcolor = pDC->SetTextColor(RGB(0xFF,0,0)); //red
        break;
    case 2:
        oldcolor = pDC->SetTextColor(RGB(0,0xFF,0)); //green
        break;
    }
```

continues

Listing 15.13 Continued

```
        int DTflags = 0;
        if (pDoc->GetHorizcenter())
        {
            DTflags |= DT_CENTER;
        }
        if (pDoc->GetVertcenter())
        {
            DTflags |= (DT_VCENTER|DT_SINGLELINE);
        }

        CRect rect;
        GetClientRect(&rect);
        pDC->DrawText(pDoc->GetString(), &rect, DTflags);
        pDC->SetTextColor(oldcolor);
}
```

When the embedded ShowString item is inactive, `CShowStringSrvrItem::OnDraw()` draws it. The code in here should be very similar to the view's `OnDraw`, but because it is a member of `CShowStringSrvrItem` rather than `CShowStringView`, it doesn't have access to the same member variables. So although there is still a `GetDocument()` function you can call, `GetClientRect` doesn't work. It's a member of the view class but not of the server item class. You use a few CDC member functions instead. It's a nice touch to draw the item slightly differently to help remind the user that it is not active, as shown in Listing 15.14. You can paste in the drawing code from the view's `OnDraw()`, but change the colors slightly to give the user a reminder.

Listing 15.14 SrvrItem.cpp—*CShowStringSrvrItem::OnDraw()*

```
BOOL CShowStringSrvrItem::OnDraw(CDC* pDC, CSize& rSize)
{
        CShowStringDoc* pDoc = GetDocument();
        ASSERT_VALID(pDoc);

        // TODO: set mapping mode and extent
        //  (The extent is usually the same as the size returned from OnGetExtent)
        pDC->SetMapMode(MM_ANISOTROPIC);
        pDC->SetWindowOrg(0,0);
        pDC->SetWindowExt(3000, 3000);

        COLORREF oldcolor;
        switch (pDoc->GetColor())
        {
        case 0:
            oldcolor = pDC->SetTextColor(RGB(0x80,0x80,0x80)); //gray
            break;
        case 1:
            oldcolor = pDC->SetTextColor(RGB(0xB0,0,0)); // dull red
            break;
        case 2:
            oldcolor = pDC->SetTextColor(RGB(0,0xB0,0)); // dull green
            break;
        }
```

```
        int DTflags = 0;
        if (pDoc->GetHorizcenter())
        {
            DTflags |= DT_CENTER;
        }
        if (pDoc->GetVertcenter())
        {
            DTflags |= (DT_VCENTER|DT_SINGLELINE);
        }

        CRect rect;
        rect.TopLeft() = pDC->GetWindowOrg();
        rect.BottomRight() = rect.TopLeft() + pDC->GetWindowExt();
        pDC->DrawText(pDoc->GetString(), &rect, DTflags);
        pDC->SetTextColor(oldcolor);

        return TRUE;
    }
```

The function starts with the boilerplate from AppWizard. With an application that doesn't just draw itself in whatever space is provided, you would want to add code to determine the extent rather than just using (3000,3000). (You'd want to add the code to OnGetExtent(), too.) But hardcoding the numbers works for this simple example.

Build the application, fix any typos or other simple errors, and then start Word and insert a ShowString document into your worksheet. ShowString should run as before, with Hello, world! in the center of the view. Convince yourself that the Options dialog box still works and that you have restored all the old functionality. Be sure to change at least one thing: the string, the color, or the centering. Then, press Esc to finish editing in place. Oops! It still draws the old Hello, world! in gray in the top left of the server area. Why?

Remember that in CShowStringDoc::OnToolsOptions(), after the user clicks OK, you tell the document that it has been changed and arrange to have the view redrawn:

```
        SetModifiedFlag();
        UpdateAllViews(NULL);
```

You need to add another line there to make sure that any containers that are containing this document are also notified:

```
        NotifyChanged();
```

Now build it again and insert a different ShowString object into a Word document. This time the changes are reflected in the inactive server display as well. Figure 15.12 shows a ShowString item being edited in place, and Figure 15.13 shows the same item inactive.

N O T E   If you turn on either centering option, the string will not appear when the item is inactive. It seems that DrawText is centering the string within a much larger rectangle than the one you pass to it. Simpler CDC functions, such as DrawEllipse, don't have this problem. It might be wise to avoid centering text with DrawText() if your inactive appearance is important. ▨

FIG. 15.12
This ShowString item is being edited in place.

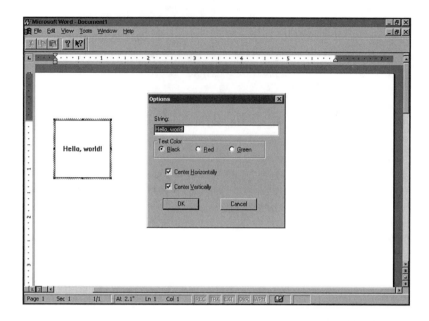

FIG. 15.13
This ShowString item is inactive.

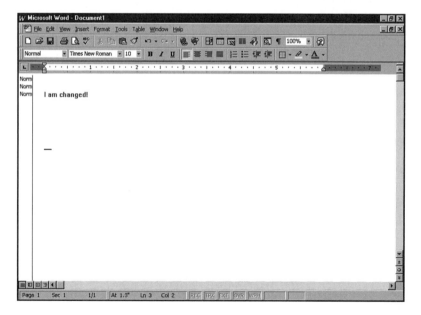

Good old ShowString has been through a lot. It's time for one more transformation.

Applications That Are Both Container and Server

As you might expect, adding container features to this version of ShowString is as difficult as adding them to the ordinary ShowString of the previous chapter. If you add these features, you gain an application that can tap the full power of ActiveX to bring extraordinary power to your work and your documents.

Building Another Version of ShowString

The way to get a ShowString that is both a container and a server is to follow these steps:

1. Build a new ShowString with AppWizard that is a container and a full server. Run AppWizard as usual but in a different directory than the one where you created the server-only ShowString. Be sure to select the Both Container And Server radio button in Step 3. In Step 4, click the Advanced button and change the filename types as you did earlier in this chapter. Finally, when asked whether you want to use the same CLSID, click No. This is a different application.

2. Make the container changes from the preceding chapter. When adding the Tools, Options menu item and accelerator, add it to the main menu, the server in-place menu, and the server-embedded menu.

3. Make the server changes from this chapter.

4. Add the ShowString functionality.

This section does not present the process of building a container and server application in detail; that is covered in the "Adding Server Capabilities to ShowString" section of this chapter and all of Chapter 14. Rather, the focus here is on the consequences of building such an application.

Nesting and Recursion Issues

After an application is both a server (meaning its documents can be embedded in other applications) and a container, it is possible to create nested documents. For example, Microsoft Word is both container and server. An Excel spreadsheet might contain a Word document, which in turn contains a bitmap, as shown in Figure 15.14.

Within Excel, you can double-click the Word document to edit it in place, as shown in Figure 15.15, but you cannot go on to double-click the bitmap and edit it in place, too. You can edit it in a window of its own, as shown in Figure 15.16. It is a limitation of ActiveX that you cannot nest in-place editing sessions indefinitely.

Active Documents

The final, important recent addition to ActiveX is Active Documents, formerly known as ActiveX Document Objects. An ordinary ActiveX server takes over the menus and interface of a container application when the document is being edited in place but does so in cooperation with the container application. An Active Document server takes over far more dramatically, as you will shortly see.

FIG. 15.14

This Excel spreadsheet contains a Word document that contains a bitmap.

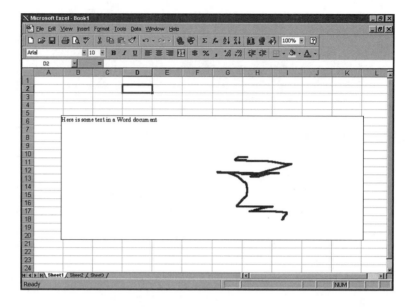

FIG. 15.15

This Word document is being edited in place.

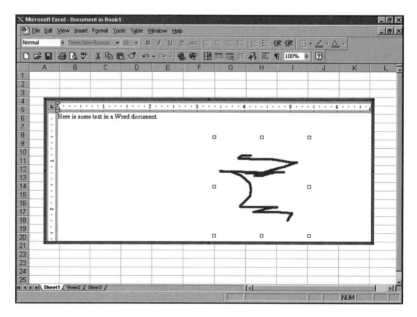

FIG. 15.16

This bitmap is nested within a Word document within an Excel spreadsheet, and so cannot be edited in place. Instead, it is edited in a separate window.

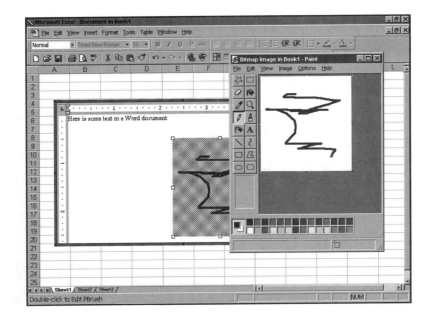

What Active Documents Do

The first application to demonstrate the use of Active Documents is the Microsoft Office Binder, shown in Figure 15.17. To the user, it appears that this application can open any Office document. In reality, the documents are opened with their own server applications while the frame around them and the list of other documents remain intact. Microsoft Internet Explorer (version 3.0 and later) is also an Active Document container—Figure 15.18 shows a Word document open in Explorer. Notice the menus are mostly Word menus, but the Explorer toolbar can still be used. For example, clicking the Back button closes this Word document and opens the document that was loaded previously.

To users, this is a complete transition to a document-centered approach. No matter what application the user is working with, any kind of document can be opened and edited, using the code written to work with that document but the interface that the user has learned for his or her own application.

Making ShowString an Active Document Server

Making yet another version of ShowString, this one as an Active Document server, is pretty simple. Follow the instructions from the "AppWizard's Server Boilerplate" section at the beginning of this chapter, with two exceptions: in AppWizard's Step 3, select Active Document Server and in AppWizard's Step 4, click the Advanced button. Fix the file type names and fill in the file extension as **.SST**, as shown in Figure 15.19. This helps Active Document containers determine what application to launch when you open a ShowString file.

FIG. 15.17
The Microsoft Office Binder makes it simple to pull Office documents together.

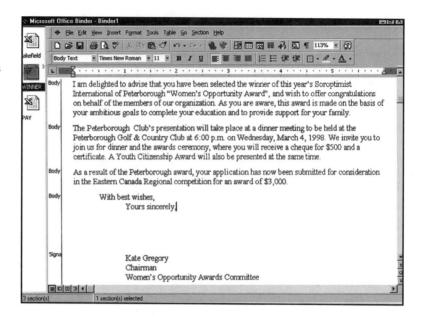

FIG. 15.18
Microsoft Internet Explorer is also a container for Active Documents.

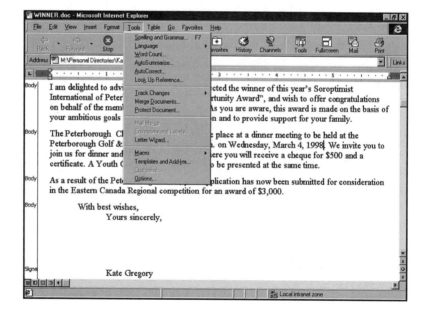

FIG. 15.19

The Advanced Options dialog box of AppWizard's Step 4 is where you specify the extension for ShowString files.

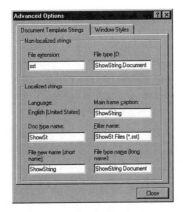

Document Extension Boilerplate   Any one of the versions of ShowString built up to this point could have had a document extension specified. AppWizard adds these lines to `CShowStringApp::InitInstance()` when you specify a document extension for an Active Document server application:

```
// Enable drag/drop open
m_pMainWnd->DragAcceptFiles();

// Enable DDE Execute open
EnableShellOpen();
RegisterShellFileTypes(TRUE);
```

It is the call to `RegisterShellFileTypes()` that matters here, though the drag and drop is a nice touch. You're able to drag files from your desktop or a folder onto the ShowString icon or an open copy of ShowString, and the file opens in ShowString.

Active Document Server Boilerplate   Selecting Active Document support makes remarkably little difference to the code generated by AppWizard. In `CShowStringApp::InitInstance()`, the versions of ShowString that were not Active Document servers had this call to update the Registry:

```
m_server.UpdateRegistry(OAT_INPLACE_SERVER);
```

The Active Document version of ShowString has this line:

```
m_server.UpdateRegistry(OAT_DOC_OBJECT_SERVER);
```

In both cases, `m_server` is a `CShowStringSrvrItem`, but now the Active Document server version has a server item that inherits from `CDocObjectServerItem`. This causes a number of little changes throughout the source and includes files for `CShowStringSrvrItem`, where base class functions are called. Similarly, the in-place frame object, `CInPlaceFrame`, now inherits from `COleDocIPFrameWnd`.

Showing Off the Newest ShowString   Restore the ShowString functionality once again as described in the section "Showing a String Again," earlier in this chapter. Also copy the OnDraw() code from an old version of ShowString to CshowStringDoc::OnDraw(). Build the application, run it once to register it, and then run Microsoft Binder (if you have Office installed). Choose Section Add to bring up the Add Section dialog box shown in Figure 15.20. On the General tab, highlight ShowString Document and click OK.

FIG. 15.20

Not many applications on the market are Active Document servers, but you can write one in minutes.

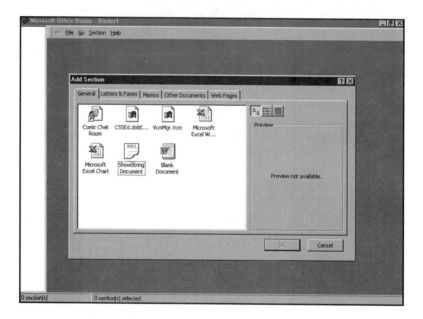

The menus include ShowString's Tools menu, as before. Choose Tools, Options and change something—for example, in Figure 15.21, the string has been changed to "Hello from the Binder" and the horizontal centering has been turned on. You have access to all of ShowString's functionality, although it doesn't look as though you are running ShowString.

Now run ShowString alone and save a document by choosing File, Save. You don't need to enter an extension: The extension .SST is used automatically. Open an Explorer window and explore until you reach the file you saved. Bring up Internet Explorer 4.0 and drag the file you saved onto Internet Explorer.

Your ShowString document opens in Explorer, as you can see in Figure 15.22. The toolbar is clearly the Explorer toolbar, but the menu has the Tools item, and you can change the string, centering, and color as before. If you use the Back button on the Explorer toolbar, you reload the document you had open. If you change the ShowString document before clicking Back, you'll even be prompted to save your changes! Microsoft plans to integrate the desktop in the next generation of Windows with the Internet Explorer interface. What you see here is a sneak preview of how that will work.

FIG. 15.21

All of ShowString's functionality is available from within the Binder.

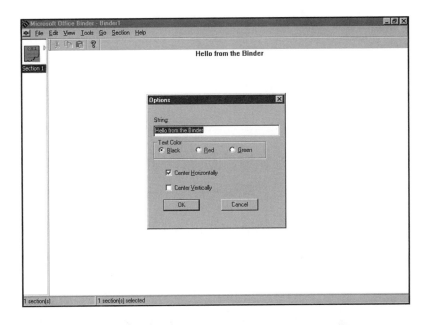

FIG. 15.22

Internet Explorer appears to be able to read and write ShowString files now.

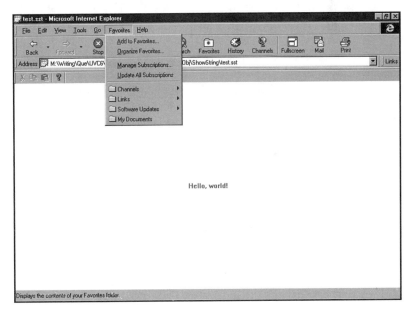

You can also arrange for your applications to be Active Document containers. Perhaps you noticed the check box on AppWizard's Step 3 where you could ask AppWizard to turn on this feature. It's not much harder to do than serving Active Documents, so you can explore it on your own. If you would like your users to be able to open Word files, Excel spreadsheets, or other Active Documents from within your application, be sure to look into this feature.

Eventually Windows will look very much like Internet Explorer; Active Documents will make that possible. ●

Building an Automation Server

Designing ShowString Again

Automation, formerly called OLE Automation and then ActiveX Automation, is about writing code that other programs can call. Other programs call your code directly, not in the insulated manner of a DLL. The jargon is that your code exposes *methods* (functions) and *properties* (variables) to other applications. The good part is that if your application is an Automation server, you don't have to create a macro language for your application; you only have to make hooks for a more universal macro language, Visual Basic for Applications, to grab on to.

All Microsoft Office applications are Automation servers, so you may have seen for yourself what a nice feature it is for a program to expose its methods and properties in this way. What's more, Developer Studio itself is an Automation server, easy to control with VBScript.

If you've been building the sample applications throughout this book, you can probably design ShowString in your sleep by now, but it's time to do it once again. This time, ShowString won't have a Tools, Options menu; instead, other programs will directly set the string and other display options. The member variables in the document will be the same, and the code in OnDraw() will be the same as in all the other implementations of ShowString.

AppWizard's Automation Boilerplate

To build the Automation server version of ShowString, first use AppWizard to create an empty shell in a different directory from your other versions of ShowString. Make almost exactly the same AppWizard choices as before: Call it ShowString and then choose an MDI application and no database support. In AppWizard's Step 3, choose No Compound Document Support (the None radio buttons at the top of the dialog box) but turn on support for Automation. Continue through the AppWizard process, selecting a docking toolbar, status bar, printing and print preview, context-sensitive help, and 3D controls. Finally, select source file comments and a shared DLL.

N O T E Even though the technology is now called ActiveX, and ActiveX Automation is starting to be known simply as Automation, the AppWizard dialog boxes refer to Compound Document Support. As well, many of the classes used throughout this chapter have Ole in their names, and comments refer to OLE. Although Microsoft has changed the name of the technology, it hasn't propagated that change throughout Visual C++ yet. You'll have to live with these contradictions until the next release of Visual C++. ■

There are just a few differences in this application from the do-nothing application without Automation support, primarily in the application object and the document.

CShowStringApp The application object, CShowStringApp, has a number of changes. In the source file, just before InitInstance(), the code shown in Listing 16.1 has been added:

Listing 16.1   ShowString.cpp—CLSID

```
// This identifier was generated to be statistically unique for your app.
// You may change it if you prefer to choose a specific identifier.

// {61C76C05-70EA-11D0-9AFF-0080C81A397C}
static const CLSID clsid =
{ 0x61c76c05, 0x70ea, 0x11d0, { 0x9a, 0xff, 0x0, 0x80, 0xc8,
    0x1a, 0x39, 0x7c } };
```

The numbers will be different in your code. This class ID identifies your Automation application.

CShowStringApp::InitInstance() has several changes. The lines of code in Listing 16.2 initialize the ActiveX (OLE) libraries.

Listing 16.2   ShowString.cpp—Initializing Libraries

```
// Initialize OLE libraries
if (!AfxOleInit())
{
    AfxMessageBox(IDP_OLE_INIT_FAILED);
    return FALSE;
}
```

As with the server application of Chapter 15, "Building an ActiveX Server Application," InitInstance() goes on to connect the document template to the COleTemplateServer after the document template is initialized:

```
m_server.ConnectTemplate(clsid, pDocTemplate, FALSE);
```

Then InitInstance() checks whether the server is being launched as an Automation server or to edit an embedded object. If so, there's no need to display the main window, so the function returns early, as shown in Listing 16.3.

Listing 16.3   ShowString.cpp—How the App Was Launched

```
// Check to see if launched as OLE server
if (cmdInfo.m_bRunEmbedded || cmdInfo.m_bRunAutomated)
{
    // Application was run with /Embedding or /Automation.  Don't show the
    //  main window in this case.
    return TRUE;
}

// When a server application is launched stand-alone, it is a good idea
//  to update the system registry in case it has been damaged.
m_server.UpdateRegistry(OAT_DISPATCH_OBJECT);
COleObjectFactory::UpdateRegistryAll();
```

If ShowString is being run as a standalone application, the code in Listing 16.3 updates the Registry as discussed in Chapter 15.

CShowStringDoc   The document class, CShowStringDoc, still inherits from CDocument rather than from any OLE document class, but that's where the similarities to the old non-OLE CShowStringDoc end. The first block of new code in ShowStringDoc.cpp is right after the message map (see Listing 16.4).

Listing 16.4   ShowStringDoc.cpp—Dispatch Map

```
BEGIN_DISPATCH_MAP(CShowStringDoc, CDocument)
     //{{AFX_DISPATCH_MAP(CShowStringDoc)
          // NOTE - the ClassWizard will add and remove mapping macros here.
          //      DO NOT EDIT what you see in these blocks of generated code!
     //}}AFX_DISPATCH_MAP
END_DISPATCH_MAP()
```

This is an empty dispatch map. A *dispatch map* is like a message map in that it maps events in the real world into function calls within this C++ class. When you expose methods and properties of this document with ClassWizard, the dispatch map will be updated.

After the dispatch map is another unique identifier, the IID (interface identifier). As Listing 16.5 shows, the IID is added as a static member, like the CLSID.

Listing 16.5   ShowStringDoc.cpp—IID

```
// Note: we add support for IID_IShowString to support typesafe binding
//  from VBA.  This IID must match the GUID that is attached to the
//  dispinterface in the .ODL file.

// {61C76C07-70EA-11D0-9AFF-0080C81A397C}
static const IID IID_IShowString =
{ 0x61c76c07, 0x70ea, 0x11d0, { 0x9a, 0xff, 0x0, 0x80,
    0xc8, 0x1a, 0x39, 0x7c } };
```

Then the interface map looks like this:

```
BEGIN_INTERFACE_MAP(CShowStringDoc, CDocument)
     INTERFACE_PART(CShowStringDoc, IID_IShowSt, Dispatch)
END_INTERFACE_MAP()
```

An *interface map* hides COM functions such as QueryInterface() from you, the programmer, and, like a message map, enables you to think at a more abstract level. ShowString won't have multiple entries in the interface map, but many applications do. ClassWizard manages entries in the interface map for you.

The document constructor has some setting up to do. The AppWizard code is in Listing 16.6.

Listing 16.6 ShowStringDoc.cpp—Constructor

```
CShowStringDoc::CShowStringDoc()
{
    // TODO: add one-time construction code here
    EnableAutomation();
    AfxOleLockApp();
}
```

`EnableAutomation()` does just what its name suggests—enables Automation for this document. `AfxOleLockApp()` is used to ensure that an application isn't closed while one of its documents is still in use elsewhere. Imagine that a user has two applications open that use ShowString objects. When the first application is closed, ShowString shouldn't be closed because it's needed by the other application. ActiveX technology implements this by keeping a count, within the framework, of the number of active objects. `AfxOleLockApp()` increases this count. If it's nonzero when users finish using a server application, the application is hidden but not actually closed.

It shouldn't be surprising, then, to see the destructor for ShowString's document:

```
CShowStringDoc::~CShowStringDoc()
{
    AfxOleUnlockApp();
}
```

`AfxOleUnlockApp()` decreases the count of active objects so that eventually ShowString can be closed.

Properties to Expose

At this point, you have an Automation server that doesn't expose any methods or properties. Also, the four member variables of the document that have been in all the previous versions of ShowString haven't been added to this version. These member variables are

- string—The string to be shown
- color—0 for black, 1 for red, and 2 for green
- horizcenter—TRUE if the string should be centered horizontally
- vertcenter—TRUE if the string should be centered vertically

These variables will be added as Automation properties, so you won't type their names into the class definition for CShowStringDoc. Bring up ClassWizard by clicking its toolbar button or choosing View, ClassWizard. Click the Automation tab (see Figure 16.1) to add properties and methods. Make sure that CShowStringDoc is selected in the Class Name box.

The first step in restoring the old ShowString functionality is to add member variables to the document class that will be exposed as properties of the Automation server. There are two ways to expose properties: as a variable and with functions. Exposing a property as a variable is like declaring a public member variable of a C++ class; other applications can look at the value of the property and change it directly. A notification function within your server is called when the variable is changed from the outside. Exposing with Get and Set functions is like implementing a private member variable with public access functions. Other applications appear to access the variable directly, but the framework arranges for a call to your functions to Get and Set the property. Your Get may make sure that the object is in a valid state (for example, that a sorted list is now sorted or that a total has been calculated) before returning the property value. Your Set function may do error checking (validation) or may calculate other variables that depend on the property that the outside application is changing. To make a property read-only, you add it as a Get/Set function property and then don't implement a Set function.

FIG. 16.1

ClassWizard's Automation page handles most of the work of building an Automation server.

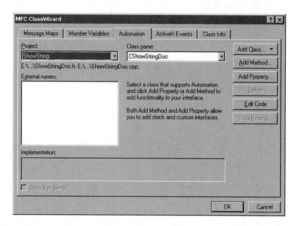

For the purposes of this chapter, you'll add the two centering flags to the CShowStringDoc class with Get and Set functions and add the string and color properties as direct-access properties. To do so, follow these steps:

1. Make sure that CShowStringDoc is the selected class, and then click the Add Property button to bring up the Add Property dialog box.

2. Type **String** in the External Name box. ClassWizard types along with you, filling in the Variable Name and Notification Function boxes for you.

3. Choose CString from the drop-down list box for Type. The dialog box should resemble Figure 16.2.

4. Click OK, click Add Property again, and then add Color as a direct-access property (see Figure 16.3). Use short as the data type.

5. Click OK, click Add Property again, and then add HorizCenter.

6. Choose BOOL for the type and then select the Get/Set Methods radio button. The Variable Name and Notification Function boxes are replaced by Get Function and Set Function, already filled in, as shown in Figure 16.4. (If the type changes from BOOL, choose BOOL again.) Click OK.

7. Add VertCenter in the same way that you added HorizCenter.

FIG. 16.2

Add String as a direct-access property.

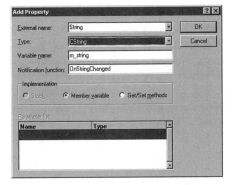

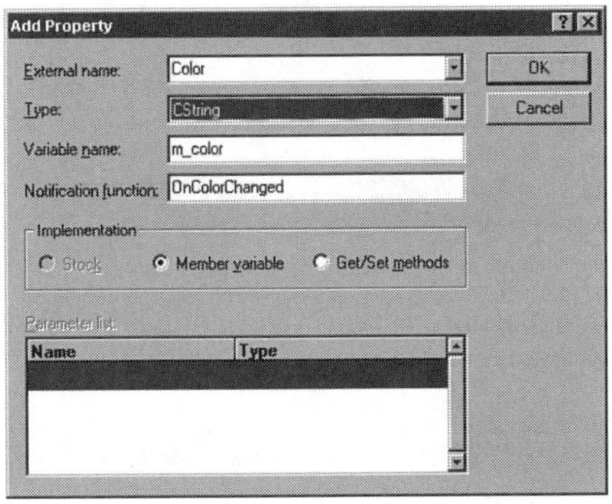

FIG. 16.3

Add Color as a direct-access property.

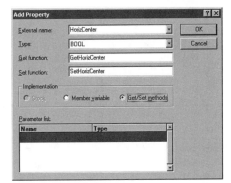

FIG. 16.4

Add HorizCenter as a Get/Set method property.

> **CAUTION**
>
> After you click OK to add a property, you can't change the type, external name, or other properties of the property. You have to delete it and then add one that has the new type, or external name, or whatever. Always look over the Add Property dialog box before clicking OK.

Figure 16.5 shows the ClassWizard summary of exposed properties and methods. The details of each property are shown in the Implementation box below the list of properties. In Figure 16.5, `VertCenter` is highlighted, and the Implementation box reminds you that `VertCenter` has a `Get` function and a `Set` function, showing their declarations. Click OK to close ClassWizard.

FIG. 16.5

ClassWizard provides a summary of the properties you've added.

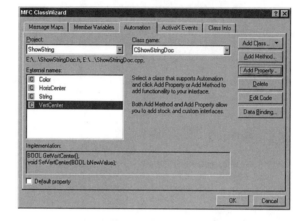

It should come as no surprise that as a result of these additions, ClassWizard has changed the header and source files for `CShowStringDoc`. Listing 16.7 shows the new dispatch map in the header file.

Listing 16.7 ShowStringDoc.h—Dispatch Map

```
//{{AFX_DISPATCH(CShowStringDoc)
CString m_string;
afx_msg void OnStringChanged();
short m_color;
afx_msg void OnColorChanged();
afx_msg BOOL GetHorizCenter();
afx_msg void SetHorizCenter(BOOL bNewValue);
afx_msg BOOL GetVertCenter();
afx_msg void SetVertCenter(BOOL bNewValue);
//}}AFX_DISPATCH
DECLARE_DISPATCH_MAP()
```

Two new member variables have been added: `m_string` and `m_color`.

N O T E It's natural to wonder whether these are actually public member variables; they aren't. Just above this dispatch map is this line:

```
DECLARE_MESSAGE_MAP()
```

That macro, when it expands, declares a number of protected variables. Because these declarations are immediately afterward, they are protected member variables and protected functions. They're accessed in just the same way that protected message-catching functions are—they're called by a member function hidden in the class that directs traffic by using these maps. ■

A block of code has been added in the source file, but it's boring, as you can see by looking at Listing 16.8.

Listing 16.8 ShowStringDoc.cpp—Notification, *Get*, and *Set* Functions

```cpp
//////////////////////////////////////////////////////////
// CShowStringDoc commands

void CShowStringDoc::OnColorChanged()
{
    // TODO: Add notification handler code

}

void CShowStringDoc::OnStringChanged()
{
    // TODO: Add notification handler code

}

BOOL CShowStringDoc::GetHorizCenter()
{
    // TODO: Add your property handler here

    return TRUE;
}

void CShowStringDoc::SetHorizCenter(BOOL bNewValue)
{
    // TODO: Add your property handler here

}

BOOL CShowStringDoc::GetVertCenter()
{
    // TODO: Add your property handler here

    return TRUE;
}

void CShowStringDoc::SetVertCenter(BOOL bNewValue)
{
    // TODO: Add your property handler here

}
```

The class still doesn't have member variables for the centering flags. (You might have decided to implement these in some other way than as two simple variables, so ClassWizard doesn't even try to guess what to add.) Add them by hand to the header file, ShowStringDoc.h, as private member variables:

```
// Attributes
private:
    BOOL m_horizcenter;
    BOOL m_vertcenter;
```

Now you can write their Get and Set functions; Listing 16.9 shows the code.

Listing 16.9   ShowStringDoc.cpp—*Get* and *Set* Functions for the Centering Flags

```
BOOL CShowStringDoc::GetHorizCenter()
{
    return m_horizcenter;
}

void CShowStringDoc::SetHorizCenter(BOOL bNewValue)
{
    m_horizcenter = bNewValue;
}

BOOL CShowStringDoc::GetVertCenter()
{
    return m_vertcenter;
}

void CShowStringDoc::SetVertCenter(BOOL bNewValue)
{
    m_vertcenter = bNewValue;
}
```

The *OnDraw()* Function

Restoring the member variables takes you halfway to the old functionality of ShowString. Changing the view's OnDraw() function will take you most of the rest of the way.

To write a version of OnDraw() that shows a string properly, you have a fair amount of background work to do. Luckily, you can open an old version of ShowString from your own work in Chapter 8, "Building a Complete Application: ShowString," and paste in the following bits of code. (If any of this code is unfamiliar to you, Chapter 8 explains it fully.) First, CShowStringDoc::OnNewDocument() in Listing 16.10 should initialize the member variables.

Listing 16.10   ShowStringDoc.cpp—*CShowStringDoc::OnNewDocument()*

```
BOOL CShowStringDoc::OnNewDocument()
{
    if (!CDocument::OnNewDocument())
        return FALSE;

    m_string = "Hello, world!";
    m_color = 0;      //black
```

```
        m_horizcenter = TRUE;
        m_vertcenter = TRUE;

        return TRUE;
}
```

Next, edit the document's Serialize function. Listing 16.11 shows the new code.

Listing 16.11   ShowStringDoc.cpp—*CShowStringDoc::Serialize()*

```
void CShowStringDoc::Serialize(CArchive& ar)
{
    if (ar.IsStoring())
    {
        ar << m_string;
        ar << m_color;
        ar << m_horizcenter;
        ar << m_vertcenter;
    }
    else
    {
        ar >> m_string;
        ar >> m_color;
        ar >> m_horizcenter;
        ar >> m_vertcenter;
    }
}
```

Finally, the view's OnDraw() function in Listing 16.12 actually shows the string.

Listing 16.12   ShowStringView.cpp—*CShowStringView::OnDraw()*

```
void CShowStringView::OnDraw(CDC* pDC)
{

    CShowStringDoc* pDoc = GetDocument();
    ASSERT_VALID(pDoc);

    COLORREF oldcolor;
    switch (pDoc->GetColor())
    {
    case 0:
        oldcolor = pDC->SetTextColor(RGB(0,0,0)); //black
        break;
    case 1:
        oldcolor = pDC->SetTextColor(RGB(0xFF,0,0)); //red
        break;
    case 2:
        oldcolor = pDC->SetTextColor(RGB(0,0xFF,0)); //green
        break;
    }
```

continues

Listing 16.12 Continued

```
    int DTflags = 0;
    if (pDoc->GetHorizcenter())
    {
        DTflags |= DT_CENTER;
    }
    if (pDoc->GetVertcenter())
    {
        DTflags |= (DT_VCENTER|DT_SINGLELINE);
    }

    CRect rect;
    GetClientRect(&rect);
    pDC->DrawText(pDoc->GetString(), &rect, DTflags);
    pDC->SetTextColor(oldcolor);

}
```

When you added `m_string`, `m_color`, `m_horizcenter`, and `m_vertcenter` to the document with ClassWizard, they were added as protected member variables. This view code needs access to them. As you can see, the view calls public functions to get to these member variables of the document.

N O T E You could have chosen instead to make the view a friend to the document so that it could access the member variables directly, but that would give view functions the capability to use and change all private and protected member variables of the document. This more limited access is more appropriate and better preserves encapsulation. Encapsulation and other object-oriented concepts are discussed in Appendix A, " C++ Review and Object-Oriented Concepts." ■

Several functions already in the document class access these variables, but they're protected functions for use by ActiveX. The four public functions you'll add won't be able to use those names, because they're taken, and will have to have not-so-good names. Add them inline, as shown in Listing 16.13, to ShowStringDoc.h.

Listing 16.13 ShowStringDoc.h—Public Access Functions

```
public:
    CString GetDocString() {return m_string;}
    int     GetDocColor() {return m_color;}
    BOOL GetHorizcenter() {return m_horizcenter;}
    BOOL GetVertcenter() {return m_vertcenter;}
```

In `CShowStringView::OnDraw()`, change the code that calls `GetColor()` to call `GetDocColor()` and then change the code that calls `GetString()` to call `GetDocString()`. Build the project to check for any typing mistakes or forgotten changes. Although it may be tempting to run ShowString now, it won't do what you expect until you make a few more changes.

Showing the Window

By default, Automation servers don't have a main window. Remember the little snippet from `CShowStringApp::InitInstance()` in Listing 16.14.

Listing 16.14 ShowString.cpp—How the App Was Launched

```
// Check to see if launched as OLE server
if (cmdInfo.m_bRunEmbedded || cmdInfo.m_bRunAutomated)
{
    // Application was run with /Embedding or /Automation.  Don't show the
    //   main window in this case.
    return TRUE;
}
```

This code returns before showing the main window. Although you could remove this test so that ShowString always shows its window, it's more common to add a `ShowWindow()` method for the controller application to call. You'll also need to add a `RefreshWindow()` method that updates the view after a variable is changed; ClassWizard makes it simple to add these functions. Bring up ClassWizard, click the Automation tab, make sure that `CShowStringDoc` is still the selected class, and then click Add Method. Fill in the External name as **ShowWindow**. ClassWizard fills in the internal name for you, and there's no need to change it. Choose `void` from the Return Type drop-down list box. Figure 16.6 shows the dialog box after it's filled in.

FIG. 16.6

ClassWizard makes it simple to add a `ShowWindow()` method.

Click OK the dialog box, and `ShowWindow()` appears in the middle of the list of properties, which turns out to be a list of properties and methods in alphabetical order. The *C* next to the properties reminds you that these properties are custom properties. The *M* next to the methods reminds you that these are methods. With `ShowWindow()` highlighted, click Edit Code and then type the function, as shown in Listing 16.15.

▶ **See** "Displaying the Current Value," **p. 399**

Listing 16.15   ShowStringDoc.cpp—*CShowStringDoc::ShowWindow()*

```
void CShowStringDoc::ShowWindow()
{
    POSITION pos = GetFirstViewPosition();
    CView* pView = GetNextView(pos);
    if (pView != NULL)
    {
        CFrameWnd* pFrameWnd = pView->GetParentFrame();
        pFrameWnd->ActivateFrame(SW_SHOW);
        pFrameWnd = pFrameWnd->GetParentFrame();
        if (pFrameWnd != NULL)
            pFrameWnd->ActivateFrame(SW_SHOW);
    }
}
```

This code activates the view and asks for it to be shown. Bring up ClassWizard again, click Add Method, and add RefreshWindow(), returning void. Click OK and then Edit Code. The code for RefreshWindow(), shown in Listing 16.16, is even simpler.

Listing 16.16   ShowStringDoc.cpp—*CShowStringDoc::RefreshWindow()*

```
void CShowStringDoc::RefreshWindow()
{
    UpdateAllViews(NULL);
    SetModifiedFlag();
}
```

This arranges for the view (now that it's active) and its parent frame to be redrawn. Because a change to the document is almost certainly the reason for the redraw, this is a handy place to put the call to SetModifiedFlag(); however, if you prefer, you can put it in each Set function and the notification functions for the direct-access properties. You'll add a call to RefreshWindow() to each of those functions now—for example, SetHorizCenter():

```
void CShowStringDoc::SetHorizCenter(BOOL bNewValue)
{
    m_horizcenter = bNewValue;
    RefreshWindow();
}
```

And OnColorChanged() looks like this:

```
void CShowStringDoc::OnColorChanged()
{
    RefreshWindow();
}
```

Add the same RefreshWindow() call to SetVertCenter() and OnStringChanged(). Now you're ready to build and test. Build the project and correct any typing errors. Run ShowString as a standalone application to register it and to test your drawing code. You can't change the string, color, or centering as you could with older versions of ShowString because this version doesn't implement the Tools, Options menu item and its dialog box. The controller application will do that for this version.

Building a Controller Application in Visual Basic

This chapter has mentioned a controller application several times, and you may have wondered where it will come from. You'll put it together in Visual Basic. Figure 16.7 shows the Visual Basic interface.

FIG. 16.7
Visual Basic makes
Automation controller
applications very
quickly.

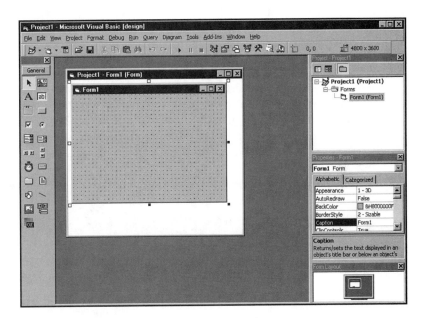

 T I P If you don't have Visual Basic but Visual C++ version 4.x or earlier, you can use DispTest, a watered-down version of Visual Basic that once came with Visual C++. It was never added to the Start menu, but you can run DISPTEST.EXE from the C:\MSDEV\BIN folder or from your old Visual C++ CD-ROM's \MSDEV\BIN folder. If you've written VBA macros in Excel and have a copy of Excel, you can use that, too. For testing OLE Automation servers, it doesn't matter which you choose.

To build a controller application for the ShowString Automation server, start by running Visual Basic. Create and empty project by choosing File, New, and double-clicking Standard EXE. In the window at the upper-right labeled Project1, click the View Code button. Choose Form from the left drop-down list box in the new window that appears; the Form_Load() subroutine is displayed. Enter the code in Listing 16.17 into that subroutine.

Listing 16.17 Form1.frm—Visual Basic Code

```
Private Sub Form_Load ()
    Set ShowTest = CreateObject("ShowString.Document")
    ShowTest.ShowWindow
    ShowTest.HorizCenter = False
    ShowTest.Color =
    ShowTest.String = "Hello from VB"
    Set ShowTest = Nothing
End Sub
```

Choose (General) from the left drop-down list box and then enter this line of code:

```
Dim ShowTest As Object
```

For those of you who don't read Visual Basic, this code will be easier to understand if you execute it one line at a time. Choose Debug, Step Into to execute the first line of code. Then repeatedly press F8 to move through the routine. (Wait after each press until the cursor is back to normal.) The line in the general code sets up an object called ShowTest. When the form is loaded (which is whenever you run this little program), an instance of the ShowString object is created. The next line calls the ShowWindow method to display the main window onscreen. Whenever the debugger pauses, the line of code that will run next is highlighted in yellow. Also notice that there is an arrow beside the highlighted line to further mark it. You will see something like Figure 16.8 with the default ShowString behavior.

FIG. 16.8

The ShowWindow method displays the main ShowString window.

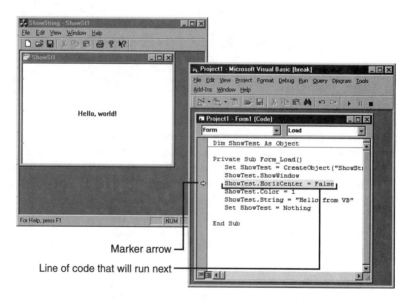

Marker arrow ⎤
Line of code that will run next ⎦

Press F8 again to run the line that turns off horizontal centering. Notice that you don't call the function SetHorizCenter. You exposed HorizCenter as a property of the OLE Automation server, and from Visual Basic you access it as a property. The difference is that the C++ framework code calls SetHorizCenter to make the change, rather than just make the change and then call a `notification` function to tell you that it was changed. After this line executes, your screen will resemble Figure 16.9 because the `SetHorizCenter` method calls `RefreshWindow()` to immediately redraw the screen.

FIG. 16.9

The Visual Basic program has turned off centering.

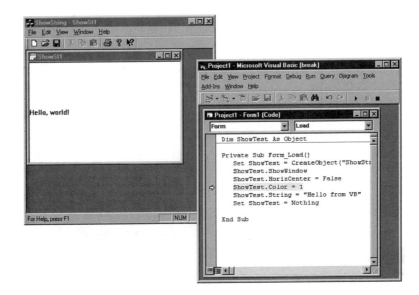

As you continue through this program, pressing F8 to move a step at a time, the string will turn red and then change to `Hello from VB`. Notice that the change to these directly exposed properties looks no different than the change to the `Get/Set` method property, `HorizCenter`. When the program finishes, the window goes away. You've successfully controlled your Automation server from Visual Basic.

Type Libraries and ActiveX Internals

Many programmers are intimidated by ActiveX, and the last thing they want is to know what's happening under the hood. There's nothing wrong with that attitude at all. It's quite object-oriented, really, to trust the already written ActiveX framework to handle the black magic of translating `ShowTest.HorizCenter = False` into a call to `CShowStringDoc::SetHorizCenter()`. If you want to know how that "magic" happens or what to do if it doesn't, you need to add one more piece to the puzzle. You've already seen the dispatch map for ShowString, but you haven't seen the *type library*. It's not meant for humans to read, but it is for ActiveX and the Registry. It's generated for you as part of a normal build from your Object Definition Language (ODL) file. This file was generated by AppWizard and is maintained by ClassWizard.

Perhaps you've noticed, as you built this application, a new entry in the ClassView pane. Figure 16.10 shows this entry expanded—it contains all the properties and methods exposed in the `IShowString` interface of your Automation server. If you right-click `IShowString` in this list, you can use the shortcut menu to add methods or properties. If you double-click any properties or methods, the .ODL file is opened for you to view. Listing 16.18 shows ShowString.odl.

FIG. 16.10
Automation servers have an entry in the ClassView for each of their interfaces.

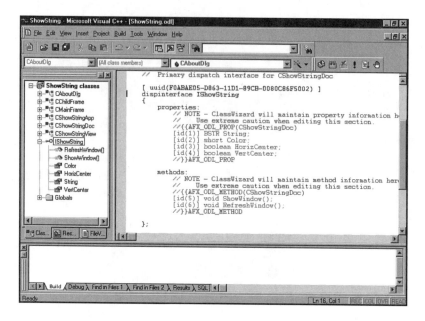

Listing 16.18 ShowString.odl—ShowString Type Library

```
// ShowString.odl : type library source for ShowString.exe

// This file will be processed by the MIDL compiler to produce the
// type library (ShowString.tlb).

[ uuid(61C76C06-70EA-11D0-9AFF-0080C81A397C), version(1.0) ]
library ShowString
{
    importlib("stdole32.tlb");

    //  Primary dispatch interface for CShowStringDoc

    [ uuid(61C76C07-70EA-11D0-9AFF-0080C81A397C) ]
    dispinterface IShowString
    {
        properties:
            // NOTE - ClassWizard will maintain property information here.
            //     Use extreme caution when editing this section.
            //{{AFX_ODL_PROP(CShowStringDoc)
            [id(1)] BSTR String;
            [id(2)] short Color;
            [id(3)] boolean HorizCenter;
            [id(4)] boolean VertCenter;
            //}}AFX_ODL_PROP

        methods:
            // NOTE - ClassWizard will maintain method information here.
            //     Use extreme caution when editing this section.
```

```
//{{AFX_ODL_METHOD(CShowStringDoc)
[id(5)] void ShowWindow();
[id(6)] void RefreshWindow();
//}}AFX_ODL_METHOD

};

//  Class information for CShowStringDoc

[ uuid(61C76C05-70EA-11D0-9AFF-0080C81A397C) ]
coclass Document
{
    [default] dispinterface IShowString;
};

//{{AFX_APPEND_ODL}}
//}}AFX_APPEND_ODL}}
};
```

This explains why Visual Basic just thought of all four properties as properties; that's how they're listed in this .ODL file. The two methods are here, too, in the methods section. You passed `"ShowString.Document"` to `CreateObject()` because there is a `coclass Document` section here. It points to a dispatch interface (`dispinterface`) called `IShowString`. Here's the interface map from ShowStringDoc.cpp:

```
BEGIN_INTERFACE_MAP(CShowStringDoc, CDocument)
    INTERFACE_PART(CShowStringDoc, IID_IShowString, Dispatch)
END_INTERFACE_MAP()
```

A call to `CreateObject("ShowString.Document")` leads to the `coclass` section of the .ODL file, which points to `IShowString`. The interface map points from `IShowString` to `CShowStringDoc`, which has a dispatch map that connects the properties and methods in the outside world to C++ code. You can see that editing any of these sections by hand could have disastrous results. Trust the wizards to do this for you.

In this chapter, you built an Automation server and controlled it from Visual Basic. Automation servers are far more powerful than older ways of application interaction, but your server doesn't have any user interaction. If the Visual Basic program wanted to enable users to choose the color, that would have to be built into the Visual Basic program. The next logical step is to allow the little embedded object to react to user events such as clicks and drags and to report to the controller program what has happened. That's what ActiveX controls do, as you'll see in the next chapter. ●

Building an ActiveX Control

Creating a Rolling-Die Control

ActiveX controls replace OLE controls, though the change affects the name more than anything else. (Much of the Microsoft documentation still refers to OLE controls.) The exciting behavior of these controls is powered by COM (the Component Object Model), which also powers OLE. This chapter draws, in part, on the work of the previous chapters. An ActiveX control is similar to an Automation server, but an ActiveX control also exposes events, and those enable the control to direct the container's behavior.

ActiveX controls take the place that VBX controls held in 16-bit Windows programming, enabling programmers to extend the control set provided by the compiler. The original purpose of VBX controls was to enable programmers to provide their users with unusual interface controls. Controls that look like gas gauges or volume knobs became easy to develop. Almost immediately, however, VBX programmers moved beyond simple controls to modules that involved significant amounts of calculation and processing. In the same way, many ActiveX controls are far more than just controls—they are components that can be used to build powerful applications quickly and easily.

The sample application for this chapter is a *die,* one of a pair of dice. Imagine a picture of a cubic die with the familiar pattern of dots indicating the current value, between 1 and 6. When the user clicks the picture, a new, randomly chosen number is shown. You might use one or more dice in any game program.

Building the Control Shell

The process of building this die control starts, as always, with AppWizard. Begin Developer Studio and then choose File, New. Click the Projects tab and then click MFC ActiveX ControlWizard, which is in the list at the left of the dialog box; fill in a project name at the top, choose an appropriate folder for the project files, and click OK. Figure 17.1 shows the completed dialog box, with the project name *Dieroll.*

FIG. 17.1

AppWizard makes creating an ActiveX control simple.

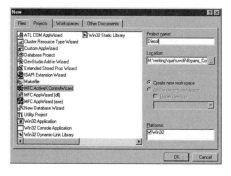

> **N O T E** Even though the technology is now called ActiveX, many classnames used throughout this chapter have Ole in their names, and comments refer to OLE. Though Microsoft has changed the technology's name, it has not yet propagated that change throughout Visual C++. You will have to live with these contradictions until the next release of Visual C++. ∎

There are two steps in the ActiveX control wizard. Fill out the first dialog box as shown in Figure 17.2: You want one control, no runtime licensing, source-file comments, and no Help files. After you have completed the dialog box, click Next.

FIG. 17.2

AppWizard's first step sets your control's basic parameters.

Part

IV

Ch

17

Runtime Licensing

Many developers produce controls as a salable product. Other programmers buy the rights to use such controls in their programs. Imagine that a developer, Alice, produces a fantastic die control and sells it to Bob, who incorporates it into the best backgammon game ever. Carol buys the backgammon game and loves the die control, and she decides that it would be perfect for a children's board game she is planning. Because the DIEROLL.OCX file is in the backgammon package, there is nothing (other than ethics) to stop her from doing this.

Runtime licensing is simple: There is a second file, DIEROLL.LIC, that contains the licensing information. Without that file, a control can't be embedded into a form or program, though a program into which the control is already embedded will work perfectly. Alice ships both DIEROLL.OCX and DIEROLL.LIC to Bob, but their licensing agreement states that only DIEROLL.OCX goes out with the backgammon game. Now Carol can admire DIEROLL.OCX, and it will work perfectly in the backgammon game, but if she wants to include it in the game she builds, she'll have to buy a license from Alice.

You arrange for runtime licensing with AppWizard when you first build the control. If you decide, after the control is already built, that you should have asked for runtime licensing after all, build a new control with licensing and copy your changes into that control.

The second and final AppWizard step enables you to set the new control's features. Make sure that Activates When Visible, Available in "Insert Object" Dialog, and Has an "About Box" are selected, as shown in Figure 17.3, and then click Finish. AppWizard summarizes your settings in a final dialog box. Click OK, and AppWizard creates 19 files for you and adds them to a project to make them easy to work with. These files are ready to compile, but they don't do anything at the moment. You have an empty shell; it's up to you to fill it.

FIG. 17.3

AppWizard's second step governs your control's appearance and behavior.

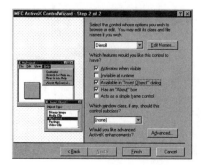

AppWizard's Code

Nineteen files sound like a lot, but they aren't. There are only three classes: CDierollApp, CDierollCtrl, and CDierollPropPage. They take up six files; the other 13 are the project file, make file, resource file, ClassWizard database, ODL file, and so on.

CDierollApp CDierollApp is a very small class. It inherits from COleControlModule and provides overrides of InitInstance() and ExitInstance() that do nothing but call the base-class versions of these functions. This is where you find _tlid, the external globally unique ID for your control, and some version numbers that make delivering upgrades of your control simpler. The lines in Dieroll.cpp that set up these identifiers are the following:

```
const GUID CDECL BASED_CODE _tlid =
        { 0x914b21a5, 0x7946, 0x11d0, { 0x9b, 0x1, 0, 0x80,
          0xc8, 0x1a, 0x39, 0x7c } };
const WORD _wVerMajor = 1;
const WORD _wVerMinor = 0;
```

CDierollCtrl The CDierollCtrl class inherits from COleControl, and it has a constructor and destructor, plus overrides for these four functions:

■ OnDraw() draws the control.

■ DoPropExchange() implements persistence and initialization.

■ OnResetState() causes the control to be reinitialized.

■ AboutBox() displays the About box for the control.

None of the code for these functions is particularly interesting. However, some of the maps that have been added to this class are of interest. There is an empty message map, ready to accept new entries, and an empty dispatch map, ready for the properties and methods that you choose to expose.

 TIP Message maps are explained in the "Message Maps" section of Chapter 3, "Messages and Commands." Dispatch maps are discussed in the "AppWizard's Automation Boilerplate" section in Chapter 16, "Building an Automation Server."

Below the empty message and dispatch maps comes a new map: the event map. Listing 17.1 shows the event map in the header file, and the source file event map is shown in Listing 17.2.

Listing 17.1 Excerpt from DierollCtl.h—Event Map

```
// Event maps
    //{{AFX_EVENT(CDierollCtrl)
        // NOTE - ClassWizard will add and remove member functions here.
        //    DO NOT EDIT what you see in these blocks of generated code !
    //}}AFX_EVENT
    DECLARE_EVENT_MAP()
```

Listing 17.2 Excerpt from DierollCtl.cpp—Event Map

```
BEGIN_EVENT_MAP(CDierollCtrl, COleControl)
    //{{AFX_EVENT_MAP(CDierollCtrl)
    // NOTE - ClassWizard will add and remove event map entries
    //    DO NOT EDIT what you see in these blocks of generated code !
    //}}AFX_EVENT_MAP
END_EVENT_MAP()
```

Part
IV

Ch
17

Event maps, like message maps and dispatch maps, link real-world happenings to your code. *Message maps* catch things the user does, such as choosing a menu item or clicking a button. They also catch messages sent from one part of an application to another. *Dispatch maps* direct requests to access properties or invoke methods of an Automation server or ActiveX control. Event maps direct notifications from an ActiveX control to the application that contains the control (and are discussed in more detail later in this chapter).

There's one more piece of code worth noting in DierollCtl.cpp. It appears in Listing 17.3.

Listing 17.3 Excerpt from DierollCtl.cpp—Property Pages

```
/////////////////////////////////////////////////////////////////////////
// Property pages

// TODO: Add more property pages as needed.  Remember to increase the count!
BEGIN_PROPPAGEIDS(CDierollCtrl, 1)
    PROPPAGEID(CDierollPropPage::guid)
END_PROPPAGEIDS(CDierollCtrl)
```

The code in Listing 17.3 is part of the mechanism that implements powerful and intuitive property pages in your controls. That mechanism is discussed later in this chapter.

CDierollPropPage   The entire `CDierollPropPage` class is the domain of ClassWizard. Like any class with a dialog box in it, it has significant data exchange components. The constructor will initialize the dialog box fields using code added by ClassWizard. Listing 17.4 shows this code.

Listing 17.4   DierollPpg.cpp—*CDierollPropPage::CDierollPropPage()*

```
CDierollPropPage::CDierollPropPage() :
    COlePropertyPage(IDD, IDS_DIEROLL_PPG_CAPTION)
{
    //{{AFX_DATA_INIT(CDierollPropPage)
    // NOTE: ClassWizard will add member initialization here
    //    DO NOT EDIT what you see in these blocks of generated code !
    //}}AFX_DATA_INIT
}
```

The DoDataExchange() function moderates the data exchange between CDierollPropPage, which represents the dialog box that is the property page, and the actual boxes on the user's screen. It, too, will have code added by ClassWizard—Listing 17.5 shows the empty map AppWizard made.

Listing 17.5   DierollPpg.cpp—*CDierollPropPage::DoDataExchange()*

```
void CDierollPropPage::DoDataExchange(CDataExchange* pDX)
{
    //{{AFX_DATA_MAP(CDierollPropPage)
    // NOTE: ClassWizard will add DDP, DDX, and DDV calls here
    //    DO NOT EDIT what you see in these blocks of generated code !
    //}}AFX_DATA_MAP
    DDP_PostProcessing(pDX);
}
```

There is, not surprisingly, a message map for CDierollPropPage, and some registration code (shown in Listing 17.6), that enables the ActiveX framework to call this code when a user edits the control's properties.

Listing 17.6   DierollPpg.cpp—*CDierollPropPageFactory::UpdateRegistry()*

```
/////////////////////////////////////////////////////////////////////////////
// Initialize class factory and guid

IMPLEMENT_OLECREATE_EX(CDierollPropPage, "DIEROLL.DierollPropPage.1",
    0x914b21a8, 0x7946, 0x11d0, 0x9b, 0x1, 0, 0x80, 0xc8, 0x1a, 0x39, 0x7c)

/////////////////////////////////////////////////////////////////////////////
// CDierollPropPage::CDierollPropPageFactory::UpdateRegistry -
// Adds or removes system registry entries for CDierollPropPage

BOOL CDierollPropPage::CDierollPropPageFactory::UpdateRegistry(BOOL bRegister)
{
    if (bRegister)
        return AfxOleRegisterPropertyPageClass(AfxGetInstanceHandle(),
            m_clsid, IDS_DIEROLL_PPG);
    else
        return AfxOleUnregisterClass(m_clsid, NULL);
}
```

Designing the Control

Typically, a control has *internal data* (properties) and shows them in some way to the user. The user provides input to the control to change its internal data and perhaps the way the control looks. Some controls present data to the user from other sources, such as databases or remote files. The only internal data that makes sense for the die-roll control, other than some appearance settings that are covered later, is a single integer between 1 and 6 that represents the current number showing in the die. Eventually, the control will show a dot pattern like a real-world die, but the first implementation of OnDraw() will simply display the digit. Another simplification is to hard-code the digit to a single value while coding the basic structure; add the code to roll the die later, while dealing with input from the user.

Displaying the Current Value

Before the value can be displayed, the control must have a value. That involves adding a property to the control and then writing the drawing code.

Adding a Property

ActiveX controls have four types of properties:

- *Stock*. These are standard properties supplied to every control, such as font or color. The developer must activate stock properties, but there is little or no coding involved.

- *Ambient*. These are properties of the environment that surrounds the control—properties of the container into which it has been placed. These can't be changed, but the control can use them to adjust its own properties. For example, it can set the control's background color to match the container's background color.

- *Extended*. These are properties that the container handles, usually involving size and placement onscreen.

- *Custom*. These are properties added by the control developer.

To add the value to the die-roll control, use ClassWizard to add a custom property called Number. Follow these steps:

1. Choose View, ClassWizard, and then click the Automation tab.
2. Make sure that the Project drop-down list box at the upper-left of the dialog box is set to Dieroll (unless you chose a different name when building the control with AppWizard) and that the Class Name drop-down list box on the right has the classname CDieRollCtrl.
3. Click the Add Property button and fill in the dialog box as shown in Figure 17.4.
4. Type **Number** into the External Name combo box and notice how ClassWizard fills in suggested values for the Variable Name and Notification Function boxes.
5. Select short for the type.
6. Click OK to close the Add Property dialog box and OK to close ClassWizard.

FIG. 17.4
ClassWizard simplifies the process of adding a custom property to your die-rolling control.

Before you can write code to display the value of the Number property, the property must have a value to display. Control properties are initialized in DoPropExchange(). This method actually implements *persistence*; that is, it enables the control to be saved as part of a document and read back in when the document is opened. Whenever a new control is created, the properties can't be read from a file, so they are set to the default values provided in this method. Controls don't have a Serialize() method.

AppWizard generated a skeleton DoPropExchange() method; this code is in Listing 17.7.

Listing 17.7   DierollCtl.cpp—CDierollCtrl::DoPropExchange()

```
void CDierollCtrl::DoPropExchange(CPropExchange* pPX)
{
    ExchangeVersion(pPX, MAKELONG(_wVerMinor, _wVerMajor));
    COleControl::DoPropExchange(pPX);

    // TODO: Call PX_ functions for each persistent custom property.

}
```

Notice the use of the version numbers to ensure that a file holding the values was saved by the same version of the control. Take away the TODO comment that AppWizard left for you, and add this line:

```
    PX_Short( pPX, "Number",  m_number, (short)3 );
```

PX_Short() is one of many property-exchange functions that you can call—one for each property type that is supported. The parameters you supply are as follows:

■ The pointer that was passed to DoPropExchange()

■ The external name of the property as you typed it on the ClassWizard Add Property dialog box

■ The member variable name of the property as you typed it on the ClassWizard Add Property dialog box

■ The default value for the property (later, you can replace this hard-coded 3 with a random value)

The following are the PX functions:

PX_Blob() (for binary large object [BLOB] types)

PX_Bool()

PX_Color() (OLE_COLOR)

PX_Currency()

PX_DATAPATH (CDataPathProperty)

PX_Double()

PX_Float()

PX_Font()

PX_IUnknown() (for LPUNKNOWN types, COM interface pointer)

PX_Long()

PX_Picture()

PX_Short()

PX_String()

PX_ULong()

PX_UShort()

PX_VBXFontConvert()

Filling in the property's default value is simple for some properties but not for others. For example, you set colors with the RGB() macro, which takes values for red, green, and blue from 0 to 255 and returns a COLORREF. Say that you had a property with the external name EdgeColor and the internal name m_edgecolor and you wanted the property to default to gray. You would code that like the following:

```
PX_Short( pPX, "EdgeColor", m_edgecolor, RGB(128,128,128) );
```

Controls with font properties should, by default, set the font to whatever the container is using. To get this font, call the COleControl method AmbientFont().

Writing the Drawing Code

The code to display the number belongs in the OnDraw() method of the control class, CDierollCtrl. (Controls don't have documents or views.) This function is called automatically whenever Windows needs to repaint the part of the screen that includes the control. AppWizard generated a skeleton of this method, too, shown in Listing 17.8.

Listing 17.8   DierollCtl.cpp—CDierollCtrl::OnDraw()

```
void CDierollCtrl::OnDraw(CDC* pdc, const CRect& rcBounds,
    const CRect& rcInvalid)
{
    // TODO: Replace the following code with your own drawing code.
    pdc->FillRect(rcBounds,
```

continues

Listing 17.8 Continued

```
                CBrush::FromHandle((HBRUSH)GetStockObject(WHITE_BRUSH)));
        pdc->Ellipse(rcBounds);
}
```

As discussed in the "Scrolling Windows" section of Chapter 5, "Drawing on the Screen," the framework passes the function a device context to draw in, a CRect describing the space occupied by your control, and another CRect describing the space that has been invalidated. The code in Listing 17.8 draws a white rectangle throughout rcBounds and then draws an ellipse inside that rectangle, using the default foreground color. You can keep the white rectangle for now, but rather than draw an ellipse on it, draw a character that corresponds to the value in Number. To do that, replace the last line in the skeletal OnDraw() with these lines:

```
    CString val; //character representation of the short value
    val.Format("%i",m_number);
    pdc->ExtTextOut( 0, 0, ETO_OPAQUE, rcBounds, val, NULL );
```

These code lines convert the short value in m_number (which you associated with the Number property on the Add Property dialog box) to a CString variable called val, using the new CString::Format() function (which eliminates one of the last uses of sprintf() in C++ programming). The ExtTextOut() function draws a piece of text—the character in val—within the rcBounds rectangle. As the die-roll control is written now, that number will always be 3.

You can build and test the control right now if you would like to see how little effort it takes to make a control that does something. Unlike the other ActiveX applications, a control isn't run as a standalone application in order to register it. Build the project and fix any typing mistakes. Choose Tools, ActiveX Control Test Container to bring up the control test container, shown in Figure 17.5.

FIG. 17.5

The ActiveX control test container is the ideal place to test your control.

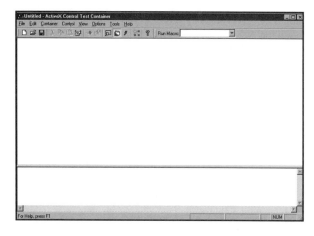

N O T E   If the Tools menu in Developer Studio doesn't include an ActiveX Control Test Container item, you can add it to the menu by following these steps:

1. Choose Tools, Customize.

2. Click the Tools tab.

3. Look at the list of tools and make sure that ActiveX Control Test Container isn't there.

4. Go to the bottom of the list and double-click the empty entry.

5. Type **Activ&eX Control Test Container** in the entry and press Enter.

6. Click the ... button to the right of the Command box and browse to your Visual C++ CD, or to the hard drive on which you installed Visual C++, and to the BIN folder beneath the Developer Studio folder. Highlight tstcon32.exe and click OK to finish browsing. On many systems the full path will be C:\Program Files\Microsoft Visual Studio\Common\Tools\TSTCON32.EXE. Your system may be different.

7. Click the rightward-pointing arrow beside the Initial Directory box and choose Target Directory from the list that appears.

8. Make sure that the three check boxes across the bottom of the directory are not selected.

9. Click the Close button.

If you haven't built a release version and your target is a release version, or if you have not built a debug version and your target is a debug version, you will receive an error message when you choose Tools, ActiveX Control Test Container. Simply build the control and you will be able to choose the menu item.

After you have installed the test container under the tools menu, you will not need to do so again. By bringing up the test container from within Developer Studio like this, you make it simpler to load your die-roll control into the test container. ■

Within the test container, choose Edit, Insert New Control and then choose Dieroll Control from the displayed list. As Figure 17.6 shows, the control appears as a white rectangle displaying a small number 3. You can move and resize this control within the container, but that little 3 stays doggedly in the upper-left corner. The next step is to make that number change when a user clicks the die.

Reacting to a Mouse Click and Rolling the Die

There are actually two things that you want your control to do when the user clicks the mouse on the control: to inform the container that the control has been clicked and to roll the die and display the new internal value.

FIG. 17.6

By adding one property and changing two functions, you have transformed the empty shell into a control that displays a 3.

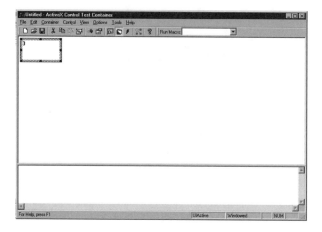

Notifying the Container

Let's first tackle using an *event* to notify a container. Events are how controls notify the container of a user action. Just as there are stock properties, there are stock events. These events are already coded for you:

- Click is coded to indicate to the container that the user clicked.
- DblClick is coded to indicate to the container that the user double-clicked.
- Error is coded to indicate an error that can't be handled by firing any other event.
- KeyDown is coded to indicate to the container that a key has gone down.
- KeyPress is coded to indicate to the container that a complete keypress (down and then up) has occurred.
- KeyUp is coded to indicate to the container that a key has gone up.
- MouseDown is coded to indicate to the container that the mouse button has gone down.
- MouseMove is coded to indicate to the container that the mouse has moved over the control.
- MouseUp is coded to indicate to the container that the mouse button has gone up.

The best way to tell the container that the user has clicked over the control is to fire a Click stock event. The first thing to do is to add it to the control with ClassWizard. Follow these steps:

1. Bring up ClassWizard by choosing View, ClassWizard, and click the ActiveX Events tab. Make sure that the selected class is CDierollCtrl.

2. Click the Add Event button and fill in the Add Event dialog box, as shown in Figure 17.7.

3. The external name is Click; choose it from the drop-down list box and notice how the internal name is filled in as FireClick.

4. Click OK to add the event, and your work is done. Close ClassWizard.

FIG. 17.7

ClassWizard helps you
add events to your
control.

You may notice the ClassView pane has a new addition: two icons resembling handles. Click
the + next to _DDierollEvents to see that Click is now listed as an event for this application, as
shown in Figure 17.8.

FIG. 17.8

ClassView displays
events as well as
classes.

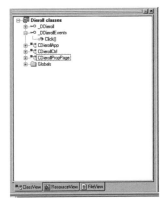

Now when the user clicks the control, the container class will be notified. If you are writing a
backgammon game, for example, the container can respond to the click by using the new value
on the die to evaluate possible moves or do some other backgammon-specific task.

The second part of reacting to clicks involves actually rolling the die and redisplaying it. Not
surprisingly, ClassWizard helps implement this. When the user clicks over your control, you
catch it with a message map entry, just as with an ordinary application. Bring up ClassWizard
and follow these steps:

1. Select the Message Maps tab this time and make sure that your control class,
   CDierollCtrl, is selected in the Class Name combo box.

2. Scroll through the Messages list box until you find the WM_LBUTTONDOWN message, which
   Windows generates whenever the left mouse button is clicked over your control.

3. Click Add Function to add a function that will be called automatically whenever this
   message is generated—in other words, whenever the user clicks your control. This
   function must always be named OnLButtonDown(), so ClassWizard doesn't give you a
   dialog box asking you to confirm the name.

4. ClassWizard has made a skeleton version of OnLButtonDown() for you; click the Edit
   Code button to close ClassWizard, and look at the new OnLButtonDown() code. Here's
   the skeleton:

   ```
   void CDierollCtrl::OnLButtonDown(UINT nFlags, CPoint point)
   {
       // TODO: Add your message handler code here and/or call default

       COleControl::OnLButtonDown(nFlags, point);
   }
   ```

5. Replace the TODO comment with a call to a new function, Roll(), that you will write in the
   next section. This function will return a random number between 1 and 6.

   ```
   m_number = Roll();
   ```

6. To force a redraw, next add this line:

   ```
   InvalidateControl();
   ```

7. Leave the call to COleControl::OnLButtonDown() at the end of the function; it handles
   the rest of the work involved in processing the mouse click.

Rolling the Die

To add Roll() to CDierollCtrl, right-click on CDierollCtrl in the ClassView pane and then
choose Add Member Function from the shortcut menu that appears. As shown in Figure 17.9,
Roll() will be a public function that takes no parameters and returns a short.

FIG. 17.9
Use the Add Member
Function dialog box to
speed routine tasks.

What should Roll() do? It should calculate a random value between 1 and 6. The C++ function
that returns a random number is rand(), which returns an integer between 0 and RAND_MAX.
Dividing by RAND_MAX + 1 gives a positive number that is always less than 1, and multiplying
by 6 gives a positive number that is less than 6. The integer part of the number will be between
0 and 5, in other words. Adding 1 produces the result that you want: a number between 1 and 6.
Listing 17.9 shows this code.

Listing 17.9   DierollCtl.cpp—CDierollCtrl::Roll()

```
short CDierollCtrl::Roll(void)
{
    double number = rand();
    number /= RAND_MAX + 1;
    number *= 6;
    return (short)number + 1;
}
```

N O T E If RAND_MAX + 1 isn't a multiple of 6, this code will roll low numbers slightly more often than high ones. A typical value for RAND_MAX is 32,767, which means that 1 and 2 will, on the average, come up 5,462 times in 32,767 rolls. However, 3 through 6 will, on the average, come up 5,461 times. You're neglecting this inaccuracy.

Some die-rolling programs use the modulo function instead of this approach, but it is far less accurate. The lowest digits in the random number are least likely to be accurate. The algorithm used here produces a much more random die roll. ■

The random number generator must be seeded before it is used, and it's traditional (and practical) to use the current time as a seed value. In DoPropExchange(), add the following line before the call to PX_Short():

```
srand( (unsigned)time( NULL ) );
```

Rather than hard-code the start value to 3, call Roll() to determine a random value. Change the call to PX_Short() so that it reads as follows:

```
PX_Short( pPX, "Number", m_number, Roll());
```

Make sure the test container is not still open, build the control, and then test it again in the test container. As you click the control, the displayed number should change with each click. Play around with it a little: Do you ever see a number less than 1 or more than 6? Any surprises at all?

Creating a Better User Interface

Now that the basic functionality of the die-roll control is in place, it's time to neaten it a little. It needs an icon, and it needs to display dots instead of a single digit.

A Bitmap Icon

Because some die-roll control users might want to add this control to the Control Palette in Visual Basic or Visual C++, you should have an icon to represent it. AppWizard has already created one, but it is simply an MFC logo that doesn't represent your control in particular. You can create a more specialized one with Developer Studio. Click the ResourceView tab of the Project Workspace window, click the + next to Bitmap, and double-click IDB_DIEROLL. You can now edit the bitmap 1 pixel at a time. Figure 17.10 shows an icon appropriate for a die. From now on, when you load the die-roll control into the test container, you will see your icon on the toolbar.

Displaying Dots

The next step in building this die-roll control is to make the control look like a die. A nice 3D effect with parts of some of the other sides showing is beyond the reach of an illustrative chapter like this one, but you can at least display a dot pattern.

Part
IV

Ch
17

FIG. 17.10

The ResourceView of Visual C++ enables you to build your own icon to be added to the Control Palette in Visual Basic.

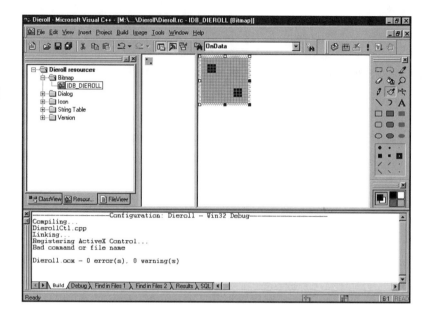

The first step is to set up a switch statement in OnDraw(). Comment out the three drawing lines and then add the switch statement so that OnDraw() looks like Listing 17.10.

Listing 17.10   DierollCtl.cpp—*CDierollCtrl::OnDraw()*

```cpp
void CDierollCtrl::OnDraw(
            CDC* pdc, const CRect& rcBounds, const CRect& rcInvalid)
{
    pdc->FillRect(rcBounds,
        CBrush::FromHandle((HBRUSH)GetStockObject(WHITE_BRUSH)));
//  CString val; //character representation of the short value
//  val.Format("%i",m_number);
//  pdc->ExtTextOut( 0, 0, ETO_OPAQUE, rcBounds, val, NULL );

    switch(m_number)
    {
    case 1:
        break;
    case 2:
        break;
    case 3:
        break;
    case 4:
        break;
    case 5:
        break;
    case 6:
        break;
    }
}
```

Now all that remains is adding code to the `case 1:` block that draws one dot, to the `case 2:` block that draws two dots, and so on. If you happen to have a real die handy, take a close look at it. The width of each dot is about one quarter of the width of the whole die's face. Dots near the edge are about one-sixteenth of the die's width from the edge. All the other rolls except 6 are contained within the layout for 5, anyway; for example, the single dot for 1 is in the same place as the central dot for 5.

The second parameter of `OnDraw()`, `rcBounds`, is a `CRect` that describes the rectangle occupied by the control. It has member variables and functions that return the control's upper-left coordinates, width, and height. The default code generated by AppWizard called `CDC::Ellipse()` to draw an ellipse within that rectangle. Your code will call `Ellipse()`, too, passing a small rectangle within the larger rectangle of the control. Your code will be easier to read (and will execute slightly faster) if you work in units that are one-sixteenth of the total width or height. Each dot will be four units wide or high. Add the following code before the `switch` statement:

```
int Xunit = rcBounds.Width()/16;
int Yunit = rcBounds.Height()/16;

int Top = rcBounds.top;
int Left = rcBounds.left;
```

Before drawing a shape by calling `Ellipse()`, you need to select a tool with which to draw. Because your circles should be filled in, they should be drawn with a brush. This code creates a brush and tells the device context `pdc` to use it, while saving a pointer to the old brush so that it can be restored later:

```
CBrush Black;
Black.CreateSolidBrush(RGB(0x00,0x00,0x00)); //solid black brush
CBrush* savebrush = pdc->SelectObject(&Black);
```

After the `switch` statement, add this line to restore the old brush:

```
pdc->SelectObject(savebrush);
```

Now you're ready to add lines to those `case` blocks to draw some dots. For example, rolls of 2, 3, 4, 5, or 6 all need a dot in the upper-left corner. This dot will be in a rectangular box that starts one unit to the right and down from the upper-left corner and extends five units right and down. The call to `Ellipse` looks like this:

```
pdc->Ellipse(Left+Xunit, Top+Yunit,
                Left+5*Xunit, Top + 5*Yunit);
```

The coordinates for the other dots are determined similarly. The `switch` statement ends up as show in Listing 17.11.

Listing 17.11 DierollCtl.cpp—CDierollCtrl::OnDraw()

```
switch(m_number)
    {
    case 1:
        pdc->Ellipse(Left+6*Xunit, Top+6*Yunit,
```

continues

Listing 17.11 Continued

```
                        Left+10*Xunit, Top + 10*Yunit); //center
        break;
    case 2:
        pdc->Ellipse(Left+Xunit, Top+Yunit,
                        Left+5*Xunit, Top + 5*Yunit);    //upper left
        pdc->Ellipse(Left+11*Xunit, Top+11*Yunit,
                        Left+15*Xunit, Top + 15*Yunit); //lower right
        break;
    case 3:
        pdc->Ellipse(Left+Xunit, Top+Yunit,
                        Left+5*Xunit, Top + 5*Yunit);    //upper left
        pdc->Ellipse(Left+6*Xunit, Top+6*Yunit,
                        Left+10*Xunit, Top + 10*Yunit); //center
        pdc->Ellipse(Left+11*Xunit, Top+11*Yunit,
                        Left+15*Xunit, Top + 15*Yunit); //lower right
        break;
    case 4:
        pdc->Ellipse(Left+Xunit, Top+Yunit,
                        Left+5*Xunit, Top + 5*Yunit);    //upper left
        pdc->Ellipse(Left+11*Xunit, Top+Yunit,
                        Left+15*Xunit, Top + 5*Yunit);  //upper right
        pdc->Ellipse(Left+Xunit, Top+11*Yunit,
                        Left+5*Xunit, Top + 15*Yunit);  //lower left
        pdc->Ellipse(Left+11*Xunit, Top+11*Yunit,
                        Left+15*Xunit, Top + 15*Yunit); //lower right
        break;
    case 5:
        pdc->Ellipse(Left+Xunit, Top+Yunit,
                        Left+5*Xunit, Top + 5*Yunit);    //upper left
        pdc->Ellipse(Left+11*Xunit, Top+Yunit,
                        Left+15*Xunit, Top + 5*Yunit);  //upper right
        pdc->Ellipse(Left+6*Xunit, Top+6*Yunit,
                        Left+10*Xunit, Top + 10*Yunit); //center
        pdc->Ellipse(Left+Xunit, Top+11*Yunit,
                        Left+5*Xunit, Top + 15*Yunit);  //lower left
        pdc->Ellipse(Left+11*Xunit, Top+11*Yunit,
                        Left+15*Xunit, Top + 15*Yunit); //lower right
        break;
    case 6:
            pdc->Ellipse(Left+Xunit, Top+Yunit,
             Left+5*Xunit, Top + 5*Yunit);    //upper left
            pdc->Ellipse(Left+11*Xunit, Top+Yunit,
             Left+15*Xunit, Top + 5*Yunit);  //upper right
            pdc->Ellipse(Left+Xunit, Top+6*Yunit,
             Left+5*Xunit, Top + 10*Yunit);  //center left
            pdc->Ellipse(Left+11*Xunit, Top+6*Yunit,
                Left+15*Xunit, Top + 10*Yunit); //center right
            pdc->Ellipse(Left+Xunit, Top+11*Yunit,
             Left+5*Xunit, Top + 15*Yunit);  //lower left
            pdc->Ellipse(Left+11*Xunit, Top+11*Yunit,
             Left+15*Xunit, Top + 15*Yunit); //lower right
            break;
    }
```

Build the OCX again and try it out in the test container. You will see something similar to Figure 17.11, which actually looks like a die!

FIG. 17.11

Your rolling-die control now looks like a die.

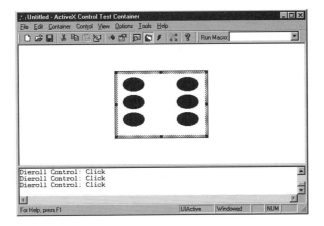

If you're sharp-eyed or if you stretch the die very small, you might notice that the pattern of dots is just slightly off-center. That's because the control's height and width are not always an exact multiple of 16. For example, if `Width()` returned 31, `Xunit` would be 1, and all the dots would be arranged between positions 0 and 16, leaving a wide blank band at the far right of the control. Luckily, the width is typically far more than 31 pixels, and so the asymmetry is less noticeable.

To fix this, center the dots in the control. Find the lines that calculate `Xunit` and `Yunit`, and then add the new lines from the code fragment in Listing 17.12.

Listing 17.12 DierollCtl.cpp—Adjusting *Xunit* and *Yunit*

```
//dots are 4 units wide and high, one unit from the edge
int Xunit = rcBounds.Width()/16;
int Yunit = rcBounds.Height()/16;
int Xleft = rcBounds.Width()%16;
int Yleft = rcBounds.Height()%16;

// adjust top left by amount left over
int Top = rcBounds.top + Yleft/2;
int Left = rcBounds.left + Xleft/2;
```

`Xleft` and `Yleft` are the leftovers in the X and Y direction. By moving `Top` and `Left` over by half the leftover, you center the dots in the control without having to change any other code.

Part
IV

Ch
17

Generating Property Sheets

ActiveX controls have property sheets that enable the user to set properties without any change to the container application. (Property sheets and pages are discussed in Chapter 12, "Property Pages and Sheets.") You set these up as dialog boxes, taking advantage of prewritten pages for font, color, and other common properties. For this control, the obvious properties to add are the following:

- A flag to indicate whether the value should be displayed as a digit or a dot pattern
- Foreground color
- Background color

N O T E   It's easy to become confused about what exactly a property page is. Is each one of the tabs on a dialog box a separate page, or is the whole collection of tabs a page? Each tab is called a *page* and the collection of tabs is called a *sheet*. You set up each page as a dialog box and use ClassWizard to connect the values on that dialog box to member variables. ■

Digits Versus Dots

It's a simple enough matter to allow the user to choose whether to display the current value as a digit or a dot pattern. Simply add a property that indicates this preference and then use the property in OnDraw(). The user can set the property, using the property page.

First, add the property using ClassWizard. Here's how: Bring up ClassWizard and select the Automation tab. Make sure that the CDierollCtrl class is selected and then click Add Property. On the Add Property dialog box, provide the external name Dots and the internal name m_dots. The type should be BOOL because Dots can be either TRUE or FALSE. Implement this new property as a member variable (direct-access) property. Click OK to complete the Add Property dialog box and click OK to close ClassWizard. The member variable is added to the class, the dispatch map is updated, and a stub is added for the notification function, OnDotsChanged().

To initialize Dots and arrange for it to be saved with a document, add the following line to DoPropExchange() after the call to PX_Short():

```
    PX_Bool( pPX, "Dots", m_dots, TRUE );
```

Initializing the Dots property to TRUE ensures that the control's default behavior is to display the dot pattern.

In OnDraw(), uncomment those lines that displayed the digit. Wrap an if around them so that the digit is displayed if m_dots is FALSE and dots are displayed if it is TRUE. The code looks like Listing 17.13.

Listing 17.13   DierollCtl.cpp—*CDierollCtrl::OnDraw()*

```
void CDierollCtrl::OnDraw(
            CDC* pdc, const CRect& rcBounds, const CRect& rcInvalid)
{
    pdc->FillRect(rcBounds,
        CBrush::FromHandle((HBRUSH)GetStockObject(WHITE_BRUSH)));

    if (!m_dots)
    {
        CString val; //character representation of the short value
        val.Format("%i",m_number);
        pdc->ExtTextOut( 0, 0, ETO_OPAQUE, rcBounds, val, NULL );
    }
    else
    {
      //dots are 4 units wide and high, one unit from the edge
        int Xunit = rcBounds.Width()/16;
        int Yunit = rcBounds.Height()/16;
        int Xleft = rcBounds.Width()%16;
        int Yleft = rcBounds.Height()%16;

        // adjust top left by amount left over
        int Top = rcBounds.top + Yleft/2;
        int Left = rcBounds.left + Xleft/2;

        CBrush Black;
        Black.CreateSolidBrush(RGB(0x00,0x00,0x00)); //solid black brush

        CBrush* savebrush = pdc->SelectObject(&Black);

        switch(m_number)
        {
        case 1:
                ...
        }
        pdc->SelectObject(savebrush);
    }
}
```

To give the user a way to set Dots, you build a property page by following these steps:

1. Click the ResourceView tab in the Project Workspace window and then click the + next to Dialog.

2. The OCX has two dialog boxes: one for the About box and one for the property page. Double-click IDD_PROPPAGE_DIEROLL to open it. Figure 17.12 shows the boilerplate property page generated by AppWizard.

3. Remove the static control with the TODO reminder by highlighting it and pressing Delete.

4. Drag a check box from the Control Palette onto the dialog box. Choose View, Properties and then pin the Property dialog box in place.

Part
IV
Ch
17

FIG. 17.12

AppWizard generates an empty property page.

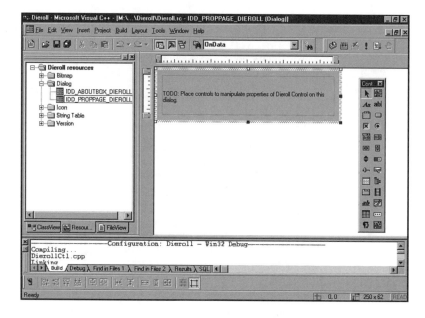

5. Change the caption to **Display Dot Pattern** and change the resource ID to **IDC_DOTS**, as shown in Figure 17.13.

FIG. 17.13

You build the property page for the die-roll control like any other dialog box.

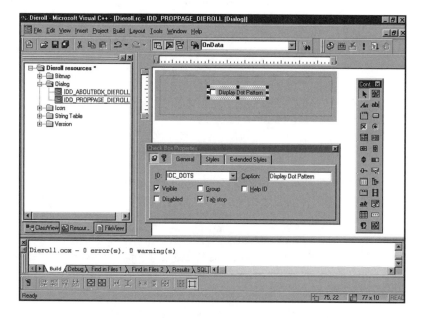

When the user brings up the property page and clicks to set or unset the check box, that doesn't directly affect the value of m_dots or the Dots property. To connect the dialog box to member variables, use ClassWizard and follow these steps:

1. Bring up ClassWizard while the dialog box is still open and on top, and then select the Member Variables tab.

2. Make sure that CDierollPropPage is the selected class and that the IDC_DOTS resource ID is highlighted, and then click the Add Variable button.

3. Fill in m_dots as the name and **BOOL** as the type, and fill in the Optional Property Name combo box with Dots, as shown in Figure 17.14.

4. Click OK, and ClassWizard generates code to connect the property page with the member variables in CDierollPropPage::DoDataExchange().

FIG. 17.14

You connect the property page to the properties of the control with ClassWizard.

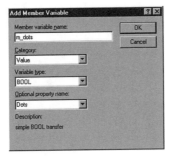

The path that data follows can be a little twisty. When the user brings up the property sheet, the value of TRUE or FALSE is in a temporary variable. Clicking the check box toggles the value of that temporary variable. When the user clicks OK, that value goes into CDierollPropPage::m_dots and also to the Automation property Dots. That property has already been connected to CDierollCtrl::m_dots, so the dispatch map in CDierollCtrl will make sure that the other m_dots is changed. Because the OnDraw() function uses CDierollCtrl::m_dots, the control's appearance changes in response to the change made by the user on the property page. Having the same name for the two member variables makes things more confusing to first-time control builders but less confusing in the long run.

This works now. Build the control and insert it into the test container. To change the properties, choose Edit, Dieroll Control Object, and Properties; your own property page will appear, as shown in Figure 17.15. (The Extended tab is provided for you, but as you can see, it doesn't really do anything. Your General tab is the important one at the moment.) Prove to yourself that the control displays dots or a digit, depending on the page's setting, by changing the setting, clicking OK, and then watching the control redraw.

When the control is displaying the value as a number, you might want to display that number in a font that's more in proportion with the control's current width and height and centered within the control. That's a relatively simple modification to OnDraw(), which you can investigate on your own.

FIG. 17.15

The control test container displays your own property page.

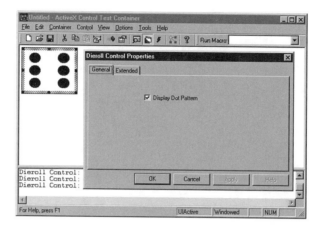

User-Selected Colors

The die you've created will always have black dots on a white background, but giving the user control to change this is remarkably simple. You need a property for the foreground color and another for the background color. These have already been implemented as stock properties: BackColor and ForeColor.

Stock Properties   Here is the complete list of stock properties available to a control that you write:

- Appearance. Specifies the control's general look
- BackColor. Specifies the control's background color
- BorderStyle. Specifies either the standard border or no border
- Caption. Specifies the control's caption or text
- Enabled. Specifies whether the control can be used
- Font. Specifies the control's default font
- ForeColor. Specifies the control's foreground color
- Text. Also specifies the control's caption or text
- hWnd. Specifies the control's window handle

Ambient Properties   Controls can also access *ambient properties,* which are properties of the environment that surrounds the control—that is, properties of the container into which you place the control. You can't change ambient properties, but the control can use them to adjust its own properties. For example, the control can set its background color to match that of the container.

The container provides all support for ambient properties. Any of your code that uses an ambient property should be prepared to use a default value if the container doesn't support that property. Here's how to use an ambient property called UserMode:

```
BOOL bUserMode;
    if( !GetAmbientProperty( DISPID_AMBIENT_USERMODE,
        VT_BOOL, &bUserMode ) )
    {
        bUserMode = TRUE;
    }
```

This code calls GetAmbientProperty() with the display ID (DISPID) and variable type (vartype) required. It also provides a pointer to a variable into which the value is placed. This variable's type must match the vartype. If GetAmbientProperty() returns FALSE, bUserMode is set to a default value.

A number of useful DISPIDs are defined in olectl.h, including these:

DISPID_AMBIENT_BACKCOLOR

DISPID_AMBIENT_DISPLAYNAME

DISPID_AMBIENT_FONT

DISPID_AMBIENT_FORECOLOR

DISPID_AMBIENT_LOCALEID

DISPID_AMBIENT_MESSAGEREFLECT

DISPID_AMBIENT_SCALEUNITS

DISPID_AMBIENT_TEXTALIGN

DISPID_AMBIENT_USERMODE

DISPID_AMBIENT_UIDEAD

DISPID_AMBIENT_SHOWGRABHANDLES

DISPID_AMBIENT_SHOWHATCHING

DISPID_AMBIENT_DISPLAYASDEFAULT

DISPID_AMBIENT_SUPPORTSMNEMONICS

DISPID_AMBIENT_AUTOCLIP

DISPID_AMBIENT_APPEARANCE

Remember that not all containers support all these properties. Some might not support any, and still others might support properties not included in the preceding list.

The vartypes include those shown in Table 17.1.

Table 17.1 Variable Types for Ambient Properties

vartype	Description
VT_BOOL	BOOL
VT_BSTR	CString
VT_I2	short

continues

Part **IV**

Ch **17**

Table 17.1 Continued

vartype	Description
VT_I4	long
VT_R4	float
VT_R8	double
VT_CY	CY
VT_COLOR	OLE_COLOR
VT_DISPATCH	LPDISPATCH
VT_FONT	LPFONTDISP

Remembering which `vartype` goes with which `DISPID` and checking the return from `GetAmbientProperty()` are a bothersome process, so the framework provides member functions of `COleControl` to get the most popular ambient properties:

- `OLE_COLOR AmbientBackColor()`
- `CString AmbientDisplayName()`
- `LPFONTDISP AmbientFont()` (Don't forget to release the font by using `Release()`.)
- `OLE_COLOR AmbientForeColor()`
- `LCID AmbientLocaleID()`
- `CString AmbientScaleUnits()`
- `short AmbientTextAlign()` (0 means general—numbers right, text left; 1 means left-justify; 2 means center; and 3 means right-justify.)
- `BOOL AmbientUserMode()` (`TRUE` means user mode; `FALSE` means design mode.)
- `BOOL AmbientUIDead()`
- `BOOL AmbientShowHatching()`
- `BOOL AmbientShowGrabHandles()`

All these functions assign reasonable defaults if the container doesn't support the requested property.

Implementing *BackColor* and *ForeColor* To add `BackColor` and `ForeColor` to the control, follow these steps:

1. Bring up ClassWizard, and select the Automation tab.
2. Make sure that `CDierollCtrl` is the selected class, and click Add Property.
3. Choose `BackColor` from the top combo box, and the rest of the dialog box is filled out for you; it is grayed out to remind you that you can't set any of these fields for a stock property. Figure 17.16 shows the values provided for you.

FIG. 17.16

ClassWizard describes stock properties for you.

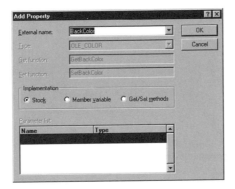

4. Click OK and then add ForeColor in the same way. After you click OK, ClassWizard's Automation tab will resemble Figure 17.17. The S next to these new properties reminds you that they are stock properties.

5. Click OK to close ClassWizard.

FIG. 17.17

An S precedes the stock properties in the OLE Automation list of properties and methods.

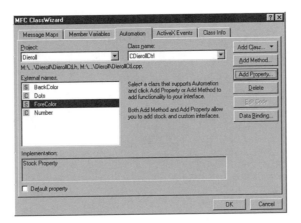

Setting up the property pages for these colors is almost as simple because there is a prewritten page that you can use. Look through DierollCtl.cpp for a block of code like Listing 17.14.

Listing 17.14 DierollCtl.cpp—Property Pages

```
/////////////////////////////////////////////////////////////
// Property pages

// TODO: Add more property pages as needed.  Remember to increase the count!
BEGIN_PROPPAGEIDS(CDierollCtrl, 1)
     PROPPAGEID(CDierollPropPage::guid)
END_PROPPAGEIDS(CDierollCtrl)
```

Part
IV

Ch
17

Remove the TODO reminder, change the count to 2, and add another PROPPAGEID so that the block looks like Listing 17.15.

Listing 17.15 DierollCtl.cpp—Property Pages

```
/////////////////////////////////////////////////////////////////////////
// Property pages

BEGIN_PROPPAGEIDS(CDierollCtrl, 2)
    PROPPAGEID(CDierollPropPage::guid)
    PROPPAGEID(CLSID_CColorPropPage)
END_PROPPAGEIDS(CDierollCtrl)
```

CLSID_CColorPropPage is a class ID for a property page that is used to set colors. Now when the user brings up the property sheet, there will be two property pages: one to set colors and the general page that you already created. Both ForeColor and BackColor will be available on this page, so all that remains to be done is using the values set by the user. You will have a chance to see that very soon, but first, your code needs to use these colors.

Changes to *OnDraw()*   In OnDraw(), your code can access the background color with GetBackColor(). Though you can't see it, this function was added by ClassWizard when you added the stock property. The dispatch map for CDierollCtrl now looks like Listing 17.16.

Listing 17.16 DierollCtl.cpp—Dispatch Map

```
BEGIN_DISPATCH_MAP(CDierollCtrl, COleControl)
    //{{AFX_DISPATCH_MAP(CDierollCtrl)
    DISP_PROPERTY_NOTIFY(CDierollCtrl, "Number", m_number,
    [ccc] OnNumberChanged, VT_I2)
    DISP_PROPERTY_NOTIFY(CDierollCtrl, "Dots", m_dots,
    [ccc] OnDotsChanged, VT_BOOL)
    DISP_STOCKPROP_BACKCOLOR()
    DISP_STOCKPROP_FORECOLOR()
    //}}AFX_DISPATCH_MAP
    DISP_FUNCTION_ID(CDierollCtrl, "AboutBox",
    [ccc]DISPID_ABOUTBOX, AboutBox, VT_EMPTY, VTS_NONE)
END_DISPATCH_MAP()
```

The macro DISP_STOCKPROP_BACKCOLOR() expands to these lines:

```
#define DISP_STOCKPROP_BACKCOLOR() \
    DISP_PROPERTY_STOCK(COleControl, "BackColor", \
    DISPID_BACKCOLOR,      COleControl::GetBackColor, \
    COleControl::SetBackColor, VT_COLOR)
```

This code is calling another macro, DISP_PROPERTY_STOCK, which ends up declaring the GetBackColor() function as a member of CDierollCtrl, which inherits from COleControl. Although you can't see it, this function is available to you. It returns an OLE_COLOR, which you translate to a COLORREF with TranslateColor(). You can pass this COLORREF to

CreateSolidBrush() and use that brush to paint the background. Access the foreground color with GetForeColor() and give it the same treatment. (Use SetTextColor() in the digit part of the code.) Listing 17.17 shows the completed OnDraw() (with most of the switch statement cropped out).

Listing 17.17   DierollCtl.cpp—CDierollCtrl::OnDraw()

```
void CDierollCtrl::OnDraw(CDC* pdc, const CRect& rcBounds,
                          const CRect& rcInvalid)
{
    COLORREF back = TranslateColor(GetBackColor());
    CBrush backbrush;
    backbrush.CreateSolidBrush(back);
    pdc->FillRect(rcBounds, &backbrush);

    if (!m_dots)
    {
        CString val; //character representation of the short value
        val.Format("%i",m_number);
        pdc->SetTextColor(TranslateColor(GetForeColor()));
        pdc->ExtTextOut( 0, 0, ETO_OPAQUE, rcBounds, val, NULL );
    }
    else
    {
        //dots are 4 units wide and high, one unit from the edge
        int Xunit = rcBounds.Width()/16;
        int Yunit = rcBounds.Height()/16;

        int Top = rcBounds.top;
        int Left = rcBounds.left;

        COLORREF fore = TranslateColor(GetForeColor());
        CBrush forebrush;
        forebrush.CreateSolidBrush(fore);

        CBrush* savebrush = pdc->SelectObject(&forebrush);

        switch(m_number)
        {
            ...
        }
        pdc->SelectObject(savebrush);
    }
}
```

Part

IV

Ch

17

Build the control again, insert it into the test container, and again bring up the property sheet by choosing Edit, Dieroll Control Object, Properties. As Figure 17.18 shows, the new property page is just fine for setting colors. Change the foreground and background colors a few times and experiment with both dots and digit display to exercise all your new code.

FIG. 17.18
Stock property pages make short work of letting the user set colors.

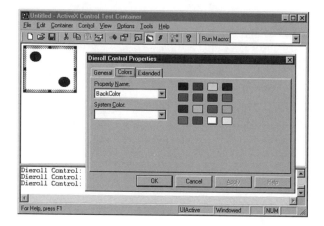

Rolling on Demand

ActiveX controls expose methods (functions) just as Automation servers do. This control rolls when the user clicks it, but you might want the container application to request a roll without the user's intervention. To do this, you add a function called DoRoll() and expose it.

Bring up ClassWizard, click the Automation tab, and then click Add Method. Name the new function **DoRoll**, select Return Type of Void, and when it is added, click Edit Code and fill it in like this:

```
void CDierollCtrl::DoRoll()
{
    m_number = Roll();
    InvalidateControl();
}
```

This simple code rolls the die and requests a redraw. Not everything about ActiveX controls needs to be difficult!

You can test this code by building the project, opening the test container, inserting a dieroll control, then choosing Control, Invoke Methods. On the Invoke Methods dialog box, shown in Figure 17.19, select DoRoll(Method) from the upper drop-down box; then click Invoke. You will see the die roll.

Future Improvements

The die-rolling control may seem complete, but it could be even better. The following sections discuss improvements that can be made to the control for different situations.

Enable and Disable Rolling

In many dice games, you can roll the die only when it is your turn. At the moment, this control rolls whenever it is clicked, no matter what. By adding a custom property called RollAllowed, you can allow the container to control the rolling. When `RollAllowed` is `FALSE`, `CDieCtrl::OnLButtonDown` should just return without rolling and redrawing. Perhaps `OnDraw` should draw a slightly different die (gray dots?) when `RollAllowed` is `FALSE`. You decide; it's your control. The container would set this property like any Automation property, according to the rules of the game in which the control is embedded.

FIG. 17.19
You can invoke your control's methods in the test container.

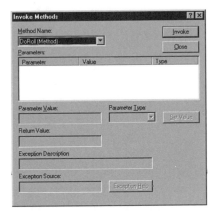

Dice with Unusual Numbers of Sides

Why restrict yourself to six-sided dice? There are dice that have 4, 8, 12, 20, and even 30 sides; wouldn't they make an interesting addition to a dice game? You'll need to get one pair of these odd dice so that you can see what they look like and change the drawing code in `CDierollCtrl::OnDraw()`. You then need to change the hard-coded 6 in `Roll()` to a custom property: an integer with the external name `Sides` and a member variable `m_sides`. Don't forget to change the property page to enable the user to set `Sides`, and don't forget to add a line to `CDieCtrl::DoPropExchange()` to make `Sides` persistent and initialize it to 6.

 There is such a thing as a two-sided die; it's commonly called a *coin*.

Arrays of Dice

If you were writing a backgammon game, you would need two dice. One approach would be to embed two individual die controls. How would you synchronize them, though, so that they both rolled at once with a single click? Why not expand the control to be an array of dice? The number of dice would be another custom property, and the control would roll the dice all at once. The `RollAllowed` flag would apply to all the dice, as would `Sides`, so that you could have two six-sided dice or three 12-sided dice, but not two four-sided dice and a 20-sider. `Number` would become an array.

 In Chapter 20, "Building an Internet ActiveX Control," you discover one way to synchronize two or more separate dice within one control container, and you'll learn some of the difficulties involved.

Internet Programming

Sockets, MAPI, and the Internet

Using Windows Sockets

There are a number of ways your applications can communicate with other applications through a network like the Internet. This chapter introduces you to the concepts involved with these programming techniques. Subsequent chapters cover some of these concepts in more detail.

Before the Windows operating system even existed, the Internet existed. As it grew, it became the largest TCP/IP network in the world. The early sites were UNIX machines, and a set of conventions called Berkeley sockets became the standard for TCP/IP communication between UNIX machines on the Internet. Other operating systems implemented TCP/IP communications, too, which contributed immensely to the Internet's growth. On those operating systems, things were becoming messy, with a wide variety of proprietary implementations of TCP/IP. Then a group of more than 20 vendors banded together to create the Winsock specification.

The Winsock specification defines the interface to a DLL, typically called WINSOCK.DLL or WSOCK32.DLL. Vendors write the code for the functions themselves. Applications can call the functions, confident that each function's name, parameter meaning, and final behavior are the same no matter which DLL is installed on the machine. For example, the DLLs included with Windows 95 and Windows NT are not the same at all, but a 32-bit Winsock application can run unchanged on a Windows 95 or Windows NT machine, calling the Winsock functions in the appropriate DLL.

N O T E Winsock isn't confined to TCP/IP communication. IPX/SPX support is the second protocol supported, and there will be others. For more information, check the Winsock specification itself. The Stardust Labs Winsock Resource Page at **http://www.stardust.com/wsresource/** is a great starting point. ■

An important concept in sockets programming is a socket's port. Every Internet site has a numeric address called an *IP address,* typically written as four numbers separated by dots: **198.53.145.3**, for example. Programs running on that machine are all willing to talk, by using sockets, to other machines. If a request arrives at **198.53.145.3**, which program should handle it?

Requests arrive at the machine, carrying a *port number*—a number from 1,024 and up that indicates which program the request is intended for. Some port numbers are reserved for standard use; for example, Web servers traditionally use port 80 to listen for Web document requests from client programs like Netscape Navigator.

Most socket work is *connection-based:* Two programs form a connection with a socket at each end and then send and receive data along the connection. Some applications prefer to send the data without a connection, but there is no guarantee that this data will arrive. The classic example is a time server that regularly sends out the current time to every machine near it without waiting until it is asked. The delay in establishing a connection might make the time sent through the connection outdated, so it makes sense in this case to use a connectionless approach.

Winsock in MFC

At first, sockets programming in Visual C++ meant making API calls into the DLL. Many developers built socket classes to encapsulate these calls. Visual C++ 2.1 introduced two new classes: `CAsyncSocket` and `CSocket` (which inherits from `CAsyncSocket`). These classes handle the API calls for you, including the startup and cleanup calls that would otherwise be easy to forget.

Windows programming is *asynchronous*: lots of different things happen at the same time. In older versions of Windows, if one part of an application was stuck in a loop or otherwise hung up, the entire application—and sometimes the entire operating system—would stick or hang with it. This is obviously something to avoid at all costs. Yet a socket call, perhaps a call to read some information through a TCP/IP connection to another site on the Internet, might take a long time to complete. (A function that is waiting to send or receive information on a socket is said to be *blocking*.) There are three ways around this problem:

- Put the function that might block in a thread of its own. The thread will block, but the rest of the application will carry on.

- Have the function return immediately after making the request, and have another function check regularly (*poll* the socket) to see whether the request has completed.

- Have the function return immediately, and send a Windows message when the request has completed.

The first option was not available until recently, and the second is inefficient under Windows. Most Winsock programming adopts the third option. The class `CAsyncSocket` implements this approach. For example, to send a string across a connected socket to another Internet site, you call that socket's `Send()` function. `Send()` doesn't necessarily send any data at all; it tries to, but if the socket isn't ready and waiting, `Send()` just returns. When the socket is ready, a message is sent to the socket window, which catches it and sends the data across. This is called *asynchronous Winsock programming*.

N O T E Winsock programming isn't a simple topic; entire books have been written on it. If you decide that this low-level sockets programming is the way to go, building standard programs is a good way to learn the process. ■

CAsyncSocket The `CAsyncSocket` class is a wrapper class for the asynchronous Winsock calls. It has a number of useful functions that facilitate using the Winsock API. Table 18.1 lists the `CAsyncSocket` member functions and responsibilities.

Table 18.1   *CAsyncSocket* Member Functions

Method Name	Description
Accept	Handles an incoming connection on a listening socket, filling a new socket with the address information.

continues

Table 18.1   Continued

Method Name	Description
AsyncSelect	Requests that a Windows message be sent when a socket is ready.
Attach	Attaches a socket handle to a CAsyncSocket instance so that it can form a connection to another machine.
Bind	Associates an address with a socket.
Close	Closes the socket.
Connect	Connects the socket to a remote address and port.
Create	Completes the initialization process begun by the constructor.
Detach	Detaches a previously attached socket handle.
FromHandle	Returns a pointer to the CAsyncSocket attached to the handle it was passed.
GetLastErro	Returns the error code of the socket. After an operation fails, call GetLastError to find out why.
GetPeerName	Finds the IP address and port number of the remote socket that the calling object socket is connected to, or fills a socket address structure with that information.
GetSockName	Returns the IP address and port number of this socket, or fills a socket address structure with that information.
GetSockOpt	Returns the currently set socket options.
IOCtl	Sets the socket mode most commonly to blocking or non-blocking.
Listen	Instructs a socket to watch for incoming connections.
OnAccept	Handles the Windows message generated when a socket has an incoming connection to accept (often overridden by derived classes).
OnClose	Handles the Windows message generated when a socket closes (often overridden by derived classes).
OnConnect	Handles the Windows message generated when a socket becomes connected or a connection attempt ends in failure (often overridden by derived classes).
OnOutOfBandData	Handles the Windows message generated when a socket has urgent, out-of-band data ready to read.
OnReceive	Handles the Windows message generated when a socket has data that can be read with Receive() (often overridden by derived classes).

Method Name	Description
OnSend	Handles the Windows message generated when a socket is ready to accept data that can be sent with Send() (often overridden by derived classes).
Receive	Reads data from the remote socket to which this socket is connected.
ReceiveFrom	Reads a datagram from a connectionless remote socket.
Send	Sends data to the remote socket to which this socket is connected.
SendTo	Sends a datagram without a connection.
SetSockOpt	Sets socket options.
ShutDown	Keeps the socket open but prevents any further Send() or Receive() calls.

If you use the CAsyncSocket class, you'll have to fill the socket address structures yourself, and many developers would rather delegate a lot of this work. In that case, CSocket is a better socket class.

CSocket CSocket inherits from CAsyncSocket and has all the functions listed for CAsyncSocket. Table 18.2 describes the new methods added and the virtual methods overridden in the derived CSocket class.

Table 18.2 *CSocket* **Methods**

Method Name	Description
Attach	Attaches a socket handle to a CAsyncSocket instance so that it can form a connection to another machine
Create	Completes the initialization after the constructor constructs a blank socket
FromHandle	Returns a pointer to the CSocket attached to the handle it was passed
IsBlocking	Returns TRUE if the socket is blocking at the moment, waiting for something to happen
CancelBlockingCal	Cancels whatever request had left the socket blocking
OnMessagePending	Handles the Windows messages generated for other parts of your application while the socket is blocking (often overridden by derived classes)

In many cases, socket programming is no longer necessary because the WinInet classes, ISAPI programming, and ActiveX controls for Web pages are bringing more and more power to

Part

V

Ch

18

Internet programmers. If you would like to explore a sample socket program, try Chatter and ChatSrvr, provided by Visual C++. Search either name in the online help to find the files.

Each session of Chatter emulates a user server. The ChatSrvr program is the server, acting as traffic manager among several clients. Each Chatter can send messages to the ChatSrvr by typing in some text, and the ChatSrvr sends the message to everyone logged on to the session. Several traffic channels are managed at once.

If you've worked with sockets before, this short overview may be all you need to get started. If not, you may not need to learn them. If you plan to write a client/server application that runs over the Internet and doesn't use the existing standard applications like mail or the Web, then learning sockets is probably in your future. But, if you want to use email, the Web, FTP, and other popular Internet information sources, you don't have to do it by writing socket programs at all. You may be able to use MAPI, the WinInet classes, or ISAPI to achieve the results you are looking for.

Using the Messaging API (MAPI)

The most popular networking feature in most offices is electronic mail. You could add code to your application to generate the right commands over a socket to transmit a mail message, but it's simpler to build on the work of others.

What Is MAPI?

MAPI is a way of pulling together applications that need to send and receive messages (*messaging applications*) with applications that know how to send and receive messages (*messaging services* and *service providers*), in order to decrease the work load of all the developers involved. Figure 18.1 shows the scope of MAPI. Note that the word *messaging* covers far more than just electronic mail: A MAPI service can send a fax or voice-mail message instead of an electronic mail message. If your application uses MAPI, the messaging services, such as email clients that the user has installed, will carry out the work of sending the messages that your application generates.

The extent to which an application uses messaging varies widely:

■ Some applications can send a message, but sending messages isn't really what the application is about. For example, a word processor is fundamentally about entering and formatting text and then printing or saving that text. If the word processor can also send the text in a message, fine, but that's incidental. Applications like this are said to be *messaging-aware* and typically use just the tip of the MAPI functionality.

■ Some applications are useful without being able to send messages, but they are far more useful in an environment where messages can be sent. For example, a personal scheduler program can manage one person's To Do list whether messaging is enabled or not. If it is enabled, a number of work group and client-contact features—such as sending email to confirm an appointment—become available. Applications like this are said to be *messaging-enabled* and use some, but not all, of the MAPI features.

■ Finally, some applications are all about messaging. Without messaging, these applications are useless. They are said to be *messaging-based,* and they use all of MAPI's functionality.

FIG. 18.1
The Messaging API includes applications that need messaging and those that provide it.

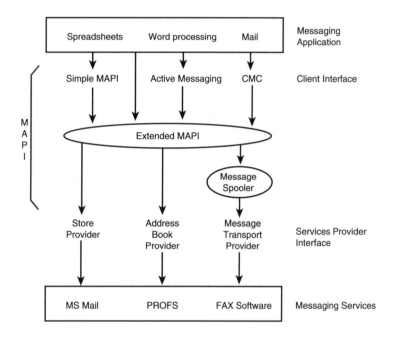

Win95 Logo Requirements

The number-one reason for a developer to make an application messaging aware is to meet the requirements of the Windows 95 Logo program. To qualify for the logo, an application must have a Send item on the File menu that uses MAPI to send the document. (Exceptions are granted to applications without documents.)

To add this feature to your applications, it's best to think of it before you create the empty shell with AppWizard. If you are planning ahead, here is a list of all the work you have to do to meet this part of the logo requirement:

1. In Step 4 of AppWizard, select the MAPI (Messaging API) check box.

That's it! The menu item is added, and message maps and functions are generated to catch the menu item and call functions that use your `Serialize()` function to send the document through MAPI. Figure 18.2 shows an application called MAPIDemo that is just an AppWizard empty shell.

No additional code was added to this application, beyond the code generated by AppWizard, and the Send item is on the File menu, as you can see. If you choose this menu item, your MAPI mail client is launched to send the message. Figures 18.2 and 18.3 were captured on a machine with Microsoft Exchange installed as an Internet mail client (Inbox), and so it is

Part
V

Ch
18

Microsoft Exchange that is launched, as shown in Figure 18.3. The message contains the current document, and it is up to you to fill in the recipient, the subject, and any text you want to send with the document.

FIG. 18.2

AppWizard adds the Send item to the File menu, as well as the code that handles the item.

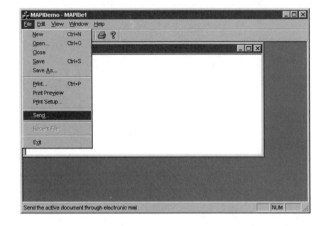

FIG. 18.3

Microsoft Mail is launched so that the user can fill in the rest of the email message around the document that is being sent.

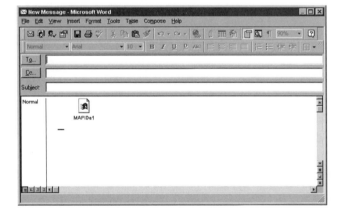

T I P If the Send item doesn't appear on your menu, make sure that you have a MAPI client installed. Microsoft Exchange is an easy-to-get MAPI client. The `OnUpdateFileSendMail()` function removes the menu item Send from the menu if no MAPI client is registered on your computer.

If you didn't request MAPI support from AppWizard when you built your application, here are the steps to manually add the Send item:

1. Add the Send item to the File menu. Use a resource ID of **`ID_FILE_SEND_MAIL`**. The prompt will be supplied for you.

2. Add these two lines to the document's message map, outside the `//AFX` comments:

```
ON_COMMAND(ID_FILE_SEND_MAIL, OnFileSendMail)
ON_UPDATE_COMMAND_UI(ID_FILE_SEND_MAIL, OnUpdateFileSendMail)
```

Adding the mail support to your application manually isn't much harder than asking AppWizard to do it.

Advanced Use of MAPI

If you want more from MAPI than just meeting the logo requirements, things do become harder. There are four kinds of MAPI client interfaces:

■ *Simple MAPI,* an older API not recommended for use in new applications

■ *Common Messaging Calls (CMC),* a simple API for messaging-aware and messaging-enabled applications

■ *Extended MAPI,* a full-featured API for messaging-based applications

■ *Active Messaging,* an API with somewhat fewer features than Extended MAPI but ideal for use with Visual C++

Common Messaging Calls   There are only ten functions in the CMC API. That makes it easy to learn, yet they pack enough punch to get the job done:

■ `cmc_logon()` connects to a mail server and identifies the user.

■ `cmc_logoff()` disconnects from a mail server.

■ `cmc_send()` sends a message.

■ `cmc_send_documents()` sends one or more files.

■ `cmc_list()` lists the messages in the user's mailbox.

■ `cmc_read()` reads a message from the user's mailbox.

■ `cmc_act_on()` saves or deletes a message.

■ `cmc_look_up()` resolves names and addresses.

■ `cmc_query_configuration()` reports what mail server is being used.

■ `cmc_free()` frees any memory allocated by other functions.

The header file XCMC.H declares a number of structures used to hold the information passed to these functions. For example, recipient information is kept in this structure:

```
/*RECIPIENT*/
typedef struct {
    CMC_string              name;
    CMC_enum                name_type;
    CMC_string              address;
    CMC_enum                role;
    CMC_flags               recip_flags;
    CMC_extension FAR       *recip_extensions;
} CMC_recipient;
```

You could fill this structure with the name and address of the recipient of a mail message by using a standard dialog box or by hard-coding the entries, like this:

```
CMC_recipient recipient = {
    "Kate Gregory",
    CMC_TYPE_INDIVIDUAL,
```

Part

V

Ch

18

```
"SMTP:kate@gregcons.com",
CMC_ROLE_TO,
CMC_RECIP_LAST_ELEMENT,
NULL };
```

The type, role, and flags use one of these predefined values:

Listing 18.1   (Excerpt from \MSDev\Include\XCMC.H) Command Definitions

```
/* NAME TYPES */
#define CMC_TYPE_UNKNOWN                    ((CMC_enum) 0)
#define CMC_TYPE_INDIVIDUAL                 ((CMC_enum) 1)
#define CMC_TYPE_GROUP                      ((CMC_enum) 2)

/* ROLES */
#define CMC_ROLE_TO                         ((CMC_enum) 0)
#define CMC_ROLE_CC                         ((CMC_enum) 1)
#define CMC_ROLE_BCC                        ((CMC_enum) 2)
#define CMC_ROLE_ORIGINATOR                 ((CMC_enum) 3)
#define CMC_ROLE_AUTHORIZING_USER           ((CMC_enum) 4)

/* RECIPIENT FLAGS */
#define CMC_RECIP_IGNORE                    ((CMC_flags) 1)
#define CMC_RECIP_LIST_TRUNCATED            ((CMC_flags) 2)
#define CMC_RECIP_LAST_ELEMENT              ((CMC_flags) 0x80000000)
```

There is a message structure you could fill in the same way or by presenting the user with a dialog box to enter the message details. This structure includes a pointer to the recipient structure you have already filled. Your program then calls `cmc_logon()`, `cmc_send()`, and `cmc_logoff()` to complete the process.

Extended MAPI   Extended MAPI is based on COM, the Component Object Model. Messages, recipients, and many other entities are defined as objects rather than as C structures. There are far more object types in Extended MAPI than there are structure types in CMC. Access to these objects is through OLE (ActiveX) interfaces. The objects expose properties, methods, and events. These concepts are discussed in Part IV, Chapter 13, "ActiveX Concepts."

Active Messaging   If you understand Automation (described in Chapter 16, "Building an Automation Server"), you will easily understand Active Messaging. Your application must be an Automation client, however, and building such a client is beyond the scope of this chapter. Various ways to use Active Messaging are in Visual Basic programming and VBA scripts for programs such as Excel. Your program would set up objects and then set their exposed properties (for example, the subject line of a message object) and invoke their exposed methods (for example, the `Send()` method of a message object).

The objects used in Active Messaging include the following:

- Session
- Message

■ Recipient

■ Attachment

Active messaging is part of the Collaboration Data Objects (CDO) library. A detailed reference of these objects, as well as their properties and methods, can be found in MSDN under Platform SDK, Database and Messaging Services, Collaboration Data Objects, CDO Library, and Reference. You'll find three articles on using Active Messaging, and sample applications, under Technical Articles, Database and Messaging Services, Microsoft Exchange Server.

Using the WinInet Classes

MFC 4.2 introduced a number of new classes that eliminate the need to learn socket programming when your applications require access to standard Internet client services. Figure 18.4 shows the way these classes relate to each other. Collectively known as the WinInet classes, they are the following:

■ CInternetSession

■ CInternetConnection

■ CInternetFile

■ HttpConnection

■ CHttpFile

■ CGopherFile

■ CFtpConnection

■ CGopherConnection

■ CFileFind

■ CFtpFileFind

■ CGopherFileFind

■ CGopherLocator

■ CInternetException

These classes help you write Internet *client* applications, with which users interact directly. If you want to write *server* applications, which interact with client applications, you'll be interested in ISAPI, discussed in the next section.

First, your program establishes a session by creating a CInternetSession. Then, if you have a uniform resource locator (URL) to a Gopher, FTP, or Web (HTTP) resource, you can call that session's OpenURL() function to retrieve the resource as a read-only CInternetFile. Your application can read the file, using CStdioFile functions, and manipulate that data in whatever way you need.

Part
V

Ch
18

FIG. 18.4

The WinInet classes make writing Internet client programs easier.

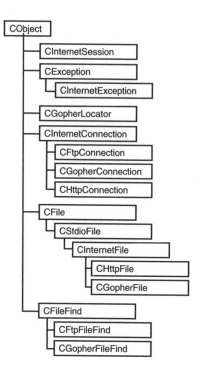

If you don't have an URL or don't want to retrieve a read-only file, you proceed differently after establishing the session. Make a connection with a specific protocol by calling the session's `GetFtpConnection()`, `GetGopherConnection()`, or `GetHttpConnection()` functions, which return the appropriate connection object. You then call the connection's `OpenFile()` function. `CFtpConnection::OpenFile()` returns a `CInternetFile`; `CGopherConnection::OpenFile()` returns a `CGopherFile`; and `CHttpConnection::OpenFile()` returns a `CHttpFile`. The `CFileFind` class and its derived classes help you find the file you want to open.

Chapter 19, "Internet Programming with the WinInet Classes," works through a sample client program using WinInet classes to establish an Internet session and retrieve information.

> **N O T E** Though email is a standard Internet application, you'll notice that the WinInet classes don't have any email functionality. That's because email is handled by MAPI. There is no support for Usenet news either, in the WinInet classes or elsewhere. ▪

Using Internet Server API (ISAPI) Classes

ISAPI is used to enhance and extend the capabilities of your HTTP (World Wide Web) server. ISAPI developers produce *extensions* and *filters*. Extensions are DLLs invoked by a user from a Web page in much the same way as CGI (common gateway interface) applications are invoked from a Web page. Filters are DLLs that run with the server and examine or change the data going to and from the server. For example, a filter might redirect requests for one file to a new location.

> **N O T E** For the ISAPI extensions and filters that you write to be useful, your Web pages must be kept on a server that is running an ISAPI-compliant server such as the Microsoft IIS Server. You must have permission to install DLLs onto the server, and for an ISAPI filter, you must be able to change the Registry on the server. If your Web pages are kept on a machine administered by your Internet service provider (ISP), you will probably not be able to use ISAPI to bring more power to your Web pages. You may choose to move your pages to a dedicated server (a powerful Intel machine running Windows NT Server 4.0 and Microsoft IIS is a good combination) so that you can use ISAPI, but this will involve considerable expense. Make sure that you understand the constraints of your current Web server before embarking on a project with ISAPI.
>
> One of the major advantages of ActiveX controls for the Internet (discussed in Chapter 20, "Building an Internet ActiveX Control") is that you don't need access to the server in order to implement them. ■

The five MFC ISAPI classes form a wrapper for the API to make it easier to use:

- `CHttpServer`
- `CHttpFilter`
- `CHttpServerContext`
- `CHttpFilterContext`
- `CHtmlStream`

Your application will have a server or a filter class (or both) that inherits from `CHttpServer` or `CHttpFilter`. These are rather like the classes in a normal application that inherit from `CWinApp`. There is only one instance of the class in each DLL, and each interaction of the server with a client takes place through its own instance of the appropriate context class. (A DLL may contain both a server and a filter but, at most, one of each.) `CHtmlStream` is a helper class that describes a stream of HTML to be sent by a server to a client.

The ISAPI Extension Wizard is an AppWizard that simplifies creating extensions and filters. To use this wizard, choose File, New (as always) and then the Project tab. Scroll down the list on the left and select ISAPI Extension Wizard (as shown in Figure 18.5). Fill in the project name and folder, and click OK.

Creating a server extension is a one-step process. That step, which is also the first step for a filter, is shown in Figure 18.6. The names and descriptions for the filter and extension are based on the project name that you chose.

If you choose to create a filter, the Next button is enabled and you can move to the second step for filters, shown in Figure 18.7. This list of parameters gives you an idea of the power of an ISAPI filter. You can monitor all incoming and outgoing requests and raw data, authenticate users, log traffic, and more.

FIG. 18.5

The ISAPI Extension Wizard is another kind of AppWizard.

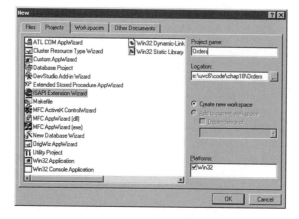

FIG. 18.6

The first step in the ISAPI Extension Wizard process is to name the components of the DLL that you are creating.

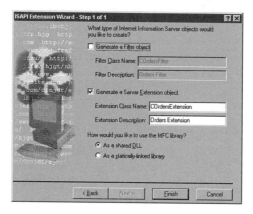

FIG. 18.7

The second step in the ISAPI Extension Wizard process is to set filter parameters.

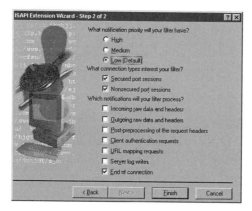

AppWizard shows you a final confirmation screen, like the one in Figure 18.8, before creating the files. When you create a server and a filter at the same time, 11 files are created for you, including source and headers for the class that inherits from CHttpServer and the class that inherits from CHttpFilter.

FIG. 18.8

The ISAPI Extension Wizard process summarizes the files that will be created.

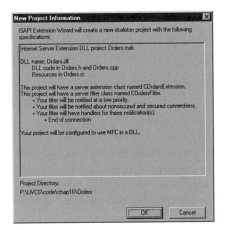

Writing a filter from this shell is quite simple. You have been provided with a stub function to react to each event for which notification was requested. For example, the filter class has a function called `OnEndOfNetSession()`, which is called when a client's session with this server is ending. You add code to this function to log, monitor, or otherwise react to this event. When the filter is complete, you edit the Registry by hand so that the server will run your DLL.

To write an extension, add one or more functions to your DLL. Each function will be passed a `CHttpContext` pointer, which can be used to gather information such as the user's IP address. If the function is invoked from an HTML form, additional parameters such as values of other fields on the form will also be passed to the function.

The details of what the function does depend on your application. If you are implementing an online ordering system, the functions involved will be lengthy and complex. Other extensions will be simpler.

When the function is complete, place the DLL in the executable folder for the server—usually the folder where CGI programs are kept—and adjust your Web pages so that they include links to your DLL, like this:

```
Now you can <A HREF=http://www.company.com/exec/orders.dll>
place an order</A> online!
```

For more information on ISAPI programming, be sure to read Que's *Special Edition Using ISAPI*. You will discover how ISAPI applications can make your Web site dynamic and interactive, learn how to write filters and extensions, and cover advanced topics including debugging ISAPI applications and writing multithreaded applications.

Adding the Internet to your applications is an exciting trend. It's going to make lots of work for programmers and create some powerful products that simplify the working life of anyone with an Internet connection. Just a year ago, writing Internet applications meant getting your fingernails dirty with sockets programming, memorizing TCP/IP ports, and reading RFCs. The new WinInet and ISAPI classes, as well as improvements to the old MAPI support, mean that today you can add amazing power to your application with just a few lines of code or by selecting a box on an AppWizard dialog box. ●

Part
V
Ch
18

Internet Programming with the WinInet Classes

Designing the Internet Query Application

Chapter 18, "Sockets, MAPI, and the Internet," introduces the WinInet classes that you can use to build Internet client applications at a fairly high level. This chapter develops an Internet application that demonstrates a number of these classes. The application also serves a useful function: You can use it to learn more about the Internet presence of a company or organization. You don't need to learn about sockets or handle the details of Internet protocols to do this.

Imagine that you have someone's email address (**kate@gregcons.com,** for example) and you'd like to know more about the domain (**gregcons.com** in this example). Perhaps you have a great idea for a domain name and want to know whether it's already taken. This application, Query, will try connecting to **gregcons.com** (or **greatidea.org**, or any other domain name that you specify) in a variety of ways and will report the results of those attempts to the user.

This application will have a simple user interface. The only piece of information that the user needs to supply is the domain name to be queried, and there is no need to keep this information in a document. You might want a menu item called Query that brings up a dialog box in which to specify the site name, but a better approach is to use a dialog-based application and incorporate a Query button into the dialog box.

A dialog-based application, as discussed in the section "A Dialog-Based Application" of Chapter 1, "Building Your First Application," has no document and no menu. The application displays a dialog box at all times; closing the dialog box closes the application. You build the dialog box for this application like any other, with Developer Studio.

To build this application's shell, choose File, New from within Developer Studio and then click the Project tab. Highlight MFC AppWizard(exe), name the application **Query**, and in Step 1 choose Dialog Based, as shown in Figure 19.1. Click Next to move to Step 2 of AppWizard.

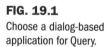

FIG. 19.1
Choose a dialog-based
application for Query.

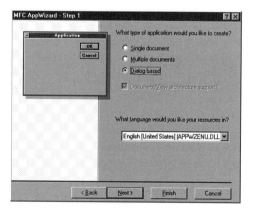

In Step 2 of AppWizard, request an About box, no context-sensitive Help, 3D controls, no automation or ActiveX control support, and no sockets support. (This application won't be calling socket functions directly.) Give the application a sensible title for the dialog box. The AppWizard choices are summarized, as shown in Figure 19.2. Click Next to move to Step 3 of AppWizard.

FIG. 19.2

This application doesn't need Help, automation, ActiveX controls, or sockets.

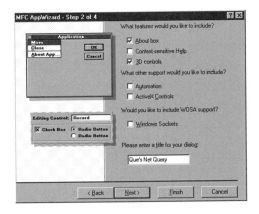

The rest of the AppWizard process will be familiar by now: You want comments, you want to link to the MFC libraries as a shared DLL, and you don't need to change any of the classnames suggested by AppWizard. When the AppWizard process is completed, you're ready to build the heart of the Query application.

Building the Query Dialog Box

AppWizard produces an empty dialog box for you to start with, as shown in Figure 19.3. To edit this dialog box, switch to the resource view, expand the Query Resources, expand the Dialogs section, and double-click the IDD_QUERY_DIALOG resource. The following steps will transform this dialog box into the interface for the Query application.

FIG. 19.3

AppWizard generates an empty dialog box for you.

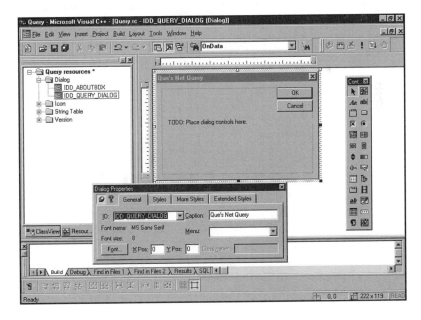

Part
V

Ch
19

T I P If working with dialog boxes is still new to you, be sure to read Chapter 2, "Dialogs and Controls."

1. Change the caption on the OK button to **Query**.

2. Change the caption on the Cancel button to **Close**.

3. Delete the TODO static text.

4. Grab a sizing handle on the right edge of the dialog box and stretch it so that the dialog box is 300 pixels wide or more. (The size of the currently selected item is in the lower-right corner of the screen.)

5. At the top of the dialog box, add an edit box with the resource ID IDC_HOST. Stretch the edit box as wide as possible.

6. Add a static label next to the edit box. Set the text to Site name.

7. Grab a sizing handle along the bottom of the dialog box and stretch it so that the dialog box is 150 pixels high, or more.

8. Add another edit box and resize it to fill as much of the bottom part of the dialog box as possible.

9. Give this edit box the resource ID IDC_OUT.

10. Click the Styles tab on the Properties box and select the Multiline, Horizontal Scroll, Vertical Scroll, Border, and Read-Only check boxes. Make sure all the other check boxes are deselected.

The finished dialog box and the Style properties of the large edit box will resemble Figure 19.4.

FIG. 19.4
Build the Query user interface as a single dialog box.

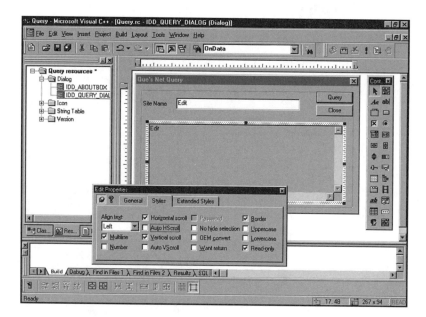

When the user clicks the Query button, this application should somehow query the site. The last step in the building of the interface is to connect the Query button to code with ClassWizard. Follow these steps to make that connection:

1. Choose View, Class Wizard to bring up ClassWizard.

2. There are three possible classes that could catch the command generated by the button click, but CQueryDlg is the logical choice because the host name will be known by that class. Make sure that CQueryDlg is the class selected in the Class Name drop-down list box.

3. Highlight ID_OK (you did not change the resource ID of the OK button when you changed the caption) in the left list box and BN_CLICKED in the right list box.

4. Click Add Function to add a function that will be called when the Query button is clicked.

5. ClassWizard suggests the name OnOK; change it to **OnQuery**, as shown in Figure 19.5, and then click OK.

FIG. 19.5

Add a function to handle a click on the Query button, still with the ID IDOK.

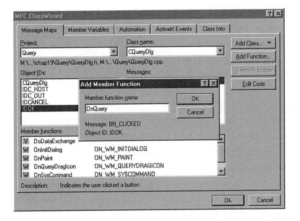

6. Click the Member Variables tab to prepare to connect the edit controls on the dialog box to member variables of the dialog class.

7. Highlight IDC_HOST and click Add Variable. As shown in Figure 19.6, you'll connect this control to a CString member variable of the dialog class m_host.

8. Connect IDC_OUT to m_out, also a CString.

Click OK to close ClassWizard. Now all that remains is to write CQueryDlg::OnQuery(), which will use the value in m_host to produce lines of output for m_out.

Part
V

Ch
19

FIG. 19.6

Connect IDC_HOST to
CQueryDlg::m_host.

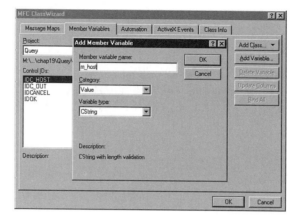

Querying HTTP Sites

The first kind of connection to try when investigating a domain's Internet presence is HTTP because so many sites have Web pages. The simplest way to make a connection using HTTP is to use the WinInet class CInternetSession and call its OpenURL() function. This will return a file, and you can display the first few lines of the file in m_out. First, add this line at the beginning of QueryDlg.cpp, after the include of stdafx.h:

```
#include "afxinet.h"
```

This gives your code access to the WinInet classes. Because this application will try a number of URLs, add a function called TryURL() to CQueryDlg. It takes a CString parameter called URL and returns void. Right-click CQueryDlg in the ClassView and choose Add Member Function to add TryURL() as a protected member function. The new function, TryURL(), will be called from CQueryDlg::OnQuery(), as shown in Listing 19.1. Edit OnQuery() to add this code.

Listing 19.1   QueryDlg.cpp—*CQueryDlg::OnQuery()*

```
void CQueryDlg::OnQuery()
{
    const CString http = "http://";

    UpdateData(TRUE);
    m_out = "";
    UpdateData(FALSE);

    TryURL(http + m_host);

    TryURL(http + "www." + m_host);
}
```

The call to UpdateData(TRUE) fills m_host with the value that the user typed. The call to UpdateData(FALSE) fills the IDC_OUT read-only edit box with the newly cleared m_out. Then come two calls to TryURL(). If, for example, the user typed **microsoft.com**, the first call would try **http://microsoft.com** and the second would try **http://www.microsoft.com**. TryURL() is shown in Listing 19.2.

Listing 19.2   QueryDlg.cpp—*CQueryDlg::TryURL()*

```
void CQueryDlg::TryURL(CString URL)
{
    CInternetSession session;

    m_out += "Trying " + URL + "\r\n";
    UpdateData(FALSE);

    CInternetFile* file = NULL;
    try
    {
        //We know for sure this is an Internet file,
        //so the cast is safe
        file = (CInternetFile*) session.OpenURL(URL);
    }
    catch (CInternetException* pEx)
    {
        //if anything went wrong, just set file to NULL
        file = NULL;
        pEx->Delete();
    }
    if (file)
    {
        m_out += "Connection established. \r\n";
        CString line;

        for (int i=0; i < 20 && file->ReadString(line); i++)
        {
            m_out += line + "\r\n";
        }
        file->Close();
        delete file;
    }
    else
    {
        m_out += "No server found there. \r\n";
    }

    m_out += "-----------------------\r\n";
    UpdateData(FALSE);
}
```

Part

V

Ch

19

The remainder of this section presents this code again, a few lines at a time. First, establish an Internet session by constructing an instance of CInternetSession. There are a number of parameters to this constructor, but they all have default values that will be fine for this application. The parameters follow:

- `LPCTSTR pstrAgent`   The name of your application. If `NULL`, it's filled in for you, using the name that you gave to AppWizard.

- `DWORD dwContext`   The context identifier for the operation. For synchronous sessions, this is not an important parameter.

- `DWORD dwAccessType`   The access type: `INTERNET_OPEN_TYPE_PRECONFIG` (default), `INTERNET_OPEN_TYPE_DIRECT`, or `INTERNET_OPEN_TYPE_PROXY`.

- `LPCTSTR pstrProxyName`   The name of your proxy, if access is `INTERNET_OPEN_TYPE_PROXY`.

- `LPCTSTR pstrProxyBypass`   A list of addresses to be connected directly rather than through the proxy server, if access is `INTERNET_OPEN_TYPE_PROXY`.

- `DWORD dwFlags`   Options that can be OR'ed together. The available options are `INTERNET_FLAG_DONT_CACHE`, `INTERNET_FLAG_ASYNC`, and `INTERNET_FLAG_OFFLINE`.

`dwAccessType` defaults to using the value in the Registry. Obviously, an application that insists on direct Internet access or proxy Internet access is less useful than one that enables users to configure that information. Making users set their Internet access type outside this program might be confusing, though. To set your default Internet access, double-click the My Computer icon on your desktop, then on the Control Panel, and then on the Internet tool in the Control Panel. Choose the Connection tab (the version for Internet Explorer under Windows 95 is shown in Figure 19.7) and complete the dialog box as appropriate for your setup. If you are using NT or Windows 98, or if your browser version is different, you might see a slightly different dialog, but you should still be able to choose your connection type.

FIG. 19.7
Set your Internet connection settings once, and all applications can retrieve them from the Registry.

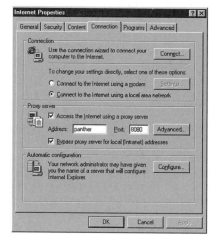

- If you dial up to the Internet, select the Dial check box and fill in the parameters in the top half of the page.

- If you connect to the Internet through a proxy server, select the Proxy check box and click the Settings button to identify your proxy addresses and ports.

- If you are connected directly to the Internet, leave both check boxes unselected.

If you want to set up an *asynchronous* (nonblocking) session, for the reasons discussed in the "Using Windows Sockets" section of Chapter 18, your options in dwFlags must include INTERNET_FLAG_ASYNC. In addition, you must call the member function EnableStatusCallback() to set up the callback function. When a request is made through the session—such as the call to OpenURL() that occurs later in TryURL()—and the response will not be immediate, a nonblocking session returns a pseudo error code, ERROR_IO_PENDING. When the response is ready, these sessions automatically invoke the callback function.

For this simple application, there is no need to allow the user to do other work or interact with the user interface while waiting for the session to respond, so the session is constructed as a blocking session and all the other default parameters are also used:

```
CInternetSession session;
```

Having constructed the session, TryURL() goes on to add a line to m_out that echoes the URL passed in as a parameter. The "\r\n" characters are *return* and *newline*, and they separate the lines added to m_out. UpdateData(FALSE) gets that onscreen:

```
m_out += "Trying " + URL + "\r\n";
UpdateData(FALSE);
```

Next is a call to the session's OpenURL() member function. This function returns a pointer to one of several file types because the URL might have been to one of four protocols:

- file:// opens a file. The function constructs a CStdioFile and returns a pointer to it.
- ftp:// goes to an FTP site and returns a pointer to a CInternetFile object.
- gopher:// goes to a Gopher site and returns a pointer to a CGopherFile object.
- http:// goes to a World Wide Web site and returns a pointer to a CHttpFile object.

Because CGopherFile and CHttpFile both inherit from CInternetFile and because you can be sure that TryURL() will not be passed a file:// URL, it is safe to cast the returned pointer to a CInternetFile.

Part

V

Ch

19

There is some confusion in Microsoft's online documentation whenever sample URLs are shown. A backslash (\) character will never appear in an URL. In any Microsoft example that includes backslashes, use forward slashes (/) instead.

If the URL would not open, file will be NULL, or OpenURL()_ will throw an exception. (For background on exceptions, see Chapter 26, "Exceptions and Templates.") Whereas in a normal application it would be a serious error if an URL didn't open, in this application you are making up URLs to see whether they work, and it's expected that some won't. As a result, you should catch these exceptions yourself and do just enough to prevent runtime errors. In this case, it's enough to make sure that file is NULL when an exception is thrown. To delete the exception and prevent memory leaks, call CException::Delete(), which safely deletes the exception. The block of code containing the call to OpenURL() is in Listing 19.3.

Listing 19.3 QueryDlg.cpp—*CQueryDlg::TryURL()*

```
CInternetFile* file = NULL;
try
{
    //We know for sure this is an Internet file,
    //so the cast is safe
    file = (CInternetFile*) session.OpenURL(URL);
}
catch (CInternetException* pEx)
{
    //if anything went wrong, just set file to NULL
    file = NULL;
    pEx->Delete();
}
```

If file is not NULL, this routine will display some of the Web page that was found. It first echoes another line to m_out. Then, in a for loop, the routine calls CInternetFile::ReadString() to fill the CString line with the characters in file up to the first \r\n, which are stripped off. This code simply tacks line (and another \r\n) onto m_out. If you would like to see more or less than the first 20 lines of the page, adjust the number in this for loop. When the first few lines have been read, TryURL() closes and deletes the file. That block of code is shown in Listing 19.4.

Listing 19.4 QueryDlg.cpp—*CQueryDlg::TryURL()*

```
if (file)
{
    m_out += "Connection established. \r\n";
    CString line;

    for (int i=0; i < 20 && file->ReadString(line); i++)
    {
        m_out += line + "\r\n";
    }
    file->Close();
    delete file;
}
```

If the file could not be opened, a message to that effect is added to m_out:

```
else
{
    m_out += "No server found there. \r\n";
}
```

Then, whether the file existed or not, a line of dashes is tacked on m_out to indicate the end of this attempt, and one last call to UpdateData(FALSE) puts the new m_out onscreen:

```
    m_out += "-----------------------\r\n";
    UpdateData(FALSE);
}
```

You can now build and run this application. If you enter **microsoft.com** in the text box and click Query, you'll discover that there are Web pages at both **http://microsoft.com** and **http://www.microsoft.com**. Figure 19.8 shows the results of that query.

FIG. 19.8

Query can find
Microsoft's Web sites.

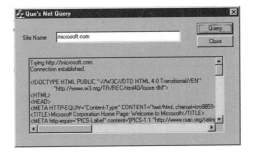

If Query doesn't find Web pages at either the domain name you provided or **www.** plus the domain name, it doesn't mean that the domain doesn't exist or even that the organization that owns the domain name doesn't have a Web page. It does make it less likely, however, that the organization both exists and has a Web page. If you see a stream of HTML, you know for certain that the organization exists and has a Web page. You might be able to read the HTML yourself, but even if you can't, you can now connect to the site with a Web browser such as Microsoft's Internet Explorer.

Querying FTP Sites

As part of a site name investigation, you should check whether there is an FTP site, too. Most FTP sites have names like **ftp.company.com**, though some older sites don't have names of that form. Checking for these sites isn't as simple as just calling `TryURL()` again because `TryURL()` assumes that the URL leads to a file, and URLs like **ftp.greatidea.org** lead to a list of files that cannot simply be opened and read. Rather than make `TryURL()` even more complicated, add a protected function to the class called `TryFTPSite(CString host)`. (Right-click `CQueryDlg` in the ClassView and choose Add Member Function to add the function. It can return `void`.)

`TryFTPSite()` has to establish a connection within the session, and if the connection is established, it has to get some information that can be added to `m_out` to show the user that the connection has been made. Getting a list of files is reasonably complex; because this is just an illustrative application, the simpler task of getting the name of the default FTP directory is the way to go. The code is in Listing 19.5.

Listing 19.5 QueryDlg.cpp—CQueryDlg::TryFTPSite()

```
void CQueryDlg::TryFTPSite(CString host)
{
    CInternetSession session;

    m_out += "Trying FTP site " + host + "\r\n";
    UpdateData(FALSE);

    CFtpConnection* connection = NULL;
    try
    {
        connection = session.GetFtpConnection(host);
    }
    catch (CInternetException* pEx)
    {
        //if anything went wrong, just set connection to NULL
        connection = NULL;
        pEx->Delete();
    }
    if (connection)
    {
        m_out += "Connection established. \r\n";
        CString line;

        connection->GetCurrentDirectory(line);
        m_out += "default directory is " + line + "\r\n";

        connection->Close();
        delete connection;
    }
    else
    {
        m_out += "No server found there. \r\n";
    }

    m_out += "----------------------\r\n";
    UpdateData(FALSE);
}
```

This code is very much like `TryURL()`, except that rather than open a file with `session.OpenURL()`, it opens an FTP connection with `session.GetFtpConnection()`. Again, exceptions are caught and essentially ignored, with the routine just making sure that the connection pointer won't be used. The call to `GetCurrentDirectory()` returns the directory on the remote site in which sessions start. The rest of the routine is just like `TryURL()`.

Add two lines at the end of `OnQuery()` to call this new function:

```
TryFTPSite(m_host);
TryFTPSite("ftp." + m_host);
```

Build the application and try it: Figure 19.9 shows Query finding no FTP site at **microsoft.com** and finding one at **ftp.microsoft.com**. The delay before results start to appear might be a little disconcerting. You can correct this by using asynchronous sockets, or *threading,* so that early results can be added to the edit box while later results are still coming in over the wire. However, for a simple demonstration application like this, just wait patiently until the results appear. It might take several minutes, depending on network traffic between your site and Microsoft's, your line speed, and so on.

FIG. 19.9

Query finds one Microsoft FTP site.

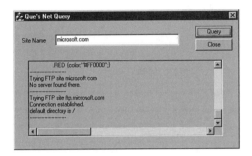

If Query doesn't find Web pages or FTP sites, perhaps this domain doesn't exist at all or doesn't have any Internet services other than email, but there are a few more investigative tricks available. The results of these investigations will definitely add to your knowledge of existing sites.

Querying Gopher Sites

As with FTP, `TryURL()` won't work when querying a Gopher site like **gopher.company.com** because this returns a list of filenames instead of a single file. The solution is to write a protected member function called `TryGopherSite()` that is almost identical to `TryFTPSite()`, except that it opens a `CGopherConnection`. Also, rather than echo a single line describing the default directory, it echoes a single line describing the Gopher locator associated with the site. Add `TryGopherSite` to `CQueryDlg` by right-clicking the classname in ClassView and choosing Add Member Function, as you did for `TryFTPSite()`. The code for `TryGopherSite()` is in Listing 19.6.

Part
V

Ch
19

Listing 19.6 QueryDlg.cpp—*CQueryDlg::TryGopherSite()*

```
void CQueryDlg::TryGopherSite(CString host)
{
    CInternetSession session;

    m_out += "Trying Gopher site " + host + "\r\n";
    UpdateData(FALSE);

    CGopherConnection* connection = NULL;
    try
    {
```

continues

Listing 19.6   Continued

```
        connection = session.GetGopherConnection(host);
    }
    catch (CInternetException* pEx)
    {
        //if anything went wrong, just set connection to NULL
        connection = NULL;
        pEx->Delete();
    }
    if (connection)
    {
        m_out += "Connection established. \r\n";
        CString line;

        CGopherLocator locator = connection->CreateLocator(NULL, NULL,
            GOPHER_TYPE_DIRECTORY);
        line = locator;
        m_out += "first locator is " + line + "\r\n";

        connection->Close();
        delete connection;
    }
    else
    {
        m_out += "No server found there. \r\n";
    }

    m_out += "----------------------\r\n";
    UpdateData(FALSE);
}
```

The call to CreateLocator() takes three parameters. The first is the filename, which might include wild cards. NULL means any file. The second parameter is a selector that can be NULL. The third is one of the following types:

```
GOPHER_TYPE_TEXT_FILE

GOPHER_TYPE_DIRECTORY

GOPHER_TYPE_CSO

GOPHER_TYPE_ERROR

GOPHER_TYPE_MAC_BINHEX

GOPHER_TYPE_DOS_ARCHIVE

GOPHER_TYPE_UNIX_UUENCODED

GOPHER_TYPE_INDEX_SERVER

GOPHER_TYPE_TELNET

GOPHER_TYPE_BINARY

GOPHER_TYPE_REDUNDANT
```

```
GOPHER_TYPE_TN3270

GOPHER_TYPE_GIF

GOPHER_TYPE_IMAGE

GOPHER_TYPE_BITMAP

GOPHER_TYPE_MOVIE

GOPHER_TYPE_SOUND

GOPHER_TYPE_HTML

GOPHER_TYPE_PDF

GOPHER_TYPE_CALENDAR

GOPHER_TYPE_INLINE

GOPHER_TYPE_UNKNOWN

GOPHER_TYPE_ASK

GOPHER_TYPE_GOPHER_PLUS
```

Normally, you don't build locators for files or directories; instead, you ask the server for them. The locator that will be returned from this call to CreateLocator() describes the locator associated with the site you are investigating.

Add a pair of lines at the end of OnQuery() that call this new TryGopherSite() function:

```
TryGopherSite(m_host);
TryGopherSite("gopher." + m_host);
```

Build and run the program again. Again, you might have to wait several minutes for the results. Figure 19.10 shows that Query has found two Gopher sites for **harvard.edu**. In both cases, the locator describes the site itself. This is enough to prove that there is a Gopher site at **harvard.edu**, which is all that Query is supposed to do.

Part

V

Ch

19

FIG. 19.10

Query finds two Harvard Gopher sites.

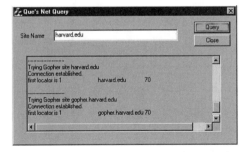

 T I P Gopher is an older protocol that has been supplanted almost entirely by the World Wide Web. As a general rule, if a site has a Gopher presence, it's been on the Internet since before the World Wide Web existed (1989) or at least before the huge upsurge in popularity began (1992). What's more, the site was probably large enough in the early 1990s to have an administrator who would set up the Gopher menus and text.

Using Gopher to Send a Finger Query

There is another protocol that can give you information about a site. It's one of the oldest protocols on the Internet, and it's called *Finger*. You can finger a single user or an entire site, and though many sites have disabled Finger, many more will provide you with useful information in response to a Finger request.

There is no MFC class or API function with the word *finger* in its name, but that doesn't mean you can't use the classes already presented. This section relies on a trick—and on knowledge of the Finger and Gopher protocols. Although the WinInet classes are a boon to new Internet programmers who don't quite know how the Internet works, they also have a lot to offer to old-timers who know what's going on under the hood.

As discussed in the "Using Windows Sockets" section of Chapter 18, all Internet transactions involve a host and a port. Well-known services use standard port numbers. For example, when you call CInternetSession::OpenURL() with an URL that begins with **http://**, the code behind the scenes connects to port 80 on the remote host. When you call GetFtpConnection(), the connection is made to port 21 on the remote host. Gopher uses port 70. If you look at Figure 19.10, you'll see that the locator that describes the **gopher.harvard.edu** site includes a mention of port 70.

The Gopher documentation makes this clear: If you build a locator with a host name, port 70, Gopher type 0 (GOPHER_TYPE_TEXT_FILE is defined to be 0), and a string with a filename, any Gopher client simply sends the string, whether it's a filename or not, to port 70. The Gopher server listening on that port responds by sending the file.

Finger is a simple protocol, too. If you send a string to port 79 on a remote host, the Finger server that is listening there will react to the string by sending a Finger reply. If the string is only \r\n, the usual reply is a list of all the users on the host and some other information about them, such as their real names. (Many sites consider this an invasion of privacy or a security risk, and they disable Finger. Many other sites, though, deliberately make this same information available on their Web pages.)

Putting this all together, if you build a Gopher locator using port 79—instead of the default 70—and an empty filename, you can do a Finger query using the MFC WinInet classes. First, add another function to CQueryDlg called TryFinger(), which takes a CString host and returns void. The code for this function is very much like TryGopherSite(), except that the connection is made to port 79:

```
connection = session.GetGopherConnection(host,NULL,NULL,79);
```

After the connection is made, a text file locator is created:

```
CGopherLocator locator = connection->CreateLocator(NULL, NULL,
    GOPHER_TYPE_TEXT_FILE);
```

This time, rather than simply cast the locator into a CString, use it to open a file:

```
CGopherFile* file = connection->OpenFile(locator);
```

Then echo the first 20 lines of this file, just as TryURL() echoed the first 20 lines of the file returned by a Web server. The code for this is in Listing 19.7.

Listing 19.7   QueryDlg.cpp—*CQueryDlg::TryFinger()* Excerpt

```
if (file)
{
    CString line;

    for (int i=0; i < 20 && file->ReadString(line); i++)
    {
        m_out += line + "\r\n";
    }
    file->Close();
    delete file;
}
```

Putting it all together, Listing 19.8 shows TryFinger().

Listing 19.8   QueryDlg.cpp—*CQueryDlg::TryFinger()*

```
void CQueryDlg::TryFinger(CString host)
{
    CInternetSession session;

    m_out += "Trying to Finger " + host + "\r\n";
    UpdateData(FALSE);

    CGopherConnection* connection = NULL;

    try
    {
        connection = session.GetGopherConnection(host,NULL,NULL,79);
    }
    catch (CInternetException* pEx)
    {
        //if anything went wrong, just set connection to NULL
        connection = NULL;
        pEx->Delete();
    }
    if (connection)
    {
        m_out += "Connection established. \r\n";

        CGopherLocator locator = connection->CreateLocator(NULL, NULL,
            GOPHER_TYPE_TEXT_FILE);

        CGopherFile* file = connection->OpenFile(locator);
        if (file)
        {
            CString line;

            for (int i=0; i < 20 && file->ReadString(line); i++)
            {
                m_out += line + "\r\n";
            }
```

continues

Listing 19.8   Continued

```
                file->Close();
                delete file;
        }

        connection->Close();
        delete connection;
    }
    else
    {
        m_out += "No server found there. \r\n";
    }

    m_out += "-----------------------\r\n";
    UpdateData(FALSE);


}
```

Add a line at the end of OnQuery() that calls this new function:

```
    TryFinger(m_host);
```

Now, build and run the application. Figure 19.11 shows the result of a query on the site **whitehouse.gov**, scrolled down to the Finger section.

FIG. 19.11

Query gets email addresses from the White House Finger server.

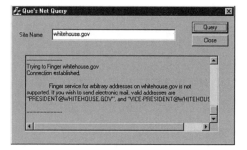

N O T E   If the site you are investigating isn't running a Finger server, the delay will be longer than usual and a message box will appear, telling you the connection timed out. Click OK on the message box if it appears. ▪

Using Gopher to Send a Whois Query

One last protocol provides information about sites. It, too, is an old protocol not supported directly by the WinInet classes. It is called *Whois*, and it's a service offered by only a few servers on the whole Internet. The servers that offer this service are maintained by the organizations that register domain names. For example, domain names that end in **.com** are registered through an organization called InterNIC, and it runs a Whois server called **rs.internic.net** (the *rs* stands for Registration Services.) Like Finger, Whois responds to a string sent on its own port; the Whois port is 43. Unlike Finger, you don't send an empty string in the locator; you send the name of the host that you want to look up. You connect to **rs.internic.net** every time. (Dedicated Whois servers offer users a chance to change this, but in practice, no one ever does.)

Add a function called TryWhois(); as usual, it takes a CString host and returns void. The code is in Listing 19.9.

Listing 19.9 QueryDlg.cpp—*CQueryDlg::TryWhois()*

```
void CQueryDlg::TryWhois(CString host)
{
    CInternetSession session;

    m_out += "Trying Whois for " + host + "\r\n";
    UpdateData(FALSE);

    CGopherConnection* connection = NULL;
    try
    {
        connection = session.GetGopherConnection
    ➥("rs.internic.net",NULL,NULL,43);
    }
    catch (CInternetException* pEx)
    {
        //if anything went wrong, just set connection to NULL
        connection = NULL;
        pEx->Delete();
    }
    if (connection)
    {
        m_out += "Connection established. \r\n";
        CGopherLocator locator = connection->CreateLocator(NULL, host,
            GOPHER_TYPE_TEXT_FILE);
        CGopherFile* file = connection->OpenFile(locator);
        if (file)
        {
            CString line;
            for (int i=0; i < 20 && file->ReadString(line); i++)
            {
                m_out += line + "\r\n";
            }
            file->Close();
            delete file;
        }
        connection->Close();
        delete connection;
    }
    else
    {
        m_out += "No server found there. \r\n";
    }
    m_out += "-----------------------\r\n";
    UpdateData(FALSE);
}
```

Part

V

Ch

19

Add a line at the end of OnQuery() to call it:

```
TryWhois(m_host);
```

Build and run the application one last time. Figure 19.12 shows the Whois part of the report for **mcp.com**—this is the domain for Macmillan Computer Publishing, Que's parent company.

FIG. 19.12

Query gets real-life addresses and names from the InterNIC Whois server.

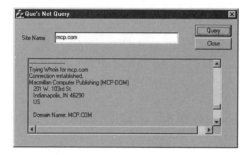

Adding code after the Finger portion of this application means that you can no longer ignore the times when the Finger code can't connect. When the call to OpenFile() in TryFinger() tries to open a file on a host that isn't running a Finger server, an exception is thrown. Control will not return to OnQuery(), and TryWhois() will never be called. To prevent this, you must wrap the call to OpenFile() in a try and catch block. Listing 19.10 shows the changes to make.

Listing 19.10   QueryDlg.cpp   Changes to *TryFinger()*

```
//replace this line:
        CGopherFile* file = connection->OpenFile(locator);
//with these lines:
        CGopherFile* file = NULL;
        try
        {
            file = connection->OpenFile(locator);
        }
        catch (CInternetException* pEx)
        {
            //if anything went wrong, just set file to NULL
            file = NULL;
            pEx->Delete();
        }
```

Change TryFinger(), build Query again, and query a site that doesn't run a Finger server, such as **microsoft.com**. You will successfully reach the Whois portion of the application.

Future Work

The Query application built in this chapter does a lot, but it could do much more. There are email and news protocols that could be reached by stretching the WinInet classes a little more and using them to connect to the standard ports for these other services. You could also connect to some well-known Web search engines and submit queries by forming URLs according to the pattern used by those engines. In this way, you could automate the sort of poking around on the Internet that most of us do when we're curious about a domain name or an organization.

If you'd like to learn more about Internet protocols, port numbers, and what's happening when a client connects to a server, you might want to read Que's *Building Internet Applications with Visual C++*. The book was written for Visual C++ 2.0, and though all the applications in the book compile and run under later versions of MFC, the applications would be much shorter and easier to write now. Still, the insight into the way the protocols work is valuable.

The WinInet classes, too, can do much more than you've seen here. Query doesn't use them to retrieve real files over the Internet. Two of the WinInet sample applications included with Visual C++ 6.0 do a fine job of showing how to retrieve files:

- FTPTREE builds a tree list of the files and directories on an FTP site.
- TEAR brings back a page of HTML from a Web site.

There are a lot more Microsoft announcements to come in the next few months. Keep an eye on the Web site **www.microsoft.com** for libraries and software development kits that will make Internet software development even easier and faster. ●

Part

V

Ch

19

Building an Internet ActiveX Control

Embedding an ActiveX Control in a Microsoft Internet Explorer Web Page

In Chapter 17, "Building an ActiveX Control," you learned how to build your own controls and include them in forms-based applications written in Visual Basic, Visual C++, and the VBA macro language. There's one other place those controls can go—on a Web page. However, the ActiveX controls generated by older versions of Visual C++ were too big and slow to put on a Web page. This chapter shows you how to place these controls on your Web pages and how to write faster, sleeker controls that will make your pages a pleasure to use.

It's a remarkably simple matter to put an ActiveX control on a Web page that you know will be loaded by Microsoft Internet Explorer 3.0 or later. You use the <OBJECT> tag, a relatively new addition to HTML that describes a wide variety of objects that you might want to insert in a Web page: a moving video clip, a sound, a Java applet, an ActiveX control, and many more kinds of information and ways of interacting with a user. Listing 20.1 shows the HTML source for a page that displays the Dieroll control from Chapter 17.

Listing 20.1   fatdie.html—Using *<OBJECT>*

```
<HEAD>
<TITLE>A Web page with a rolling die</TITLE>
</HEAD>
<BODY>
<OBJECT ID="Dieroll1"
CLASSID="CLSID:46646B43-EA16-11CF-870C-00201801DDD6"
CODEBASE="dieroll.cab#Version=1,0,0,1"
WIDTH="200"
HEIGHT="200">
<PARAM NAME="ForeColor" VALUE="0">
<PARAM NAME="BackColor" VALUE="16777215">
If you see this text, your browser does not support the OBJECT tag.
<BR>
</OBJECT>
<BR>
Here is some text after the die
</BODY>
</HTML>
```

The only ugly thing here is the CLSID, and the easiest way to get that, because you're a software developer, is to cut and paste it from dieroll.odl, the Object Description Library. Open the dieroll project you built in Chapter 17 and use FileView to open dieroll.odl quickly. Here's the section in dieroll.odl that includes the CLSID:

```
// Class information for CDierollCtrl

[ uuid(46646B43-EA16-11CF-870C-00201801DDD6),
  helpstring("Dieroll Control"), control ]
```

This section is at the end of dieroll.odl—the earlier CLSIDs do not refer to the whole control, only to portions of it. Copy the uuid from inside the brackets into your HTML source.

> **TIP** Microsoft has a product called the *Control Pad* that gets CLSIDs from the Registry for you and makes life easier for Web page builders who are either intimidated by instructions like "open the ODL file" or don't have the ODL file because it's not shipped with the control. Because you're building this control and know how to open files in Developer Studio, this chapter will not describe the Control Pad tool. If you're curious, see Microsoft's Control Pad Web page at **http://www.microsoft.com/workshop/ author/cpad/** for more details.

The CODEBASE attribute of the OBJECT tag specifies where the OCX file is kept, so if the user doesn't have a copy of the ActiveX control, one will be downloaded automatically. The use of the CLSID means that if this user has already installed this ActiveX control, there is no download time; the control is used immediately. You can simply specify an URL to the OCX file, but to automate the DLL downloading, this CODEBASE attribute points to a CAB file. Putting your control in a CAB file will cut your download time by nearly half. You can learn more about CAB technology at **http://www.microsoft.com/intdev/cab/**. That page is written for Java developers, but the technology works just as well to cut the download time for ActiveX controls.

> **TIP** If you don't have access to a Web server in which to put controls while you're developing them, use a **file://** URL in the CODEBASE attribute that points to the control's location on your hard drive.

The remaining OBJECT tag attributes will be intuitive if you've built a Web page before: ID is used by other tags on the page to refer to this control; WIDTH and HEIGHT specify the size, in pixels, of the control's appearance; and HSPACE and VSPACE are horizontal and vertical blank spaces, in pixels, around the entire control.

Everything after the <OBJECT ...> tag and before the </OBJECT> tag is ignored by browsers that understand the OBJECT tag. (The <OBJECT...> tag is usually many lines long and contains all the information to describe the object.) Browsers that don't understand the OBJECT tag ignore the <OBJECT ...> tag and the </OBJECT> tag and display the HTML between them (in this case, a line of text pointing out that this browser doesn't support the tag). This is part of the specification for a Web browser: It should ignore tags it doesn't understand.

Figure 20.1 shows this page displayed in Microsoft Explorer 3.0. Clicking the die rolls it, and everything works beautifully. Things certainly look simple and amazing, but two flaws appear immediately:

- Not all browsers support the OBJECT tag.
- It can take a long time to download the control.

Part
V

Ch
20

FIG. 20.1

Microsoft Internet Explorer can show ActiveX controls.

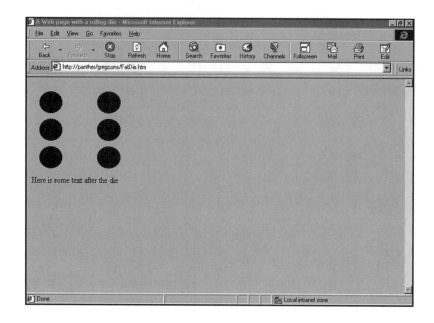

Figure 20.2 shows the same page displayed in Netscape Navigator 3.0. It doesn't support the OBJECT tag, so it doesn't show the die. Also, Netscape Navigator is used by more than half the people who browse the Web! Does that mean it's not worth writing ActiveX controls for Web pages? Not at all. As you'll see in the very next section, there's a way that Navigator users can use the same controls as Explorer users.

FIG. 20.2

Netscape Navigator can't show ActiveX controls.

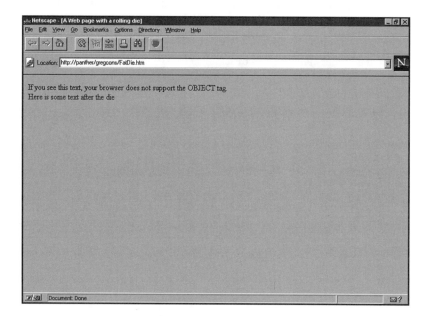

The size issue is a bigger worry. The release version of the Dieroll control, as built for Chapter 17, is 26KB. Many designers put a 50KB limit per Web page for graphics and other material to be downloaded, and this simple control uses half that limit. A more powerful control would easily exceed it. The majority of this chapter deals with ways to reduce that size or otherwise minimize the download time for ActiveX controls. Web page designers can then tap the controls' full power without worrying that users will label their pages as slow, one of the worst knocks against any Web site.

There's a third flaw that you won't notice because you have Visual C++ installed on your computer. The control requires the MFC DLL. The user must download it and install it before the controls can run. The mechanism that automatically downloads and installs controls doesn't automatically download and install this DLL, though using a CAB file as discussed earlier can make it possible.

 For an example of a Web page that includes a CAB file for the Dieroll control and the MFC DLLs, come to **http://www.gregcons.com/dieroll.htm**.

N O T E It might occur to you to try linking the MFC Library statically into your control. It seems easy enough to do: Choose Project, Settings, and on the General tab there is a drop-down list box inviting you to choose static linking. If you do that and build, you'll get hundreds of linker errors: The `COleControl` and `CPropPage` functions are not in the DLL that is linked statically. (That's because Microsoft felt it would be foolish to link the MFC functions statically in a control.) Setting up another library to link in those functions is beyond the scope of this chapter, especially because all this work would lead to an enormous (more than 1MB) control that would take far too long to download the first time. ■

Embedding an ActiveX Control in a Netscape Navigator Web Page

NCompass Labs (**www.ncompasslabs.com**) has produced a Netscape plug-in, called ScriptActive, that enables you to embed an ActiveX control in a page to be read with Netscape Navigator. The HTML for the page must be changed, as shown in Listing 20.2. (Resist the temptation to get the plug-in and load this HTML into Netscape yourself until you have registered the control as safe for initializing and scripting in the next section.)

Part
V

Ch

20

 You can download a demonstration version of the plug-in for a free 30-day trial from the NCompass Labs Web site.

Listing 20.2   fatdie2.html—Using *<OBJECT>* and *<EMBED>*

```
<HTML>
<HEAD>
<TITLE>A Web page with a rolling die</TITLE>
</HEAD>
<BODY>
<OBJECT ID="Dieroll1"
CLASSID="CLSID:46646B43-EA16-11CF-870C-00201801DDD6"
CODEBASE="dieroll.cab#Version=1,0,0,1"
WIDTH="200"
HEIGHT="200">
<PARAM NAME="ForeColor" VALUE="0">
<PARAM NAME="BackColor" VALUE="16777215">
<PARAM NAME="Image" VALUE="beans.bmp">
<EMBED LIVECONNECT NAME="Dieroll1"
WIDTH="200"
HEIGHT="200"
CLASSID="CLSID:46646B43-EA16-11CF-870C-00201801DDD6"
TYPE="application/oleobject"
CODEBASE="dieroll.cab#Version=1,0,0,1"
PARAM_ForeColor="0"
PARAM_BackColor="16777215">
</OBJECT>
<BR>
Here is some text after the die
</BODY>
</HTML>
```

It is the <EMBED> tag that brings up the plug-in. Because it's inside the <OBJECT>...</OBJECT> tag, Microsoft Internet Explorer and other browsers that know the OBJECT tag will ignore the EMBED. This means that this HTML source will display the control equally well in Netscape Navigator and in Explorer. You'll probably want to include a link on your page to the NCompass page to help your readers find the plug-in and learn about it.

Microsoft is committed to establishing ActiveX controls as a cross-platform, multibrowser solution that will, in the words of its slogan, "Activate the Internet." The ActiveX control specification is no longer a proprietary document but has been released to a committee that will maintain the standard. Don't pay any attention to people who suggest you should only build these controls if your readers use Internet Explorer!

Registering as Safe for Scripting and Initializing

For any of your readers who operate with a Medium safety level, the control should be registered as safe for scripting and initializing. This assures anyone who wants to view a page containing the control that no matter what functions are called from a script or what parameters are initialized through the PARAM attribute, nothing unsafe will happen. For an example of a control that isn't safe, think of a control that deletes a file on your machine when it executes. The default file is one you won't miss or that probably won't exist. A page that put this control in a script, or that initialized the filename with PARAM attributes, might order the control to delete a very important file or files, based on guesses about where most people keep documents. It would be simple to delete C:\MSOFFICE\WINWORD\WINWORD.EXE, for example, and that would be annoying for Word users. Figure 20.3 shows the error message displayed in Explorer when you are using the Medium safety level and load a page featuring a control that isn't registered as `script-safe` or `init-safe`. The NCompass Labs plug-in, ScriptActive, also refuses to load controls that are not registered as `script-safe` and `init-safe`.

FIG. 20.3

Explorer alerts you to controls that might run amok.

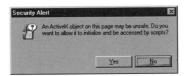

First, you need to add three functions to DierollCtl.cpp. (They come unchanged from the ActiveX SDK.) These functions are called by code presented later in this section. Don't forget to add declarations of these functions to the header file, too. The code is in Listing 20.3.

Listing 20.3 DierollCtl.cpp—New Functions to Mark the Control as Safe

```
///////////////////////////////////////////////////////////////
// Copied from the ActiveX SDK
// This code is used to register and unregister a
// control as safe for initialization and safe for scripting

HRESULT CreateComponentCategory(CATID catid, WCHAR* catDescription)
{
    ICatRegister* pcr = NULL ;
    HRESULT hr = S_OK ;

    hr = CoCreateInstance(CLSID_StdComponentCategoriesMgr,
            NULL, CLSCTX_INPROC_SERVER, IID_ICatRegister, (void**)&pcr);
    if (FAILED(hr))
            return hr;

    // Make sure the HKCR\Component Categories\{..catid...}
    // key is registered
    CATEGORYINFO catinfo;
    catinfo.catid = catid;
    catinfo.lcid = 0x0409 ; // english

    // Make sure the provided description is not too long.
    // Only copy the first 127 characters if it is
    int len = wcslen(catDescription);
    if (len>127)
            len = 127;
    wcsncpy(catinfo.szDescription, catDescription, len);
    // Make sure the description is null terminated
    catinfo.szDescription[len] = '\0';
```

continues

Part
V

Ch
20

Listing 20.3   Continued

```
        hr = pcr->RegisterCategories(1, &catinfo);
        pcr->Release();

        return hr;
}

HRESULT RegisterCLSIDInCategory(REFCLSID clsid, CATID catid)
{
    // Register your component categories information.
    ICatRegister* pcr = NULL ;
    HRESULT hr = S_OK ;
    hr = CoCreateInstance(CLSID_StdComponentCategoriesMgr,
            NULL, CLSCTX_INPROC_SERVER, IID_ICatRegister, (void**)&pcr);
    if (SUCCEEDED(hr))
    {
        // Register this category as being "implemented" by
        // the class.
        CATID rgcatid[1] ;
        rgcatid[0] = catid;
        hr = pcr->RegisterClassImplCategories(clsid, 1, rgcatid);
    }

    if (pcr != NULL)
        pcr->Release();

    return hr;
}

HRESULT UnRegisterCLSIDInCategory(REFCLSID clsid, CATID catid)
{
    ICatRegister* pcr = NULL ;
    HRESULT hr = S_OK ;
    hr = CoCreateInstance(CLSID_StdComponentCategoriesMgr,
            NULL, CLSCTX_INPROC_SERVER, IID_ICatRegister, (void**)&pcr);
    if (SUCCEEDED(hr))
    {
        // Unregister this category as being "implemented" by
        // the class.
        CATID rgcatid[1] ;
        rgcatid[0] = catid;
        hr = pcr->UnRegisterClassImplCategories(clsid, 1, rgcatid);
    }

    if (pcr != NULL)
    pcr->Release();

    return hr;
}
```

Second, add two #include statements at the top of DierollCtl.cpp:

```
#include "comcat.h"
#include "objsafe.h"
```

Finally, modify UpdateRegistry() in DierollCtl.cpp to call these new functions. The new code calls CreateComponentCategory() to create a category called CATID_SafeForScripting and adds this control to that category. Then it creates a category called CATID_SafeForInitializing and adds the control to that category as well. Listing 20.4 shows the new version of UpdateRegistry().

Listing 20.4   DierollCtl.cpp—*CDierollCtrl::CDierollCtrlFactory::UpdateRegistry()*

```
BOOL CDierollCtrl::CDierollCtrlFactory::UpdateRegistry(BOOL bRegister)
{
    // TODO: Verify that your control follows apartment-model threading rules.
    // Refer to MFC TechNote 64 for more information.
    // If your control does not conform to the apartment-model rules, then
    // you must modify the code below, changing the 6th parameter from
    // afxRegInsertable | afxRegApartmentThreading to afxRegInsertable.

    if (bRegister)
    {
        HRESULT hr = S_OK ;

        // register as safe for scripting
        hr = CreateComponentCategory(CATID_SafeForScripting,
                L"Controls that are safely scriptable");

        if (FAILED(hr))
            return FALSE;

        hr = RegisterCLSIDInCategory(m_clsid, CATID_SafeForScripting);

        if (FAILED(hr))
            return FALSE;

        // register as safe for initializing
        hr = CreateComponentCategory(CATID_SafeForInitializing,
                L"Controls safely initializable from persistent data");

        if (FAILED(hr))
            return FALSE;

        hr = RegisterCLSIDInCategory(m_clsid, CATID_SafeForInitializing);

        if (FAILED(hr))
            return FALSE;

        return AfxOleRegisterControlClass(
            AfxGetInstanceHandle(),
            m_clsid,
            m_lpszProgID,
            IDS_DIEROLL,
            IDB_DIEROLL,
            afxRegInsertable | afxRegApartmentThreading,
            _dwDierollOleMisc,
```

Part

V

Ch

20

continues

Listing 20.4 Continued

```
            _tlid,
            _wVerMajor,
            _wVerMinor);

    else
    {
    HRESULT hr = S_OK ;
    hr = UnRegisterCLSIDInCategory(m_clsid, CATID_SafeForScripting);

    if (FAILED(hr))
        return FALSE;

    hr = UnRegisterCLSIDInCategory(m_clsid, CATID_SafeForInitializing);

    if (FAILED(hr))
        return FALSE;

        return AfxOleUnregisterClass(m_clsid, m_lpszProgID);
    }
}
```

To confirm that this works, open Explorer and set your safety level to Medium. Load the HTML page that uses the control; it should warn you the control is unsafe. Then make these changes, build the control, and reload the page. The warning will not reappear.

Choosing Between ActiveX and Java Applets

Java is an application development language as well as an applet development language, which means you can develop ActiveX controls in Java if you choose to, using a tool like Microsoft's Visual J++ integrated into Developer Studio. When most people frame a showdown like ActiveX versus Java, though, they mean ActiveX versus Java *applets*, which are little, tightly contained applications that run on a Web page and can't run standalone.

Many people are concerned about the security of running an application they did not code, when they do not know the person or organization supplying the application. The Java approach attempts to restrict the actions that applets can perform so that even malicious applets can't do any real damage. However, regular announcements of flaws in the restriction approach are damaging Java's credibility. Even if a Java applet were guaranteed to be safe, these same restrictions prevent it from doing certain useful tasks, since they cannot read or write files, send email, or load information from other Internet sites.

The approach taken by Microsoft with ActiveX is the trusted supplier approach, which is extendable to Java and any other code that can execute instructions. Code is digitally signed so that you are sure who provided it and that it has not been changed since it was signed. This won't prevent bad things from happening if you run the code, but it will guarantee that you know who is to blame if bad things do occur. This is just the same as buying shrink-wrapped software from the shelf in the computer store. For more details, look at

http://www.microsoft.com/ie/most/howto/trusted.htm and follow some of the links from that page.

Probably the biggest difference between the ActiveX approach and the Java applet approach is downloading. Java code is downloaded every time you load the page that contains it. ActiveX code is downloaded once, unless you already have the control installed some other way (perhaps a CD-ROM was sent to you in a magazine, for example) and then never again. A copy is stored on the user's machine and entered in the Registry. The Java code that is downloaded is small because most of the code involved is in the Java Virtual Machine installed on your computer, probably as part of your browser.

The ActiveX code that's downloaded can be much larger, though the optimizations discussed in the next section can significantly reduce the size by relying on DLLs and other code already on the user's computer. If users come to this page once and never again, they might be annoyed to find ActiveX controls cluttering their disk and Registry. On the other hand, if they come to the same page repeatedly, they will be pleased to find that there is no download time: The control simply activates and runs.

There are still other differences. Java applets can't fire events to notify the container that something has happened. Java applets can't be licensed and often don't distinguish between design-time and runtime use. Java applets can't be used in Visual Basic forms, VC++ programs, or Word documents in the same way that ActiveX controls can. ActiveX controls are nearly 10 times faster than Java applets. In their favor, Java applets are genuinely multiplatform and typically smaller than the equivalent ActiveX control.

Using AppWizard to Create Faster ActiveX Controls

Microsoft did not develop OCX controls to be placed in Web pages, and changing their name to ActiveX controls didn't magically make them faster to load or smaller. So the AppWizard that comes with Visual C++ has a number of options available to achieve those ends. This chapter changes these options in the Dieroll control that was already created, just to show how it's done. Because Dieroll is already a lean control and loads quickly, these simple changes won't make much difference. It's worth learning the techniques, though, for your own controls, which will surely be fatter than Dieroll.

The first few options to reduce your control's size have always been available on Step 2 of the ActiveX ControlWizard:

- Activates When Visible
- Invisible at Runtime
- Available in Insert Object Dialog Box
- Has an About Box
- Acts as a Simple Frame Control

If you are developing your control solely for the Web, many of these settings won't matter anymore. For example, it doesn't matter whether your control has an About box; users won't be able to bring it up when they are viewing the control in a Web page.

The Activates When Visible option is very important. Activating a control takes a lot of over-head activity and should be postponed as long as possible so that your control appears to load quickly. If your control activates as soon as it is visible, you'll add to the time it takes to load your control. To deselect this option in the existing Dieroll code, open the Dieroll project in Developer Studio if it isn't still open, and open DierollCtl.cpp with FileView. Look for a block of code like the one in Listing 20.5.

Listing 20.5   Excerpt from DierollCtl.cpp—Setting Activates When Visible

```
/////////////////////////////////////////////////////////////////////////////
// Control type information

static const DWORD BASED_CODE _dwDierollOleMisc =
    OLEMISC_ACTIVATEWHENVISIBLE ¦
    OLEMISC_SETCLIENTSITEFIRST ¦
    OLEMISC_INSIDEOUT ¦
    OLEMISC_CANTLINKINSIDE ¦
    OLEMISC_RECOMPOSEONRESIZE;

IMPLEMENT_OLECTLTYPE(CDierollCtrl, IDS_DIEROLL, _dwDierollOleMisc)
```

Delete the `OLEMISC_ACTIVATEWHENVISIBLE` line. Build a release version of the application. Though the size of the Dieroll OCX file is unchanged, Web pages with this control should load more quickly because the window isn't created until the user first clicks on the die. If you re-load the Web page with the die in it, you'll see the first value immediately, even though the control is inactive. The window is created to catch mouse clicks, not to display the die roll.

There are more optimizations available. Figure 20.4 shows the list of advanced options for ActiveX ControlWizard, reached by clicking the Advanced button on Step 2. You can choose each of these options when you first build the application through the ControlWizard. They can also be changed in an existing application, saving you the trouble of redoing AppWizard and adding your own functionality again. The options are

■ Windowless Activation
■ Unclipped Device Context
■ Flicker-Free Activation
■ Mouse Pointer Notifications When Inactive
■ Optimized Drawing Code
■ Loads Properties Asynchronously

FIG. 20.4
The Advanced button on Step 2 of the ActiveX ControlWizard leads to a choice of optimizations.

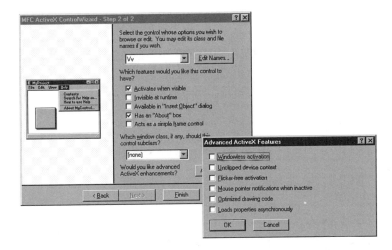

Windowless activation is going to be very popular because of the benefits it provides. If you want a transparent control or one that isn't a rectangle, you must use windowless activation. However, because it reduces code size and speeds execution, every control should consider using this option. Modern containers provide the functionality for the control. In older containers, the control creates the window anyway, denying you the savings but ensuring that the control still works.

To implement the Windowless Activation option in Dieroll, override `CDierollCtrl::GetControlFlags()` like this:

```
DWORD CDierollCtrl::GetControlFlags()
{
    return COleControl::GetControlFlags()¦ windowlessActivate;
}
```

Add the function quickly by right-clicking `CDierollCtrl` in ClassView and choosing Add Member Function. If you do this to Dieroll, build it, and reload the Web page that uses it, you'll notice no apparent effect because Dieroll is such a lean control. You'll at least notice that it still functions perfectly and doesn't mind not having a window.

The next two options, Unclipped Device Context and Flicker-Free Activation, are not available to windowless controls. In a control with a window, choosing Unclipped Device Context means that you are completely sure that you never draw outside the control's client rectangle. Skipping the checks that make sure you don't means your control runs faster, though it could mean trouble if you have an error in your draw code. If you were to do this in Dieroll, the override of `GetControlFlags()` would look like this:

```
DWORD CDierollCtrl::GetControlFlags()
{
    return COleControl::GetControlFlags()& ~clipPaintDC;
}
```

Don't try to combine this with windowless activation: It doesn't do anything.

Part
V

Ch
20

Flicker-free activation is useful for controls that draw their inactive and active views identically. (Think back to Chapter 15, "Building an ActiveX Server Application," in which the server object was drawn in dimmed colors when the objects were inactive.) If there is no need to redraw, because the drawing code is the same, you can select this option and skip the second draw. Your users won't see an annoying flicker as the control activates, and activation will be a tiny bit quicker. If you were to do this in Dieroll, the `GetControlFlags()` override would be

```
DWORD CDierollCtrl::GetControlFlags()
{
    return COleControl::GetControlFlags()¦ noFlickerActivate;
}
```

Like unclipped device context, don't try to combine this with windowless activation: It doesn't do anything.

Mouse pointer notifications, when inactive, enable more controls to turn off the Activates When Visible option. If the only reason to be active is to have a window to process mouse interactions, this option will divert those interactions to the container through an `IPointerInactive` interface. To enable this option in an application that is already built, you override `GetControlFlags()`again:

```
DWORD CDierollCtrl::GetControlFlags()
{
    return COleControl::GetControlFlags()¦ pointerInactive;
}
```

Now your code will receive WM_SETCURSOR and WM_MOUSEMOVE messages through message map entries, even though you have no window. The container, whose window your control is using, will send these messages to you through the `IPointerInactive` interface.

The other circumstance under which you might want to process window messages while still inactive, and so without a window, is if the user drags something over your control and drops it. The control needs to activate at that moment so that it has a window to be a drop target. You can arrange that with an override to `GetActivationPolicy()`:

```
DWORD CDierollCtrl::GetActivationPolicy()
{
    return POINTERINACTIVE_ACTIVATEONDRAG;
}
```

Don't bother doing this if your control isn't a drop target, of course.

The problem with relying on the container to pass on your messages through the `IPointerInactive` interface is that the container might have no idea such an interface exists and no plans to pass your messages on with it. If you think your control might end up in such a container, don't remove the OLEMISC_ACTIVATEWHENVISIBLE flag from the block of code shown previously in in Listing 20.5

Instead, combine another flag, OLEMISC_IGNOREACTIVATEWHENVISIBLE, with these flags using the bitwise or operator. This oddly named flag is meaningful to containers that understand `IPointerInactive` and means, in effect, "I take it back— don't activate when visible after all."

Containers that don't understand IPointerInactive don't understand this flag either, and your control will activate when visible and thus be around to catch mouse messages in these containers.

Optimized drawing code is only useful to controls that will be sharing the container with a number of other drawing controls. As you might recall from Chapter 5, "Drawing on the Screen," the typical pattern for drawing a view of any kind is to set the brush, pen, or other GDI object to a new value, saving the old. Then you use the GDI object and restore it to the saved value. If there are several controls doing this in turn, all those restore steps can be skipped in favor of one restore at the end of all the drawing. The container saves all the GDI object values before instructing the controls to redraw and afterwards restores them all.

If you would like your control to take advantage of this, you need to make two changes. First, if a pen or other GDI object is to remain connected between draw calls, it must not go out of scope. That means any local pens, brushes, and fonts should be converted to member variables so that they stay in scope between function calls. Second, the code to restore the old objects should be surrounded by an if statement that calls COleControl::IsOptimizedDraw() to see whether the restoration is necessary. A typical draw routine would set up the colors and proceed like this:

```
...
if(!m_pen.m_hObject)
{
    m_pen.CreatePen(PS_SOLID, 0, forecolor);
}
if(!m_brush.m_hObject)
{
    m_brush.CreateSolidBrush(backcolor);
}

CPen* savepen = pdc->SelectObject(&m_pen);
CBrush* savebrush = pdc->SelectObject(&m_brush);

...
// use device context
...
if(!IsOptimizedDraw())
{
    pdc->SelectObject(savepen);
    pdc->SelectObject(savebrush);
}
...
```

The device context has the addresses of the member variables, so when it lets go of them at the direction of the container, their m_hObject member becomes NULL. As long as it isn't NULL, there is no need to reset the device context, and if this container supports optimized drawing code, there is no need to restore it either.

If you select this optimized drawing code option from the Advanced button in AppWizard Step 2, the if statement with the call to IsOptimizedDraw() is added to your draw code, with some comments to remind you what to do.

The last optimization option, Loads Properties Asynchronously, is covered in the next section.

Speeding Control Loads with Asynchronous Properties

Asynchronous refers to spreading out activities over time and not insisting that one activity be completed before another can begin. In the context of the Web, it's worth harking back to the features that made Netscape Navigator better than Mosaic, way back when it was first released. The number one benefit cited by people who were on the Web then was that the Netscape browser, unlike Mosaic, could display text while pictures were still loading. This is classic asynchronous behavior. You don't have to wait until the huge image files have transferred, to see what the words on the page are and whether the images are worth waiting for.

Faster Internet connections and more compact image formats have lessened some of the concerns about waiting for images. Still, being asynchronous is a good thing. For one thing, waiting for video clips, sound clips, and executable code has made many Web users long for the good old days when they had to wait only 30 seconds for pages to find all their images.

Properties

The die that comes up in your Web page is the default die appearance. There's no way for the user to access the control's properties. The Web page developer can, using the <PARAM> tag inside the <OBJECT> tag. (Browsers that ignore OBJECT also ignore PARAM.) Here's the PARAM tag to add to your HTML between <OBJECT> and </OBJECT> to include a die with a number instead of dots:

```
<PARAM NAME="Dots" value="0">
```

The PARAM tag has two attributes: NAME provides a name that matches the external ActiveX name (Dots), and value provides the value (0, or FALSE). The die displays with a number.

To demonstrate the value of asynchronous properties, Dieroll needs to have some big properties. Because this is a demonstration application, the next step is to add a big property. A natural choice is to give the user more control over the die's appearance. The user (which means the Web page designer if the control is being used in a Web page) can specify an image file and use that as the background for the die. Before you learn how to make that happen, imagine what the Web page reader will have to wait for when loading a page that uses Dieroll:

- The HTML has to be loaded from the server.
- The browser lays out the text and nontext elements and starts to display text.
- The browser searches the Registry for the control's CLSID.
- If necessary, the control is downloaded, using the CODEBASE parameter.
- The control properties are initialized, using the PARAM tags.
- The control runs and draws itself.

When Dieroll gains another property—an image file that might be quite large—there will be another delay while the image file is retrieved from wherever it is kept. If nothing happens in the meantime, the Web page reader will eventually tire of staring at an empty square and go to another page. Using asynchronous properties means that the control can roughly draw itself and start to be useful, even while the large image file is still being downloaded. For Dieroll, drawing the dots on a plain background, using `GetBackColor()`, will do until the image file is ready.

Using BLOBs

A *BLOB* is a binary large object. It's a generic name for things like the image file you are about to add to the Dieroll control. The way a control talks to a BLOB is through a *moniker*. That's not new. It's just that monikers have always been hidden away inside OLE. If you already understand them, you still have a great deal more to learn about them because things are changing with the introduction of asynchronous monikers. If you've never heard of them before, no problem. Eventually there will be all sorts of asynchronous monikers, but at the moment only URL monikers have been implemented. These are a way for ActiveX to connect BLOB properties to URLs. If you're prepared to trust ActiveX to do this for you, you can achieve some amazing things. The remainder of this subsection explains how to work with URL monikers to load BLOB properties asynchronously.

Remember, the idea here is that the control will start drawing itself even before it has all its properties. Your `OnDraw()` code will be structured like this:

```
// prepare to draw
if(AllPropertiesAreLoaded)
{
    // draw using the BLOB
}
else
{
    // draw without the BLOB
}
//cleanup after drawing
```

There are two problems to solve here. First, what will be the test to see whether all the properties are loaded? Second, how can you arrange to have `OnDraw()` called again when the properties are ready, if it's already been called and has already drawn the control the BLOBless way?

The first problem has been solved by adding two new functions to `COleControl`. `GetReadyState()` returns one of these values:

- ■ `READYSTATE_UNINITIALIZED` means the control is completely unitialized.
- ■ `READYSTATE_LOADING` means the control properties are loading.
- ■ `READYSTATE_LOADED` means the properties are all loaded.
- ■ `READYSTATE_INTERACTIVE` means the control can talk to the user but isn't fully loaded yet.
- ■ `READYSTATE_COMPLETE` means there is nothing more to wait for.

The function `InternalSetReadyState()` sets the ready state to one of these values.

The second problem, getting a second call to `OnDraw()` after the control has already been drawn without the BLOB, has been solved by a new class called `CDataPathProperty` and its derived class `CCachedDataPathProperty`. These classes have a member function called `OnDataAvailable()` that catches the Windows message generated when the property has been retrieved from the remote site. The `OnDataAvailable()` function invalidates the control, forcing a redraw.

Changing Dieroll

Make a copy of the Dieroll folder you created in Chapter 17 and change it to windowless activation as described earlier in this chapter. Now you're ready to begin. There is a lot to do to implement asynchronous properties, but each step is straightforward.

Add the *CDierollDataPathProperty* Class   Bring up ClassWizard, click the Automation tab, and click the Add Class button. From the drop-down menu that appears under the button, choose New. This brings up the Create New Class dialog box. Name the class `CDierollDataPathProperty`. Click the drop-down box for Base Class and choose `CCachedDataPathProperty`. The dialog box will resemble Figure 20.5. Click OK to create the class and add it to the project.

FIG. 20.5
Create a new class to handle asynchronous properties.

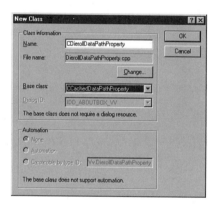

The reason that the new class should inherit from `CCachedDataProperty` is that it will load the property information into a file, which is an easier way to handle the bitmap. If the control has a property that was downloaded because it changed often (for example, current weather), `CDataPathProperty` would be a better choice.

Add the *Image* Property to *CDierollCtrl*   With the new `CDierollDataPathProperty` class added to the Dieroll control, add the property to the original `CDierollCtrl` class that you copied: In ClassWizard, on the Automation tab, make sure that `CDierollCtrl` is selected in the far right drop-down box. Click Add Property and fill out the dialog as shown in Figure 20.6. The external name you choose is the one that will appear in the HTML: `Image` is simple and doesn't require a lot of typing. The type should be `BSTR`—that choice won't be in the drop-down box for type until you change the Implementation to Get/Set Methods.

FIG. 20.6

The image file is added as a BSTR property.

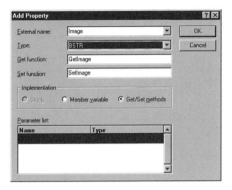

ClassWizard adds the Get and Set functions to your control class, but the TODO comments (see Listing 20.6) are cryptic.

Listing 20.6 DierollCtl.cpp—*Get* and *Set* Functions

```
BSTR CDierollCtrl::GetImage()
{
    CString strResult;
    // TODO: Add your property handler here

    return strResult.AllocSysString();
}

void CDierollCtrl::SetImage(LPCTSTR lpszNewValue)
{
    // TODO: Add your property handler here

    SetModifiedFlag();
}
```

As with other Get and Set properties, you'll have to add a member variable to the control class and add code to these functions to get or set its value. It is an instance of the new CDierollDataPathProperty class. Right-click CDierollCtrl in ClassView and choose Add Member Variable. Figure 20.7 shows how to fill in the dialog box to declare the member variable mdpp_image. (The dpp in the name is to remind you that this is a data path property.)

Part

V

Ch

20

FIG. 20.7

The image file member variable is an instance of the new class.

Now you can finish the Get and Set functions, as shown in Listing 20.7.

Listing 20.7   DierollCtl.cpp—Completed *Get* and *Set* Functions

```
BSTR CDierollCtrl::GetImage()
{
    CString strResult;
    strResult = mdpp_image.GetPath();
    return strResult.AllocSysString();
}

void CDierollCtrl::SetImage(LPCTSTR lpszNewValue)
{
    Load(lpszNewValue, mdpp_image);
    SetModifiedFlag();
}
```

At the top of the header file for CDierollCtrl, add this include statement:

```
#include "DierollDataPathProperty.h"
```

Now there are some bits and pieces to deal with because you are changing an existing control rather than turning on asynchronous properties when you first built Dieroll. First, in CDierollCtrl::DoPropExchange(), arrange persistence and initialization for mdpp_image by adding this line:

```
PX_DataPath( pPX, _T("Image"), mdpp_image);
```

Second, add a line to the stub of CDierollCtrl::OnResetState() that ClassWizard provided, to reset the data path property when the control is reset. Listing 20.8 shows the function.

Listing 20.8   DierollCtl.cpp—*CDierollCtrl::OnResetState()*

```
/////////////////////////////////////////////////////////////////////////
// CDierollCtrl::OnResetState - Reset control to default state

void CDierollCtrl::OnResetState()
{
    COleControl::OnResetState();  // Resets defaults found in DoPropExchange

    mdpp_image.ResetData();
}
```

Add the *ReadyStateChange* Event and the *ReadyState* Property   Use ClassWizard to add the stock event ReadyStateChange. In ClassWizard, click the ActiveX Events tab, then the Add Event button. Choose ReadyStateChange from the drop-down box and click OK. Figure 20.8 shows the Add Event dialog box for this event. Events, as discussed in Chapter 17, notify the control's container that something has happened within the control. In this case, what has happened is that the rest of the control's data has arrived and the control's state of readiness has changed.

FIG. 20.8

Add a stock event to notify the container of a change in the control's readiness.

Use ClassWizard to add a property to CDierollCtrl for the ready state. In ClassWizard, click the Automation tab, then the Add Property button. Choose ReadyState from the drop-down box, and because this is a stock property, the rest of the dialog box is filled in for you, as shown in Figure 20.9. Click OK to finish adding the property and then close ClassWizard. ClassWizard doesn't add a stub function for GetReadyState() because CDierollCtrl will inherit this from COleControl.

FIG. 20.9

Add a stock property to track the control's readiness.

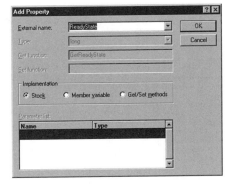

Add code to the constructor to connect the cached property to this control and to initialize the member variable in COleControl that is used in COleControl::GetReadyState() and set by COleControl::InternalSetReadyState(). Because the control can be used right away, the readiness state should start at READYSTATE_INTERACTIVE. Listing 20.9 shows the new constructor.

Part
V

Ch
20

Listing 20.9   DierollCtl.cpp—*CDierollCtrl::CDierollCtrl()*

```
CDierollCtrl::CDierollCtrl()
{
    InitializeIIDs(&IID_DDieroll, &IID_DDierollEvents);
    mdpp_image.SetControl(this);
    m_lReadyState = READYSTATE_INTERACTIVE;
}
```

Implement *CDierollDataPathProperty* There is some work to do in
CDierollDataPathProperty before changing CDierollCtrl::OnDraw(). This class loads a
bitmap, and this chapter isn't going to explain most of what's involved in reading a BMP file
into a CBitmap object. The most important function is OnDataAvailable(), which is in Listing
20.10. Add this function to the class by right-clicking CDierollCtrl in ClassView and choosing
Add Virtual Function. Select OnDataAvailable from the list on the left, and click Add and Edit;
then type this code.

Listing 20.10   DierollDataPathProperty.cpp—*OnDataAvailable()*

```
void CDierollDataPathProperty::OnDataAvailable(DWORD dwSize, DWORD grfBSCF)
{
    CCachedDataPathProperty::OnDataAvailable(dwSize, grfBSCF);

    if(grfBSCF & BSCF_LASTDATANOTIFICATION)
    {
        m_Cache.SeekToBegin();
        if (ReadBitmap(m_Cache))
        {
            BitmapDataLoaded = TRUE;
            // safe because this control has only one property:
            GetControl()->InternalSetReadyState(READYSTATE_COMPLETE);
            GetControl()->InvalidateControl();
        }
    }
}
```

Every time a block of data is received from the remote site, this function is called. The first line
of code uses the base class version of the function to deal with that block and set the flag called
grfBSCF. If, after dealing with the latest block, the download is complete, the ReadBitmap()
function is called to read the cached data into a bitmap object that can be displayed as the
control background. (The code for ReadBitmap() isn't presented or discussed here, though it is
on the Web site for you to copy into your application.) After the bitmap has been read, the
control's ready state is complete and the call to InvalidateControl() arranges for a redraw.

Revise *CDierollCtrl::OnDraw()* The structure of CDierollCtrl::OnDraw() was laid out long
ago. In this block of code, the background is filled in before the code that checks whether to
draw dots or a number:

```
COLORREF back = TranslateColor(GetBackColor());
CBrush backbrush;
backbrush.CreateSolidBrush(back);
pdc->FillRect(rcBounds, &backbrush);
```

Replace that block with the one in Listing 20.11.

Listing 20.11 DierollDataPathProperty.cpp—New Code for *OnDraw()*

```
CBrush backbrush;
BOOL drawn = FALSE;
if (GetReadyState() == READYSTATE_COMPLETE)
{
    CBitmap* image = mdpp_image.GetBitmap(*pdc);
    if (image)
    {
        CDC memdc;
        memdc.CreateCompatibleDC(pdc);
        memdc.SelectObject(image);
        BITMAP bmp;                           // just for height and width
        image->GetBitmap(&bmp);
        pdc->StretchBlt(0,                    // upper left
                        0,                    // upper right
                        rcBounds.Width(),     // target width
                        rcBounds.Height(),    // target height
                        &memdc,               // the image
                        0,                    // offset into image -x
                        0,                    // offset into image -y
                        bmp.bmWidth,          // width
                        bmp.bmHeight,         // height
                        SRCCOPY);             // copy it over

        drawn = TRUE;
    }
}
if (!drawn)
{
    COLORREF back = TranslateColor(GetBackColor());
    backbrush.CreateSolidBrush(back);
    pdc->FillRect(rcBounds, &backbrush);
}
```

The BOOL variable drawn ensures that if the control is complete, but something goes wrong with the attempt to use the bitmap, the control will be drawn the old way. If the control is complete, the image is loaded into a CBitmap* and then drawn into the device context. Bitmaps can only be selected into a memory device context and then copied over to an ordinary device context. Using StretchBlt() will stretch the bitmap during the copy, though a sensible Web page designer will have specified a bitmap that matches the HEIGHT and WIDTH attributes of the OBJECT tag. The old drawing code is still here, used if drawn remains FALSE.

Testing and Debugging Dieroll

Having made all those changes, build the control, which will register it. One way to test it would be to bring up that HTML page in Explorer again, but you might prefer to debug the control. It is possible to debug a control even though you can't run it standalone. Normally, a developer would arrange to debug the control in the test container, but you can use any application that can contain the control.

Part
V

Ch
20

In Developer Studio, choose Project Settings. Click the Debug tab and make sure that all the lines in the far left list box are selected. Select General in the top drop-down box, and in the edit box labeled Executable for Debug Session, enter the full path to Microsoft Internet Explorer on your computer. (If there's a shortcut to Microsoft Internet Explorer on your desktop, right-click it and choose Properties to get the path to the executable. Otherwise, use the Find utility on the Start menu to find iexplore.exe. Figure 20.10 shows an example.) Now when you choose Build, Start Debug, Go or click the Go toolbar button, Explorer will launch. Open a page of HTML that loads the control, and the control will run in the debugger. You can set breakpoints, step through code, and examine variables, just as with any other application.

FIG. 20.10

Arrange to run Explorer when you debug the control.

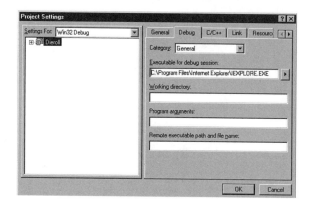

Here's the syntax for an OBJECT tag that sets the Image property:

```
<OBJECT
CLASSID="clsid:46646B43-EA16-11CF-870C-00201801DDD6"
CODEBASE="http://www.gregcons.com/test/dieroll.ocx"
ID=die1
WIDTH=200
HEIGHT=200
ALIGN=center
HSPACE=0
VSPACE=0
>
<PARAM NAME="Dots" VALUE="1">
<PARAM NAME="Image" VALUE="http://www.gregcons.com/test/beans.bmp">
If you see this text, your browser does not support the OBJECT tag. </BR>
</OBJECT>
```

TIP   Remember, don't just copy these HTML samples to your own machine if you are building Dieroll yourself. You need to use your own CLSID, an URL to the location of your copy of the OCX, and the image file you are using.

Figure 20.11 shows the control with a background image of jelly beans. It takes 30–60 seconds to load this 40KB image through the Web, and while it is loading, the control is perfectly usable as a plain die with no background image. That's the whole point of asynchronous properties, and that's what all the effort of the previous sections achieves.

FIG. 20.11

Now the die displays on a field of jelly beans or on any other image you choose.

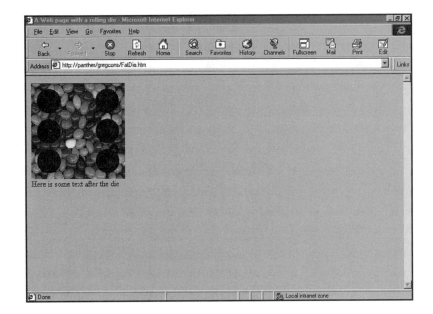

The Active Template Library

The Active Template Library (ATL) is a collection of C++ class templates that you can use to build ActiveX controls. These small controls generally don't use MFC, the Microsoft Foundation Classes, at all. Writing an ActiveX control with ATL requires a lot more knowledge of COM and interfaces than writing an MFC ActiveX control, because MFC protects you from a lot of low-level COM concepts. Using ATL is not for the timid, but it pays dividends in smaller, tighter controls. This chapter rewrites the Dieroll control of Chapter 17, "Building an ActiveX Control," and Chapter 20, "Building an Internet ActiveX Control," by using ATL rather than MFC as in those chapters. You will learn the important COM/ActiveX concepts that were skimmed over while you were using MFC.

Why Use the ATL?

Building an ActiveX Control with MFC is simple, as you saw in Chapters 17 and 20. You can get by without knowing what a COM interface is or how to use a type library. Your control can use all sorts of handy MFC classes, such as CString and CWnd, can draw itself by using CDC member functions, and more. The only downside is that users of your control need the MFC DLLs, and if those DLLs aren't on their system already, the delay while 600KB or so of CAB file downloads will be significant.

The alternative to MFC is to obtain the ActiveX functionality from the ATL and to call Win32 SDK functions, just as C programmers did when writing for Windows in the days before Visual C++ and MFC. The Win32 SDK is a lot to learn and won't be fully covered in this chapter. The good news is that if you're familiar with major MFC classes, such as CWnd and CDC, you will recognize a lot of these SDK functions, even if you've never seen them before. Many MFC member functions are merely wrappers for SDK functions.

How much download time can you save? The MFC control from Chapter 20 is nearly 30KB plus, of course, the MFC DLLs. The ATL control built in this chapter is, at most, 100KB and is fully self-contained. With a few tricks, you could reduce it to 50KB of control and 20KB for the ATL DLL—one-tenth the size of the total control and DLL from Chapter 20!

Using AppWizard to Get Started

There's an AppWizard that knows how to make ATL controls, and it makes your job much simpler than it would be without the wizard. As always, choose File, New and click the Projects tab on the New dialog. Fill in an appropriate directory and name the project **DieRollControl**, as shown in Figure 21.1. Click OK.

N O T E It's tempting to name the project *DieRoll*, but later in this process you will be inserting a control into the project—that control will be called *DieRoll*, so to avoid name conflicts, choose a longer name for the project. ▪

FIG. 21.1

AppWizard makes creating an ATL control simple.

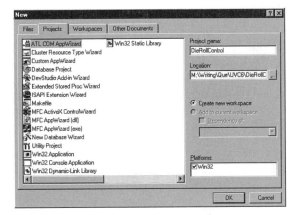

There is only one step in the ATL COM AppWizard, and it is shown in Figure 21.2. The default choices—DLL control, no merging proxy/stub code, no MFC support, no MTS support—are the right ones for this project. The file extension will be DLL rather than OCX, as it was for MFC controls, but that's not an important difference. Click Finish.

FIG. 21.2

Create a DLL control.

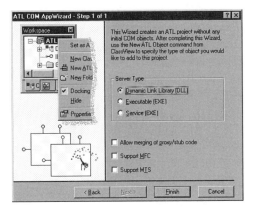

The New Project Information dialog box, shown in Figure 21.3, confirms the choices you have made. Click OK to create the project.

Using the Object Wizard

The ATL COM AppWizard created 13 files, but you don't have a skeleton control yet. First, you have to follow the instructions included in the Step 1 dialog box and insert an ATL object into the project.

Adding a Control to the Project

Choose Insert, New ATL Object from the menu bar. This opens the ATL Object Wizard, shown in Figure 21.4.

FIG. 21.3

Your ATL choices are summarized before you create the project.

FIG. 21.4

Add an ATL control to your project.

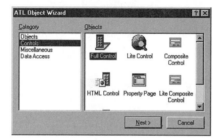

You can add several kinds of ATL objects to your project, but at the moment you are interested only in controls, so select Controls in the list box on the left. The choices in the list box on the left include Full Control, Lite Control, and Property Page. If you know for certain that this control will be used only in Internet Explorer, perhaps as part of an intranet project, you could choose Lite Control and save a little space. This DieRoll control might end up in any browser, a Visual Basic application, or anywhere else for that matter, so a Full Control is the way to go. You will add a property page later in this chapter. Select Full Control and click Next.

Naming the Control

Now the ATL Object Wizard Properties dialog box appears. The first tab is the Names tab. Here you can customize all the names used for this control. Enter **DieRoll** for the Short Name of DieRoll, and the rest will default to names based on it, as shown in Figure 21.5. You could change these names if you want, but there is no need. Note that the Type, DieRoll Class, is the name that will appear in the Insert Object dialog box of most containers. Because the MFC version of DieRoll is probably already in your Registry, having a different name for this version is a good thing. On other projects, you might consider changing the type name.

FIG. 21.5
Set the names of the
files and the control.

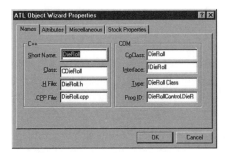

Setting Control Attributes

Click the Attributes tab. Leave the default values: Apartment Threading Model, Dual Interface,
and Yes for Aggregation. Select the check boxes Support ISupportErrorInfo and Support Connection Points. Leave Free Threaded Marshaler deselected, as shown in Figure 21.6. Each of
these choices is discussed in the paragraphs that follow.

FIG. 21.6
Set the COM properties
of your control.

Threading Models   Avoid selecting the Single Threading Model, even if your controls don't
have any threading. To be sure that no two functions of such a control are running at the same
time, all calls to methods of a single-threaded control must be marshalled through a proxy,
which significantly slows execution. The Apartment setting is a better choice for new controls.

The Apartment model refers to STA (Single-Threaded Apartment model). This means that
access to any resources shared by instances of the control (globals and statics) is through
serialization. Instance data—local automatic variables and objects dynamically allocated on the
heap—doesn't need this protection. This makes STA controls faster than single-threaded controls. Internet Explorer exploits STA in controls it contains.

TIP   If the design for your control includes a lot of globals and statics, it might be a great deal of work to
use the Apartment model. This isn't a good reason to write a single-threaded control; it's a good reason
to redesign your control as a more object-oriented system.

The Free Threading (Multithreaded Apartment or MTA) Model refers to controls that are threaded and that already include protection against thread collisions. Although writing a multithreaded control might seem like a great idea, using such a control in a nonthreaded or STA container will result in marshalling again, this time to protect the container against having two functions called at once. This, too, introduces inefficiencies. Also, you, the developer, will do a significant amount of extra work to create a free-threaded control, because you must add the thread collision protection.

The Both option in the Threading Model column asks the wizard to make a control that can be STA or MTA, avoiding inefficiences when used in a container that is single-threaded or STA, and exploiting the power of MTA models when available. You will have to add the threading-protection work, just as when you write an MTA control.

At the moment, controls for Internet Explorer should be STA. DCOM controls that might be accessed by several connections at once can benefit from being MTA.

Dual and Custom Interfaces   COM objects communicate through *interfaces*, which are collections of function names that describe the possible behavior of a COM object. To use an interface, you obtain a pointer to it and then call a member function of the interface. All Automation servers and ActiveX controls have an IDispatch interface in addition to any other interfaces that might be specific to what the server or control is for. To call a method of a control, you can use the Invoke() method of the IDispatch interface, passing in the dispid of the method you want to invoke. (This technique was developed so that methods could be called from Visual Basic and other pointerless languages.)

Simply put, a *dual-interface* control lets you call methods both ways: by using a member function of a custom interface or by using IDispatch. MFC controls use only IDispatch, but this is slower than using a custom interface. The Interface column on this dialog box lets you choose Dual or Custom: Custom leaves IDispatch out of the picture. Select Dual so that the control can be used from Visual Basic, if necessary.

Aggregation   The third column, Aggregation, governs whether another COM class can use this COM class by containing a reference to an instance of it. Choosing Yes means that other COM objects can use this class, No means they can't, and Only means they must—this object can't stand alone.

Other Control Settings   Selecting support for ISupportErrorInfo means that your control will be able to return richer error information to the container. Selecting support for Connection Points is vital for a control, like this one, that will fire events. Selecting Free-Threaded Marshaler isn't required for an STA control.

Click the Miscellaneous tab and examine all the settings, which can be left at their default values (see Figure 21.7). The control should be Opaque with a Solid Background and should use a normalized DC, even though that's slightly less efficient, because your draw code will be much easier to write.

T I P If you'd like to see how a DC is normalized for an ATL control, remember that the entire ATL source is available to you, just as the MFC source is. In Program Files\Microsoft Visual Studio\VC98\ATL\ Include\\ATLCTL.CPP, you will find `CComControlBase::OnDrawAdvanced()`, which normalizes a DC and calls `OnDraw()` for you.

FIG. 21.7
Leave the Miscellaneous properties at the defaults.

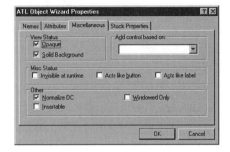

Supporting Stock Properties

Click the Stock Properties tab to specify which stock properties the control will support. To add support for a stock property, select it in the Not Supported list box; then click the > button, and it will be moved to the Supported list on the right. Add support for Background Color and Foreground Color, as shown in Figure 21.8. If you plan to support a lot of properties, use the >> button to move them all to the supported list and then move back the ones you don't want to support.

FIG. 21.8
Support Background Color and Foreground Color.

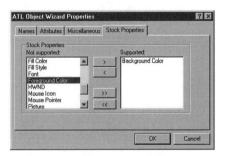

Click OK on the Object Wizard to complete the control creation. At this point, you can build the project if you want, though the control does nothing at the moment.

Adding Properties to the Control

The MFC versions of DieRoll featured three stock properties: `BackColor`, `ForeColor`, and `ReadyState`. The first two have been added already, but the `ReadyState` stock properties must be added by hand. Also, there are two custom properties, `Number` and `Dots`, and an asynchronous property, `Image`.

Part
V

Ch
21

Code from the Object Wizard

A COM class that implements or uses an interface does so by inheriting from a class representing that interface. Listing 21.1 shows all the classes that CDieRoll inherits from.

Listing 21.1   Excerpt from DieRoll.h in the DieRollControl Project—Inheritance

```
class ATL_NO_VTABLE CDieRoll :
    public CComObjectRootEx<CComSingleThreadModel>,
    public CStockPropImpl<CDieRoll, IDieRoll, &IID_IDieRoll,
    ➥&LIBID_DIEROLLCONTROLLib>,
    public CComControl<CDieRoll>,
    public IPersistStreamInitImpl<CDieRoll>,
    public IOleControlImpl<CDieRoll>,
    public IOleObjectImpl<CDieRoll>,
    public IOleInPlaceActiveObjectImpl<CDieRoll>,
    public IViewObjectExImpl<CDieRoll>,
    public IOleInPlaceObjectWindowlessImpl<CDieRoll>,
    public ISupportErrorInfo,
    public IConnectionPointContainerImpl<CDieRoll>,
    public IPersistStorageImpl<CDieRoll>,
    public ISpecifyPropertyPagesImpl<CDieRoll>,
    public IQuickActivateImpl<CDieRoll>,
    public IDataObjectImpl<CDieRoll>,
    public IProvideClassInfo2Impl<&CLSID_DieRoll,
    ➥&DIID__IDieRollEvents, &LIBID_DIEROLLCONTROLLib>,
    public IPropertyNotifySinkCP<CDieRoll>,
    public CComCoClass<CDieRoll, &CLSID_DieRoll>,
```

Now you can see where the *T* in ATL comes in: All these classes are template classes. (If you aren't familiar with templates, read Chapter 26, "Exceptions and Templates.") You add support for an interface to a control by adding another entry to this list of interface classes from which it inherits.

N O T E   Notice that some names follow the pattern IxxxImpl: That means that this class implements the Ixxx interface. Classes inheriting from IxxxImpl inherit code as well as function names. For example, CDieRoll inherits from ISupportErrorInfo, not ISupportErrorInfoImpl<CDieRoll>, even though such a template does exist. That is because the code in that template implementation class isn't appropriate for an ATL control, so the control inherits only the names of the functions from the original interface and provides code for them in the source file, as you will shortly see. ■

Farther down the header file, you will find the COM map shown in Listing 21.2.

Listing 21.2   Excerpt from DieRollControl.h—COM Map

```
BEGIN_COM_MAP(CDieRoll)
    COM_INTERFACE_ENTRY_IMPL(IConnectionPointContainer)
    COM_INTERFACE_ENTRY(IDieRoll)
```

```
    COM_INTERFACE_ENTRY(IDispatch)
    COM_INTERFACE_ENTRY(IViewObjectEx)
    COM_INTERFACE_ENTRY(IViewObject2)
    COM_INTERFACE_ENTRY(IViewObject)
    COM_INTERFACE_ENTRY(IOleInPlaceObjectWindowless)
    COM_INTERFACE_ENTRY(IOleInPlaceObject)
    COM_INTERFACE_ENTRY2(IOleWindow, IOleInPlaceObjectWindowless)
    COM_INTERFACE_ENTRY(IOleInPlaceActiveObject)
    COM_INTERFACE_ENTRY(IOleControl)
    COM_INTERFACE_ENTRY(IOleObject)
    COM_INTERFACE_ENTRY(IPersistStreamInit)
    COM_INTERFACE_ENTRY2(IPersist, IPersistStreamInit)
    COM_INTERFACE_ENTRY(ISupportErrorInfo)
    COM_INTERFACE_ENTRY(IConnectionPointContainer)
    COM_INTERFACE_ENTRY(ISpecifyPropertyPages)
    COM_INTERFACE_ENTRY(IQuickActivate)
    COM_INTERFACE_ENTRY(IPersistStorage)
    COM_INTERFACE_ENTRY(IDataObject)
    COM_INTERFACE_ENTRY(IProvideClassInfo)
    COM_INTERFACE_ENTRY(IProvideClassInfo2)
  END_COM_MAP()
```

This COM map is the connection between `IUnknown::QueryInterface()` and all the interfaces supported by the control. All COM objects must implement `IUnknown`, and `QueryInterface()` can be used to determine what other interfaces the control supports and obtain a pointer to them. The macros connect the `Ixxx` interfaces to the `IxxxImpl` classes from which `CDieRoll` inherits.

 T I P IUnknown and QueryInterface are discussed in Chapter 13, "ActiveX Concepts," in the section titled "The Component Object Model."

Looking back at the inheritance list for `CDieRoll`, most templates take only one parameter, the name of this class, and come from AppWizard. This entry came from ObjectWizard:

```
public CStockPropImpl<CDieRoll, IDieRoll, &IID_IDieRoll,
  ➥&LIBID_DIEROLLCONTROLLib>,
```

This line is how ObjectWizard arranged for support for stock properties. Notice that there is no indication which properties are supported. Farther down the header file, two member variables have been added to `CDieRoll`:

```
OLE_COLOR m_clrBackColor;
OLE_COLOR m_clrForeColor;
```

The ObjectWizard also updated DieRollControl.idl, the interface definition file, to show these two stock properties, as shown in Listing 21.3. (Double-click on the interface, `IDieRoll`, in ClassView to edit the .IDL file.)

Part

V

Ch

21

Listing 21.3   Excerpt from DieRollControl.idl—Stock Properties

```
[
    object,
    uuid(2DE15F32-8A71-11D0-9B10-0080C81A397C),
    dual,
    helpstring("IDieRoll Interface"),
    pointer_default(unique)
]
interface IDieRoll : IDispatch
{
[propput, id(DISPID_BACKCOLOR)]
    HRESULT BackColor([in]OLE_COLOR clr);
[propget, id(DISPID_BACKCOLOR)]
    HRESULT BackColor([out,retval]OLE_COLOR* pclr);
[propput, id(DISPID_FORECOLOR)]
    HRESULT ForeColor([in]OLE_COLOR clr);
[propget, id(DISPID_FORECOLOR)]
    HRESULT ForeColor([out,retval]OLE_COLOR* pclr);
};
```

This class will provide all the support for the get and put functions and will notify the container when one of these properties changes.

Adding the *ReadyState* Stock Property

Although ReadyState wasn't on the stock property list in the ATL Object Wizard, it's supported by CStockPropImpl. You can add another stock property by editing the header and idl files. In the header file, immediately after the lines that declare m_clrBackColor and m_clrForeColor, declare another member variable:

```
long m_nReadyState;
```

This property will be used in the same way as the ReadyState property in the MFC version of DieRoll: to implement Image as an asynchronous property. In DieRollControl.idl, add these lines to the IDispatch block, after the lines for BackColor and ForeColor:

```
[propget, id(DISPID_READYSTATE)]
HRESULT ReadyState([out,retval]long* prs);
```

You don't need to add a pair of lines to implement put for this property, because external objects can't update ReadyState. Save the header and idl files to update ClassView—if you don't, you won't be able to add more properties with ClassView. Expand CDieRoll and IDieRoll in ClassView to see that the member variable has been added to CDieRoll and a ReadyState() function has been added to IDieRoll.

Adding Custom Properties

To add custom properties, you will use an ATL tool similar to the MFC ClassWizard. Right-click on IDieRoll (the top-level one, not the one under CDieRoll) in ClassView to open the shortcut menu shown in Figure 21.9, and choose Add Property.

FIG. 21.9

ATL projects have a different ClassView shortcut menu than MFC projects.

The Add Property to Interface dialog box, shown in Figure 21.10, appears. Choose **short** for the type and fill in **Number** for the name. Deselect Put Function because containers won't need to change the number showing on the die. Leave the rest of the settings unchanged and click OK to add the property.

FIG. 21.10

Add **Number** as a read-only property.

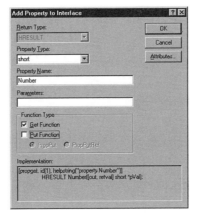

Repeat this process for the BOOL Dots, which should have both get and put functions. (Leave the Put radio button at PropPut.) The ClassView now shows entries under both CDieRoll and IDieRoll related to these new properties. Try double-clicking the new entries. For example, double-clicking get_Dots() under the IDieRoll that is under CDieRoll opens the source (cpp) file scrolled to the get_Dots() function. Double-clicking Dots() under the top-level IDieRoll opens the idl file scrolled to the propget entry for Dots.

Although a number of entries have been added to CDieRoll, no member variables have been added. Only you can add the member variables that correspond to the new properties. Although in many cases it's safe to assume that the new properties are simply member variables of the control class, they might not be. For example, Number might have been the dimension of some array kept within the class rather than a variable of its own.

Add the following to the header file, after the declarations of m_clrBackColor, m_clrForeColor, and m_nReadyState:

```
short m_sNumber;
BOOL m_bDots;
```

Part
V

Ch
21

In the idl file, the new propget and propput entries use hard-coded dispids of 1 and 2, like this:

```
[propget, id(1), helpstring("property Number")]
    HRESULT Number([out, retval] short *pVal);
[propget, id(2), helpstring("property Dots")]
    HRESULT Dots([out, retval] BOOL *pVal);
[propput, id(2), helpstring("property Dots")]
    HRESULT Dots([in] BOOL newVal);
```

To make the code more readable, use an enum of dispids. Adding the declaration of the enum to the idl file will make it usable in both the idl and header file. Add these lines to the beginning of DieRollControl.idl:

```
typedef enum propertydispids
    {
        dispidNumber = 1,
        dispidDots = 2,
    }PROPERTYDISPIDS;
```

Now you can change the propget and propput lines:

```
[propget, id(dispidNumber), helpstring("property Number")]
    HRESULT Number([out, retval] short *pVal);
[propget, id(dispidDots), helpstring("property Dots")]
    HRESULT Dots([out, retval] BOOL *pVal);
[propput, id(dispidDots), helpstring("property Dots")]
    HRESULT Dots([in] BOOL newVal);
```

The next step is to code the get and set functions to use the member variables. Listing 21.4 shows the completed functions. (If you can't see these in ClassView, expand the IDieRoll under CDieRoll.)

Listing 21.4   Excerpt from DieRoll.cpp—*get* and *set* Functions

```
STDMETHODIMP CDieRoll::get_Number(short * pVal)
{
    *pVal = m_sNumber;
    return S_OK;
}

STDMETHODIMP CDieRoll::get_Dots(BOOL * pVal)
{
    *pVal = m_bDots;
    return S_OK;
}

STDMETHODIMP CDieRoll::put_Dots(BOOL newVal)
{
    if (FireOnRequestEdit(dispidDots) == S_FALSE)
    {
        return S_FALSE;
    }
    m_bDots = newVal;
```

```
        SetDirty(TRUE);
        FireOnChanged(dispidDots);
        FireViewChange();

        return S_OK;
    }
```

The code in the two get functions is simple and straightforward. The put_dots() code is more complex because it fires notifications. FireOnRequestEdit() notifies all the IPropertyNotifySink interfaces that this property is going to change. Any one of these interfaces can deny the request, and if one does, this function will return S_FALSE to forbid the change.

Assuming the change is allowed, the member variable is changed, and the control is marked as modified (dirty) so that it will be saved. The call to FireOnChange() notifies the IPropertyNotifySink interfaces that this property has changed, and the call to FireViewChange() tells the container to redraw the control.

Initializing the Properties

Having added the code to get and set these properties, you should now change the CDieRoll constructor to initialize all the stock and custom properties, as shown in Listing 21.5. A stub for the constructor is in the header file for you to edit.

Listing 21.5   Excerpt from DieRoll.h—Constructor

```
CDieRoll()
{
    srand( (unsigned)time( NULL ) );
    m_nReadyState = READYSTATE_COMPLETE;
    m_clrBackColor = 0x80000000 | COLOR_WINDOW;
    m_clrForeColor = 0x80000000 | COLOR_WINDOWTEXT;
    m_sNumber = Roll();
    m_bDots = TRUE;
}
```

At the top of the header, add this line to bring in a declaration of the time() function:

```
#include "time.h"
```

Just as you did in the MFC version of this control, you initialize m_sNumber to a random number between 1 and 6, returned by the Roll() function. Add this function to CDieRoll by right-clicking on the classname in ClassView and choosing Add Member Function from the shortcut menu. Roll() is protected takes no parameters and returns a short. The code for Roll() is in Listing 21.6 and is explained in Chapter 17.

Part

V

Ch

21

Listing 21.6   *CDieRoll::Roll()*

```
short CDieRoll::Roll()
{
    double number = rand();
    number /= RAND_MAX + 1;
    number *= 6;
    return (short)number + 1;
}
```

It's a good idea to build the project at this point to be sure you haven't made any typos or missed any steps.

Adding the Asynchronous Property

Just as in Chapter 20, the Image property represents a bitmap to be loaded asynchronously and used as a background image. Add the property to the interface just as **Number** and **Dots** were added. Use **BSTR** for the type and **Image** for the name. Update the enum in the idl file so that **dispidImage** is 3, and edit the **propget** and **propput** lines in the idl file to use the enum value:

```
[propget, id(dispidImage), helpstring("property Image")]
    HRESULT Image([out, retval] BSTR *pVal);
[propput, id(dispidImage), helpstring("property Image")]
    HRESULT Image([in] BSTR newVal);
```

Add a member variable, m_bstrImage, to the class after the five properties you have already added:

```
CComBSTR m_bstrImage;
```

CComBSTR is an ATL wrapper class with useful member functions for manipulating a BSTR.

A number of other member variables must be added to handle the bitmap and the asynchronous loading. Add these lines to DieRoll.h after the declaration of m_bstrImage:

```
HBITMAP hBitmap;
BITMAPINFOHEADER bmih;
char *lpvBits;
BITMAPINFO *lpbmi;
HGLOBAL hmem1;
HGLOBAL hmem2;
BOOL BitmapDataLoaded;
char *m_Data;
unsigned long m_DataLength;
```

The first six of these new variables are used to draw the bitmap and won't be discussed. The last three combine to achieve the same behavior as the data path property used in the MFC version of this control.

Add these three lines to the constructor:

```
m_Data = NULL;
m_DataLength = 0;
BitmapDataLoaded = FALSE;
```

Add a destructor to `CDieRoll` (in the header file) and add the code in Listing 21.7.

Listing 21.7   *CDieRoll::~CDieRoll()*

```
~CDieRoll()
{
    if (BitmapDataLoaded)
    {
        GlobalUnlock(hmem1);
        GlobalFree(hmem1);
        GlobalUnlock(hmem2);
        GlobalFree(hmem2);
        BitmapDataLoaded = FALSE;
    }

    if (m_Data != NULL)
    {
        delete m_Data;
    }
}
```

The `Image` property has `get` and `put` functions. Code them as in Listing 21.8.

Listing 21.8   DieRoll.cpp—*get_Image()* and *put_Image()*

```
STDMETHODIMP CDieRoll::get_Image(BSTR * pVal)
{
    *pVal = m_bstrImage.Copy();
    return S_OK;
}

STDMETHODIMP CDieRoll::put_Image(BSTR newVal)
{
    USES_CONVERSION;

    if (FireOnRequestEdit(dispidImage) == S_FALSE)
    {
        return S_FALSE;
    }

// if there was an old bitmap or data, delete it
    if (BitmapDataLoaded)
    {
        GlobalUnlock(hmem1);
        GlobalFree(hmem1);
        GlobalUnlock(hmem2);
        GlobalFree(hmem2);
        BitmapDataLoaded = FALSE;
    }
```

Part

V

Ch

21

continues

Listing 21.8 Continued

```
    if (m_Data != NULL)
    {
        delete m_Data;
    }

    m_Data = NULL;
    m_DataLength = 0;

    m_bstrImage = newVal;
    LPSTR string = W2A(m_bstrImage);

    if (string != NULL && strlen(string) > 0)
    {
        // not a null string so try to load it
        BOOL relativeURL = FALSE;
        if (strchr(string, ':') == NULL)
        {
            relativeURL = TRUE;
        }

      m_nReadyState = READYSTATE_LOADING;

        HRESULT ret = CBindStatusCallback<CDieRoll>::Download(this,
            OnData, m_bstrImage, m_spClientSite, relativeURL);
}
    else
    {
        // was a null string so don't try to load it
        m_nReadyState = READYSTATE_COMPLETE;
        FireViewChange();

    }

    SetDirty(TRUE);
    FireOnChanged(dispidImage);
    return S_OK;
}
```

As with Numbers and Dots, the get function is straightforward, and the put function is more complicated. The beginning and end of the put function are like put_Dots(), firing notifications to check whether the variable can be changed and then other notifications that it was changed. In between is the code unique to an asynchronous property.

To start the download of the asynchronous property, this function will call CBindStatusCallback<CDieRoll>::Download(), but first it needs to determine whether the URL in m_bstrImage is a relative or absolute URL. Use the ATL macro W2A to convert the wide BSTR to an ordinary C string so that the C function strchr() can be used to search for a : character in the URL. An URL with no : in it is assumed to be a relative URL.

N O T E   A BSTR is a wide (double-byte) character on all 32-bit Windows platforms. It is a narrow
(single-byte) string on a PowerMac. ■

In the MFC version of the DieRoll control with an asynchronous image property, whenever a
block of data came through, the OnDataAvailable() function was called. The call to Down-
load() arranges for a function called OnData() to be called when data arrives. You will write
the OnData() function. Add it to the class with the other public functions and add the implementation shown in Listing 21.9 to DieRoll.cpp.

Listing 21.9   DieRoll.cpp—*CDieRoll::OnData()*

```
void CDieRoll::OnData(CBindStatusCallback<CDieRoll>* pbsc,
                      BYTE * pBytes, DWORD dwSize)
{

    char *newData = new char[m_DataLength + dwSize];

    memcpy(newData, m_Data, m_DataLength);
    memcpy(newData+m_DataLength, pBytes, dwSize);
    m_DataLength += dwSize;

    delete m_Data;
    m_Data = newData;

    if (ReadBitmap())
    {
        m_nReadyState = READYSTATE_COMPLETE;
        FireViewChange();
    }
}
```

Because there is no realloc() when using new, this function uses new to allocate enough
chars to hold the data that has already been read (m_DataLength) and the new data that is
coming in (dwSize); it then copies m_Data to this block, and the new data (pBytes) after m_Data.
Then it attempts to convert into a bitmap the data that has been received so far. If this succeeds, the download must be complete, so the ready state notifications are sent, and the call to
FireViewChange() sends a notification to the container to redraw the view. You can obtain the
ReadBitmap() function from the Web site and add it to your project. It's much like the MFC
version, but it doesn't use any MFC classes such as CFile. Add the function and its code to
CDieRoll.

Once again, build the control, just to be sure you haven't missed any steps or made any typos.

Part
V

Ch
21

Drawing the Control

Now that all the properties have been added, you can code OnDraw(). Although the basic structure of this function is the same as in the MFC version of Chapter 20. A lot more work must be done because you can't rely on MFC to do some of it for you. A more detailed explanation of the OnDraw() design is in Chapter 20.

The structure of OnDraw() is

```
HRESULT CDieRoll::OnDraw(ATL_DRAWINFO& di)
// if the bitmap is ready, draw it
// else draw a plan background using BackColor
// if !Dots draw a number in ForeColor
// else draw the dots
```

First, you need to test whether the bitmap is ready and to draw it, if possible. This code is in Listing 21.10: Add it to dieroll.cpp and remove the OnDraw()code left in dieroll.h by AppWizard. (Leave the declaration of OnDraw() in the header file.) Notice that if ReadyState is READYSTATE_COMPLETE, but the call to CreateDIBitmap() doesn't result in a valid bitmap handle, the bitmap member variables are cleared away to make subsequent calls to this function give up a little faster. This chapter doesn't discuss how to draw bitmaps.

Listing 21.10   *CDieRoll::OnDraw()*—Use the Bitmap

```
HRESULT CDieRoll::OnDraw(ATL_DRAWINFO& di)
{
    int width = (di.prcBounds->right - di.prcBounds->left + 1);
    int height = (di.prcBounds->bottom - di.prcBounds->top + 1);

    BOOL drawn = FALSE;
    if (m_nReadyState == READYSTATE_COMPLETE)
    {
        if (BitmapDataLoaded)
        {
            hBitmap = ::CreateDIBitmap(di.hdcDraw, &bmih, CBM_INIT, lpvBits,
                lpbmi, DIB_RGB_COLORS);

            if (hBitmap)
            {
                HDC hmemdc;
                hmemdc = ::CreateCompatibleDC(di.hdcDraw);
                ::SelectObject(hmemdc, hBitmap);
                DIBSECTION ds;
                ::GetObject(hBitmap,sizeof(DIBSECTION),(LPSTR)&ds);
                ::StretchBlt(di.hdcDraw,
                            di.prcBounds->left, // left
                            di.prcBounds->top,  // top
                            width, // target width
                            height, // target height
                            hmemdc,         // the image
                            0,              //offset into image -x
                            0,              //offset into image -y
                            ds.dsBm.bmWidth, // width
```

```
                            ds.dsBm.bmHeight, // height
                            SRCCOPY);    //copy it over

                    drawn = TRUE;
                    ::DeleteObject(hBitmap);
                    hBitmap = NULL;
                    ::DeleteDC(hmemdc);
                }
                else
                {
                    GlobalUnlock(hmem1);
                    GlobalFree(hmem1);
                    GlobalUnlock(hmem2);
                    GlobalFree(hmem2);
                    BitmapDataLoaded = FALSE;
                }
            }
        }
    }
    return S_OK;
    }
```

If the bitmap wasn't drawn because ReadyState is not READYSTATE_COMPLETE yet or there was a problem with the bitmap, OnDraw() draws a solid background by using the BackColor property, as shown in Listing 21.11. Add this code at the end of OnDraw(), before the return statement. The SDK calls are very similar to the MFC calls used in the MFC version of DieRoll—for example, ::OleTranslateColor() corresponds to TranslateColor().

Listing 21.11 *CDieRoll::OnDraw()*—Draw a Solid Background

```
    if (!drawn)
    {
        COLORREF back;
        ::OleTranslateColor(m_clrBackColor, NULL, &back);
        HBRUSH backbrush = ::CreateSolidBrush(back);
        ::FillRect(di.hdcDraw, (RECT *)di.prcBounds, backbrush);
        ::DeleteObject(backbrush);
    }
```

With the background drawn, as a bitmap image or a solid color, OnDraw() must now tackle the foreground. Getting the foreground color is simple. Add these two lines at the end of OnDraw() before the return statement:

```
COLORREF fore;
::OleTranslateColor(m_clrForeColor, NULL, &fore);
```

The project should build successfully at this point if you want to be sure you've entered all this code correctly.

If Dots is FALSE, the die should be drawn with a number on it. Add the code in Listing 21.12 to OnDraw() before the return statement as usual. Again, the SDK functions do the same job as the similarly named MFC functions used in the MFC version of DieRoll.

Part
V

Ch
21

Listing 21.12 *CDieRoll::OnDraw()—Draw a Number*

```
if (!m_bDots)
{
    _TCHAR val[20]; //character representation of the short value
    _itot(m_sNumber, val, 10);
        ::SetTextColor(di.hdcDraw, fore);
    ::ExtTextOut(di.hdcDraw, 0, 0, ETO_OPAQUE,
        (RECT *)di.prcBounds, val, _tcslen(val), NULL );
}
```

The code that draws dots is in Listing 21.13. Add it to OnDraw() before the return statement to complete the function. This code is long but is explained in Chapter 17. As in the rest of OnDraw(), MFC function calls have been replaced with SDK calls.

Listing 21.13 *CDieRoll::OnDraw()—Draw Dots*

```
else
{
    //dots are 4 units wide and high, one unit from the edge
    int Xunit = width/16;
    int Yunit = height/16;
    int Xleft = width%16;
    int Yleft = height%16;

    // adjust top left by amount left over
    int Top = di.prcBounds->top + Yleft/2;
    int Left = di.prcBounds->left + Xleft/2;

    HBRUSH forebrush;
    forebrush = ::CreateSolidBrush(fore);

    HBRUSH savebrush = (HBRUSH)::SelectObject(di.hdcDraw, forebrush);

    switch(m_sNumber)
    {
    case 1:
        ::Ellipse(di.hdcDraw, Left+6*Xunit, Top+6*Yunit,
                    Left+10*Xunit, Top + 10*Yunit); //center
        break;
    case 2:
        ::Ellipse(di.hdcDraw, Left+Xunit, Top+Yunit,
                    Left+5*Xunit, Top + 5*Yunit);    //upper left
        ::Ellipse(di.hdcDraw, Left+11*Xunit, Top+11*Yunit,
                    Left+15*Xunit, Top + 15*Yunit); //lower right
        break;
    case 3:
        ::Ellipse(di.hdcDraw, Left+Xunit, Top+Yunit,
                    Left+5*Xunit, Top + 5*Yunit);    //upper left
        ::Ellipse(di.hdcDraw, Left+6*Xunit, Top+6*Yunit,
                    Left+10*Xunit, Top + 10*Yunit); //center
```

```
            ::Ellipse(di.hdcDraw, Left+11*Xunit, Top+11*Yunit,
                        Left+15*Xunit, Top + 15*Yunit); //lower right
        break;
    case 4:
        ::Ellipse(di.hdcDraw, Left+Xunit, Top+Yunit,
                        Left+5*Xunit, Top + 5*Yunit);   //upper left
        ::Ellipse(di.hdcDraw, Left+11*Xunit, Top+Yunit,
                        Left+15*Xunit, Top + 5*Yunit);  //upper right
        ::Ellipse(di.hdcDraw, Left+Xunit, Top+11*Yunit,
                        Left+5*Xunit, Top + 15*Yunit);  //lower left
        ::Ellipse(di.hdcDraw, Left+11*Xunit, Top+11*Yunit,
                        Left+15*Xunit, Top + 15*Yunit); //lower right
        break;
    case 5:
        ::Ellipse(di.hdcDraw, Left+Xunit, Top+Yunit,
                        Left+5*Xunit, Top + 5*Yunit);   //upper left
        ::Ellipse(di.hdcDraw, Left+11*Xunit, Top+Yunit,
                        Left+15*Xunit, Top + 5*Yunit);  //upper right
        ::Ellipse(di.hdcDraw, Left+6*Xunit, Top+6*Yunit,
                        Left+10*Xunit, Top + 10*Yunit); //center
        ::Ellipse(di.hdcDraw, Left+Xunit, Top+11*Yunit,
                        Left+5*Xunit, Top + 15*Yunit);  //lower left
        ::Ellipse(di.hdcDraw, Left+11*Xunit, Top+11*Yunit,
                        Left+15*Xunit, Top + 15*Yunit); //lower right
        break;
    case 6:
        ::Ellipse(di.hdcDraw, Left+Xunit, Top+Yunit,
                Left+5*Xunit, Top + 5*Yunit);   //upper left
        ::Ellipse(di.hdcDraw, Left+11*Xunit, Top+Yunit,
                Left+15*Xunit, Top + 5*Yunit);  //upper right
        ::Ellipse(di.hdcDraw, Left+Xunit, Top+6*Yunit,
                Left+5*Xunit, Top + 10*Yunit);  //center left
        ::Ellipse(di.hdcDraw, Left+11*Xunit, Top+6*Yunit,
                    Left+15*Xunit, Top + 10*Yunit); //center right
        ::Ellipse(di.hdcDraw, Left+Xunit, Top+11*Yunit,
                Left+5*Xunit, Top + 15*Yunit);  //lower left
        ::Ellipse(di.hdcDraw, Left+11*Xunit, Top+11*Yunit,
                Left+15*Xunit, Top + 15*Yunit); //lower right
        break;
    }

    ::SelectObject(di.hdcDraw, savebrush);
    ::DeleteObject(forebrush);
}
```

Again, build the project to be sure you haven't missed anything. If you look in your project folder now, you should see a file called DieRoll.htm (it doesn't show up in FileView). This HTML is generated for you to test your control. Try loading it into Internet Explorer now, and a die should display, as in Figure 21.11. It will not have an image background and it will not roll when you click it.

FIG. 21.11
Your control can draw itself in a browser.

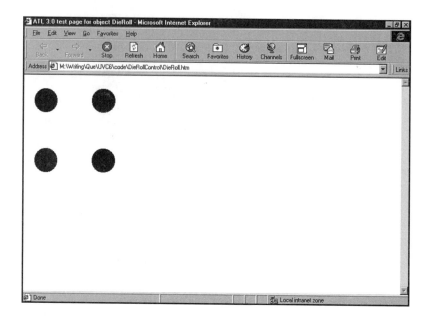

Persistence and a Property Page

The properties have been added to the control and used in the drawing of the control. Now all that remains is to make the properties persistent and to add a property page.

Adding a Property Page

To add a property page to this control, follow these steps:

1. Choose Insert, New ATL Object from the menu bar to open the ATL Object Wizard.
2. Select Controls in the left pane and Property Page in the right pane; then click Next.
3. On the Names tab, enter **DieRollPPG** for the Short Name.
4. Click the Strings tab (the settings on the Attributes tab will not be changed). Enter **General** for the Title and **DieRoll Property Page** for the Doc String. Blank out the Helpfile Name.
5. Click OK to add the property page to the project.

Developer Studio will switch to ResourceView and open the dialog IDD_DIEROLLPPG. Add a check box with the resource ID IDC_DOTS and the caption Display Dot Pattern and an edit box with the resource ID **IDC_IMAGE** labelled Image URL, as shown in Figure 21.12.

At the top of DieRollPPG.h, add this line:

```
#include "DieRollControl.h"
```

You need to connect the controls on this property page to properties of the DieRoll control. The first step is to add three lines to the message map in DieRollPPG.h so that it resembles Listing 21.14.

FIG. 21.12

Add two controls to the property page.

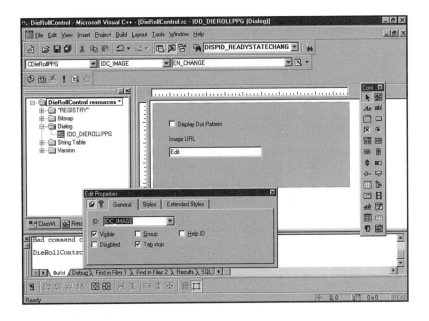

Listing 21.14   DieRollPPG.h—Message Map

```
BEGIN_MSG_MAP(CDieRollPPG)
    MESSAGE_HANDLER(WM_INITDIALOG, OnInitDialog)
    COMMAND_HANDLER(IDC_DOTS, BN_CLICKED, OnDotsChanged)
    COMMAND_HANDLER(IDC_IMAGE, EN_CHANGE, OnImageChanged)
    CHAIN_MSG_MAP(IPropertyPageImpl<CDieRollPPG>)
END_MSG_MAP()
```

These new lines ensure that `OnInitDialog()` will be called when the dialog box is initialized and that `OnDotsChanged()` or `OnImageChanged()` will be called whenever `Dots` or `Image` are changed (the other properties don't have `put` methods and so can't be changed).

Add the code in Listing 21.15 to the header file to declare and implement `OnInitDialog()`. Put it after the constructor, so it will be public as well.

Listing 21.15   DieRollPPG.h—*CDieRollPPG::OnInitDialog()*

```
LRESULT OnInitDialog(UINT uMsg, WPARAM wParam, LPARAM lParam,
                     BOOL & bHandled)
{
    USES_CONVERSION;

    CComQIPtr<IDieRoll, &IID_IDieRoll> pDieRoll(m_ppUnk[0]);

    BOOL dots;
    pDieRoll->get_Dots(&dots);
    ::SendDlgItemMessage(m_hWnd, IDC_DOTS, BM_SETCHECK, dots, 0L);
```

continues

Listing 21.15 Continued

```
        BSTR image;
        pDieRoll->get_Image(&image);
        LPTSTR image_URL = W2T(image);
        SetDlgItemText(IDC_IMAGE, image_URL);

        return TRUE;
    }
```

This code begins by declaring a pointer to an IDieRoll interface using the CComQIPtr template class and initializing it to the first element of the m_ppUnk array in this class, CDieRollPPG. (A property page can be associated with multiple controls.) The constructor for the CComQIPtr template class uses the QueryInterface() method of the IUnknown pointer that was passed in to the constructor to find a pointer to an IDieRoll interface. Now you can call member functions of this interface to access the properties of the DieRoll control.

Finding the value of the Dots property of the CDieRoll object is simple enough: Call get_Dots(). To use that value to initialize the check box on the property page, send a message to the control using the SDK function ::SendDlgItemMessage(). The BM_SETCHECK parameter indicates that you are setting whether the box is checked (selected). Passing dots as the fourth parameter ensures that IDC_DOTS will be selected if dots is TRUE and deselected if dots is FALSE. Similarly, obtain the URL for the image with get_Image(), convert it from wide characters, and then use SetDlgItemText() to set the edit box contents to that URL.

OnDotsChanged() and OnImageChanged() are simple: Add the code for them both, as presented in Listing 21.16, to the header file, after OnInitDialog().

Listing 21.16 DieRollPPG.h—The *OnChanged* Functions

```
    LRESULT OnDotsChanged(WORD wNotify, WORD wID, HWND hWnd, BOOL& bHandled)
    {
        SetDirty(TRUE);
        return FALSE;
    }

    LRESULT OnImageChanged(WORD wNotify, WORD wID, HWND hWnd, BOOL& bHandled)
    {
        SetDirty(TRUE);
        return FALSE;
    }
```

The calls to SetDirty() in these functions ensure that the Apply() function will be called when the user clicks OK on the property page.

The ObjectWizard generated a simple Apply() function, but it doesn't affect the Dots or Number properties. Edit Apply() so that it resembles Listing 21.17.

Listing 21.17 DieRollPPG.h—*CDieRollPPG::Apply()*

```
STDMETHOD(Apply)(void)
{
    USES_CONVERSION;
    BSTR image = NULL;
    GetDlgItemText(IDC_IMAGE, image);

    BOOL dots = (BOOL)::SendDlgItemMessage(m_hWnd, IDC_DOTS,
            BM_GETCHECK, 0, 0L);

    ATLTRACE(_T("CDieRollPPG::Apply\n"));
    for (UINT i = 0; i < m_nObjects; i++)
    {
        CComQIPtr<IDieRoll, &IID_IDieRoll> pDieRoll(m_ppUnk[i]);

        if FAILED(pDieRoll->put_Dots(dots))
        {
            CComPtr<IErrorInfo> pError;
            CComBSTR          strError;
            GetErrorInfo(0, &pError);
            pError->GetDescription(&strError);
            MessageBox(OLE2T(strError), _T("Error"), MB_ICONEXCLAMATION);
            return E_FAIL;
        }

        if FAILED(pDieRoll->put_Image(image))
        {
            CComPtr<IErrorInfo> pError;
            CComBSTR          strError;
            GetErrorInfo(0, &pError);
            pError->GetDescription(&strError);
            MessageBox(OLE2T(strError), _T("Error"), MB_ICONEXCLAMATION);
            return E_FAIL;
        }
    }
    m_bDirty = FALSE;
    return S_OK;
}
```

Apply starts by getting dots and image from the dialog box. Notice in the call to ::SendDlgItemMessage() that the third parameter is BM_GETCHECK, so this call ascertains the selected state (TRUE or FALSE) of the check box. Then a call to ATLTRACE prints a trace message to aid debugging. Like the trace statements discussed in Chapter 24, "Improving Your Application's Performance," this statement disappears in a release build.

The majority of Apply() is a for loop that is executed once for each control associated with this property page. It obtains an IDieRoll interface pointer, just as in OnInitDialog(), and tries calling the put_Dots() and put_Image() member functions of that interface. If either call fails, a message box informs the user of the problem. After the loop, the m_bDirty member variable can be set to FALSE.

Build the project at this point to be sure you have no errors.

Connecting the Property Page to *CDieRoll*

The changes to CDieRollPPG are complete. You need to make some changes to CDieRoll to connect it to the property page class. Specifically, the property map needs some more entries. Add the first two entries for Dots and Image so that it looks like Listing 21.18.

Listing 21.18   DieRoll.h—Property Map

```
BEGIN_PROP_MAP(CDieRoll)
    PROP_ENTRY( "Dots", dispidDots, CLSID_DieRollPPG)
    PROP_ENTRY( "Image", dispidImage, CLSID_DieRollPPG)
    PROP_DATA_ENTRY("_cx", m_sizeExtent.cx, VT_UI4)
    PROP_DATA_ENTRY("_cy", m_sizeExtent.cy, VT_UI4)
    PROP_ENTRY("BackColor", DISPID_BACKCOLOR, CLSID_StockColorPage)
    PROP_ENTRY("ForeColor", DISPID_FORECOLOR, CLSID_StockColorPage)
END_PROP_MAP()
```

Persistence in a Property Bag

In a number of different ways, Internet Explorer can get property values out of some HTML and into a control wrapped in an <OBJECT> tag. With stream persistence, provided by default, you use a DATA attribute in the <OBJECT> tag. If you would like to use <PARAM> tags, which are far more readable, the control must support property bag persistence through the IPersistPropertyBag interface.

Add another class to the list of base classes at the start of the CDieRoll class:

```
public IPersistPropertyBagImpl<CDieRoll>,
```

Add this line to the COM map:

```
COM_INTERFACE_ENTRY(IPersistPropertyBag)
```

Now you can use <PARAM> tags to set properties of the control.

Using the Control in Control Pad

You've added a lot of code to CDieRoll and CDieRollPPG, and it's time to build the control. After fixing any typos or minor errors, you can use the control.

You are going to build the HTML to display this control in Microsoft's Control Pad. If you don't have Control Pad, it's downloadable free from **http://www.microsoft.com/workshop/author/cpad/download.htm**. If you have a copy of Control Pad from before January 1997, find the latest one. If you use the old version, the init safe and script safe work you will do later in this chapter will appear to malfunction.

N O T E   Control Pad used to serve two purposes: It simplified building <OBJECT> tags for ActiveX controls and helped developers use the HTML Layout control. Now that the functionality of the Layout control is in Internet Explorer 4.0, it's just a handy way to make <OBJECT> tags. ▪

When you start Control pad, it makes an empty HTML document. With the cursor between <BODY> and </BODY>, choose Edit, Insert ActiveX Control. The Insert ActiveX Control dialog appears: Choose DieRoll Class from the list (you might recall from Figure 21.5 that the type name for this control is DieRoll Class) and click OK. The control and a Properties dialog appear. Click on the Image property and enter the full path to the image file you want to use in the edit box at the top of the Properties dialog. (You can use any bmp file you have handy, including one you make yourself in the Paint program that comes with Windows, or get beans.bmp from the Web site.) Click Apply, and the control redraws with a background image, such as the jelly beans shown in Figure 21.13. Close the Properties dialog and the Edit ActiveX Control dialog, and you will see the HTML generated for you, including the <PARAM> tags that were added because Control Pad could determine that DieRoll supports the IPersistPropertyBag interface. Close Control Pad; you can save the HTML if you want.

FIG. 21.13
Inserting the control into Control Pad displays it for you.

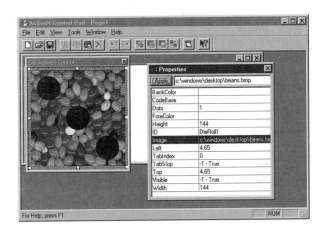

The control doesn't have its full functionality yet: It doesn't roll itself when you click it. The next section will add events.

Adding Events

Two events must be added: one when the user clicks on the control and one when the ready state changes. The Click event is discussed in Chapter 17 and the ReadyStateChanged event is discussed in Chapter 20.

Adding Methods to the Event Interface

In ClassView, right-click the _IDieRollEvents interface. Choose Add Method and fill in the Return Type as **void** and the Method Name as **Click**; leave the parameters blank. Figure 21.14 shows the completed dialog. Click OK to add the method.

Part
V

Ch
21

FIG. 21.14

Add the Click method
to the event interface.

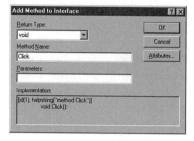

In the same way, add `ReadyStateChange()`, returning `void` and taking no parameters, to the
event interface. The `dispinterface` section in the idl file should now look like this:

```
dispinterface _IDieRollEvents
{
    properties:
    methods:
    [id(DISPID_CLICK), helpstring("method Click")] void Click();
    [id(DISPID_READYSTATECHANGE),
➡helpstring("method ReadyStateChange")] void ReadyStateChange();
};
```

If the dispids appear as 1 and 2 rather than `DISPID_CLICK` and `DISPID_READYSTATECHANGE`, edit
them to match this code.

Implementing the *IConnectionPoint* Interface

To fire events, you implement the `IConnectionPoint` interface. The Connection Point Wizard
will get you started, but first, save the idl file and build the project so that the typelib associated
with the project is up-to-date.

In ClassView, right-click `CDieRoll` and choose Implement Connection Point. Select
`_IDieRollEvents`, as in Figure 21.15, and click OK to generate a *proxy class* for the connection
point. This class will have methods you can call to fire an event.

FIG. 21.15

The Connection Point
Wizard makes short
work of adding events.

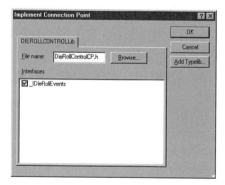

Look for the new class, CProxy_IDieRollEvents, in ClassView. Expand it, and you will see it has two functions, Fire_Click() and Fire_ReadyStateChange().

Firing the *Click* Event

When the user clicks the control, it should fire a Click event. Right-click CDieRoll in ClassView and choose Add Windows Message Handler. Select WM_LBUTTONDOWN from the long list on the left and click Add Handler; then click OK. You will see a new entry in the message map:

```
MESSAGE_HANDLER(WM_LBUTTONDOWN, OnLButtonDown)
```

Edit the member function OnLButtonDown() that has been added to CDieRoll, so that it looks like Listing 21.19.

Listing 21.19   *CDieRoll::OnLButtonDown()*

```
LRESULT OnLButtonDown(UINT uMsg, WPARAM wParam, LPARAM lParam, BOOL & bHandled)
{
    m_sNumber = Roll();
    FireOnChanged(dispidNumber);
    Fire_Click();
    FireViewChange();
    return 0;
}
```

This code rolls the die, fires a notification that Number has changed, fires a Click event, and notifies the container that the control should be redrawn. Build the control again and load the dieroll.htm page that was generated for you into Internet Explorer. Click the die a few times and watch the displayed number change. Close Internet Explorer, or later you'll have trouble building the project because the DLL will be locked by Explorer.

Firing the *ReadyStateChange* Event

Now put_Image() and OnData() can fire events when the ready state changes. There are two ways to tell containers that ReadyState has changed: Fire_ReadyStateChange() for older containers and, for Internet Explorer 4.0 and above, a FireOnChanged() call exactly like the ones you've already coded for dispidImage and dispidDots.

In ClassView, expand CDieRoll and then expand IDieRoll underneath it. Double-click put_Image() to edit it, and look for a line like this:

```
m_nReadyState = READYSTATE_LOADING;
```

Add immediately after that line:

```
Fire_ReadyStateChange();
FireOnChanged(DISPID_READYSTATE);
```

Part

V

Ch

21

Then, later in `put_Image()` find this line:

`m_nReadyState = READYSTATE_COMPLETE;`

Add the same two lines after this line as well. In `OnData()`, find this line:

`m_nReadyState = READYSTATE_COMPLETE;`

Add the same two lines immediately after it.

Build the control again and insert it into a new page in Control Pad. Be sure to assign the Image property so that you can see what happens while the image loads. Click the die in the Edit ActiveX Control window, and it will roll a new number each time that you click. Save the HTML, load it into Explorer, and see if you can roll the die while the image loads. Click Refresh and you'll see that the image redraws itself even if you don't click anything. As another test, open the ActiveX Control Test container (available from the Tools menu in Developer Studio) and insert a DieRoll control; then use the event log to confirm that `Click` and `ReadyStateChange` events are being fired.

Probably the easiest and most relevant way to test the control is in Internet Explorer 4. To do this, you specify Explorer as the executable for debug. First, you must turn off the Active Desktop if you have it installed, because under the Active Desktop, Explorer is always running.

To remove the Active desktop, first close any applications you have open, because you're going to restart your system as part of the process. Choose Start, Settings, Control Panel and double-click Add/Remove Programs. On the Install/Uninstall tab, choose Microsoft Internet Explorer 4.0 and click Add/Remove. Choose the last radio button, which says Remove the Windows Desktop Update Component, But Keep the Internet Explorer 4.0 Web Browser. Click OK. Setup will adjust the Registry and restart your system.

After the restart, open Developer Studio; load the DieRollControl project again; choose Project, Settings; and click the Debug tab. If Internet Explorer 4 is your default browser, click the arrow next to Executable for Debug Session and choose Default Web Browser. If it's not, enter **C:\Program Files\Internet Explorer\IEXPLORE.EXE** (or the path to Explorer on your system, if it's different) in the edit box. Under Program Arguments, enter the path to the HTML you developed with Control Pad to test the control. Click OK, and now whenever you choose Build, Start Debug, Go, or click the Go button on the toolbar, Explorer will be launched, and the page that holds the control will be loaded. Choose Debug, Stop Debugging, and Explorer will close.

Exposing the *DoRoll()* Function

The next stage in the development of this control is to expose a function that will enable the container to roll the die. One use for this is to arrange for the container to roll one die whenever the other is clicked. Right-click the `IDieRoll` interface in ClassView and choose Add Method. Enter **DoRoll** for Method Name and leave the Parameters section blank. Click OK.

Functions have a dispid just as properties do. Add an entry to the `enum` of dispids in the idl file so that `dispidDoRoll` is 4. This ensures that if you add another property later, you won't collide with the default dispid of 1 for DoRoll(). When you added the function to the interface, a line was added to the .idl file after the get and put entries for the properties. Change it to use the new dispid so that it looks like this:

```
[id(dispidDoRoll), helpstring("method DoRoll")] HRESULT DoRoll();
```

The code for DoRoll() is in Listing 21.20. Add it to the function stub that has been created in DieRoll.cpp.

Listing 21.20 *CDieRoll::DoRoll()*

```
STDMETHODIMP CDieRoll::DoRoll()
{
    m_sNumber = Roll();
    FireOnChanged(dispidNumber);
    FireViewChange();
    return S_OK;
}
```

This code is just like OnLButtonDown but doesn't fire a Click event. Build the control again.

One way to test this method is with the Test Container. Open it by choosing Tools, ActiveX Control Test Container and choose Edit, Insert New Control. Find DieRoll Class in the list and double-click it to insert a dieroll; then choose Control, Invoke Methods. From the drop-down box at the top, choose DoRoll and then click Invoke a few times. Figure 21.16 shows the Invoke Methods dialog. In the background, Test Container is reporting that the Number property has changed.

FIG. 21.16
The Invoke Methods
dialog box.

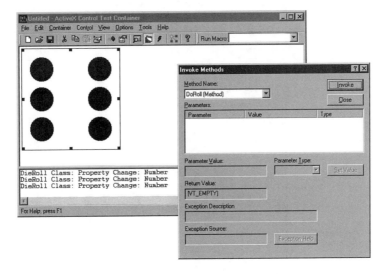

Part
V

Ch
21

Registering as *init* Safe and *script* Safe

In Chapter 20 you added Registry entries to indicate that the control was safe to accept parameters in a Web page and to interact with a script. For an ATL control, you can achieve this by supporting the IObjectSafety interface. A container will query this interface to see whether the control is safe.

Add the following line to the inheritance list for CDieRoll:

```
    public IObjectSafetyImpl<CDieRoll,
INTERFACESAFE_FOR_UNTRUSTED_CALLER | INTERFACESAFE_FOR_UNTRUSTED_DATA>,
,
```

Add this line to the COM map in dieroll.h:

```
COM_INTERFACE_ENTRY(IObjectSafety)
```

This will automatically make the control script and init safe.

Preparing the Control for Use in Design Mode

When a developer is building a form or dialog box in an application such as Visual Basic or Visual C++, a control palette makes it simple to identify the controls to be added. Building the icon used on that palette is the next step in completing this control.

Switch to ResourceView, expand the resources, expand bitmaps, and double-click **IDB_DIEROLL** to edit it. Change it to the much simpler icon shown in Figure 21.17.

FIG. 21.17

Draw an icon for the control.

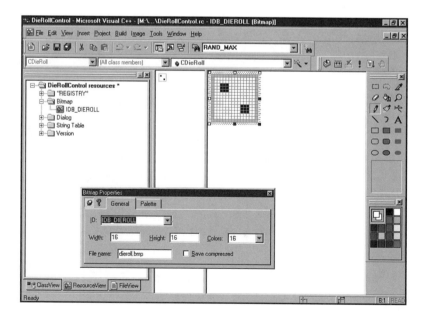

The Registry Script for this control refers to this icon by resource number. To discover what number has been assigned to IDB_DIEROLL, choose View, Resource Symbols and note the numeric value associated with IDB_DIEROLL. (On the machine where this sample was written, it's 202.) Open DieRoll.rgs (the script file) from FileView and look for this line:

```
ForceRemove 'ToolboxBitmap32' = s '%MODULE%, 101'
```

Change it to the following:

```
ForceRemove 'ToolboxBitmap32' = s '%MODULE%, 202'
```

Be sure to use your value rather than 202. Build the control again. To see the fruits of your labors, run the Control Pad again and choose File, New HTML Layout. Select the Additional tab on the Toolbox palette and then right-click on the page. From the shortcut menu that appears, choose Additional Controls. Find DieRoll Class on the list and select it; then click OK. The new icon appears on the Additional tab, as shown in Figure 21.18.

FIG. 21.18

Add the DieRoll class to the HTML Layout toolbox.

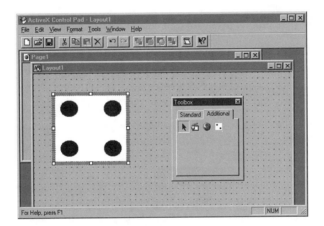

Minimizing Executable Size

Until now, you have been building debug versions of the control. Dieroll.dll is more than 420KB. Although that's much smaller than the 600KB of CAB file for the MFC DLLs that the MFC version of DieRoll might require, it's a lot larger than the 30KB or so that the release version of dieroll.ocx takes up. With development complete, it's time to build a release version.

Choose Build, Set Active Configuration to open the Set Active Project Configuration dialog shown in Figure 21.19. You will notice that there are twice as many release versions in an ATL project as in an MFC project. In addition to choosing whether you support Unicode, you must choose MinSize or MinDependency.

Part

V

Ch

21

FIG. 21.19

Choose a build type
from the Set Active
Project Configuration
dialog box.

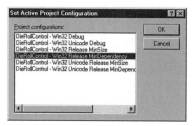

The minimum size release version makes the control as small as possible by linking dynamically to an ATL DLL and the ATL Registrar. The minimum dependencies version links to these statically, which makes the control larger but self-contained. If you choose minimum size, you will need to set up cab files for the control and the DLLs, as discussed in Chapter 20 for the MFC DLLs. At this early stage of ATL acceptance, it's probably better to choose minimum dependencies.

If you choose minimum dependency and build, you will receive these error messages from the linker:

```
Linking...
   Creating library ReleaseMinDependency/DieRollControl.lib and
  ➥object ReleaseMinDependency/DieRollControl.exp
LIBCMT.lib(crt0.obj) : error LNK2001: unresolved external symbol _main
ReleaseMinDependency/DieRollControl.dll :
  ➥fatal error LNK1120: 1 unresolved externals
Error executing link.exe.

DieRollControl.dll - 2 error(s), 0 warning(s)
```

This error isn't due to any mistake on your part. By default, ATL release builds use a tiny version of the C runtime library (CRT) so that they will build as small a DLL as possible. This minimal CRT doesn't include the `time()`, `rand()`, and `srand()` functions used to roll the die. The linker finds these functions in the full-size CRT, but that library expects a `main()` function in your control. Because there isn't one, the link fails.

This behavior is controlled with a linker setting. Choose Project, Settings. From the drop-down box at the upper left, choose Win32 Release MinDependency. Click the C/C++ tab on the right. Select Preprocessor from the Category drop-down box, click in the Preprocessor definitions box, and press the END key to move to the end of the box. Remove the `_ATL_MIN_CRT` flag, highlighted in Figure 21.20, and the comma immediately before it. Click OK, build the project again, and the linker errors disappear.

If you comment out the calls to `rand()`, `srand()`, and `time()` so that the control no longer works, it will link with `_ATL_MIN_CRT` into a 57KB DLL. With `_ATL_MIN_CRT` removed, it is 86KB—a significant increase but still substantially smaller than the MFC control and its DLLs. A minimum size release build with `_ATL_MIN_CRT` removed is 75KB: The saving is hardly worth the trouble to package up the ATL DLLs. With `rand()`, `srand()`, and `time()` commented out, a minimum size release build with `_ATL_MIN_CRT` left in is only 46KB.

FIG. 21.20
Turn off the flag that links in only a tiny version of the C runtime library.

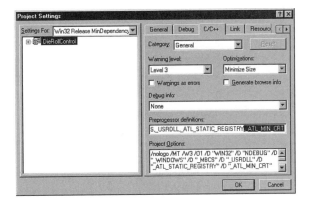

Removing the `_ATL_MIN_CRT` flag increases the control's size by almost 30KB. Although there's no way to rewrite this control so that it doesn't need the `rand()`, `srand()`, and `time()` functions, you could write your own versions of them and include them in the project so that the control would still link with the `_ATL_MIN_CRT` flag. You can find algorithms for random number generators and their seed functions in books of algorithms. The SDK `GetSystemTime()` function can substitute for `time()`. If you were writing a control that would be used for the first time by many users in a time-sensitive application, this extra work might be worth it. Remember that the second time a user comes to a Web page with an ActiveX control, the control doesn't need to be downloaded again.

Using the Control in a Web Page

This control has a slightly different name and different CLSID than the MFC version built in Chapter 20. You can use them together in a single Web page to compare them. Listing 21.21 presents some HTML that puts the two controls in a table. (Use your own CLSID values when you create this page—you might want to use Control Pad as described earlier.) Figure 21.21 shows this page in Explorer.

Listing 21.21   dieroll.htm

```
</HEAD>
<BODY>
<TABLE CELLSPACING=15>
<TR>
<TD>
Here's the MFC die:<BR>
<OBJECT ID="MFCDie"
  CLASSID="CLSID:46646B43-EA16-11CF-870C-00201801DDD6"
  WIDTH="200" HEIGHT="200">
    <PARAM NAME="ForeColor" VALUE="0">
    <PARAM NAME="BackColor" VALUE="16777215">
    <PARAM NAME="Image" VALUE="beans.bmp">
```

Part
V

Ch
21

continues

Listing 21.21   Continued

```
If you see this text, your browser doesn't support the OBJECT tag.
</OBJECT>
</TD>
<TD>
Here's the ATL die:<BR>
<OBJECT ID="ATLDie" WIDTH=200 HEIGHT=200
  CLASSID="CLSID:2DE15F35-8A71-11D0-9B10-0080C81A397C">
    <PARAM NAME="Dots" VALUE="1">
    <PARAM NAME="Image" VALUE="beans.bmp">
    <PARAM NAME="Fore Color" VALUE="2147483656">
    <PARAM NAME="Back Color" VALUE="2147483653">
</OBJECT>
</TD>
</TR>
</TABLE>
</BODY>
</HTML>
```

FIG. 21.21

The ATL control can be used wherever the MFC control was used.

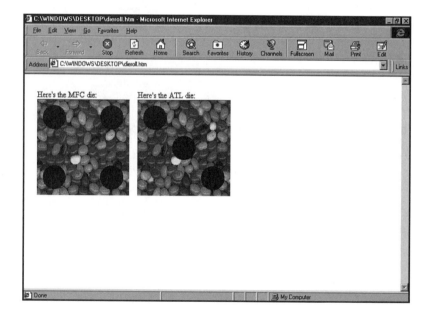

You can edit HTML files in Developer Studio as easily as source files, and with syntax coloring, too! Simply choose File, New and then select HTML Page from the list on the File tab. When you have typed in the HTML, right-click in the editor area and choose Preview to launch Explorer and load the page.

VI

Advanced Programming Techniques

Database Access

Without a doubt, databases are one of the most popular computer applications. Virtually every business uses databases to keep track of everything from its customer list to the company payroll. Unfortunately, there are many different types of database applications, each of which defines its own file layouts and rules. In the past, programming database applications was a nightmare because it was up to the programmer to figure out all the intricacies of accessing the different types of database files. As a Visual C++ developer, you have a somewhat simpler task because MFC includes classes built on the ODBC (Open Database Connectivity) and DAO (Data Access Objects) systems. Other Microsoft database technologies are gaining MFC support as well.

Believe it or not, by using AppWizard, you can create a simple database program without writing even a single line of C++ code. More complex tasks do require some programming, but not as much as you might think.

This chapter gives you an introduction to programming with Visual C++'s ODBC classes. You will also learn about the similarities and differences between ODBC and DAO. Along the way, you will create a database application that can not only display records in a database but also update, add, delete, sort, and filter records.

Understanding Database Concepts

Before you can write database applications, you have to know a little about how databases work. Databases have come a long way since their invention, so there's much you can learn about them. This section provides a quick introduction to basic database concepts, including the two main types of databases: flat and relational.

Using the Flat Database Model

Simply put, a *database* is a collection of records. Each record in the database is composed of fields, and each field contains information related to that specific record. For example, suppose you have an address database. In this database, you have one record for each person. Each record contains six fields: the person's name, street address, city, state, zip code, and phone number. A single record in your database might look like this:

```
NAME: Ronald Wilson
STREET: 16 Tolland Dr.
CITY: Hartford
STATE: CT
ZIP: 06084
PHONE: 860-555-3542
```

Your entire database will contain many records like this one, with each record containing information about a different person. To find a person's address or phone number, you search for the name. When you find the name, you also find all the information that's included in the record with the name.

This type of database system uses the *flat database model*. For home use or for small businesses, the simple flat database model can be a powerful tool. However, for large databases that must track dozens, or even hundreds, of fields of data, a flat database can lead to repetition and wasted space. Suppose you run a large department store and want to track some information about your employees, including their name, department, manager's name, and so on. If you have 10 people in Sporting Goods, the name of the Sporting Goods manager is repeated in each of those 10 records. When Sporting Goods hires a new manager, all 10 records have to be updated. It would be much simpler if each employee record could be *related* to another database of departments and manager names.

Using the Relational Database Model

A *relational database* is like several flat databases linked together. Using a relational database, you can not only search for individual records, as you can with a flat database but also relate one set of records to another. This enables you to store data much more efficiently. Each set of records in a relational database is called a *table*. The links are accomplished through *keys*, values that define a record. (For example, the employee ID might be the key to an employee table.)

The sample relational database that you use in this chapter was created using Microsoft Access. The database is a simple system for tracking employees, managers, and the departments for which they work. Figures 22.1, 22.2, and 22.3 show the tables: The Employees table contains information about each store employee, the Managers table contains information about each store department's manager, and the Departments table contains information about the departments themselves. (This database is very simple and probably not usable in the real world.)

FIG. 22.1

The Employees table contains data fields for each store employee.

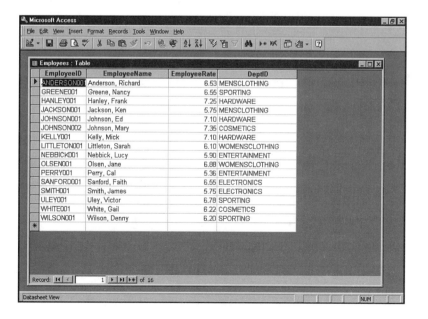

FIG. 22.2

The Managers table contains information about each store department's manager.

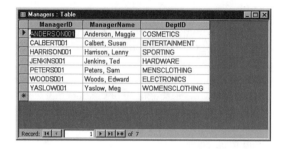

FIG. 22.3

The Departments table contains data about each store department.

Accessing a Database

Relational databases are accessed by using some sort of database scripting language. The most commonly used database language is the Structured Query Language (SQL), which is used to manage not only databases on desktop computers but also huge databases used by banks, schools, corporations, and other institutions with sophisticated database needs. By using a language such as SQL, you can compare information in the various tables of a relational database and extract results made up of data fields from one or more tables combined.

Most developers pronounce SQL as *Sequel*.

Learning SQL, though, is a large task, one that is beyond the scope of this book (let alone this chapter). In fact, entire college-level courses are taught on the design, implementation, and manipulation of databases. Because there isn't space in this chapter to cover relational databases in any useful way, you will use the Employee table (refer to Figure 22.1) of the Department Store database in the sample database program you will soon develop. When you finish creating the application, you will have learned one way to update the tables of a relational database without knowing even a word of SQL. (Those of you who live and breathe SQL will enjoy Chapter 23, "SQL and the Enterprise Edition.")

The Visual C++ ODBC Classes

When you create a database program with Visual C++'s AppWizard, you end up with an application that draws extensively on the various ODBC classes that have been incorporated into MFC. The most important of these classes are CDatabase, CRecordset, and CRecordView.

AppWizard automatically generates the code needed to create an object of the CDatabase class. This object represents the connection between your application and the data source that you will be accessing. In most cases, using the CDatabase class in an AppWizard-generated program is transparent to you, the programmer. All the details are handled by the framework.

AppWizard also generates the code needed to create a CRecordset object for the application. The CRecordset object represents the actual data currently selected from the data source, and its member functions manipulate the data from the database.

Finally, the CRecordView object in your database program takes the place of the normal view window you're accustomed to using in AppWizard-generated applications. A CRecordView window is like a dialog box that's being used as the application's display. This dialog box–type of window retains a connection to the application's CRecordset object, hustling data back and forth between the program, the window's controls, and the recordset. When you first create a new database application with AppWizard, it's up to you to add edit controls to the CRecordView window. These edit controls must be bound to the database fields they represent so that the application framework knows where to display the data you want to view.

In the next section, you will see how these various database classes fit together as you build the Employee application step by step.

Creating an ODBC Database Program

Although creating a simple ODBC database program is easy with Visual C++, there are a number of steps you must complete:

1. Register the database with the system.

2. Use AppWizard to create the basic database application.

3. Add code to the basic application to implement features not automatically supported by AppWizard.

In the following sections, you will see how to perform these steps as you create the Employee application, which enables you to add, delete, update, sort, and view records in the Employees table of the sample Department Store database.

Registering the Database

Before you can create a database application, you must register the database that you want to access as a data source that you can access through the ODBC driver. Follow these steps to accomplish this important task:

1. Create a folder called **Database** on your hard disk and copy the file named DeptStore.mdb from this book's Web site to the new Database folder. If you don't have Web access, you can type the three tables into Microsoft Access. If you don't have Access, you can use a different database program, but you will have to connect to the data source for that program.

   The DeptStore.mdb file is a database created with Microsoft Access. You will use this database as the data source for the Employee application.

2. From the Windows Start menu, click Settings and then Control Panel. When the Control Panel dialog appears, double-click the 32-Bit ODBC icon. The ODBC Data Source Administrator dialog box appears, as shown in Figure 22.4.

FIG. 22.4

Connecting a data source to your application starts with the ODBC Data Source Administrator.

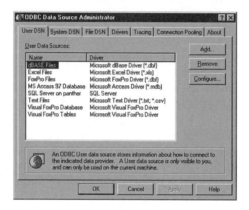

3. Click the Add button. The Create New Data Source dialog box appears. Select the Microsoft Access Driver from the list of drivers, as shown in Figure 22.5, and click Finish.

   The Microsoft Access Driver is now the ODBC driver that will be associated with the data source you create for the Employee application.

FIG. 22.5

Creating a new data source is as simple as choosing Access from a list of drivers.

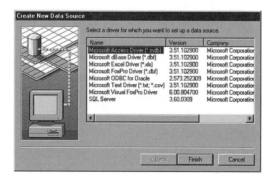

4. When the ODBC Microsoft Access 97 Setup dialog box appears, enter **Department Store** in the Data Source Name text box and **Department Store Sample** in the Description text box, as shown in Figure 22.6.

The Data Source Name is a way of identifying the specific data source you're creating. The Description field enables you to include more specific information about the data source.

FIG. 22.6

Name your data source whatever you like.

5. Click the Select button. The Select Database file selector appears. Use the selector to locate and select the DeptStore.mdb file (see Figure 22.7).

FIG. 22.7

Browse your way to the .mdb file that holds your data.

6. Click OK to finalize the database selection and then, in the ODBC Microsoft Access 97 Setup dialog box, click OK to finalize the data-source creation process. Finally, click OK in the ODBC Data Source Administrator dialog box and close the Control Panel.

Your system is now set up to access the DeptStore.mdb database file with the Microsoft Access ODBC driver.

Creating the Basic Employee Application

Now that you have created and registered your data source, it's time to create the basic Employee application. The steps that follow lead you through this process. After you complete these steps, you will have an application that can access and view the Employees table of the Department Store database:

1. Select File, New from Developer Studio's menu bar. Click the Projects tab.

2. Select MFC AppWizard (exe) and type **Employee** in the Project Name box, as shown in Figure 22.8. Click OK. The Step 1 dialog box appears.

FIG. 22.8
Create an ordinary MFC application with AppWizard.

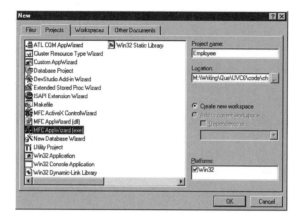

3. Select Single Document, as shown in Figure 22.9, to ensure that the Employee application doesn't allow more than one window to be open at a time. Click Next.

FIG. 22.9
Create a single-document application.

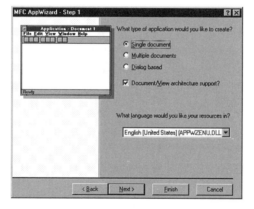

4. Select the Database View Without File Support option, as shown in Figure 22.10, so that AppWizard will generate the classes you need in order to view the contents of a database. This application will not use any supplemental files besides the database, so it doesn't need file (serializing) support. Click the Data Source button to connect the application to the data source you set up earlier.

FIG. 22.10

Arrange for a database view but no other file support.

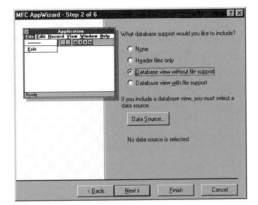

5. In the Database Options dialog box, drop down the ODBC list and select the Department Store data source, as shown in Figure 22.11. Click OK.

FIG. 22.11

Choose the Department Store data source.

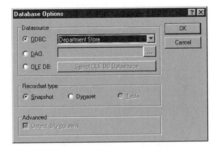

6. In the Select Database Tables dialog box, select the Employees table, as shown in Figure 22.12, and click OK. The Step 2 dialog box reappears, filled in as shown in Figure 22.13.

You've now associated the Employees table of the Department Store data source with the Employee application. Click Next to move to Step 3.

FIG. 22.12

Select which tables from the data source you want to use in this application.

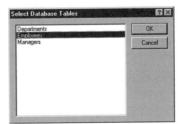

FIG. 22.13

After selecting the data source, the Step 2 dialog box looks like this.

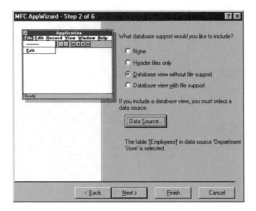

7. Accept the default (None) no compound document support and click Next.

8. In the Step 4 dialog box, turn off the Printing and Print Preview option so that the dialog box resembles Figure 22.14. Click Next.

FIG. 22.14

Turn off print support.

9. Accept the defaults for Step 5 by clicking Next. In Step 6, click Finish to finalize your selections for the Employee application. Figure 22.15 shows the New Project Information dialog box that appears.

10. Click OK, and AppWizard creates the basic Employee application.

At this point, you can compile the application by clicking the Build button on Developer Studio's toolbar, by selecting the Build, Build command from the menu bar, or by pressing F7 on your keyboard. After the program has compiled, select the Build, Execute command from the menu bar or press Ctrl+F5 to run the program. When you do, you see the window shown in Figure 22.16. You can use the database controls in the application's toolbar to navigate from one record in the Employee table to another. However, nothing appears in the window because you've yet to associate controls with the fields in the table that you want to view. You will do that in the following section.

FIG. 22.15

The application summary mentions the data source as well as the usual information.

FIG. 22.16

The basic Employee application looks nice but doesn't do much.

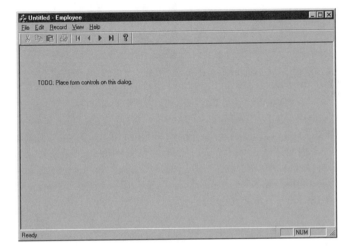

Creating the Database Display

The next step in creating the Employee database application is to modify the form that displays data in the application's window. Because this form is just a special type of dialog box, it's easy to modify with Developer Studio's resource editor, as you will discover while completing the following steps:

1. In the workspace window, select the Resource View tab to display the application's resources.

2. Open the resource tree by clicking + next to the Employee resources folder. Then, open the Dialog resource folder the same way. Double-click the IDD_EMPLOYEE_FORM dialog box ID to open the dialog box into the resource editor, as shown in Figure 22.17.

FIG. 22.17

Open the dialog box in the resource editor.

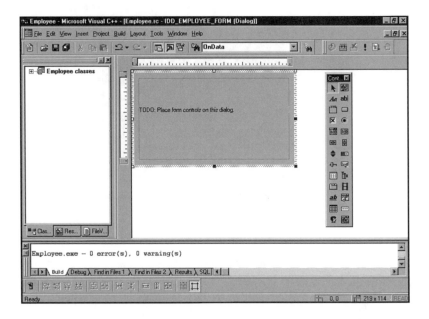

3. Click the static string in the center of the dialog box to select it, and then press the Delete key to remove the string from the dialog box.

4. Use the dialog box editor's tools to create the dialog box, shown in Figure 22.18, by adding edit boxes and static labels. (Editing dialog boxes is introduced in Chapter 2, "Dialogs and Controls.") Give the edit boxes the following IDs: **IDC_EMPLOYEE_ID**, **IDC_EMPLOYEE_NAME**, **IDC_EMPLOYEE_RATE**, and **IDC_EMPLOYEE_DEPT**. Set the Read-Only style (found on the Styles page of the Edit Properties property sheet) of the IDC_EMPLOYEE_ID edit box.

   Each of these edit boxes will represent a field of data in the database. The first edit box is read-only because it will hold the database's primary key, which should never be modified.

FIG. 22.18

Create a dialog box to be used in your database form.

5. Choose View, ClassWizard to open ClassWizard, and click the Member Variables tab.

6. With the IDC_EMPLOYEE_DEPT resource ID selected, click the Add Variable button. The Add Member Variable dialog box appears.

7. Click the arrow next to the Member Variable Name drop-down list and select m_pSet->m_DeptID, as shown in Figure 22.19. Leave the type as CString and click OK to add the variable.

FIG. 22.19

Connect the IDC_EMPLOYEE_DEPT control with the m_DeptID member variable of the recordset.

8. Associate other member variables (m_pSet->EmployeeID, m_pSet->EmployeeName, and m_pSet->EmployeeRate) with the edit controls in the same way. When you're finished, the Member Variables page of the MFC ClassWizard property sheet will look like Figure 22.20.

By selecting member variables of the application's CEmployeeSet class (derived from MFC's CRecordset class) as member variables for the controls in Database view, you're establishing a connection through which data can flow between the controls and the data source.

FIG. 22.20

All four controls are connected to member variables.

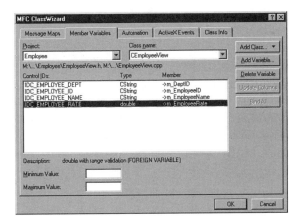

9. Click the OK button in the MFC ClassWizard property sheet to finalize your changes.

You've now created a data display form for the Employee application. Build and execute the program again, and you will see the window shown in Figure 22.21. Now the application displays the contents of records in the Employee database table. Use the database controls in the application's toolbar to navigate from one record in the Employee table to another.

FIG. 22.21

The Employee application now displays data in its window.

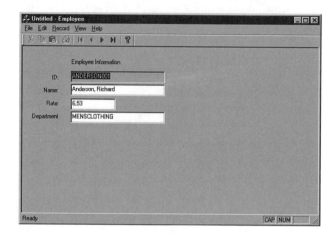

After you've examined the database, try updating a record. To do this, simply change one of the record's fields (except the employee ID, which is the table's primary key and can't be edited). When you move to another record, the application automatically updates the modified record. The commands in the application's Record menu also enable you to navigate through the records in the same manner as the toolbar buttons.

Notice that you've created a sophisticated database-access program without writing a single line of C++ code—an amazing feat. Still, the Employee application is limited. For example, it can't add or delete records. As you may have guessed, that's the next piece of the database puzzle, which you will add.

Adding and Deleting Records

When you can add and delete records from a database table, you will have a full-featured program for manipulating a flat (that is, not a relational) database. In this case, the flat database is the Employees table of the Department Store relational database. Adding and deleting records in a database table is an easier process than you might believe, thanks to Visual C++'s

CRecordView and CRecordSet classes, which provide all the member functions you need in order to accomplish these common database tasks. You will need to add some menu items to the application, as first discussed in Chapter 8, "Building a Complete Application: ShowString." Follow these steps to include add and delete commands in the Employee application:

1. Select the ResourceView tab, open the Menu folder, and double-click the IDR_MAINFRAME menu ID. The menu editor appears, as shown in Figure 22.22.

FIG. 22.22

Developer Studio's menu editor is in the pane on the right.

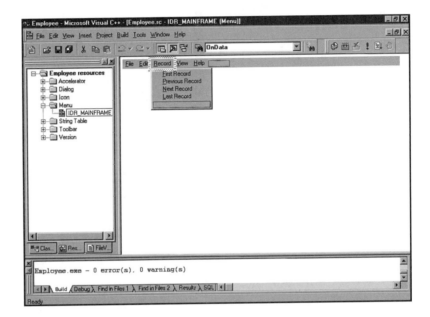

2. Click the Record menu item to open it, and click the blank menu item at the bottom of the menu. Choose View, Properties and pin the Menu Item Properties dialog box in place.

3. In the ID edit box, enter **ID_RECORD_ADD** and in the Caption box, enter **&Add Record**, as shown in Figure 22.23. This adds a new command to the Record menu.

4. In the next blank menu item, add a delete command with the ID **ID_RECORD_DELETE** and the caption **&Delete Record**.

FIG. 22.23

Add a menu item that adds a record to the Employee table.

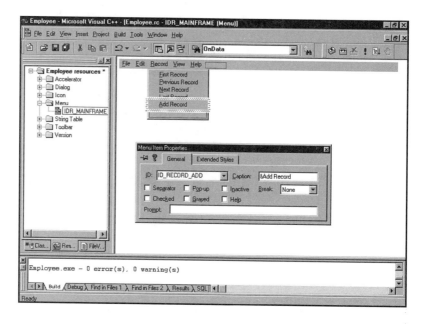

Next, you will connect these commands to toolbar buttons, as first discussed in Chapter 9, "Status Bars and Toolbars." Follow these steps:

1. In the ResourceView pane, open the Toolbar folder and then double-click the IDR_MAINFRAME ID. The application's toolbar appears in the resource editor.

2. Click the blank toolbar button to select it, and then use the editor's tools to draw a red plus on the button.

3. Double-click the new button in the toolbar. The Toolbar Button Properties property sheet appears. Select ID_RECORD_ADD in the ID box to connect this button to the menu, as shown in Figure 22.24.

4. Select the blank button again and draw a red minus sign, giving the button the ID_RECORD_DELETE ID, as you can see in Figure 22.25. Drag and drop the Add and Delete buttons to the left of the Help (question mark) button.

Now that you have added the menu items and the toolbar buttons, you need to arrange for code to catch the command message sent when the user clicks the button or chooses the menu item. Background information on this process is in Chapter 3, "Messages and Commands," and in Chapter 8 and Chapter 9. Because it is the view that is connected to the database, the view will catch these messages. Follow these steps:

1. Open ClassWizard and select the Message Maps tab.

FIG. 22.24
Add a button and
connect it to the menu
item.

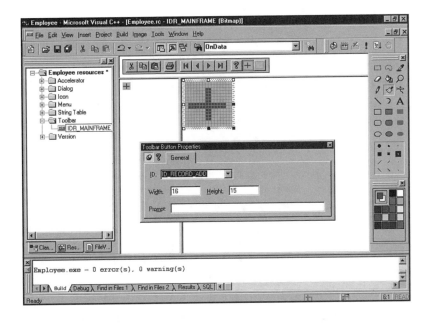

FIG. 22.25
The minus-sign button
will control the
Delete() function.

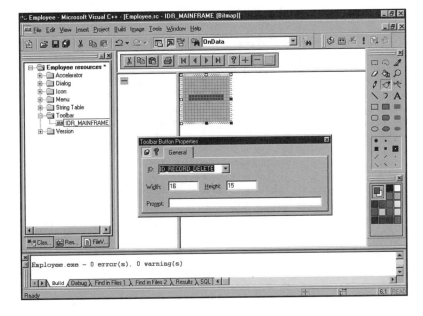

2. Set the Class Name box to `CEmployeeView`, click the `ID_RECORD_ADD` ID in the Object IDs box, and then double-click `COMMAND` in the Messages box. The Add Member Function dialog box appears, as shown in Figure 22.26.

FIG. 22.26

Add a function to catch the message.

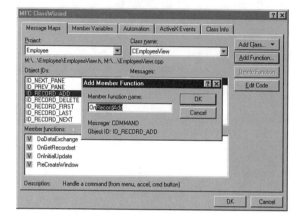

3. Click the OK button to accept the default name for the new function. The function appears in the Member Functions box at the bottom of the ClassWizard dialog box.

4. Add a member function for the `ID_RECORD_DELETE` command in the same way. The list of functions should resemble Figure 22.27. Click OK to close ClassWizard.

FIG. 22.27

The new functions appear in the Member Functions box.

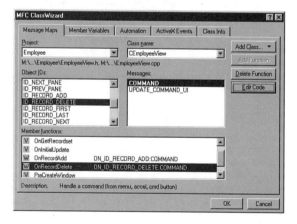

5. Open the EmployeeView.h file by double-clicking `CEmployeeView` in the ClassView pane. In the Attributes section of the class's declaration, add the following lines:

```
protected:
  BOOL m_bAdding;
```

6. Double-click the CEmployeeView constructor in ClassView to edit it, and add this line at the bottom of the function:

```
m_bAdding = FALSE;
```

7. Double-click the OnRecordAdd() function and edit it so that it looks like Listing 22.1. This code is explained in the next section.

Listing 22.1 CEmployeeView::OnRecordAdd()

```
void CEmployeeView::OnRecordAdd()
{
    m_pSet->AddNew();
    m_bAdding = TRUE;
    CEdit* pCtrl = (CEdit*)GetDlgItem(IDC_EMPLOYEE_ID);
    int result = pCtrl->SetReadOnly(FALSE);
    UpdateData(FALSE);
}
```

8. Right-click CEmployeeView in ClassView and choose Add Virtual Function. Select OnMove from the list on the left, as shown in Figure 22.28, and then click the Add and Edit button to add the function and to edit the skeleton code immediately.

FIG. 22.28

Override the OnMove() function.

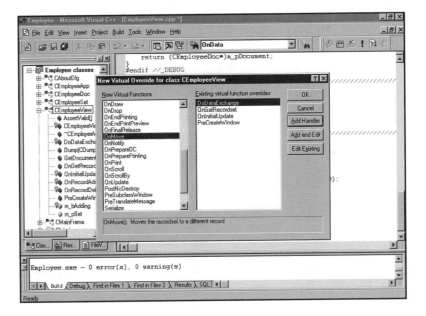

9. Edit the OnMove() function so that it has the code in Listing 22.2. This code is explained in the next section.

Listing 22.2   *CEmployeeView::OnMove()*

```
BOOL CEmployeeView::OnMove(UINT nIDMoveCommand)
{
    if (m_bAdding)
    {
        m_bAdding = FALSE;
        UpdateData(TRUE);
        if (m_pSet->CanUpdate())
            m_pSet->Update();
        m_pSet->Requery();
        UpdateData(FALSE);
        CEdit* pCtrl = (CEdit*)GetDlgItem(IDC_EMPLOYEE_ID);
        pCtrl->SetReadOnly(TRUE);
        return TRUE;
    }
    else
        return CRecordView::OnMove(nIDMoveCommand);
}
```

10. Double-click the OnRecordDelete() function and edit it so that it looks like Listing 22.3. This code is explained in the next section.

Listing 22.3   *CEmployeeView::OnRecordDelete()*

```
void CEmployeeView::OnRecordDelete()
{
    m_pSet->Delete();
    m_pSet->MoveNext();

    if (m_pSet->IsEOF())
        m_pSet->MoveLast();
    if (m_pSet->IsBOF())
        m_pSet->SetFieldNull(NULL);

    UpdateData(FALSE);
}
```

You've now modified the Employee application so that it can add and delete, as well as update, records. After compiling the application, run it by selecting the Build, Execute command from Developer Studio's menu bar or by pressing Ctrl+F5. When you do, you see the Employee application's main window, which doesn't look any different than it did in the preceding section. Now, however, you can add new records by clicking the Add button on the toolbar (or by selecting the Record, Add Record command on the menu bar) and delete records by clicking the Delete button (or by clicking the Record, Delete Record command).

When you click the Add button, the application displays a blank record. Fill in the fields for the record; then when you move to another record, the application automatically updates the database with the new record. To delete a record, just click the Delete button. The current record (the one on the screen) vanishes and is replaced by the next record in the database.

Examining the *OnRecordAdd()* Function

You might be wondering how the C++ code you added to the application works. OnRecordAdd() starts with a call to the AddNew() member function of CEmployeeSet, the class derived from CRecordSet. This sets up a blank record for the user to fill in, but the new blank record doesn't appear on the screen until the view window's UpdateData() function is called. Before that happens, you have a few other things to tackle.

After the user has created a new record, the database will need to be updated. By setting a flag in this routine, the move routine will be able to determine whether the user is moving away from an ordinary database record or a newly added one. That's why m_bAdding is set to TRUE here.

Now, because the user is entering a new record, it should be possible to change the contents of the Employee ID field, which is currently set to read-only. To change the read-only status of the control, the program first obtains a pointer to the control with GetDlgItem() and then calls the control's SetReadOnly() member function to set the read-only attribute to FALSE.

Finally, the call to UpdateData() will display the new blank record.

Examining the *OnMove()* Function

Now that the user has a blank record on the screen, it's a simple matter to fill in the edit controls with the necessary data. To add the new record to the database, the user must move to a new record, an action that forces a call to the view window's OnMove() member function. Normally, OnMove() does nothing more than display the next record. Your override will save new records as well.

When OnMove() is called, the first thing the program does is check the Boolean variable m_bAdding to see whether the user is in the process of adding a new record. If m_bAdding is FALSE, the body of the if statement is skipped and the else clause is executed. In the else clause, the program calls the base class (CRecordView) version of OnMove(), which simply moves to the next record.

If m_bAdding is TRUE, the body of the if statement is executed. There, the program first resets the m_bAdding flag and then calls UpdateData() to transfer data out of the view window's controls and into the recordset class. A call to the recordset's CanUpdate() method determines whether it's okay to update the data source, after which a call to the recordset's Update() member function adds the new record to the data source.

To rebuild the recordset, the program must call the recordset's Requery() member function, and then a call to the view window's UpdateData() member function transfers new data to the window's controls. Finally, the program sets the Employee ID field back to read-only, with another call to GetDlgItem() and SetReadOnly().

Examining the *OnRecordDelete()* Function

Deleting a record is simple. OnRecordDelete() just calls the recordset's Delete() function. When the record is deleted, a call to the recordset's MoveNext() arranges for the record that follows to be displayed.

A problem might arise, though, when the deleted record was in the last position or when the deleted record was the only record in the recordset. A call to the recordset's IsEOF() function will determine whether the recordset was at the end. If the call to IsEOF() returns TRUE, the recordset needs to be repositioned on the last record. The recordset's MoveLast() function takes care of this task.

When all records have been deleted from the recordset, the record pointer will be at the beginning of the set. The program can test for this situation by calling the recordset's IsBOF() function. If this function returns TRUE, the program sets the current record's fields to NULL.

Finally, the last task is to update the view window's display with another call to UpdateData().

Sorting and Filtering

In many cases when you're accessing a database, you want to change the order in which the records are presented, or you may even want to search for records that fit certain criteria. MFC's ODBC database classes feature member functions that enable you to sort a set of records on any field. You can also call member functions to limit the records displayed to those whose fields contain given information, such as a specific name or ID. This latter operation is called *filtering*. In this section, you will add sorting and filtering to the Employee application. Just follow these steps:

1. Add a Sort menu to the application's menu bar, as shown in Figure 22.29. Let Developer Studio set the command IDs.

2. Use ClassWizard to arrange for CEmployeeView to catch the four new sorting commands, using the function names suggested by ClassWizard. Figure 22.30 shows the resultant ClassWizard property sheet.

FIG. 22.29

The Sort menu has four commands for sorting the database.

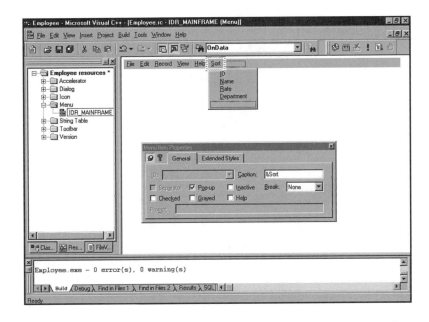

FIG. 22.30

After you add the four new functions, ClassWizard looks like this.

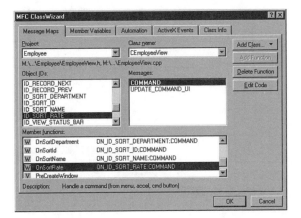

3. Add a Filter menu to the application's menu bar, as shown in Figure 22.31. Let Developer Studio set the command IDs.

4. Use ClassWizard to arrange for CEmployeeView to catch the four new filtering commands, using the function names suggested by ClassWizard.

5. Create a new dialog box by choosing Insert, Resource and double-clicking Dialog; then edit the dialog so that it resembles the dialog box shown in Figure 22.32. Give the edit control the ID **IDC_FILTERVALUE**. Give the entire dialog the ID **IDD_FILTER**.

FIG. 22.31

The Filter menu has four commands.

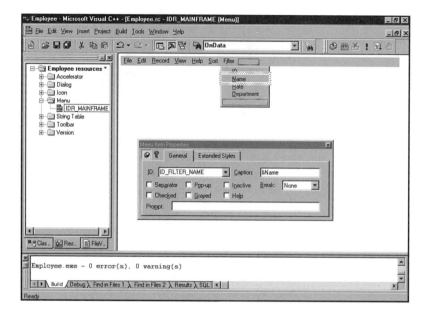

FIG. 22.32

Create a filter dialog box.

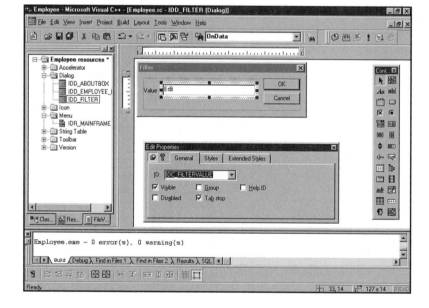

6. Start ClassWizard while the new dialog box is on the screen. The Adding a Class dialog box appears. Select the Create a New Class option and click OK.

7. The New Class dialog box appears. In the Name box, type `CFilterDlg`, as shown in Figure 22.33. Click OK to add the class.

FIG. 22.33

Create a dialog class
for the Filter dialog box.

8. Click ClassWizard's Member Variables tab. Connect the IDC_FILTERVALUE control to a member variable called m_filterValue. Click the OK button to dismiss ClassWizard.

Now that the menus and dialogs have been created and connected to skeleton functions, it's time to add some code to those functions. Double-click OnSortDepartment() in ClassView and edit it to look like Listing 22.4.

Listing 22.4 *CEmployeeView::OnSortDepartment()*

```
void CEmployeeView::OnSortDepartment()
{
        m_pSet->Close();
        m_pSet->m_strSort = "DeptID";
        m_pSet->Open();
        UpdateData(FALSE);
}
```

Double-click OnSortID() in ClassView and edit it to look like Listing 22.5. Double-click OnSortName() in ClassView and edit it to look like Listing 22.6. Double-click OnSortRate() in ClassView and edit it to look like Listing 22.7.

Listing 22.5 *CEmployeeView::OnSortId()*

```
void CEmployeeView::OnSortId()
{
        m_pSet->Close();
        m_pSet->m_strSort = "EmployeeID";
        m_pSet->Open();
        UpdateData(FALSE);
}
```

Listing 22.6 *CEmployeeView::OnSortName()*

```
void CEmployeeView::OnSortName()
{
        m_pSet->Close();
        m_pSet->m_strSort = "EmployeeName";
        m_pSet->Open();
        UpdateData(FALSE);
}
```

Listing 22.7 **LST14_07.TXT: Code for the** *OnSortRate()* **Function**

```
void CEmployeeView::OnSortRate()
{
        m_pSet->Close();
        m_pSet->m_strSort = "EmployeeRate";
        m_pSet->Open();
        UpdateData(FALSE);
}
```

At the top of EmployeeView.cpp, add the following line after the other `#include` directives:

```
#include "FilterDlg.h"
```

Edit `OnFilterDepartment()`, `OnFilterID()`, `OnFilterName()`, and `OnFilterRate()`, using Listing 22.8.

Listing 22.8 **The Four Filtering Functions**

```
void CEmployeeView::OnFilterDepartment()
{
        DoFilter("DeptID");
}

void CEmployeeView::OnFilterId()
{
        DoFilter("EmployeeID");
}

void CEmployeeView::OnFilterName()
{
        DoFilter("EmployeeName");
}

void CEmployeeView::OnFilterRate()
{
        DoFilter("EmployeeRate");
}
```

All four functions call `DoFilter()`. You will write this function to filter the database records represented by the recordset class. Right-click `CEmployeeView` in ClassView and choose Add Member Function. The Function Type is `void`, and the declaration is `DoFilter(CString col)`. It's a protected member function because it's called only from other member functions of `CEmployeeView`. Click OK to close the Add Member Function dialog box. Add the code from Listing 22.9.

Listing 22.9   *CEmployeeView::DoFilter()*

```
void CEmployeeView::DoFilter(CString col)
{
    CFilterDlg dlg;
    int result = dlg.DoModal();

    if (result == IDOK)
    {
        CString str = col + " = '" + dlg.m_filterValue + "'";
        m_pSet->Close();
        m_pSet->m_strFilter = str;
        m_pSet->Open();
        int recCount = m_pSet->GetRecordCount();

        if (recCount == 0)
        {
            MessageBox("No matching records.");
            m_pSet->Close();
            m_pSet->m_strFilter = "";
            m_pSet->Open();
        }

        UpdateData(FALSE);
    }

}
```

You've now added the capability to sort and filter records in the employee database. Build the application and run it. When you do, the application's main window appears, looking the same as before. Now, however, you can sort the records on any field, by selecting a field from the Sort menu. You can also filter the records by selecting a field from the Filter menu and then typing the filter string into the Filter dialog box that appears. You can tell how the records are sorted or filtered by moving through them one at a time. Try sorting by department or rate, for example. Then try filtering on one of the departments you saw scroll by.

Examining the *OnSortDept()* Function

All the sorting functions have the same structure. They close the recordset, set its `m_strSort` member variable, open it again, and then call `UpdateData()` to refresh the view with the values from the newly sorted recordset. You don't see any calls to a member function with `Sort` in its name. Then when does the sort happen? When the recordset is reopened.

A `CRecordset` object (or any object of a class derived from `CRecordset`, such as this program's `CEmployeeSet` object) uses a special string, called `m_strSort`, to determine how the records should be sorted. When the recordset is being created, the object checks this string and sorts the records accordingly.

Examining the *DoFilter()* Function

Whenever the user selects a command from the Filter menu, the framework calls the appropriate member function, either `OnFilterDept()`, `OnFilterID()`, `OnFilterName()`, or `OnFilterRate()`. Each of these functions does nothing more than call the local member function `DoFilter()` with a string representing the field on which to filter.

`DoFilter()` displays the same dialog box, no matter which filter menu item was chosen, by creating an instance of the dialog box class and calling its `DoModal()` function.

If `result` doesn't equal `IDOK`, the user must have clicked Cancel: The entire `if` statement is skipped, and the `DoFilter()` function does nothing but return.

Inside the `if` statement, the function first creates the string that will be used to filter the database. Just as you set a string to sort the database, so, too, do you set a string to filter the database. In this case, the string is called `m_strFilter`. The string you use to filter the database must be in a form like this:

```
ColumnID = 'ColumnValue'
```

The column ID was provided to `DoFilter()` as a `CString` parameter, and the value was provided by the user. If, for example, the user chooses to filter by department and types **hardware** in the filter value box, `DoFilter()` would set str to `DeptID = 'hardware'`.

With the string constructed, the program is ready to filter the database. As with sorting, the recordset must first be closed; then `DoFilter()` sets the recordset's filter string and reopens the recordset.

What happens when the given filter results in no records being selected? Good question. The `DoFilter()` function handles this by obtaining the number of records in the new recordset and comparing them to zero. If the recordset is empty, the program displays a message box telling the user of the problem. Then the program closes the recordset, resets the filter string to an empty string, and reopens the recordset. This restores the recordset to include all the records in the Employees table.

Finally, whether the filter resulted in a subset of records or the recordset had to be restored, the program must redisplay the data—by calling `UpdateData()`, as always.

Choosing Between ODBC and DAO

In the preceding section, you read an introduction to Visual C++'s ODBC classes and how they're used in an AppWizard-generated application. Visual C++ also features a complete set of DAO classes that you can use to create database applications. DAO is, in many ways, almost a superset of the ODBC classes, containing most of the functionality of the ODBC classes and adding a great deal of its own. Unfortunately, although DAO can read ODBC data sources for which ODBC drivers are available, it's not particularly efficient at the task. For this reason, the DAO classes are best suited for programming applications that manipulate Microsoft's .mdb database files, which are created by Microsoft Access. Other file formats that DAO can read directly are those created by Fox Pro and Excel. If you are writing an application that uses an Access database and always will, you might want to use DAO for its extra functionality. If, as is more likely, your application uses another database format now or will move to another format in the future, use ODBC instead.

The DAO classes, which use the Microsoft Jet Database Engine, are so much like the ODBC classes that you can often convert an ODBC program to DAO simply by changing the classnames in the program: CDatabase becomes CDaoDatabase, CRecordset becomes CDaoRecordset, and CRecordView becomes CDaoRecordView. One big difference between ODBC and DAO, however, is the way in which the system implements the libraries. ODBC is implemented as a set of DLLs, whereas DAO is implemented as COM objects. Using COM objects makes DAO a bit more up to date, at least as far as architecture goes, than ODBC.

Although DAO is implemented as COM objects, you don't have to worry about directly dealing with those objects. The MFC DAO classes handle all the details for you, providing data and function members that interact with the COM objects. The CDaoWorkspace class provides more direct access to the DAO database-engine object through static member functions. Although MFC handles the workspace for you, you can access its member functions and data members to explicitly initialize the database connection.

Another difference is that the DAO classes feature a more powerful set of methods that you can use to manipulate a database. These more powerful member functions enable you to perform sophisticated database manipulations without having to write a lot of complicated C++ code or SQL statements.

In summary, ODBC and DAO similarities are the following:

- ODBC and DAO both can manipulate ODBC data sources. However, DAO is less efficient at this task because it's best used with .mdb database files.

- AppWizard can create a basic database application based on either the ODBC or DAO classes. Which type of application you want to create depends, at least in some part, on the type of databases with which you will be working.

- ODBC and DAO both use objects of an MFC database class to provide a connection to the database being accessed. In ODBC, this database class is called CDatabase, whereas in DAO, the class is called CDaoDatabase. Although these classes have different names, the DAO database class contains some members similar to those found in the ODBC class.

- ODBC and DAO both use objects of a recordset class to hold the currently selected records from the database. In ODBC, this recordset class is called CRecordset, whereas in DAO, the class is called CDaoRecordset. Although these classes have different names, the DAO recordset class contains not only almost the same members as the ODBC class but also a large set of additional member functions.

■ ODBC and DAO use similar procedures for viewing the contents of a data source. That is, in both cases, the application must create a database object, create a recordset object, and then call member functions of the appropriate classes to manipulate the database.

Some differences between ODBC and DAO include the following:

■ Although both ODBC and DAO MFC classes are much alike (very much, in some cases), some similar methods have different names. In addition, the DAO classes feature many member functions not included in the ODBC classes.

■ ODBC uses macros and enumerations to define options that can be used when opening recordsets. DAO, on the other hand, defines constants for this purpose.

■ Under ODBC, snapshot recordsets are the default, whereas under DAO, dynamic recordsets are the default.

■ The many available ODBC drivers make ODBC useful for many different database file formats, whereas DAO is best suited to applications that need to access only .mdb files.

■ ODBC is implemented as a set of DLLs, whereas DAO is implemented as COM objects.

■ Under ODBC, an object of the CDatabase class transacts directly with the data source. Under DAO, a CDaoWorkspace object sits between the CDaoRecordset and CDaoDatabase objects, thus enabling the workspace to transact with multiple database objects.

OLE DB

OLE DB is a collection of OLE (COM) interfaces that simplify access to data stored in nondatabase applications such as email mailboxes or flat files. An application using OLE DB can integrate information from DBMS systems such as Oracle, SQL Server, or Access with information from nondatabase systems, using the power of OLE (COM).

OLE DB applications are either *consumers* or *providers*. A provider knows the format for a specific kind of file (such as an ODBC data source or a proprietary format) and provides access to those files or data sources to other applications. A consumer wants to access a database. For example, you might choose to rewrite the Employees example of this chapter as an OLE DB consumer application.

You will receive some help from AppWizard if you choose to go this route. On Step 2, when you select your data source, one of the choices is an OLE DB data source. Your application will be a little more complex to write than the ODBC example presented here, but you will be able to manipulate the data in a way very similar to the methods just covered. For example, the MFC class COleDBRecordView is the OLE DB equivalent of CRecordView.

A full treatment of OLE DB is outside the scope of this chapter. You need to be comfortable with OLE interfaces and with templates in order to use this powerful tool. An OLE DB Programmer's Reference is in the Visual C++ online documentation. When you are familiar with OLE and ActiveX concepts and have used templates, that's a great place to start. ●

SQL and the Enterprise Edition

What's in the Enterprise Edition?

The Enterprise Edition of Visual C++ was developed for those of you who are integrating SQL databases and C++ programs, especially if you use stored procedures. It's sold as a separate edition of the product: You can buy a copy of the Enterprise Edition instead of the Professional Edition. If you already own a Professional or Subscription Edition, you can upgrade to the Enterprise Edition for a reduced price.

The Enterprise Edition of Visual C++ includes several extra features within Visual Studio:

- SQL debugging
- Extended Stored Procedure Wizard
- OLE DB support for AS 400 access

Also, a number of separate development tools are included:

- Visual SourceSafe
- SQL Server 6.5 (Developer Edition, SP 3)
- Visual Modeler
- Microsoft Transaction Server
- Internet Information Server 4.0

If you do database programming, if you develop large projects and produce object model diagrams, and if you work in teams and need to prevent revision collision, you need the features of the Enterprise Edition.

Understanding SQL

Structured Query Language (SQL) is a way to access databases, interactively or in a program, that is designed to read as though it were English. Most SQL statements are *queries*—requests for information from one or more databases—but it's also possible to use SQL to add, delete, and change information. As mentioned in Chapter 22, "Database Access," SQL is an enormous topic. This section reviews the most important SQL commands so that even if you haven't used it before, you can understand these examples and see how powerful these tools can be.

SQL is used to access a relational database, which contains several tables. A table is made up of rows, and a row is made up of columns. Table 23.1 lists some names used in database research or in some other kinds of databases for tables, rows, and columns.

Table 23.1   Database Terminology

SQL	Also Known As
Table	Entity
Row	Record, Tuple
Column	Field, Attribute

Here's a sample SQL statement:

```
SELECT au_fname, au_lname FROM authors
```

It produces a list of authors' first and last names from a table called `authors`. (This table is included in the sample pubs database that comes with SQL Server, which you will be using in this chapter.) Here's a far more complicated SQL statement:

```
SELECT item, SUM(amount) total, AVG(amount) average FROM ledger
    WHERE action = 'PAID'
    GROUP BY item
having AVG(amount) > (SELECT avg(amount) FROM ledger
                        WHERE action = 'PAID')
```

Part
VI
Ch
23

A SQL statement is put together from keywords, table names, and column names. The keywords include the following:

- `SELECT` returns the specific column of the database. Secondary keywords including `FROM`, `WHERE`, `LIKE`, `NULL`, and `ORDER BY` restrict the search to certain records within each table.

- `DELETE` removes records. The secondary keyword `WHERE` specifies which records to delete.

- `UPDATE` changes the value of columns (specified with `SET`) in records specified with `WHERE`. It can be combined with a `SELECT` statement.

- `INSERT` inserts a new record into the database.

- `COMMIT` saves any changes you have made to the database.

- `ROLLBACK` undoes all your changes back to the most recent `COMMIT`.

- `EXEC` calls a stored procedure.

Like C++, SQL supports two kinds of comments:

```
/* This comment has begin and end symbols */
— This is a from-here-to-end-of-line comment
```

Working with SQL Databases from C++

As you saw in Chapter 22, "Database Access," an ODBC program using `CDatabase` and `CRecordset` can already access a SQL Server database or any database that supports SQL queries. What's more, with the `ExecuteSQL` function of `CDatabase`, you can execute any line of SQL from within your program. Most of the time, the line of SQL that you execute is a *stored procedure*—a collection of SQL statements stored with the database and designed to be executed on-the-fly by the database server.

There are lots of reasons not to hard-code your SQL into your C++ program. The three most compelling are

- Reuse
- Skill separation
- Maintainability

Many programmers accessing a SQL database from a C++ application are building on the work of other developers who have been building the database and its stored procedures for years. Copying those procedures into your code would be foolish indeed. Calling them from within your code lets you build slick user interfaces, simplify Internet access, or take advantage of the speed of C++, while retaining all the power of the stored procedures previously written.

Highly skilled professionals are always in demand, and sometimes the demand exceeds the supply. Many companies find it hard to recruit solid C++ programmers and equally as hard to recruit experienced database administrators who can learn the structure of a database and write in SQL. Imagine how difficult it would be to find a single individual who can do both— almost as difficult as having two developers work on the parts of the program that called SQL from C++. A much better approach is to have the C++ programmer call well-documented SQL stored procedures and the SQL developer build those stored procedures and keep the database running smoothly.

Separating the C++ and SQL parts of your application has another benefit: Changes to one might not affect the other. For example, a minor C++ change that doesn't involve the SQL will compile and link more quickly because the C++ part of the application is a little smaller without the SQL statements in it. Also, changes to the SQL stored procedure, if they don't involve the parameters to the function or the values it returns, will take effect without compiling and linking the C++ program.

There is a downside, however. It can be very difficult to track down problems when you are unsure whether they are in the C++ or the SQL part of your program. When one developer is doing both parts, learning two different tools and switching between them makes the job harder than it would be in a single tool. Also, the tools available for working with SQL lack many features that Visual C++ has offered C++ programmers.

Now, with the Enterprise Edition of Visual C++, you can have the best of both worlds. You can separate your C++ and SQL for reuse and maintenance but use the editor, syntax coloring, and even the debugger from Visual C++ to work on your SQL stored procedures.

Exploring the Publishing Application

One sample database that comes with SQL Server is called *pubs*. It tracks the sales of books and the royalties paid to their authors. In this chapter you will write a new stored procedure and display the records returned by it in a simple record view dialog box. SQL Server should be up and running before you start to build the application.

Setting Up the Data Source

Before you create the project, you need to create a data source to which it will connect. On your real projects, this data source might already exist.

Choose Start, Settings, Control Panel and then double-click ODBC. Select the User DSN tab, as in Figure 23.1, and click the Add button to add a new data source name (DSN).

FIG. 23.1

Add a user data source
name.

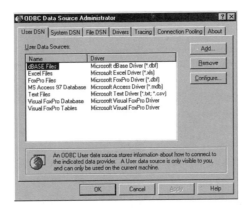

On the next dialog box, choose SQL Server, as in Figure 23.2, and click Finish. You're several
steps away from finishing, no matter what the button says.

FIG. 23.2

Connect to a SQL
Server.

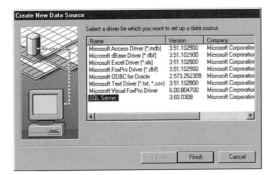

On the next dialog box, fill in a name and description for the data source. Then drop down the
Server box; choose your server or type its name. Figure 23.3 shows the completed dialog box
for a test system with only the sample databases installed. Click Next.

FIG. 23.3

Specify the server.

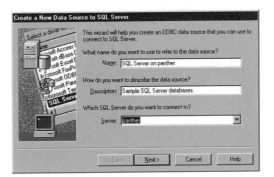

You can choose to connect to the server by using NT authentication or SQL Server authentication. If you're not sure, talk to your system administrator. Because this sample was developed on a test machine, SQL Server authentication—with the default account of sa and no password—is acceptable. Figure 23.4 shows the completed dialog box. Click Next.

FIG. 23.4

Security can be lax on test machines but not in the real world.

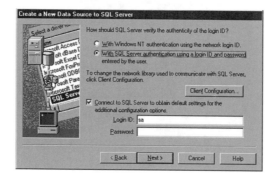

At this point, you can choose whether to connect this data source name to a single database on the server or to the server as a whole. If you want to associate this DSN with only one database, select the top check box and choose your database. If not, leave the top check box deselected. In either case, leave the rest of the dialog at the defaults, shown in Figure 23.5. Click Next.

FIG. 23.5

This DSN is connected to the entire server, not just one database.

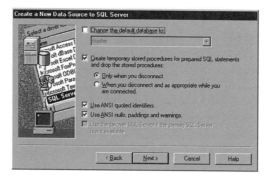

Accept the default on the next dialog box, shown in Figure 23.6, and click Next.

Leave both check boxes deselected on the last dialog, shown in Figure 23.7. Click Finish, and the process really is over.

Figure 23.8 shows the summary of settings from this connection process. It's a very good idea to test your connection before moving on.

FIG. 23.6

Character translations and regional settings need no special treatment in this example.

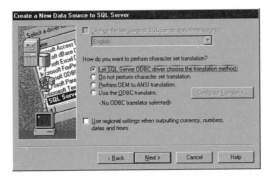

FIG. 23.7

There's no need to log slow queries or driver statistics in this example.

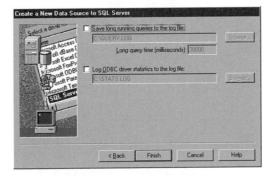

FIG. 23.8

Confirm your choices for the ODBC SQL connection.

Part

VI

Ch

23

Click Test Data Source, and you should see something like Figure 23.9. If you don't, click Cancel to return to the final step of the process and click Back until you are back to the step you need to adjust. Then come forward again with Next.

FIG. 23.9

Make sure your DSN connects properly.

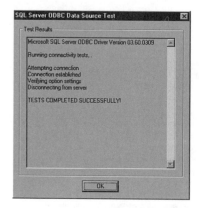

When you have tested the connection successfully, click OK on the summary dialog and then OK on the ODBC Data Source Administrator. Close Control Panel.

Building the Application Shell

Open Developer Studio and choose File, New and then click the Projects tab. Select MFC AppWizard (exe) and name the project Publishing, as shown in Figure 23.10. Click OK to start the AppWizard process.

FIG. 23.10

Start AppWizard in the usual way.

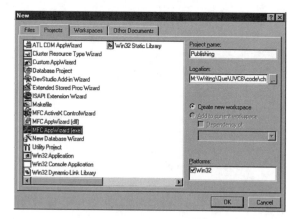

In Step 1 of AppWizard, choose an SDI application. Click Next to move to Step 2 of AppWizard. As shown in Figure 23.11, select the Database View Without File Support option. Click Data Source to connect a data source to your application.

Select the ODBC option and from the drop-down box next to it, select the DSN you just created, as shown in Figure 23.12. Leave the Recordset Type as Snapshot and click OK to specify the exact data source.

FIG. 23.11

This application needs database support but will not have a document.

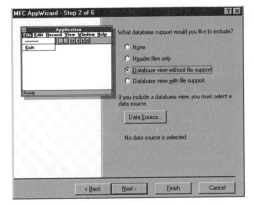

FIG. 23.12

Your data source is an ODBC data source name.

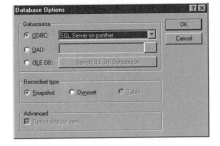

The SQL Server login dialog appears. Click the Options button to show the enlarged dialog of Figure 23.13. Choose pubs from the Database drop-down box and enter your login ID and password at the top of the dialog. Click OK.

FIG. 23.13

Connect to the sample pubs database.

The Select Database Tables dialog, shown in Figure 23.14, appears. Click on dbo.authors, dbo.titleauthor, and dbo.titles. Click OK.

Part

VI

Ch

23

FIG. 23.14

Choose the authors, titles, and authortitle tables.

You are back to Step 2 of AppWizard. Click Next to move to Step 3. Choose No Support for Compound Documents or ActiveX Controls and click Next to move to Step 4. Click Next to accept the Step 4 defaults and then Next again to accept the Step 5 defaults. On Step 6, click Finish. The New Project Information summary, shown in Figure 23.15, appears. Click OK to create the project.

FIG. 23.15

Confirm that your choices are correct before clicking OK.

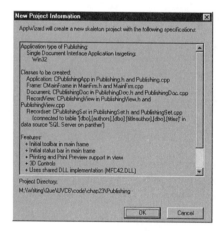

You have now completed a shell of an application that displays database values in a record view, much like the one discussed in Chapter 22. Nothing you have done so far has been specific to the Enterprise Edition. That is about to change.

Making a Data Connection

The database tables you specified are connected to your record set, but they aren't available for use with the SQL features of the Enterprise Edition. You need to make a data connection to connect the database to your application. Follow these steps to make the connection:

1. Choose Project, Add to Project, New.

2. Click the Projects tab.

3. As shown in Figure 23.16, select a Database Project, name it **PubDB**, and select the Add to Current Workspace radio button. Click OK.

FIG. 23.16

Create a subproject within this project.

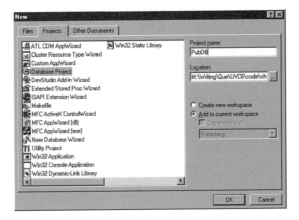

4. The Select Data Source dialog appears. Click the Machine Data Source tab, choose the DSN you created (shown in Figure 23.17), and click OK.

FIG. 23.17

Connect to the local server.

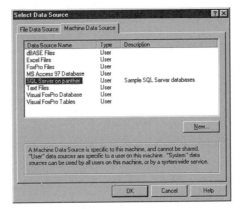

5. The SQL Server Login dialog appears. As before, specify your login ID and password and make sure the pubs database is selected. Click OK to complete the data connection.

In the Workspace pane on the left of the screen, a new tab has appeared. Figure 23.18 shows the new DataView. Expand the Tables section and expand authors to show the columns within the table. Double-click the authors table, and you can see your data on the right in Figure 23.18.

Also featured in Figure 23.18 is the Query toolbar, with the following buttons:

■ *Show Diagram Pane* toggles the Query Designer diagram pane (discussed in the next section).

■ *Show Grid Pane* toggles the Query Designer grid pane (discussed in the next section).

■ *Show SQL Pane* toggles the Query Designer SQL pane (discussed in the next section).

Part

VI

Ch

23

FIG. 23.18
The DataView shows you the database structure and can display your data in the working area.

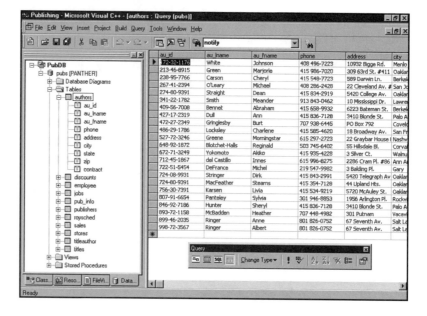

- *Show Results Pane* toggles the Query Designer results pane (discussed in the next section).

- *Change Type* creates a SELECT, INSERT, UPDATE, or DELETE query in the four panes of Query Designer.

- *Run* executes your SQL.

- *Verify SQL Syntax* checks the syntax of the SQL you have written.

- *Sort Ascending* displays records from the low value of a selected column to high.

- *Sort Descending* displays records from the high value of a selected column to low.

- *Remove Filter* shows all the records instead of only those that meet the filter specifications.

- *Group By* adds a GROUP BY condition to the query being built.

- *Properties* displays information about a column or table.

Working with Query Designer

When you double-click a table name, such as authors, in the DataView to display all the columns and all the records, you are actually executing a simple SQL query, as follows:

```
SELECT authors.* FROM authors
```

The results of this query appear in the results pane, which is the only one of the four Query Designer panes to be displayed, by default. This query was built for you by Query Designer and means *show all the columns and records of the* authors *table.* Figure 23.19 shows the four panes of Query Designer as they appear when you first make the data connection. To see all four panes, use the toolbar buttons to toggle them on. You can adjust the vertical size of each pane but not the horizontal.

To change your query, deselect * (All Columns) in the diagram pane (at the top of Figure 23.19) and then select au_lname, au_fname, and phone. The values in the results pane become gray to remind you that these aren't the results of the query you are now building. As you make these selections in the diagram pane, the other panes update automatically, as shown in Figure 23.20.

FIG. 23.19

The DataView shows you the database structure and can display your data in the working area.

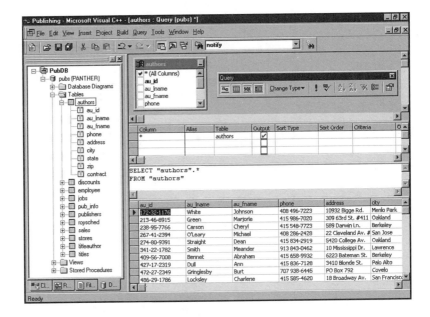

Highlight phone in the diagram pane and click the Sort Ascending button on the Query toolbar. This will sort the results by phone number. Click the Run button on the Query toolbar to execute the SQL that has been built for you. Figure 23.21 shows what you should see, including the new values in the results pane.

Stored Procedures

The capability to create simple SQL queries quickly, even if your SQL skills aren't strong, is an amazing aspect of the Enterprise Edition. However, using stored procedures is where the real payoff of this software becomes apparent.

FIG. 23.20

You can build simple queries even if you don't know any SQL.

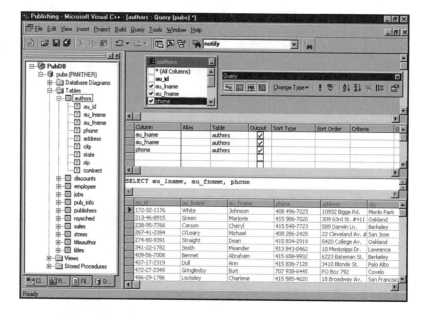

FIG. 23.21

Running your SQL queries is a matter of a single click.

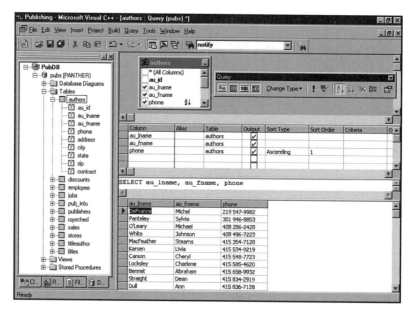

Collapse the tables section in the DataView and expand the Stored Procedures section. This shows all the stored procedures that are kept in the database and are available for you to use. Double-click reptq2 to display the procedure. One thing you probably notice immediately is the syntax coloring in the editor window. The colors used are

- *Blue* for keywords such as PRINT and SELECT
- *Green* for both styles of comment
- *Black* for other kinds of text

To run a stored procedure, choose Tools, Run; or right-click the stored procedure name in DataView and choose Run; or right-click in the editor and choose Run. The results appear in the Results pane of the Output window—don't confuse this with the Results pane of Query Designer. Figure 23.22 shows the Output window stretched very large to show some results of reptq2.

FIG. 23.22
You can see the results of any stored procedure from within Developer Studio.

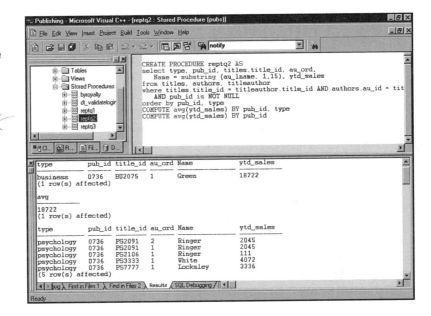

Some stored procedures take parameters. For example, double-click reptq3; its code looks like this:

```
CREATE PROCEDURE reptq3 @lolimit money, @hilimit money,
@type char(12)
AS
select pub_id, type, title_id, price
from titles
where price >@lolimit AND price <@hilimit AND type = @type
     OR type LIKE '%cook%'
order by pub_id, type
COMPUTE count(title_id) BY pub_id, type
```

This stored procedure takes three parameters: `lolimit`, `hilimit`, and `type`. If you run it, the dialog box shown in Figure 23.23 appears: Enter parameter values and click OK to run the procedure. See the results in the Output window.

FIG. 23.23

Providing parameters to stored procedures is simple.

It might be nice if the `type` parameter were a drop-down box, enabling you to see all the `type` values in the table before submitting the query rather than having to type `business` yourself. That sort of capability is exactly what you can build into a C++ program that uses SQL stored procedures. To see how, in the next section you will write a new stored procedure and call it from your C++ program.

Writing a New Stored Procedure

To create a new stored procedure, right-click Stored Procedures in DataView and choose New Stored Procedure. This code appears in the editor:

```
Create Procedure /*Procedure_Name*/
As
     return (0)
```

Edit this code so that it looks like Listing 23.1. Save the stored procedure by choosing File, Save—there's no need to specify the name because it's in the first line. After the procedure has been saved, its name appears in the DataView.

Listing 23.1   *author_ytd*, the New Stored Procedure

```
CREATE PROCEDURE author_ytd @sales int
AS
SELECT authors.au_lname, authors.au_fname, titles.title, ytd_sales
   FROM authors, titles, titleauthor
   WHERE ytd_sales > @sales
      AND authors.au_id = titleauthor.au_id
      AND titleauthor.title_id = titles.title_id
ORDER BY ytd_sales DESC
```

This SQL code gathers information from three tables, using the `au_id` and `title_id` columns to connect `authors` to `titles`. It takes one parameter, `sales`, which is an integer value. Run the procedure to see the results immediately. Listing 23.2 shows the results, using 4000 as the value for `sales`.

Listing 23.2 *author_ytd* results (*@sales* = 4000)

```
Running Stored Procedure dbo.author_ytd ( @sales = 4000 ).
au_lname          au_fname  title                                     ytd_sales
--------------    --------  ------------------------------------      ------
DeFrance          Michel    The Gourmet Microwave                       22246
Ringer            Anne      The Gourmet Microwave                       22246
Green             Marjorie  You Can Combat Computer Stress!             18722
Blotchet-Halls    Reginald  Fifty Years in Buckingham Palace Kitchens   15096
Carson            Cheryl    But Is It User Friendly?                     8780
Green             Marjorie  The Busy Executive's Database Guide          4095
Bennet            Abraham   The Busy Executive's Database Guide          4095
Straight          Dean      Straight Talk About Computers                4095
Dull              Ann       Secrets of Silicon Valley                    4095
Hunter            Sheryl    Secrets of Silicon Valley                    4095
O'Leary           Michael   Sushi, Anyone?                               4095
Gringlesby        Burt      Sushi, Anyone?                               4095
Yokomoto          Akiko     Sushi, Anyone?                               4095
White             Johnson   Prolonged Data Deprivation: Four Case Studies 4072
 (14 row(s) affected)
Finished running dbo.author_ytd.
RETURN_VALUE = 0
```

Connecting the Stored Procedure to C++ Code

At the moment, you have an empty C++ application that uses a recordset and would display members of that recordset in a record view if you added fields to the dialog to do so. The recordset contains all the columns from the three tables (`authors`, `titleauthor`, and `titles`) that you specified during the AppWizard process. That's arranged by a function called `CPublishingSet::GetDefaultSQL()` that AppWizard wrote for you, shown in Listing 23.3.

Listing 23.3 *CPublishingSet::GetDefaultSQL()* from AppWizard

```cpp
CString CPublishingSet::GetDefaultSQL()
{
    return _T("[dbo].[authors],[dbo].[titleauthor],[dbo].[titles]");
}
```

You're going to change this default SQL so that it calls your stored procedure, which is now part of the pubs database. First, choose Project, Set Active Project and select Publishing. Switch to ClassView in the Workspace pane, expand `CPublishingSet`, and double-click `GetDefaultSQL()` to edit it. Replace the code with that in Listing 23.4.

Listing 23.4 *CPublishingSet::GetDefaultSQL()* to Call Your Stored Procedure

```cpp
CString CPublishingSet::GetDefaultSQL()
{
    return _T("{CALL author_ytd(4000)}");
}
```

Part
VI

Ch
23

N O T E Normally you would not hard-code the parameter value like this. Adding member variables to the class to hold parameters and passing them to the SQL is a topic you can explore in the online help when you are more familiar with the Enterprise Edition. ■

The records returned from this query will go into your recordset. The query returns four columns (au_lname, au_fname, title, and ytd_sales), but the recordset is expecting far more than that. You can use ClassWizard to edit your recordset definition. Follow these steps:

1. Open ClassWizard by choosing View, ClassWizard.

2. Click the Member Variables tab. You should see something like Figure 23.24, showing all the member variables of the recordset connected to table columns.

FIG. 23.24

ClassWizard manages your recordset definition.

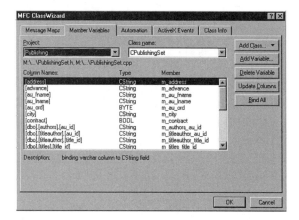

3. Highlight [address] and click Delete Variable.

4. In the same way, delete all the variables except au_lname, au_fname, title, and ytd_sales.

5. Click OK to close ClassWizard.

Your application can compile and run now, but until you edit the Record View dialog box, you won't be able to see the records and columns that are returned by another query. Editing the dialog box is covered in Chapter 22 and uses skills first demonstrated in Chapter 2, "Dialogs and Controls," so the description here will be brief.

Click the ResourceView tab, expand the resources, expand Dialogs, and double-click IDD_PUBLISHING_FORM. This dialog box was created for you by AppWizard but has no controls on it yet. Delete the static text reminding you to add controls, and add four edit boxes and their labels so that the dialog resembles Figure 23.25. Use sensible resource IDs for the edit boxes, not the defaults provided by Developer Studio. Name them IDC_QUERY_LNAME, IDC_QUERY_FNAME, IDC_QUERY_TITLE, and IDC_QUERY_YTDSALES.

FIG.23.25

Edit your Record View dialog box.

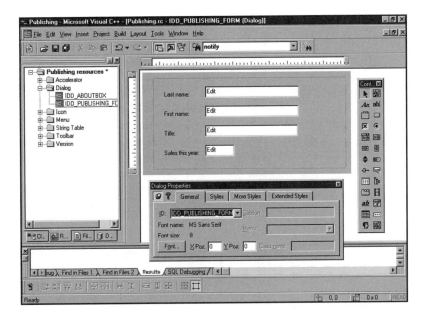

There is one task left: Connect these fields to member variables. Here's how to make that connection:

1. Open ClassWizard while this dialog box has focus.
2. Click the Member Variables tab.
3. Select IDC_QUERY_FNAME and click Add Variable to open the Add Member Variable dialog box.
4. From the drop-down box labeled Member Variable Name, choose m_pSet->m_au_fname and click OK.
5. In the same way, connect IDC_QUERY_LNAME to m_pSet->m_au_lname, IDC_QUERY_TITLE to m_pSet->m_title, and IDC_QUERY_YTDSALES to m_pSet->m_ytd_sales.
6. Figure 23.26 shows the ClassWizard dialog box when all four controls have been connected. Click OK to close ClassWizard.

In ClassView, double-click the function DoFieldExchange() under CPublishingSet and look at the code that was generated for you. The order in which the variables appear in this code is important: It must match the order in which the fields are coming back from your stored procedure. Figure 23.27 shows DoFieldExchange() and the stored procedure together. Adjust the order of the fields in the SELECT statement, if required.

Build your project and run it. You should see a record view like Figure 23.28 (you might have to go through the SQL login procedure again first), and if you scroll through the record view with the arrow buttons, you should see every author from the report in Listing 23.2.

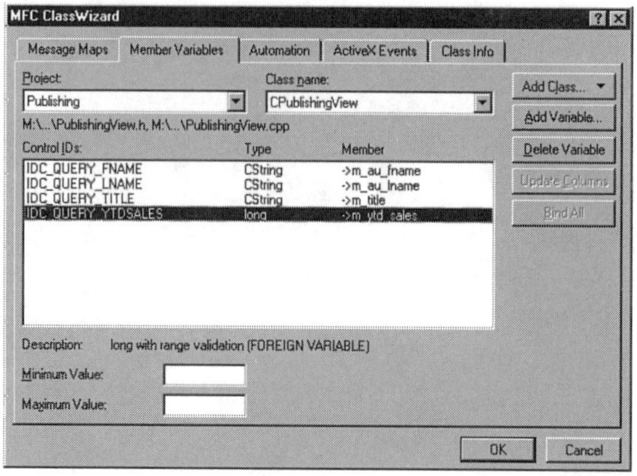

FIG. 23.26

Connect the record view controls to member variables of the recordset.

FIG. 23.27

Make sure that the fields are in the same order in `DoFieldExchange()` as in your stored procedure.

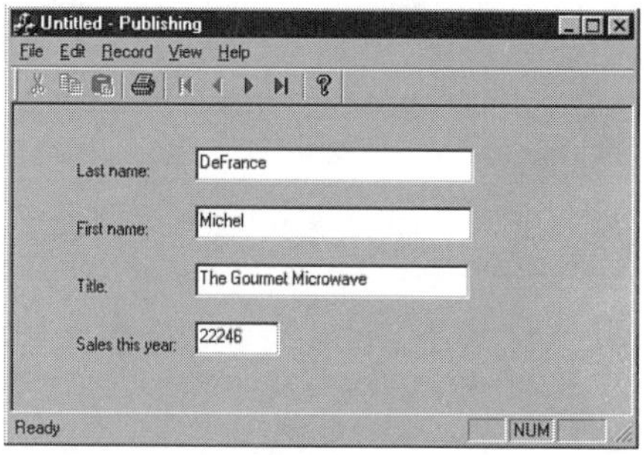

FIG. 23.28

Your application displays the results of the stored procedure's query.

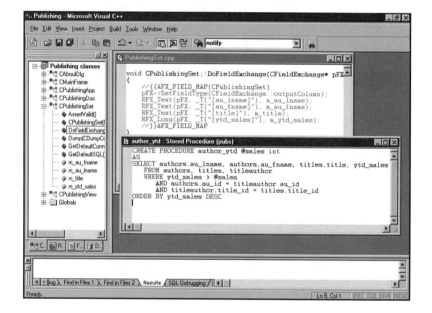

T I P Make sure you have saved the SQL stored procedure before you build. Because the stored procedures are in a subproject of Publishing, building Publishing will not trigger any saves in the subproject.

This application doesn't do much at the moment: It calls a stored procedure and neatly presents the results. With a little imagination, you can probably see how your SQL-based C++ programs can wrap stored procedures in user-friendly interfaces and how easy it is to develop and maintain these stored procedures by using Developer Studio. You can even debug your SQL by using the Developer Studio debugger.

Working with Your Database

The DataView gives you full control over not only the contents of your SQL database but also its design. A raft of graphical tools makes it easy to see how the database works or to change any aspect of it.

Database Designer

Return to the DataView, right-click the authors table, and choose Design. With the Database Designer, shown in Figure 23.29, you can change the key column, adjust the width, apply constraints on valid values, and more.

FIG. 23.29
The Database Designer lets you change any aspect of your database's design.

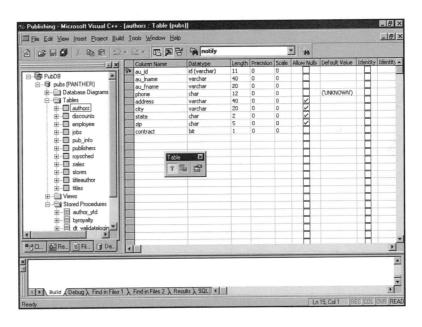

For example, to open the property sheet shown in Figure 23.30, click the Properties button at the far right of the Table toolbar while au_id is selected. The constraint shown here means that au_id must be a 9-digit number. Clicking the Relationship tab, shown in Figure 23.31, shows that au_id is used to connect the authors table to the titleauthor table.

FIG. 23.30
It's simple to specify
column constraints.

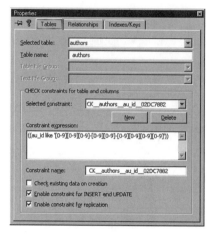

FIG. 23.31
The Relationships tab
makes it simple to see
how tables are related.

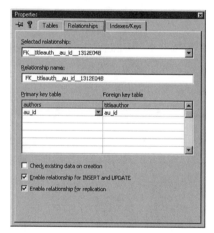

Database Diagrams

One of the easiest ways to quickly present information to people is with a diagram. Figure
23.32 shows a diagram that explains the relationships between the three tables used throughout this chapter. To create the same diagram yourself, follow these steps:

1. Right-click Database Diagrams in DataView and choose New Diagram.
2. Click `authors` and drag it into the working area.
3. Click `titleauthor` and drag it into the working area. Wait a moment for a link between
   `authors` and `titleauthor` to appear.
4. Click `titles` and drag it into the working area. Wait for the link to appear.
5. Rearrange the tables so that their keys are aligned as in Figure 23.32.

6. Drag the links up or down until they run from one key to another, as they do in Figure 23.32.

FIG. 23.32

A picture is worth a thousand words when it's time to explain your database design.

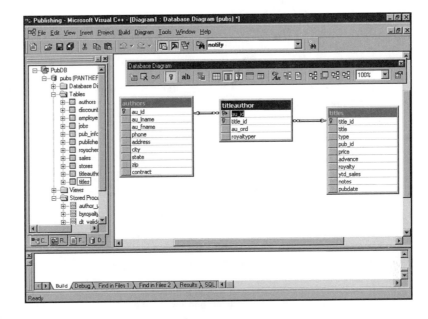

If you want, you can save this diagram in the database. Just click the Save button on the standard toolbar and provide a name. The diagrams will be available to any other developers who use the Enterprise Edition to access this database.

If you're a database developer, you probably can't wait to open your own database in the Database Designer and set to work. Be sure to take advantage of the many features on the Database Diagram toolbar. For example, you can add a note or explanation with the New Text Annotation button; this note can be moved wherever you want. Four buttons grouped together control how much detail is shown for each table. The first, Column Properties, shows all the details that were in the table view. The second, Column Names, is the default in the diagram view. Keys shows only those columns that are keys, and Name Only shrinks the grid to a tiny column showing only the table's name. This is useful for diagrams representing the relationships of many tables or of tables from other projects.

To change any design decision about these tables, open the shortcut menu and choose Column Properties; then edit these properties as you did in the Database Designer. How's that for an easy way to design and administer a SQL database?

Understanding Microsoft Transaction Server

Microsoft Transaction Server is a completely separate product that comes with the Enterprise Edition of Visual C++ but is not integrated with it. MTS enables you to use a collection of COM objects called *components* to securely execute distributed transactions within enterprise-scale database applications. Applications that use MTS can be written in any language that produces ActiveX applications, including Visual C++, Visual J++, and Visual Basic.

To work with MTS, you must be comfortable doing under-the-hood ActiveX and COM programming, working directly with interfaces. If you've always relied on MFC to hide interfaces from you, you should probably read Chapter 21, "The Active Template Library," to gain an introduction to the way that interfaces are used.

Like ODBC, you can use MTS with almost any kind of database, including ordinary file systems. Certainly SQL databases work with MTS, but so do a huge variety of other resource managers. This enables you access to the power of MTS without having to change your database system at all.

An MTS component is a COM object. It can do any specific task within your system, and often several components are involved in a given *transaction*. Components are gathered together into packages, which are installed as a unit onto your system.

A *transaction* is a unit of work that should succeed or fail as a whole. For example, if a customer is transferring money from one bank account to another, the money should be withdrawn from one account and deposited to the other. It doesn't make sense for one step in this process to fail and the other to proceed to completion. This would either unfairly take money away from customers or unfairly give money to customers. Database programmers have long realized this and have developed ways of rolling back transactions that are partially completed when a step fails or of checking conditions to ensure that all the steps will succeed before starting. However, these techniques are much more difficult to implement in a large, distributed system—too difficult to implement by hand.

For example, imagine that two systems are about to take money (say, $100) from a customer's bank account. The first checks the balance, and there is enough money. Both systems are connected through a network to the system that keeps the balance for that account. The first system asks for the balance and receives the reply: $150. Moments later, the second asks and is also told $150. The first confidently sends the request for $100 and succeeds; only a fraction of a second later, the second asks for $100 and fails. Any portions of a transaction involving this customer that were already completed by the second system will now have to be rolled back. A transactional system such as MTS makes this process much simpler for developers by providing system services to support these tasks.

Sound good? Then install the product and get going in the online help. Two good sample systems are included: a simple banking application and a game. You can also check out Microsoft's Transaction Server Web site at **http://www.microsoft.com/transaction**.

Using Visual SourceSafe

If you work as part of a team of developers, a revision control system isn't a nicety—it's a necessity. For too many teams, the revision control system consists of sticking your head into the hall and telling your fellow programmers that you will be working on fooble.h and fooble.cpp for a while and to leave these alone. Perhaps it's more about demanding to know who saved his changes to fooble.h over your changes because you both had the file open at once, and somebody saved after you did. There is a better way.

Revision control systems are not a new idea. They all implement these concepts:

■ *Check out a file*—By bringing a copy of a file to your desktop from a central library or repository, you mark the file as unavailable to others who might want to change it. (Some systems allow changes to source files by several developers at once and can later merge the changes.)

■ *Check in a file*—When your changes are complete, you return the file to the library. You provide a brief description of what you've done, and the RCS automatically adds your name, the date, and other files affected by this change.

■ *Merge changes*—Some RCS systems can accept check-ins by different developers on the same file and will make sure that both sets of changes appear in the central file.

■ *Change tracking*—Some RCS systems can reconstruct earlier versions of a file by working backwards through a change log.

■ *History*—The information added at check-in can form a nice summary of what was done to each file, when, and why.

Microsoft's Visual SourceSafe is a good revision control system that many developers use to keep their code in order. What sets Visual SourceSafe apart from other RCS systems? It's project oriented, it hooks into Visual C++ (through the new SCCI interface, some other RCS systems can also hook in), and it comes with the Enterprise Edition of Visual C++.

When you install Visual SourceSafe, choose a custom installation and select Enable SourceSafe Integration. Doing this adds a cascading menu to Developer Studio's Project menu, shown in Figure 23.33. To enable the items on the menu, you must add your project to source control by choosing Add to Source Control and logging into Visual SourceSafe.

Part

VI

Ch

23

FIG. 23.33

Installing Visual SourceSafe adds a cascading menu to the Project menu.

The items on the menu are as follows:

- *Get Latest Version*—For selected files, replace your copies with newer copies from the library.
- *Check Out*—Start to work on a file.
- *Check In*—Finish working on a file and make your changed versions available to everyone.
- *Undo Check Out*—Give back a file without making any changes or an entry in the history.
- *Add to Source Control*—Enable source control for this project.
- *Remove from Source Control*—Disable source control for this project.
- *Show History*—Display the changes made to selected files.
- *Show Differences*—Display the differences between old and new files.
- *SourceSafe Properties*—See information that SourceSafe keeps about your files.
- *Share from SourceSafe*—Allow other developers to work on selected files.
- *Refresh Status*—Update your display with status changes made by other developers.
- *SourceSafe*—Run Visual SourceSafe to see reports and summaries.

You must have an account and password set up in Visual SourceSafe before you can put a project under source control and use these features. Run Visual SourceSafe from this menu to perform any administrative tasks that haven't already been taken care of for you.

Unless you are the only developer who will work on your project, you simply must use a revision control system. Visual SourceSafe is good: It works from within Developer Studio, and if you have the Enterprise Edition of Visual C++, it's free. What more could you want? Install it, learn it, use it. You won't regret it.

TIP Revision control systems work on Web pages, database contents, documentation, bug lists, and spreadsheets as well as they do on code and program files. After you get in the habit and see the benefits, you won't stop.

Improving Your Application's Performance

When developing a new application, there are various challenges developers must meet. You need your application to compile, to run without blowing up, and you must be sure that it does what you want it to do. On some projects, there is time to determine whether your application can run faster and use less memory or whether you can have a smaller executable file. The performance improvement techniques discussed in this chapter can prevent your program from blowing up and eliminate the kind of thinkos that result in a program calculating or reporting the wrong numbers. These improvements are not merely final tweaks and touch-ups on a finished product.

You should form the habit of adding an ounce of prevention to your code as you write and the habit of using the debugging capabilities that Developer Studio provides you to confirm what's going on in your program. If you save all your testing to the end, both the testing and the bug-fixing will be much harder than if you had been testing all along. Also, of course, any bug you manage to prevent will never have to be fixed at all!

Preventing Errors with *ASSERT* and *TRACE*

The developers of Visual C++ did not invent the concepts of asserting and tracing. Other languages support these ideas, and they are taught in many computer science courses. What is exciting about the Visual C++ implementation of these concepts is the clear way in which your results are presented and the ease with which you can suppress assertions and TRACE statements in release versions of your application.

ASSERT: Detecting Logic Errors

The ASSERT macro enables you to check a condition that you logically believe should always be TRUE. For example, imagine you are about to access an array like this:

```
array[i] = 5;
```

You want to be sure that the index, i, isn't less than zero and larger than the number of elements allocated for the array. Presumably you have already written code to calculate i, and if that code has been written properly, i must be between 0 and the array size. An ASSERT statement will verify that:

```
ASSERT( i > 0 && i < ARRAYSIZE)
```

N O T E　There is no semicolon (;) at the end of the line because ASSERT is a macro, not a function. Older C programs may call a function named assert(), but you should replace these calls with the ASSERT macro because ASSERT disappears during a release build, as discussed later in this section. ▪

You can check your own logic with ASSERT statements. They should never be used to check for user input errors or bad data in a file. Whenever the condition inside an ASSERT statement is FALSE, program execution halts with a message telling you which assertion failed. At this point, you know you have a logic error, or a developer error, that you need to correct.

Here's another example:

```
// Calling code must pass a non-null pointer
void ProcessObject( Foo * fooObject )
{
        ASSERT( fooObject )
        // process object
}
```

This code can dereference the pointer in confidence, knowing execution will be halted if the pointer is NULL.

You probably already know that Developer Studio makes it simple to build debug and release versions of your programs. The debug version #defines a constant, _DEBUG, and macros and other pre-processor code can check this constant to determine the build type. When _DEBUG isn't defined, the ASSERT macro does nothing. This means there is no speed constraint in the final code, as there would be if you added if statements yourself to test for logic errors. There is no need for you to go through your code, removing ASSERT statements when you release your application, and, in fact, it's better to leave them there to help the developers who work on version 2. They document your assumptions, and they'll be there when the debugging work starts again. In addition, ASSERT can't help you if there is a problem with the release version of your code because it is used to find logic and design errors before you release version 1.0 of your product.

TRACE: Isolating Problem Areas in Your Program

As discussed in Appendix D, "Debugging," the power of the Developer Studio debugger is considerable. You can step through your code one line at a time or run to a breakpoint, and you can see any of your variables' values in watch windows as you move through the code. This can be slow, however, and many developers use TRACE statements as a way of speeding up this process and zeroing in on the problem area. Then they turn to more traditional step-by-step debugging to isolate the bad code.

In the old days, isolating bad code meant adding lots of print statements to your program, which is problematic in a Windows application. Before you start to think up workarounds, such as printing to a file, relax. The TRACE macro does everything you want, and like ASSERT, it magically goes away in release builds.

There are several TRACE macros: TRACE, TRACE0, TRACE1, TRACE2, and TRACE3. The number-suffix indicates the number of parametric arguments beyond a simple string, working much like printf. The different versions of TRACE were implemented to save data segment space.

When you generate an application with AppWizard, many ASSERT and TRACE statements are added for you. Here's a TRACE example:

```
if (!m_wndToolBar.Create(this)
    || !m_wndToolBar.LoadToolBar(IDR_MAINFRAME))
{
    TRACE0("Failed to create toolbar\n");
    return -1;      // fail to create
}
```

Part
VI

Ch
24

If the creation of the toolbar fails, this routine will return -1, which signals to the calling program that something is wrong. This will happen in both debug and release builds. In debug builds, though, a trace output will be sent to help the programmer understand what went wrong.

All the TRACE macros write to afxDump, which is usually the debug window, but can be set to stderr for console applications. The number-suffix indicates the parametric argument count, and you use the parametric values within the string to indicate the passed data type—for example, to send a TRACE statement that includes the value of an integer variable:

```
TRACE1("Error Number: %d\n", -1 );
```

or to pass two arguments, maybe a string and an integer:

```
TRACE2("File Error %s, error number: %d\n", __FILE__, -1 );
```

The most difficult part of tracing is making it a habit. Sprinkle TRACE statements anywhere you return error values: before ASSERT statements and in areas where you are unsure that you constructed your code correctly. When confronted with unexpected behavior, add TRACE statements first so that you better understand what is going on before you start debugging.

Adding Debug-Only Features

If the idea of code that isn't included in a release build appeals to you, you may want to arrange for some of your own code to be included in debug builds but not in release builds. It's easy. Just wrap the code in a test of the _DEBUG constant, like this:

```
#ifdef _DEBUG
    // debug code here
#endif
```

In release builds, this code will not be compiled at all.

All the settings and configurations of the compiler and linker are kept separately for debug and release builds and can be changed independently. For example, many developers use different compiler warning levels. To bump your warning level to 4 for debug builds only, follow these steps:

1. Choose Project, Settings, which opens the Project Settings dialog box, shown in Figure 24.1.

2. Choose Debug or Release from the drop-down list box at the upper left. If you choose All Configurations, you'll change debug and release settings simultaneously.

3. Click the C/C++ tab and set the Warning Level to Level 4, as shown in Figure 24.2. The default is Level 3, which you will use for the release version (see Figure 24.3).

Warning level 4 will generate a lot more errors than level 3. Some of those errors will probably come from code you didn't even write, such as MFC functions. You'll just have to ignore those warnings.

FIG. 24.1
The Project Settings dialog box enables you to set configuration items for different phases of development.

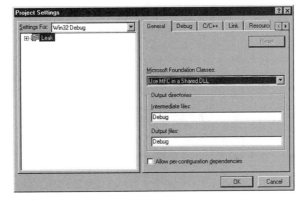

FIG. 24.2
Warning levels can be set higher during development.

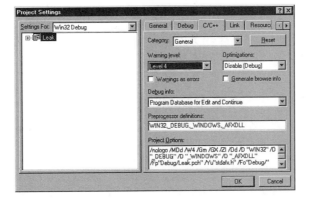

FIG. 24.3
Warning levels are usually lower in a production release.

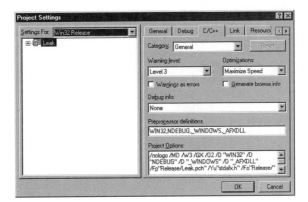

Sealing Memory Leaks

A memory leak can be the most pernicious of errors. Small leaks may not cause any execution errors in your program until it is run for an exceptionally long time or with a larger-than-usual data file. Because most programmers test with tiny data files or run the program for only a few minutes when they are experimenting with parts of it, memory leaks may not reveal themselves in everyday testing. Alas, memory leaks may well reveal themselves to your users when the program crashes or otherwise misbehaves.

Common Causes of Memory Leaks

What does it mean when your program has a memory leak? It means that your program allocated memory and never released it. One very simple cause is calling new to allocate an object or an array of objects on the heap and never calling delete. Another cause is changing the pointer kept in a variable without deleting the memory the pointer was pointing to. More subtle memory leaks arise when a class with a pointer as a member variable calls new to assign the pointer but doesn't have a copy constructor, assignment operator, or destructor. Listing 24.1 illustrates some ways that memory leaks are caused.

Listing 24.1 Causing Memory Leaks

```
// simple pointer leaving scope
{
  int * one = new int;
  *one = 1;
} // one is out of scope now, and wasn't deleted

// mismatched new and delete: new uses delete and new[] uses delete[]
{
float * f = new float[10];
// use array
delete f; // Oops! Deleted f[0] correct version is delete [] f;
}

// pointer of new memory goes out of scope before delete
{
    const char * DeleteP = "Don't forget P";
    char * p = new char[strlen(DeleteP) + 1];
    strcpy( p, DeleteP );
} // scope ended before delete[]

class A
{
   public:
      int * pi;
}

A::A()
{
   pi = new int();
   *pi = 3;
```

```
}

//  ..later on, some code using this class..

A firsta;   //allocates an int for first.pi to point to
B seconda;  //allocates another int for seconda.pi

seconda=firsta;

// will perform a bitwise (shallow) copy. Both objects
// have a pi that points to the first int allocated.
// The pointer to the second int allocated is gone
// forever.
```

The code fragments all represent ways in which memory can be allocated and the pointer to that memory lost before deallocation. After the pointer goes out of scope, you can't reclaim the memory, and no one else can use it either. It's even worse when you consider exceptions, discussed in Chapter 26, "Exceptions and Templates," because if an exception is thrown, your flow of execution may leave a function before reaching the delete at the bottom of the code. Because destructors are called for objects that are going out of scope as the stack unwinds, you can prevent some of these problems by putting delete calls in destructors. This, too, is discussed in more detail in Chapter 26, in the "Placing the catch Block" section.

Like all bugs, the secret to dealing with memory leaks is to prevent them—or to detect them as soon as possible when they occur. You can develop some good habits to help you:

- If a class contains a pointer and allocates that pointer with new, be sure to code a destructor that deletes the memory. Also, code a copy constructor and an operator (=).
- If a function will allocate memory and return something to let the calling program access that memory, it must return a pointer instead of a reference. You can't delete a reference.
- If a function will allocate memory and then delete it later in the same function, allocate the memory on the stack, if at all possible, so that you don't forget to delete it.
- Never change a pointer's value unless you have first deleted the object or array it was pointing to. Never increment a pointer that was returned by new.

Debug *new* and *delete*

MFC has a lot to offer the programmer who is looking for memory leaks. In debug builds, whenever you use new and delete, you are actually using special debug versions that track the filename and line number on which each allocation occurred and match up deletes with their news. If memory is left over as the program ends, you get a warning message in the output section, as shown in Figure 24.4.

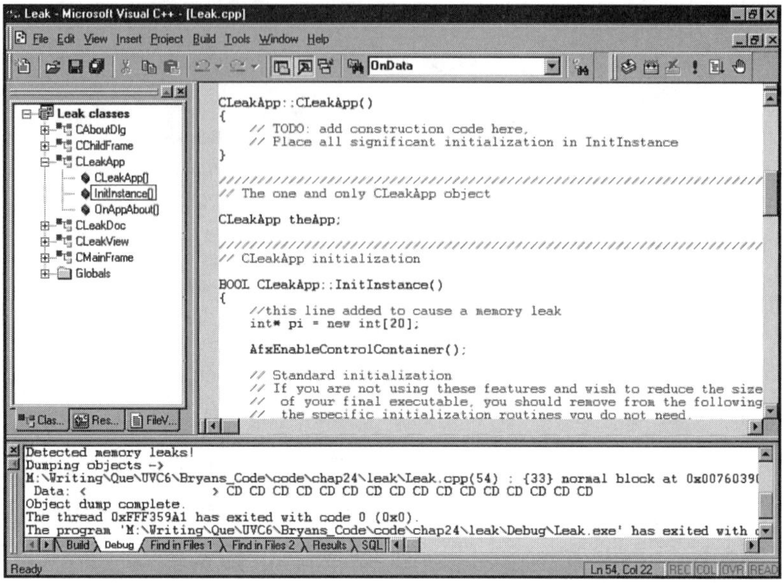

FIG. 24.4

Memory leaks are
detected automatically
in debug builds.

To see this for yourself, create an AppWizard MDI application called Leak, accepting all the defaults. In the `InitInstance()` function of the application class (`CLeakApp` in this example), add this line:

```
int* pi = new int[20];
```

Build a debug version of the application and run it by choosing Build, Start Debug, and Go, or click the Go button on the Build minibar. You will see output like Figure 24.4. Notice that the filename (Leak.cpp) and line number where the memory was allocated are provided in the error message. Double-click that line in the output window, and the editor window displays Leak.cpp with the cursor on line 54. (The coordinates in the lower-right corner always remind you what line number you are on.) If you were writing a real application, you would now know what the problem is. Now you must determine where to fix it (more specifically, where to put the `delete`).

Automatic Pointers

When a program is executing within a particular scope, like a function, all variables allocated in that function are allocated on the stack. The *stack* is a temporary storage space that shrinks and grows, like an accordion. The stack is used to store the current execution address before a function call, the arguments passed to the function, and the local function objects and variables.

When the function returns, the *stack pointer* is reset to that location where the prior execution point was stored. This makes the stack space after the reset location available to whatever else needs it, which means those elements allocated on the stack in the function are gone. This process is referred to as *stack unwinding*.

N O T E Objects or variables defined with the keyword `static` are not allocated on the stack. ∎

Stack unwinding also happens when an exception occurs. To reliably restore the program to its state before an exception occurred in the function, the stack is unwound. Stack-wise variables are gone, and the destructors for stack-wise objects are called. Unfortunately, the same is not true for dynamic objects. The handles (for example, pointers) are unwound, but the unwinding process doesn't call `delete`. This causes a memory leak.

In some cases, the solution is to add `delete` statements to the destructors of objects that you know will be destructed as part of the unwinding, so they can use these pointers before they go out of scope. A more general approach is to replace simple pointers with a C++ class that can be used just like a pointer but contains a destructor that deletes any memory at the location where it points. Don't worry, you don't have to write such a class: One is included in the Standard Template Library, which comes with Visual C++. Listing 24.2 is a heavily edited version of the `auto_ptr` class definition, presented to demonstrate the key concepts.

Part VI

Ch 24

T I P If you haven't seen template code before, it's explained in Chapter 26.

Listing 24.2 A Scaled-Down Version of the *auto_ptr* Class

```
// This class is not complete. Use the complete definition in
//the Standard Template Library.
 template <class T>
 class auto_ptr
 {
 public:
         auto_ptr( T *p = 0) : rep(p) {}
         // store pointer in the class
         ~auto_ptr(){ delete rep; }              // delete internal rep
         // include pointer conversion members
         inline T* operator->() const { return rep; }
         inline T& operator*() const { return *rep; }
    private:
         T * rep;
 };
```

The class has one member variable, a pointer to whatever type that you want a pointer to. It has a one-argument constructor to build an `auto_ptr` from an `int*` or a `Truck*` or any other pointer type. The destructor deletes the memory pointed to by the internal member variable. Finally, the class overrides `->` and `*`, the dereferencing operators, so that dereferencing an `auto_ptr` feels just like dereferencing an ordinary pointer.

If there is some class `C` to which you want to make an automatic pointer called `p`, all you do is this:

```
auto_ptr<C> p(new C());
```

Now you can use p as though it were a C*—for example:

```
p->Method();   // calls C::Method()
```

You never have to delete the C object that p points to, even in the event of an exception, because p was allocated on the stack. When it goes out of scope, its destructor is called, and the destructor calls delete on the C object that was allocated in the new statement.

You can read more about managed pointers and exceptions in Chapter 26.

Using Optimization to Make Efficient Code

There was a time when programmers were expected to optimize their code themselves. Many a night was spent arguing about the order in which to test conditions or about which variables should be register instead of automatic storage. These days, compilers come with optimizers that can speed execution or shrink program size far beyond what a typical programmer can accomplish by hand.

Here's a simple example of how optimizers work. Imagine you have written a piece of code like this:

```
for (i=0;i<10;i++)
{
    y=2;
    x[i]=5;
}
for (i=0; i<10; i++)
{
    total += x[i];
}
```

Your code will run faster, with no effect on the final results, if you move the y=2 in front of the first loop. In addition, you can easily combine the two loops into a single loop. If you do that, it's faster to add 5 to total each time than it is to calculate the address of x[i] to retrieve the value just stored in it. Really bright optimizers may even realize that total can be calculated outside the loop as well. The revised code might look like this:

```
y=2;
for (i=0;i<10;i++)
{
    x[i]=5;
}
    total += 50;
```

Optimizers do far more than this, of course, but this example gives you an idea of what's going on behind the scenes. It's up to you whether the optimizer focuses on speed, occasionally at the expense of memory usage, or tries to minimize memory usage, perhaps at a slighter lower speed.

To set the optimization options for your project, select the Project, Settings command from Developer Studio's menu bar. The Project Settings property sheet, first shown in Figure 24.1, appears. Click the C/C++ tab and make sure you are looking at the Release settings; then select Optimizations in the Category box. Keep optimization turned off for debug builds because the code in your source files and the code being executed won't match line for line, which will confuse you and the debugger. You should turn on some kind of optimization for release builds. Choose from the drop-down list box, as shown in Figure 24.5.

FIG. 24.5

Select the type of optimization you want.

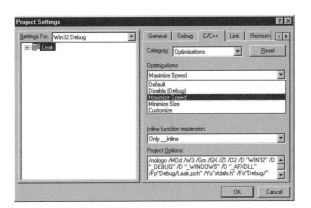

Part

VI

Ch

24

If you select the Customize option in the Optimizations box, you can select from the list of individual optimizations, including Assume No Aliasing, Global Optimizations, Favor Fast Code, Generate Intrinsic Functions, Frame-Pointer Omission, and more. However, as you can tell from these names, you really have to know what you're doing before you set up a custom optimization scheme. For now, accept one of the schemes that have been laid out for you.

Finding Bottlenecks by Profiling

Profiling an application lets you discover *bottlenecks*, pieces of code that are slowing your application's execution and deserve special attention. It's pointless to hand-optimize a routine unless you know that the routine is called often enough for its speed to matter.

Another use of a profiler is to see whether the test cases you have put together result in every one of your functions being called or in each line of your code being executed. You may think you have selected test inputs that guarantee this; however, the profiler can confirm it for you.

Visual C++ includes a profiler integrated with the IDE: All you need to do is use it. First, adjust your project settings to include profiler information. Bring up the Project Settings property sheet as you did in the preceding section and click the Link tab. Check the Enable Profiling check box. Click OK and rebuild your project. Links will be slower now because you can't do an incremental link when you are planning to profile, but you can go back to your old settings after you've learned a little about the way your program runs. Choose Build, Profile and the Profile dialog box, shown in Figure 24.6, appears.

FIG. 24.6

A profiler can gather many kinds of information.

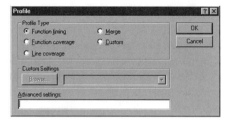

If you aren't sure what any of the radio buttons on this dialog box mean, click the question mark in the upper-right corner and then click the radio button. You'll receive a short explanation of the option. (If you would like to add this kind of context-sensitive Help to your own applications, be sure to read Chapter 11, "Help.")

You don't profile as a method to catch bugs, but it can help to validate your testing or show you the parts of your application that need work, which makes it a vital part of the developer's toolbox. Get in the habit of profiling all your applications at least once in the development cycle. ●

CHAPTER 25

Achieving Reuse with the Gallery and Your Own AppWizards

In these days of complex programs, *reusability* has become more than a buzzword. It's become a survival technique for programmers who find themselves with the awesome task of creating hundreds of thousands of lines of working source code in a minimum amount of time. Visual C++ is packed with ways to let you reuse the work of programmers who have gone before you, such as AppWizard, ClassWizard, and of course the Microsoft Foundation Classes. The tools discussed in this chapter enable you to contribute code to the future, ready to be reused quickly and easily by some future coworker—or better yet, by you.

Reviewing the Benefits of Writing Reusable Code

If you have a job to do, it's easy to see how reusing someone else's code, dialog boxes, or design simplifies your work and lets you finish faster. As long as you can trust the provider of the material you reuse, the more you can reuse, the better. As a result, there's a market for reusable bits and pieces of programs.

In fact, there are two markets: one formal one, with vendors selling project parts such as controls or templates, and another informal one within many large companies, with departments developing reusable parts for brownie points or bragging rights, or other intangibles. Some companies even have a reuse budget to which you can charge the time you spend making parts of your project reusable, or they award reuse credits if someone else in the company reuses one of your parts. If yours doesn't, maybe it should: Reuse can save as much as 60% of your software budget, but only if someone is noble or charitable enough to develop with reuse in mind or if company policy inspires everyone to develop with reuse in mind.

Most newcomers to reuse think only of reusing code, but there are other parts of a project that can save you far more time than you can save with code reuse only. These include the following:

- *Design.* The Document/View paradigm, first discussed in Chapter 4, "Documents and Views," is a classic example of a design decision that is reused in project after project.

- *Interface Resources.* You can reuse controls, icons, menus, toolbars, or entire dialog boxes and reduce training time for your users as well as development time for your programmers.

- *Project Settings.* Whether it's an obscure linker setting or the perfect arrangement of toolbars, your working environment must be right for you, and getting it right is faster on every project you do because you reuse the decisions you made the last time.

- *Documentation.* As you read in Chapter 11, "Help," help text for standard commands like File, Open is generated for you by AppWizard. You can reuse your own help text from project to project and save even more time.

Using Component Gallery

Component Gallery is one way that Developer Studio helps support reuse. Component Gallery gives you instant access to everything from reusable classes and OLE controls to wizards.

You can even create your own components and add them to Component Gallery. In fact, in its default installation, Developer Studio automatically adds a category to Component Gallery for new AppWizard applications that you create.

Adding a Component to the Gallery

Suppose you have a dialog box that you use frequently in projects. You can create this dialog box once, add it to Component Gallery, and then merge it into new projects whenever you need it. To see how this works, follow these steps:

1. Start a new Custom AppWizard project workspace called App1. (Click Finish on Step 1 to use all the default AppWizard settings; then click OK to create the project.)

2. Add a new dialog box to the project by choosing Insert, Resource and double-clicking Dialog.

3. Using the techniques first presented in Chapter 2, "Dialogs and Controls," build the dialog-box resource shown in Figure 25.1, giving the dialog box the resource ID IDD_NAMEDLG.

FIG. 25.1
Build a dialog box to add to Component Gallery.

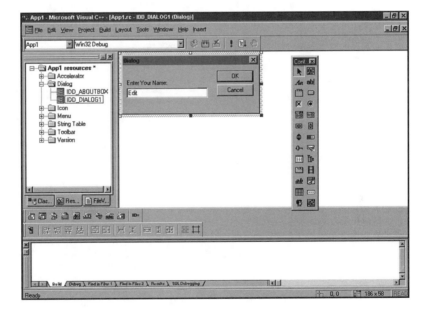

4. While the dialog box has focus, bring up ClassWizard and agree to create a new class. Call the new class **CNameDlg**.

5. Close ClassWizard.

6. Right-click CNameDlg in ClassView and choose Add To Gallery from the shortcut menu.

Although nothing appears to happen, the class `CNameDlg` and the associated resource have been added to the Gallery. Minimize Developer Studio and browse your hard drive, starting at My Computer, until you display C:\Program Files\Microsoft VisualStudio\Common\ MSDev98\Gallery (if you installed Visual C++ in another directory, look in that directory for the MSDev98 folder and continue down from there). As you can see in Figure 25.2, there is now an App1 folder in the Gallery.

FIG. 25.2

The Gallery uses your project name as the folder name when you add a class.

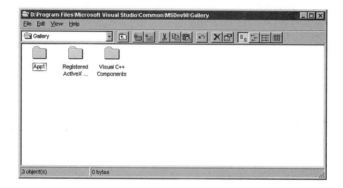

Double-click the App1 folder and you'll see it contains one file, Name Dlg.ogx, as shown in Figure 25.3. The .ogx extension signifies a Gallery component.

FIG. 25.3

The filename for your Gallery component is based on the classname.

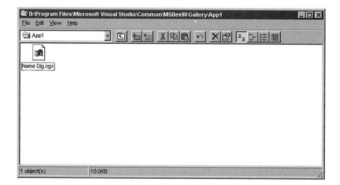

Using Gallery Components in Your Projects

Now that you've added the resource and associated class to the Gallery, a logical next step is to make another project that will use them. Create a MFC AppWizard (exe) application, called App2, with AppWizard. Again, click Finish on Step 1 to accept all the defaults and then OK to create the project.

Click the ClassView tab and expand the App2 classes. There are six: `CAboutDlg`, `CApp2App`, `CApp2Doc`, `CApp2View`, `CChildFrame`, and `CMainFrame`.

Choose Project, Add To Project, and Components and Controls. The Gallery dialog box, shown in Figure 25.4, appears.

FIG. 25.4

Gallery components are arranged in folders.

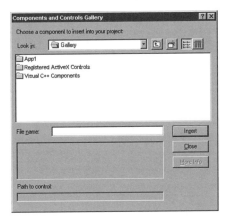

Double-click App1 and you'll see Name Dlg.ogx again. Double-click it. When prompted, confirm that you want to insert this component in your project. Click Close to close the Gallery.

Look at ClassView again. CNameDlg has been added. Check FileView and you'll see that NameDlg.cpp and NameDlg.h have been added to the project. Switch to ResourceView to confirm that the dialog box IDD_NAMEDLG has been added. You can use this resource in App2 in just the way you used it in App1.

Part
VI

Ch
25

Exploring the Gallery

You can use Component Gallery to manage many other component types, including those that you might get from a friend or buy from a third-party supplier. Component Gallery can add, delete, import, and edit components in a variety of ways, depending on the type of component with which you're working. Take some time to experiment with Component Gallery, and you'll soon see how easy it is to use.

Figure 25.5 shows the contents of the Registered ActiveX Controls folder, reached by choosing Project, Add to Project, Components and Controls. Both the ATL and MFC versions of the Dieroll control are here: DieRoll Class was built in Chapter 21, "The Active Template Library," and Dieroll Control was built in Chapter 17, "Building an ActiveX Control." Before this shot was taken, DBGrid Control was highlighted and the More Info button was clicked. Components can be bundled with a Help file that is reached from the More Info button.

Introducing Custom AppWizards

AppWizard is a sensational tool for starting projects effortlessly. However, because of its general nature, AppWizard makes many assumptions about the way you want a new project created. Sometimes you may need a special type of AppWizard project that isn't supported by the default AppWizard. If this special project is a one-time deal, you'll probably just create the project by hand. However, if you need to use this custom project type again and again, you might want to consider creating a custom AppWizard.

FIG. 25.5

All ActiveX controls are available through the Gallery.

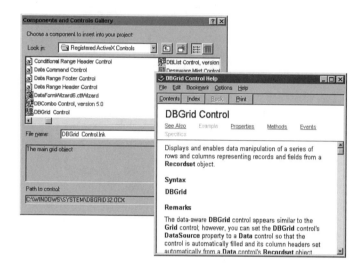

You can create a custom AppWizard in three ways: using the existing AppWizard steps as a starting point, using an existing project as a starting point, or starting completely from scratch. However, no matter what method you choose, creating a custom AppWizard can be a complicated task, requiring that you understand and be able to write script files by using the macros and commands that Visual C++ provides for this purpose.

The following tackles the very simplest case first, creating an AppWizard to reproduce an existing project with a different name. Follow these steps:

1. Create a project in the usual way. Call it **Original** and click Finish on Step 1 to accept all the AppWizard defaults.

2. Edit the About box to resemble Figure 25.6.

FIG. 25.6

Customize your About box.

3. Choose File, New and click the Projects tab. Select Custom AppWizard and enter **OrigWiz**, as shown in Figure 25.7. Click OK.

4. The first of two custom AppWizard dialog boxes appears, as shown in Figure 25.8. Select An Existing Project to base your wizard on the project you created in steps 1 and 2. Do not edit the wizard's name. Click Next.

FIG. 25.7

Create a custom AppWizard.

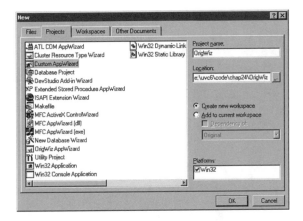

FIG. 25.8

Base your wizard on an existing project.

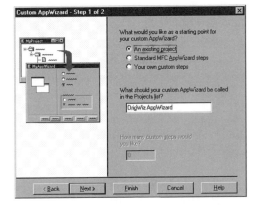

5. The second custom AppWizard dialog box appears. Browse to the project file for the Original project, Original.dsp. Click Finish.

6. The New Project Information dialog box, shown in Figure 25.9, confirms your choices. Click OK.

You are now working on the OrigWiz project, and in many cases you would add code at this point. Because this is an example, just build the project immediately.

To use your custom AppWizard, choose File, New again and click the Projects tab. As shown in Figure 25.10, OrigWizard has been added to the list of choices on the left. Select it and enter **App3** for the name of the project. Click OK.

N O T E When you compile the custom AppWizard, Developer Studio creates the final files and stores them in your C:\Program Files\Microsoft Visual Studio\Common\MSDev98\ Template directory. The next time you choose to start a new project workspace, your custom AppWizard will be listed in the project types. To remove the custom AppWizard, delete the wizard's .awx and .pdb files from your C:\Program Files\Microsoft Visual Studio\Common\MSDev98\Template directory. ■

FIG. 25.9

Your custom AppWizard creates copies of the Original project with different names.

FIG. 25.10

Your custom AppWizard has been added to the list of AppWizards.

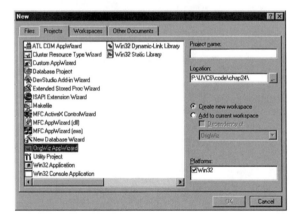

Figure 25.11 shows one of the tasks that you normally complete before you build the AppWizard: generating the text for the New Project Information dialog box. Click OK.

Look at the classnames and the code—App3 looks like any of the projects created in this chapter that accept all the AppWizard defaults, but you didn't have to go through any dialog steps. Switch to ResourceView and edit IDD_ABOUTBOX. As Figure 25.12 shows, it contains the extra text (based on Original 1.0) that you added, but the application name on the top line of the box has been correctly changed to App3. This is one smart wizard.

When you build a wizard from an existing project, all the classes, resources, and code that you added will be incorporated in the new projects you generate with the wizard. It's a great time-saver.

FIG. 25.11

You have to write the text for the New Project Information dialog box.

FIG. 25.12

AppWizard copied your custom About box to the new project.

You can also build custom AppWizards that present dialog boxes for you to fill out. Before you do that, you should be comfortable writing wizards that are not AppWizards, like the ones discussed in Chapter 12, "Property Pages and Sheets." You should also have generated lots of different types of applications so that you have a feel for the sort of work AppWizard does. When you're ready, check the section in the online help titled "Creating Custom AppWizards."

This whole book demonstrates the value of using other people's designs, classes, code, controls, dialog boxes, and other project parts. This chapter shows two simple ways to arrange for other people (or you, in the future) to reuse your code, which benefits your customers or employer by saving significant development time. Your job will be more enjoyable when repetitive tasks, such as building a dialog box and associating it with a class, are taken care of, freeing you to do the fun stuff. ●

Exceptions and Templates

C++ is an evolving language and frequently undergoes review and improvement. Two important features that were added to C++ after many developers had already learned the language are exceptions and templates. Although most programmers delay learning these concepts until they have six months to a year of Visual C++ programming experience, you should consider learning them now. These concepts are not much more difficult than the ones covered earlier in this book and can add extra power to your programs.

Understanding Exceptions

When writing applications using Visual C++, sooner or later you're going to run into error-handling situations that don't seem to have a solution. Perhaps you are writing a function that returns a numeric value and need a way to send back an error response. Sometimes you can come up with one special return value, perhaps 0 or -1, that indicates a problem. Other times there doesn't seem to be a way to signal trouble. Perhaps you use special return values but find yourself writing code that starts out like this:

```
while (somefunction(x))
{
    for (int i=0; i<limit; i++)
    {
        y = someotherfunction(i);
    }
}
```

After writing that, perhaps you realize that if `someotherfunction()` returns -1, you should not move on to the next i, and you should leave the `while` loop. Your code becomes the following:

```
int timetostop = 0;
while (somefunction(x) && !timetostop)
{
    for (int i=0; i<limit && !timetostop; i++)
    {
        if ( (y = someotherfunction(i)) == -1)
            timetostop = 1;
    }
}
```

This isn't bad, but it is hard to read. If there are two or three things that could go wrong, your code becomes unmanageably complex.

Exceptions are designed to handle these sorts of problems. The exception mechanism allows programs to signal each other about serious and unexpected problems. Three places in your code participate in most exceptions:

- The `try` *block* marks the code you believe might run into difficulty.
- The `catch` *block* immediately follows the `try` block and holds the code that deals with the problem.
- The `throw` *statement* is how the code with a problem notifies the calling code.

Simple Exception Handling

The mechanism used by exception-handling code is simple. Place the source code that you want guarded against errors inside a try block. Then construct a catch program block that acts as the error handler. If the code in the try block (or any code called from the try block) throws an exception, the try block immediately ceases execution, and the program continues inside the catch block.

For example, memory allocation is one place in a program where you might expect to run into trouble. Listing 26.1 shows a nonsensical little program that allocates some memory and then immediately deletes it. Because memory allocation could fail, the code that allocates the memory is enclosed in a try program block. If the pointer returned from the memory allocation is NULL, the try block throws an exception. In this case, the exception object is a string.

N O T E The sample applications in this chapter are console applications, which can run from a DOS prompt and don't have a graphical interface. This keeps them small enough to be shown in their entirety in the listings. To try them, create a console application as discussed in Chapter 28, "Future Explorations," add a file to the project, and add the code shown here. ■

Listing 26.1   EXCEPTION1.CPP—Simple Exception Handling

```
#include <iostream.h>

int main()
{
    int* buffer;

    try
    {
        buffer = new int[256];

        if (buffer == NULL)
            throw "Memory allocation failed!";
        else
            delete buffer;
    }
    catch(char* exception)
    {
        cout << exception << endl;
    }

    return 0;
}
```

Part
VI

Ch
26

When the program throws the exception, program execution jumps to the first line of the catch program block. (The remainder of the code inside the try block is not executed.) In the case of Listing 26.1, this line prints out a message, after which the function's return line is executed and the program ends.

If the memory allocation is successful, the program executes the entire `try` block, deleting the buffer. Then program execution skips over the `catch` block completely, in this case going directly to the `return` statement.

N O T E   The `catch` program block does more than direct program execution. It actually catches the exception object thrown by the program. For example, in Listing 26.1, you can see the exception object being caught inside the parentheses following the `catch` keyword. This is very similar to a parameter being received by a method. In this case, the type of the "parameter" is `char*` and the name of the parameter is `exception`. ■

Exception Objects

The beauty of C++ exceptions is that the exception object thrown can be just about any kind of data structure you like. For example, you might want to create an exception class for certain kinds of exceptions that occur in your programs. Listing 26.2 shows a program that defines a general-purpose exception class called `MyException`. In the case of a memory-allocation failure, the main program creates an object of the class and throws it. The `catch` block catches the `MyException` object, calls the object's `GetError()` member function to get the object's error string, and then displays the string on the screen.

Listing 26.2   EXCEPTION2.CPP—Creating an Exception Class

```cpp
#include <iostream.h>

class MyException
{
protected:
    char* m_msg;

public:
    MyException(char *msg) { m_msg = msg; }

    ~MyException(){}

    char* GetError() {return m_msg; };
};

int main()
{
    int* buffer;

    try
    {
        buffer = new int[256];

        if (buffer == NULL)
        {
            MyException* exception =
                new MyException("Memory allocation failed!");
            throw exception;
```

```
    }
    else
        delete buffer;
}
catch(MyException* exception)
{
    char* msg = exception->GetError();
    cout << msg << endl;
}

return 0;
}
```

An exception object can be as simple as an integer error code or as complex as a fully developed class. MFC provides a number of exception classes, including CException and several classes derived from it. The abstract class CException has a constructor and three member functions: Delete(), which deletes the exception, GetErrorMessage(), which returns a string describing the exception, and ReportError(), which reports the error in a message box.

Placing the *catch* Block

The catch program block doesn't have to be in the same function as the one in which the exception is thrown. When an exception is thrown, the system starts "unwinding the stack," looking for the nearest catch block. If the catch block is not found in the function that threw the exception, the system looks in the function that called the throwing function. This search continues up the function-call stack. If the exception is never caught, the program halts.

Listing 26.3 is a short program that demonstrates this concept. The program throws the exception from the AllocateBuffer() function but catches the exception in main(), which is the function from which AllocateBuffer() is called.

Part
VI

Ch
26

Listing 26.3 EXCEPTION3.CPP—Catching Exceptions Outside the Throwing Function

```
#include <iostream.h>

class MyException
{
protected:
    char* m_msg;

public:
    MyException(char *msg) { m_msg = msg;}
    ~MyException(){}
    char* GetError() {return m_msg;}
};
```

continues

Listing 26.3   Continued

```cpp
class BigObject
{
private:
    int* intarray;
public:
    BigObject() {intarray = new int[1000];}
    ~BigObject() {delete intarray;}
};

int* AllocateBuffer();

int main()
{
    int* buffer;

    try
    {
        buffer = AllocateBuffer();
        delete buffer;
    }
    catch (MyException* exception)
    {
        char* msg = exception->GetError();
        cout << msg << endl;
    }

    return 0;
}

int* AllocateBuffer()
{
    BigObject bigarray;
    float* floatarray = new float[1000];
    int* buffer = new int[256];

    if (buffer == NULL)
    {
        MyException* exception =
            new MyException("Memory allocation failed!");
        throw exception;
    }

    delete floatarray;
    return buffer;
}
```

When the exception is thrown in `AllocateBuffer()`, the remainder of the function is not executed. The dynamically allocated floatarray will not be deleted. The BigObject that was allocated on the stack will go out of scope, and its destructor will be executed, deleting the intarray member variable that was allocated with new in the constructor. This is an important concept to grasp: Objects created on the stack will be destructed as the stack unwinds. Objects created on the heap will not. Your code must take care of these. For example, `AllocateBuffer()` should include code to delete `floatarray` before throwing the exception, like this:

```
if (buffer == NULL)
    {
        MyException* exception =
            new MyException("Memory allocation failed!");
        delete floatarray;
        throw exception;
    }
```

In many cases, using an object with a carefully written destructor can save significant code duplication when you are using exceptions. If you are using objects allocated on the heap, you may need to catch and rethrow exceptions so that you can delete them. Consider the code in Listing 26.4, in which the exception is thrown right past an intermediate function up to the catching function.

Listing 26.4 EXCEPTION4.CPP—Unwinding the Stack

```cpp
#include <iostream.h>

class MyException
{
protected:
    char* m_msg;

public:
    MyException(char *msg) { m_msg = msg;}
    ~MyException(){}
    char* GetError() {return m_msg;}
};

class BigObject
{
private:
    int* intarray;
public:
    BigObject() {intarray = new int[1000];}
    ~BigObject() {delete intarray;}
};

int* AllocateBuffer();
int* Intermediate();

int main()
{
    int* buffer;

    try
    {
        buffer = Intermediate();
        delete buffer;
```

Part

VI

Ch

26

continues

Listing 26.4   Continued

```
    }
    catch (MyException* exception)
    {
        char* msg = exception->GetError();
        cout << msg << endl;
    }

    return 0;
}

int* Intermediate()
{
    BigObject bigarray;
    float* floatarray = new float[1000];
    int* retval = AllocateBuffer();
    delete floatarray;
    return retval;
}

int* AllocateBuffer()
{
    int* buffer = new int[256];

    if (buffer == NULL)
    {
        MyException* exception =
            new MyException("Memory allocation failed!");
        throw exception;
    }

    return buffer;
}
```

If the exception is thrown, execution of AllocateBuffer() is abandoned immediately. The stack unwinds. Because there is no catch block in Intermediate(), execution of that function will be abandoned after the call to AllocateBuffer(). The delete for floatarray will not happen, but the destructor for bigarray will be executed. Listing 26.5 shows a way around this problem.

Listing 26.5   Rethrowing Exceptions

```
int* Intermediate()
{
    BigObject bigarray;
    float* floatarray = new float[1000];
    int* retval = NULL;
    try
    {
    retval = AllocateBuffer();
    }
    catch (MyException e)
```

```
  {
    delete floatarray;
  throw;
  }
  delete floatarray;
  return retval;
}
```

This revised version of `Intermediate()` catches the exception so that it can delete `floatarray` and throw it farther up to the calling function. (Notice that the name of the exception is not in this `throw` statement; it can throw only the exception it just caught.) There are a few things you should notice about this revised code:

- The line that deletes `floatarray` has been duplicated.

- The declaration of `retval` has had to move out of the `try` block so that it will still be in scope after the `try` block.

- `retval` has been initialized to a default value.

This is really starting to get ugly. Through this entire process, the `BigObject` called `bigarray` has been quietly handled properly and easily, with an automatic call to the destructor no matter which function allocated it or where the exception was called. When you write code that uses exceptions, wrapping all your heap-allocated objects in classes such as `BigObject` makes your life easier. `BigObject` uses a *managed pointer*: When a `BigObject` object such as `bigarray` goes out of scope, the memory it pointed to is deleted. A very flexible approach to managed pointers is described at the end of the section on templates in this chapter.

Handling Multiple Types of Exceptions

Often, a block of code generates more than one type of exception, so you may want to use multiple `catch` blocks with a `try` block. You might, for example, need to be on the lookout for both `CException` and `char*` exceptions. Because a `catch` block must receive a specific type of exception object, you need two different `catch` blocks to watch for both `CException` and `char*` exception objects. You can also set up a `catch` block to catch whatever type of exception hasn't been caught yet, by placing ellipses (…) in the parentheses, rather than a specific argument. The problem with this sort of multipurpose `catch` block is that you have no access to the exception object received and so must handle the exception in a general way.

Listing 26.6 is a program that generates three different types of exceptions based on a user's input. (In a real program, you shouldn't use exceptions to deal with user errors. It's a slow mechanism, and checking what the user typed can usually be handled more efficiently in another way.)

Running the program, you're instructed to enter a value between 4 and 8, except for 6. If you enter a value less than 4, the program throws a `MyException` exception; if you enter a value greater than 8, the program throws a `char*` exception; and, finally, if you happen to enter 6, the program throws the entered value as an exception.

Although the program throws the exceptions in the `GetValue()` function, the program catches them all in `main()`. The `try` block in `main()` is associated with three `catch` blocks. The first catches the `MyException` object, the second catches the `char*` object, and the third catches any other exception that happens to come down the pike.

> **N O T E** Similar to `if...else` statements, the order in which you place `catch` program blocks can have a profound effect on program execution. You should always place the most specific `catch` blocks first. For example, in Listing 26.6, if the `catch(...)` block were first, none of the other `catch` blocks would ever be called. This is because the `catch(...)` is as general as you can get, catching every single exception that the program throws. In this case (as in most cases), you want to use `catch(...)` to receive only the leftover exceptions. ■

Listing 26.6 EXCEPTION6.CPP—Using Multiple *catch* Blocks

```cpp
#include <iostream.h>

class MyException
{
protected:
    char* m_msg;

public:
    MyException(char *msg) { m_msg = msg;}
    ~MyException(){}
    char* GetError() {return m_msg;}
};

int GetValue();


int main()
{
    try
    {
        int value = GetValue();
        cout << "The value you entered is okay." << endl;
    }
    catch(MyException* exception)
    {
        char* msg = exception->GetError();
        cout << msg << endl;
    }
    catch(char* msg)
    {
        cout << msg << endl;
    }
    catch(...)
    {
        cout << "Caught unknown exception!" << endl;
    }
```

```
    return 0;
}

int GetValue(){
    int value;

    cout << "Type a number from 4 to 8 (except 6):" << endl;
    cin >> value;

    if (value < 4)
    {
        MyException* exception =
            new MyException("Value less than 4!");
        throw exception;
    }
    else if (value > 8)
    {
        throw "Value greater than 8!";
    }
    else if (value == 6)
    {
        throw value;
    }
    return value;
}
```

The Old Exception Mechanism

Before try, catch, and throw were added to Visual C++, there was a rudimentary form of exception handling available to both C and C++ programmers through macros called TRY, CATCH, and THROW. These macros are a little slower than the standard exception mechanisms and can throw only exceptions that are objects of a class derived from CException. Don't use these in your programs. If you have an existing program that uses them, you may want to convert to the new mechanism. There's a helpful article on this topic in the Visual C++ documentation: search for TRY and you'll find it.

Part
VI

Ch
26

Exploring Templates

It's a good guess that, at one time or another, you wished you could develop a single function or class that could handle any kind of data. Sure, you can use function overloading to write several versions of a function, or you can use inheritance to derive several different classes from a base class. But, in these cases, you still end up writing many different functions or classes. If only there were a way to make functions and classes a little smarter so that you could write just one function that handled any kind of data you wanted to throw at it. There is a way to accomplish this seemingly impossible task. You need to use something called *templates,* the focus of this section.

Introducing Templates

A *template* is a kind of blueprint for a function or class. You write the template in a general way, supplying placeholders, called *parameters*, for the data objects that the final function or class will manipulate. A template always begins with the keyword `template` followed by a list of parameters between angle brackets, like this:

```
template<class Type>
```

You can have as many parameters as you need, and you can name them whatever you like, but each must begin with the `class` keyword and must be separated by commas, like this:

```
template<class Type1, class Type2, class Type3>
```

As you may have guessed from previous discussion, there are two types of templates: function and class. The following sections describe how to create and use both types of templates.

Creating Function Templates

A function template starts with the `template` line you just learned about, followed by the function's declaration, as shown in Listing 26.7. The `template` line specifies the types of arguments that will be used when calling the function, whereas the function's declaration specifies how those arguments are to be received as parameters by the function. Every parameter specified in the `template` line must be used by the function declaration. Notice the `Type1` immediately before the function name. `Type1` is a placeholder for the function's return type, which will vary, depending on how the template is used.

Listing 26.7   The Basic Form of a Function Template

```
template<class Type1, class Type2>
Type1 MyFunction(Type1 data1, Type1 data2, Type2 data3)
{
    // Place the body of the function here.
}
```

An actual working example will help you understand how function templates become functions. A common example is a `Min()` function that can accept any type of arguments. Listing 26.8 is a short program that defines a template for a `Min()` function and then uses that function in `main()`. When you run the program, the program displays the smallest value of whatever data is sent as arguments to `Min()`. This is possible because the compiler takes the template and creates functions for each of the data types that are compared in the program.

Listing 26.8   TEMPLATE1.CPP—Using a Typical Function Template

```
#include <iostream.h>

template<class Type>
Type Min(Type arg1, Type arg2)
{
```

```
    Type min;

    if (arg1 < arg2)
        min = arg1;
    else
        min = arg2;

    return min;
}

int main()
{
    cout << Min(15, 25) << endl;
    cout << Min(254.78, 12.983) << endl;
    cout << Min('A', 'Z') << endl;

    return 0;
}
```

N O T E Notice how, in Listing 26.8, the Min() template uses the data type Type not only in its parameter list and function argument list but also in the body of the function in order to declare a local variable. This illustrates how you can use the parameter types just as you would use any specific data type such as int or char. ■

Because function templates are so flexible, they often lead to trouble. For example, in the Min() template, you have to be sure that the data types you supply as parameters can be compared. If you tried to compare two classes, your program would not compile unless the classes overloaded the < and > operators.

Another way you can run into trouble is when the arguments you supply to the template are not used as you think. For example, what about adding the following line to main() in Listing 26.6?

```
cout << Min("APPLE", "ORANGE") << endl;
```

If you don't think about what you're doing in the previous line, you may jump to the conclusion that the returned result will be APPLE. The truth is that the preceding line may or may not give you the result you expect. Why? Because the "APPLE" and "ORANGE" string constants result in pointers to char. This means that the program will compile smoothly, with the compiler creating a version of Min() that compares char pointers. But there's a big difference between comparing two pointers and comparing the data to which the pointers point. If "ORANGE" happens to be stored at a lower address than "APPLE", the preceding call to Min() results in "ORANGE".

A way to avoid this problem is to provide a specific replacement function for Min() that defines exactly how you want the two string constants compared. When you provide a specific function, the compiler uses that function rather than create one from the template. Listing 26.9 is a short program that demonstrates this important technique. When the program needs to compare the two strings, it doesn't call a function created from the template but instead uses the specific replacement function.

Listing 26.9   TEMPLATE2.CPP—Using a Specific Replacement Function

```cpp
#include <iostream.h>
#include <string.h>

template<class Type>
Type Min(Type arg1, Type arg2)
{
    Type min;

    if (arg1 < arg2)
        min = arg1;
    else
        min = arg2;

    return min;
}

char* Min(char* arg1, char* arg2)
{
    char* min;

    int result = strcmp(arg1, arg2);

    if (result < 0)
        min = arg1;
    else
        min = arg2;

    return min;
}

int main()
{
    cout << Min(15, 25) << endl;
    cout << Min(254.78, 12.983) << endl;
    cout << Min('A', 'Z') << endl;
    cout << Min("APPLE", "ORANGE") << endl;

    return 0;
}
```

Creating Class Templates

Just as you can create abstract functions with function templates, so too can you create abstract classes with class templates. A class template represents a class, which in turn represents an object. When you define a class template, the compiler takes the template and creates a class. You then declare (instantiate) objects of the class. As you can see, class templates add another layer of abstraction to the concept of classes.

You define a class template much as you define a function template—by supplying the template line followed by the class's declaration, as shown in Listing 26.10. Notice that, just as with a function template, you use the abstract data types given as parameters in the `template` line in the class's body. They might be the types for member variables, return types, and other data objects.

Listing 26.10 Defining a Class Template

```
template<class Type>
class CMyClass
{
protected:
    Type data;

public:
    CMyClass(Type arg) { data = arg; }
    ~CMyClass() {};
};
```

When ready to instantiate objects from the template class, you must supply the data type that will replace the template parameters. For example, to create an object of the `CMyClass` class, you might use a line like this:

```
CMyClass<int> myClass(15);
```

The preceding line creates a `CMyClass` object that uses integers in place of the abstract data type. If you wanted the class to deal with floating-point values, you'd create an object of the class something like this:

```
CMyClass<float> myClass(15.75);
```

For a more complete example, suppose you want to create a class that stores two values and has member functions that compare those values. Listing 26.11 is a program that does just that. First, the listing defines a class template called `CCompare`. This class stores two values that are supplied to the constructor. The class also includes the usual constructor and destructor, as well as member functions for determining the larger or smaller of the values, or whether the values are equal.

Part
VI

Ch
26

Listing 26.11 TEMPLATE3.CPP—Using a Class Template

```
#include <iostream.h>

template<class Type>
class CCompare
{
protected:
    Type arg1;
    Type arg2;

public:
    CCompare(Type arg1, Type arg2)
    {
```

continues

Listing 26.11   Continued

```
            CCompare::arg1 = arg1;
            CCompare::arg2 = arg2;
        }

        ~CCompare() {}

        Type GetMin()
        {
            Type min;

            if (arg1 < arg2)
                min = arg1;
            else
                min = arg2;

            return min;
        }

        Type GetMax()
        {
            Type max;

            if (arg1 > arg2)
                max = arg1;
            else
                max = arg2;

            return max;
        }

        int Equal()
        {
            int equal;

            if (arg1 == arg2)
                equal = 1;
            else
                equal = 0;

            return equal;
        }
};

int main()
{
    CCompare<int> compare1(15, 25);
    CCompare<double> compare2(254.78, 12.983);
    CCompare<char> compare3('A', 'Z');

    cout << "THE COMPARE1 OBJECT" << endl;
    cout << "Lowest: " << compare1.GetMin() << endl;
    cout << "Highest: " << compare1.GetMax() << endl;
    cout << "Equal: " << compare1.Equal() << endl;
    cout << endl;
```

```
    cout << "THE COMPARE2 OBJECT" << endl;
    cout << "Lowest: " << compare2.GetMin() << endl;
    cout << "Highest: " << compare2.GetMax() << endl;
    cout << "Equal: " << compare2.Equal() << endl;
    cout << endl;

    cout << "THE COMPARE2 OBJECT" << endl;
    cout << "Lowest: " << compare3.GetMin() << endl;
    cout << "Highest: " << compare3.GetMax() << endl;
    cout << "Equal: " << compare3.Equal() << endl;
    cout << endl;

    return 0;
}
```

The main program instantiates three objects from the class template: one that deals with integers, one that uses floating-point values, and one that stores and compares character values. After creating the three CCompare objects, main() calls the objects' member functions in order to display information about the data stored in each object. Figure 26.1 shows the program's output.

FIG. 26.1

The template3 program creates three different objects from a class template.

You can pass as many parameters as you like to a class template, just like a function template. Listing 26.12 shows a class template that uses two different types of data.

Listing 26.12 Using Multiple Parameters with a Class Template

```
template<class Type1, class Type2>
class CMyClass
{
protected:
    Type1 data1;
    Type2 data2;
```

continues

Part
VI

Ch
26

Listing 26.12 Continued

```
public:
    CMyClass(Type1 arg1, Type2 arg2)
    {
        data1 = arg1;
        data2 = arg2;
    }

    ~CMyClass() {}
};
```

To instantiate an object of the CMyClass class, you might use a line like this:

```
CMyClass<int, char> myClass(15, 'A');
```

Finally, you can use specific data types, as well as the placeholder data types, as parameters in a class template. Just add the specific data type to the parameter list, as you add any other parameter. Listing 26.13 is a short program that creates an object from a class template, using two abstract parameters and one specific data type.

Listing 26.13 Using Specific Data Types as Parameters in a Class Template

```
#include <iostream.h>

template<class Type1, class Type2, int num>
class CMyClass
{
protected:
    Type1 data1;
    Type2 data2;
    int data3;

public:
    CMyClass(Type1 arg1, Type2 arg2, int num)
    {
        data1 = arg1;
        data2 = arg2;
        data3 = num;
    }

    ~CMyClass() {}
};

int main()
{
    CMyClass<int, char, 0> myClass(15, 'A', 10);

    return 0;
}
```

The Standard Template Library

Before running off to write templates that implement linked lists, binary trees, sorting, and other common tasks, you might like to know that somebody else already has. Visual C++ incorporates the Standard Template Library (STL), which includes hundreds of function and class templates to tackle common tasks. Would you like a stack of ints or a stack of floats? Don't write lots of different stack classes. Don't even write one stack class template. Simply use the stack template included in the STL. This applies to almost every common data structure.

Managed Pointer Templates: *auto_ptr*

Earlier in this chapter you saw applications that use exceptions and allocate memory on the heap (dynamic allocation with new) can run into trouble when exceptions are thrown. If the delete statement for that memory gets bypassed, the memory will leak. If there were an object on the stack whose destructor called delete for the memory, you would prevent this problem. STL implements a managed pointer called auto_ptr. Here's the declaration:

```
template<class T>
    class auto_ptr {
public:
    typedef T element_type;
    explicit auto_ptr(T *p = 0) ;
    auto_ptr(const auto_ptr<T>& rhs) ;
    auto_ptr<T>& operator=(auto_ptr<T>& rhs);
    ~auto_ptr();
    T& operator*() const ;
    T *operator->() const;
    T *get() const ;
    T *release() const;
    };
```

After you create a pointer to an int, float, Employee, or any other type of object, you can make an auto_ptr and use that like a pointer. For example, imagine a code fragment like this:

```
// ...
    Employee* emp = new Employee(stuff);
    emp->ProcessEmployee;
    delete emp;
// ...
```

When you realize that ProcessEmployee() might throw an EmployeeException, you can change this code to read like this:

```
// ...
    Employee* emp = new Employee(stuff);
    try
    {
        emp->ProcessEmployee;
    }
    catch (EmployeeException e)
    {
```

```
        delete emp;
        throw;
    }
    delete emp;
// ...
```

But you think this is ugly and hard to maintain, so you go with an `auto_ptr` instead:

```
#include <memory>
// ...
    auto_ptr<Employee> emp (new Employee(stuff));
    emp->ProcessEmployee;
// ...
```

This looks like the first example, but it works like the second: Whether you leave this code snippet normally or because of an exception, `emp` will go out of scope, and when it does, the Employee object that was allocated on the heap will be deleted for you automatically. No extra `try` or `catch` blocks, and as an extra bonus you don't even have to remember to delete the memory in the routine—it's done for you.

Look again at the functions declared in the template: a constructor, a copy constructor, an address-of (&) operator, a destructor, a contents of (*) operator, a dereferencing (->) operator, and functions called `get()` and `release()`. These work together to ensure that you can treat your pointer exactly as though it were an ordinary pointer.

Other Useful STL Templates

STL is especially useful to ATL programmers, who may not be using MFC. Why drag in all of MFC because you want to do a little string manipulation or manage a lookup table or linked list? Use the STL versions of these common data structures instead. The full details are in the online documentation, but be sure to look for these classes or functions:

- ▓ `deque`
- ▓ `list`
- ▓ `map`
- ▓ `multimap`
- ▓ `set`
- ▓ `multiset`
- ▓ `vector`
- ▓ `basic_string`
- ▓ `stack`
- ▓ `swap`
- ▓ `min, max`

There are many more, but these will give you an idea of the amount of work you can save with templates, especially with templates you don't have to write.

Understanding Namespaces

A *namespace* defines a scope in which duplicate identifiers cannot be used. For example, you already know that you can have a global variable named `value` and then also define a function with a local variable called `value`. Because the two variables are in different namespaces, your program knows that it should use the local `value` when inside the function and the global `value` everywhere else.

Namespaces, however, do not extend far enough to cover some very thorny problems. One example is duplicate names in external classes or libraries. This issue crops up when a programmer is using several external files within a single project. None of the external variables and functions can have the same name as other external variables or functions. To avoid this type of problem, third-party vendors frequently add prefixes or suffixes to variable and function names in order to reduce the likeliness of some other vendor using the same name.

Obviously, the C++ gurus have come up with a solution to such scope-resolution problems. The solution is user-defined namespaces.

Defining a Namespace

In its simplest form, a namespace is not unlike a structure or a class. You start the namespace definition with the `namespace` keyword, followed by the namespace's name and the declaration of the identifiers that will be valid within the scope of that namespace.

Listing 26.16 shows a namespace definition. The namespace is called A and includes two identifiers, i and j, and a function, `Func()`. Notice that the `Func()` function is completely defined within the namespace definition. You can also choose to define the function outside the namespace definition. In that case, you must preface the function definition's name with the namespace's name, much as you would preface a class's member-function definition with the class's name. Listing 26.17 shows this form of namespace function definition.

Part
VI

Ch
26

Listing 26.16   Defining a Namespace

```
namespace A
{
    int i;
    int j;

    int Func()
    {
        return 1;
    }
}
```

Listing 26.17   Defining a Function Outside the Namespace Definition

```
namespace A
{
    int i;
    int j;

    int Func();
}

int A::Func()
{
    return 1;
}
```

N O T E   Namespaces must be defined at the file level of scope or within another namespace definition. They cannot be defined, for example, inside a function. ■

Namespace Scope Resolution

Namespaces add a new layer of scope to your programs, but this means that you need some way of identifying that scope. The identification is, of course, the namespace's name, which you must use in your programs to resolve references to identifiers. For example, to refer to the variable i in namespace A, you'd write something like this:

```
A::i = 0;
```

You can nest one namespace definition within another, as shown in Listing 26.18. In that case, however, you have to use more complicated scope resolutions in order to differentiate between the i variable declared in A and B, like this:

```
A::i = 0;
A::B::i = 0;
```

Listing 26.18   Nesting Namespace Definitions

```
namespace A
{
    int i;
    int j;

    int Func()
    {
        return 1;
    }

    namespace B
    {
        int i;
    }
}
```

If you're going to frequently reference variables and functions within namespace A, you can avoid using the A:: resolution by preceding the program statements with a using line, as shown in Listing 26.19. This is very common in programs that use STL templates, most of which are in the std namespace.

Listing 26.19 Resolving Scope with the *using* Keyword

```
using namespace A;
i = 0;
j = 0;
int num1 = Func();
```

Unnamed Namespaces

To thoroughly confuse you, Visual C++ allows you to have unnamed namespaces. You define an unnamed namespace exactly as you would any other namespace, without attaching a name. Listing 26.20 shows the definition of an unnamed namespace. It lets you arrange variables whose names are valid only within one namespace and cannot be accessed from elsewhere because no other code can know the name of the unnamed namespace.

Listing 26.20 Defining an Unnamed Namespace

```
namespace
{
    int i;
    int j;

    int Func()
    {
        return 1;
    }
}
```

Part
VI

Ch
26

Refer to the identifiers in the unnamed namespace without any sort of extra scope resolution, like this:

```
i = 0;
j = 0;
int num1 = Func();
```

Namespace Aliases

Often you run into namespaces that have long names. In these cases, having to use the long name over and over in your program in order to access the identifiers defined in the namespace can be a major chore. To solve this problem, Visual C++ enables you to create *namespace aliases*, which are just replacement names for a namespace. You create an alias like this:

```
namespace A = LongName;
```

LongName is the original name of the namespace, and A is the alias. After the preceding line executes, you can access the LongName namespace, using either A or LongName. You can think of an alias as a nickname or short form. Listing 26.21 is a short program that demonstrates namespace aliases.

Listing 26.21 Using a Namespace Alias

```
namespace ThisIsANamespaceName
{
    int i;
    int j;

    int Func()
    {
        return 2;
    }
}

int main()
{
    namespace ns = ThisIsANamespaceName;

    ns::i = 0;
    ns::j = 0;
    int num1 = ns::Func();

    return 0;
}
```

CHAPTER 27

Multitasking with Windows Threads

When using Windows 95 (and other modern operating systems), you know that you can run several programs simultaneously. This capability is called *multitasking*. What you may not know is that many of today's operating systems also enable *threads,* which are separate processes that are not complete applications. A thread is a lot like a subprogram. An application can create several threads—several different flows of execution—and run them concurrently. Threads give you the ability to have multitasking inside multitasking. The user knows that he can run several applications at a time. The programmer knows that each application can run several threads at a time. In this chapter, you'll learn how to create and manage threads in your applications.

Understanding Simple Threads

A thread is a path of execution through a program. In a multithreaded program, each thread has its own stack and operates independently of other threads running within the same program. MFC distinguishes between *UI threads*, which have a message pump and typically perform user interface tasks, and *worker threads*, which do not.

> **N O T E** Any application always has at least one thread, which is the program's primary or main thread. You can start and stop as many additional threads as you need, but the main thread keeps running as long as the application is active. ▪

A thread is the smallest unit of execution, much smaller than a *process*. Generally each running application on your system is a process. If you start the same application (for example, Notepad) twice, there will be two processes, one for each instance. It is possible for several instances of an application to share a single process: for example, if you choose File, New Window in Internet Explorer, there are two applications on your taskbar, and they share a process. The unfortunate consequence is that if one instance crashes, they all do.

To create a worker thread using MFC, all you have to do is write a function that you want to run parallel with the rest of your application. Then call AfxBeginThread() to start a thread that will execute your function. The thread remains active as long as the thread's function is executing: When the thread function exits, the thread is destroyed. A simple call to AfxBeginThread() looks like this:

```
AfxBeginThread(ProcName, param, priority);
```

In the preceding line, ProcName is the name of the thread's function, param is any 32-bit value you want to pass to the thread, and priority is the thread's priority, which is represented by a number of predefined constants. Table 27.1 shows those constants and their descriptions.

Table 27.1 Thread Priority Constants

Constant	Description
THREAD_PRIORITY_ABOVE_NORMAL	Sets a priority one point higher than normal.
THREAD_PRIORITY_BELOW_NORMAL	Sets a priority one point lower than normal.
THREAD_PRIORITY_HIGHEST	Sets a priority two points above normal.
THREAD_PRIORITY_IDLE	Sets a base priority of 1. For a REALTIME_PRIORITY_CLASS process, this sets a priority of 16.
THREAD_PRIORITY_LOWEST	Sets a priority two points below normal.
THREAD_PRIORITY_NORMAL	Sets normal priority.
THREAD_PRIORITY_TIME_CRITICAL	Sets a base priority of 15. For a REALTIME_PRIORITY_CLASS process, this sets a priority of 30.

N O T E A thread's priority determines how often the thread takes control of the system, relative to the other running threads. Generally, the higher the priority, the more running time the thread gets, which is why the value of THREAD_PRIORITY_TIME_CRITICAL is so high. ▪

To see a simple thread in action, build the Thread application as detailed in the following steps.

1. Start a new AppWizard project workspace called **Thread**, as shown in Figure 27.1.

FIG. 27.1

Start an AppWizard project workspace called **Thread**.

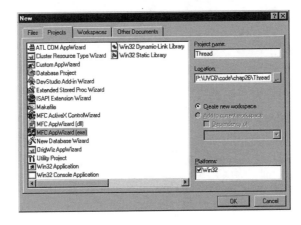

2. Give the new project the following settings in the AppWizard dialog boxes. The New Project Information dialog box will then look like Figure 27.2.

Step 1: Single document

Step 2: Default settings

Step 3: Default settings

Step 4: Turn off all options

Step 5: Default settings

Step 6: Default settings

FIG. 27.2

These are the AppWizard settings for the Thread project.

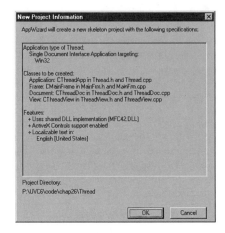

3. Use the resource editor to add a Thread menu to the application's IDR_MAINFRAME menu. Give the menu one command called **Start Thread** with a command ID of **ID_STARTTHREAD**, and enter a sensible prompt and ToolTip, as shown in Figure 27.3.

FIG. 27.3

Add a Thread menu with a Start Thread command.

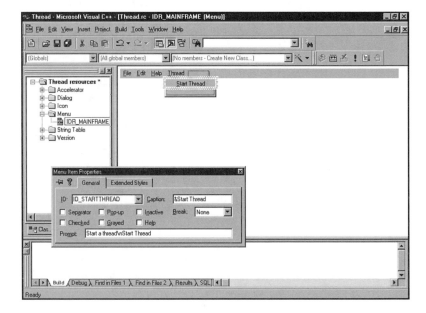

4. Use ClassWizard to associate the ID_STARTTHREAD command with the OnStartthread() message-response function, as shown in Figure 27.4. Make sure that you have **CThreadView** selected in the Class Name box before you add the function.

FIG. 27.4

Add the OnStartthread() message-response function to the view class.

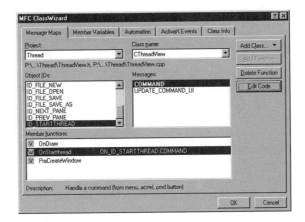

5. Click the Edit Code button and then add the following lines to the new OnStartthread() function, replacing the TODO: Add your command handler code here comment:

```
HWND hWnd = GetSafeHwnd();
AfxBeginThread(ThreadProc, hWnd, THREAD_PRIORITY_NORMAL);
```

This code will call a function called ThreadProc within a worker thread of its own. Next, add ThreadProc, shown in Listing 27.1, to ThreadView.cpp, placing it right before the OnStartthread() function. Note that ThreadProc() is a global function and not a member function of the CThreadView class, even though it is in the view class's implementation file.

Listing 27.1   ThreadView.cpp—*ThreadProc()*

```
UINT ThreadProc(LPVOID param)
{
    ::MessageBox((HWND)param, "Thread activated.", "Thread", MB_OK);

    return 0;
}
```

Part
VI

Ch
27

This threaded function doesn't do much, just reports that it was started. The SDK function MessageBox() is very much like AfxMessageBox(), but because this isn't a member function of a class derived from CWnd, you can't use AfxMessageBox().

TIP The double colons in front of a function name indicate a call to a global function, instead of an MFC class member function. For Windows programmers, this usually means an API or SDK call. For example, inside an MFC window class, you can call `MessageBox("Hi, There!")` to display *Hi, There!* to the user. This form of `MessageBox()` is a member function of the MFC window classes. To call the original Windows version, you write something like `::MessageBox(0, "Hi, There!", "Message", MB_OK)`. Notice the colons in front of the function name and the additional arguments.

When you run the Thread program, the main window appears. Select the Thread, Start Thread command, and the system starts the thread represented by the `ThreadProc()` function and displays a message box, as shown in Figure 27.5.

FIG. 27.5

The simple secondary thread in the Thread program displays a message box and then ends.

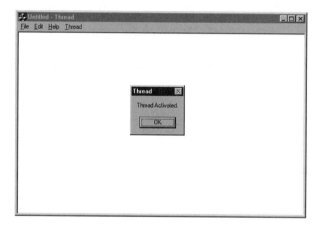

Understanding Thread Communication

Usually, a secondary thread performs some sort of task for the main program, which implies that there needs to be a channel of communication between the program (which is also a thread) and its secondary threads. There are several ways to accomplish these communications tasks: with global variables, event objects, and messages. In this section, you'll explore these thread-communication techniques.

Communicating with Global Variables

Suppose you want your main program to be able to stop the thread. You need a way, then, to tell the thread when to stop. One method is to set up a global variable and then have the thread monitor the global variable for a value that signals the thread to end. Because the threads share the same address space, they have the same global variables. To see how this technique works, modify the Thread application as follows:

1. Use the resource editor to add a **Stop Thread** command to the application's Thread menu. Give this new command the **ID_STOPTHREAD** ID, as shown in Figure 27.6.

FIG. 27.6

Add a Stop Thread command to the Thread menu.

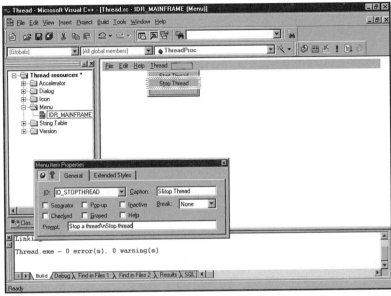

2. Use ClassWizard to associate the ID_STOPTHREAD command with the OnStopthread() message-response function, as shown in Figure 27.7. Make sure that you have **CThreadView** selected in the Class Name box before you add the function. Add the following line to the OnStopthread() function, replacing the TODO: Add your command handler code here comment:

```
threadController = 0;
```

FIG. 27.7

Add the OnStopthread() message-response function.

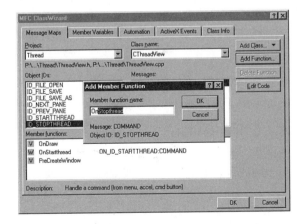

This refers to a new global variable you are about to declare.

3. Add the following line to the top of the ThreadView.cpp file, right after the endif directive:

```
volatile int threadController;
```

The `volatile` keyword means that you expect this variable will be changed from outside a thread that uses it. The keyword requests that the compiler not cache the variable in a register or in any way count on the value staying unchanged just because code in one thread doesn't seem to change it.

4. Add the following line to the `OnStartthread()` function, before the two lines you added earlier:

   ```
   threadController = 1;
   ```

   By now, perhaps, you've guessed that the value of `threadController` determines whether the thread will continue. Replace the `ThreadProc()` function with the one shown in Listing 27.2.

Listing 27.2   The New *ThreadProc()* Function

```
UINT ThreadProc(LPVOID param)
{
    ::MessageBox((HWND)param, "Thread activated.", "Thread", MB_OK);

    while (threadController == 1)
    {
        ;
    }

    ::MessageBox((HWND)param, "Thread stopped.", "Thread", MB_OK);

    return 0;
}
```

Now the thread first displays a message box, telling the user that the thread is starting. Then a `while` loop continues to check the `threadController` global variable, waiting for its value to change to `0`. Although this `while` loop is trivial, it is here that you would place the code that performs whatever task you want the thread to perform, making sure not to tie things up for too long before rechecking the value of `threadController`.

Try a test: Build and run the program, and choose Thread, Start Thread to start the secondary thread. When you do, a message box appears, telling you that the new thread was started. To stop the thread, select the Thread, Stop Thread command. Again, a message box appears, this time telling you that the thread is stopping.

> **CAUTION**
>
> Using global variables to communicate between threads is, to say the least, an unsophisticated approach to thread communication and can be a dangerous technique if you're not sure how C++ handles variables from an assembly-language level. Other thread-communication techniques are safer and more elegant.

Communicating with User-Defined Messages

Now you have a simple, albeit unsophisticated, method for communicating information from your main program to your thread. How about the reverse? That is, how can your thread communicate with the main program? The easiest method to accomplish this communication is to incorporate user-defined Windows messages into the program.

The first step is to define a user message, which you can do easily, like this:

```
const WM_USERMSG = WM_USER + 100;
```

The `WM_USER` constant, defined by Windows, holds the first available user-message number. Because other parts of your program may use some user messages for their own purposes, the preceding line sets `WM_USERMSG` to `WM_USER+100`.

After defining the message, you call `::PostMessage()` from the thread to send the message to the main program whenever you need to. (Message handling was discussed in Chapter 3, "Messages and Commands." Sending your own messages allows you to take advantage of the message-handling facility built into MFC.) A typical call to `::PostMessage()` might look like this:

```
::PostMessage((HWND)param, WM_USERMSG, 0, 0);
```

`PostMessage()`'s four arguments are the handle of the window to which the message should be sent, the message identifier, and the message's `WPARAM` and `LPARAM` parameters.

Modify the Thread application according to the next steps to see how to implement posting user messages from a thread.

1. Add the following line to the top of the ThreadView.h header file, right before the beginning of the class declaration:

   ```
   const WM_THREADENDED = WM_USER + 100;
   ```

2. Still in the header file, add the following line to the message map, right after the `//{{AFX_MSG(CThreadView)` comment and before `DECLARE_MESSAGE_MAP`:

   ```
   afx_msg LONG OnThreadended(WPARAM wParam, LPARAM lParam);
   ```

3. Switch to the ThreadView.cpp file and add the following line to the class's message map, making sure to place it right *after* the `}}AFX_MSG_MAP` comment:

   ```
   ON_MESSAGE(WM_THREADENDED, OnThreadended)
   ```

4. Replace the `ThreadProc()` function with the one shown in Listing 27.3.

Part
VI

Ch
27

Listing 27.3   The Message-Posting *ThreadProc()*

```
UINT ThreadProc(LPVOID param)
{
    ::MessageBox((HWND)param, "Thread activated.", "Thread", MB_OK);

    while (threadController == 1)
    {
```

continues

Listing 27.3   Continued

```
        ;
    }

    ::PostMessage((HWND)param, WM_THREADENDED, 0, 0);

    return 0;
}
```

---

5. Add the function shown in Listing 27.4 to the end of the ThreadView.cpp file.

Listing 27.4   *CThreadView::OnThreadended()*

```
LONG CThreadView::OnThreadended(WPARAM wParam, LPARAM lParam)
{
    AfxMessageBox("Thread ended.");
    return 0;
}
```

When you run the new version of the Thread program, select the Thread, Start Thread command to start the thread. When you do, a message box appears, telling you that the thread has started. To end the thread, select the Thread, Stop Thread command. Just as with the previous version of the program, a message box appears, telling you that the thread has ended.

Although this version of the Thread application seems to run identically to the previous version, there's a subtle difference. Now the program displays the message box that signals the end of the thread in the main program rather than from inside the thread. The program can do this because, when the user selects the Stop Thread command, the thread sends a WM_THREADENDED message to the main program. When the program receives that message, it displays the final message box.

Communicating with Event Objects

A slightly more sophisticated method of signaling between threads is to use *event objects,* which under MFC are represented by the CEvent class. An event object can be in one of two states: signaled and nonsignaled. Threads can watch for events to be signaled and so perform their operations at the appropriate time. Creating an event object is as easy as declaring a global variable, like this:

```
CEvent threadStart;
```

Although the CEvent constructor has a number of optional arguments, you can usually get away with creating the default object, as shown in the previous line of code. On creation, the event object is automatically in its nonsignaled state. To signal the event, you call the event object's SetEvent() member function, like this:

```
threadStart.SetEvent();
```

After the preceding line executes, the `threadStart` event object will be in its signaled state. Your thread should be watching for this signal so that the thread knows it's okay to get to work. How does a thread watch for a signal? By calling the Windows API function, `WaitForSingleObject()`:

```
::WaitForSingleObject(threadStart.m_hObject, INFINITE);
```

This function's two arguments are

■ The handle of the event for which to check (stored in the event object's `m_hObject` data member)

■ The length of time the function should wait for the event

The predefined `INFINITE` constant tells `WaitForSingleObject()` not to return until the specified event is signaled. In other words, if you place the preceding line at the beginning of your thread, the system suspends the thread until the event is signaled. Even though you've started the thread execution, it's halted until whatever you need to happen happens. When your program is ready for the thread to perform its duty, you call the `SetEvent()` function, as previously described.

When the thread is no longer suspended, it can go about its business. However, if you want to signal the end of the thread from the main program, the thread must watch for this next event to be signaled. The thread can do this by polling for the event. To poll for the event, you again call `WaitForSingleObject()`, only this time you give the function a wait time of `0`, like this:

```
::WaitForSingleObject(threadEnd.m_hObject, 0);
```

In this case, if `WaitForSingleObject()` returns `WAIT_OBJECT_0`, the event has been signaled. Otherwise, the event is still in its nonsignaled state.

To better see how event objects work, follow these steps to further modify the Thread application:

1. Add the following line to the top of the ThreadView.cpp file, right after the line `#include "ThreadView.h"`:

   ```
   #include "afxmt.h"
   ```

2. Add the following lines near the top of the ThreadView.cpp file, after the `volatile int threadController` line that you placed there previously:

   ```
   CEvent threadStart;
   CEvent threadEnd;
   ```

3. Delete the `volatile int threadController` line from the file.

4. Replace the `ThreadProc()` function with the one shown in Listing 27.5.

Listing 27.5   Yet Another *ThreadProc()*

```
UINT ThreadProc(LPVOID param)
{
    ::WaitForSingleObject(threadStart.m_hObject, INFINITE);
    ::MessageBox((HWND)param, "Thread activated.",
        "Thread", MB_OK);

    BOOL keepRunning = TRUE;
    while (keepRunning)
    {
        int result =
            ::WaitForSingleObject(threadEnd.m_hObject, 0);
        if (result == WAIT_OBJECT_0)
            keepRunning = FALSE;
    }

    ::PostMessage((HWND)param, WM_THREADENDED, 0, 0);

    return 0;
}
```

5. Replace all the code in the OnStartthread() function with the following line:

   ```
   threadStart.SetEvent();
   ```

6. Replace the code in the OnStopthread() function with the following line:

   ```
   threadEnd.SetEvent();
   ```

7. Use ClassWizard to add an OnCreate() function that handles the WM_CREATE message, as shown in Figure 27.8. Make sure that you have **CThreadView** selected in the Class Name box before you add the function.

FIG. 27.8

Use ClassWizard to add the OnCreate() function.

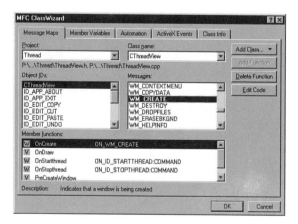

8. Add the following lines to the OnCreate() function, replacing the TODO: Add your specialized creation code here comment:

```
HWND hWnd = GetSafeHwnd();
AfxBeginThread(ThreadProc, hWnd);
```

Again, this new version of the program seems to run just like the preceding version. However, the program is now using both event objects and user-defined Windows messages to communicate between the main program and the thread. No more messing with clunky global variables.

One big difference from previous versions of the program is that the secondary thread is begun in the OnCreate() function, which is called when the application first runs and creates the view. However, because the first line of the thread function is the call to WaitForSingleObject(), the thread immediately suspends execution and waits for the threadStart event to be signaled.

When the threadStart event object is signaled, the thread is free to display the message box and then enter its while loop, where it polls the threadEnd event object. The while loop continues to execute until threadEnd is signaled, at which time the thread sends the WM_THREADENDED message to the main program and exits. Because the thread is started in OnCreate(), after the thread ends, it can't be restarted.

Using Thread Synchronization

Using multiple threads can lead to some interesting problems. For example, how do you prevent two threads from accessing the same data at the same time? What if, for example, one thread is in the middle of trying to update a data set when another thread tries to read that data? The second thread will almost certainly read corrupted data because only some of the data set will have been updated.

Trying to keep threads working together properly is called *thread synchronization*. Event objects, about which you just learned, are a form of thread synchronization. In this section, you'll learn about *critical sections, mutexes,* and *semaphores*—thread synchronization objects that make your thread programming even safer.

Using Critical Sections

Critical sections are an easy way to ensure that only one thread at a time can access a data set. When you use a critical section, you give your threads an object that they have to share. Whichever thread possesses the critical-section object has access to the guarded data. Other threads have to wait until the first thread releases the critical section, after which another thread can grab the critical section to access the data in turn.

Because the guarded data is represented by a single critical-section object and because only one thread can own the critical section at any given time, the guarded data can never be accessed by more than a single thread at a time.

To create a critical-section object in an MFC program, you create an instance of the CCriticalSection class, like this:

```
CCriticalSection criticalSection;
```

Part
VI

Ch
27

Then, when program code is about to access the data that you want to protect, you call the critical-section object's Lock() member function, like this:

```
criticalSection.Lock();
```

If another thread doesn't already own the critical section, Lock() gives the object to the calling thread. That thread can then access the guarded data, after which it calls the critical-section object's Unlock() member function:

```
criticalSection.Unlock();
```

Unlock() releases the ownership of the critical-section object so that another thread can grab it and access the guarded data.

The best way to implement something like critical sections is to build the data you want to protect into a thread-safe class. When you do this, you no longer have to worry about thread synchronization in the main program; the class handles it all for you. As an example, look at Listing 27.6, which is the header file for a thread-safe array class.

Listing 27.6   COUNTARRAY.H—The *CCountArray* Class Header File

```
#include "afxmt.h"

class CCountArray
{
private:
    int array[10];
    CCriticalSection criticalSection;

public:
    CCountArray() {};
    ~CCountArray() {};

    void SetArray(int value);
    void GetArray(int dstArray[10]);
};
```

The header file starts by including the MFC header file, afxmt.h, which gives the program access to the CCriticalSection class. Within the CCountArray class declaration, the file declares a 10-element integer array, which is the data that the critical section will guard, and declares the critical-section object, here called criticalSection. The CCountArray class's public member functions include the usual constructor and destructor, as well as functions for setting and reading the array. These latter two member functions must deal with the critical-section object because these functions access the array.

Listing 27.7 is the CCountArray class's implementation file. Notice that, in each member function, the class takes care of locking and unlocking the critical-section object. This means that any thread can call these member functions without worrying about thread synchronization. For example, if thread 1 calls SetArray(), the first thing SetArray() does is call criticalSection.Lock(), which gives the critical-section object to thread 1. The complete for loop then executes, without any fear of being interrupted by another thread. If thread 2 calls `SetArray()` or `GetArray()`, the call to `criticalSection.Lock()` suspends thread 2 until thread 1 releases the critical-section object, which it does when `SetArray()` finishes the `for` loop and executes the `criticalSection.Unlock()` line. Then the system wakes up thread 2 and gives it the critical-section object. In this way, all threads have to wait politely for their chance to access the guarded data.

Listing 27.7 COUNTARRAY.CPP—The *CCountArray* Class Implementation File

```cpp
#include "stdafx.h"
#include "CountArray.h"

void CCountArray::SetArray(int value)
{
    criticalSection.Lock();

    for (int x=0; x<10; ++x)
        array[x] = value;

    criticalSection.Unlock();
}

void CCountArray::GetArray(int dstArray[10])
{
    criticalSection.Lock();

    for (int x=0; x<10; ++x)
        dstArray[x] = array[x];

    criticalSection.Unlock();
}
```

Now that you've had a chance to see what a thread-safe class looks like, it's time to put the class to work. Perform the following steps, which modify the Thread application to test the `CCountArray` class:

1. Use the File, New command to add a new C++ header file called **CountArray.h** to the project, as shown in Figure 27.9. Enter the code from Listing 27.6.

2. Again choose File, New, and create a new C++ source file called **CountArray.cpp** in this project. Enter the code from Listing 27.7.

3. Switch to ThreadView.cpp and add the following line near the top of the file, after the line `#include "afxmt.h"`, which you placed there previously:
   ```cpp
   #include "CountArray.h"
   ```

4. Add the following line near the top of the file, after the `CEvent threadEnd` line you placed there previously:
   ```cpp
   CCountArray countArray;
   ```

5. Delete the `CEvent threadStart` and `CEvent threadEnd` lines from the file.

FIG. 27.9

Add CountArray.h to the Thread project.

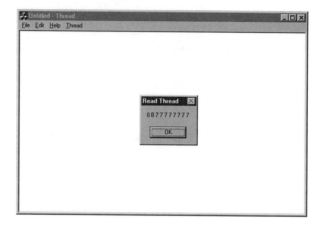

6. Delete the lines ON_MESSAGE(WM_THREADENDED, OnThreadended), ON_COMMAND(ID_STOPTHREAD, OnStopthread), and ON_WM_CREATE() from the message map.

7. Replace the ThreadProc() function with the thread functions shown in Listing 27.8.

Listing 27.8   *WriteThreadProc()* and *ReadThreadProc()*

```
UINT WriteThreadProc(LPVOID param)
{
    for(int x=0; x<10; ++x)
    {
        countArray.SetArray(x);
        ::Sleep(1000);
    }

    return 0;
}

UINT ReadThreadProc(LPVOID param)
{
    int array[10];

    for (int x=0; x<20; ++x)
    {
        countArray.GetArray(array);
        char str[50];
        str[0] = 0;
        for (int i=0; i<10; ++i)
        {
            int len = strlen(str);
            wsprintf(&str[len], "%d ", array[i]);
        }
        ::MessageBox((HWND)param, str, "Read Thread", MB_OK);
    }

    return 0;
}
```

8. Replace all the code in the `OnStartthread()` function with the following lines:

```
HWND hWnd = GetSafeHwnd();
AfxBeginThread(WriteThreadProc, hWnd);
AfxBeginThread(ReadThreadProc, hWnd);
```

9. Delete the `OnStopthread()`, `OnThreadended`, and `OnCreate()` functions from the file.

10. Switch to the ThreadView.h file and delete the line `const WM_THREADENDED = WM_USER + 100` from the listing.

11. Also, in ThreadView.h, delete the lines `afx_msg LONG OnThreadended(WPARAM wParam, LPARAM lParam)`, `afx_msg void OnStopthread()`, and `afx_msg int OnCreate(LPCREATESTRUCT lpCreateStruct)` from the message map.

12. Using the resource editor, remove the Stop Thread command from the Thread menu.

Now build and run the new version of the Thread application. When you do, the main window appears. Select the Thread, Start Thread command to get things hopping. The first thing you'll see is a message box (see Figure 27.10) displaying the current values in the guarded array. Each time you dismiss the message box, it reappears with the array's new contents. The message box will reappear 20 times. The values listed in the message box depend on how often you dismiss the message box. The first thread is writing new values into the array once a second, even as you're viewing the array's contents in the second thread.

FIG. 27.10

This message box displays the current contents of the guarded array.

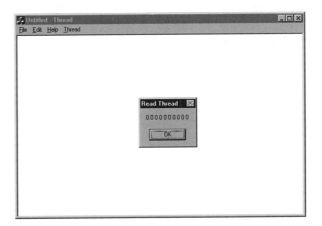

The important thing to notice is that at no time does the second thread interrupt when the first thread is changing the values in the array. You can tell that this is true because the array always contains 10 identical values. If the first thread were interrupted as it modified the array, the 10 values in the array would not be identical, as shown in Figure 27.11.

If you examine the source code carefully, you'll see that the first thread, named `WriteThreadProc()`, is calling the array class's `SetArray()` member function 10 times within a `for` loop. Each time through the loop, `SetArray()` gives the thread the critical-section object, changes the array contents to the passed number, and then takes the critical-section object away again. Note the call to the `Sleep()` function, which suspends the thread for the number of milliseconds given as the function's single argument.

FIG. 27.11

Without thread synchronization, you might see something like this in the message box.

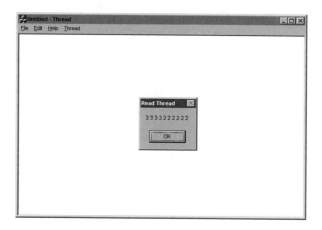

The second thread, named `ReadThreadProc()`, is also trying to access the same critical-section object to construct a display string of the values contained in the array. However, if `WriteThreadProc()` is currently trying to fill the array with new values, `ReadThreadProc()` has to wait. The inverse is also true. That is, `WriteThreadProc()` can't access the guarded data until it can regain ownership of the critical section from `ReadThreadProc()`.

If you really want to prove that the critical-section object is working, remove the `criticalSection.Unlock()` line from the end of the `CCountArray` class's `SetArray()` member function. Then compile and run the program. This time when you start the threads, no message box appears. Why? Because `WriteThreadProc()` takes the critical-section object and never lets it go, which forces the system to suspend `ReadThreadProc()` forever (or at least until you exit the program).

Using Mutexes

Mutexes are a lot like critical sections but a little more complicated because they enable safe sharing of resources, not only between threads in the same application but also between threads of different applications. Although synchronizing threads of different applications is beyond the scope of this chapter, you can get a little experience with mutexes by using them in place of critical sections.

Listing 27.9 is the `CCountArray2` class's header file. Except for the new classname and the mutex object, this header file is identical to the original CountArray.h. Listing 27.10 is the modified class's implementation file. As you can see, the member functions look a lot different when they are using mutexes instead of critical sections, even though both objects provide essentially the same type of services.

Listing 27.9 CCOUNTARRAY2.H—The *CCountArray2* Class Header File

```
#include "afxmt.h"

class CCountArray2
{
private:
    int array[10];
    CMutex mutex;

public:
    CCountArray2() {};
    ~CCountArray2() {};

    void SetArray(int value);
    void GetArray(int dstArray[10]);
};
```

Listing 27.10 COUNTARRAY2.CPP—The *CCountArray2* Class Implementation File

```
#include "stdafx.h"
#include "CountArray2.h"

void CCountArray2::SetArray(int value)
{
    CSingleLock singleLock(&mutex);
    singleLock.Lock();

    for (int x=0; x<10; ++x)
        array[x] = value;
}

void CCountArray2::GetArray(int dstArray[10])
{
    CSingleLock singleLock(&mutex);
    singleLock.Lock();

    for (int x=0; x<10; ++x)
        dstArray[x] = array[x];
}
```

Part
VI

Ch
27

To access a mutex object, you must create a CSingleLock or CMultiLock object, which performs the actual access control. The CCountArray2 class uses CSingleLock objects because this class is dealing with only a single mutex. When the code is about to manipulate guarded resources (in this case, the array), you create a CSingleLock object, like this:

```
CSingleLock singleLock(&mutex);
```

The constructor's argument is a pointer to the thread-synchronization object that you want to control. Then, to gain access to the mutex, you call the CSingleLock object's Lock() member function:

```
singleLock.Lock();
```

If the mutex is unowned, the calling thread becomes the owner. If another thread already owns the mutex, the system suspends the calling thread until the mutex is released, at which time the waiting thread is awakened and takes control of the mutex.

To release the mutex, you call the CSingleLock object's Unlock() member function. However, if you create your CSingleLock object on the stack (rather than on the heap, using the new operator) as shown in Listing 27.10, you don't have to call Unlock() at all. When the function exits, the object goes out of scope, which causes its destructor to execute. The destructor automatically unlocks the object for you.

To try out the new CCountArray2 class in the Thread application, add new CountArray2.h and CountArray2.cpp files to the Thread project and then delete the original CountArray.h and CountArray.cpp files. Finally, in ThreadView.cpp, change all references to CCountArray to CCountArray2. Because all the thread synchronization is handled in the CCountArray2 class, no further changes are necessary to use mutexes instead of critical sections.

Using Semaphores

Although semaphores are used like critical sections and mutexes in an MFC program, they serve a slightly different function. Rather than enable only one thread to access a resource at a time, semaphores enable multiple threads to access a resource, but only to a point. That is, semaphores enable a maximum number of threads to access a resource simultaneously.

When you create the semaphore, you tell it how many threads should be allowed simultaneous access to the resource. Then, each time a thread grabs the resource, the semaphore decrements its internal counter. When the counter reaches 0, no further threads are allowed access to the guarded resource until another thread releases the resource, which increments the semaphore's counter.

You create a semaphore by supplying the initial count and the maximum count, like this:

```
CSemaphore Semaphore(2, 2);
```

Because in this section you'll be using a semaphore to create a thread-safe class, it's more convenient to declare a CSemaphore pointer as a data member of the class and then create the CSemaphore object dynamically in the class's constructor, like this:

```
semaphore = new CSemaphore(2, 2);
```

You should do this because you have to initialize a data member in the constructor rather than at the time you declare it. With the critical-section and mutex objects, you didn't have to supply arguments to the class's constructors, so you were able to create the object at the same time you declared it.

After you have created the semaphore object, it's ready to start counting resource access. To implement the counting process, you first create a CSingleLock object (or CMultiLock, if you're dealing with multiple thread-synchronization objects), giving it a pointer to the semaphore you want to use, like this:

```
CSingleLock singleLock(semaphore);
```

Then, to decrement the semaphore's count, you call the CSingleLock object's Lock() member function:

```
singleLock.Lock();
```

At this point, the semaphore object has decremented its internal counter. This new count remains in effect until the semaphore object is released, which you can do explicitly by calling the object's Unlock() member function:

```
singleLock.Unlock();
```

Alternatively, if you've created the CSingleLock object locally on the stack, you can just let the object go out of scope, which not only automatically deletes the object but also releases the hold on the semaphore. In other words, both calling Unlock() and deleting the CSingleLock object increment the semaphore's counter, enabling a waiting thread to access the guarded resource.

Listing 27.11 is the header file for a class called CSomeResource. CSomeResource is a mostly useless class whose only calling is to demonstrate the use of semaphores. The class has a single data member, which is a pointer to a CSemaphore object. The class also has a constructor and destructor, as well as a member function called UseResource(), which is where the semaphore will be used.

Listing 27.11 SOMERESOURCE.H

```
#include "afxmt.h"

class CSomeResource
{
private:
    CSemaphore* semaphore;

public:
    CSomeResource();
    ~CSomeResource();

    void UseResource();
};
```

Part
VI

Ch
27

Listing 27.12 shows the CSomeResource class's implementation file. You can see that the CSemaphore object is constructed dynamically in the class's constructor and deleted in the destructor. The UseResource() member function simulates accessing a resource by attaining a count on the semaphore and then sleeping for five seconds, after which the hold on the semaphore is released when the function exits and the CSingleLock object goes out of scope.

Listing 27.12 SOMERESOURCE.CPP

```
#include "stdafx.h"
#include "SomeResource.h"

CSomeResource::CSomeResource()
{
    semaphore = new CSemaphore(2, 2);
}

CSomeResource::~CSomeResource()
{
    delete semaphore;
}

void CSomeResource::UseResource()
{
    CSingleLock singleLock(semaphore);
    singleLock.Lock();

    Sleep(5000);
}
```

If you modify the Thread application to use the `CSomeResource` object, you can watch semaphores at work. Follow these steps:

1. Delete any `CountArray` files that are still in the project. (In FileView, click the file once to select it; then press Del to delete the file from the project.)

2. Create the new empty **SomeResource.h** and **SomeResource.cpp** files in the project.

3. Add the code from Listings 27.11 and 27.12 to these empty files.

4. Load ThreadView.cpp and replace the line `#include "CountArray2.h"` with the following:

    ```
    #include "SomeResource.h"
    ```

5. Replace the line `CCountArray2 countArray` with the following:

    ```
    CSomeResource someResource;
    ```

6. Replace the `WriteThreadProc()` and `ReadThreadProc()` functions with the functions shown in Listing 27.13.

Listing 27.13 *ThreadProc1(), ThreadProc2(), and ThreadProc3()*

```
UINT ThreadProc1(LPVOID param)
{
    someResource.UseResource();

    ::MessageBox((HWND)param,
        "Thread 1 had access.", "Thread 1", MB_OK);

    return 0;
}
```

```
UINT ThreadProc2(LPVOID param)
{
    someResource.UseResource();

    ::MessageBox((HWND)param,
        "Thread 2 had access.", "Thread 2", MB_OK);

    return 0;
}

UINT ThreadProc3(LPVOID param)
{
    someResource.UseResource();

    ::MessageBox((HWND)param,
        "Thread 3 had access.", "Thread 3", MB_OK);

    return 0;
}
```

7. Replace the code in the `OnStartthread()` function with that shown in Listing 27.14.

Listing 27.14   LST27_14.TXT—New Code for the *OnStartthread()* Function

```
HWND hWnd = GetSafeHwnd();
AfxBeginThread(ThreadProc1, hWnd);
AfxBeginThread(ThreadProc2, hWnd);
AfxBeginThread(ThreadProc3, hWnd);
```

Now compile and run the new version of the Thread application. When the main window appears, select the Thread, Start Thread command. In about five seconds, two message boxes will appear, informing you that thread 1 and thread 2 had access to the guarded resource. About five seconds after that, a third message box will appear, telling you that thread 3 also had access to the resource. Thread 3 took five seconds longer because thread 1 and thread 2 grabbed control of the resource first. The semaphore is set to allow only two simultaneous resource accesses, so thread 3 had to wait for thread 1 or thread 2 to release its hold on the semaphore.

N O T E   Although the sample programs in this chapter have demonstrated using a single thread-synchronization object, you can have as many synchronization objects as you need in a single program. You can even use critical sections, mutexes, and semaphores all at once to protect different data sets and resources in different ways. ▪

Part

VI

Ch

27

For complex applications, threads offer the capability to maintain fast and efficient data processing. You no longer have to wait for one part of the program to finish its task before moving on to something else. For example, a spreadsheet application could use one thread to update the calculations while the main thread continues accepting entries from the user. Using threads, however, leads to some interesting problems, not the least of which is the need to control access to shared resources. Writing a threaded application requires thought and careful consideration of how the threads will be used and what resources they'll access. ●

Future Explorations

There are a number of topics that have not been covered elsewhere in this book, but that are well known to experienced Visual C++ programmers. They are best explored after you have experience with Developer Studio, MFC, and C++ programming. This chapter has just enough to show you how interesting these topics are, and to encourage you to explore them yourself in the months and years to come.

Creating Console Applications

A console application looks very much like a DOS application, though it runs in a resizable window. It has a strictly character-based interface with cursor keys rather than mouse movement. You use the Console API and character-based I/O functions such as `printf()` and `scanf()` to interact with the user.

Creating a Console Executable

A console application is executed from the DOS command line or by choosing Start, Run and typing the full name (including the path) of the application. Console applications are probably still among the easiest programs to create, and this version of the compiler supports them directly.

Let's walk together through the few steps necessary to create a basic console application, and then we'll explore some beneficial uses of creating these applications. The first console application we'll create is a spin on the classic "Hello, World!" that Kernighan and Ritchie (the creators of C++'s ancestor C) created in the 1970s.

Open the Microsoft Developer Studio and follow these steps to create a console application:

1. In the Microsoft Developer Studio, select File, New.
2. In the New dialog box, click the Projects tab to bring up the now familiar New project dialog box. (If it isn't familiar, go back to Chapter 1, "Building Your First Windows Application.")
3. Name the project HelloWorld, set an appropriate folder for the project, and choose `Win32 Console Application` from the list on the left.
4. Click OK.
5. AppWizard asks whether you want to create An Empty Project, A Simple Application, A "Hello World" Application, or An Application that uses MFC. Select An Empty Project so that you can create our slightly simpler HelloWorld by yourself.
6. Click Finish.

The project is created immediately but has no file added to it. You create source and header files and add them to the project. This sample will all fit in one file. Follow these steps:

1. Select File, New from the File menu and click the File tab.
2. Leave the Add to Project box selected; the new file will be added to the project.

3. Choose C++ Source File from the box on the left.

4. Enter **HelloWorld** as the filename—the extension .cpp will be added automatically.

5. The New dialog box should resemble Figure 28.1. Click OK.

FIG. 28.1
Create a C++ source file for your console application.

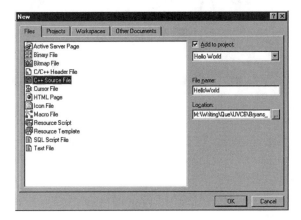

A blank text file is created and named for you and added to the project, all in one step. Add the code in Listing 28.1 to the new file.

Listing 28.1   HelloWorld.cpp

```
#include <iostream.h>
int main()
{
    cout << "Hello from the console!"<< endl;
    return 0;
}
```

Choose Build, Execute to compile, link, and execute the program. (A dialog will ask you to confirm that you want to build the project before executing.) You should see a DOS box appear that resembles Figure 28.2. The line Press any key to continue is generated by the system and gives you a chance to read your output before the DOS box disappears.

Writing an Object-Oriented Console Application

The HelloWorld application is clearly C++ and would not compile in a C compiler, which doesn't support stream-based I/O with cout, but it's not object oriented—there's not an object in it. Replace the code in HelloWorld.cpp with the lines in Listing 28.2.

Part
VI

Ch

28

FIG. 28.2

Your application appears to be a DOS program.

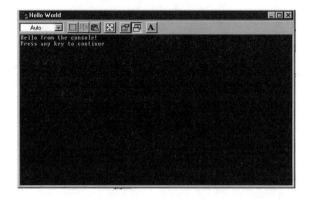

Listing 28.2 HelloWorld.cpp—With Objects

```cpp
// HelloWorld.cpp
//

#include <iostream.h>
#include <afx.h>

class Hello
{
private:
    CString message;

public:
    Hello();
    void display();
};

Hello::Hello()
{
    message = "Hello from the console!";
}

void Hello::display()
{
    cout << message << endl;
}

int main()
{
    Hello hello;
    hello.display();

    return 0;

}
```

Now this is an object-oriented program, and what's more, it uses CString, an MFC class. To do so, it must include <afx.h>. If you build the project now, you will get linker error messages that refer to _beginthreadex and _endthreadex. By default, console applications are single-threaded, but MFC is multithreaded. By including afx.h and bringing in MFC, this application is making itself incompatible with the single-threaded default. To fix this, choose Project Settings and click the C/C++ tab. From the drop-down box at the top of the dialog box, choose Code Generation. In the drop-down list box labeled Use Run-Time Library, choose Debug Multithreaded. (The completed dialog box is shown in Figure 28.3.) Click OK and rebuild the project.

FIG. 28.3

Make your console application multithreaded so that it can use MFC.

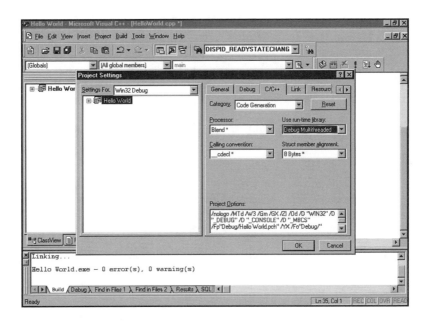

The output of this object-oriented program is just like that of the preceding program—this is just a sample. But you see that console applications can use MFC, be built around objects, and be quite small. They must have a main() function, and it is this function that is called by the operating system when you run the application.

N O T E Although this application is small, Visual C++ creates a lot of overhead files. The Debug directory occupies about 7.8MB, of which about 1.3MB is HelloWorld.exe. The rest is the MFC libraries—they aren't small. ▪

Scaffolding Discrete Algorithms

One important reason to build a console application these days is to *scaffold* small code fragments or single objects. This refers to building a temporary framework around the code you want to test. (Some developers call this a *test harness*.) The simplest possible framework is a console application like the one you just built: In fact, you'll build a scaffold later in this chapter.

To scaffold an object or function, you should do the following:

1. Create a new console application just for the scaffolding process.
2. Add a `main()` function to the .CPP file you plan to scaffold.
3. Include the header file for the object or function to be tested.
4. Add code to `main()` that exercises the function or object in a variety of test cases.

Having followed those steps, you can now test the code thoroughly, focusing only on the performance characteristics and correctness of this small piece of your large project. Scaffolding holds true to the canon of software development that states, "Design in the large and program in the small."

By applying a scaffold to any algorithm, you are helping to ensure the accuracy in the small. Remember there are additional benefits involved, too: By placing the scaffold code directly into the module, you are clearly documenting that the code has been tested and how to use it. You make it available for further testing, debugging, or extending at a later date.

Creating and Using a 32-Bit Dynamic Link Library

Dynamic link libraries (DLLs) are the backbone of the Windows 95 and Windows NT operating systems. Windows 95 uses Kernel32.dll, User32.dll, and Gdi32.dll to perform the vast majority of its work, and you can use them as well. The Visual C++ online help is a good source of information for these three DLLs.

A good tool for poking around in Windows applications is the DumpBin utility, usually found in \Program Files\Microsoft Visual Studio\VC98\Bin. DumpBin is a command line program that shows you the imports and exports of executable files and dynamic link libraries. The following listing is an excerpted example of the output produced when using DumpBin to examine the executable file for Spy++, one of the utilities provided with Visual C++.

Listing 28.3   Output from DumpBin

```
dumpbin -imports spyxx.exe
Microsoft (R) COFF Binary File Dumper Version 6.00.8047
Copyright  Microsoft Corp 1992-1998. All rights reserved.


Dump of file spyxx.exe

File Type: EXECUTABLE IMAGE

  Section contains the following imports:

    MFC42.DLL
                44B138 Import Address Table
                452B8C Import Name Table
```

```
              0 time date stamp
              0 Index of first forwarder reference

                 Ordinal   818
                 Ordinal  4424

        ... 392 similar lines omitted ...

MSVCRT.dll
           44B7A4 Import Address Table
           4531F8 Import Name Table
              0 time date stamp
              0 Index of first forwarder reference

             81  __set_app_type
             6F  __p__fmode
             6A  __p__commode
             9D  _adjust_fdiv
             83  __setusermatherr
            10F  _initterm
             58  __getmainargs
             8F  _acmdln
            249  exit
            2B5  sscanf
             49  __CxxFrameHandler
            298  memmove
            1B9  _splitpath
            134  _itoa
            159  _mbscmp
            2C9  strtoul
            100  _getmbcp
            168  _mbsnbcpy
             8E  _access
            161  _mbsinc
            192  _purecall
            2B2  sprintf
             A5  _beginthread
             C4  _endthread
            25E  free
            15F  _mbsicmp
             B7  _controlfp
            291  malloc
            158  _mbschr
             F1  _ftol
            1F3  _wcsupr
            2EB  wcsrchr
             63  __p___argv
             62  __p___argc
            2D4  toupper
            272  iscntrl
            2D0  time
             55  __dllonexit
            186  _onexit
```

Part
VI

Ch
28

continues

Listing 28.3   Continued

```
                 CA   _except_handler3
                 2E   ?terminate@@YAXXZ
                 D3   _exit
                 48   _XcptFilter
                 1AA  _setmbcp

MSVCIRT.dll
             44B75C Import Address Table
             4531B0 Import Name Table
                  0 time date stamp
                  0 Index of first forwarder reference

                194  ?str@strstreambuf@@QAEPADXZ
                11F  ?freeze@strstreambuf@@QAEXH@Z
                10F  ?ends@@YAAAVostream@@AAV1@@Z
                171  ?seekp@ostream@@QAEAAV1@J@Z
                 8B  ??6ostream@@QAEAAV0@K@Z
                 87  ??6ostream@@QAEAAV0@G@Z
                 50  ??1ostrstream@@UAE@XZ
                 14  ??0ios@@IAE@XZ
                 31  ??0ostrstream@@QAE@XZ
                1BB  _mtlock
                1BC  _mtunlock
                 47  ??1ios@@UAE@XZ
                 8A  ??6ostream@@QAEAAV0@J@Z
                 89  ??6ostream@@QAEAAV0@I@Z
                 88  ??6ostream@@QAEAAV0@H@Z
                 85  ??6ostream@@QAEAAV0@E@Z
                 93  ??6ostream@@QAEAAV0@PBD@Z

KERNEL32.dll
             44B084 Import Address Table
             452AD8 Import Name Table
                  0 time date stamp
                  0 Index of first forwarder reference

                246  SetEvent
                136  GetProfileStringA
                10F  GetModuleFileNameA
                 32  CreateFileA
                 19  CloseHandle
                2AC  WideCharToMultiByte
                1CB  MultiByteToWideChar
                 93  FindResourceA
                272  SizeofResource
                168  GlobalAlloc
                173  GlobalLock
                1AE  LoadResource
                1BC  LockResource
                17A  GlobalUnlock
                16F  GlobalFree

        ... 29 similar lines omitted ...
```

```
USER32.dll
          44B8AC Import Address Table
          453300 Import Name Table
               0 time date stamp
               0 Index of first forwarder reference

          2A5  wsprintfA
          160  GetWindowWord
          253  SetWindowLongA
          158  GetWindowPlacement
          1CF  OffsetRect
          189  IsIconic
          16E  InflateRect
          240  SetRectEmpty
           CF  EnumWindows
           BC  EnumChildWindows
          218  SetActiveWindow
           EE  GetClientRect

       ... 77 similar lines omitted ...


GDI32.dll
          44B024 Import Address Table
          452A78 Import Name Table
               0 time date stamp
               0 Index of first forwarder reference

          167  Rectangle
          121  GetStockObject
          17A  SelectObject
           3D  CreatePen
          19D  SetROP2
           30  CreateFontIndirectA
           36  CreateHatchBrush
           41  CreateRectRgn
           72  FrameRgn
           1D  CreateBitmap
           E8  GetDeviceCaps
          137  GetTextMetricsA
          130  GetTextExtentPoint32A
           3C  CreatePatternBrush
          14E  PatBlt
          161  PtInRegion
           46  CreateSolidBrush
           4C  DeleteObject
          111  GetObjectA
           23  CreateCompatibleDC
            D  BitBlt
          118  GetPixel
           6B  ExtTextOutA

ADVAPI32.dll
          44B000 Import Address Table
          452A54 Import Name Table
```

Part

VI

Ch

28

continues

Listing 28.3 Continued

```
              0 time date stamp
              0 Index of first forwarder reference

            148  RegCreateKeyA
            15B  RegOpenKeyA
            160  RegQueryInfoKeyA
            149  RegCreateKeyExA
            170  RegSetValueExA
            15C  RegOpenKeyExA
            165  RegQueryValueExA
            145  RegCloseKey

  Summary

      17000 .data
       A000 .rdata
      10000 .rsrc
      4A000 .text
```

As you can see, the utility program Spy++ uses the C Runtime and Windows DLLs extensively.

You can call functions from the Windows DLLs in any of your programs, and more importantly, you can write DLLs of your own.

Making a 32-Bit DLL

There are two kinds of DLLs in Visual C++: Those that use MFC and those that don't. Each kind of DLL has its own AppWizard, as you will see shortly.

If you gather three or four functions into a DLL, your DLL *exports* those functions for other programs to use. Quite often a DLL will also *import* functions from other DLLs to get its work done.

Importing and Exporting Functions   To designate a symbol as exportable, use the following syntax:

```
__declspec(dllexport) data_type int var_name; // for variables
```

or

```
__declspec(ddlexport) return_type func_name( [argument_list ] );
// for functions
```

Importing functions is almost identical: Simply replace the keyword tokens, `__declspec(dllexport)` with `__declspec(dllimport)`. Use an actual function and variable to demonstrate the syntax this time:

```
__declspec(dllimport) int referenceCount;
__declspec(dllimport) void DiskFree( lpStr Drivepath );
```

T I P   Two underscores precede the keyword `__declspec`.

By convention, Microsoft uses a header file and a preprocessor macro to make the inclusion of DLL declarations much simpler. The technique requires that you make a preprocessor token using a unique token—the header filename works easily and requires very little in the way of memorization—and define a macro that will replace the token with the correct import or export statement. Thus, assuming a header file named Diskfree.h, the preprocessor macro in the header file would be as follows.

Listing 28.4   Diskfree.h

```
// DISKFREE.H - Contains a simpler function for returning the amount of
// free disk space.
#ifndef __DISKFREE_H
#define __DISKFREE_H

#ifndef __DISKFREE__
#define DISKFREELIB __declspec(dllimport)
#else
#define DISKFREELIB __declspec(dllexport)
#endif
// Use the macro to control an import or export declaration.
DISKFREELIB unsigned long DiskFree( unsigned int drive );
// (e.g. 0 = A:, 1 = B:, 2 = C:
#endif
```

By including the header file, you can let the preprocessor decide whether DiskFree is being imported or exported. Now you can share the header file for the DLL developer and the DLL user, and that means fewer maintenance headaches.

Creating the DiskFree DLL   The DiskFree utility provides a simple way to determine the amount of free disk space for any given drive. The underlying functionality is the GetDiskFreeSpace() function found in Kernel32.dll.

To create a non-MFC DLL, choose File, New, click the Projects tab, select Win32 Dynamic Link Library from the list on the left, and enter DiskFree for the project name. Click OK and the AppWizard dialog box, shown in Figure 28.4, appears. Choose An Empty DLL project, and your project is created with no files in it.

Add a C++ header file called DiskFree.h to the project and type in the code from Listing 28.5. Add a C++ source file called DiskFree.cpp and type in the code from Listing 28.6.

Listing 28.5   DiskFree.h

```
#ifndef __DISKFREE_H
#define __DISKFREE_H
#ifndef __DISKFREE__
#define __DISKFREELIB__ __declspec(dllimport)
#else
#define __DISKFREELIB__ __declspec(dllexport)
#endif
```

Part

VI

Ch

28

continues

Listing 28.5 Continued

```
// Returns the amount of free space on drive number (e.g. 0 = A:, 1= B:,
// 2 = c:)
__DISKFREELIB__ unsigned long DiskFree( unsigned int drive );
#endif
```

Listing 28.6 DiskFree.cpp

```
#include <afx.h>
#include <winbase.h>        // Declares kernel32 GetDiskFreeSpace
#define __DISKFREE__        // Define the token before including the library
#include "diskfree.h"
// Returns the amount of free space on drive number
// (e.g. 0 = A:, 1= B:, 2 = c:)
__DISKFREELIB__ unsigned long DiskFree( unsigned int drive )
{
    unsigned long bytesPerSector, sectorsPerCluster,
        freeClusters, totalClusters;
    char DrivePath[4] = { char( drive + 65 ), ':', '\\', '\0' };
    if( GetDiskFreeSpace( DrivePath, &sectorsPerCluster,
        &bytesPerSector, &freeClusters, &totalClusters ))
    {
        return sectorsPerCluster * bytesPerSector * freeClusters;
    }
    else
    {
        return 0;
    }
}
```

Now you can build the DLL. In the next section, you will see how to use 32-bit DLLs in general and how Windows finds DLLs on your system.

FIG. 28.4

Creating a non-MFC DLL project is a one-step process.

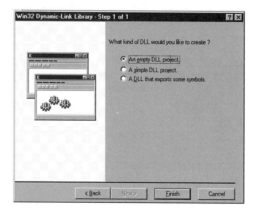

The most common use of a DLL is to provide extended, reusable functionality and let Windows implicitly load the DLL. Topics that aren't discussed in this book, which you might want to explore for yourself, include the following:

- Dynamic versus static linking of MFC
- Implicit versus explicit DLL loading, which requires the use of LoadLibrary and FreeLibrary
- Multithreading DLLs
- Sharing data across DLL boundaries
- Calling conventions for DLLs that will be used by other languages (_stdcall, WINAPI, …)

In this chapter you are going to use a default compile of DiskFree, using an implicit DllMain (the compiler added one) and an implicit loading of the DLL, allowing Windows to manage loading and unloading the library.

Using 32-Bit DLLs

Many DLLs are loaded implicitly, and their loading and unloading are managed by Windows. Libraries loaded in this fashion are searched for like executables: First the directory of the application loading the DLL is searched, followed by the current directory, the Windows\System directory for Windows 95 or 98, Winnt\System or Winnt\System32 for NT, the Windows directory, and finally each directory specified in the path.

It is a common practice to place a DLL in the Windows or Windows\System directory after the application is shipped, but in the meantime, you can use the development directory of the executable for temporary storage. One thing to safeguard against is that you don't end up with multiple versions of the DLL in each of the Windows, Windows\System, or project directories.

Using a DLL   Implicitly loading and using a DLL is about as simple as using any other function. This is especially true if you created the header file as described in the "Creating the DiskFree DLL" section. When you compile your DLL, Microsoft Visual C++ creates a .LIB file. (So, DISKFREE.DLL has a DISKFREE.LIB created by the compiler.) The library (.LIB) file is used to resolve the load address of the DLL and specify the full pathname of the dynamic link library, and the header file provides the declaration.

All you have to do is include the header in the file using the DLL functionality and add the .LIB name to the Project Settings dialog box, on the Link tab (see Figure 28.5), in the Object/Library Modules edit field.

To test the DiskFree DLL, create a console application called TestDiskFree as An Empty Project and add a C++ source file called TestDiskFree.cpp. Add the code from Listing 28.7 to this file. Copy DiskFree.h to this folder and add it to the project by choosing Project, Add To Project, Files, and selecting DiskFree.h. Copy DiskFree.dll and DiskFree.Lib to the TestDiskFree folder also. (You'll find them in DiskFree\Debug.) Change the project settings as just described to include the DiskFree.Lib file, and build the project.

Part
VI

Ch
28

FIG. 28.5

Add your LIB file to the project settings.

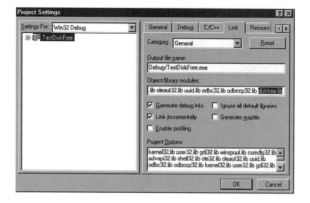

Listing 28.7 TestDiskFree.cpp

```
#include <iostream.h>
#include "diskfree.h"
#define CodeTrace(arg) \
     cout << #arg << endl;\
     arg
int main()
{
     CodeTrace( cout << DiskFree(2) << endl );
     return 0;
}
```

This code brings in the DLL by including DiskFree.h and then uses it. The CodeTrace macro simply prints out a line of code before executing it. All this application does is call the DiskFree() function to ask how much space is free on drive 2. Drive 0 is A:, drive 1 is B:, and drive 2 is C:. If you build and execute the program, you should see output like Figure 28.6.

FIG. 28.6

Your little application calls the DLL.

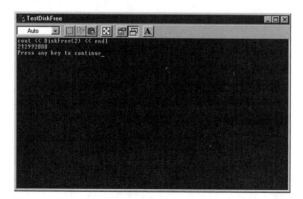

According to TestDiskFree, the C: drive on the machine used for these samples has more than 200MB of free disk space. This number is correct.

Now you know how to write real functions in a DLL and use them yourself or make them available for others.

Sending Messages and Commands

As discussed in Chapter 3, "Messages and Commands," messages are the heart of Windows. Everything that happens in a Windows application happens because a message showed up to make it happen. When you move your mouse and click a button, a huge number of messages are generated, including WM_MOUSEMOVE for each movement of the mouse, WM_LBUTTONDOWN when the button goes down, WM_LBUTTONCLICK when the button is released, and higher-level, more abstract messages such as the WM_COMMAND message with the button's resource ID as one of its parameters. You can ignore the lower-level messages if you want; many programmers do.

What you may not know is that *you* can generate messages, too. There are two functions that generate messages: CWnd::SendMessage() and CWnd::PostMessage(). Each of these gets a message to an object that inherits from CWnd. An object that wants to send a message to a window using one of these functions must have a pointer to the window, and the window must be prepared to catch the message. A very common approach to this situation is to have a member variable in the sending object that stores a pointer to the window that will receive the message and another that stores the message to be sent:

```
CWnd* m_messagewindow;
UINT m_message;
```

Messages are represented by unsigned integers. They appear to have names only because names like WM_MOUSEMOVE are connected to integers with #define statements.

The sending class has a member function to set these member variables, typically very short:

```
void Sender::SetReceiveTarget(CWnd *window, UINT message)
{
    m_messagewindow = window;
    m_message = message;
}
```

When the sending class needs to get a message to the window, it calls SendMessage():

```
    m_messagewindow->SendMessage(m_message, wparam, lparam);
```

or PostMessage():

```
    m_messagewindow->PostMessage(m_message, wparam, lparam);
```

The difference between sending and posting a message is that SendMessage() does not return until the message has been handled by the window that received it, but PostMessage() just adds the message to the message queue and returns right away. If, for example, you build an object, pass that object's address as the lparam, and then delete the object, you should choose SendMessage() because you can't delete the object until you are sure that the message-handling code has finished with it. If you aren't passing pointers, you can probably use PostMessage() and move on as soon as the message has been added to the queue.

The meaning of the `wparam` and `lparam` values depends on the message you are sending. If it is a defined system message like `WM_MOUSEMOVE`, you can read the online documentation to learn what the parameters are. If, as is more likely, you are sending a message that you have invented, the meaning of the parameters is entirely up to you. You are the one who is inventing this message and writing the code to handle it when it arrives at the other window.

To invent a message, add a defining statement to the header file of the class that will catch it:

```
#define WM_HELLO WM_USER + 300
```

`WM_USER` is an unsigned integer that marks the start of the range of message numbers available for user-defined messages. In this release of MFC, its value is `0x4000`, though you should not depend on that. User-defined messages have message numbers between `WM_USER` and `0x7FFF`.

Then add a line to the message map, in both the header and source file, outside the ClassWizard comments. The source file message map might look like this:

```
BEGIN_MESSAGE_MAP(CMainFrame, CMDIFrameWnd)
    //{{AFX_MSG_MAP(CMainFrame)
        // NOTE - the ClassWizard will add and remove mapping macros here.
        //    DO NOT EDIT what you see in these blocks of generated code!
    //}}AFX_MSG_MAP
    ON_MESSAGE(WM_HELLO, OnHello)
END_MESSAGE_MAP()
```

The entry added outside the `//AFX_MSG_MAP` comments catches the `WM_HELLO` message and arranges for the `OnHello()` function to be called. The header file message map might look like this:

```
// Generated message map functions
protected:
    //{{AFX_MSG(CMainFrame)
    afx_msg int OnCreate(LPCREATESTRUCT lpCreateStruct);
        // NOTE - the ClassWizard will add and remove member functions here.
        //    DO NOT EDIT what you see in these blocks of generated code!
    //}}AFX_MSG
    afx_msg LRESULT OnHello(WPARAM wParam, LPARAM lParam);
    DECLARE_MESSAGE_MAP()
```

Then you add an implementation of `OnHello()` to the source file to complete the process.

Considering International Software Development Issues

International boundaries are shrinking at incredible rates. As the Internet and other methods of cheap international software distribution continue to grow, so will the demand for components built by vendors worldwide. Even in-house software development will less frequently be able to ignore international markets. The rise in popularity of the Internet has expanded the reach of many developers into countries where languages other than English and character sets other than ASCII predominate. This means your applications should be able to communicate with users in languages other than English, and in characters sets other than the typical Western character set.

Microcomputers were invented in the United States, which explains why we have 8-bit character-based operating systems. There are only 26 letters in our alphabet and 10 digits, which leaves plenty of room (about 220 characters worth) for punctuation and other miscellaneous characters. But countries like Japan and China require a character set in the thousands.

Unicode is one way to tackle the character set problem. The Unicode standard was developed and is supported by a consortium of some of the biggest players in the international computing markets. Among these are Adobe, Aldus, Apple, Borland, Digital, IBM, Lotus, Microsoft, Novell, and Xerox. (For more information, check **www.unicode.org**.)

Unicode uses two bytes for each character, whereas ASCII uses only one. One byte (8 bits) can represent 2^8 or 256 characters. Two bytes (16 bits) can represent 65,536 characters. This is enough not just for one language, but for all the character sets in general use. For example, the Japanese character set, one of the largest, needs about 5,000 characters. Most require far less. The Unicode specification sets aside different ranges for different character sets and can cover almost every language on Earth in one universal code—a Unicode.

MFC has full Unicode support, with Unicode versions of almost every function. For example, consider the function `CWnd::SetWindowText()`. It takes a string and sets the title of the window, or the caption of a button, to that string. What kind of string it takes depends on whether you have Unicode support turned on in your application. In reality, two different functions set the window text one—a Unicode version and a non-Unicode version—and in WINUSER.H, the block of code shown in Listing 28.8 changes the function name that you call to `SetWindowTextA` if you are not using Unicode or to `SetWindowTextW` if you are.

Listing 28.8 Microsoft's WINUSER.H Implementing Unicode Support

```
WINUSERAPI BOOL WINAPI SetWindowTextA(HWND hWnd, LPCSTR lpString);
WINUSERAPI BOOL WINAPI SetWindowTextW(HWND hWnd, LPCWSTR lpString);

#ifdef UNICODE
#define SetWindowText   SetWindowTextW
#else
#define SetWindowText   SetWindowTextA
#endif // !UNICODE
```

The difference between these two functions is the type of the second parameter: `LPCSTR` for the A version and `LPCWSTR` for the W (Wide) version.

If you are using Unicode, whenever you pass a literal string (such as "Hello") to a function, wrap it in the `_T` macro, like this:

```
pWnd->SetWindowText(_T("Hello"));
```

Part
VI

Ch
28

If you can deal with the annoyance of wrapping all text strings in _T macros, just like that, your application is Unicode aware. When you prepare your Greek or Japanese version of the application, life will be much simpler.

> **N O T E**   Windows 95 was built on earlier versions of Windows, so it was not built using Unicode. This means that if you use Unicode in your Windows 95 programs, you are going to suffer performance penalties because the Windows 95 kernel will have to convert Unicode strings back to ordinary strings. Windows NT was designed at Microsoft from scratch, so it is completely compatible with Unicode.
>
> If you are developing for several platforms with C++ and using Unicode, your Win95 version may seem sluggish in comparison to the Windows NT version. ■

Appendixes

C++ Review and Object-Oriented Concepts

Working with Objects

C++ is an object-oriented programming language. You can use it to write programs that are not object-oriented, like the "Hello World!" example in Chapter 28, "Future Explorations," but its real power comes from the way it helps you to implement your applications as objects rather than procedures. As a Visual C++ programmer, you will make extensive use of MFC, the Microsoft Foundation Classes: These are implementations of objects almost every application uses.

 TIP If you never worked with C++ before you picked up this book, you are likely to need more help than one chapter can provide. As an introduction, consider using any of Jesse Liberty's books on C++: *Sams Teach Yourself C++ in 24 Hours*, *Sams Teach Yourself C++ in 21 Days*, or *Sams Teach Yourself C++ in 21 Days: Complete Compiler Edition*.

What Is an Object?

An object is a bundle, a clump, a gathering together of items of information that belong to-gether, and functions that work on those items of information. For example, a `BankAccount` object might gather up a customer number, account number, and current balance—these three pieces of information are required for all bank accounts. Many languages provide a way to group related information together into *structures* or *records* or whatever the language calls the feature. However, where an object differs from these is in including functions, or behavior, as well as information. Our `BankAccount` object will have `Deposit()`, `Withdraw()`, and `GetBalance()` functions, for example. Figure A.1 shows one way of looking at the design of an object.

FIG. A.1
Objects combine information (variables) and behavior (functions).

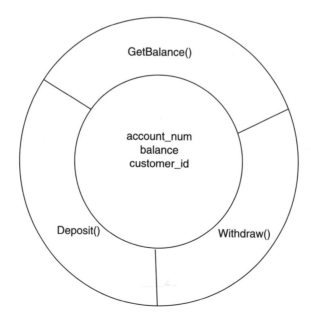

Why Use Objects?

There are many advantages to an object-oriented approach to application development, but the two most important are maintanability and robustness. That's what you call them when you're persuading your manager to switch to C++. In your day-to-day life, they mean you can change one thing without breaking anything else, and you don't have to count on remembering to always do step B whenever you do step A. Both these benefits arise because code from outside our `BankAccount` object can't directly access any information inside the object, only through the functions you've added to the object. For example, imagine that some piece of code creates a bank account like this:

```
BankAccount account;
```

That code can now deposit or withdraw money or find out the balance in the account, like this:

```
account.Deposit(100.00);
account.Withdraw(50.00);
float newbalance = account.GetBalance();
```

That code cannot work on the balance directly, like this:

```
account.balance = 100.00;
account.balance -= 50.00;
float newbalance = account.balance;
```

This information hiding doesn't seek to protect the numeric value of the account balance—the three lines of code that work are obviously using and affecting that value. Instead, information hiding protects design decisions made by the programmer, and it leaves you free to change them later.

As an example, say you decide to use a floating point number to represent the account balance, the number of dollars in the account. Later, you change your mind, deciding that using an integer that represents the number of pennies in the account would be faster, or more accurate, or less of a burden on available memory. Of course, you will have to change the code for `Deposit()` and `Withdraw()`, which will still take floating point arguments, to convert from dollars to pennies. After you do that, all the code that other people wrote that called those functions will work perfectly: They'll never know you changed anything. If you're the one writing the whole project, you'll know that you have no work to do other than the changes within your `BankAccount` object. If other code could talk to `balance` directly, as in the second set of three lines, you'd have to find every place in the whole application that does so and change it to convert from dollars to pennies or from pennies to dollars. What a nightmare!

What if you never make such a fundamental change as that? After all, it's rare to change the type of a variable partway through the project. Well then, imagine a change in the business rules governing withdrawals. When the project started, you were told that accounts couldn't be overdrawn, so you wrote code for the `Withdraw()` function that looked like this:

```
balance -= amounttowithdraw;
if (balance < 0)
    balance += amounttowithdraw; //reverse transaction
```

Then, just as the application was almost complete, you were told that, in fact, many accounts have overdraft protection and you should have written the following:

```
balance -= amounttowithdraw;
if (balance < -overdraftlimit)
    balance += amounttowithdraw; //reverse transaction
```

If all withdrawals go through the Withdraw() function, your life is easy: Make one change in the function, and everything's taken care of. If lots of other places in the code were processing withdrawals themselves, by just lowering the value of balance, you would have to find all those places and fix the overdraft check in each place. If you missed one, your program would have a strange and subtle bug that missed overdrafts in some situations and caught them in others. The object-oriented way is much safer.

What Is a Class?

In any bank, there are many bank accounts: yours, mine, and thousands of others. They all have fundamental things in common: They have a balance and a customer, and certain kinds of transactions are allowed with them. In a banking application, you will have perhaps thousands of bank account objects, and each will be an instance of the BankAccount class.

When you define a class, you define what it means to be a BankAccount (or a Truck, or an Employee, or whatever). You list the information that is kept by objects of this class in the form of member variables, and the things objects of this class can do, in the form of member functions. Also, you make it clear which parts of the class you want to protect with information hiding. Listing A.1 shows a declaration for the class BankAccount.

Listing A.1 Declaring the *BankAccount* Class

```
class BankAccount
{
    private:
        float balance;
        char[8] customer_id;
        char[8] account_num;

    public:
        float GetBalance();
        void Withdraw(float amounttowithdraw);
        void Deposit(float amounttodeposit);
};
```

← put in header .h file (handwritten annotation)

The keyword private before the three variables directs the compiler not to compile code that accesses these variables, unless that code is within a member function of BankAccount. The keyword public before the three functions tells the compiler any code at all can call them. This is a typical arrangement for a well-designed object-oriented program: All the variables are private, and all the functions are public.

TIP Occasionally, you might write a function for an object that is used to perform some repetitive task. It's not always appropriate for other objects to use that function to direct your object to perform that task. In this case, you can make the function private. Many developers make variables public to save the bother of writing public functions to access the variable. There's rarely a good reason to do this; it's just laziness.

Now if certain code declares two bank accounts, `mine` and `yours`, each will have its own `balance`, `customer_id`, and `account_num` variables. Depositing money into my bank account will not affect your balance. Listing A.2 shows some code that creates bank accounts and then exercises their functions.

Listing A.2 Using *BankAccount* Objects

```
BankAccount mine, yours;
mine.Deposit(1000);
yours.Deposit(100);
mine.Withdraw(500);
float mybalance = mine.GetBalance();
float yourbalance = yours.GetBalance();
```

Where Are the Functions?

The three member functions—`Deposit()`, `Withdraw()`, and `GetBalance()`—must be written, and their code must be compiled. You can put the code for these functions in two places: inside the class declaration (called *inline code*) or outside the class declaration, usually in a separate file. Only very short and simple functions should have inline code because long functions here make the class declaration hard to read. If all three functions in this sample class had inline code, the class declaration would be as shown in Listing A.3.

Listing A.3 *BankAccount* with Inline Code

```
class BankAccount
{
    private:
        float balance;
        char[8] customer_id;
        char[8] account_num;

    public:
        float GetBalance() { return balance;}
        void Withdraw(float amounttowithdraw)
            {
              balance -= amounttowithdraw;
              if (balance < 0)
                  balance += amounttowithdraw; //reverse transaction
            }
        void Deposit(float amounttodeposit) {balance += amounttodeposit;}
};
```

Notice that the semicolon after the function names in Listing A.1 has been replaced by the function body, surrounded by braces. The `Withdraw()` function is a little too long to include in the class declaration like this and would be better placed outside the class. Because all functions in an object-oriented program belong to a class, when you provide the code, you must indicate the name of the class to which the function belongs. Listing A.4 shows the code for `Withdraw()` as it might appear outside the class declaration. The two colons (::) between the classname and the function name are called the *scope resolution operator.*

Listing A.4   *BankAccount's Withdraw() Function*

```
void BankAccount::Withdraw(float amounttowithdraw)
    {
    balance -= amounttowithdraw;
    if (balance < 0)
        balance += amounttowithdraw; //reverse transaction
    }
```

N O T E   Usually, the class declaration is placed in a file of its own with a name such as BankAccount.h so that it can be used by all the other code that makes BankAccount objects or calls BankAccount functions. This file is generally referred to as the *header file.* Typically, the rest of the code is placed in another file with a name such as BankAccount.cpp, referred to as the *implementation file.* ▪

Inline Functions

It's easy to confuse inline code, such as that in Listing A.3, with inline functions. The compiler can choose to make any function an inline function, which provides tremendous performance improvements for small functions. Because it can harm performance for long functions, generally the compiler, not the programmer, makes the decision about inlining. When you provide inline code, you are suggesting to the compiler that the function be inlined. Another way to make this suggestion is to use the keyword `inline` with the code outside the class declaration, like this:

```
inline void BankAccount::Withdraw(float amounttowithdraw)
    {
    balance -= amounttowithdraw;
    if (balance < 0)
        balance += amounttowithdraw; //reverse transaction
    }
```

If this function will be called from other objects, don't inline it like this in the .cpp file. Leave it in the header file or make a separate file for inline functions, an .inl file, and `#include` it into each file that calls the member functions. That way the compiler will be able to find the code.

The compiler might not inline a function, even though it has inline code (in the class declaration) or you use the `inline` keyword. If you know what you're doing, the `__forceinline` keyword introduced in Visual C++ 6 enables you to insist that a function be inlined. (Notice that this keyword, like all nonstandard compiler keywords, starts with two underscores.) Because this can cause code bloat and slow your application, use this feature only when you have an almost complete application and are looking for performance improvements. This is a Visual C++–only keyword that won't work with other compilers.

Perhaps you've already seen one of the other advantages of C++. Functions generally require much fewer parameters. In another language, you might pass the account number into each of these three functions to make it clear which balance you want to know about or change. Perhaps you would pass the balance itself into a Withdraw() function that checks the business rules and then approves or denies the withdrawal. However, because these BankAccount functions are member functions, they have all the member variables of the object to work with and don't require them as parameters. That makes all your code simpler to read and maintain.

How Are Objects Initialized?

In C, you can just declare a variable, like this:

```
int i;
```

If you prefer, you can declare it and initialize it at the same time, like this:

```
int i = 3;
```

A valid bank account needs values for its customer_id and account_num member variables. You can probably start with a balance of 0, but what sensible defaults can you use for the other two? More importantly, where would you put the code that assigns these values to the variables? In C++, every object has an initializer function called a *constructor*, and it handles this work. A constructor is different from ordinary member functions in two ways: Its name is the name of the class, and it doesn't have a return type, not even void. Perhaps you might write a constructor like the one in Listing A.5 for the BankAccount class.

Listing A.5 *BankAccount* Constructor

```
BankAccount::BankAccount(char* customer, char* account, float startbalance)
    {
      strcpy(customer_id, customer);
      strcpy(account_num, account);
      balance = startbalance;
    }
```

TIP strcpy() is a function from the C runtime library, available to all C and C++ programs, that copies strings. The code in Listing A.5 copies the strings that were passed to the constructor into the member variables.

add to header
prototype
no class needed

After writing the BankAccount constructor, you would add its declaration to the class by adding this line to the class declaration:

```
BankAccount(char* customer, char* account, float startbalance);
```

Notice that there is no return type. You don't need the class name and scope resolution operator because you are in the class definition, and the semicolon at the end of the line indicates that the code is outside the class declaration.

Now, when you declare a BankAccount object, you can initialize by providing constructor parameters, like this:

```
BankAccount account("AB123456","11038-30",100.00);
```

What Is Overloading?

Imagine the banking application you are writing also deals with credit cards and that there is a CreditCard class. You might want a GetBalance() function in that class, too. In C, functions weren't associated with classes. They were all global, and you couldn't have two functions with the same name. In C++ you can. Imagine that you write some code like this:

```
BankAccount account("AB123456","11038-30",100.00);
float accountbalance = account.GetBalance();
CreditCard card("AB123456", "4500 000 000 000", 1000.00);
card.GetBalance();
```

ex.1

Most developers can see that the second line will call the BankAccount GetBalance() function, whose full name is BankAccount::GetBalance(), and the fourth line will call CreditCard::GetBalance(). In a sense, these functions don't have the same name. This is one example of overloading, and it's a really nice thing for developers because it lets you use a simple and intuitive name for all your functions, instead of one called GetBankAccountBalance() and another called GetCreditCardBalance().

There's another, even nicer situation in which you might want two functions with the same name, and that's within a single class. Take, for example, that BankAccount constructor you saw a little earlier in this chapter. It might be annoying to pass in a zero balance all the time. What if you could have two constructors, one that takes the customer identifier, account number, and starting balance and another that takes only the customer and account identifiers? You might add them to the class declaration like this:

ex 2

```
BankAccount(char* customer, char* account, float startbalance);
BankAccount(char* customer, char* account);
```

As Listing A.6 shows, the code for these functions would be very similar. You might feel that you need different names for them, but you don't. The compiler tells them apart by their *signature*: the combination of their full names and all the parameter types that they take. This isn't unique to constructors: All functions can be overloaded as long as at least one aspect of the signature is different for the two functions that have the same name.

TIP Two functions in the same class, with the same name, must differ in the type or number of parameters. If they differ only in the return type, that is not a valid overload.

Listing A.6   Two *BankAccount* Constructors

```
BankAccount::BankAccount(char* customer, char* account, float startbalance)
        {
          strcpy(customer_id, customer);
          strcpy(account_num, account);
          balance = startbalance;
        }
BankAccount::BankAccount(char* customer, char* account)
        {
          strcpy(customer_id, customer);
          strcpy(account_num, account);
          balance = 0;
        }
```

Reusing Code and Design with Inheritance

Maintainability and robustness, thanks to information hiding, are two of the features that inspire people to switch to object-oriented programming. Another is reuse. You can reuse other people's objects, calling their public functions and ignoring their design decisions, by simply making an object that is an instance of the class and calling the functions. The hundreds of classes that make up MFC are a good example. C++ enables another form of reuse as well, called *inheritance*.

What Is Inheritance?

To stick with the banking example, imagine that after you have BankAccount implemented, tested, and working perfectly, you decide to add checking and savings accounts to your system. You would like to reuse the code you have already written for BankAccount, not just copy it into each of these new classes. To see whether you should reuse by making an object and calling its functions or reuse by inheriting, you try saying these sample sentences:

A checking account IS a bank account.

A checking account HAS a bank account part.

A savings account IS a bank account.

A savings account HAS a bank account part.

Most people agree that the IS sentences sound better. In contrast, which of the following would you choose?

A car IS an engine (with some seats and wheels)

A car HAS an engine (and some seats and wheels)

If the IS sentences don't sound silly, inheritance is the way to implement your design. Listing A.7 contains possible class declarations for the two new classes.

> **T I P**   The class reusing code in this way is called a *derived* class or sometimes a *subclass*. The class providing the code is called the *base* class or sometimes the *superclass*.

Listing A.7   *CheckingAccount* and *SavingsAccount*

```
class SavingsAccount: public BankAccount
{
    private:
      float interestrate;

    public:
      SavingsAccount(char* customer, char* account,
                     float startbalance, float interest);
      void CreditInterest(int days);
};
class CheckingAccount: public BankAccount
{

    public:
      Checking(char* customer, char* account, float startbalance);
      void PrintStatement(int month);
};
```

Now, if someone makes a CheckingAccount object, he can call functions that CheckingAccount inherited from BankAccount or functions that were written specially for CheckingAcount. Here's an example:

```
CheckingAccount ca("AB123456","11038-30",100.00);
ca.Deposit(100);
ca.PrintStatement(5);
```

What's terrific about this is what happens when someone changes the business rules. Perhaps management notices that there are no service charges in this system and instructs you to add them. You will charge 10 cents for each deposit and withdrawal, and subtract the service charges on instruction from some monthly maintenance code that another developer is writing. You open up BankAccount.h and add a private member variable called servicecharges. You set this to zero in the constructor and increase it by 0.1 in both Deposit() and Withdraw(). Then you add a public function called ApplyServiceCharges() that reduces the balance and resets the charges to zero.

At this point in most other languages, you'd have to repeat all this for CheckingAccount and SavingsAccount. Not in C++! You have to add a line to the constructors for these classes, but you don't change anything else. You can reuse your changes as easily as you reused your BankAccount class in the first place.

What Is Protected Access?

Without writing all of CheckingAccount::PrintStatement(), you can assume it will need to know the balance of the account. To spare any hard-to-read code that would put that number onscreen, consider this line of code:

```
float bal = balance;
```

This line, inside CheckingAccount::PrintStatement(), will not compile. balance is a private member variable, and no code can access it, other than code in BankAccount member functions. Though this probably seems outrageous, it's actually very useful. Remember the possible design decision that would change the type of balance from float to int? How would the BankAccount programmer know all the classes out there that inherited from BankAccount and rely on the type of the balance member variable? It's much simpler to prevent access by any other code. After all, CheckingAccount::PrintStatement() can use a public function, GetBalance(), to achieve the desired result.

If you want to grant code in derived classes direct access to a member variable, and you're confident that you will never need to find all these classes to repeat some change in all of them, you can make the variable protected rather than private. The class declaration for BankAccount would start like this:

```
class BankAccount
{
    protected:   ← allows inheriting classes to change directly
        float balance;
    private:
        char[8] customer_id;
        char[8] account_num;

    // ...
};
```

What Is Overriding? — inheriting class writes (overwrites) another fn in super class.

At times, your class will inherit from a base class that already provides a function you need, but the code for that function isn't quite what you want. For example, BankAccount might have a Display() function that writes onscreen the values of the three member variables: customer_id, account_num, and balance. Other code could create BankAccount, CheckingAccount, or SavingsAccount objects and display them by calling this function. No problem. Well, there is one little problem: All SavingsAccount objects have an interestrate variable as well, and it would be nice if the Display() function showed its value, too. You can write your own code for SavingsAccount::Display(). This is called an override of the function from the base class.

You want SavingsAccount::Display() to do everything that BankAccount::Display() does and then do the extra things unique to savings accounts. The best way to achieve this is to call BankAccount::Display() (that's its full name) from within SavingsAccount::Display(). Besides saving you time typing or copying and pasting, you won't have to recopy later if someone changes the base class Display().

What Is Polymorphism?

Polymorphism is a tremendously useful feature of C++, but it doesn't sneak up on you. You can use it only if you are using inheritance and pointers, and then only if the base class in your inheritance hierarchy deliberately activates it. Consider the code in Listing A.8.

TIP If you haven't worked with pointers before, you may find the &, *, and -> operators used in this code example confusing. & means *address of* and obtains a pointer from a variable. * means *contents of* and uses a pointer to access the variable it points to. -> is used when the pointer has the address of an object rather than an integer, float, or other fundamental type.

Listing A.8   Inheritance and Pointers

```
BankAccount ba("AB123456","11038-30",100.00);
CheckingAccount ca("AB123456","11038-32",200.00);
SavingsAccount sa("AB123456","11038-39",1000.00, 0.03);

BankAccount* pb = &ba;
CheckingAccount* pc = &ca;
SavingsAccount* ps = &sa;

pb->Display();
pc->Display();
ps->Display();

BankAccount* pc2 = &ca;
BankAccount* ps2 = &sa;

pc2->Display();
ps2->Display();

};
```

In this example, there are three objects and five pointers. pb, pc, and ps are straightforward, but pc2 and ps2 represent what is often called an *upcast*: A pointer that points to a derived class object is being carried around as a pointer to a base class object. Although there doesn't seem to be any use at all in doing such a thing in this code example, it would be very useful to be able to make an array of BankAccount pointers and then pass it to a function that wouldn't have to know that SavingsAccount or CheckingAccount objects even existed. You will see an example of that in a moment, but first you need to be clear about what's happening in Listing A.8.

The call to pb->Display() will execute the BankAccount::Display() function, not surprisingly. The call to pc->Display() would execute CheckingAccount::Display() if you had written one, but because CheckingAccount only inherits the base class code, this call will be to BankAccount::Display(), also. The call to ps->Display() will execute the override, SavingsAccount::Display(). This is exactly the behavior you want. Each account will be displayed completely and properly.

Things aren't as simple when it comes to pc2 and ps2, however. These pointers, though they point to a CheckingAccount object and a SavingsAccount object, are declared to be of type pointer-to-BankAccount. Each of the display calls will execute the BankAccount::Display() function, which is not what you want at all. To achieve the desired behavior, you must include the keyword virtual in your declaration of BankAccount::Display(). (The keyword must appear in the base class declaration of the function.) When you do so, you are asking for polymorphism, asking that the same line of code sometimes do quite different things. To see how this can happen, consider a function such as this one:

```
void SomeClass::DisplayAccounts(BankAccount* a[], int numaccounts)
{
    for (int i = 0; i < numaccounts; i++)
    {
        a[i]->Display();
    }
}
```

This function takes an array of BankAccount pointers, goes through the array, and displays each account. If, for example, the first pointer is pointing to a CheckingAccount object, BankAccount::Display() will be executed. If the second pointer is pointing to a SavingsAccount object, and Display() is virtual, SavingsAccount::Display() will be executed. You can't tell by looking at the code which lines will be executed, and that's polymorphism.

It's a tremendously useful feature. Without it, you'd have to write switch statements that decide which function to call, and every time you add another kind of BankAccount, you'd have to find those switch statements and change them. With it, you can add as many new kinds of BankAccount classes as you want, and you never have to change SomeClass::DisplayAccounts() to accommodate that.

Managing Memory

When you declare an object in a block of code, it lasts only until the last line of code in the block has been executed. Then the object goes out of scope, and its memory is reclaimed. If you want some cleanup task taken care of, you write a *destructor* (the opposite of a constructor) for the object, and the system will call the destructor before reclaiming the memory.

Often you want to create an object that will continue to exist past the lifetime of the function that created it. You must, of course, keep a pointer to the object somewhere. A very common situation is to have the pointer as a member variable of a class: The constructor for the class allocates the memory, and the destructor releases it.

Allocating and Releasing Memory

In C, you allocate memory like this with the malloc() function. For example, to allocate enough memory for a single integer, you would write

```
int *pi = (int *) malloc ( sizeof(int) );
```

However, when you allocate memory for an object, you want the constructor to run. `malloc()`, written long before C++ was developed, can't call constructors. Therefore, you use an operator called new to allocate and initialize the memory, like this:

```
BankAccount* pb = new BankAccount("AB123456","11038-30",100.00);
```

(handwritten margin note) like Java will allocate mem

The parameters after the classname are passed along to the constructor, as they were when you allocated a `BankAccount` within a block. Not only does new call the constructor, but you also don't have to calculate the number of bytes you need with `sizeof`, and you don't have to cast the pointer you receive back. This is a handy operator.

> **TIP**
>
> The place where this memory is allocated is technically called the *free store*. Many C++ developers call it the *heap*. On the other hand, variables allocated within a block are said to be *on the stack*.

When you're finished with the object you allocated with new, you use the `delete` operator to get rid of it, like this:

(handwritten margin note) free up mem

```
delete pb;
```

(handwritten margin note) malloc(), free new w/ delete

`delete` will call the destructor and then reclaim the memory. The older C function, `free()`, must never be used to release memory that was allocated with new. If you allocate some other memory (say, a dynamic array of integers) with `malloc()`, you must release it with `free()` rather than `delete`. Many developers find it simpler to leave `free()` and `malloc()` behind forever and use new and delete exclusively.

new can be used for array allocation, like this:

```
int * numbers = new int[100];
```

When you are finished with memory that was allocated like this, always use the array form of delete to release it:

```
delete[] numbers;
```

Pointers as Member Variables

It's common to use pointers within objects. Consider the `BankAccount` class that's been the example throughout this chapter. Why should it carry around a character string representing a customer identifier? Wouldn't it be better to carry around a pointer to an object that is an instance of the class `Customer`? This is easy to do. Remove the private `customer_id` variable and add a `Customer` pointer to the class declaration, like this:

```
Customer* pCustomer;
```

You would have to write code in the constructor that finds the right `Customer` object using only the customer identifer passed to the constructor, and you would probably add two new constructors that take `Customer` pointers. You can't take away a public function after you've written it, because someone might be relying on it. If you are sure no one is, you could remove it.

Now a `BankAccount` can do all sorts of useful things by delegating to the `Customer` object it is associated with. Need to print the customer's name and address at the top of the statement? No problem, have the `Customer` object do it:

```
pCustomer->PrintNameandAddress();
```

This is a terrific way to reuse all the work that went into formatting the name and address in the `Customer` class. It also completely isolates you from changes in that format later.

 TIP This kind of reuse is generally called *aggregation* or *containment* and is contrasted with inheritance. It corresponds to the HAS sentences presented in the inheritance section.

Dynamic Objects

A `BankAccount` is always associated with exactly one `Customer` object. However, there are other things about a `BankAccount` that might or might not exist. Perhaps an account is associated with a `CreditCard`, and if so, possible overdrafts are covered from that card.

To implement this in code, you would add another private member variable to the `BankAccount` class:

```
CreditCard *pCard;
```

All the constructors written so far would set this pointer to NULL to indicate that it doesn't point to a valid `CreditCard`:

```
pCard = NULL;
```

You could then add a public function such as `AddCreditCard()` that would set the pointer. The code could be inline, like this:

```
void AddCreditCard(CreditCard* card) {pCard = card;}
```

The new code for `Withdraw()` would probably look like this:

```
void BankAccount::Withdraw(float amounttowithdraw)
{
    balance -= amounttowithdraw;
    if (balance < 0)
        {
        if (pCard)
            {
            int hundreds = - (int) (balance / 100);
            hundreds++;
            pCard->CashAdvance(hundreds * 100);
            balance += hundreds * 100;
            }
        else
            balance += amounttowithdraw; //reverse transaction
        }
}
```

This rounds the overdraft (not the withdrawal) to the nearest hundred and obtains that amount from the credit card. If this account has no associated card, it reverses the transaction, as before.

Destructors and Pointers

When a BankAccount object is thrown away, the Customer or CreditCard objects to which it might have had pointers continue to exist. That means BankAccount doesn't need a destructor at the moment. Many times, objects with pointers as member variables do need destructors.

Consider the situation of ordering new checks. When the checks arrive, the charge is taken out of the account. Perhaps you will make a CheckOrder object to gather up the information and will add a function to CheckingAccount to make one of these. Without taking this example too far afield by trying to design CheckOrder, the OrderChecks() function might look like this:

```
CheckingAccount::OrderChecks()
{
    pOrder = new CheckOrder( /* whatever parameters the constructor takes */);
}
```

You would add pOrder as a private member variable of CheckingAccount:

```
CheckOrder* pOrder;
```

In the constructor for CheckingAccount, you would set pOrder to NULL because a brand new account doesn't have an outstanding check order.

When the checks arrive, whatever outside code called OrderChecks() could call ChecksArrive(), which would look like this:

```
CheckingAccount::ChecksArrive()
{
    balance -= pOrder.GetCharge();
    delete pOrder;
    pOrder = NULL;
}
```

N O T E   This function will be able to access balance directly like this only if balance was protected in BankAccount rather than private, as discussed earlier. ◼

The delete operator will clean up the order object by running its destructor and then reclaim the memory. You set the pointer to NULL afterwards to make sure that no other code tries to use the pointer, which no longer points to a valid CheckOrder object.

What if a CheckingAccount is closed while an order is outstanding? If you throw away the pointer, the memory occupied by the CheckOrder object will never be reclaimed. You will have to write a destructor for CheckingAccount that cleans this up. Remember that constructors always have the same name as the class. Destructor names are always a tilde (~) followed by the name of the class. CheckingAccount::~CheckingAccount() would look like this:

```
CheckingAccount::~CheckingAccount()
{
    delete pOrder;
}
```

Running Destructors Accidentally *call by ref.*

When a class has a destructor that does something destructive, you have to be very careful to make sure that it isn't unexpectedly called and causes you trouble. Look at the code in Listing A.9. It makes a CheckingAccount object, orders checks, passes the object to some function or another, and then tells the account that the checks have arrived.

Listing A.9   Accidental Destruction

```
CheckingAccount ca("AB123456","11038-32",200.00);
ca.OrderChecks();
SomeFunction(ca);
ca.ChecksArrive();
```

This looks harmless enough. However, when you pass the CheckingAccount object to SomeFunction(), the system makes a copy of it to give to the function. This copy is identical to ca: It has a pointer in it that points to the same CheckOrder as ca. When the call to SomeFunction() returns, the copy is no longer needed, so the system runs the destructor and reclaims the memory. Unfortunately, the destructor for the temporary CheckingAccount object will delete its CheckOrder, which is also ca's CheckOrder. The call to ChecksArrive() can't work because the CheckOrder object is gone.

There are two ways to deal with this problem. The first is to change SomeFunction() so that it takes a pointer to a CheckingAccount or a reference to a CheckingAccount. The second is to write a function called a *copy constructor* that controls the way the temporary CheckingAccount is made. References and copy constructors are beyond the scope of this chapter. If the function takes a pointer, no copy is made, and there can be no accidental destruction.

What Else Should I Know?

If you bought a book solely on C++ or attended a week-long introductory course, you would learn a number of other C++ features, including the following:

- Default parameter values
- Constructor initializer line
- The const keyword
- Passing parameters by reference
- Returning values by reference
- Static member variables and static member functions
- Copy constructors
- Operator overloading

Two topics not always covered in introductory material are exceptions and templates. These are discussed in Chapter 26, "Exceptions and Templates."

Windows Programming Review and a Look Inside *CWnd*

In this appendix

The Microsoft Foundation Classes were written for one single purpose: to make Windows programming easier by providing classes with methods and data that handle tasks common to all Windows programs. The classes that are in MFC are designed to be useful to a Windows programmer specifically. The methods within each class perform tasks that Windows programmers often need to perform. Many of the classes have a close correspondence to structures and *window classes*, in the old Windows sense of the word *class*. Many of the methods correspond closely to API (Application Programming Interface) functions already familiar to Windows programmers, who often refer to them as the Windows SDK or as SDK functions.

Programming for Windows

If you've programmed for Windows in C, you know that the word *class* was used to describe a window long before C++ programming came to Windows. A window class is vital to any Windows C program. A standard structure holds the data that describes this window class, and the operating system provides a number of standard window classes. A programmer usually builds a new window class for each program and registers it by calling an API function, `RegisterClass()`. Windows that appear onscreen can then be created, based on that class, by calling another API function, `CreateWindow()`.

A C-Style Window Class

The WNDCLASS structure, which describes the window class, is equivalent to the WNDCLASSA structure, which looks like Listing B.1.

Listing B.1   *WNDCLASSA* Structure from WINUSER.H

```
typedef struct tagWNDCLASSA {
    UINT        style;
    WNDPROC     lpfnWndProc;
    int         cbClsExtra;
    int         cbWndExtra;
    HINSTANCE   hInstance;
    HICON       hIcon;
    HCURSOR     hCursor;
    HBRUSH      hbrBackground;
    LPCSTR      lpszMenuName;
    LPCSTR      lpszClassName;
} WNDCLASSA, *PWNDCLASSA, NEAR *NPWNDCLASSA, FAR *LPWNDCLASSA;
```

WINUSER.H sets up two very similar window class structures: WNDCLASSA for programs that use normal strings and WNDCLASSW for Unicode programs. Chapter 28, "Future Explorations," covers Unicode programs in the "Unicode" section.

TIP WINUSER.H is code supplied with Developer Studio. It's typically in the folder \Program Files\ Files\Microsoft Visual Studio\VC98\include.

If you were creating a Windows program in C, you would need to fill a WNDCLASS structure. The members of the WNDCLASS structure are as follows:

- **style**—A number made by combining standard styles, represented with constants like CS_GLOBALCLASS or CS_OWNDC, with the bitwise or operator (¦). A perfectly good class can be registered with a style value of 0; the other styles are for exceptions to normal procedure.

- **lpfnWndProc**—A pointer to a function that is the Windows Procedure (generally called the WindProc) for the class. Refer to Chapter 3, "Messages and Commands," for a discussion of this function.

- **cbClsExtra**—The number of extra bytes to add to the window class. It's usually 0, but C programmers would sometimes build a window class with extra data in it.

- **cbWndExtra**—The number of extra bytes to add to each instance of the window, usually 0.

- **hInstance**—A handle to an instance of an application, the running program that is registering this window class. For now, think of this as a way for the window class to reach the application that uses it.

- **hIcon**—An icon to be drawn when the window is minimized. Typically, this is set with a call to another API function, LoadIcon().

- **hCursor**—The cursor that displays when the mouse is over the screen window associated with this window class. Typically, this is set with a call to the API function LoadCursor().

- **hbrBackground**—The brush to be used for painting the window background. The API call to GetStockObject() is the usual way to set this variable.

- **lpszMenuName**—A long pointer to a string that is zero terminated and contains the name of the menu for the window class.

- **lpszClassName**—The name for this window class, to be used by CreateWindow(), when a window (an instance of the window class) is created. You make up a name.

Window Creation

If you've never written a Windows program before, having to fill out a WNDCLASS structure might intimidate you. This is the first step, though, in Windows programming in C. However, you can always find simple sample programs to copy, like this one:

```
WNDCLASS wcInit;

wcInit.style = 0;
wcInit.lpfnWndProc = (WNDPROC)MainWndProc;
wcInit.cbClsExtra = 0;
wcInit.cbWndExtra = 0;
wcInit.hInstance = hInstance;
wcInit.hIcon = LoadIcon (hInstance, MAKEINTRESOURCE(ID_ICON));
wcInit.hCursor = LoadCursor (NULL, IDC_ARROW);
```

```
wcInit.hbrBackground = GetStockObject (WHITE_BRUSH);
wcInit.lpszMenuName = "DEMO";
wcInit.lpszClassName ="NewWClass";

return (RegisterClass (&wcInit));
```

Hungarian Notation

You might wonder what kind of variable name `lpszClassName` is or why it's `wcInit` and not just `Init`. The reason for this is Microsoft programmers use a variable naming convention called *Hungarian Notation*. It is so named because a Hungarian programmer named Charles Simonyi popularized it at Microsoft (and probably because at first glance, the variable names seem to be written in another language).

In Hungarian Notation, the variable is given a descriptive name, like `Count` or `ClassName`, that starts with a capital letter. If it is a multiword name, each word is capitalized. Then, before the descriptive name, letters are added to indicate the variable type—for example, `nCount` for an integer or `bFlag` for a Boolean (`TRUE` or `FALSE`) variable. In this way, the programmer should never forget a variable type or do something foolish such as pass a signed variable to a function that is expecting an unsigned value.

The style has gained widespread popularity, although some people hate it. If you long for the good old days of arguing where to put the braces, or better still whether to call them brace, face, or squiggle brackets, but can't find anyone to rehash those old wars anymore, you can probably find somebody to argue about Hungarian Notation instead. The arguments in favor boil down to "you catch yourself making stupid mistakes," and the arguments against it to "it's ugly and hard to read." The practical truth is that the structures used by the API and the classes defined in MFC all use Hungarian Notation, so you might as well get used to it. You'll probably find yourself doing it for your own variables, too. The prefixes are as follows:

Prefix	Variable Type	Comment
a	Array	
b	Boolean	
d	Double	
h	Handle	
i	Integer	"index into"
l	Long	
lp	Long pointer to	
lpfn	Long pointer to function	
m_	Member variable	
n	Integer	"number of"
p	Pointer to	
s	String	
sz	Zero-terminated string	

u   Unsigned integer

c   Class

Many people add their own type conventions to variable names; the wc in wcInit stands for *window class.*

Filling the wcInit structure and calling RegisterClass is standard stuff: registering a class called NewWClass with a menu called DEMO and a WindProc called MainWndProc. Everything else about it is ordinary to an experienced Windows C programmer. After registering the class, when those old-time Windows programmers wanted to create a window onscreen, out popped some code like this:

```
HWND hWnd;
hInst = hInstance;
hWnd = CreateWindow (
"NewWClass",
"Demo 1",
WS_OVERLAPPEDWINDOW,
CW_USEDEFAULT,
CW_USEDEFAULT,
CW_USEDEFAULT,
CW_USEDEFAULT,
NULL,
NULL,
hInstance,
NULL);

if (! hWnd)
return (FALSE);

ShowWindow (hWnd, nCmdShow);
UpdateWindow (hWnd);
```

This code calls CreateWindow(), then ShowWindow(), and UpdateWindow(). The parameters to the API function CreateWindow() are as follows:

- lpClassName—A pointer to the classname that was used in the RegisterClass() call.

- lpWindowName—The window name. You make this up.

- dwStyle—The window style, made by combining #define constants with the ¦ operator. For a primary application window like this one, WS_OVERLAPPEDWINDOW is standard.

- x—The window's horizontal position. CW_USEDEFAULT lets the operating system calculate sensible defaults, based on the user's screen settings.

- y—The window's vertical position. CW_USEDEFAULT lets the operating system calculate sensible defaults, based on the user's screen settings.

- nWidth—The window's width. CW_USEDEFAULT lets the operating system calculate sensible defaults, based on the user's screen settings.

- nHeight—The window's height. CW_USEDEFAULT lets the operating system calculate sensible defaults, based on the user's screen settings.

- hWndParent—The handle of the parent or owner window. (Some windows are created by other windows, which own them.) NULL means that there is no parent to this window.
- hMenu—The handle to a menu or child-window identifier, in other words a window owned by this window. NULL means that there are no children.
- hInstance—The handle of the application instance that is creating this window.
- lpParam—A pointer to any extra parameters. None are needed in this example.

CreateWindow()returns a window handle—everybody calls his window handles hWnd—and this handle is used in the rest of the standard code. If it's NULL, the window creation failed. If the handle returned has any non-NULL value, the creation succeeded and the handle is passed to ShowWindow() and UpdateWindow(), which together draw the actual window onscreen.

Handles

A *handle* is more than just a pointer. Windows programs refer to resources such as windows, icons, cursors, and so on, with a handle. Behind the scenes there is a handle table that tracks the resource's address as well as information about the resource type. It's called a *handle* because a program uses it as a way to "get hold of" a resource. Handles are typically passed to functions that need to use resources and are returned from functions that allocate resources.

There are a number of basic handle types: HWND for a window handle, HICON for an icon handle, and so on. No matter what kind of handle is used, remember that it's a way to reach a resource so that you can use the resource.

Encapsulating the Windows API

API functions create and manipulate windows onscreen, handle drawing, connect programs to Help files, facilitate threading, manage memory, and much more. When these functions are encapsulated into MFC classes, your programs can accomplish these same basic Windows tasks, with less work on your part.

There are literally thousands of API functions, and it can take six months to a year to get a good handle on the API, so this book doesn't attempt to present a minitutorial on the API. In the "Programming for Windows" section earlier in this chapter, you were reminded about two API functions, RegisterClass() and CreateWindow(). These illustrate what was difficult about C Windows programming with the API and how the MFC classes make it easier. Documentation on the API functions is available on MSDN, which comes with Visual C++.

Inside *CWnd*

CWnd is an enormously important MFC class. Roughly a third of all the MFC classes use it as a base class—classes such as CDialog, CEditView, CButton, and many more. It serves as a wrapper for the old-style window class and the API functions that create and manipulate window classes. For example, the only public member variable is m_hWnd, the member variable that stores the window handle. This variable is set by the member function CWnd::Create() and used by almost all the other member functions when they call their associated API functions.

You might think that the call to the API function CreateWindow() would be handled automatically in the CWnd constructor, CWnd::CWnd, so that when the constructor is called to initialize a CWnd object, the corresponding window on the screen is created. This would save you, the programmer, a good deal of effort because you can't forget to call a constructor. In fact, that's not what Microsoft has chosen to do. The constructor looks like this:

```
CWnd::CWnd()
{
 AFX_ZERO_INIT_OBJECT(CCmdTarget);
}
```

AFX_ZERO_INIT_OBJECT is just a macro, expanded by the C++ compiler's preprocessor, that uses the C function memset to zero out every byte of every member variable in the object, like this:

```
#define AFX_ZERO_INIT_OBJECT(base_class)
➥ memset(((base_class*)this)+1, 0, sizeof(*this)
➥ - sizeof(class base_class));
```

The reason why Microsoft chose not to call CreateWindow() in the constructor is that constructors can't return a value. If something goes wrong with the window creation, there are no elegant or neat ways to deal with it. Instead, the constructor does almost nothing, a step that essentially can't fail, and the call to CreateWindow() is done from within the member function Cwnd::Create()or the closely related CWnd::CreateEx(), which looks like the one in Listing B.2.

Listing B.2 *CWnd::CreateEx()* from WINCORE.CPP

```
BOOL CWnd::CreateEx(DWORD dwExStyle, LPCTSTR lpszClassName,
 LPCTSTR lpszWindowName, DWORD dwStyle,
 int x, int y, int nWidth, int nHeight,
 HWND hWndParent, HMENU nIDorHMenu, LPVOID lpParam)
{
 // allow modification of several common create parameters
 CREATESTRUCT cs;
 cs.dwExStyle = dwExStyle;
 cs.lpszClass = lpszClassName;
 cs.lpszName = lpszWindowName;
 cs.style = dwStyle;
 cs.x = x;
 cs.y = y;
 cs.cx = nWidth;
 cs.cy = nHeight;
 cs.hwndParent = hWndParent;
 cs.hMenu = nIDorHMenu;
 cs.hInstance = AfxGetInstanceHandle();
 cs.lpCreateParams = lpParam;
```

continues

Part
VII
App
B

Listing B.2 Continued

```
if (!PreCreateWindow(cs))
{
PostNcDestroy();
return FALSE;
}

AfxHookWindowCreate(this);
HWND hWnd = ::CreateWindowEx(cs.dwExStyle, cs.lpszClass,
cs.lpszName, cs.style, cs.x, cs.y, cs.cx, cs.cy,
cs.hwndParent, cs.hMenu, cs.hInstance, cs.lpCreateParams);

#ifdef _DEBUG
if (hWnd == NULL)
{
TRACE1("Warning: Window creation failed: Â
GetLastError returns 0x%8.8X\n",
GetLastError());
}
#endif

if (!AfxUnhookWindowCreate())
PostNcDestroy();
// cleanup if CreateWindowEx fails too soon

if (hWnd == NULL)
return FALSE;
ASSERT(hWnd == m_hWnd); // should have been set in send msg hook
return TRUE;
}
```

TIP WINCORE.CPP is code supplied with Developer Studio. It's typically in the folder \Program Files\Microsoft Visual Studio\VC98\mfc\src.

This sets up a CREATESTRUCT structure very much like a WNDCLASS and fills it with the parameters that were passed to CreateEx(). It calls PreCreateWindow, AfxHookWindowCreate(), ::CreateWindow(), and AfxUnhookWindowCreate() before checking hWnd and returning.

TIP The AFX prefix on many useful MFC functions dates back to the days when Microsoft's internal name for its class library was Application Framework. The :: in the call to CreateWindow identifies it as an API function, sometimes referred to as an SDK function in this context. The other functions are member functions of CWnd that set up other background boilerplate for you.

On the face of it, there doesn't seem to be any effort saved here. You declare an instance of some CWnd object, call its Create() function, and have to pass just as many parameters as you did in the old C way of doing things. What's the point? Well, CWnd is really a class from which to inherit. Things become much simpler in the derived classes. Take CButton, for example, a class that encapsulates the concept of a button on a dialog box. A button is just a tiny window, but its behavior is constrained—for example, the user can't resize a button. Its `Create()` member function looks like this:

```
BOOL CButton::Create(LPCTSTR lpszCaption, DWORD dwStyle,
 const RECT& rect, CWnd* pParentWnd, UINT nID)
{
 CWnd* pWnd = this;
 return pWnd->Create(_T("BUTTON"), lpszCaption, dwStyle, rect, pParentWnd, nID);
}
```

That amounts to a lot fewer parameters. If you want a button, you create a button and let the class hierarchy fill in the rest.

Getting a Handle on All These MFC Classes

There are more than 200 MFC classes. Why so many? What do they do? How can any normal human keep track of them and know which one to use for what? Good questions. Questions that will take a large portion of this book to answer. The first half of this book presents the most commonly used MFC classes. This section looks at some of the more important base classes.

CObject

Figure B.1 shows a high-level overview of the inheritance tree for the classes in MFC. Only a handful of MFC classes do not inherit from `CObject`. `CObject` contains the basic functionality that all the MFC classes (and most of the new classes you create) will be sure to need, such as persistence support and diagnostic output. As well, classes derived from `CObject` can be contained in the MFC container classes, discussed in Appendix F, "Useful Classes."

FIG. B.1
Almost all the classes in MFC inherit from `CObject`.

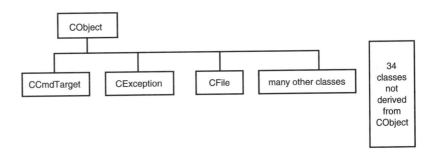

CCmdTarget

Some of the classes that inherit from `CObject`, such as `CFile` and `CException`, and their derived classes don't need to interact directly with the user and the operating system through messages and commands. All the classes that do need to receive messages and commands inherit from `CCmdTarget`. Figure B.2 shows a bird's-eye view of `CCmdTarget`'s derived classes, generally called *command targets*.

FIG. B.2

Any class that will receive a command must inherit from CCmdTarget.

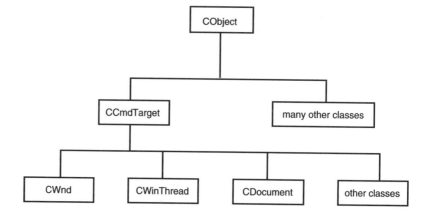

CWnd

As already mentioned, CWnd is an extremely important class. Only classes derived from CWnd can receive messages; threads and documents can receive commands but not messages.

TIP   Chapter 3, "Messages and Commands," explores the distinction between commands and messages. Chapter 4, "Documents and Views," explains documents, and Chapter 27, "Multitasking with Windows Threads," explains threads.

CWnd provides window-oriented functionality, such as calls to CreateWindow and DestroyWindow, functions to handle painting the window onscreen, processing messages, talking to the Clipboard, and much more—almost 250 member functions in all. Only a handful of these will need to be overridden in derived classes. Figure B.3 shows the classes that inherit from CWnd; there are so many control classes that to list them all would clutter up the diagram, so they are lumped together as control classes.

All Those Other Classes

So far you've seen 10 classes in these three figures. What about the other 200+? You'll meet them in context throughout the book. If there's a specific class you're wondering about, check the index. Check the online help, too, because every class is documented there. Also, don't forget that the full source for MFC is included with every copy of Visual C++. Reading the source is a hard way to figure out how a class works, but sometimes you need that level of detail.

FIG. B.3
Any class that will
receive a message must
inherit from CWnd,
which provides lots of
window-related
functions.

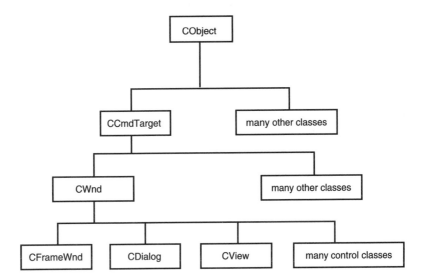

The Visual Studio User Interface, Menus, and Toolbars

In this chapter

Reviewing Developer Studio: An Integrated Development Environment

When you buy Microsoft Visual C++, you actually get Microsoft Developer Studio with the Visual C++ component activated. Developer Studio is far more than just a compiler, and you have far more to learn than you may think. The interface is very visual, which means that there are many possibilities greeting you when you first run Visual C++.

Microsoft Visual C++ is one component of the Microsoft Developer Studio. The capabilities of this one piece of software are astonishing. It is called an *integrated development environment (IDE)* because within a single tool, you can perform the following:

- Generate starter applications without writing code.
- View a project several different ways.
- Edit source and include files.
- Build the visual interface (menus and dialog boxes) of your application.
- Compile and link.
- Debug an application while it runs.

Visual C++ is, technically speaking, just one component of Developer Studio. You can buy, for example, Microsoft's Visual J++ compiler and use it in Developer Studio as well. Looking at it another way, Visual C++ is more than just Developer Studio because the *Microsoft Foundation Classes (MFC)* that are becoming the standard for C++ Windows programming are a class library and not related to the development environment. In fact, the major C++ compilers all use MFC now. However, for most people, Visual C++ and Developer Studio mean the same thing, and in this book the names are used interchangeably.

Choosing a View

The user interface of Developer Studio encourages you to move from view to view in your project, looking at your resources, classes, and files. The main screen is divided into panes that you can resize to suit your own needs. There are many shortcut menus, reached by right-clicking different places on the screen, that simplify common tasks.

With Visual C++, you work on a single application as a *workspace*, which contains one or more projects. A *project* is a collection of files: source, headers, resources, settings, and configuration information. Developer Studio is designed to enable work on all aspects of a single workspace at once. You create a new application by creating a new project. When you want to work on your application, open the workspace (a file with the extension .DSW) rather than each code file independently. The interface of \revdttm1176855283 Developer Studio, shown in Figures C.1 and C.2, is designed to work with a workspace and is divided into several zones.

FIG. C.1

The Developer Studio interface presents a lot of information. The Workspace window is on the left.

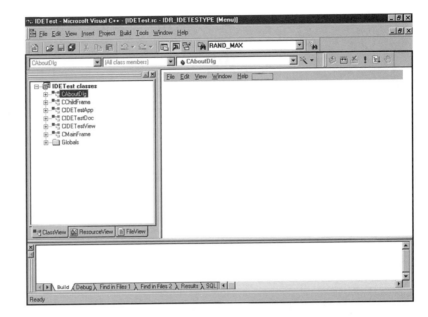

FIG. C.2

When the Workspace window is narrowed, the words on the tabs are replaced with icons.

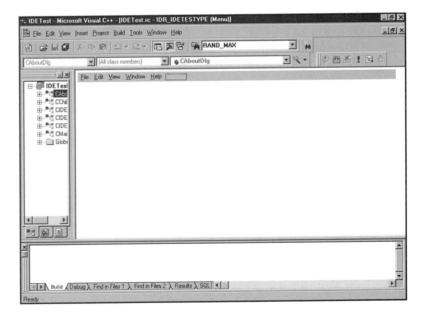

The zones that make up the Developer Studio interface are as follows:

- Across the top: menus and toolbars. These are discussed in the second half of this chapter.
- On the left: the Workspace window.

- On the right: your main working area where you edit files.
- Across the bottom: the output window and status bar.

TIP Open Developer Studio and try to resize the panes and follow along as functions are described in this chapter. If you want an application to follow along with, you can build a very simple one as described in Chapter 1, "Building Your First Windows Application."

The Workspace window determines which way you look at your project and what is in the main working area: code or resources (menus, icons, and dialog boxes). Each of these views is discussed in detail in a separate section in this chapter, including the following:

- The ResourceView is discussed in the "Looking at Interface Elements" section.
- The ClassView is discussed in the "Looking at Your Code, Arranged by Class" section.
- The FileView is discussed in the "Looking at Your Code, Arranged by File" section.

Developer Studio uses two different files to keep track of all the information about your project. The *project workspace file*, with a .DSW extension, contains the names of all the files in the project, what directories they are in, compiler and linker options, and other information required by everyone who may work on the project. There is also a *project file*, with a .DSP extension, for each project within the workspace. *The workspace options file*, with an .OPT extension, contains all your personal settings for Developer Studio—colors, fonts, toolbars, which files are open and how their MDI windows are sized and located, breakpoints from your most recent debugging session, and so on. If someone else is going to work on your project, you give that person a copy of the project workspace file and project file but not the project options file.

To open the project, open the project workspace file. The other files are opened automatically.

Looking at Interface Elements

After you've opened or created a workspace, clicking the ResourceView tab in the Workspace window opens an expandable and collapsible outline of the visual elements of your program: accelerators, dialog boxes, icons, menus, the string table, toolbars, and version information. These resources define the way users interact with your program. Chapter 2, "Dialogs and Controls;" Chapter 8, "Building a Complete Application: ShowString;" and Chapter 9, "Status Bars and Toolbars" cover the work involved in creating and editing these resources. The next few sections cover the way in which you can look at completed resources.

TIP Open one of the projects that was built in this book, or a sample project from Visual C++, and follow along as functions are described in this section. ShowString, the sample application from Chapter 8, is a good choice because it uses most of the features described in this section.

Accelerators

Accelerators associate key combinations with menu items. Figure C.3 shows an accelerator resource created by AppWizard. All these accelerator combinations are made for you when you create a new application. You can add accelerators for specific menu items, if necessary.

FIG. C.3

Accelerators associate key combinations with menu items.

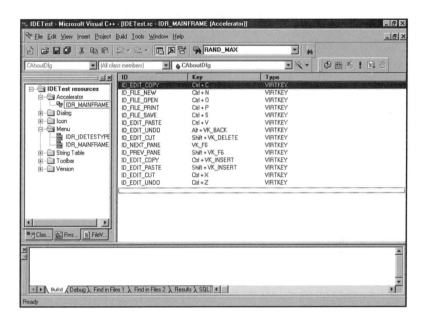

Part

VII

App

C

Dialog Boxes

Your application receives information from users through *dialog boxes*. When a dialog resource is being displayed in the main working area, as in Figure C.4, a control palette floats over the working area. (If it's not displayed, right-click the menu bar and check Controls to display it.) Each small icon on the palette represents a control (edit box, list box, button, and so on) that can be inserted onto your dialog box. By choosing View, Properties, the Dialog Properties box shown in Figure C.4 is displayed. Here the behavior of a control or of the whole dialog box can be controlled.

 TIP Click the pushpin at the top left of the Properties box to keep it displayed, even when a different item is highlighted. The box displays the properties of each item you click.

This method of editing dialog boxes is one of the reasons for the name *Visual C++*. In this product, if you want a button to be a little lower on a dialog box, you click it with the mouse, drag it to the new position, and release the mouse button. Similarly, if you want the dialog box larger or smaller, grab a corner or edge and drag it to the new size, like any other sizable window. Before Visual C++ was released, the process involved coding and pixel counting and took many minutes rather than just a few seconds. This visual approach to dialog box building made Windows programming accessible to many more programmers.

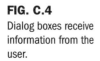

FIG. C.4

Dialog boxes receive information from the user.

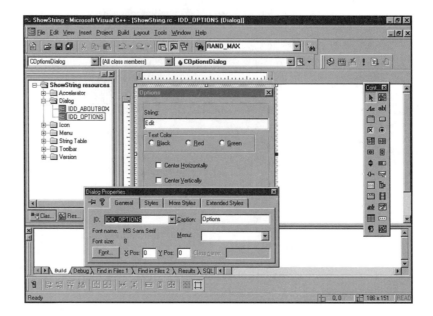

Icons

Icons are small bitmaps that represent your program or its documents. For example, when a program is minimized, an icon is used to represent it. A larger version of that icon is used to represent both the program and its documents within an Explorer window. When an MDI window is minimized within your application, the minimized window is represented by an icon. Figure C.5 shows the default icon provided by AppWizard for minimized MDI windows. One of your first tasks after building any application is to replace this with an icon that more clearly represents the work your program performs.

An icon is a 32×32 pixel bitmap that can be edited with any number of drawing tools, including the simple bitmap editor included in Developer Studio. The interface is very similar to Microsoft Paint or Microsoft Paintbrush in Zoom mode. You can draw one pixel at a time by clicking, or freehand lines by clicking and dragging. You can work on the small or zoomed versions of the icon and see the effects at once in both places.

Menus

With *menus,* users can tell your program what to do. *Keyboard shortcuts* (accelerators) are linked to menu items, as are toolbar buttons. AppWizard creates the standard menus for a new application, and you edit those and create new ones in this view. Later, you'll use ClassWizard to connect menu items to functions within your code. Figure C.6 shows a menu displayed in the ResourceView. Choose View, Properties to display the Menu \revised Properties box for the menu item. Every menu item has the following three components:

FIG. C.5

Icons represent your application and its documents.

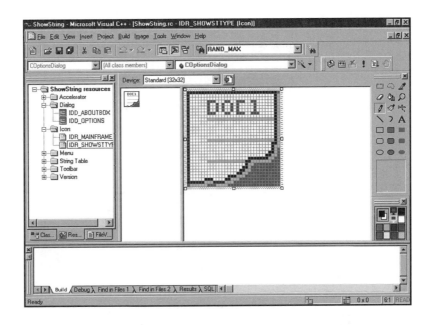

- *Resource ID.* This uniquely identifies this menu item. Accelerators and toolbar buttons are linked to resource IDs. The convention is to build the ID from the menu choices that lead to the item. In Figure C.6, the resource ID is ID_FILE_OPEN.

- *Caption.* This is the text that appears for a menu choice. In Figure C.6, the caption is &Open…\tCtrl+O. The & means that the O will appear underlined, and the menu item can be selected by typing **O** when the menu is displayed. The \t is a tab, and the Ctrl+O is the accelerator for this menu item, as defined in Figure C.3.

- *Prompt.* A prompt appears in the status bar when the highlight is on the menu item or the cursor is over the associated toolbar button. In Figure C.6, the prompt is Open an existing document\nOpen. Only the portion before the newline (\n) is displayed in the status bar. The second part of the prompt, Open, is the text for the ToolTip that appears if the user pauses the mouse over a toolbar button with this resource ID. All this functionality is provided for you automatically by the framework of Visual C++ and MFC.

The String Table

The *string table* is a list of strings within your application. Many strings, such as the static text on dialog boxes or the prompts for menu items, can be accessed in far simpler ways than through the string table, but some are reached only through it. For example, a default name or value can be kept in the string table and changed without recompiling any code, though the resources will have to be compiled and the project linked. Each of these could be hard-coded into the program, but then changes would require a full recompile.

Figure C.7 shows the string table for a sample application. To change a string, open the String Table Properties dialog box and change the caption. Strings cannot be changed within the main working area.

FIG. C.6

Your application receives commands through menus.

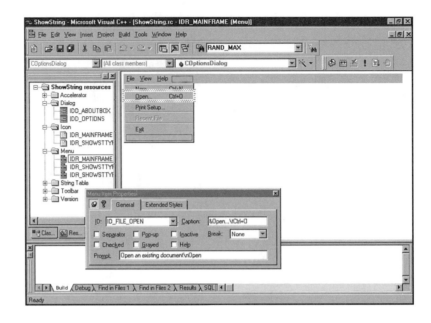

FIG. C.7

The string table stores all the prompts and text in your application.

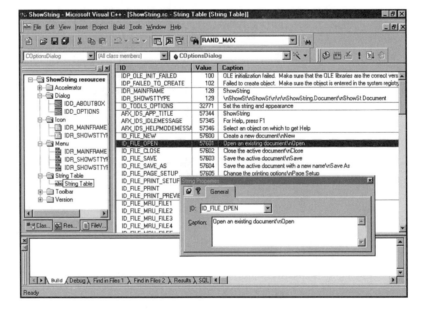

Toolbars

Toolbars are the lines of small buttons typically located directly underneath the menus of an application. Each button is linked to a menu item, and its appearance depends on the state of the menu item. If a menu item is grayed, the corresponding toolbar button is grayed as well. If a menu item is checked, the corresponding toolbar button is typically drawn as a pushed-in button. In this way, toolbar buttons serve as indicators as well as mechanisms for giving commands to the application.

A toolbar button has two parts: a bitmap of the button and a resource ID. When a user clicks the button, it is just as though the menu item with the same resource ID was chosen. Figure C.8 shows a typical toolbar and the properties of the File, Open button on that toolbar. In this view, you can change the resource ID of any button and edit the bitmap with the same tools used to edit icons.

FIG. C.8

Toolbar buttons are associated with menu items through a resource ID.

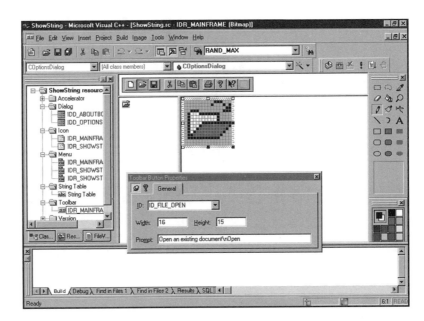

Part

VII

App

C

Version Information

Good installation programs use the version information resource when installing your application on a user's machine. For example, if a user is installing an application that has already been installed, the installation program may not have to copy as many files. It may alert the user if an old version is being installed over a new version, and so on.

When you create an application with AppWizard, version information like that in Figure C.9 is generated for you automatically. Before attempting to change any of it, make sure you understand how installation programs use it.

FIG. C.9
Version information
is used by install
programs.

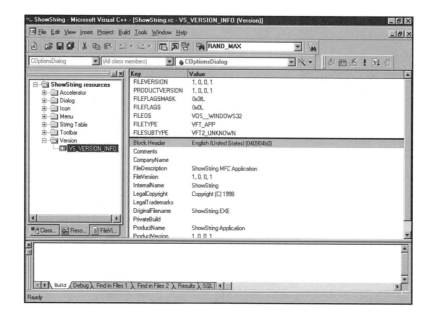

Looking at Your Code, Arranged by Class

The ClassView shows the classes in your application. Under each class, the member variables
and functions are shown, as demonstrated in Figure C.10. Member functions are shown first
with a purple icon next to them, followed by member variables with a turquoise icon. Protected
members have a key next to the icon, whereas private members have a padlock.

FIG. C.10
The ClassView shows
the functions and
variables in each class
in your application.

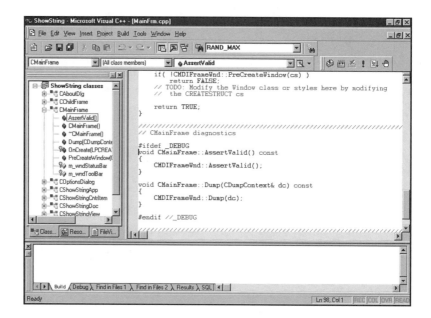

Double-clicking a function name opens the source for that function in the main working area, as shown in Figure C.10. Double-clicking a variable name opens the file in which the variable is declared.

Right-clicking a classname opens a shortcut menu, shown in Figure C.11, with these items:

- *Go to Definition.* Opens the header (.h) file at the definition of this class.

- *Go to Dialog Editor.* For classes associated with a dialog box, opens the dialog box in the resource editor.

- *Add Member Function.* Opens the Add Member Function dialog box shown in Figure C.12. This adds a declaration of the function to the header file, and the stub of a definition to the source file.

FIG. C.11

Common commands related to classes are on the ClassView shortcut menu for a class.

Part
VII

App
C

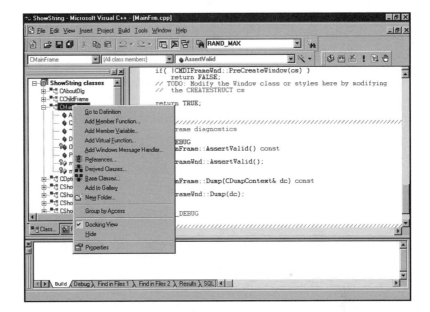

FIG. C.12

Never again forget to add part of a function declaration or definition when you use the Add Member Function shortcut.

- *Add Member Variable.* Opens the Add Member Variable dialog box shown in Figure C.13. This adds a declaration of the variable to the header file.

FIG. C.13

Simplify adding member variables with this shortcut.

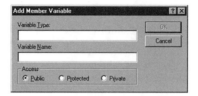

- *Add Virtual Function.* Opens the New Virtual Override dialog box, discussed in Chapter 3, "Messages and Commands."

- *Add Windows Message Handler.* Opens the New Windows Message and Event Handlers dialog box, discussed in Chapter 3.

- *References.* Opens a list of the places where the classname is mentioned within your application. Typically the classname occurs in declarations of instances of the class, but this will also find places where the classname is passed as a parameter to a function or macro.

- *Derived Classes.* Opens a list of all the member functions and member variables of this class, a list of other classes that use this class as a base class, and the references information.

- *Base Classes.* Opens a list of all the member functions and member variables of this class, a list of the base classes of this class, and the references information.

- *Add to Gallery.* Adds this class to the Component Gallery, discussed in Chapter 25, "Achieving Reuse with the Gallery and Your Own AppWizards."

- *New Folder.* Creates a folder you can drag classes into. This helps to organize projects with large numbers of classes.

- *Group by Access.* Rearranges the order of the list. By default, functions are listed in alphabetical order, followed by data members in alphabetical order. With this option toggled on, functions come first (public, then protected, then private functions, alphabetically in each section) followed by data members (again public, then protected, then private data members, alphabetically in each section).

- *Docking View.* Keeps the project workspace window docked at the side of the main working area or undocks it if it was docked.

- *Hide.* Hides the project workspace window. To redisplay it, choose View, Workspace.

- *Properties.* Displays the properties of the class (name, base class).

T I P   Menu items that appear on a toolbar have their toolbar icon next to them on the menu. Make note of the icon; the next time you want to choose that item, perhaps you can use a toolbar instead.

Right-clicking the name of a member function opens a substantial shortcut menu, with the following menu items:

- *Go To Definition.* Opens the source (.cpp) file at the code for this function.

- *Go To Declaration.* Opens the header (.h) file at the declaration of this function.

■ *Delete*. Removes the function from the class.

■ *Set Breakpoint*. Sets a breakpoint. Breakpoints are discussed in Appendix D, "Debugging."

■ *References*. Opens a list of the places where the function is called within your application.

■ *Calls*. Displays a collapsible and expandable outline of all the functions that this function calls. Figure C.14 shows a sample Call Graph window.

FIG. C.14

The Call Graph window lists all the functions that your function calls, and all the functions they call, and so on.

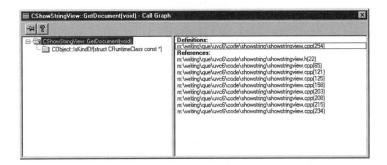

Part

VII

App

C

■ *Called By*. Displays a Callers Graph listing the functions this function is called by.

■ *New Folder*. Creates a folder you can drag classes into. This helps organize projects with large numbers of classes.

■ *Group by Access*. Rearranges the order of the list. By default, functions are listed in alphabetical order, followed by data members in alphabetical order. With this option toggled on, functions come first (public, then protected, then private functions, alphabetically in each section) followed by data members (again public, then protected, then private data members, alphabetically in each section).

■ *Docking View*. Keeps the workspace window docked at the side of the main working area.

■ *Hide*. Hides the workspace window. To redisplay it, choose View, Workspace.

■ *Properties*. Displays the properties of the function (name, return type, parameters).

Right-clicking the name of a member variable opens a shortcut menu with less menu items. The items are as follows:

■ *Go To Definition*. Opens the header (.h) file at the declaration of this variable.

■ *References*. Opens a list of the places where the variable is used within your application.

■ *New Folder*. Creates a folder you can drag classes into. This helps organize projects with large numbers of classes.

■ *Group by Access*. Rearranges the order of the list. By default, functions are listed in alphabetical order, followed by data members in alphabetical order. With this option toggled on, functions come first (public, then protected, then private functions, alphabetically in each section) followed by data members (again public, then protected, then private data members, alphabetically in each section).

■ *Docking View*. Keeps the workspace window docked at the side of the main working area.

■ *Hide*. Hides the workspace window. To redisplay it, choose View, Workspace.

■ *Properties*. Displays the properties of the variable (name and type).

When the main working area is displaying a source or header file, you can edit your code as described in the later section "Editing Your Code."

Looking at Your Code, Arranged by File

The FileView is much like the ClassView in that you can display and edit source and header files (see Figure C.15). However, it gives you access to parts of your file that are outside class definitions and makes it easy to open non-code files like resources and plain text.

The project workspace window contains a tree view of the source files in your project. The default categories used are Source Files, Header Files, Resource Files, Help Files (if you project has Help) and External Dependencies. You can add your own categories by right-clicking anywhere in the FileView and choosing New Folder, and then specifying which file extensions belong in the new category.

FIG. C.15
The FileView displays source and header files.

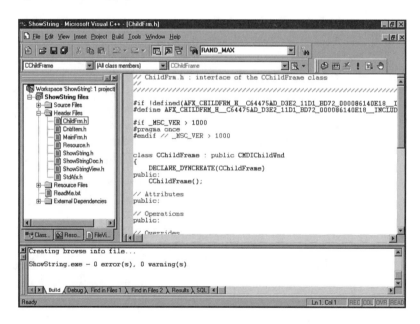

Double-clicking a file name displays that file in the main working area. You can then edit the file (even if it isn't a source or header file) as described in the later section "Editing Your Code."

Output and Error Messages

Across the bottom of the Developer Studio screen is the Output view. This is a tabbed view that shows output and error messages from a variety of Developer Studio functions.

 T I P   If there is no Output view on your screen, choose View, Output from the menu to restore the view.

The five tabs in the Output view are the following:

- *Build*. Displays the results of compiling and linking.
- *Debug*. Used when debugging, as discussed in Appendix D.
- *Find in Files 1*. Displays the results of the Find in Files search, discussed later in this chapter.
- *Find in Files 2*. An alternative display window for Find in Files results so that you can preserve earlier results.
- *Results*. Displays results of tools like the profiler, discussed in Chapter 24, "Improving Your Application's Performance."

If you have installed the Enterprise Edition of Visual C++, there is a sixth tab, SQL Debugging. For more information, see Chapter 23, "SQL and the Enterprise Edition."

Part

VII

App

C

Editing Your Code

For most people, editing code is the most important task you do in a development environment. If you've used any other editor or word processor before, you can handle the basics of the Developer Studio editor right away. You should be able to type in code, fix your mistakes, and move around in source or header files by using the basic Windows techniques you would expect to be able to use. Because this is a programmer's editor, there are some nice features you should know about.

Basic Typing and Editing

To add text to a file, click where you want the text to go and start typing. By default, the editor is in Insert mode, which means your new text pushes the old text over. To switch to Overstrike mode, press the Insert key. Now your text types over the text that is already there. The OVR indicator on the status bar reminds you that you are in Overstrike mode. Pressing Insert again puts you back in Insert mode. Move around in the file by clicking with the mouse or use the cursor keys. To move a page or more at a time, use the Page Up and Page Down keys or the scrollbar at the right side of the main working area.

By default, the window for the file you are editing is maximized within the main working area. You can click the Restore button at the top right, just under the Restore button for all of Developer Studio, to show the file in a smaller window. If you have several files open at once, you can arrange them so that you can see them side by side, as shown in Figure C.16.

FIG. C.16

Your files are in MDI
windows, so you can
edit several at once,
side by side.

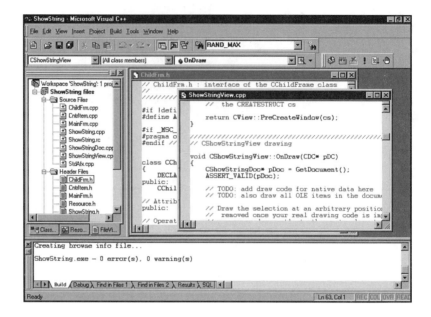

Working with Blocks of Text

Much of the time, you will want to perform an action on a block of text within the editor. First, select the block by clicking at one end of it and, holding the mouse button down, moving the mouse to the other end of the block, then releasing the mouse button. This should be familiar from so many other Windows applications. Not surprisingly, at this point you can copy or cut the block to the Clipboard, replace it with text you type, replace it with the current contents of the Clipboard, or delete it.

 T I P   To select columns of text, as shown in Figure C.17, hold down the Alt key as you select the block.

Syntax Coloring

You may have noticed the color scheme used to present your code. Developer Studio highlights the elements of your code with *syntax coloring*. By default, your code is black, with comments in green and keywords (reserved words in C++ such as public, private, new, or int) in blue. You can also arrange for special colors for strings, numbers, or operators (such as + and -) if you want, using the Format tab of the Options dialog box, reached by choosing Tools, Options.

Syntax coloring can help you spot silly mistakes. If you forget to close a C-style comment, the huge swath of green in your file points out the problem right away. If you type **inr** where you meant to type **int**, the inr isn't blue, and that alerts you to a mistyped keyword. This means you can prevent most compiler errors before you even compile.

FIG. C.17

Selecting columns makes fixing indents much simpler. Hold down the Alt key as you select the block.

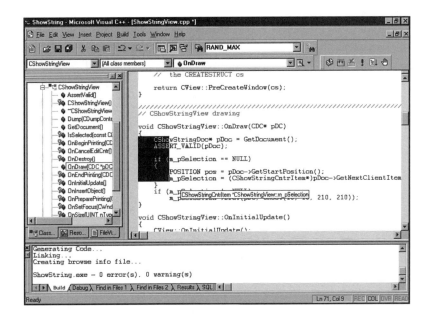

 TIP If you build Web pages and still use Notepad from time to time so that you can see the tags, you're in for a pleasant surprise. Open an HTML file in Developer Studio and see HTML syntax coloring in action. You'll never go back to Notepad.

Shortcut Menu

Many of the actions you are likely to perform are available on the shortcut menu that appears when you right-click within a file you are editing. The items on that menu are as follows:

- *Cut.* Cuts the selected text to the Clipboard.

- *Copy.* Copies the selected text to the Clipboard.

- *Paste.* Replaces the selected text with the Clipboard contents, or if no text is selected, inserts the Clipboard contents at the cursor.

- *Insert File Into Project.* Adds the file you are editing to the project you have open.

- *Check Out.* If you're using Visual Source Safe, marks the file as being changed by you.

- *Open.* Opens the file whose name is under the cursor. Especially useful for header files because you don't need to know what folder they are in.

- *List members.* Lists the member variables and functions of the object under the cursor.

- *Type Info.* Pops up a tip to remind you of the type of a variable or function.

- *Parameter Info.* Pops up a tip to remind you the parameters a function takes.

- *Complete Word.* "Wakes up" AutoComplete to help with a variable or function name that is partially typed.

Part
VII

App
C

■ *Go To Definition.* Opens the file where the item under the cursor is defined (header for a variable, source for a function) and positions the cursor at the definition of the item.

■ *Go To Reference.* Positions the cursor at the next reference to the variable or function whose name is under the cursor.

■ *Insert/Remove Breakpoint.* Inserts a breakpoint at the cursor or removes one that is already there.

■ *Enable Breakpoint.* Enables a disabled breakpoint (breakpoints are discussed in Appendix D).

■ *ClassWizard.* Opens ClassWizard.

■ *Properties.* Opens the property sheet.

Not all the items are enabled at once—for example, Cut and Copy are only enabled when there is a selection. Insert File into Project is enabled only when the file you're editing is not in the project you have open. All these actions have menu and toolbar equivalents and are discussed more fully later in this chapter.

Learning the Menu System

Developer Studio has many menus. Some commands are three or four levels deep under the menu structure. In most cases, there are far quicker ways to accomplish the same task, but for a new user, the menus are an easier way to learn because you can rely on reading the menu items as opposed to memorizing shortcuts. There are nine menus on the Developer Studio menu bar, as follows:

■ *File.* For actions related to entire files, such as opening, closing, and printing.

■ *Edit.* For copying, cutting, pasting, searching, and moving about.

■ *View.* For changing the appearance of Developer Studio, including toolbars and subwindows such as the Workspace window.

■ *Insert.* For adding files or components to your project.

■ *Project.* For dealing with your entire project.

■ *Build.* For compiling, linking, and debugging.

■ *Tools.* For customizing the Developer Studio and accessing standalone utilities.

■ *Window.* To change which window is maximized or has focus.

■ *Help.* To use the InfoViewer system (not the usual online help).

The following section presents each Developer Studio menu in turn and mentions keyboard shortcuts and toolbar buttons where they exist.

Using the File Menu

The File menu, shown in Figure C.18, collects most of the commands that affect entire files or the entire project.

FIG. C.18

The File menu has
actions for files like
Open, Close, and Print.

File New (Ctrl+N)   Choosing this menu item opens the New dialog box, shown in Figure C.19. This tabbed dialog box is used to create new files, projects, workspaces, or other documents. The Project tab is used to start AppWizard, discussed for the first time in Chapter 1, "Building Your First Windows Application."

FIG. C.19

The New dialog box is
used to create new files
or workspaces.

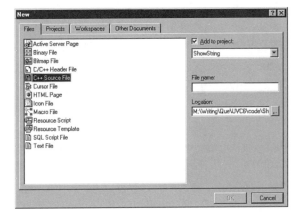

This dialog box is an easy way to create a blank file, give it a name, and insert it into your project all in one step.

File Open (Ctrl+O)   Choosing this item opens the Open dialog box, as shown in Figure C.20. (It's the standard Windows File Open dialog box, so it should be familiar.) The file type defaults to Common Files with .C, .CPP, .CXX, .TLI, .H, .TLH, .INL, or .RC extensions. By clicking the drop-down box, you can open almost any kind of file, including executables and workspaces.

 Don't forget the list of recently opened files further down the File menu. That can save a lot of typing or clicking.

FIG. C.20

The familiar File Open dialog box is used to open a variety of file types.

File Close   Choosing the File, Close item closes the file that has focus; if no file has focus, the item is grayed. You can also close a file by clicking the cancel button, depicted by an X, in the top-right corner. You may also close the window by double-clicking the icon in the upper-left corner. (The icon used to be the system menu, shown with a minus on a button.)

File Open Workspace   Use this item to open a workspace. (You can use File, Open and change the file type to Project Workspaces, but using File, Open Workspace is quicker.)

File Save Workspace   Use this item to save a workspace and all the files within it.

File Close Workspace   Use this item to close a workspace. The current workspace is closed automatically when you create a new project or open another workspace, so you won't use this menu item very often.

File Save (Ctrl+S)   Use this item to save the file that has focus at the moment; if no file has focus, the item is grayed. There is a Save button on the Standard toolbar as well.

File Save As   Use this item to save a file and change its name at the same time. It saves the file that has focus at the moment; if no file has focus, the item is grayed.

File Save All   This item saves all the files that are currently open. All files are saved just before a compile and when the application is closed, but if you aren't compiling very often and are making a lot of changes, it's a good idea to save all your files every 15 minutes or so. (You can do it less often if the idea of losing that amount of work doesn't bother you.)

File Page Setup   This item opens the Page Setup dialog box, shown in Figure C.21. Here you specify the header, footer, and margins—left, right, top, and bottom. The header and footer can contain any text including one or more special fields, which you add by clicking the arrow next to the edit box or entering the codes yourself. The codes are

- *Filename.* The name of the file being printed (&f).
- *Page Number.* The current page number (&p).
- *Current Time.* The time the page was printed (&t).

- *Current Date.* The date the page was printed (&d).
- *Left Align.* Align this portion to the left (&l).
- *Right Align.* Align this portion to the right (&c).
- *Center.* Center this portion (this is the default alignment) (&c).

FIG. C.21

The Page Setup dialog box lays out your printed pages the way you want.

File Print (Ctrl+P)   Choosing this item prints the file with focus according to your Page Setup settings. (The item is grayed if no file has focus.) The Print dialog box, shown in Figure C.22, has you confirm the printer you want to print on. If you have some text highlighted, the Selection radio button is enabled. Choosing it lets you print just the selected text; otherwise, only the All radio button is enabled, which prints the entire file. If you forget to set the headers, footers, and margins before choosing File, Print, the Setup button opens the Page Setup dialog box discussed in the previous section. There is no way to print only certain pages or to cancel printing after it has started.

FIG. C.22

The Print dialog box confirms your choice to print a file.

Recent Files and Recent Workspaces   The recent files and workspaces items, between Print and Exit, each lead to a cascading menu. The items on the secondary menus are the names of files and workspaces that have been opened most recently, up to the last four of each. These are real time-savers if you work on several projects at once. Whenever you want to open a file, before you click that toolbar button and prepare to point and click your way to the file, think first whether it might be on the File menu. Menus aren't always the slower way to go.

File Exit   Probably the most familiar Windows menu item of all, this closes Developer Studio. You can also click the X in the top-right corner or double-click what used to be the system menu in the top left. If you have made changes without saving, you get a chance to save each file on your way out.

Edit

The Edit menu, shown in Figure C.23, collects actions related to changing text in a source file.

Edit Undo (Ctrl+Z)   The Undo item reverses whatever you just did. Most operations, like text edits and deleting text, can be undone. When Undo is disabled, it is an indication that nothing needs to be undone or you cannot undo the last operation.

Part

VII

App

C

FIG. C.23

The Edit menu holds items that change the text in a file.

There is an Undo button on the Standard toolbar. Clicking the arrow next to the button displays a stack (reverse order list from most recent to least recent) of operations that can be undone. You must select a contiguous range of undo items including the first, second, and so on. You cannot pick and choose.

Edit Redo (Ctrl+Y) As you undo actions, the name given to the operations move from the Undo to the Redo list (Redo is next to Undo on the toolbar). If you undo a little too much, choose Edit, Redo to un-undo them (if that makes sense).

Edit Cut (Ctrl+X) This item cuts the currently highlighted text to the Clipboard. That means a copy of it goes to the Clipboard, and the text itself is deleted from your file. The Cut button (represented as scissors) is on the Standard toolbar.

Edit Copy (Ctrl+C) Editing buttons on the toolbar are grouped next to the scissors (Cut). Edit, Copy copies the currently selected text or item to the Windows Clipboard.

Edit Paste (Ctrl+V) Choosing this item copies the Clipboard contents at the cursor or replaces the highlighted text with the Clipboard contents if any text is highlighted. The Paste item and button are disabled if there is nothing in the Clipboard in a format appropriate for pasting to the focus window. In addition to text, you can copy and paste menu items, dialog box items, and other resources. The Paste button is on the Standard toolbar.

Edit Delete (Delete) Edit, Delete clears the selected text or item. If what you deleted is undeletable, the Undo button is enabled, and the last operation is added to the Undo button combo box. Deleted material does not go to the Clipboard and cannot be retrieved except by undoing the delete.

Edit Select All (Ctrl+A) This item selects everything in the file with focus that can be selected. For example, if a text file has focus, the entire file is selected. If a dialog box has focus, every control on it is selected.

To select many items on a dialog box, you can click the first item and then Ctrl+click each remaining item. It is often faster to use Edit, Select All to select everything and then Ctrl+click to deselect the few items you do not want highlighted.

Edit Find (Ctrl+F) The Find dialog box shown in Figure C.24 enables you to search for text within the file that currently has the focus. Enter a word or phrase into the Find What edit box. The following check boxes set the options for the search:

- *Match Whole Word Only.* If this is checked, `table` in the Find What box matches only `table`, not `suitable` or `tables`.

- *Match Case.* If this is checked, `Chapter` in the Find What box matches only `Chapter`, not `chapter` or `CHAPTER`. Uppercase and lowercase must match.

- *Regular Expression.* The Find What box is treated as a regular expression if this box is checked.

- *Search All Open Documents.* Expands your search to all the documents you have open at the moment.

- *Direction.* Choose the Up radio button to search backwards and the Down radio button to search forwards through the file.

Part
VII

App
C

FIG. C.24
The Find dialog box is used to find a string within the file that has focus.

 TIP If you highlight a block of text before selecting Edit, Find, that text is put into the Find What box for you. If no text is highlighted, the word or identifier under the cursor is put into the Find What box.

A typical use for the Find dialog box is to enter some text and click the Find Next button until you find the precise occurrence of the text for which you are searching. You may want to combine the Find feature with bookmarks (discussed a little later in this section) and put a bookmark on each line that has an occurrence of the string. Click the Mark All button in the Find dialog box to add temporary, unnamed bookmarks on match lines; they are indicated with a blue oval in the margin.

There is a Find edit box on the Standard toolbar. Enter the text you want to search for in the box and press Enter to search forward. Regular expressions are used if you have turned them on using the Find dialog box. To repeat a search, click in the search box and press Enter. You may wish to add the Find Next or Find Previous buttons to the Standard toolbar using the Tools, Customize menu item described later in this chapter.

Regular Expressions

Many of the find and replace operations within Developer Studio can be made more powerful with regular expressions. For example, if you want to search for a string only at the end of a line, or one of several similar strings, you can do so by constructing an appropriate regular expression, entering it in the Find dialog box, and instructing Developer Studio to use regular expressions for the search. A regular expression is some text combined with special characters that represent things that can't be typed, such as "the end of a line" or "any number" or "three capital letters."

When regular expressions are being used, some characters give up their usual meaning and instead stand in for one or more other characters. Regular expressions in Developer Studio are built from ordinary characters mixed in with these special entries, shown in Table C.1.

You don't have to type these in if you have trouble remembering them. Next to the Find What box is an arrowhead pointing to the right. Click there to open a shortcut menu of all these fields, and click any one of them to insert it into the Find What box. (You need to be able to read these symbols to understand what expression you are building, and there's no arrowhead on the toolbar's Find box.) Remember to select the Regular Expressions box so that these regular expressions are evaluated properly.

Here are some examples of regular expressions:

- `^test$` matches only `test` alone on a line.
- `doc[1234]` matches doc1, doc2, doc3, or doc4 but not doc5.
- `doc[1-4]` matches the same strings as above but requires less typing.
- `doc[^56]` matches doca, doc1, and anything else that starts with doc and is not doc5 or doc6.
- `H\~e` matches `Hillo` and `Hxllo` (and lots more) but not `Hello`. `H[^e]llo` has the same effect.
- `[xy]z` matches xz and yz.
- `New *York` matches `New York` but also `NewYork` and `New        York`.
- `New +York` matches `New York` and `New        York` but not NewYork.
- `New.*k` matches `Newk`, `Newark`, and `New York`, plus lots more.
- `\:n` matches `0.123`, `234`, and `23.45` (among others) but not `-1C`.
- `World$` matches `World` at the end of a line, but `World\$` matches only `World$` anywhere on a line.

Table C.1   Regular Expression Entries

Entry	Matches
^	Start of the line.
$	End of the line.
.	Any single character.

Entry	Matches
[]	Any one of the characters within the brackets (use - for a range, ^ for "except").
\~	Anything except the character that follows next.
*	Zero or more of the next character.
+	One or more of the next character.
{ }	Doesn't match specially, but saves part of the match string to be used in the replacement string. Up to nine portions can be tagged like this.
[]	Either of the characters within the [].
\:a	A single letter or number.
\:b	Whitespace (tabs or spaces).
\:c	A single letter.
\:d	A single numerical digit.
\:n	An unsigned number.
\:z	An unsigned integer.
\:h	A hexadecimal number.
\:i	A string of characters that meets the rules for C++ identifiers (starts with a letter, number, or underscore).
\:w	A string of letters only.
\:q	A quoted string surrounded by double or single quotes.
\	Removes the special meaning from the character that follows.

Edit Find in Files   This useful command searches for a word or phrase within a large number of files at once. In its simplest form, shown in Figure C.25, you enter a word or phrase into the Find What edit box, restrict the search to certain types of files in the In Files /File Types box, and choose the folder to conduct the search within the In Folder edit box. The following check boxes in the bottom half of the dialog box set the options for the search:

FIG. C.25

The simplest Find In Files approach searches for a string within a folder and its subfolders.

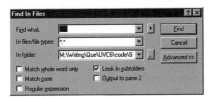

- *Match Whole Word Only.* If this is checked, `table` in the Find What box matches only `table`, not `suitable` or `tables`.

■ *Match Case.* If this is checked, Chapter in the Find What box matches only Chapter, not chapter or CHAPTER. Uppercase and lowercase must match.

■ *Regular Expression.* The Find What box is treated as a regular expression (see the sidebar "Regular Expressions") if this box is checked.

■ *Look in Subfolders.* Work through all the subfolders of the chosen folder if this is checked.

■ *Output to Pane 2.* Sends the results to the Find in Files 2 pane of the output window, so as not to wipe out the results of an earlier search.

Using Advanced Text Finding Features   At the bottom right of the Find in Files dialog box is the Advanced button. Clicking it expands the dialog box shown in Figure C.26 and allows you to search several different folders at once.

FIG. C.26

Advanced Find in Files searches for a string within several folders and their subfolders.

If you highlight a block of text before selecting Find in Files, that text is put into the Find What box for you. If no text is highlighted, the word or identifier under the cursor is put into the Find What box.

The results of the Find in Files command appear in the Find in Files 1 tab (unless you ask for pane 2) of the output window; the output window will be visible after this operation if it was not already. You can resize this window like any other window, by holding the mouse over the border until it becomes a sizing cursor, and you can scroll around within the window in the usual way. Double-clicking a filename in the output list opens that file with the cursor on the line where the match was found.

Edit Replace (Ctrl+H)   This item opens the Replace dialog box, shown in Figure C.27. It is very similar to the Find dialog box but is used to replace the found text with new text. Enter one string into the Find What edit box and the replacement string into the Replace With edit box. The three check boxes—Regular Expression, Match Case, and Match Whole Word Only—have the same meaning as on the Find dialog box (discussed in the previous section). The Replace In radio buttons enable you to restrict the search-and-replace operation to a block of highlighted text, if you prefer.

FIG. C.27

The Replace dialog box is used to replace one string with another.

To see the next match before you agree to replace it, click Find Next. To replace the next match or the match you have just found, click Replace. If you are confident that there won't be any false matches, you can click Replace All to do the rest of the file all at once. (If you realize after you click Replace All that you were wrong, there is always Edit, Undo.)

Edit Go To (Ctrl+G)   The Go To dialog box (see Figure C.28) is a central navigation point. It enables you to go to a particular line number (the default), address, reference, or bookmark, among other things. To use the Go To dialog box, select something from the Go To What list on the left; if Line is selected, enter a line number; if Bookmark is selected, pick the particular bookmark from the combo box; and so on.

Part

VII

App

C

FIG. C.28

The Go To dialog box moves you around within your project.

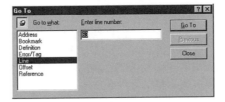

The Go To What box contains the following choices:

- *Address.* In the Memory or Disassembly windows, as explained in Appendix D, you can go to an address given by a debugger expression.

- *Bookmark.* In a text file, you can go to a bookmark, though you are more likely to choose Edit, Bookmarks or the bookmark-related buttons on the Edit toolbar.

- *Definition.* If the cursor is over the name of a function, this opens the source (.cpp) file at its definition. If the cursor is over a variable, it opens the include (.h) file.

- *Error/Tag.* After a compile, you can move from error to error by double-clicking them within the output window by using this dialog box or (most likely) by pressing F4.

- *Line.* This is the default selection. The line number that is filled in for you is your current line.

- *Offset.* Enter an offset address (in hexadecimal).

- *Reference.* Enter a name, such as a function or object name, and the cursor will be placed on the line of code where the name is defined, in your code or in the MFC libraries.

T I P   The pushpin in the upper-left corner of this dialog box is used to "pin" it to the screen so that it stays in place after you have gone to the requested location. Click the pin to unpin the dialog box from the screen so that it goes away after the jump.

Edit Bookmarks (Alt+F2)   This item is used to manage the bookmarks within your text files. The bookmark list is shown in Figure C.29. Note that temporary bookmarks set by the Find command are not included in this list.

FIG. C.29

The Bookmark dialog box manages the bookmarks you have set in text files.

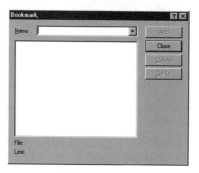

To add a named bookmark for the line you are on and have it saved with the file, type a name in the Name box and click Add. To go to a named bookmark, choose it from the list box and click Go To. There are buttons on the Edit toolbar to add or delete a bookmark at the cursor, move to the next or preceding bookmark, and clear all bookmarks in the file.

Edit ActiveX Control in HTML   If you have Visual InterDev installed and are working with an ActiveX control, this menu item will let you edit its settings. Building ActiveX controls is discussed in Chapter 17, "Building an ActiveX Control."

Edit HTML Layout   This item is used to edit an HTML layout with Visual InterDev.

Edit Advanced   Choosing this item opens a cascading menu with the following items:

- *Incremental Search*. This is a faster search than opening the Find dialog box discussed earlier. You enter your search string directly on the status bar. As you type each letter, Developer Studio finds the string you have built so far. For example, in a header file, if you choose Edit, Advanced, Incremental Search and then type **p**, the cursor will jump to the first instance of the letter p, probably in the keyword `public`. If you then type **r**, the cursor will jump to the first pr, probably in the keyword `protected`. This can save you typing the entire word you are looking for.

- *Format Selection*. This item adjust the indenting of a selection using the same rules that apply when you are entering code.

- *Tabify Selection*. Converts spaces to tabs.

- *Untabify Selection*. Converts tabs to spaces.

- *Make Selection Uppercase*. Converts the selected text to capital letters.

- *Make Selection Lowercase*. Converts the selected text to lowercase letters.

- *View Whitespace*. Inserts small placeholder characters (. for space and >> for tab) to show all the whitespace in your document.

Edit Breakpoints (Alt+F9)   A *breakpoint* pauses program execution. The Edit, Breakpoints item displays the Breakpoints dialog box, shown in Figure C.30 and discussed in Appendix D.

FIG. C.30

The Breakpoints dialog box is used in debugging your application.

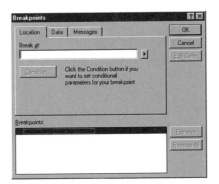

Part

VII

App

C

Edit List Members (Ctrl+Alt+T)   This item is used to "reawaken" Autocomplete for code you have already typed. It opens a list of member variables and functions for the class whose implementation you are editing, as well as global variables and functions. This list is generally too long to be useful.

Edit Type Info (Ctrl+T)   This pops up a little window telling you the type of variable the cursor is on. You can get this window much more easily by pausing the mouse over the variable and waiting a second or two.

Edit Parameter Info (Ctrl+Shift+Space)   This pops up a window reminding you of the parameters taken by the function the cursor is on. Again, this information will pop up if you just pause the mouse over the function name.

Edit Complete Word (Ctrl+Space)   This asks Autocomplete to fill in the word you are typing. If you haven't typed much of it, you may get a dialog box from which to choose the word you want. The Autocomplete dialog box generally only appears after you have typed -> or . to indicate you are looking for a member function or variable. When the function you want to call is a member of the class you are editing, it's annoying to type this--> just to open Autocomplete. Use Ctrl+Space instead.

N O T E   If these options are disabled, check your AutoComplete settings by choosing Tools, Options and clicking the Editor tab, shown in Figure C.55. ■

Using the View Menu

The View menu, shown in Figure C.31, collects actions that are related to the appearance of Developer Studio—which windows are open, what toolbars are visible, and so on.

View ScriptWizard   This InterDev-related command is used to edit Web page scripts.

View ClassWizard (Ctrl+W)   ClassWizard is probably the most used tool in Developer Studio.

FIG. C.31

The View menu controls the appearance of Developer Studio.

Whenever you add a resource (menu, dialog box, control, and so on), you connect it to your code with ClassWizard. When you are working with ActiveX, you use ClassWizard to set up properties, methods, and events. If you use custom messages, you use ClassWizard to arrange for them to be caught. You learn how to use ClassWizard starting in Chapter 2.

> **CAUTION**
>
> All changed files are saved when you open ClassWizard, just as they are saved before a compile. If you have been making changes that you may not want saved, don't open ClassWizard.

View Resource Symbols   This item opens the Resource Symbols dialog box, shown in Figure C.32. It displays the resource IDs, such as ID_EDIT_COPY, used in your application. The large list box at the top of the dialog box lists resource IDs, and the smaller box below it reminds you where this resource is used—on a menu, in an accelerator, in the string table, and so on. The buttons along the right side are used to make changes. Click New to create a new resource ID, Delete to delete this resource ID (if it's not in use), Change to change the ID (if it's in use by only one resource), and View Use to open the resource (menu, string table, and so on) that is highlighted in the lower list.

FIG. C.32

The Resource Symbols dialog box displays resource IDs.

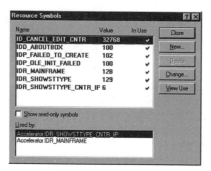

View Resource Includes   Choosing this item opens the Resource Includes dialog box, as shown in Figure C.33. It is unusual for you to need to change this generated material. In the rare cases where the resource.h file generated for you is not quite what you need, you can add extra lines with this dialog box.

FIG. C.33

The Resource Includes dialog box lets you insert extra instructions into the file that describes the resources of your project.

View Full Screen   This item hides all the toolbars, menus, Output window, and Project Workspace window, giving you the entire screen as the main working area. One small toolbar appears whose only button is Toggle Full Screen. Click that button or press the Esc key to restore the menus, toolbars, and windows.

View Workspace (Alt+0)   Choosing this item opens the Workspace window, if it is hidden. It does not take away the Workspace window. To hide it, right-click the window and choose Hide, or press Shift+Esc while the window has focus. There is a Workspace button on the Standard toolbar, which hides or displays the window.

View Output (Alt+2)   This item opens the Output window, if it is hidden. To hide the Output window, right-click it and choose Hide, or press Shift+Esc while the window has focus. The Output window opens automatically when you build your project or use Find in Files.

View Debug Windows   This cascading menu deals with windows used while debugging, which are discussed in Appendix D. It contains the following items:

- Watch
- Call Stack
- Memory

- Variables
- Registers
- Disassembly

View Properties (Alt+Enter)   Choosing this item opens a property sheet. The property sheets for different items vary widely, as shown in Figures C.34, C.35, and C.36, which illustrate the property sheet for an entire source file, an accelerator table selected in the Project Workspace window, and one key in that accelerator table, respectively.

Property sheets are a powerful way of editing non-source file entities, such as resources. For functions and variables, however, it's usually easier to make the changes in the source file. Some rather obscure effects can only be achieved through property sheets. For example, to turn off syntax coloring for a file, use the property sheet to set the language to None. (The effect will be observed after the window is repainted by Windows.)

 TIP   The property normally disappears as soon as you click something else. If you click the pushpin button in the top-left corner, it stays "pinned" to the screen as you work, displaying the properties of all the entities you are working with.

Part

VII

App

C

FIG. C.34

The property sheet for a
source file reminds you
of the name and size
and lets you set the
language (used for
syntax coloring) and tab
size.

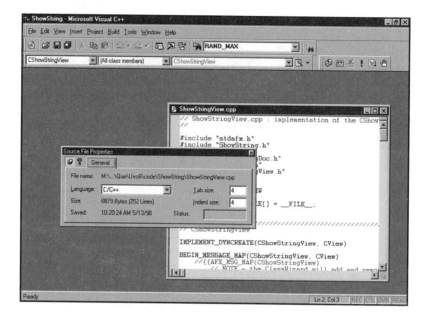

FIG. C.35

The property sheet for
an accelerator table is
where you set the
language, enabling you
to include multiple
tables in one
application.

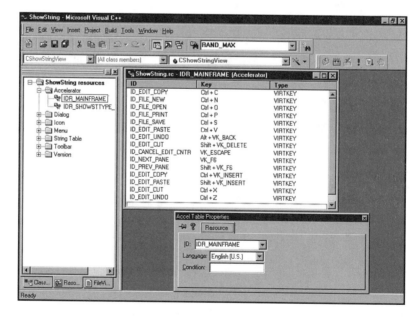

FIG. C.36

The property sheet for an entry in an accelerator table gives you full control over the keystrokes associated with the resource ID.

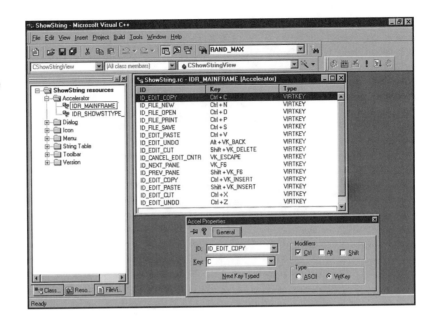

Insert

The Insert menu, shown in Figure C.37, collects actions related to inserting something into your project or one of its files.

FIG. C.37

The Insert menu is one way to add items to a project or a file.

Insert New Class   Use this item to create a header and source file for a new class and add it to this project. The New Class dialog box is shown in Figure C.38. Note the drop-down box that makes specifying the base class simpler.

Insert New Form   This item generates a CFormView and attaches it to your application. A CFormView can contain controls, such as a combination of a dialog and a view.

Insert Resource (Ctrl+R)   Use this item to add a new resource to your project. The Insert Resource dialog box, shown in Figure C.39, appears. Choose the type of resource to be added and click New.

There are buttons on the Resource toolbar to add a new dialog box, menu, cursor, icon, bitmap, toolbar, accelerator, string table, or version.

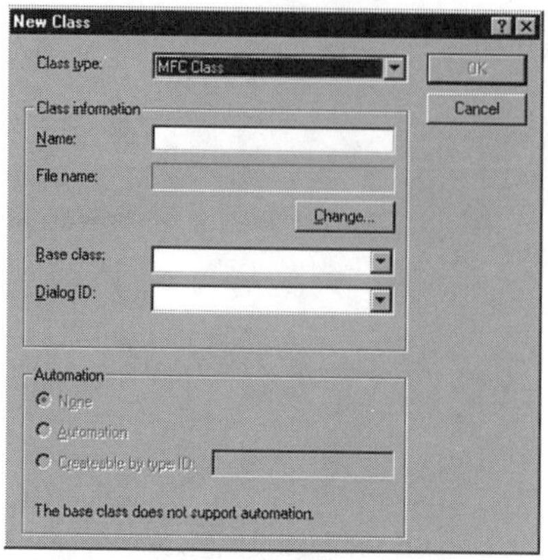

FIG. C.38

The New Class dialog box simplifies creating a new class.

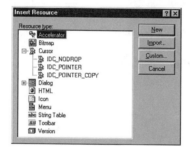

FIG. C.39

The Insert Resource dialog box is one way to add resources to your project.

Insert Resource Copy   Use this item to copy an existing resource, changing only the language (for example, from US English to Canadian French) or the condition (for example, building a debug version of a dialog box). Your project will have different language versions of the resource, allowing you to use compiler directives to determine which resource is compiled into the executable.

Insert File As Text   This item reads an entire file from the hard drive into the file you are editing. The text is inserted at the current cursor position.

Insert New ATL Object   When you are creating an ActiveX control with the Active Template Library (ATL), use this item to insert ATL objects into your project. See Chapter 21, "The Active Template Library."

Project

The Project menu, shown in Figure C.40, holds items associated with project maintenance. The items in this menu are listed in the following sections.

Project Set Active Project   If you have several projects in your workspace, this item sets which project is active.

FIG. C.40

The Project menu simplifies project maintenance.

Project Add to Project   This item opens a cascading menu with the following choices:

- *New.* Opens the same dialog box as File, New with the Add to Project box selected.
- *New Folder.* Creates a new folder to organize the classes in the project.
- *Files.* Opens the Insert Files into Project dialog box shown in Figure C.41.
- *Data Connection.* Available in the Enterprise Edition discussed in Chapter 23, this item connects your project to a data source.
- *Components and Controls.* Opens the Components and Control Gallery, discussed in Chapter 25.

Part

VII

App

C

FIG. C.41

The Insert Files into Project dialog box looks very much like a File Open dialog box.

Project Source Control   This item gathers together a number of tasks related to tracking and controlling revisions to your project source.

▶ **See** "Using Visual Source Safe," **p. 583**

Project Dependencies   This item allows you to make one project dependent on another so that when one project is changed, its dependents are rebuilt.

Project Settings (Alt+F7)   This item opens the Project Settings dialog box, which has the following 10 tabs:

- *General.* Change the static versus shared DLL choice you made when AppWizard built this project, and change the directory where intermediate (source and object) or output (EXE, DLL, OCX) files are kept (see Figure C.42).
- *Debug.* These settings are discussed in Appendix D.

FIG. C.42

The General tab of the Project Settings dialog box governs where files are kept.

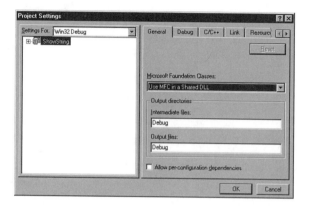

- *C/C++*. These are your compiler settings. The Category combo box has General selected by default. To change the settings category, select a category from the combo box. Figure C.43 shows the General category. You can change the optimization criteria (your choices are Default, Maximize Speed, Minimize Size, Customize, or Disable if your debugging is being thrown off by the optimizer) or the warning level. This tab is discussed in more detail in Chapter 24.

FIG. C.43

The C/C++ tab of the Project Settings dialog box governs compiler settings in eight categories, starting with General.

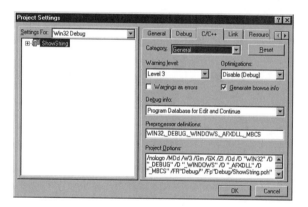

- *Link*. This tab controls linker options, which you are unlikely to need to change. The settings are divided into five categories; the General category is shown in Figure C.44.

- *Resources*. This tab, shown in Figure C.45, is used to change the language you are working in. This tab enables you to change which resources are compiled into your application, and other resource settings.

- *MIDL*. This tab is used by programmers who are building a type library (TLB) from an object description (ODL) file. ODL files are discussed in Chapter 16, "Building an Automation Server."

FIG. C.44

The Link tab of the Project Settings dialog box governs linker settings in five categories, starting with General.

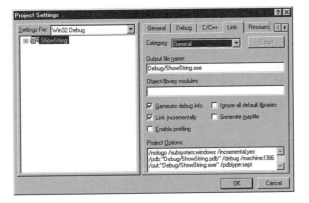

FIG. C.45

The Resources tab of the Project Settings dialog box governs resources settings, including language.

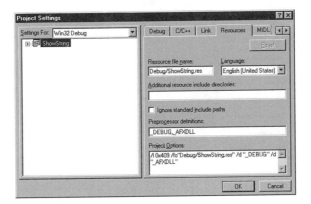

■ *Browse Info.* This tab, shown in Figure C.46, controls the Browse Info (.BSC) file used for Go To Definition, Go To Declaration, and similar menu items. If you never use these, your links will be quicker if you don't generate browse information. If you want browse information, in addition to checking Build Browse Info File Name on this tab, check Generate Browse Info in the General category of the C/C++ tab.

FIG. C.46

The Browse Info tab of the Project Settings dialog box turns on or off the powerful browse feature.

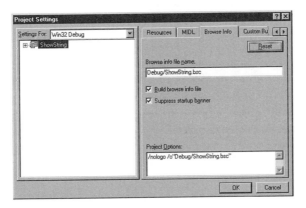

- *Custom Build.* These settings allow you to add your own steps to be performed as part of every build process.

- *Pre-Link Step.* You can add your own steps just before the link step.

- *Post-Build Step.* You can add your own steps to be performed after everything else has successfully completed.

To see the last few tabs, click the right-pointing arrow at the end of the list of tabs. You can adjust the settings for each configuration (Debug, Release, and so on) separately or all at once. Many of the panes have a Reset button that restores the settings to those you chose when you first created the project.

Build

The Build menu, shown in Figure C.47, holds all the actions associated with compiling, running, and debugging your application.

FIG. C.47

The Build menu is used to compile, link, and debug your application.

The Build menu will be a hub of activity when your are ready to compile and debug. The Build menu item names are listed in the following sections.

Build Compile (Ctrl+F7)   Choosing this item compiles the file with focus. This is a very useful thing to do when you are expecting to find errors or warnings, such as the first time you compile after a lot of changes. For example, if there is an error in a header file that is included in many source files, a typical build produces error messages related to that header file over and over again as each source file is compiled. If there are warnings in one of your source files, a typical build links the project, but you might prefer to stop and correct the warnings. There is a Compile button on the Build toolbar, represented by a stack of papers with an arrow pointing downward.

Build Build (F7)   This item compiles all the changed files in the project and then links them. There is a Build button on the Build toolbar.

Build Rebuild All   This item compiles all files in the project, even those that have not been changed since the last build, and then links them. There are times when a typical build misses a file that should be recompiled; using this item corrects the problem.

Build Batch Build   Typically a project contains at least two *configurations*: Debug and Release. Usually you work with the Debug configuration, changing, building, testing, and changing the project again until it is ready to be released, and then you build a Release version. If you ever need to build several configurations at once, use this menu item to open the Batch Build dialog box shown in Figure C.48. Choose Build to compile only changed files and Rebuild All to compile all files. If the compiles are successful, links follow. Choose Clean to delete intermediate and output files, leaving only source files.

FIG. C.48

The Batch Build dialog box builds several configurations of your project at once.

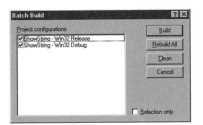

Build Clean   This item deletes all the intermediate and output files so that your project directory contains only source files.

Build Start Debug   Debugging is a lengthy topic, discussed in Appendix D.

Build Debugger Remote Connection   It is possible to run a program on one computer and debug it on another. As part of that process, you use this menu item to connect the two computers. This is discussed in Appendix D.

Build Execute (Ctrl+F5)   Choosing the Build, Execute item runs your application without opening the debugger.

Build Set Active Configuration   The Set Active Project Configuration dialog box, shown in Figure C.49, sets which of your configurations is active (typically Debug and Release). The active configuration is built by the Build commands.

FIG. C.49

The Set Active Project Configuration dialog box sets the default configuration.

Build Configurations   Choosing this item opens the Configurations dialog box, shown in Figure C.50. Here you can add or remove configurations. Use Project Settings to change the settings for the new configuration.

FIG. C.50
The Configurations dialog box lets you add to the standard Debug and Release configurations.

Build Profiler   The profiler is a powerful tool to identify bottlenecks in your applications. It is discussed in Chapter 24.

Tools

The Tools menu, shown in Figure C.51, simplifies access to add-in tools and holds some odds-and-ends leftover commands that don't fit on any other menu.

FIG. C.51
The Tools menu organizes add-in tools.

Tools Source Browser (Alt+F12)   The browser is a very powerful addition to Developer Studio; you use it whenever you go to a definition or reference, check a call graph, or otherwise explore the relationships among the classes, functions, and variables in your project. However, it's unusual to access the browser through this menu item, which opens the Browse dialog box shown in Figure C.52. You are more likely to use Edit, Go To, a Go To item from the right-click menu, or one of the 11 buttons on the Browse toolbar.

FIG. C.52
The Browse dialog box is a less common way to browse your objects, functions, and variables.

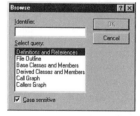

Tools Close Source Browser File   Whenever you rebuild your project, your browse file is rebuilt, too. If you rebuild your project outside Developer Studio with a tool such as NMAKE, you should close the browse file first (with this menu choice) so that it can be updated by that tool.

Accessory Tools A number of tools are added to the Tools menu when you install Visual C++, and you can add more tools with the Customize menu item, discussed next.

Tools Customize Choosing this option opens the Customize dialog box. The Commands pane of that dialog box is shown in Figure C.53 with the File buttons showing. The 11 buttons correspond to items on the File menu, and if you would like one of those items on any toolbar, simply drag it from the dialog box to the appropriate place on the toolbar and release it. The list box on the left side of the Toolbar tab lets you choose other menus, each with a collection of toolbar buttons you can drag to any toolbar. Remember that the menu bar is also a toolbar to which you can drag buttons, if you want.

FIG. C.53

The Commands pane of the Customize dialog box lets you build your own toolbars.

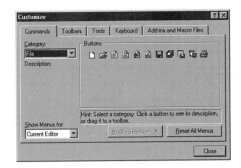

Part

VII

App

C

 T I P If your toolbars are messed up, with extra buttons or missing buttons or both, the Reset All Menus button on this dialog box returns objects to their normal state.

The Toolbars pane, shown in Figure C.54, is one way to control which toolbars are displayed. As you can see, you can also suppress ToolTips if they annoy you or turn on larger toolbar buttons if you have the space for them. (The standard toolbar in Figure C.54 has large buttons.)

FIG. C.54

The Toolbars tab of the Customize dialog box is one way to turn a toolbar on or off, and the only way to govern ToolTips and button size.

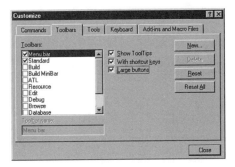

The Tools tab lets you add programs to the Tools menu, and the Keyboard tab lets you change the keyboard shortcuts for commands or add shortcuts for commands without them. The Add-Ins and Macro Files tab lets you add *macros*, which are written in VBScript and can automate many Developer Studio tasks, or *add-ins*, which can be written in any language and also automate Developer Studio tasks, to your workspace.

Tools Options   This item gathers up a great number of settings and options that relate to Developer Studio itself. For example, Figure C.55 shows the Editor tab of the Options dialog box. If there is a feature of Developer Studio you don't like, you can almost certainly change it within this large dialog box.

FIG. C.55

The Editor tab of the Options dialog box is where you change editor settings.

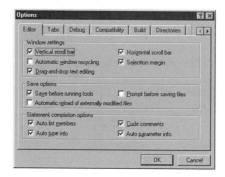

The tabs are as follows:

- *Editor.* Chooses scrollbars, enables drag and drop, sets automatic saving and loading, and controls the AutoComplete suite of features
- *Tabs.* Sets options related to tabs (inserted when you press the Tab key) and indents (inserted by the editor on new lines after language elements such as braces)
- *Debug.* Determines what information is displayed during debugging
- *Compatibility.* Lets you choose to emulate another editor (Brief or Epsilon) or just one portion of that editor's interface
- *Build.* Generates an external makefile or a build log
- *Directories.* Sets directories in which to look for include, executable, library, and source files
- *Source Control.* Sets options related to Visual SourceSafe, discussed in Chapter 23
- *Workspace.* Shown in Figure C.56, sets docking windows, status bar, and project reloading
- *Data View.* (Enterprise Edition only) Governs the appearance of the DataView
- *Macros.* Sets the rules for reloading a changed macro
- *Help System.* Determines the information displayed by the help system, typically MSDN
- *Format.* Sets the color scheme, including syntax coloring, for source windows

Part
VII
App
C

FIG. C.56
The Workspace tab of the Options dialog box sets which views dock and which float, as well as reload options.

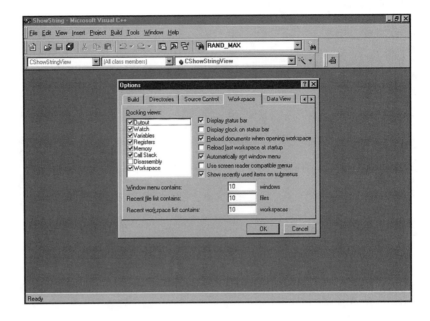

TIP If you work on the same project all the time, check the Reload Last Workspace at Startup box on the Workspace tab of the Option dialog box. Loading the Developer Studio and the last project then becomes a one-step process; simply loading the Developer Studio will load the last project, too. If you work on a variety of different projects, uncheck this box so that Developer Studio comes up more quickly.

Tools Macro   This item opens the Macro dialog box, shown in Figure C.57. Here you can record or play back simple macros, or edit a set of recorded keystrokes by adding VBScript statements.

Tools Record Quick Macro   If you don't want to name your macro and use it in many different projects but want to speed up a task right now, record a quick macro and you won't have to name it, describe it, or save it in a file. You can have only one "quick macro" at a time: Recording a new one will wipe out the old one.

Tools Play Quick Macro   This item plays your most recently recorded quick macro.

Window

The Window menu, shown in Figure C.58, controls the windows in the main working area of Developer Studio.

Window New Window   Choosing this item opens another window containing the same source file as the window with focus. The first window's title bar is changed, with :1 added after the filename; in the new window, :2 is added after the filename. Changes made in one window are immediately reflected in the other. The windows can be scrolled, sized, and closed independently.

FIG. C.57

The Macro dialog box is the nerve center for creating, editing, and using macros.

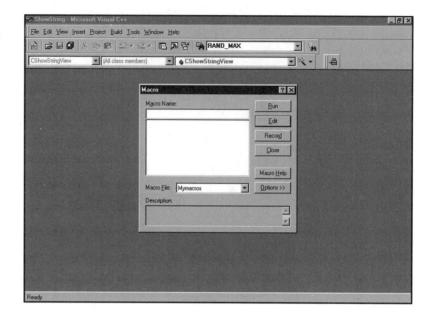

FIG. C.58

The Window menu controls the windows in the main working area.

Window Split   Choosing this window puts cross hairs over the file with focus; when you click the mouse, the window is split into four panes along the lines of these cross hairs. You can drag these boundaries about in the usual way if they are not in the right place. Scrolling one pane scrolls its companion pane as well so that the views stay in sync. To unsplit a window, drag a boundary right to the edge of the window and it disappears. Drag away both the horizontal and vertical boundaries, and the window is no longer split.

Window Docking View (Alt+F6)   This menu item governs whether the window with focus is a docking view. It is disabled when the main working area has focus.

Window Close   Choosing this item closes the window with focus and its associated file. If you have any unsaved changes, you are asked whether to save them.

Window Close All   Choosing this item closes all the windows in the main working area. If you have any unsaved changes, you are asked whether to save them.

Window Next (Ctrl+Tab) This item switches focus to the next window. The order of the windows can be determined by looking at the list of open windows at the bottom of the menu. If you have a number of windows open at once, you can cycle among them using Ctrl+Tab. This is a great way to get back to where you were after going to another file to look at something or copy some code.

Window Previous (Ctrl+Shift+Tab) This item switches focus to the previous window.

Window Cascade This item arranges all the windows in the main working area in the familiar cascade pattern, like the one shown in Figure C.59. Minimized windows are not restored and cascaded.

FIG. C.59

Arranging windows in a cascade makes it easy to switch between them.

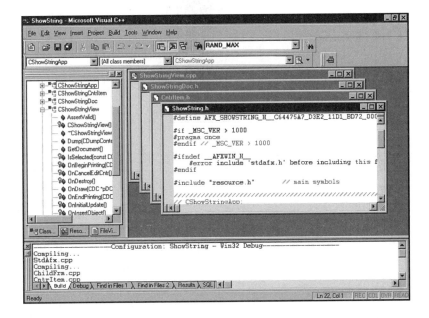

Window Tile Horizontally This item arranges all the windows in the main working area so that each is the full width of the working area, as shown in Figure C.60. The file that had focus when you chose this item is at the top.

Window Tile Vertically This item arranges all the windows in the main working area so that each is the full height of the working area, as shown in Figure C.61. The file that had focus when you chose this item is at the left.

Open Windows The bottom section of this menu lists the windows in the main working area so that you can move among them even when they are maximized. If there are more than nine open windows, only the first nine are listed. The rest can be reached by choosing Window, Windows.

FIG. C.60

When windows are tiled horizontally, each is the full width of the main working area.

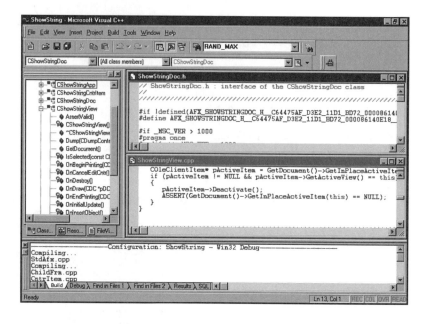

FIG. C.61

When windows are tiled vertically, each is the full height of the main working area.

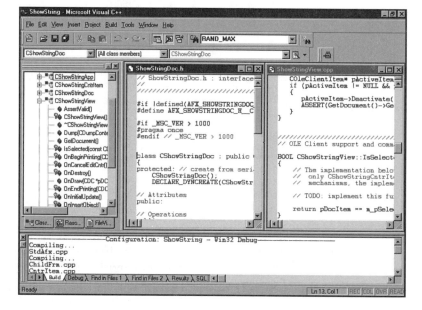

Window Windows   This item opens the Windows dialog box, shown in Figure C.62. From here you can close, save, or activate any window.

FIG. C.62

The Windows dialog box allows access to any window in the main working area.

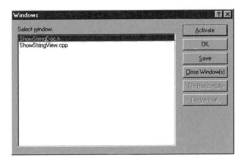

Help

The Help system for Developer Studio is a separate product. Choosing items on this menu, shown in Figure C.63, or pressing F1 activates the Help system, typically the Microsoft Developer Network, MSDN.

FIG. C.63

The Help menu is your doorway to the help system.

Help Contents   This item starts MSDN if it is not running, or switches focus to MSDN and displays the Table of Contents tab.

Help Search   This item starts MSDN if it is not running, or switches focus to MSDN and displays the Search tab.

Help Index   This item starts MSDN if it is not running, or switches focus to MSDN and displays the Index tab.

Help Use Extension Help   This item, when set, triggers a different Help system instead of MSDN. It's a good way for your group to include your own documentation, but you'll want to toggle extension help off again so that F1 will search MSDN for your error messages or classnames.

Help Readme   This item displays the "read me" file for Visual C++.

Help Keyboard Map   This item does not involve MSDN. Choosing it opens the Help Keyboard dialog box, shown in Figure C.64. Use the drop-down box at the top to choose the commands for which you want to see keystrokes: Bound commands (those with keystrokes assigned), All commands, or commands from the File, Edit, View, Insert, Build, Debug, Tools, Window, or Help menus. Commands related to Images and Layout are also available.

FIG. C.64

The Help Keyboard dialog box displays the keystrokes associated with commands.

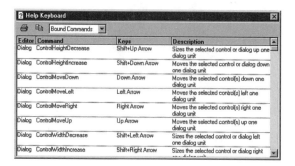

Click the title bars across the top of the table to sort the display by that column. Keystrokes cannot be changed here; choose Tools, Customize and use the Keyboard tab to change keystrokes.

Help Tip of the Day   Choosing this item opens the Tip of the Day, like that in Figure C.65. Some are Windows tips; others are specific to Developer Studio. If you can't wait to see a new tip each time you open Developer Studio, click Next Tip to scroll through the list. If you are annoyed by these tips on startup, deselect the Show Tips at Startup box.

FIG. C.65

The Tip of the Day is a great way to learn more about Developer Studio.

Help Technical Support   If you think you need technical support, start here. Not only do you learn how to get that support, but you may also find the answer to your question.

Help Microsoft on the Web   One of the ways Microsoft supplies information about Developer Studio and other products is through the World Wide Web. Choosing this item opens a cascading menu with a list of Web sites. Choosing any of these displays the pages in your default Web browser.

Help About Visual C++   Choosing this item opens the About box for Visual C++, which includes, among other information, your Product ID.

Reviewing Toolbars

After you are familiar with the sorts of actions you are likely to request of Developer Studio, the toolbars save you a lot of time. Instead of choosing File, Open, which takes two clicks and a mouse move, it is simpler to just click the Open button on the toolbar. There are, however, 11 toolbars plus a menu bar in this product, and that means a lot of little icons to learn. In this section, you will see each toolbar and which menu items the buttons correspond to.

Figure C.66 shows all the toolbars that are available in Developer Studio. The quickest way to turn several toolbars on and off is with the Toolbars dialog box, which you can also use to turn ToolTips on or off and set whether the tips include the shortcut keys for the command. Any of these toolbars can dock against any of the four edges of the working area, as shown in Figure C.67. To move a docked toolbar, drag it by the *wrinkles*—the two vertical bars at the far right. You move an undocked toolbar like any other window. When it nears the edge of the main working area, the shape change shows you it will dock. Take some time to experiment moving toolbars around until you find a configuration that suits you.

FIG. C.66
Developer Studio has 11 toolbars and a menu bar, shown here floating.

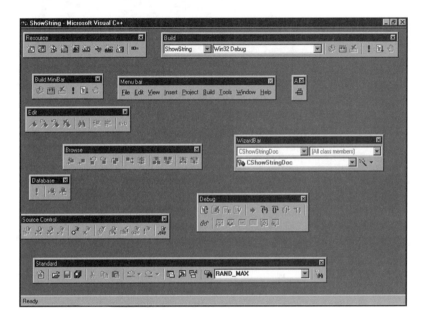

Two of the most important toolbars are the Standard and the Build Mini-bar. These are discussed in the sections that follow. For a full description of what each button does, refer to the section earlier in this chapter for the corresponding menu item.

Standard Toolbar

The Standard Toolbar helps you maintain and edit text and files in your workspace. Table C.2 names each Standard tool button and its equivalent menu operation.

FIG. C.67

Developer Studio toolbars can dock against any edge.

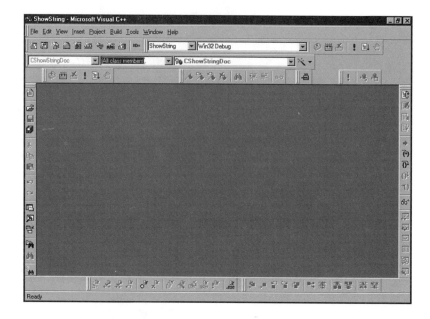

Table C.2   Standard Toolbar Buttons and Equivalent Menu Operations

Button Name	Menu Equivalent
New Text File	File, New
Open	File, Open
Save	File, Save
Save All	File, Save All
Cut	Edit, Cut
Copy	Edit, Copy
Paste	Edit, Paste
Undo	Edit, Undo
Redo	Edit, Redo
Workspace	View, Workspace
Output	View, Output
Window List	Window, Windows
Find in Files	Edit, Find in Files
Find	Edit, Find
Search	Help, Search

Build Mini-bar

The names for the Build Mini-bar buttons, which are related to compiling and debugging, are defined in Table C.3.

Table C.3   Build Mini-Bar Buttons and Equivalent Menu Commands

Button Name	Menu Equivalent
Compile	Build, Compile
Build	Build, Build
Stop Build	Build, Stop Build
Execute	Build, Execute
Go	Build, Start Debug, Go
Insert/Remove Breakpoint	N/A

Part

VII

App

C

Using Other Toolbars

You can display any or all of the toolbars, add and remove buttons to them, and generally make Developer Studio into a product that works the way you work. Experiment and see what simplifies your software development effort.

Debugging

Debugging is a vital part of programming. Whenever a program doesn't do what you expect, even if it doesn't blow up, you should turn to the debugger to see what's really going on. Some of the philosophies and techniques of debugging have been explained elsewhere in this book, especially in Chapter 24, "Improving Your Application's Performance." This appendix concentrates on the nuts and bolts of how to use the debugger: the menus, toolbars, and windows that were not covered in Appendix C, "The Visual Studio User Interface, Menus, and Toolbars."

Debugging Vocabulary

Probably the most important word in debugging is *breakpoint*. A breakpoint is a spot in your program, a single line of code, where you would like to pause. Perhaps you are wondering how many times a loop is executed, whether control transfers inside a certain if statement, or whether a function is even called. Setting a breakpoint on a line will make execution stop when that line is about to be executed. At that point you may want the program to be off and running again or want to move through your code a line or so at a time. You may want to know some of your variables' values or see how control transferred to this point by examining the call stack. Often, you'll spot the cause of a bug and correct your code on the spot.

When it's time to move along, there are a number of ways you might like execution to resume. These are explained in the following list:

- *Go*—Execute to the next breakpoint or, if there are no more breakpoints, until the program completes.
- *Restart*—Start again from the beginning.
- *Step Over*—Execute only the next statement, and then pause again. If it is a function call, run the whole function and pause after returning from it.
- *Step Into*—Execute just the next statement, but if it is a function, go into it and pause before executing the first statement in the function.
- *Step Out*—Execute the rest of the current function and pause in the function that called this one.
- *Run to Cursor*—Start running and stop a few (or many) lines from here, where the cursor is positioned.

Most information made available to you by the debugger is in the form of new windows. These are discussed in the following sections.

Debugging Commands and Windows

Developer Studio has a powerful debugger with a rich interface. There are menu items, toolbar buttons, and windows (output areas) that are used only when debugging.

Menu Items

The user interface for debugging starts with items on some ordinary menus that are used only in debugging and are not discussed in Appendix C. These include

- Edit, Breakpoints
- View, Debug Windows, Watch
- View, Debug Windows, Call Stack
- View, Debug Windows, Memory
- View, Debug Windows, Variables
- View, Debug Windows, Registers
- View, Debug Windows, Disassembly
- Build, Start Debug, Go
- Build, Start Debug, Step Into
- Build, Start Debug, Run to Cursor
- Build, Start Debug, Attach to Process
- Build, Debugger Remote Connection

These are not the only menu items you'll use, of course. For example, the Edit, Go To dialog box can be used to scroll the editor to a specific breakpoint as easily as a line, bookmark, or address. Many menu items you've already learned about are useful during debugging.

When you start debugging, the Build menu disappears and a Debug menu appears. The items on that menu are as follows:

- Debug, Go
- Debug, Restart
- Debug, Stop Debugging
- Debug, Break
- Debug, Apply Code Changes
- Debug, Step Into
- Debug, Step Over
- Debug, Step Out
- Debug, Run to Cursor
- Debug, Step into Specific Function
- Debug, Exceptions
- Debug, Threads
- Debug, Show Next Statement
- Debug, QuickWatch

Part

VII

App

D

As you can see, some items from the Build, Start Debug cascading menu are also on the Debug menu, along with many other items. The sections that follow discuss the individual items.

Setting Breakpoints

Probably the simplest way to set a breakpoint is to place the cursor on the line of code where you would like to pause. Then, toggle a breakpoint by pressing F9 or by clicking the Insert/Remove Breakpoint button on the Build MiniBar, which looks like an upraised hand (you're supposed to think "Stop!"). A red dot appears in the margin to indicate you have placed a breakpoint here, as shown in Figure D.1.

FIG. D.1

The F9 key toggles a breakpoint on the line containing the cursor.

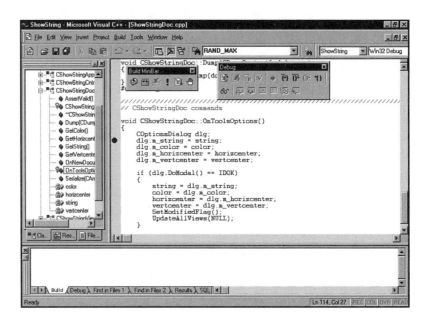

N O T E   The application being debugged throughout this appendix is ShowString, as built in Chapter 8, "Building a Complete Application: ShowString." ▪

Choosing Edit, Breakpoints displays a tabbed dialog box to set simple or conditional breakpoints. For example, you may want to pause whenever a certain variable's value changes. Searching through your code for lines that change that variable's value and setting breakpoints on them all is tiresome. Instead, use the Data tab of the Breakpoints dialog box, shown in Figure D.2. When the value of the variable changes, a message box tells you why execution is pausing; then you can look at code and variables, as described next.

You can also set conditional breakpoints, such as `break on this line when i exceeds 100`, that spare you from mindlessly clicking Go, Go, Go until you have been through a loop 100 times.

FIG. D.2

You can arrange for execution to pause whenever a variable or expression changes value.

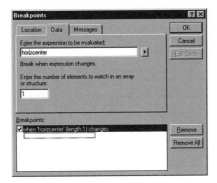

Examining Variable Values

When you set a breakpoint and debug the program, everything proceeds normally until the breakpoint line of code is about to execute. Then Developer Studio comes up on top of your application, with some extra windows in the display and a yellow arrow in the red margin dot that indicates your breakpoint, as shown in Figure D.3. This shows you the line of code that is about to execute.

Part

VII

App

D

FIG. D.3

A yellow arrow indicates the line of code about to execute.

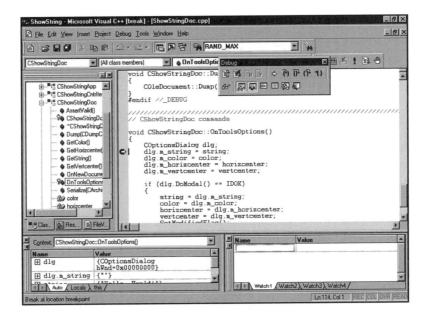

Move the mouse over a variable name, like color or horizcenter. A DataTip appears, telling you the current value of this variable. You can check as many local variables as you want like this, then continue executing, and check them again. There are other ways, though, to examine variable values.

You could click on the variable (or move the cursor to it some other way) and choose Debug, QuickWatch or click the QuickWatch button (a pair of glasses) on the toolbar. This brings up the QuickWatch window, which shows you the value of a variable or expression and lets you add it to the Watch window, if you want. You're probably wondering why anyone uses this feature now that DataTips will show you a variable's value without even clicking. DataTips can't handle expressions, even simple ones like `dlg.m_horizcenter`, but QuickWatch can, as you see in Figure D.4. You can also change a variable's value with this dialog box to recover from horrible errors and see what happens.

FIG. D.4

The QuickWatch dialog box evaluates expressions. You add them to the Watch window by clicking Add Watch.

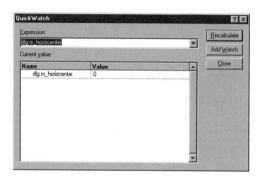

Figure D.5 shows a debug session after running forward a few lines from the original breakpoint (you'll see how to do this in a moment). The Watch and Variable windows have been undocked to show more clearly which is which, and two watches have been added: one for `horizcenter` and one for `dlg.m_horizcenter`. The program is paused immediately after the user clicks OK on the Options dialog, and in this case the user changed the string, the color, and both kinds of centering.

The Watch window simply shows the values of the two variables that were added to it. `horizcenter` is still TRUE (1) because the line of code that sets it has not yet been executed. `dlg.m_horizcenter` is FALSE (0) because the user deselected the check box associated with the member variable. (Dialogs, controls, and associating controls with member variables are discussed in Chapter 2, "Dialogs and Controls.")

The Variables window has a lot more information in it, which sometimes makes it harder to use. The local variable `dlg` and the pointer to the object for whom this member function was invoked, `this`, are both in the Variables window in tree form: Click on a + to expand the tree and on a – to collapse it. In addition, the return value from `DoModal()`, 1, is displayed.

At the top of the Variables window is a drop-down box labeled *Context*. Dropping it down shows how control got here: It lists the names of a series of functions. The top entry is the function in which the line about to be executed is contained, `CShowStringDoc::OnToolsOptions()`. The second entry is the function that called this one, `_AfxDispatchCmdMsg()`, which dispatches command messages. Chapter 3, "Messages and Commands," introduces commands and messages and discusses the way that control passes to a message-handling function like `OnToolsOptions()`. Here, the debugger gives proof of this process right before your eyes.

FIG. D.5

The Watch window and the Variable window make it easy to know the values of all your variables.

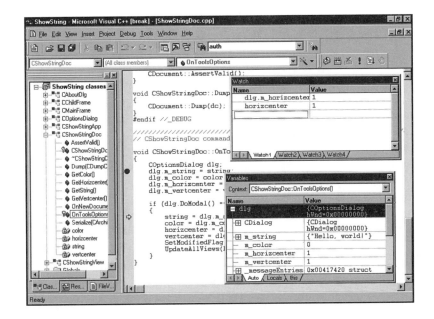

Click on any function name in the drop-down box and the code for that function is displayed. You can look at variables local to that function, and so on.

The Call Stack window, shown in Figure D.6, is easier to examine than the drop-down box in the Variables window, and it shows the same information. As well as the function names, you can see the parameters that were passed to each function. You may notice the number 32771 recurring in most of the function calls. Choose View, Resource Symbols, and you'll see that 32771 means ID_TOOLS_OPTIONS, the resource ID associated with the menu item Tools, Options in ShowString (see Figure D.7).

FIG. D.6

The Call Stack window shows how you arrived here.

Stepping Through Code

Double-clicking a function name in the call stack or the context drop-down box of the Variables window doesn't make any code execute: It simply gives you a chance to examine the local variables and code of the functions that called the function now executing. After you've looked at everything you want to look at, it's time to move on. Although there are items on the Debug menu to Step Over, Step Into, and so on, most developers use the toolbar buttons or the keyboard shortcuts. The Debug toolbar can be seen in Figures D.1, D.3, and D.5. Pause your mouse over each button to see the command it is connected to and a reminder of the keyboard shortcut. For example, the button showing an arrow going down into a pair of braces is Step Into, and the shortcut key is F11.

FIG. D.7

The number 32771 corresponds to ID_TOOLS_OPTIONS.

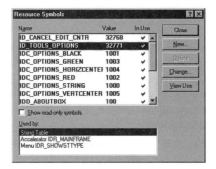

As you move through code, the yellow arrow in the margin moves with you to show which line is about to execute. Whenever the program is paused, you can add or remove breakpoints, examine variables, or resume execution. These are the mechanics of debugging.

Edit and Continue

Most developers are familiar with the cycle of debugging work. You build your project, you run it, and something unusual happens. You debug for a while to understand why. You find the bad code, change it, rebuild, rerun, and either find another bug or convince yourself that the application works. Sometimes you think you've fixed it, but you haven't. As your project grows, these rebuilds can take a very long time, and they break the rhythm of your work. It can also take a significant amount of time to run the application to the trouble spot each time. It's very boring to enter the same information every time on a dialog box, for example, trying to set up an error condition.

In version 6.0 of Visual C++, in many cases you can keep right on debugging after making a code change—without rebuilding and without rerunning. This feature is called Edit and Continue and is sure to be a major time-saver.

To use Edit and Continue, you should start by confirming that it's enabled both for the product as a whole and for this specific project. First, choose Tools, Options and click the Debug tab. Make sure that Debug commands Invoke Edit and Continue is selected, as in Figure D.8. Second, choose Project, Settings and click the C/C++ tab. In the left pane, make sure you are editing your Debug settings. Ensure that the Debug Info drop-down box contains Program Database for Edit and Continue. If not, drop the box down, select this option, as in Figure D.9 (it's last on the list), and then rebuild the project after exiting the Project Settings dialog. Always check the project settings when you start a new project, to confirm that Edit and Continue is enabled.

FIG. D.8

Enable Edit And
Continue on the Debug
tab of the Options
dialog.

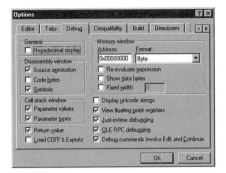

FIG. D.9

Your project must
generate Edit and
Continue information.

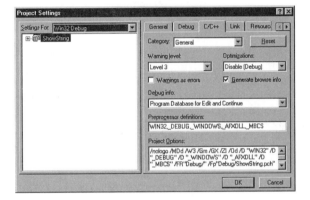

Now, debug as you always did, but don't automatically click Build after making a code change: Try to step to the next line. If it's not possible to continue without a build, you will receive a line of output in the Build tab of the Output window telling you so and the familiar One or More Files Are out of Date message box offering you a chance to rebuild your project. If it's possible to continue, you will have saved a tremendous amount of time.

Most simple code changes, such as changing the condition in an if or for statement or changing the value to which you set a variable, should work immediately. More complex changes will require a rebuild. For example, you must rebuild after any one of these changes:

- Any change to a header file, including changing code in an inline function
- Changing a C++ class definition
- Changing a function prototype
- Changing the code in a global (nonmember) function or a static member function

Try it yourself: Imagine that you can't remember why the string originally displayed by ShowString is black, and you'd like it to be red. You suspect that the OnNewDocument() function is setting it, so you expand CShowStringDoc in the ClassView and double-click OnNewDocument(). Then you place a breakpoint (F9) on this line:

```
string = "Hello, world!";
```

Click Go (F5), or choose Build, Start Debug, Go; ShowString will run, create a new document, and stop at your breakpoint. Change the next line of code to read

```
color = 1;    //red
```

Click Go again and wait. Watch your output window and you will see that showstringdoc.cpp is recompiling. After a short wait, the familiar Hello, world! will appear—in red. Your changes went into effect immediately.

When you finish your debugging session, it's a good idea to do a build because the changes used by Edit and Continue may be in memory only and not written out to your executable file.

Other Debug Windows

Three debug windows have not yet been mentioned: Memory, Registers, and Disassembly. These windows provide a level of detail rarely required in ordinary debugging. With each release of Visual C++, the circumstances under which these windows are needed dwindle. For example, the Registers window used to be the only way to see the value just returned from a function call. Now that information is in the Variables window in a more accessible format.

The Memory Window   This window, shown in Figure D.10, shows you the hex values in every byte of the memory space from 0x00000000 to 0xFFFFFFFF. It's a very long list, which makes the dialog box hard to scroll—use the Address box to enter an address that interests you. Typically, these addresses are copied (through the Clipboard, not by hand) from the Variables window. It is a handy way to look through a large array or to track down subtle platform-dependent problems.

FIG. D.10

You can examine raw memory, though you'll rarely need to.

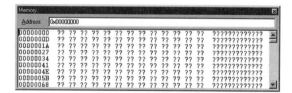

The Registers Window   If you are debugging at the assembler level, it might be useful to examine the registers. Figure D.11 shows the Registers window. This shot was taken at the same point of execution as Figure D.5, and you can see that the EAX register contains the value 1, which is the return value from DoModal().

FIG. D.11

All the registers are available for examination.

The Disassembly Window By default, the Disassembly window comes up full screen, replacing the C++ code in the main working area. You can see the assembly language statements generated for your C++ code, shown in Figure D.12. Debugging at the assembly level is beyond the scope of this book, though perhaps you might be curious to see the assembly code generated for parts of your program.

FIG. D.12

You can debug the assembler that was generated for you.

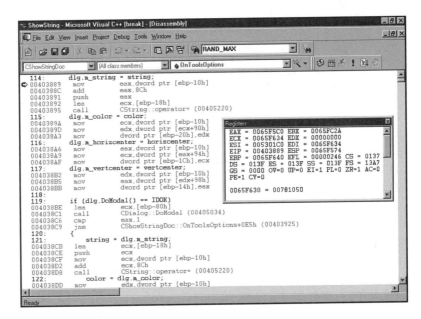

Using MFC Tracer

The MFC Tracer utility is a standalone application with an integrated menu item in the Developer Studio. To run it, choose Tools, MFC Tracer. Figure D.13 shows the Tracer dialog that appears.

FIG. D.13

A standalone utility simplifies setting trace flags.

Tracer doesn't do very much: It's just an easy way to set trace flags that govern the kind of debug output you get. Try setting all the flags on and running ShowString, simply starting it up and shutting it down. Turn off a few flags and see how the output changes.

With all the trace flags on, your application will be slow. Use Tracer to set only the ones you're interested in, while you're interested in them. It's much easier than changing a variable on-the-fly.

Defining a *Dump* Member Function

All MFC classes have a Dump() member function. When things go wrong, some error-handling code calls this function to show you the object's contents. You can write Dump() functions for your objects, too. Although you won't normally call these functions yourself, you could do so as part of your own error handling.

MFC classes inherit Dump() from Cobject, where it is defined like this:

```
virtual void Dump(CDumpContext& dc ) const;
```

The keyword virtual suggests you should override the method in your derived classes, and const indicates that Dump() will not modify the object state.

Like trace and assert statements, the Dump() member function disappears in a release build. This saves users seeing output they can't deal with and makes a smaller, faster, release version for you. You have to make this happen yourself for any Dump() function you write, with conditional compilation, as discussed in the "Adding Debug-Only Features" section of Chapter 24.

In the header file, declare Dump() like this:

```
class CNewClass : public CObject
{
public:
    // other class stuff
    #ifdef _DEBUG
    virtual void Dump( CDumpContext& dc) const
    #endif
    // ...
};
```

In the implementation file, the definition, which includes a code body, might look like this:

```
#include "cnewclass.h"

#ifdef _DEBUG
void CNewClass::Dump( CDumpContext& dc ) const
{
    CObject::Dump( dc );      // Dump parent;
    // perhaps dump individual members, works like cout
    dc << "member: " << /* member here */ endl;
}

#endif
```

As you see in the code for the Dump() function, writing the code is much like writing to standard output with the cout object or serializing to an archive. You are provided with a CDumpContext object called dc, and you send text and values to that object with the << operator. If this is unfamiliar to you, read Chapter 7, "Persistence and File I/O."

An Example Using *CDumpContext, CFile,* and *axfDump*

The sample application in this section uses the MFC debugging class CDumpContext and the global axfDump object. The debug window output from this demo and the output CFile code are in Listing D.1. To run this application yourself, create a console application as described in Chapter 28, "Future Explorations," and create an empty C++ source file called Dump.cpp. Enter this code, build, and run a debug version of the project.

When linking a debug version of this product, if you receive error messages that refer to _beginthreadex and _endthreadex, you need to change some settings. By default, console applications are single-threaded, but MFC is multithreaded. By including afx.h and bringing in MFC, this application is making itself incompatible with the single-threaded default. To fix this, choose Project Settings and click the C/C++ tab. From the drop-down box at the top of the dialog box, choose Code Generation. In the drop-down box labeled Use Runtime Library, choose Debug Multithreaded. (Figure D.15 shows the completed dialog.) Click OK and rebuild the project. You should usually change the settings for release as well, but because the calls to Dump() aren't surrounded by tests of _DEBUG, this code won't compile a release version anyway.

Listing D.1 Dump.Cpp—Demonstrating the MFC Debugging Class *CDumpContext* and the Output *CFile* Code

```
#include <afx.h>
// _DEBUG defined for debug build

class CPeople : public CObject
{
public:
    // constructor
        CPeople( const char * name );
        // destructor
        virtual ~CPeople();
        #ifdef _DEBUG
            virtual void Dump(CDumpContext& dc) const;
        #endif
    private:
        CString * person;
    };

    // constructor
    CPeople::CPeople( const char * name) : person( new CString(name)) {};
    // destructor
    CPeople::~CPeople(){ delete person; }

#ifdef _DEBUG
    void CPeople::Dump( CDumpContext& dc ) const
    {
        CObject::Dump(dc);
        dc << person->GetBuffer( person->GetLength() + 1);
```

continues

Listing D.1   Continued

```
    }
#endif

int main()
    {
        CPeople person1("Kate Gregory");
        CPeople person2("Clayton Walnum");
        CPeople person3("Paul Kimmel");

        // Use existing afxDump with virtual dump member function
        person1.Dump( afxDump );

        // Instantiate a CFile object
        CFile dumpFile("dumpout.txt", CFile::modeCreate |
            CFile::modeWrite);

        if( !dumpFile )
        {
            afxDump << "File open failed.";
        }
        else
        {
            // Dump with other CDumpContext
            CDumpContext context(&dumpFile);
            person2.Dump(context);
        }

        return 0;
    }
```

This single file contains a class definition, all the code for the class member functions, and a main() function to run as a console application. Each of these parts of the file is explained in the next few paragraphs. The class is a simple wrapper around a CString pointer, which allocates the CString with new in the constructor and deletes it in the destructor. It's so simple that it's actually useless for anything other than demonstrating the Dump() function.

First, the <afx.h> header file is included, which contains the CObject class definition and provides access to afxDump.

Next, this code defines the class CPeople derived from CObject. Notice the placement of the override of the virtual Dump() method and the conditional compiler wrap. (Any calls to Dump() should be wrapped in the same way, or that code will not compile in a release build.)

Following the constructor and destructor comes the code for CPeople::Dump(). Notice how it, too, is wrapped in conditional compiler directives. The call to CObject::Dump() takes advantage of the work done by the MFC programmers, dumping information all objects keep.

Finally, the main() function exercises this little class. It creates three instances of the CPeople class and dumps the first one.

For the second CPeople object, this code creates and opens a CFile object by passing a text string to the constructor. If the open succeeds, it creates a CDumpContextObject from the file and passes this context to Dump instead of the usual afxDump().

If you run this program, you'll see output like that in Figure D.14. The file dumpout.txt will contain these lines:

```
a CObject at $71FDDC
Clayton Walnum
```

FIG. D.14

Using the afxDump context sends your output to the Debug window.

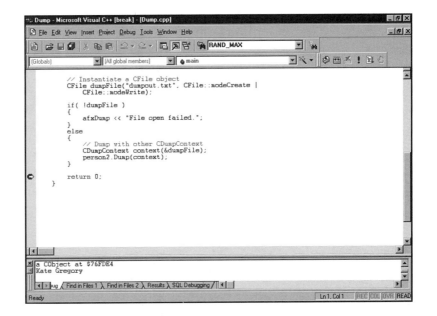

The first line of the output, to both the debug window and the file, came from CObject::Dump() and gives you the object type and the address. The second line is from your own code and is simply the CString kept within each CPeople.

FIG. D.15

To use MFC in a console application, change to the multithreaded runtime library.

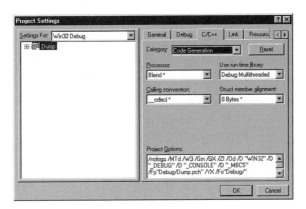

Now that you've seen the basic tools of debugging in action, you're ready to put them to work in your own applications. You'll find errors quickly, understand other people's code, and see with your own eyes just how message-routing and other behind-the-scenes magic really occur. If you find yourself enjoying debugging, don't worry—no one else has to know!

MFC Macros and Globals

In this appendix

When you're writing programs, you must use many types of data and operations again and again. Sometimes, you have to do something as simple as creating a portable integer data type. Other times, you need to do something a little more complex, such as extracting a word from a long word value or storing the position of the mouse pointer. As you might know, when you compile your program with Visual C++, many constants and variables are already defined. You can use these in your programs to save time writing code and to make your programs more portable and more readable for other programmers. In the following tables, you'll have a look at the most important of these globally available constants, macros, and variables.

Because there are so many constants, macros, and global variables, it is helpful to divide them into the following ten categories. The next sections describe each of these categories and the symbols they define:

- Application information and management
- ClassWizard comment delimiters
- Collection class helpers
- CString formatting and message-box display
- Data types
- Diagnostic services
- Exception processing
- Message maps
- Runtime object model services
- Standard command and window IDs

Application Information and Management Functions

Because a typical Visual C++ application contains only one application object but many other objects created from other MFC classes, you frequently need to obtain information about the application in different places in a program. Visual C++ defines a set of global functions that return this information to any class in a program. These functions, listed in Table E.1, can be called from anywhere within an MFC program. For example, you frequently need to get a pointer to an application's main window. The following function call accomplishes that task:

```
CWnd* pWnd = AfxGetMainWnd();
```

Table E.1   Application Information and Management

Function	Description
AfxBeginThread()	Creates a new thread (see Chapter 27, "Multitasking with Windows Threads")
AfxEndThread()	Terminates a thread
AfxGetApp()	Gets the application's CWinApp pointer

Function	Description
AfxGetAppName()	Gets the application's name
AfxGetInstanceHandle()	Gets the application's instance handle
AfxGetMainWnd()	Gets a pointer to the application's main window
AfxGetResourceHandle()	Gets the application's resource handle
AfxGetThread()	Gets a pointer to a CWinThread object
AfxRegisterClass()	Registers a window class in an MFC DLL
AfxRegisterWndClass()	Registers a Windows window class in an MFC application
AfxSetResourceHandle()	Sets the instance handle that determines where to load the application's default resources
AfxSocketInit()	Initializes Windows Sockets (see Chapter 18, "Sockets, MAPI, and the Internet")

ClassWizard Comment Delimiters

Visual C++ defines a number of delimiters that ClassWizard uses to keep track of what it's doing, as well as to locate specific areas of source code. Although you'll rarely, if ever, use these macros yourself, you will see them embedded in your AppWizard applications, so you might like to know exactly what they do. Table E.2 fills you in.

Table E.2   ClassWizard Delimiters

Delimiter	Description
AFX_DATA	Starts and ends member variable declarations in header files that are associated with dialog data exchange
AFX_DATA_INIT	Starts and ends dialog data exchange variable initialization in a dialog class's constructor
AFX_DATA_MAP	Starts and ends dialog data exchange function calls in a dialog class's DoDataExchange() function
AFX_DISP	Starts and ends Automation declarations in header files
AFX_DISP_MAP	Starts and ends Automation mapping in implementation files
AFX_EVENT	Starts and ends ActiveX event declarations in header files
AFX_EVENT_MAP	Starts and ends ActiveX events in implementation files
AFX_FIELD	Starts and ends member variable declarations in header files that are associated with database record field exchange

Part

VII

App

E

continues

Table E.2 Continued

Delimiter	Description
AFX_FIELD_INIT	Starts and ends record field exchange member variable initialization in a record set class's constructor
AFX_FIELD_MAP	Starts and ends record field exchange function calls in a record set class's DoFieldExchange() function
AFX_MSG	Starts and ends ClassWizard entries in header files for classes that use message maps
AFX_MSG_MAP	Starts and ends message map entries
AFX_VIRTUAL	Starts and ends virtual function overrides in header files

Collection Class Helper Functions

Because certain types of data structures are so commonly used in programming, MFC defines collection classes that enable you to get these common data structures initialized quickly and manipulated easily. MFC includes collection classes for arrays, linked lists, and mapping tables. (See Appendix F, "Useful Classes," for more on these constructs.) Each of these types of collections contains elements that represent the individual pieces of data that compose the collection. To make it easier to access these elements, MFC defines a set of functions created from templates (see Chapter 26, "Exceptions and Templates," for more on templates.) Table E.3 shows the functions, and you provide the implementation for each particular data type.

For example, if you want to keep a sorted list, the functions that insert new items into the list must be able to compare two Truck objects or two Employee objects to decide where to put a new Truck or Employee. You implement CompareElements() for the Truck class or Employee class, and then the collection class code can use this function to decide where to put new additions to the collection.

Table E.3 Collection Class Helper Functions

Function	Description
CompareElements()	Checks elements for equality
ConstructElements()	Constructs new elements (works similar to a class constructor)
DestructElements()	Destroys elements (works similar to a class destructor)
DumpElements()	Provides diagnostic output in text form
HashKey()	Calculates hashing keys
SerializeElements()	Saves or loads elements to or from an archive

CString Formatting and Message-Box Display

If you've done much Visual C++ programming, you know that MFC features a special string class, called CString, that makes string handling under C++ less cumbersome. CString objects are used extensively throughout MFC programs and are discussed in Appendix F. There are times when CString is not the right class, though, such as when dealing with strings in a resource's string table. These global functions, which replace format characters in string tables, provide the CString Format() capability for resource strings. There's also a global function for displaying a message box.

Table E.4   *CString* Formatting and Message-Box Functions

Function	Description
AfxFormatString1()	Replaces the format characters (such as %1) in a string resource with a given string
AfxFormatString2()	Replaces the format characters %1 and %2 in a string resource with the given strings
AfxMessageBox()	Displays a message box

Data Types

The most commonly used constants are those that define a portable set of data types. You've seen tons of these constants (named in all uppercase letters) used in Windows programs. You'll recognize many of these from the Windows SDK. Others are included only as part of Visual C++. You use these constants exactly as you would any other data type. For example, to declare an unsigned integer variable, you'd write something like this:

```
UINT flag;
```

Table E.5 lists the most commonly used data types defined by Visual C++ for Windows 95/98 and NT. Searching in the help index on any one of these types will lead you to a page in the online help that lists all the data types used in MFC and the Windows SDK.

Table E.5   Commonly Used Data Types

Data Type	Description
BOOL	Boolean value
BSTR	32-bit pointer to character data
BYTE	8-bit unsigned integer
COLORREF	32-bit color value
DWORD	32-bit unsigned integer

continues

Part
VII

App
E

Table E.5   Continued

Data Type	Description
LONG	32-bit signed integer
LPARAM	32-bit window-procedure parameter
LPCRECT	32-bit constant RECT structure pointer
LPCSTR	32-bit string-constant pointer
LPSTR	32-bit string pointer
LPVOID	32-bit void pointer
LRESULT	32-bit window-procedure return value
POSITION	The position of an element in a collection
UINT	32-bit unsigned integer
WNDPROC	32-bit window-procedure pointer
WORD	16-bit unsigned integer
WPARAM	32-bit window-procedure parameter

Diagnostic Services

When you have written your program, you're far from finished. Then comes the grueling task of testing, which means rolling up your sleeves, cranking up your debugger, and weeding out all the gotchas hiding in your code. Luckily, Visual C++ provides many macros, functions, and global variables for incorporating diagnostic abilities into your projects. By using these tools, you can print output to a debugging window, check the integrity of memory blocks, and much more. Table E.6 lists these valuable diagnostic macros, functions, and global variables. Many are discussed in Chapter 24, "Improving Your Application's Performance," and Appendix D, "Debugging."

Table E.6   Diagnostic Macros, Functions, and Global Variables

Symbol	Description
AfxCheckMemory()	Verifies the integrity of allocated memory.
AfxDoForAllClasses()	Calls a given iteration function for all classes that are derived from CObject and that incorporate runtime type checking.
AfxDoForAllObjects()	Calls a given iteration function for all objects derived from CObject and allocated with the new operator.

Symbol	Description
afxDump	A global `CDumpContext` object that enables a program to send information to the debugger window.
AfxDump()	Dumps an object's state during a debugging session.
AfxEnableMemoryTracking()	Toggles memory tracking.
AfxIsMemoryBlock()	Checks that memory allocation was successful.
AfxIsValidAddress()	Checks that a memory address range is valid for the program.
AfxIsValidString()	Checks string pointer validity.
afxMemDF	A global variable that controls memory-allocation diagnostics. It can be set to `allocMemDF`, `DelayFreeMemDF`, or `checkAlwaysMemDF`.
AfxSetAllocHook()	Sets a user-defined hook function that is called whenever memory allocation is performed.
afxTraceEnabled	A global variable that enables or disables `TRACE` output.
afxTraceFlags	A global variable that enables the MFC reporting features.
ASSERT	Prints a message and exits the program if the `ASSERT` expression is `FALSE` (see Chapter 24).
ASSERT_VALID	Validates an object by calling the object's `AssertValid()` function.
DEBUG_NEW	Used in place of the `new` operator to trace memory-leak problems (see Chapter 23).
TRACE	Creates formatted strings for debugging output (see Chapter 23).
TRACE0	Same as `TRACE` but requires no arguments in the format string.
TRACE1	Same as `TRACE` but requires one argument in the format string.
TRACE2	Same as `TRACE` but requires two arguments in the format string.
TRACE3	Same as `TRACE` but requires three arguments in the format string.
VERIFY	Like `ASSERT`, but `VERIFY` evaluates the `ASSERT` expression in both the debug and release versions of MFC. If the assertion fails, a message is printed and the program is halted only in the debug version.

Part
VII

App
E

Exception Processing

Exceptions give a program greater control over how errors are handled (see Chapter 26). Before exceptions were part of the language, MFC developers used macros to achieve the same results. Now that exceptions are firmly established in Visual C++, a number of functions make it easier to throw exceptions of various types. These macros and functions are listed in Table E.7.

Table E.7   Exception Macros and Functions

Symbol	Description
AfxAbort()	Terminates an application upon a fatal error
AfxThrowArchiveException()	Throws an archive exception
AfxThrowDAOException()	Throws a CDAOException
AfxThrowDBException()	Throws a CDBException
AfxThrowFileException()	Throws a file exception
AfxThrowMemoryException()	Throws a memory exception
AfxThrowNotSupportedException()	Throws a not-supported exception
AfxThrowOleDispatchException()	Throws an OLE automation exception
AfxThrowOleException ()	Throws an OLE exception
AfxThrowResourceException()	Throws a resource-not-found exception
AfxThrowUserException()	Throws an end user exception
AND_CATCH	Begins code that will catch specified exceptions not caught in the preceding TRY block
AND_CATCH_ALL	Begins code that will catch all exceptions not caught in the preceding TRY block
CATCH	Begins code for catching an exception
CATCH_ALL	Begins code for catching all exceptions
END_CATCH	Ends CATCH or AND_CATCH code blocks
END_CATCH_ALL	Ends CATCH_ALL code blocks
THROW	Throws a given exception
THROW_LAST	Throws the most recent exception to the next handler
TRY	Starts code that will accommodate exception handling

Message-Map Macros

Windows is an event-driven operating system, which means that every Windows application must handle a flood of messages that flow between an application and the system. MFC does away with the clunky `switch` statements that early Windows programmers had to construct to handle messages and replaces those statements with a message map. A *message map* is nothing more than a table that matches a message with its message handler (see Chapter 3, "Messages and Commands"). To simplify the declaration and definition of these tables, Visual C++ defines a set of message-map macros. Many of these macros, which are listed in Table E.8, will already be familiar to experienced MFC programmers.

Table E.8   Message-Map Macros

Macro	Description
BEGIN_MESSAGE_MAP	Begins a message-map definition
DECLARE_MESSAGE_MAP	Starts a message-map declaration
END_MESSAGE_MAP	Ends a message-map definition
ON_COMMAND	Begins a command-message message-map entry
ON_COMMAND_RANGE	Begins a command-message message-map entry that maps multiple messages to a single handler
ON_CONTROL	Begins a control-notification message-map entry
ON_CONTROL_RANGE	Begins a control-notification message-map entry that maps multiple control IDs to a single handler
ON_MESSAGE	Begins a user-message message-map entry
ON_REGISTERED_MESSAGE	Begins a registered user-message message-map entry
ON_UPDATE_COMMAND_UI	Begins a command-update message-map entry
ON_UPDATE_COMMAND_UI_RANGE	Begins a command-update message-map entry that maps multiple command-update messages to a single handler

Runtime Object Model Services

Frequently in your programs, you need access to information about classes at runtime. MFC supplies a macro for obtaining this type of information in a `CRuntimeClass` structure. In addition, the MFC application framework relies on a set of macros to declare and define runtime abilities (such as object serialization and dynamic object creation). If you've used AppWizard at all, you've seen these macros in the generated source-code files. If you're an advanced MFC programmer, you might have even used these macros yourself. Table E.9 lists the runtime macros and their descriptions.

Table E.9 Runtime Services Macros

Macro	File	Description
DECLARE_DYNAMIC	Class declaration(.h)	Enables runtime class information access
DECLARE_DYNCREATE	Class declaration(.h)	Enables the class (derived from CObject) to be created dynamically and also enables runtime class information access
DECLARE_OLECREATE	Class declaration (.h)	Enables object creation with OLE automation
DECLARE_SERIAL	Class declaration (.h)	Enables object serialization, as well as runtime class information access
IMPLEMENT_DYNAMIC	Class implementation (.cpp)	Enables runtime class information access
IMPLEMENT_DYNCREATE	Class implementation (.cpp)	Enables dynamic creation of the object and runtime information access
IMPLEMENT_OLECREATE	Class implementation (.cpp)	Enables object creation with OLE
IMPLEMENT_SERIAL	Class implementation (.cpp)	Enables object serialization and runtime class information access
RUNTIME_CLASS		Returns a CRuntimeClass structure for the given class

Standard Command and Window IDs

A Windows application user can generate myriad standard messages. For example, whenever the user selects a menu command from a standard menu like File or Edit, the program sends a message. Each standard command is represented by an ID. To relieve the programmer of having to define the dozens of IDs often used in a Windows application, Visual C++ defines these symbols in a file called AFXRES.H. Some of these IDs have obvious purposes (for example, ID_FILE_OPEN), but many others are used internally by MFC for everything from mapping standard Windows messages to their handlers, to defining string-table IDs, to assigning IDs to toolbar and status bar styles.

There are far too many of these identifiers to list here. However, if you're interested in seeing them, just open the AFXRES.H file from your Visual C++ installation folder.

Useful Classes

MFC includes a lot more than classes for programming the Windows graphical user interface. It also features many utility classes for handling such things as lists, arrays, times and dates, and mapped collections. By using these classes, you gain extra power over data in your programs and simplify many operations involved in using complex data structures such as lists.

For example, because MFC's array classes can change their size dynamically, you are relieved of creating oversized arrays in an attempt to ensure that the arrays are large enough for the application. In this way, you save memory. You don't have to worry about resizing the arrays yourself, and you avoid many of the subtle bugs and memory leaks that occur from mistakes in array-resizing code. The other collection classes provide many other similar conveniences.

The Array Classes

MFC's array classes enable you to create and manipulate one-dimensional array objects that can hold virtually any type of data. These array objects work much like the standard arrays that you're familiar with using in your programs, except that MFC can enlarge or shrink an array object dynamically at runtime. This means that you don't have to be concerned with dimensioning your array just right when it's declared. Because MFC's arrays can grow dynamically, you can forget about the memory waste that often occurs with conventional arrays, which must be dimensioned to hold the maximum number of elements needed in the program, whether or not you actually use every element.

The array classes include CByteArray, CDWordArray, CObArray, CPtrArray, CUIntArray, CWordArray, and CStringArray. As you can tell from the classnames, each class is designed to hold a specific type of data. For example, the CUIntArray, which is used in this section's examples, is an array class that can hold unsigned integers. The CPtrArray class, on the other hand, represents an array of pointers to void, and the CObArray class represents an array of objects. The array classes are all nearly identical, differing only in the type of data that they store. When you've learned to use one of the array classes, you've learned to use them all. Table F.1 lists the member functions of the array classes and their descriptions.

Table F.1   Member Functions of the Array Classes

Function	Description
Add()	Appends a value to the end of the array, increasing the size of the array, as needed.
ElementAt()	Gets a reference to an array element's pointer.
FreeExtra()	Releases unused array memory.
GetAt()	Gets the value at the specified array index.
GetSize()	Gets the number of elements in the array.
GetUpperBound()	Gets the array's *upper bound,* which is the highest valid index at which a value can be stored.
InsertAt()	Inserts a value at the specified index, shifting existing elements upward, as necessary, to accommodate the insert.

Function	Description
RemoveAll()	Removes all the array's elements.
RemoveAt()	Removes the value at the specified index.
SetAt()	Places a value at the specified index. Because this function will not increase the array's size, the index must be currently valid.
SetAtGrow()	Places a value at the specified index, increasing the array's size, as needed.
SetSize()	Sets the array's initial size and the amount by which it grows when needed. By allocating more than one element's worth of space at a time, you save time but might waste memory.

Array Templates

Because the only difference between all these array classes is the type of data they hold, they seem like an obvious use for templates. In fact, they predate the implementation of templates in Visual C++. There is a vector template in the Standard Template Library, discussed in Chapter 26, "Exceptions and Templates," which holds simple lists of any single data type. Many developers find the MFC array classes much easier to use than templates. There are also MFC collection templates, discussed later in this chapter.

Introducing the Array Application

To illustrate how the array classes work, this chapter includes the Array application. When you run the program, you see the window shown in Figure F.1. The window displays the array's current contents. Because the application's array object (which is an instance of CUIntArray) starts off with 10 elements, the values for these elements (indexed as 0 through 9) are displayed onscreen. The application enables you to change, add, or delete elements in the array and see the results.

FIG. F.1

The Array application enables you to experiment with MFC's array classes.

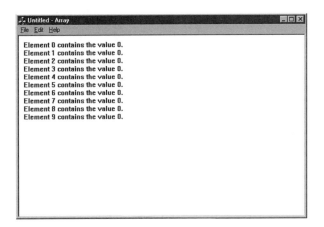

You can add an element to the array in several ways. To see these choices, click in the application's window. The dialog box shown in Figure F.2 appears. Type an array index in the Index box and the new value in the Value box. Then select whether you want to set, insert, or add the element. When you choose Set, the value of the element you specify in the Index field is changed to the value in the Value field. The Insert operation creates a new array element at the location specified by the index, pushing succeeding elements forward. Finally, the Add operation tacks the new element on the end of the array. In this case, the program ignores the Index field of the dialog box.

FIG. F.2

The Add to Array dialog box enables you to add elements to the array.

Suppose, for example, that you enter **3** in the dialog box's Index field and **15** in the Value field, leaving the Set radio button selected. Figure F.3 shows the result: The program has placed the value 15 in element 3 of the array, overwriting the previous value. Now type **2** in Index, **25** in Value, select the Insert radio button, and click OK. Figure F.4 shows the result: The program stuffs a new element in the array, shoving the other elements forward.

FIG. F.3

The value 15 has been placed in array element 3.

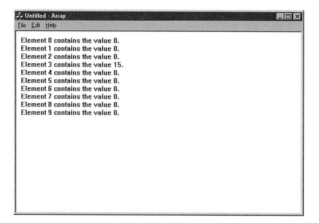

An interesting thing to try—something that really shows how dynamic MFC's arrays are—is to set an array element beyond the end of the array. For example, given the program's state shown in Figure F.4, if you type **20** in Index and **45** in Value and then choose the Set radio button, you get the results shown in Figure F.5. Because there was no element 20, the array class created the new elements that it needed to get to 20. You don't need to keep track of how many elements are in the array. Try that with an old-fashioned array.

FIG. F.4

The screen now shows the new array element, giving 11 elements in all.

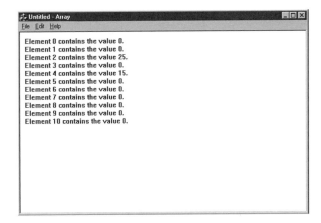

FIG. F.5

The array class has added the elements needed to set element 20.

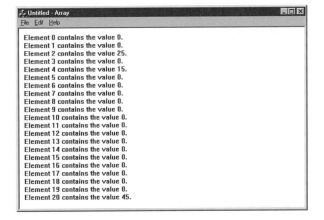

Besides adding new elements to the array, you can also delete elements in one of two ways. To do this, first right-click in the window. When you do, you see the dialog box shown in Figure F.6. If you type an index in the Remove field and then click OK, the program deletes the selected element from the array. This has the opposite effect of the Insert command because the Remove command shortens the array, rather than lengthen it. If you want, you can select the Remove All option in the dialog box. Then the program deletes all elements from the array, leaving it empty.

FIG. F.6

The Remove From Array dialog box enables you to delete elements from the array.

Declaring and Initializing the Array

Now you'd probably like to see how all this array trickery works. It's really pretty simple. First, the program declares the array object as a data member of the view class, like this:

```
CUIntArray array;
```

Then, in the view class's constructor, the program initializes the array to 10 elements:

```
array.SetSize(10, 5);
```

The SetSize() function takes as parameters the number of elements to give the array initially and the number of elements by which the array should grow whenever it needs to. You don't need to call SetSize() to use the array class. If you don't, MFC adds elements to the array one at a time, as needed, which can be slow. Unless you're doing some heavy processing, though, you're not likely to notice any difference in speed. If your application doesn't often add elements to its arrays and you are concerned about memory consumption, don't use SetSize(). If your application repeatedly adds elements and you have lots of memory available, using SetSize() to arrange for many elements to be allocated at once will reduce the number of allocations performed, giving you a faster application.

Adding Elements to the Array

After setting the array size, the program waits for the user to click the left or right mouse buttons in the window. When the user does, the program springs into action, displaying the appropriate dialog box and processing the values entered in the dialog box. Listing F.1 shows the Array application's OnLButtonDown() function, which handles the left mouse button clicks.

 Chapter 3, "Messages and Commands," shows you how to catch mouse clicks and arrange for a message handler such as OnLButtonDown() to be called.

Listing F.1   *CArrayView::OnLButtonDown()*

```
void CArrayView::OnLButtonDown(UINT nFlags, CPoint point)
{
    ArrayAddDlg dialog(this);
    dialog.m_index = 0;
    dialog.m_value = 0;
    dialog.m_radio = 0;
    int result = dialog.DoModal();
    if (result == IDOK)
    {
        if (dialog.m_radio == 0)
            array.SetAtGrow(dialog.m_index, dialog.m_value);
        else if (dialog.m_radio == 1)
            array.InsertAt(dialog.m_index, dialog.m_value, 1);
        else
            array.Add(dialog.m_value);
        Invalidate();
    }
    CView::OnLButtonDown(nFlags, point);
}
```

This code starts by creating a dialog object and initializing it, as discussed in Chapter 2, "Dialogs and Controls." If the user exits the dialog box by clicking the OK button, the `OnLButtonDown()` function checks the value of the dialog box's `m_radio` data member. A value of `0` means that the first radio button (Set) is selected, `1` means that the second button (Insert) is selected, and `2` means that the third button (Add) is selected.

 Chapter 2, "Dialogs and Controls," discusses displaying dialog boxes and getting values from them.

If the user wants to set an array element, the program calls `SetAtGrow()`, giving the array index and the new value as arguments. Unlike the regular `SetAt()` function, which you can use only with a currently valid index number, `SetAtGrow()` will enlarge the array as necessary to set the specified array element. That's how the extra array elements were added when you chose to set element `20`.

When the user has selected the Insert radio button, the program calls the `InsertAt()` function, giving the array index and new value as arguments. This causes MFC to create a new array element at the index specified, shoving the other array elements forward. Finally, when the user has selected the Add option, the program calls the `Add()` function, which adds a new element to the end of the array. This function's single argument is the new value to place in the added element. The call to `Invalidate()` forces the window to redraw the data display with the new information.

Reading Through the Array

So that you can see what's happening as you add, change, and delete array elements, the Array application's `OnDraw()` function reads through the array, displaying the values that it finds in each element. Listing F.2 shows the code for this function.

 Chapter 5, "Drawing on the Screen," shows you how to write an `OnDraw()` function and how it is called.

Listing F.2 *CArrayView::OnDraw()*

```
void CArrayView::OnDraw(CDC* pDC)
{
    CArrayDoc* pDoc = GetDocument();
    ASSERT_VALID(pDoc);

    // Get the current font's height.
    TEXTMETRIC textMetric;
    pDC->GetTextMetrics(&textMetric);
    int fontHeight = textMetric.tmHeight;
    // Get the size of the array.
    int count = array.GetSize();
    int displayPos = 10;
```

Part
VII

App
F

continues

Listing F.2   Continued

```
    // Display the array data.
    for (int x=0; x<count; ++x)
    {
        UINT value = array.GetAt(x);
        char s[81];
        wsprintf(s, "Element %d contains the value %u.", x, value);
        pDC->TextOut(10, displayPos, s);
        displayPos += fontHeight;
    }
}
```

Here, the program first gets the current font's height so that it can properly space the lines of text that it displays in the window. It then gets the number of elements in the array by calling the array object's GetSize() function. Finally, the program uses the element count to control a for loop, which calls the array object's GetAt() member function to get the value of the currently indexed array element. The program converts this value to a string for display purposes.

Removing Elements from the Array

Because it is a right button click in the window that brings up the Remove from Array dialog box, it is the program's OnRButtonDown() function that handles the element-deletion duties. Listing F.3 shows this function.

Listing F.3   CArrayView::OnRButtonDown()

```
void CArrayView::OnRButtonDown(UINT nFlags, CPoint point)
{
    ArrayRemoveDlg dialog(this);
    dialog.m_remove = 0;
    dialog.m_removeAll = FALSE;
    int result = dialog.DoModal();
    if (result == IDOK)
    {
        if (dialog.m_removeAll)
            array.RemoveAll();
        else
            array.RemoveAt(dialog.m_remove);
        Invalidate();
    }

    CView::OnRButtonDown(nFlags, point);
}
```

In this function, after displaying the dialog box, the program checks the value of the dialog box's m_removeAll data member. A value of TRUE means that the user has checked this option and wants to delete all elements from the array. In this case, the program calls the array object's RemoveAll() member function. Otherwise, the program calls RemoveAt(), whose single argument specifies the index of the element to delete. The call to Invalidate() forces the window to redraw the data display with the new information.

The List Classes

Lists are like fancy arrays. The MFC list classes use *linked lists*, which use pointers to link their elements (called *nodes*) rather than depend on contiguous memory locations to order values. Lists are a better data structure to use when you need to be able to insert and delete items quickly. However, finding items in a list can be slower than finding items in an array because a list often needs to be traversed sequentially to follow the pointers from one item to the next.

When using lists, you need to know some new vocabulary. Specifically, you need to know that the *head* of a list is the first node in the list and the *tail* of the list is the last node in the list (see Figure F.7). Each node knows how to reach the *next* node, the one after it in the list. You'll see these terms used often as you explore MFC's list classes.

FIG. F.7
A linked list has a head and a tail, with the remaining nodes in between.

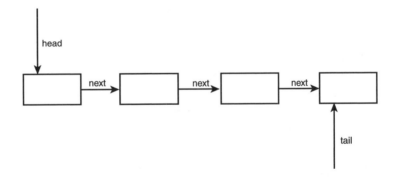

MFC provides three list classes that you can use to create your lists. These classes are CObList (which represents a list of objects), CPtrList (which represents a list of pointers), and CStringList (which represents a list of strings). Each of these classes has similar member functions, and the classes differ in the type of data that they can hold in their lists. Table F.2 lists and describes the member functions of the list classes.

Part VII

App F

Table F.2   Member Functions of the List Classes

Function	Description
AddHead()	Adds a node to the head of the list, making the node the new head
AddTail()	Adds a node to the tail of the list, making the node the new tail
Find()	Searches the list sequentially to find the given object pointer and returns a POSITION value

continues

Table F.2   Continued

Function	Description
FindIndex()	Scans the list sequentially, stopping at the node indicated by the given index, and returns a POSITION value for the node
GetAt()	Gets the node at the specified position
GetCount()	Gets the number of nodes in the list
GetHead()	Gets the list's head node
GetHeadPosition()	Gets the head node's position
GetNext()	Gets the next node in the list when iterating over a list
GetPrev()	Gets the previous node in the list when iterating over a list
GetTail()	Gets the list's tail node
GetTailPosition()	Gets the tail node's position
InsertAfter()	Inserts a new node after the specified position
InsertBefore()	Inserts a new node before the specified position
IsEmpty()	Returns TRUE if the list is empty and returns FALSE otherwise
RemoveAll()	Removes all nodes from a list
RemoveAt()	Removes a single node from a list
RemoveHead()	Removes the list's head node
RemoveTail()	Removes the list's tail node
SetAt()	Sets the node at the specified position

List Templates

Linked lists are another good use for templates. There is a list and a deque (double-ended queue) in the Standard Template Library, discussed in Chapter 26, "Exceptions and Templates." Many developers find the MFC list classes much easier to use than templates. There are also MFC collection templates, discussed later in this chapter.

Introducing the List Application

As you've no doubt guessed, now that you know a little about list classes and their member functions, you're going to get a chance to see lists in action—in the List application. When you run the application, you see the window shown in Figure F.8. The window displays the values of the single node with which the list begins. Each node in the list can hold two different values, both of which are integers.

FIG. F.8

The List application begins with one node in its list.

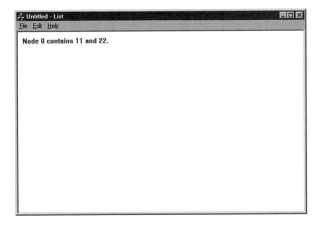

Using the List application, you can experiment with adding and removing nodes from a list. To add a node, left-click in the application's window. You then see the dialog box shown in Figure F.9. Enter the two values that you want the new node to hold and then click OK. When you do, the program adds the new node to the tail of the list and displays the new list in the window. For example, if you enter the values **55** and **65** in the dialog box, you see the display shown in Figure F.10.

FIG. F.9

A left click in the window brings up the Add Node dialog box.

FIG. F.10

Each node you add to the list can hold two different values.

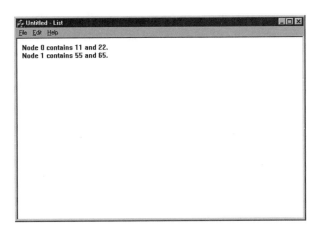

You can also delete nodes from the list. To do this, right-click in the window to display the Remove Node dialog box (see Figure F.11). Using this dialog box, you can choose to remove the head or tail node. If you exit the dialog box by clicking OK, the program deletes the specified node and displays the resulting list in the window.

> **N O T E**   If you try to delete nodes from an empty list, the List application displays a message box,
> warning you of your error. If the application didn't catch this possible error, the program
> could crash when it tries to delete a nonexistent node. ■

FIG. F.11

Right-click in the
window to delete a
node.

Declaring and Initializing the List

Declaring a list is as easy as declaring any other data type. Just include the name of the class
you're using, followed by the name of the object. For example, the List application declares its
list like this:

```
CPtrList list;
```

Here, the program is declaring an object of the CPtrList class. This class holds a linked list of
pointers, which means that the list can reference nearly any type of information.

Although there's not much you need to do to initialize an empty list, you do need to decide
what type of information will be pointed to by the pointers in the list. That is, you need to declare exactly what a node in the list will look like. The List application declares a node as shown
in Listing F.4.

Listing F.4   *CNode* Structure

```
struct CNode
{
    int value1;
    int value2;
};
```

Here, a node is defined as a structure holding two integer values. However, you can create any
type of data structure you like for your nodes. To add a node to a list, you use the new operator
to create a node structure in memory, and then you add the returned pointer to the pointer list.
The List application begins its list with a single node, which is created in the view class's constructor, as shown in Listing F.5.

Listing F.5   *CMyListView* Constructor

```
CMyListView::CMyListView()
{
    CNode* pNode = new CNode;
    pNode->value1 = 11;
    pNode->value2 = 22;
    list.AddTail(pNode);
}
```

In Listing F.5, the program first creates a new CNode structure on the heap and then sets the node's two members. After initializing the new node, a quick call to the list's AddTail() member function adds the node to the list. Because the list was empty, adding a node to the tail of the list is the same as adding the node to the head of the list. That is, the program could have also called AddHead() to add the node. In either case, the new single node is now both the head and tail of the list.

Adding a Node to the List

Although you can insert nodes at any position in a list, the easiest way to add to a list is to add a node to the head or tail, making the node the new head or tail. In the List application, you left-click in the window to bring up the Add Node dialog box, so you'll want to examine the OnLButtonDown() function, which looks like Listing F.6.

Listing F.6 *CMyListView::OnLButtonDown()*

```cpp
void CMyListView::OnLButtonDown(UINT nFlags, CPoint point)
{
    // Create and initialize the dialog box.
    AddNodeDlg dialog;
    dialog.m_value1 = 0;
    dialog.m_value2 = 0;
    // Display the dialog box.
    int result = dialog.DoModal();
    // If the user clicked the OK button...
    if (result == IDOK)
    {
        // Create and initialize the new node.
        CNode* pNode = new CNode;
        pNode->value1 = dialog.m_value1;
        pNode->value2 = dialog.m_value2;
        // Add the node to the list.
        list.AddTail(pNode);
        // Repaint the window.
        Invalidate();
    }
    CView::OnLButtonDown(nFlags, point);
}
```

Part
VII

App
F

In Listing F.6, after displaying the dialog box, the program checks whether the user exited the dialog with the OK button. If so, the user wants to add a new node to the list. In this case, the program creates and initializes the new node, as it did previously for the first node that it added in the view class's constructor. The program adds the node in the same way, too, by calling the AddTail(). If you want to modify the List application, one thing you could try is to give the user a choice between adding the node at the head or the tail of the list, instead of just at the tail.

Deleting a Node from the List

Deleting a node from a list can be easy or complicated, depending on where in the list you want to delete the node. As with adding a node, dealing with nodes other than the head or tail requires that you first locate the node that you want and then get its position in the list. You'll learn about node positions in the next section, which demonstrates how to iterate over a list. To keep things simple, however, this program enables you to delete nodes only from the head or tail of the list, as shown in Listing F.7.

Listing F.7 *CMyListView::OnRButtonDown()*

```
void CMyListView::OnRButtonDown(UINT nFlags, CPoint point)
{
    // Create and initialize the dialog box.
    RemoveNodeDlg dialog;
    dialog.m_radio = 0;
    // Display the dialog box.
    int result = dialog.DoModal();
    // If the user clicked the OK button...
    if (result == IDOK)
    {
        CNode* pNode;
        // Make sure the list isn't empty.
        if (list.IsEmpty())
            MessageBox("No nodes to delete.");
        else
        {
            // Remove the specified node.
            if (dialog.m_radio == 0)
                pNode = (CNode*)list.RemoveHead();
            else
                pNode = (CNode*)list.RemoveTail();
            // Delete the node object and repaint the window.
            delete pNode;
            Invalidate();
        }
    }
    CView::OnRButtonDown(nFlags, point);
}
```

Here, after displaying the dialog box, the program checks whether the user exited the dialog box via the OK button. If so, the program must then check whether the user wants to delete a node from the head or tail of the list. If the Remove Head radio button was checked, the dialog box's m_radio data member will be 0. In this case, the program calls the list class's RemoveHead() member function. Otherwise, the program calls RemoveTail(). Both of these functions return a pointer to the object that was removed from the list. Before calling either of these member functions, however, notice how the program calls IsEmpty() to determine whether the list contains any nodes. You can't delete a node from an empty list.

N O T E Notice that when removing a node from the list, the List application calls `delete` on the pointer returned by the list. It's important to remember that when you remove a node from a list, the node's pointer is removed from the list, but the object to which the pointer points is still in memory, where it stays until you delete it. ■

Iterating Over the List

Often, you'll want to *iterate over* (read through) a list. For example, you might want to display the values in each node of the list, starting from the head of the list and working your way to the tail. The List application does exactly this in its `OnDraw()` function, as shown in Listing F.8.

Listing F.8 *CMyListView::OnDraw()*

```
void CMyListView::OnDraw(CDC* pDC)
{
    CListDoc* pDoc = GetDocument();
    ASSERT_VALID(pDoc);
// Get the current font's height.
    TEXTMETRIC textMetric;
    pDC->GetTextMetrics(&textMetric);
    int fontHeight = textMetric.tmHeight;
    // Initialize values used in the loop.
    POSITION pos = list.GetHeadPosition();
    int displayPosition = 10;
    int index = 0;
    // Iterate over the list, displaying each node's values.
    while (pos != NULL)
    {
        CNode* pNode = (CNode*)list.GetNext(pos);
        char s[81];
        wsprintf(s, "Node %d contains %d and %d.",
            index, pNode->value1, pNode->value2);
        pDC->TextOut(10, displayPosition, s);
        displayPosition += fontHeight;
        ++index;
    }
}
```

In Listing F.8, the program gets the position of the head node by calling the `GetHeadPosition()` member function. The position is a value that many of the list class's member functions use to quickly locate nodes in the list. You must have this starting position value to iterate over the list.

In the `while` loop, the iteration actually takes place. The program calls the list object's `GetNext()` member function, which requires as its single argument the position of the node to retrieve. The function returns a pointer to the node and sets the position to the next node in the list. When the position is `NULL`, the program has reached the end of the list. In Listing F.8, this `NULL` value is the condition that's used to terminate the `while` loop.

Cleaning Up the List

There's one other time when you need to iterate over a list. That's when the program is about to terminate and you need to delete all the objects pointed to by the pointers in the list. The List application performs this task in the view class's destructor, as shown in Listing F.9.

Listing F.9   *CMyListView* **Destructor**

```
CMyListView::~CMyListView()
{
    // Iterate over the list, deleting each node.
    while (!list.IsEmpty())
    {
        CNode* pNode = (CNode*)list.RemoveHead();
        delete pNode;
    }
}
```

The destructor in Listing F.9 iterates over the list in a while loop until the IsEmpty() member function returns TRUE. Inside the loop, the program removes the head node from the list (which makes the next node in the list the new head) and deletes the node from memory. When the list is empty, all the nodes that the program allocated have been deleted.

CAUTION

Don't forget that you're responsible for deleting every node that you create with the new operator. If you fail to delete nodes, you might cause a memory leak. In a small program like this, a few wasted bytes don't matter, but in a long-running program adding and deleting hundreds or thousands of list nodes, you could create serious errors in your program. It's always good programming practice to delete any objects you allocate in memory.

TIP   Chapter 24, "Improving Your Application's Performance," discusses memory management and preventing memory leaks.

The Map Classes

You can use MFC's mapped collection classes for creating lookup tables. For example, you might want to convert digits to the words that represent the numbers. That is, you might want to use the digit 1 as a key to find the word *one*. A mapped collection is perfect for this sort of task. Thanks to the many MFC map classes, you can use various types of data for keys and values.

The MFC map classes are CMapPtrToPtr, CMapPtrToWord, CMapStringToOb, CMapStringToPtr, CMapStringToString, CMapWordToOb, and CMapWordToPtr. The first data type in the name is the key, and the second is the value type. For example, `CMapStringToOb` uses strings as keys and objects as values, whereas `CMapStringToString`, which this section uses in its examples, uses strings as both keys and values. All the map classes are similar and so have similar member functions, which are listed and described in Table F.3.

Table F.3   Functions of the Map Classes

Function	Description
GetCount()	Gets the number of map elements
GetNextAssoc()	Gets the next element when iterating over the map
GetStartPosition()	Gets the first element's position
IsEmpty()	Returns TRUE if the map is empty and returns FALSE otherwise
Lookup()	Finds the value associated with a key
RemoveAll()	Removes all the map's elements
RemoveKey()	Removes an element from the map
SetAt()	Adds a map element or replaces an element with a matching key

Map Templates

Maps and lookup tables are another good use for templates. There are set, multiset, map, and multimap templates in the Standard Template Library, discussed in Chapter 26, "Exceptions and Templates." Many developers find the MFC map classes much easier to use than templates. There are also MFC collection templates, discussed later in this chapter.

Introducing the Map Application

This section's sample program, Map, displays the contents of a map and enables you to retrieve values from the map by giving the program the appropriate key. When you run the program, you see the window shown in Figure F.12.

The window displays the contents of the application's map object, in which digits are used as keys to access the words that represent the numbers. To retrieve a value from the map, click in the window. You then see the dialog box shown in Figure F.13. Type the digit that you want to use for a key and click OK. The program finds the matching value in the map and displays it in another message box. For example, if you type **8** as the key, you see the message box shown in Figure F.14. If the key doesn't exist, the program's message box tells you so.

FIG. F.12

The Map application
displays the contents
of a map object.

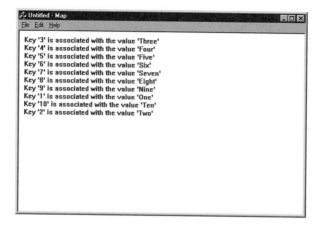

FIG. F.13

The Get Map Value
dialog box enables you
to match a key with the
key's value in the map.

FIG. F.14

This message box
displays the requested
map value.

Creating and Initializing the Map

The Map application begins with a 10-element map. The map object is declared as a data member of the view class, like this:

```
CMapStringToString map;
```

This is an object of the CMapStringToString class, which means that the map uses strings as keys and strings as values.

Declaring the map object doesn't, of course, fill it with values. You have to do that on your own, which the Map application does in its view class constructor, shown in Listing F.10.

Listing F.10   *CMapView* Constructor

```
CMapView::CMapView()
{
    map.SetAt("1", "One");
    map.SetAt("2", "Two");
    map.SetAt("3", "Three");
    map.SetAt("4", "Four");
    map.SetAt("5", "Five");
```

```
    map.SetAt("6", "Six");
    map.SetAt("7", "Seven");
    map.SetAt("8", "Eight");
    map.SetAt("9", "Nine");
    map.SetAt("10", "Ten");
}
```

The SetAt() function takes as parameters the key and the value to associate with the key in the map. If the key already exists, the function replaces the value associated with the key with the new value given as the second argument.

Retrieving a Value from the Map

When you click in Map's window, the Get Map Value dialog box appears, so it's probably not surprising that the view class OnLButtonDown() member function comes into play somewhere. Listing F.11 shows this function.

Listing F.11 *CMapView::OnLButtonDown()*

```
void CMapView::OnLButtonDown(UINT nFlags, CPoint point)
{
// Initialize the dialog box.
    GetMapDlg dialog(this);
    dialog.m_key = "";
    // Display the dialog box.
    int result = dialog.DoModal();
    // If the user exits with the OK button...
    if (result == IDOK)
    {
        // Look for the requested value.
        CString value;
        BOOL found = map.Lookup(dialog.m_key, value);
        if (found)
            MessageBox(value);
        else
            MessageBox("No matching value.");
    }
    CView::OnLButtonDown(nFlags, point);
}
```

Part VII

App F

In OnLButtonDown(), the program displays the dialog box in the usual way, checking whether the user exited the dialog box by clicking the OK button. If the user did, the program calls the map object's Lookup() member function, using the key that the user entered in the dialog box as the first argument. The second argument is a reference to the string in which the function can store the value it retrieves from the map. If the key can't be found, the Lookup() function returns FALSE; otherwise, it returns TRUE. The program uses this return value to determine whether it should display the string value retrieved from the map or a message box indicating an error.

Iterating Over the Map

To display the keys and values used in the map, the program must iterate over the map, moving from one entry to the next, retrieving and displaying the information for each map element. As with the array and list examples, the Map application accomplishes this in its OnDraw() function, which is shown in Listing F.12.

Listing F.12 CMapView::OnDraw()

```
void CMapView::OnDraw(CDC* pDC)
{
    CMapDoc* pDoc = GetDocument();
    ASSERT_VALID(pDoc);
    TEXTMETRIC textMetric;
    pDC->GetTextMetrics(&textMetric);
    int fontHeight = textMetric.tmHeight;
    int displayPosition = 10;
    POSITION pos = map.GetStartPosition();
    CString key;
    CString value;
    while (pos != NULL)
    {
        map.GetNextAssoc(pos, key, value);
        CString str = "Key '" + key +
            "' is associated with the value '" +
            value + "'";
        pDC->TextOut(10, displayPosition, str);
        displayPosition += fontHeight;
    }
}
```

Much of this OnDraw() function is similar to other versions that you've seen in this chapter. The map iteration, however, begins when the program calls the map object's GetStartPosition() member function, which returns a position value for the first entry in the map (not necessarily the first entry that you added to the map). Inside a while loop, the program calls the map object's GetNextAssoc() member function, giving the position returned from GetStartPosition() as the single argument. GetNextAssoc() retrieves the key and value at the given position and then updates the position to the next element in the map. When the position value becomes NULL, the program has reached the end of the map.

Collection Class Templates

MFC includes class templates that you can use to create your own special types of collection classes. (For more information on templates, please refer to the section "Exploring Templates" in Chapter 26.) Although the subject of templates can be complex, using the collection class templates is easy enough. For example, suppose that you want to create an array class that can hold structures of the type shown in Listing F.13.

Listing F.13   A Sample Structure

```
struct MyValues
{
    int value1;
    int value2;
    int value3;
};
```

The first step is to use the template to create your class, like this:

```
CArray<MyValues, MyValues&> myValueArray;
```

Here, CArray is the template you use for creating your own array classes. The template's two arguments are the type of data to store in the array and the type of data that the new array class's member functions should use as arguments where appropriate. In this case, the type of data to store in the array is structures of the MyValues type. The second argument specifies that class member functions should expect references to MyValues structures as arguments, where needed.

To build your array, you optionally set the array's initial size:

```
myValueArray.SetSize(10, 5);
```

Then you can start adding elements to the array, like this:

```
MyValues myValues;
myValueArray.Add(myValues);
```

After you create your array class from the template, you use the array as you do any of MFC's array classes, described earlier in this chapter. Other collection class templates you can use are CList and CMap. This means you can take advantage of all the design work put in by the MFC team to create an array of Employee objects, or a linked list of Order objects, or a map linking names to Customer objects.

The String Class

There are few programs that don't have to deal with text strings of one sort or another. Unfortunately, C++ is infamous for its weak string-handling capabilities, whereas languages such as BASIC and Pascal have always enjoyed superior power when it comes to these ubiquitous data types. MFC's CString class addresses C++'s string problems by providing member functions that are as handy to use as those found in other languages. Table F.4 lists the commonly used member functions of the CString class.

Part
VII

App
F

Table F.4 Commonly Used Member Functions of the *CString* Class

Function	Description
Compare()	A case-sensitive compare of two strings
CompareNoCase()	Not a case-sensitive compare of two strings
Empty()	Clears a string
Find()	Locates a substring
Format()	"Prints" variables in a CString much like the C sprintf function
GetAt()	Gets a character at a specified position in the string
GetBuffer()	Gets a pointer to the string's contents
GetLength()	Gets the number of characters in the string
IsEmpty()	Returns TRUE if the string holds no characters
Left()	Gets a string's left segment
MakeLower()	Lowercases a string
MakeReverse()	Reverses a string's contents
MakeUpper()	Uppercases a string
Mid()	Gets a string's middle segment
Right()	Gets a string's right segment
SetAt()	Sets a character at a specified position in the string
TrimLeft()	Removes leading whitespace characters from a string
TrimRight()	Removes trailing whitespace characters from a string

Besides the functions listed in the table, the CString class also defines a full set of operators for dealing with strings. Using these operators, you can do things like *concatenate* (join together) strings with the plus sign (+), assign values to a string object with the equal sign (=), access the string as a C-style string with the LPCTSTR operator, and more.

Creating a string object is quick and easy, like this:

```
CString str = "This is a test string";
```

Of course, there are lots of ways to construct your string object. The previous example is only one possibility. You can create an empty string object and assign characters to it later, you can create a string object from an existing string object, and you can even create a string from a repeating character. The one thing you don't have to do is decide the size of your string as you make it. Managing the memory isn't your problem any more.

After you have created the string object, you can call its member functions and manipulate the string in a number of ways. For example, to convert all the characters in the string to uppercase, you'd make a function call like this:

```
str.MakeUpper();
```

To lengthen a string, use the + or += operators, like this:

```
CString sentence = "hello " + str;
sentence += " there."
```

To compare two strings, you'd make a function call like this:

```
str.Compare("Test String");
```

You can also compare two CString objects:

```
CString testStr = "Test String";
str.Compare(testStr);
```

or neater still:

```
if (testStr == str)
```

If you peruse your online documentation, you'll find that most of the other CString member functions are equally easy to use.

The Time Classes

If you've ever tried to manipulate time values returned from a computer, you'll be pleased to learn about MFC's CTime and CTimeSpan classes, which represent absolute times and elapsed times, respectively. The use of these classes is straightforward, so there's no sample program for this section. However, the following sections get you started with these handy classes. Before you start working with the time classes, look over Table F.5, which lists the member functions of the CTime class, and Table F.6, which lists the member functions of the CTimeSpan class.

Part
VII

App

F

Table F.5   Member Functions of the *CTime* Class

Function	Description
Format()	Constructs a string representing the time object's time.
FormatGmt()	Constructs a string representing the time object's GMT (or UTC) time. This is Greenwich Mean Time.
GetCurrentTime()	Creates a CTime object for the current time.
GetDay()	Gets the time object's day as an integer.
GetDayOfWeek()	Gets the time object's day of the week, starting with 1 for Sunday.

continues

Table F.5   Continued

Function	Description
GetGmtTm()	Gets a time object's second, minute, hour, day, month, year, day of the week, and day of the year as a tm structure.
GetHour()	Gets the time object's hour as an integer.
GetLocalTm()	Gets a time object's local time, returning the second, minute, hour, day, month, year, day of the week, and day of the year in a tm structure.
GetMinute()	Gets the time object's minutes as an integer.
GetMonth()	Gets the time object's month as an integer.
GetSecond()	Gets the time object's second as an integer.
GetTime()	Gets the time object's time as a time_t value.
GetYear()	Gets the time object's year as an integer.

Table F.6   Member Functions of the *CTimeSpan* Class

Function	Description
Format()	Constructs a string representing the time-span object's time
GetDays()	Gets the time-span object's days
GetHours()	Gets the time-span object's hours for the current day
GetMinutes()	Gets the time-span object's minutes for the current hour
GetSeconds()	Gets the time-span object's seconds for the current minute
GetTotalHours()	Gets the time-span objects total hours
GetTotalMinutes()	Gets the time-span object's total minutes
GetTotalSeconds()	Gets the time-span object's total seconds

Using a *CTime* Object

Creating a CTime object for the current time is a simple matter of calling the GetCurrentTime() function, like this:

```
CTime time = CTime::GetCurrentTime();
```

Because GetCurrentTime() is a static member function of the CTime class, you can call it without actually creating a CTime object. You do, however, have to include the class's name as part of the function call, as shown in the preceding code. As you can see, the function returns a

CTime object. This object represents the current time. If you wanted to display this time, you could call on the Format() member function, like this:

```
CString str = time.Format("DATE: %A, %B %d, %Y");
```

The Format() function takes as its single argument a format string that tells the function how to create the string representing the time. The previous example creates a string that looks like this:

```
DATE: Saturday, April 19, 1998
```

The format string used with Format() is not unlike the format string used with functions like the old DOS favorite, printf(), or the Windows conversion function wsprintf(). That is, you specify the string's format by including literal characters along with control characters. The literal characters, such as the "DATE:" and the commas in the previous string example, are added to the string exactly as you type them, whereas the format codes are replaced with the appropriate values. For example, the %A in the previous code example will be replaced by the name of the day, and the %B will be replaced by the name of the month. Although the format-string concept is the same as that used with printf(), the Format() function has its own set of format codes, which are listed in Table F.7.

Table F.7 Format Codes for the *Format()* Function

Code	Description
%a	Day name, abbreviated (such as Sat for Saturday)
%A	Day name, no abbreviation
%b	Month name, abbreviated (such as Mar for March)
%B	Month name, no abbreviation
%c	Localized date and time (for the U.S., that would be something like 03/17/98 12:15:34)
%d	Day of the month as a number (01–31)
%H	Hour in the 24-hour format (00–23)
%I	Hour in the normal 12-hour format (01–12)
%j	Day of the year as a number (001–366)
%m	Month as a number (01–12)
%M	Minute as a number (00–59)
%p	Localized a.m./p.m. indicator for 12-hour clock
%S	Second as a number (00–59)
%U	Week of the year as a number (00–51, considering Sunday to be the first day of the week)

Part
VII

App
F

continues

Table F.7 Continued

Code	Description
%w	Day of the week as a number (0–6, with Sunday being 0)
%W	Week of the year as a number (00–51, considering Monday to be the first day of the week)
%x	Localized date representation
%X	Localized time representation
%y	Year without the century prefix as a number (00–99)
%Y	Year with the century prefix as a decimal number (such as 1998)
%z	Name of time zone, abbreviated
%Z	Name of time zone, not abbreviated
%%	Percent sign

Other `CTime` member functions such as `GetMinute()`, `GetYear()`, and `GetMonth()` are obvious in their use. However, you may like an example of using a function like `GetLocalTm()`, which is what the following shows:

```
struct tm* timeStruct;
timeStruct = time.GetLocalTm();
```

The first line of the previous code declares a pointer to a `tm` structure. (The `tm` structure is defined by Visual C++ and shown in Listing F.14.) The second line sets the pointer to the `tm` structure created by the call to `GetLocalTm()`.

Listing F.14 The *tm* Structure

```
struct tm {
        int tm_sec;     /* seconds after the minute - [0,59] */
        int tm_min;     /* minutes after the hour - [0,59] */
        int tm_hour;    /* hours since midnight - [0,23] */
        int tm_mday;    /* day of the month - [1,31] */
        int tm_mon;     /* months since January - [0,11] */
        int tm_year;    /* years since 1900 */
        int tm_wday;    /* days since Sunday - [0,6] */
        int tm_yday;    /* days since January 1 - [0,365] */
        int tm_isdst;   /* daylight saving time flag */
        };
```

N O T E The `CTime` class features a number of overloaded constructors, enabling you to create `CTime` objects in various ways and using various times. ■

Using a *CTimeSpan* Object

A CTimeSpan object is nothing more complex than the difference between two times. You can use CTime objects in conjunction with CTimeSpan objects to easily determine the amount of time that's elapsed between two absolute times. To do this, first create a CTime object for the current time. Then, when the time you're measuring has elapsed, create a second CTime object for the current time. Subtracting the old time object from the new one gives you a CTimeSpan object representing the amount of time that has elapsed. The example in Listing F.15 shows how this process works.

Listing F.15   Calculating a Time Span

```
CTime startTime = CTime::GetCurrentTime();
   //.
   //. Time elapses...
   //.
CTime endTime = CTime::GetCurrentTime();
CTimeSpan timeSpan = endTime - startTime;
```

Part
VII

App
F

Index

X-Y-Z

FREE ISSUE!

The Ultimate Add-on Tool for Microsoft Visual Basic

As part of your purchase, you are eligible to receive a free issue of *Visual Basic Programmer's Journal*, the leading magazine for Visual Basic programmers.

There's a lot to know about Visual Basic and its improved development tools. And *VBPJ* is the only magazine devoted to giving you the timely information you need with articles on subjects like:

- When—and how—to use the latest data access technologies
- How DHTML and the Web affect the way you develop and deploy apps
- Which new Visual Basic features save time—and which to avoid
- Creating reusable code with Visual Basic classes

But don't let the development information stop with your free issue. When you subscribe to *VBPJ*, we'll also send you a **FREE** CD-ROM – with three issues of *VBPJ* in electronically readable format, plus all the source code & sample apps from each issue.

Filled with hands-on articles and indispensable tips, tricks and utilities, *Visual Basic Programmer's Journal* will save your hours of programming time. And, *VBPJ* is the only magazine devoted to making VB programmers more productive.

A single tip can more than pay for a year's subscription.

Send for your free issue today.

MY GUARANTEE

If at any time I do not agree that *Visual Basic Programmer's Journal* is the best, most useful source of information on Visual Basic, I can cancel my subscription and receive a full refund.

☐ **YES!** Please rush me the next issue of *Visual Basic Programmer's Journal* to examine without obligation. If I like it, I'll pay the low rate of $22.9 for a full year—eleven additional issues plus the annual *Buyers Guide* and *Enterprise* issue, (for a total of fourteen). Also, with my paid subscription, I receive a **FREE** gift—three issues (with sample apps and code) of *VBPJ* on CD-ROM! if I choose not to subscribe, I'll simply write cancel on my bill and owe nothing. The free issue is mine to keep with your compliments.

Name: _____

Company: _____

Address: _____

_____

City: _____ State: _____ Zip: _____

* Basic annual subscription rate is $34.97. Your subscription is for 12 monthly issues plus two bonus issues. Canad Mexico residents please add $18/year for surface delivery. All other countries please add $44/year for air mail deli Canadian GST included. Send in this card or fax your order to 415.853.0230. Microsoft and Visual Basic are registered trademarks and ActiveX is a trademark of Microsoft Corporation.

FREE ISSUE!

Find out for yourself what *Visual Basic Programmer's Journal* can do for you.

Visual Basic is the most productive Windows development environment. Get the most out of it by learning from the experts that write for ***Visual Basic Programmer's Journal.***

Check out select articles online at http://www.devx.com